Switzerland

a Lonely Planet travel survival kit

Mark Honan

Switzerland

2nd edition

Published by
    Lonely Planet Publications
    Head Office: PO Box 617, Hawthorn, Vic 3122, Australia
    Branches: 155 Filbert St, Suite 251, Oakland, CA 94607, USA
                  10 Barley Mow Passage, Chiswick, London W4 4PH, UK
                  71 bis rue du Cardinal Lemoine, 75005 Paris, France

Printed by
    SNP Printing Pte Ltd, Singapore

Photographs by

Mark Honan	Max Weiss, St Moritz	Vevey Tourist Office
Glenn van der Knijff	Tourist Office,	Tony Wheeler
Kandersberg Tourist Office	Vaud Tourist Office	Zermatt Tourist Office
James Lyon	Verbier Tourist Office	

Front cover: Matterhorn meadows, The Alps (Jeff Hunter, The Image Bank)

First Published
    January 1994

This Edition
    May 1997

National Library of Australia Cataloguing in Publication Data

    Honan, Mark.
      Switzerland.

      2nd ed.
      Includes index.
      ISBN 0 86442 404 3.

      1. Switzerland – Guidebooks. I Title. (Series: Lonely
      Planet travel survival kit).

    914.940473

Mark Honan

After a university degree in philosophy opened up a glittering career as an office clerk, Mark soon decided that there was more to life than form-filling and data-entry. He set off on a two-year trip round the world, armed with a backpack and a vague intent to sell travel stories and pictures upon his return to England. Astonishingly, this inchoate plan succeeded and Mark became the travel correspondent for a London-based magazine. He toured Europe in a campervan, mailing back articles to the magazine and gathering the experience that would later enable him to contribute to the 1st edition of Lonely Planet's *Western Europe on a shoestring*. Mark has been writing regularly for Lonely Planet ever since.

He has written guides to *Switzerland, Austria* and *Vienna,* as well as contributing to an edition of *Central America on a shoestring* and the next two editions of *Western Europe.* He is currently updating the guide to the *Solomon Islands.* Although more than happy not to be a clerk anymore, he finds, curiously, that life as a travel writer still entails a good deal of form-filling and data-entry.

From the Author

At Switzerland Tourism, many thanks to Heidi Reisz and Evelyn Lafone in London and John Geissler in Zürich for answering my diverse, often obscure enquiries with good humour and diligence. Generous support and encouragement were received from friends in Switzerland – Beata & Jim Pukhely in Zürich, Sue Mallen and Jim Pittendrigh in Geneva, Beat Schild in Basel and the Donikian family in Zofingen. Clem Lindenmayer, who acknowledged my 1st edition in his *Walking in Switzerland* guide for Lonely Planet, needs to be thanked in turn. Seeing Switzerland from his hiker's perspective helped me strengthen a few sections for this edition. Thanks to the RAC and AA for providing road information.

From the Publisher

This book was coordinated and edited by Cathy Oliver, and proofed by Jane Fitzpatrick. Jenny Jones drew the maps with assistance from Tony Fankhauser, Lyndell Taylor, Ann Jeffree and Michael Signal. Jenny also coordinated the design, layout and colour-wraps, and drew the majority of the illustrations. Additional illustrations were drawn by Reita Wilson, Geoff Stringer, Kay Dancey and Ann Jeffree. Simon Bracken designed the cover, Michael Signal drew the back cover map, and Marcel Gaston designed the climate charts.

Warning & Request

Things change – prices go up, schedules change, good places go bad and bad places go bankrupt – nothing stays the same. So, if you find things better or worse, recently opened or long since closed, please tell us and help make the next edition even more accurate and useful.

We value all of the feedback we receive from travellers. Julie Young coordinates a small team who read and acknowledge every letter, postcard and email, and ensure that every morsel of information finds its way to the appropriate authors, editors and publishers.

Everyone who writes to us will find their

name in the next edition of the appropriate guide and will also receive a free subscription to our quarterly newsletter, *Planet Talk*. The very best contributions will be rewarded with a free Lonely Planet guide.

Excerpts from your correspondence may appear in updates (which we add to the end pages of reprints); new editions of this guide; in our newsletter, *Planet Talk*; or in the Postcards section of our Web site – so please let us know if you don't want your letter published or your name acknowledged.

Thanks

Many thanks to the travellers who used the last edition and wrote to us with helpful hints, useful advice and interesting anecdotes :

Susan Bean Aycock, Raphael Birchmeier, EM Bland, Dianne Dinsmore, Nick Doyle, G Eagle, RP Eischens, Diana Hanoar, S Hunt, Rita Karaoguz, Joan & Thomas Kearns, Iris King, Rebecca Lyon, Betty McGeever, Lyn & Donald Miller, Madelou Peck, Sally Seed, Gary Spinks, Mandy Taggart, Sue Tanck, Fran Wells, Harold White.

Contents

INTRODUCTION 11

FACTS ABOUT THE COUNTRY 13

History 13   Government & Politics 23   Society & Conduct....................28
Geography 19   Economy...................................24   Religion.....................................29
Climate 20   Population & People..................25   Language...................................29
Ecology & Environment 21   Education 27
Flora & Fauna..........................22   Arts..27

FACTS FOR THE VISITOR 32

Planning....................................32   Photography & Video 43   Business Hours 50
Suggested Itineraries 33   Time 43   Public Holidays.........................50
Highlights 33   Electricity..................................43   Special Events...........................51
Tourist Offices 34   Weights & Measures..................44   Activities...................................51
Visas & Documents 35   Laundry......................................44   Courses......................................54
Embassies 35   Health..44   Work..54
Customs 35   Toilets..47   Accommodation.........................55
Money.......................................36   Women Travellers......................47   Food..58
Post & Communications 39   Student Travellers......................47   Drinks..61
Books..41   Gay & Lesbian Travellers.........48   Entertainment............................61
Online Services.........................42   Disabled Travellers....................48   Spectator Sport..........................62
Newspapers & Magazines.........42   Senior Travellers.......................48   Things to Buy............................62
Radio & TV 42   Travel with Children..................49
Video Systems 43   Dangers & Annoyances 49

GETTING THERE & AWAY 63

Air..63   Bicycle 73   Departure Taxes 74
Bus...68   Hitching 74   Organised Tours 75
Train...69   Mountain Escapes......................74   Warning.....................................75
Car & Motorcycle.....................71   Boat...74

GETTING AROUND... 76

Air 77   Bicycle 82   Mountain Transport 82
Bus...77   Hitching 82   Local Transport.........................83
Train...77   Walking.....................................82   Organised Tours 83
Car & Motorcycle 79   Boat...82

BERNESE MITTELLAND.. 84

Bern..................................... 85   Around Biel 98
Biel 95   **Emmental Region ....** 99

BERNESE OBERLAND 100

Interlaken...................... 100   Kleine Scheidegg....................117   **East Bernese Oberland..** 124
Jungfrau Region 107   Jungfraujoch 117   Meiringen..................................124
Grindelwald 109   **The Lakes ....** 118   Alpine Pass Tours 126
Lauterbrunnen 113   Thun...118   **West Bernese Oberland..** 126
Gimmelwald 114   Spiez 120   Stockhorn 126
Mürren 114   Around Lake Thun.....................121   Niesen 127
Schilthorn 115   Giessbach Falls 122   Kandersteg 127
Wengen 115   Brienz..122   Gstaad 128
Männlichen...............................116   Freilichtmuseum Ballenberg .. 123

CENTRAL SWITZERLAND 130

Lucerne............................ 132	Schwyz Canton.............. 149	Zug................................... 152
Lake Lucerne.................. 138	Schwyz....................................149	Andermatt 154
Engelberg 145	Einsiedeln 151	

ZÜRICH CANTON 156

Zürich............................... 156	Around Zürich 172	Winterthur 173

NORTH-WEST SWITZERLAND... 176

Basel 176	The Black Forest 185	Aargau Canton................ 188
Around Basel 185	Solothurn.......................... 186	Baden 189
Augusta Raurica 185	Around Solothurn 188	Zofingen.................................190

FRIBOURG, NEUCHÂTEL & JURA... 191

Fribourg Canton.............. 193	Broc...202	Neuchâtel Montagnes 211
Fribourg 193	Neuchâtel Canton........... 203	Jura Canton 213
Murten 198	Neuchâtel...............................203	Franches Montagnes 213
Gruyères 200	Around Neuchâtel..................207	
Bulle 202	La Chaux-de-Fonds 208	

GENEVA 214

LAKE GENEVA REGION 230

Lausanne........................ 232	Around Montreux 245	Château d'Oex 251
Around Lausanne 239	North-West Vaud............. 245	Leysin 252
Swiss Riviera................... 239	Grandson.................................248	Les Diablerets 252
Vevey 240	Sainte Croix 248	Villars 253
Around Vevey 241	Vallorbe..................................249	Bex 253
Montreux 241	Vaud Alps 250	

VALAIS 254

Lower Valais.................... 256	Verbier....................................266	Brig..271
Sion...256	Mauvoisin Dam 268	Brigerbad................................273
Around Sion 260	Sierre......................................268	Visp 273
Martigny 260	Anniviers Valley 269	Zermatt....................................274
Around Martigny.....................263	Upper Valais..................... 270	Saas Fee..................................278
Mont Blanc 264	Leukerbad...............................270	Aletsch Glacier 281

TICINO 283

Bellinzona....................... 285	Campione d'Italia 294	Locarno 296
Lugano............................. 288	Monte Generoso 295	Around Locarno......................301
Around Lugano...................... 293	Ceresio....................................295	Northern Valleys 302
Lake Lugano.................... 294	Mendrisio................................296	
Gandria 294	Meride.....................................296	

GRAÜBUNDEN 303

Chur 306	Sils..319	Bernina Pass Road......... 328
Around Chur.................... 309	Silvaplana...............................320	Pontresina...............................329
Lenzerheide & Valbella..........309	St Moritz.................................320	Chünetta 330
Flims 309	Celerina..................................325	Diavolezza 330
Arosa.......................................311	Zuoz..325	Piz Lagalb 330
Davos............................... 312	Zernez.....................................326	Alp Grüm................................330
Klosters....................................316	Müstair....................................327	Bregaglia Valley............. 330
Engadine Valley 317	Guarda....................................327	Soglio 330
Maloja......................................319	Scuol 327	

NORTH-EAST SWITZERLAND 332

St Gallen Canton............. 334
St Gallen 334
Rapperswil.............................. 338
Walensee 339
Appenzellerland 339
Appenzell................................ 339
Stein 340
Säntis 341

Schaffhausen Canton..... 342
Schaffhausen........................... 342
The Rhine Falls (Rheinfall).... 344
Stein am Rhein........................ 344
Lake Constance 346
Constance................................ 349
Kreuzlingen 349
Romanshorn............................. 350

Arbon 350
Horn 350
Rorschach.................................. 351
Bregenz 351
Lindau 352
Friedrichshafen 352
Meersburg 352

LIECHTENSTEIN.. 354

Facts about the Country 354
Facts for the Visitor 356
Getting There & Away..... 356

Getting Around 356
Vaduz 357
Around Vaduz 359

Malbun 359

Appendix I – Alternative Place Names 361

Appendix II – Acronyms 362

Language Guide 363

INDEX 371
Maps 371   Text 371

Boxed Asides

Bank Accounts 25
Birth of Dada 157
Circuit of Mont Blanc 265
Cow Fights 262
Crime & Drugs................... 161
Defence................................. 19
Doing Time in the Bern
  Patent Office 90
Ferdinand Hodler 187
First Hippie 182
Glaciers 279
Jung Ideas......................... 160
Le Corbusier...................... 209
Making of Chocolate 202

Mountain Myths &
  Legends.........................140
Mt Rigi & 19th Century
  Tourism 41
Müsli....................................60
Nein Merci...........................30
On the Piste: Top Swiss Ski
  Resorts 52
Royal Race 314
Rules for Life......................50
St Mo-RITZY Guests........ 322
Swiss Cheese 341
Swiss Flag 150
Switzerland Goes Green......21

Swiss National
  Character.......................... 26
Tell: a Tale from the Dawn
  of the Confederation...... 145
Thomas Cook.................... 110
Ticinese Cuisine 285
Tourist Spending.................. 37
26 Countries in One 218
Valais Wine........................ 256
WWII & the Schaffhausen
  Bombings 342
Zürich's Transport
  System 171

Map Index

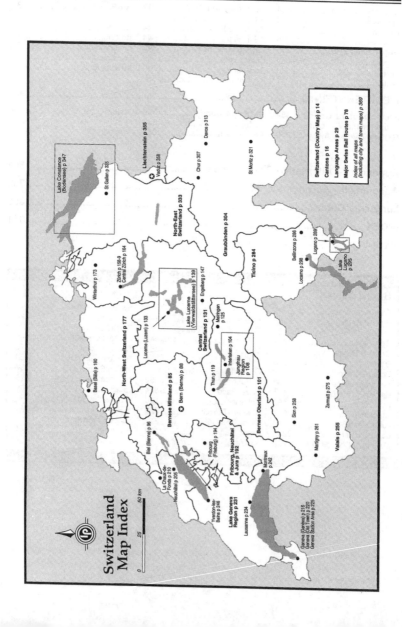

Switzerland Map Index

0   25   50 km

Switzerland (Country Map) p 14
Cantons p 16
Language Areas p 29
Major Swiss Rail Routes p 78
Index of all maps
(including city and town maps) p 389

Lake Constance (Bodensee) p 347

St Gallen p 335

Liechtenstein p 355

Vaduz p 358

Davos p 313

Chur p 307

St Moritz p 321

North-East Switzerland p 333

Graubünden p 304

Bellinzona p 286

Ticino p 284

Locarno p 298

Lugano p 289

Lake Lugano p 285

Winterthur p 173

Zürich p 158-9
Central Zürich p 164

Engelberg p 147

Lake Lucerne (Vierwaldstättersee) p 139

North-West Switzerland p 177

Luzern (Lucern) p 133

Meiringen p 125

Basel (Bâle) p 180

Central Switzerland p 131

Interlaken p 104

Jungfrau Region p 108

Thun p 119

Bernese Mitteland p 85

Bern (Berne) p 88

Bernese Oberland p 101

Sion p 258

Zermatt p 275

Valais p 255

Biel (Bienne) p 96

Fribourg (Freiburg) p 194

Fribourg, Neuchâtel & Jura p 192

Martigny p 261

La Chaux-de-Fonds p 210

Neuchâtel p 205

Montreux p 242

Yverdon-les-Bains p 246

Lake Geneva Region p 231

Lausanne p 234

Genève (Geneva) p 216
Geneva Old Town p 220
Geneva Station Area p 225

Map Legend

BOUNDARIES

- International Boundary
- Regional Boundary

ROUTES

- Motorway
- Major Road
- Minor Road
- Unsealed Road or Track
- City Road
- City Street
- Railway
- Underground Railway
- Tram
- Walking Track
- Walking Tour
- Ferry Route
- Cable Car or Chairlift

AREA FEATURES

- Parks
- Built-Up Area
- Pedestrian Mall
- Market
- Cemetery
- Reef
- Beach or Desert
- Rocks

HYDROGRAPHIC FEATURES

- Coastline
- River, Creek
- Intermittent River or Creek
- Rapids, Waterfalls
- Lake, Intermittent Lake
- Canal
- Swamp

SYMBOLS

✪ CAPITAL		National Capital
◉ Capital		Regional Capital
⬤ CITY		Major City
● City		City
● Town		Major Town
● Town		Minor Town
■	▼	Place to Stay, Place to Eat
⬛	🍴	Cafe, Pub or Bar
✉	☎	Post Office, Telephone
❶	❾	Tourist Information, Bank
◐	🅿	Transport, Parking
🏛	🏠	Museum, Youth Hostel
⛺	🏕	Caravan Park, Camping Ground
✝	✚	Church, Cathedral
☪	✡	Mosque, Synagogue
卍	🕉	Buddhist Temple, Hindu Temple
✛	★	Hospital, Police Station

◐	🅱	Embassy, Petrol Station
✈	✝	Airport, Airfield
▭	✿	Swimming Pool, Gardens
❖	🐘	Shopping Centre, Zoo
⚘	🌲	Winery or Vineyard, Picnic Site
←	A25	One Way Street, Route Number
🏛	🗿	Stately Home, Monument
⛩	◼	Castle, Tomb
⌒	⌂	Cave, Hut or Chalet
▲	☀	Mountain or Hill, Lookout
🗼	⚓	Lighthouse, Shipwreck
)(	◎	Pass, Spring
🏄	🏄	Beach, Surf Beach
	∴	Archaeological Site or Ruins
		Ancient or City Wall
		Cliff or Escarpment, Tunnel
		Railway Station

Note: not all symbols displayed above appear in this book

Introduction

What is it about Switzerland that so fascinates? Is it the idea that 700 years ago a band of woodsmen, a bunch of parochial William Tells, were able to repel the might of the all-conquering Habsburgs and thereby make possible the formation of the Swiss Confederation? Is it that such a militarily efficient nation as this could have avoided international warfare for so long? Could it be that (as Orson Welles/Harry Lime points out in the film *The Third Man*) 500 years of Swiss democracy and peace has produced nothing more than the cuckoo clock?

Actually Orson Welles' character was wrong on more than one count. For one thing, the Swiss didn't invent the cuckoo clock: that came from the German Black Forest. But the Swiss are a brainy lot, and per capita have produced more Nobel Prize winners and registered more patents than any other country. Milk chocolate, DDT, life insurance, the pump-turbine – all are Swiss inventions. They also came up with the Alp horn, an instrument several metres long and about as portable as a posse of elephants – hardly ideal for carrying up and down the sides of mountains.

The Swiss have a way of making the unexpected work. Like successfully knitting together people from four language groups into one small nation. When travelling around the country, the visitor gets a flavour of Germany, France and Italy, but always seasoned with a unique Swissness. The Swiss political system is one of the most complicated in the world, yet citizens dutifully inform themselves of the issues and vote regularly in a whole host of referenda.

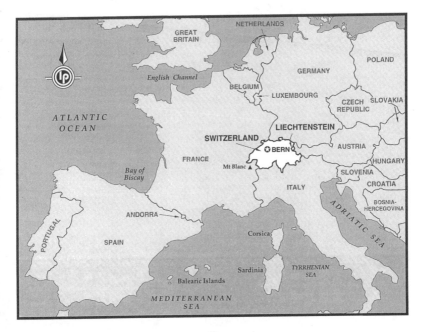

Every adult male has an army rifle at home but nobody goes around blowing people's heads off. British trains are late if a few leaves fall on the line in autumn, yet Swiss trains go over, round, and through the Alps and still generally arrive minute-perfect. Things work in Switzerland – and work well.

And the Alps! They are sufficient reason alone for visiting Switzerland. The countryside is visually stunning. Breathtaking views inspire peace and tranquillity and provide many sporting possibilities for the more adventurous. Skiers and hikers find paradise in the Alps. But you don't have to be a sportsperson to enjoy yourself; dreamers find their niche, and have done for centuries. The Romantics such as Byron and Shelley were drawn to the mountains for inspiration, as were many other writers, artists and musicians before and since.

Beyond the Alps and the chalet-style mountain resorts there are the towns and cities. Sober, responsible banker's towns like Zürich, Geneva and Lugano, which are nevertheless attractively situated and packed with interesting sights and fine museums. There's the enigmatic capital, Bern, that looks more like a museum piece than a seat of power. And there are many places, such as Lucerne, Murten and Stein am Rhein, that have old town centres so apparently unchanged by time that they could have been preserved under glass, like parts of a watch (yes, they make watches in Switzerland, too).

So here we have the fundamental dichotomy of things Swiss – the untamed, majestic, adventuresome Alpine landscape, set against the tidy, just-so, watch-precision towns and cities. Goethe summed it up succinctly in his description of Switzerland as a combination of 'the colossal and the well-ordered'. It's two different sides of a highly valued coin. Spend it at your leisure.

Facts about the Country

HISTORY

Switzerland is seen as the ultimate neutral state, a paragon of virtue, too pure and too clever to sully its hands in the base conflicts that plague the rest of the world. Yet in 1845 the Austrian Chancellor, Metternich, wrote:

The (Swiss) Confederation staggers from evils into upheavals and represents for itself and for its neighbours an inexhaustible spring of unrest and disturbance.

Maybe that was true. Or maybe Metternich was simply still smarting from the way the Austrians had been booted out of Switzerland centuries before.

Pre-Confederation

The first inhabitants of the region were Celtic tribes. The most important of these were the Helvetii, who lived in the Jura and the Mittelland plain, and the Rhaetians, located in the Alpine region that became Graubünden. The Romans appeared on the scene in 107 BC by way of the Great St Bernard Pass, but their attempted conquest was indecisive owing to the difficulty of the terrain. Nevertheless, under Julius Caesar they defeated the Gauls in 58 BC, thereby gaining control of Gaul and present-day Switzerland. Two centuries of prosperity followed, in which Aventicum (now the site of Avenches) was established as the capital of Roman Switzerland.

In 260 AD the Germanic Alemanni tribe began the first of many incursions southwards, and by around 400, succeeded in driving the Romans from the northern side of the Alps altogether. The Alemanni settled in eastern Switzerland, and were joined by another Germanic tribe, the Burgundians, who settled in the west. The latter adopted Christianity and the Latin language, thereby starting the division between what became French-speaking and German-speaking Switzerland. The Franks conquered both tribes in the 6th century, but the two areas were torn asunder when Charlemagne's empire was partitioned in 870.

The territory was united under the Holy Roman Empire in 1032 but central control was never very tight, allowing neighbouring nobles to contest each other for local influence. One of the most successful of these was the Zähringen family, who founded and fortified towns as a means of securing their scattered possessions. In the 1300s they founded Fribourg, Bern and Murten, and built a castle at Thun. They were not alone in this policy; the Savoy family established a ring of castles around Lake Geneva, most notably the Château de Chillon.

The internal fighting of the nobles was all changed by the Germanic Habsburg family, which gradually extended its power throughout central Europe. Habsburg expansion was spearheaded by Rudolph I, who became the Holy Roman Emperor in 1273. He installed heavy-handed bailiffs to take care of the local administration of Swiss territories, and in this way gradually brought the squabbling nobles to heel.

The Swiss Confederation

Habsburg domination was deeply resented, and upon the death of Rudolph I in 1291, local leaders saw a chance to gain independence. The forest communities of Uri, Schwyz and Nidwalden formed an alliance on 1 August 1291. Central to the agreement was the assertion that they would not recognise any external judge or law. Their pact of mutual assistance is seen as the origin of the Swiss Confederation and the inaugural document is still preserved in the canton of Schwyz. The Latin name for the confederation, Confederatio Helvetica, survives in the 'CH' abbreviation for Switzerland (used on car number plates). The efforts of the founding cantons to free themselves from the yoke of the Habsburgs is personified in the tale of William Tell, who in all probability never actually existed as an individual. According

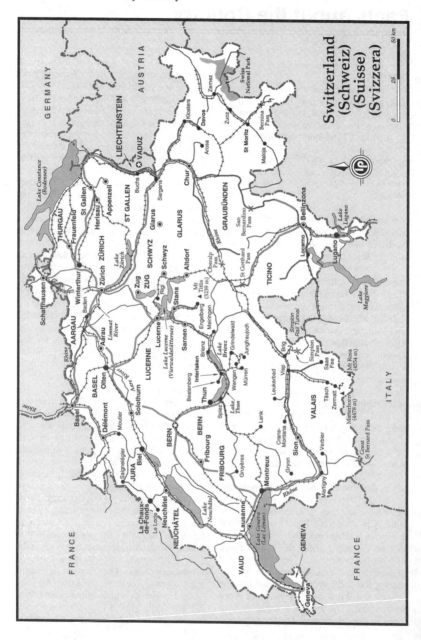

to the legend, it was the Habsburg bailiff, Gessler, who compelled Tell to shoot the apple off his son's head, in what must be the most famous episode in Swiss history. Tell got his revenge by later murdering Gessler at Küssnacht, by Lake Lucerne.

Duke Leopold responded to the Swiss shenanigans by dispatching a powerful Austrian army in 1315. The duke must have anticipated a straightforward victory against such ill-equipped forest folk, but his army was thoroughly defeated by the Swiss at Morgarten. The effective action of the union soon prompted other communities to join. Lucerne (1332) was followed by Zürich (1351), Glarus and Zug (1352), and Bern (1353). Further defeats of the Habsburgs followed at Sempach (1386) and Näfels (1388).

Encouraged by these successes, the Swiss gradually acquired a taste for territorial expansion themselves. Further land was seized from the Habsburgs. They took on Charles the Bold (the Duke of Burgundy) and defeated him at Grandson and Murten. Fribourg, Solothurn, Basel, Schaffhausen and Appenzell joined the Confederation, and the Swiss gained independence from Holy Roman Emperor Maximilian I after their victory at Dornach in 1499.

In 1513 the Confederation was at the peak of its territorial influence, and even had Milan under its protection, but finally the Swiss over-reached themelves. They squared up against a superior combined force of French and Venetians at Marignano in 1515 and lost. The Swiss army in the battle had been compiled without the support of several cantons, most noticeably the all-powerful Bern. This first defeat gave the Swiss cause for thought. In order to ensure that future armies would be full-strength, it would be necessary to curtail the autonomy of the cantons, something they were not prepared to do. Another consideration was that weaponry had advanced – soldiers had to be equipped with the new weapons – firearms – which was a very expensive proposition as the Swiss fighting reputation had been previously built on the use of the halberd, a combination axe, pick and pike on the end of a long staff.

The Swiss therefore decided to withdraw from the international scene by renouncing expansionist policies and declaring their neutrality. Not being a nation to waste useful skills, Swiss mercenaries continued to serve in other armies for centuries to come, and earned an unrivalled reputation for their skill and courage. (Even today the pope is protected by the Swiss Guard.) The mercenary policy (effectively, exporting war) actually helped to preserve Swiss neutrality, in at least two ways. It provided an outlet for aggression without ever involving the country in international disputes under in its own colours, and it showed the Swiss the economic sense of keeping war beyond its own borders – to feed off war rather than suffer from it. The policy only ceased when Swiss soldiers increasingly found themelves fighting on opposing sides, such as during the War of the Spanish Succession in 1709.

The Reformation

The Reformation in the 16th century caused upheaval throughout Europe. Ulrich Zwingli, from eastern Switzerland, started teaching the Protestant word in Zürich in 1519. The new faith spread rapidly, but

Ulrich Zwingli

central Switzerland remained Catholic. The result was conflict, and Zwingli was killed in fighting between the factions in 1531. But Zwingli's death did not halt the spread of the Reformation in the Confederation, and in the meantime, Calvin and Farel were thumping the Protestant pulpit in Geneva and Neuchâtel.

The Catholic church responded with the Counter Reformation, and while the rest of Europe was fighting it out in the Thirty Years' War, the Swiss closed ranks and kept out of trouble. They even prospered during the conflict, trading in food and materials which the fighting nations were unable to provide for themelves. At the end of the war in 1648 they were recognised in the Treaty of Westphalia as a neutral state.

Peasant unrest, fuelled by the burgeoning powers of the urban upper class over the rural areas, was quashed in 1653. However, religious disputes dragged on in Switzerland, in the Villmergen Wars of 1656 and 1712. At this time the Catholic cantons were sucked into a dangerous alliance with France that could have split the Confederation beyond repair had matters really come to a head. But the Catholic factions reluctantly agreed to

religious freedom and the country was able to get on with the serious business of making money. Switzerland gradually prospered as a financial and intellectual centre; the economic aspect driven to a great extent by the textile industry in the north-east.

The French invaded Switzerland in 1798 and established the Helvetic Republic. The new regime was liberal in many ways – sovereignty was invested in the people and cantonal frontiers were abolished – but the Swiss did not take too kindly to such centralised control. Internal fighting prompted Napoleon (who had now assumed power in France) to restore the former Confederation of cantons in 1803 (the Act of Mediation), but with France retaining overall jurisdiction. Further cantons also joined the Confederation at this time: Aargau, St Gallen, Graubünden, Ticino, Thurgau and Vaud. Napoleon was finally sent packing following his defeat by the British and Prussians at Waterloo. In 1815 the Congress of Vienna guaranteed Switzerland's independence and permanent neutrality, as well as adding the cantons of Valais, Geneva, and Neuchâtel. But politically the country had moved backwards, with the aristocrats

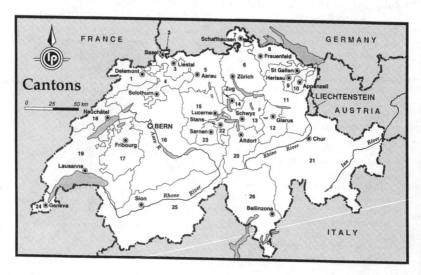

regaining most of their old powers in the Confederation.

Towards a Modern Constitution

The July Revolution in Paris in 1830 sparked off similar forces in several cantons so that the liberals came to power. Lucerne was particularly volatile; coup was followed by counter-coup, and the liberals were appalled when the Jesuits were invited to take over cantonal education. Civil war broke out in 1847 when the Protestant army, led by General Dufour, quickly crushed the Catholic cantons (including Lucerne) who had formed a separatist league (the Sonderbund). Victory by liberal forces was quickly underlined with the creation of a new federal constitution in 1848, which is largely still in place today. Various civil liberties were granted, such as equality before the law, freedom of association and freedom of place of residence.

The constitution was a neat compromise between advocates of central control and conservative forces wanting cantonal authority to be retained. Throughout the

```
CANTONS
 1   Jura (JU)
 2   Basel Town (BS)
 3   Basel District (BL)
 4   Solothurn (SO)
 5   Aargau (AG)
 6   Zürich (ZH)
 7   Schaffhausen (SH)
 8   Thurgau (TG)
 9   Appenzel Ausserrhoden (AR)
10   Appenzel Innerrhoden (AI)
11   St Gallen (SG)
12   Glarus (GL)
13   Schwyz (SZ)
14   Zug (ZG)
15   Lucerne (LU)
16   Bern (BE)
17   Fribourg (FR)
18   Neuchâtel (NE)
19   Vaud (VD)
20   Uri (UR)
21   Graubünden (GR)
22   Nidwalden (NW)
23   Obwalden (OW)
24   Geneva (GE)
25   Valais (VS)
26   Ticino (TI)
```

gradual move towards one nation, each canton remained fiercely independent, even to the extent of controlling its own currency and postal services and levying its own custom duties. All these powers were transferred to federal authority, but cantons nevertheless retained legislative (Grand Council) and executive (State Council) powers to deal with local matters. Furthermore, the federal assembly that was set up to take care of national issues was composed of two chambers, one of which gave the cantons their voice. The consent of both houses was required to pass a federal law (see the Government section later in this chapter). Bern was established as the capital and the seat of power.

Having achieved political stability, Switzerland was able to concentrate on economic and social matters. Relatively poor in mineral resources, it developed industries predominantly dependent on highly skilled labour. Industry was mainly of the cottage type, based upon peasants supplementing dwindling earnings from the land. A network of railways and roads was built, opening up previously inaccessible Alpine regions and helping the development of tourism. Between 1850 and 1860, six new commercial banks were set up. The International Red Cross was founded in Geneva in 1863 by Henri Dunant, and compulsory free education was introduced.

Many of the new political leaders had fingers in various economic pies, and patronage and nepotism became the standard way to conduct government. Movements towards greater democracy soon gathered momentum in the cantons, particularly in Zürich, and made it inevitable that there would be some change at the national level. In 1874 the constitution was revised to enable citizens to partake in direct democracy. In the years that followed, political battle lines gradually moved from struggles between liberals and Catholics to one between workers and the bourgeoisie.

The 20th Century

During WWI, Switzerland came quite close

to violating its much vaunted neutrality. German-speaking Switzerland (but not the French or Italian parts) was pro-Germany, and secret military information was passed to the German side. In 1917 Hermann Hoffmann, a federal councillor, even tried to bring about a separate peace between Germany and Russia. He was forced to resign when the plan became public. In physical term, Switzerland's only involvement in WWI lay in the organising of Red Cross units, although the civilian army was ready to defend the country's borders if need arose. After peace was restored, Switzerland joined the League of Nations under the proviso that its involvement would be purely financial and economic rather than entailing any possible military sanctions.

Swiss industry profited during the war, but the rewards did not filter down to the working classes. Mobilisation of the civilian army affected wages, and food prices more than doubled during the period. In November 1918 a general strike brought the country to a halt. The paralysis was only temporary: the army was called in and within three days the strike leaders had capitulated. But the strike was not a waste of time. It eased the passage of a referendum on proportional representation, and some of the strikers' demands were subsequently accepted by the Federal Council: a 48-hour week was introduced, collective contract-bargaining between workers and employers was developed, and the social security system was extended.

The conciliatory mood spread and in 1937 the Swiss Metalworkers and Watchmakers' Union created the *Arbeitsfrieden* with the Federation of Metal and Machine Industry Employers, under which all future disputes would be solved by agreement. One side would abandon strikes, and the other would no longer use such tactics as 'lockouts' and 'scab' labour. This contract has been periodically renewed, and subsequently imitated by other Swiss industries, giving the country an envied industrial relations record ever since. Not one full day was lost to strikes in 1987.

Switzerland was left largely unscathed by WWII. Again the civilian army was mobilised; Henri Guisan was elected as the general. Surrounded by Axis powers, Switzerland was in a very vulnerable position in 1940. In July of that year, Guisan, in a symbolic but effective move, called all top military personnel to the Rütli meadow (the site of the 1291 Oath of Allegiance), and instilled in those present and the world at large the Swiss determination to defend its soil at all costs. Swiss neutrality remained unbreached (barring some accidental bombing in 1940, 1944 and 1945), and its territory proved to be a safe haven for escaping Allied prisoners. For more on Switzerland during WWII, see the boxed aside near Schaffhausen in the North-East Switzerland chapter.

Post WWII

While the rest of Europe underwent the painful process of rebuilding from the ravages of war, Switzerland was able to expand from an already powerful commercial, financial and industrial base. Zürich developed as an international banking and insurance centre. The World Health Organisation, the World Council of Churches, and many other international organisations based their headquarters in Geneva. Social reform were also introduced, such as old-age pensions in 1948.

Post-war prosperity was largely built on the backs of foreign workers, who mostly had menial jobs, while Swiss workers were often elevated to supervisory roles. In 1945 foreigners made up 5% of residents in Switzerland; by 1974 this figure had grown to 17%. Foreign workers had (and have) few political rights, and in theory, could have their residency status rescinded in times of economic hardship. Indeed, tens of thousands left (voluntarily) in the depression of 1974-5.

Afraid that its neutrality would be compromised, Switzerland declined to become a member of the United Nations, NATO or the EEC (European Economic Community as the European Union was then called). It did,

Defence

Despite the fact that Switzerland has managed to avoid international conflicts for over 400 years, every able-bodied male starts national service at age 20. After 15 weeks of training he is released, but remains attached to a unit and eligible for call-up until the age of 32. From 33 to 42 (52 for officers) he remains in the military reserves, and has to attend a three-week refresher course every two years. Throughout this period he keeps his rifle, ammunition and full kit (including gas mask) at home, and has to attend target practice sessions. The army is subject to Federal Council control, and a general is only appointed as commander-in-chief of the armed forces in times of national emergency. Within 48 hours over 400,000 civilian soldiers can be mobilised. Switzerland's army previously numbered 600,000, but the number was diminished in 1995 by reducing the stint in the reserves.

In December 1989 a surprisingly large number of people (35.6%) voted in favour of abolishing the army, yet conscientious objectors were still getting sentenced to imprisonment by military courts. Civil service as an alternative to military service for objectors was rejected in an earlier referendum in 1984, but finally got through in 1991.

In the last 55 years, Switzerland has made comprehensive preparations against foreign aggression. Besides the civilian army, a whole infrastructure is in place to repel any invasion. After military service, men then have to undertake civil protection service until age 60, requiring more training courses and assignment of duties in the event of attack. Roads and bridges have built-in recesses at key points so that they can be primed for explosion without delay. All new buildings must have a substantial air-raid capacity, and underground car parks can be instantly converted to bunkers.

Over 90% of the population can currently be sheltered underground; this figure will reach 100% at the end of the decade. Fully equipped emergency hospitals, unused yet maintained, await underneath ordinary hospitals. Food and raw materials have been stockpiled. It's a sobering thought, as you explore the countryside, to realise that those apparently undisturbed mountains and lakes hide a network of military installations and storage depots. The message that comes across today is the same as that dealt out by the country's fearless mercenaries of centuries ago: don't mess with the Swiss. ∎

however, join UNESCO (the United Nations Educational, Scientific and Cultural Organisation) and EFTA (the European Free Trade Association).

In the face of other EFTA nations applying for EU (European Union) membership, Switzerland finally made its own application in 1992. This was a pre-emptive move by the parliament, because in the meantime, it was necessary to hold a referendum on membership of the EEA (European Economic Area). The EEA was seen as a sort of halfway house towards the EU composed of EFTA members, under which there would be the free trade advantages of the EU without the political commitment. A majority of citizens and a majority of cantons had to vote in favour in order for EEA membership to be ratified.

Despite the strong support of industry and political parties, Swiss citizens were unimpressed, and the motion failed on both counts in the vote in December 1992. Although in percentage term the defeat was a narrow one

(49.7% voted 'yes', 50.3% voted 'no'), only seven cantons were in favour when at least 12 were needed. Those in favour included all the French-speaking cantons (Geneva, Vaud, Neuchâtel, Jura, Fribourg and Valais) and only one German-speaking canton (Basel). Overall, French-speakers were three to one in favour of joining, and there was bitter resentment towards German-speakers for keeping Switzerland isolated.

All this rather upset plans to join the EU. In consequence of the EEA vote, Switzerland's EU application has been put on ice, without actually being withdrawn. In the meantime the pro-EEA and EU lobby has not given up hope, and is pushing to re-start EEA negotiations in 1998. The government has ruled out new EU negotiations before the year 2000, but talks are continuing with the EU to try to win economic concessions for Switzerland in the meantime.

GEOGRAPHY

Above all, Switzerland is known as an

Alpine country. The Alps and Pre-Alps make up 60% of Switzerland's 41,285 sq km. The Jura Mountains account for 10% and the Swiss Mittelland (also called the Central Plateau) comprises the remaining 30%. The land is 45% meadow and pasture, 24% forest and 6% arable. Farming of cultivated land is intensive and cows graze on the upper slopes in the summer as soon as the retreating snow line permits.

The Alps occupy the central and southern regions of the country. The Dufour summit (4634m) of Monte Rosa is the highest point, although the Matterhorn (4478m) is better known. A series of high passes in the south provide overland access into Italy. Glaciers account for an area of 2000 sq km; most notable is the Aletsch Glacier, which at 169 sq km is the largest valley glacier in Europe.

The St Gotthard Massif in the centre of Switzerland is the source of many lakes and rivers, such as the Rhine and the Rhône. The Jura Mountains straddle the northern border with France. These mountains peak at around 1700m and are less steep and less severely eroded than the Alps.

The Bernese Mittelland is between the two mountain systems, running in a band from Lake Geneva in the south-west to Lake Constance in the north-east. It is a region of hills crisscrossed by rivers, ravines and winding valleys. This area has spawned the most populous cities and is where much of the agricultural activity takes place. The one canton entirely south of the Alps is Ticino, home to the northern part of Lake Maggiore: at 193m the lake is the lowest point in the country.

Lakes are dotted throughout the country, except in the Jura where the substrata rock is mostly too brittle and porous. The majority of lakes, including all those in the Bernese Mittelland, were created from the depressions and basins left by glacial ice or moraines (the debris from melting glaciers) after the ice age.

CLIMATE

The mountains are mainly responsible for the variety of local and regional micro-

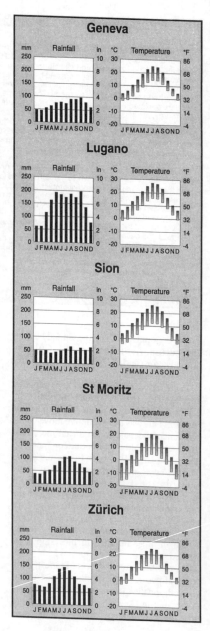

climates enjoyed (or suffered) by Switzerland. Air currents waft in from the four points of the compass, each bringing a different type of weather. Ticino in the south has a hot, Mediterranean climate. Most of the rest of the country has a central European climate, with temperatures typically around 20 to 25°C in summer and 2 to 6°C in winter, with spring and autumn hovering around the 7 to 14°C mark. Valais in the south-west is noted for being dry. Staldenried in Valais gets just 53 cm of precipitation per year, as opposed to 257 cm at Rochers de Naye, Vaud, under 75 km away as the cloud flies. The coldest area is the Jura, and in particular the Brevine Valley, a natural trap for cold air.

Summer tends to bring a lot of sunshine, but also the most rain. You will need to be prepared for a range of temperatures dependent on altitude. Look out for the *Föhn*, a hot, dry wind that sweeps down into the valleys and can be oppressively uncomfortable (though some find its warming effect refreshing). It can strike at any time of the year, but especially in spring and autumn. Daily weather reports covering 25 resorts are displayed in major train stations.

Statistics can be used to back up all sorts of meteorological claims. The sun obviously gets about a bit: La Chaux-de-Fonds, Sierre, Andermatt, Locarno and Crans-Montana are all said to enjoy the sunniest climate in Switzerland.

ECOLOGY & ENVIRONMENT

Since the 1950s, the Federal Government has introduced measures to protect forests, lakes and marshland from environmental damage. Mountain areas have fragile ecosystems and are extremely vulnerable to pollution and environmental damage. Switzerland, along with its Alpine neighbours, signed the Alpine Convention in 1991, which seeks to reduce damage caused by motor traffic and tourism. Switzerland's reluctance to lift its weight limit for transit lorries through the Alps from 28 tonnes to 40 tonnes has been a major sticking point with its negotiations for closer ties with the EU. The Alp Action Group (☎ 022-735 92 95) is based in Geneva. It was created to try to protect the Alpine environment, which annually receives 120 million visitors. Many mountain resorts now have a policy of

Switzerland Goes Green

Switzerland produces 450 kg of waste per annum per person, half the figure for the Americans, but 28% more than the average for the EU. A Federal Office for the Environment slogan advocates 'Reduction, Recovery and Recycling' with some success – the Swiss are amongst the most diligent recyclers in the world.

Paper is collected regularly from households, provided it is tied in neat bundles (it invariably is!). Colour-coded recycling bins are common, accepting glass, aluminium, PET plastic, and used oil. Switzerland ranks third in the world in terms of bottle recycling: around 60% of non-returnable drinks bottles are recycled, as compared to about 12% in Britain. One-litre beer bottles are invariably deposit-refundable, as are bottles for many of the cheaper cap-topped wines. Many supermarkets have automatic bottle-return machines *(Flaschen Rüchnahmne)* that will give you a credit note against your shopping. A returnable bottle may be re-used 50 times. A few years ago, the use of phosphate-containing detergents was banned in Switzerland, and since 1986 battery retailers have had to provide containers for the collection of used batteries. A law designed to reduce excess packaging entitles customers to unwrap unnecessary packaging on site (and many do) and leave it for the shop to dispose of.

Swiss diligence in regard to recycling is encouraged by financial considerations. Most cantons have introduced specially marked bags that must be used for all rubbish that is not recycled. These bags are extremely expensive (Sfr1.50 to Sfr5 *each!*) so they are used only when necessary (and as much is crammed in as possible). The high price covers incineration costs, but not all Swiss are prepared to pay this environmental tariff. The phenomenon of 'rubbish tourism' has recently appeared, by which households take a day out to a canton that has not yet introduced the bag tariff, see the sights...and dump their rubbish. ■

upgrading existing facilities rather than expanding them.

The country also has an efficient recycling industry; households dutifully separate their waste into different categories prior to collection. See also the boxed aside.

FLORA & FAUNA

Climatic variation means that vegetation ranges from palm trees in Ticino to nordic flora in the Alps. At higher elevations, flowers start to bloom from April to July, depending on the species. The famous Edelweiss, with star-shaped flowers, grows at up to 3500m. Alpine rhododendrons, known locally as Alpenroses, are numerous at 2500m. Spring gentians are small, violet-blue flowers. White crocuses are early bloomers (from March) at lower elevations. Alpine flowers are usually protected and should not be picked.

In the Swiss Mittelland, trees are a mixture of deciduous and conifers. At altitude of 800m conifers become more numerous. The red spruce is common at lower levels; the larch and arolla pine mostly take over higher up. At around 2000m , tall trees are replaced by bushes and scrub which finally yield to Alpine meadows (these can be rich in flora, despite the altitude). Like in most of the rest of the continent, forests are being depleted by pollution and acid rain, increasing the risk of avalanches and landslides.

Despite strong environmental legislation, animal life is on the retreat in Switzerland. But there have been some success stories – species that were once extinct in the wild have been reintroduced and are thriving, not least in the protected environs of the Swiss National Park (see the Graubünden chapter). Eighty-one species of bird are currently threatened with extinction.

A bird often seen fluttering around at mountain tops is the *Alpendohle*, a relative of the crow; it has jet-black feathers and yellow beak. Rather larger Alpine birds, with a wingspan reaching 2.5m or more, are the golden eagle and the bearded vulture.

The Edelweiss is the national floral emblem of Switzerland.

The Red Spruce is especially abundant throughout northern Switzerland. Once favoured by farmers for its usefulness, it has now become susceptible to acid rain and the bark beetle.

The *Alpendohle* is often seen hunting for food scraps at mountain-top restaurants.

The most distinctive Alpine animal is the ibex, a mountain goat which has huge, curved and ridged horns. There are about 12,000 left in Switzerland, and they can migrate up to 3000m. The chamois (a horned antelope) is more timid but equally at home scampering around on the peaks – it can leap four metres vertically. Roe deer or the larger red deer can also be seen in forested regions and Alpine pastures. Marmots (chunky rodents related to the squirrel) are other famous residents. These hibernating, monogamous creatures live in colonies within complex labyrinthine burrows that can take generations to build. They mark their territory and recognise co-colonists by smell. A sentry, which will raise itself to its hind legs to scan the horizon, is often posted to repel alien marmots and warn of predators.

GOVERNMENT & POLITICS

The modern Swiss Confederation is made up of 23 cantons; three are subdivided, bringing the total to 26. Each has its own constitution and legislative body for dealing with local issues, and has a great deal of independent autonomy. The Jura achieved full cantonal status as late as 1979, after a protracted struggle with its former ruler, Bern.

National legislative power is in the hands of the Federal Assembly, which consists of two chambers. The lower chamber, the National Council *(Nationalrat)*, has 200 members. Seats are allocated to cantons in proportion to population size, though each canton gets at least one. The upper chamber, the States Council *(Ständerat)*, is composed of 46 members, two per canton (one per half-canton). The Federal Assembly elects seven members to form the Federal Council, which holds executive power. All elections are for a four-year term except for the posts of president and vice-president of the Confederation, which are rotated annually. The holder of these posts has no special authority over the rest of the Federal Council. The vice-president always succeeds the president. In this way the governing body is not dominated by any one individual. In fact,

many Swiss would be hard-pressed to name their president.

Elected members of parliament are usually part-timers, and receive payment only for expenses. Incredibly, the cost of running the parliament is a mere Sfr7 per person per annum (no wonder they don't want to join the bureaucratic EU). At the last general election, in October 1995, both the left-wing Social Democrats (54 National seats, 5 States seats) and the right-wing Swiss People's Party, formerly the Farmers' Party (29 National, 5 States) made gains, while the Radical Democrats (45 National, 17 States) held steady and the Christian Democrats (34 National, 16 States) fell back slightly. Other parties with national seats include the Evangelical Party, the Free Party (formerly the Motorist's Party) and environmentalist groups. The composition of the Federal Council adheres to a 'magic formula' unchanged since 1959: two members each from the Radical, Christian and Social Democrats and one from the Swiss People's Party.

Laws can actually be influenced directly by the Swiss people, provided enough signatures can be collected from active citizens: 50,000 to force a full referendum on proposed laws, and 100,000 to initiate legislation. In any case important federal decisions are generally subject to a referendum. The system is known as direct democracy, and is one that tends to lead to a government based on compromise. Surprisingly for such a democratic people, women only won the right to vote in federal elections in 1971. In some cantons women gained a local vote only in the last few years. A few cantons still vote by a show of hands in an open-air parliament *(Landsgemeinde)*.

As if these two tiers of government weren't enough, each Swiss citizen is also the member of a commune *(Gemeinde)*, the smallest political unit. There are around 3000 in the whole country. Even communes have significant autonomy to act independently. Citizens regularly have to turn out to vote on issues at all three levels: federal, cantonal and communal. The commune has its own councillors with responsibility for finances, fire services, taxes, welfare, schools and civil defence. Most adults get involved in community service in one way or another.

The Swiss political system works from the bottom upwards, and it is actually membership of a commune that invests constituents with Swiss citizenship, rather than vice versa. The electorate (ie private individuals) is viewed as holding ultimate authority, and is often referred to as the 'sovereign', as in 'the sovereign has decided' when a referendum has been accepted or rejected. Subsidiarity *(Subsidiarität)* is a principle that has guided Swiss politics for centuries. It describes the view that the lowest level of authority that can effectively perform a task should be left alone to do so. A new constitution for Switzerland is planned for 1998.

ECONOMY

Switzerland has a mixed economy with the emphasis on private ownership. The only industries nationalised outright are the telephone, telegraph, post and some railways (though privatisation plans are afoot for the telephone and railway). Other than municipal enterprises, everything else is in private hands and operates according to capitalist principles, with the occasional subsidy thrown in. A good proportion of the wealth generated is channelled back into the community via social welfare programmes. The overall result is very efficient and strikes are rare. But even Switzerland is not immune from economic downturns. Like much of the rest of the world, the Swiss economy went into recession in the early 1990s. In 1996, unemployment was over 4% (unusually high for Switzerland), partially caused by Swiss firms relocating abroad to seek lower costs. Inflation was under 2% and expected to stay that way.

Agriculture occupies 5.5% of the working population, and Swiss farmers enjoy one of the highest levels of protection in the world, keeping prices high. Cartel agreements in other sectors of the economy also contribute to general high prices and restrict competition. Over 60% of workers are employed in

service areas as compared to around 34% in industry. In the absence of other raw materials, hydro-electric power is now the main source of energy (59%). Nuclear energy production (36%) is high but diminishing, following a referendum initiative to freeze construction of nuclear power stations. Chemicals, machine tools, watches and clocks are the most important exports. Silks and embroidery, also important, are produced to a high quality.

SMH (Société Suisse de Micro-élelectronique et d'Horlogerie) unleashed the Swatch onto the world. This innovative product revitalised the Swiss watch-making industry, which had been taking a battering at the hands of cheap Japanese models. At the top end of the watch market (where watches cost thousands in any currency you care to name) Swiss domination was never broken, and it has a 90% worldwide share. Swiss breakthroughs in science and industry include vitamins, DDT, gas turbines and milk chocolate. They also, for their sins, developed the modern formula for life insurance.

Swiss banks are a magnet for foreign funds, attracted by political and monetary stability. The three biggest banks are the Union Bank of Switzerland, the Swiss Bank Corporation, and Credit Suisse. The country is the fourth most important financial centre in the world, after New York, London and Tokyo. In most cantons there are more banks than dentists, and Switzerland is one of the world leaders for private banking.

Tourism is important to the economy – it's the third biggest export with a turnover of over Sfr20 billion. The Swiss aim to make things as easy as possible for foreign visitors. (It's certainly easy to spend money.) Based on the number of overnight stays, Graubünden is easily the most popular holiday region, followed by Valais, Central Switzerland and the Bernese Oberland. Summer brings nearly 50% more foreign tourists than winter.

Switzerland's most important trading partner is Germany, responsible for 33% of imports and 23% of exports. EU countries as

Bank Accounts

Voltaire once said: 'If you see a Swiss banker jump out of a window, follow him. There is surely money to be made.' There's certainly no shortage of bankers to follow: the country has 630 domestic banks and over 200 foreign banks. The Swiss are great savers, storing away an unusually high level of their income. Banks have a long tradition, but really took off after WWII, thanks to their reputation for discretion and secrecy.

Numbered bank accounts are a well-known Swiss institution. These are where the account is identified purely by a number, rather than being linked to a name, so anonymity is assured. The anonymity brings the risk of attracting funds of dubious origin, or money that is simply trying to avoid the attention of the tax inspectors.

Numbered accounts were introduced in WWII, allegedly to provide cover for funds escaping from Nazi control. In 1995 Swiss banks received bad press for not doing enough to trace the owners of numerous deposit boxes and secret accounts, dormant since WWII. The banks owned up to finding US$34 million and have been quite happy to hang on to these assets all these years. But Israeli sources claim that up to US$6.7 billion worth of cash and valuables could be involved, seized from holocaust victims and deposited by Nazis. For years Swiss banks have been a favourite destination for funds spirited away by corrupt African leaders. It is believed that the deposed dictator of Mali, Moussa Traore, deposited at least US$1 billion – this from one of the poorest countries in the world. President Mobutu of Zaïre is estimated to have US$8 billion hidden away.

Perfectly legitimate money flows in too, of course, attracted by the stability of the country. When Iraq invaded Kuwait in 1990 there was a huge influx of money into Switzerland from the Middle East. That was also the year that a new law against money laundering was introduced. There is now an obligation for the banks to identify the true owner of the monies deposited with them in the event of an investigation, and they can be prosecuted if they hinder the identification of suspected 'dirty money' (proceeds from drug or arms trafficking, etc). The legislation was inspired by the arrest in Switzerland in 1988

Typical dress of an 18th century banker from Geneva.

of two drug traffickers who deposited Sfr1.5 billion in a Zürich bank (the deposit drew attention as it was marginally higher than the average Swiss salary cheque).

In practice, anybody can still open a Swiss bank account, numbered or otherwise. All you have to do is sign a form declaring that the money is rightfully yours. Responding to such a question with an untruth would hardly cause great pangs of conscience in the average underworld boss. ■

a whole account for 79% of imports and 62% of exports, which is why most economists (but not all) agree that there will be an economic cost if Switzerland stays out of the EU. The country usually has a negative visible trade balance, which is offset by earnings from investment income and the current account. The national income per capita is the second highest in the world (behind Luxembourg) at US$37,180.

POPULATION & PEOPLE

With a population of 7,019,000, Switzerland averages 170 inhabitants per sq km. The Alpine districts are sparsely populated, meaning that the Mittelland is densely settled, especially round the shores of the larger lakes. Zürich is the largest city, with 363,000 inhabitants; next comes Basel (190,000), Geneva (175,000) and Bern (133,000). Most people are of Germanic origin, as indicated by the breakdown of languages spoken in Switzerland. German speakers account for 66% of the population, French 18%, Italian 10% and Romansch under 1%.

As many as 18.9% of people living in the country are residents but not Swiss citizens – over 1.33 million. This figure does *not* include the many seasonal workers, tempo-rary residents and international civil servants and administrators. Most of the permanent residents arrived after WWII: initially from Italy and Spain, and subsequently from the rest of southern Europe.

The other side of the equation is the Swiss community living abroad, numbering about 528,000. Historically, Swiss left the country because of domestic food shortages (thou-

The Swiss National Character

Some people believe that the magnificent, untamed Swiss landscape is wasted on the native dwellers. There's an old joke that imagines that heaven and hell are run by a number of European nations. In heaven, the Swiss are the organisers (and the French are the lovers). In hell, the Swiss are the lovers (and the Italians are the organisers). This joke illustrates the oft-expressed view that the people are a dull, serious, colourless, undemonstrative lot, somewhat petty, yet extremely efficient. Like many generalisa-tions, this picture of the Swiss character is an inadequate one. The Swiss people are as varied as the languages they speak. To make a few more generalisations: the French Swiss make a habit of kissing each other on both cheeks upon meeting (a custom the undemonstrative British would have a hard time adapting to); the Italian Swiss have a Mediterranean complexion and outlook in a canton where *dolce vita* competes with the *Arbeit* ethos; in the valleys of south-east Switzerland, many villagers still speak Romansch, a language with its roots in ancient Latin that well reflects their enduring, rural lifestyle.

Traditional men's attire from the Appenzell region.

But what about the majority, the German Swiss, I hear you ask. They are what we mean by the typical Swiss; efficient and honest yet conventional, pedan-tic and sticklers for the rules. It's true they do exist – the term *Bünzli* describes them, but every society has such people. Ask any German Swiss about the German Swiss national character and they'll probably tell you in great detail how the people in their town, their street, their house, are different to all other Swiss. I know somebody who goes to university in Zürich; she complains the Zürichers are cold and money-oriented, not like the people of Basel who are much more friendly and open.

The people of Appenzellerland have a reputation among other Swiss for being simple folk with intellects that could blunt the sharpest knife. The Bernese are considered slow and parochial. You may encounter many other regional differences if you travel with an open mind. Of course, you may also find that your preconceptions about the Swiss are confirmed, but travel is always more enjoyable if you allow yourself the possibility of being surprised by the people you meet. ■

Traditional ceremonial dress from the Appenzell region is characterised by a coif (headdress).

sands died of hunger in 1817) and through mercenary service (halted in 1859). Nowadays emigration is more due to the expansion of Swiss firms abroad.

EDUCATION

Control of education is at the cantonal level, with the consequence that there are 26 different systems in operation. They all adhere to a greater or lesser extent to a national standard, but there are variations in types of schools, curricula, and teaching methods. It wasn't even until the referendum in 1985 that it was agreed to universally start the school year at the end of summer.

Most children attend nursery school from age four. Compulsory schooling starts at age six or seven and continues for eight or (usually) nine years. Towards the end of this period students are eased into different streams: apprenticeship, vocational, or academic. The latter two streams usually continue with two to three years of post-compulsory education, leading to entry into a vocational college (medicine, teaching etc) or a general university or institute. There are eight cantonal universities.

Apprenticeships are given in private companies, and at the same time the trainee usually attends part-time courses in a college. There remains a shortage of skilled labour in the country, forcing some Swiss firms to expand abroad. Switzerland is one of the highest spenders on research and development in the world (2.7% of GDP).

ARTS

Switzerland does not have a very strong tradition in the arts, even though many foreign writers and artists (such as Voltaire, Byron, Shelley and Turner) have visited and settled, attracted by the beauty and tranquillity of the mountains and lakes. The 18th century writings of Rousseau in Geneva played an important part in the development of democracy. Influential artists settled in Zürich in the early 20th century and created the Dada movement.

In contrast, many creative Swiss left the country to make their name abroad, such as the film director Jean-Luc Godard, the artist Paul Klee and the architect Le Corbusier.

Writers & Artists

Few Swiss writers have gained international attention. Hermann Hesse is by far the best known novelist, though he was German born and naturalised Swiss. The linguistic diversity in the country makes it very hard to have a literary tradition. Carl Spitteler (1845-1924) won the Nobel prize in 1919 for his writings in German. Max Frisch, writing a generation later, has been translated into English and often dwells on the restrictions of Swiss society.

Paul Klee work can be seen in the art museum in Bern. He was born in Bern yet he never actually acquired Swiss citizenship and did most of his work in Germany. Klee (1879-1940) created abstract works which used colour, line and form to evoke a variety of sensations.

Alberto Giacometti (1901-66), a sculptor from Graubünden who settled in Paris, dabbled in cubism and surrealism before developing his distinctive stick-like figures (expressive, apparently, of individual isolation). His father, Giovanni, and his uncle, Augusto, are also well known artists. You can see much of their work in the art museums in Chur and Zürich.

The most 'Swiss' artist in lineage, residence and the subject matter of his work is Ferdinand Hodler (see the North-West Switzerland chapter for more information about him). The motorised sculptures of Jean Tinguely, mostly cobbled together from discards, can be seen especially in Basel and Fribourg.

Music & Theatre

Until the 17th century, folk music and religious music were the only genres that developed in Switzerland. The country still lacks famous exponents: Arthur Honegger (1892-1955) is the only Swiss composer of note. He settled in Paris and co-founded the avant-garde 'Les Six'.

Despite this dearth, music is strongly emphasised: there is a full-sized symphony orchestra in every main city. Music festivals are held throughout the year: two of the most famous are the Lucerne International Music Festival and the Montreux Jazz Festival.

The theatre scene flourishes, even in English in Geneva and Zürich. Go to Bern to visit small-scale, atmospheric cellar *(Keller)* theatres, where plays are often performed in dialect.

Architecture

Gothic and Renaissance architecture are evident in urban areas, especially Bern. Rural Swiss houses vary according to region, but the typical chalet-style is generally characterised by steep, ridged roofs with wide, overhanging eaves, and balconies and verandahs which are usually enlivened by colourful floral displays, particularly of geraniums. Anybody interested in regional architecture should visit the Ballenberg Museum outside Brienz (see the Freilichtmuseum Ballenberg section in the Bernese Overland chapter). The region of Ticino offers an architectural itinerary exploring more modern styles. Le Corbusier is the country's best known architectural export (see the La Chaux-de-Fonds section in the Neuchâtel, Fribourg & Jura chapter).

SOCIETY & CONDUCT
Traditional Culture

In a few mountain regions such as Valais, people still wear traditional rural costumes, but dressing up is usually reserved for festivals. Every spring, hardy herders climb to Alpine pastures with their cattle and live in summer huts while tending their herds. They gradually descend back to village level as the grassland is grazed. Both the departure and the return is a cause for celebrations and processions through the village. Cows are decorated with garlands of flowers for the processions to and from the pastures, and they each have a bell with a distinct ring hung around their necks, which help them to be found.

Yodelling and playing the Alp horn are also part of the Alpine tradition. Swiss wrestling is another event that is featured in frequent festivals.

Festivals and carnivals crop up in urban as well as rural areas. Sometimes ancient traditions and customs are inherent in the celebrations.

Dos & Don'ts

In general the Swiss are a law-abiding nation; even minor transgressions such as littering can cause offence. Always shake hands when being introduced to a Swiss, and again when leaving. This is standard behaviour, even with young and casual people. Formal titles should also be used, except among youngsters – *Herr* for men and *Frau* for women. It is also customary to greet the proprietor upon entering a shop, bar or café, and to say goodbye when leaving. Public displays of affection are fine, but are more common in French Switzerland than in the slightly more formal German-speaking parts. Exchanging kisses (three times, alternating cheeks) upon meeting is a common ritual in French Switzerland.

The Swiss are punctual, and will expect you to be too. At the dinner table, everybody waits for the host to make a toast prior to drinking, and before your impatient lips stretch for that soothing libation, you must chink glasses with all present while looking them in the eye. Before tucking into the food, the cry of *en Guete* or *bon appétit* is heard. Most Swiss go to bed early so don't overstay your welcome if you're invited to somebody's home (and if you do get invited, take a gift), and don't telephone anybody after about 9 pm.

On the beach, nude bathing is usually limited to restricted areas, but topless bathing is common in many parts. Women should be wary of taking their tops off as a matter of course. The rule is, if nobody else seems to be doing it, don't. You're not there to educate the locals.

Dress codes are pretty relaxed in Switzerland. It's not unusual to see office workers, bank clerks and tourist office staff wearing casual clothes like jeans. But men would be advised to wear a jacket and tie when dining in some of the top restaurants mentioned in this book. It is no problem for men to wear shorts away from the beach.

Sport

The number one activity is walking, with 40% of the population regularly taking walks in the countryside. Skiing is of course very popular, and Swiss competitors usually win a good haul of medals at international winter sports events. Swimming, mountaineering, cycling, fishing and football are also favourite pastimes.

Shooting and gymnastic clubs are popular with male adults. The interest in shooting is a spillover from the need to maintain a minimum standard with service weapons while in the reserves. There are 3600 shooting clubs in Switzerland. There is a strange running race, unique to Switzerland, called the *Waffenlaufen*, where runners complete a course of between 18 and 42 km, dressed in military uniform, complete with rucksack and rifle.

RELIGION

The country is split pretty evenly between Protestantism (in decline since WWII, now down to 40%) and Roman Catholicism (46%). Most of the rest of the population are 'unaffiliated'. The predominant faith varies between cantons. Bern is a Protestant stronghold, followed by Vaud, Zürich, Thurgau, Neuchâtel and Glarus. Strong Catholic areas are Valais, Ticino, Uri, Unterwalden and Schwyz, followed by Fribourg, Lucerne, Zug and the Jura. Curiously, the two half-cantons of Appenzell are at odds: Ausserrhoden is strongly Protestant while nine out of 10 people in Innerrhoden are Catholic. Some churches are supported entirely by donations from the public while others receive state subsidies.

LANGUAGE

Located in the corner of Europe where the German, French and Italian language areas meet, the linguistic melting pot that is Switzerland (Schweiz, Suisse, Svizzera) has three official federal languages: German (spoken by about 64% of the population), French (19%) and Italian (8%). A fourth language, Rhaeto-Romanic, or Romansch, is spoken by under 1% of the population, mainly in the canton of Graubünden. Derived from Latin, it's a linguistic relic which, along with Friulian and Ladin across the border in Italy, has survived in the isolation of mountain valleys. In 1938, Romansch was recognised as an official national language by referendum. In 1996, a further referendum gave Romansch partial status as an official federal language, together with guarantees for its preservation and promotion.

Being Understood in English

The English language is not a compulsory subject in Swiss schools. That's surprising, as generally the Swiss speak English very well, especially in German Switzerland. Ask a German-speaking Swiss if they speak English and you normally get one of two answers: 'a little' means they speak it fluently, but a philosophical discussion on etymology and epistemology in English would probably be beyond their grasp; a simple 'yes' means that your ego is about to get a battering – they speak English better than you do, and no doubt know what those obscure 'ology' words mean into the bargain. Most people working in 'service' areas (tourist office staff, telephone operators, hotel and office receptionists, restaurant staff, shopkeepers) speak some English.

Nevertheless, don't automatically assume that everyone you meet does speak English,

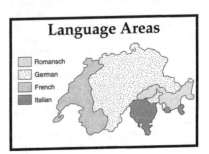

Language Areas

Romansch
German
French
Italian

especially in smaller, less-touristy towns where English has less penetration. It is simple courtesy to greet people with *Grüezi* (hello) and to enquire *Sprechen Sie Englisch?* (Do you speak English?) before launching into English. And don't feel discouraged if your clumsy attempts at speaking German immediately elicit a response in English – your efforts will still be appreciated.

In French Switzerland you shouldn't have too many problems being understood either, though the locals' grasp of English is likely to be less complete than that of German speakers. Italian Switzerland is where you will have the greatest difficulty. Most locals speak some French and/or German in addition to Italian, but English has a lower priority. Even so, you will find that the majority of restaurants and hotels have at least one English-speaking staff member.

In the Romansch-speaking parts of Graubünden, those involved in the tourist industry usually speak English, but ordinary country folk probably won't. Instead, they may offer you one of the other three national languages, usually German.

Swiss Languages
For pronunciation guidelines, and a useful table of conversational vocabulary and phrases, turn to the Language Guide at the back of this book.

Swiss German Though German-speaking Swiss have little trouble with standard High German, they use Swiss German, or *Schwyzertütsch*, in private conversation and in most unofficial situations. Contrary to the worldwide trend of erosion of dialects, its usage is actually increasing. Swiss German covers a wide variety of melodic dialects that can differ quite markedly from High German, often more closely resembling the German of hundreds of years ago than the modern version. It's as different to High German as is Dutch. Swiss German is an oral language, rarely written down, and indeed there is no standard written form (in fact, they can't even agree on how to spell

Nein Merci
Some of the uneasiness between French and German speakers in Switzerland is due to difficulties with Schwyzertütsch, though there are other factors (eg the geographical line separating French and German speakers has been coined the *Röstigraben* – Rösti ditch – to reflect the culinary difference). French Swiss learn High German at school, and are completely at a loss when their German-speaking compatriots lapse into Schwyzertütsch. The German speakers don't have that difficulty when French is spoken, but they do have a different problem. They are happier and more fluent in Schwyzertütsch than in High German, and feel acutely disadvantaged when encountering articulate Germans. This is one factor behind the Swiss Germans' reluctance to become part of a German-dominated EU, much to the dismay of the pro-EU Swiss French. ■

'Schwyzertütsch'). Newspapers and books almost invariably use High German and it is also used in news broadcasts, schools, and the federal parliament. But people are more comfortable with their own Swiss German, and may even attempt a completely different language when speaking to foreigners rather than resort to High German.

Germans themselves often have trouble understanding Schwyzertütsch. To English-speakers' ears High German sounds like it's full of rasping 'ch' sounds, but even Germans think that Schwyzertütsch sounds like a lot of throat-clearing. A reason for this is that the Germanic 'k' becomes 'ch' in High German only at the middle and end of words, whereas in Swiss German it also applies at the beginning. Hence the relatively manageable *Küchen-kästchen* (kitchen cupboard) in High German become the almost unpronounceable *chuchichäschtli* in Swiss German.

To make matters even more complicated, regional dialects are strongly differentiated for a small country, thanks to the isolating effect of mountain ranges (and the lack of a written 'standard'). In the south, such as in Upper Valais, an older form of dialect has been preserved. Eastern dialects have words in common with all other German vernaculars, whereas in western dialects, some Old Alemannic names have been retained. For example, *meadow* is *Wiese* in High German, *wise* in eastern dialects and *matte* in the west. The letters 'b', 'd 'and 'g' are voiceless in Swiss German, and hardened in eastern dialects into an unaspirated 'p', 't' and 'gg', hence the High German *bitte, danke* and *Gans* (please, thank you and goose) become *pitte, tankche* and *ggans. St* is always pronounced as *scht*. Visitors will probably note the frequent use of the suffix *-li* to indicate the diminutive, or as a term of endearment.

As there is no written form and so many dialects, it is impossible to provide a proper vocabulary for Swiss German. Commonly used greetings are *Grüezi* meaning 'Hello' and *Uf Wiederluege*, meaning 'Goodbye'. Tram is *Tram* not *Strassenbahn*, holiday is *Ferien* not *Urlaub*. Versions of French words are often used: thank you is not *danke* but *merci* (though pronounced 'mer-ci' rather than the correct French, 'mair-ci'); bicycle is *vélo* not *Fahrrad*; ice cream is *glace*, not *Sahneneis*. In pronunciation, double vowel sounds are common – 'good' sounds more like 'gu-et' than the High German *gut*.

For more information, read *Dialect and High German in German-Speaking Switzerland* (paperback, published by Pro Helvetia).

High German Words that you'll often encounter on maps and throughout this book include: *Altstadt* (old city), *Bahnhof* (station), *Brücke* (bridge), *Hauptbahnhof* (main train station), *Markt* (market, often the central square in old towns), *Platz* (square)

and *Rathaus* (town hall). One distinctive feature of German is that all nouns are written with a capital letter.

Swiss French Neuchâtel is where the purest form of French is spoken, yet you won't find very much difference from standard French wherever you go. Of course there are some local expressions and regional accents. A female waitress is a *sommelière* not a *serveuse,* a postal box is a *case postale* not a *bôite postale*. Although the normal French numbers are understood, some locals use *septante* for 70, *huitante* for 80, and *nonante* for 90. Swiss Romande is a term used to refer to French-speaking Switzerland.

Swiss Italian There are some differences in Ticinese dialect compared to standard Italian, but they are not very significant. You may come across some people saying *bun di* instead of *buon giorno* (good morning/day) or *buona noc* (pronounced 'nockh') instead of *buona notte* (goodnight).

Romansch Romansch dialects tend to be restricted to their own particular mountain valley. Usage is gradually being undermined by the steady encroachment of German, and linguists fear that the language may eventually disappear altogether. There are so many dialects that not all the words listed in the back of this book will be understood. See the Graubünden chapter for some examples of regional variations. The main street in villages is usually called Via Maistra.

Facts for the Visitor

PLANNING
When to Go

You can visit Switzerland at any time of the year. Summer lasts roughly from June to September, and offers the most pleasant climate for outdoor pursuits. Unfortunately, you won't be the only tourist during summer – prices can be high, accommodation fully booked, and the sights packed. You'll find much better deals, and less crowds, in the shoulder seasons either side of summer: in April and May or September and October. In Ticino, flowers are in bloom as early as March and hints of summer warmth are already seeping through.

On the other hand, if you're keen on winter sports, resorts in the Alps begin operating in early December and move into full swing around Christmas, closing down again when the snows begin to melt around April. Alpine resorts all but shut down in May and November. July and August is their summer high season.

See Climate in the Facts about the Country chapter for weather considerations. Any time of year, as you travel around the country you'll hit many different climactic conditions. The continental climate in the Alps tends to show the greatest extremes between summer and winter. Mid-August to late October generally has fairly settled weather, and is a good period for hiking trips.

Maps

There are several good map publishers based in Switzerland. Hallwag produces clear country maps, including a ring-bound map book designed for drivers. Kümmerly + Frey (K+F) is another major Swiss map publisher; its Swiss Atlas is also a good buy for drivers – it contains a country map and 35 town plans. K+F publishes a comprehensive series of maps for hikers, mostly on a 1:60,000 scale. Swiss Hiking Federation maps (1:50,000 scale, with orange covers) are an

even better buy. The Swiss Travel System brochure, free from Switzerland Tourism, contains a clear A3 map of bus and rail routes, though for more detail buy the SBB (Swiss Federal Railway) rail map from a Swiss train station.

Once you're in Switzerland, it usually pays to go directly to the local tourist information office to stock up on their free maps and brochures. Another excellent source of free maps is the Swiss Bank Corporation (SBC), which has decent maps of most towns and cities (surprisingly, not of Lucerne), including a street index. Its tourist map of all Switzerland has town plans on the reverse. Other banks, such as the Union Bank of Switzerland (UBS), occasionally have maps. All the bank maps are free – just ask at the counters.

What to Bring

Pack as lightly as you can. Anything you forget to bring you can easily buy in Switzerland, though prices are high. Allow for colder weather in winter and at high altitudes (several layers of thin clothing are better than one thick one). Even if they prefer to dress informally, men should consider packing proper shoes (not trainers or running shoes), smart trousers (not jeans) and a tie for formal outings, such as to top restaurants, though dress codes are usually pretty relaxed at places like nightclubs. Being able to present a smart appearance helps when dealing with officialdom (like at border controls).

Whether to take suitcases or a backpack is a matter of personal choice. If you're travelling by car it doesn't really matter what you take, but a backpack is better if you plan to do much walking. Unfortunately, it doesn't offer too much protection for your valuables; the straps tend to get caught on things and some airlines may refuse to be responsible if the pack is damaged or broken into. Travel packs are a nifty combination of backpack

MARK HONAN

VEVEY TOURIST OFFICE

MARK HONAN

MARK HONAN

MARK HONAN

VEVEY TOURIST OFFICE

MARK HONAN

A	B	C
D	E	
F	G	

A: Bell foundry, La Chaux-de-Fonds
B: Organ grinder, Vevey
C: Onion market, Bern
D: Modern cheese-making, Gruyères
E: Traditional cheese-making
   at Le Chalet, Château d'Oex
F: Wine-tasting, Vevey
G: Alp horn blowing, Bärenplatz, Bern

MARK HONAN

ZERMATT TOURIST OFFICE

VERBIER TOURIST OFFICE

VAUD TOURIST OFFICE

MARK HONAN

Top Left: Curling at Arosa, Graubünden
Top Right: Powder skiing near Zermatt, Valais
Middle Left: Para-gliding above Verbier, Valais
Middle Right: Ballooning at Château d'Oex, Lake Geneva Region
Bottom: Ice-hockey, St Moritz, Graubünden

and shoulder bag, where the backpack straps zip away inside the pack. During city sightseeing, a small daypack is better than a shoulder bag for deterring bag snatchers.

A padlock and chain is useful to lock your bag to a train or bus luggage rack, and may also be needed to secure a youth hostel locker. Swiss Army knives are the most versatile pocket knives available; get one with at least a bottle opener and corkscrew (yes, you can buy them in Switzerland).

Other items that might be useful include a compass, a flashlight (torch), an alarm clock or watch alarm, an adapter plug for electrical appliances, a universal bath/sink plug (a film canister sometimes works, too), sunglasses, clothes pegs and string (impromptu clothesline). Some rural hostels charge extra for sheets so you may save money if you have your own. If you take a water bottle you won't have to keep buying expensive drinks when sightseeing. Consider also acquiring a cup water heater to make your own hot beverages. A supply of passport photos is useful for visas for onward travel, rail/bus passes etc. Tampons and condoms are widely available in Switzerland.

SUGGESTED ITINERARIES

Depending on the length of your stay, you might want to see and do the following things:

Two days
Visit the sights in Geneva and take a trip on the lake. Don't miss Chillon Castle in Montreux.
One week
Visit Geneva and Montreux. Take the Panoramic Express to Interlaken and explore the Jungfrau Region. Finish up with Lucerne and Zürich.
Two weeks
As above, but spend longer in the mountains. Visit the Gruyères cheese dairy after Montreux. Detour to Bern and Basel.
One month
As above, but after Zürich, explore St Gallen and eastern Switzerland before looping down to take in Graubünden, Ticino and Valais.
Two months
As above, but take your time. Visit Neuchâtel and the Jura from Bern.

HIGHLIGHTS
Castles & Churches
There are many interesting castles scattered through the country. The Château de Chillon is one of the most famous (see the Montreux section in the Lake Geneva chapter). Also try and take a day tour of the castles around Lake Thun. Basel and Bern both have fine cathedrals. The most impressive abbey churches in the country, quite breathtaking in their scale, are those in Einsiedeln and St Gallen.

Museums & Galleries
Basel and Zürich each have an excellent art museum, the Kunstmuseum and the Kunsthaus. Getting away from the mainstream, my personal favourite is the bizarre l'Art Brut collection in Lausanne. Zürich's national museum (Schweizerisches Landesmuseum) gives the most complete rundown of Swiss life and times, making all but redundant equivalent regional museums. The sprawling Art and History Museum in Geneva covers a bit of everything. The best clock and watch museum is probably the Museum of Horology in La Chaux-de-Fonds. For food fans there are various show cheese dairies (eg at Gruyères and Stein), or visit the Lindt & Sprüngli chocolate factory in Zürich.

Picturesque Town Centres
Rathausplatz in Stein am Rhein is harmonious and perfectly preserved; the main street in Gruyères is almost as photogenic. Lucerne is worthy of its fame. Schaffhausen and St Gallen sport historic centres bristling with oriel windows. Bern is unbelievably quaint for a capital city. Murten, and to a lesser extent, Estavayer-le-Lac, proudly display ancient centres ringed by fortifications, virtually unchanged by time.

Scenery & Ski Resorts
In a country so blessed with beautiful vistas it is difficult to select favourites. You can't get much better than the view from Schilthorn, or from its neighbour across the valley,

Jungfrau. The three or four-pass tour (see the Bernese Oberland chapter) is unforgettable on a fine day. The mountains and lakes combination seen from one of the summits round Lake Lucerne (Mt Pilatus, Mt Rigi, Mt Stanserhorn) is as seductive as views from higher peaks. The ski resorts invariably provide great panoramas to go with the pistes. Zermatt has excellent skiing and inspiring views of the Matterhorn. Davos and Verbier offer some of the best skiing in the world.

TOURIST OFFICES

Switzerland Tourism abroad and local tourist offices in Switzerland are extremely helpful and have plenty of literature (in English) to give out. They usually also have specialised information for travellers with special requirements. Switzerland Tourism brochures are often glossy sales-pitches, but the offices have good practical information too. For specific and detailed resort information, you're better off contacting the local tourist office direct. Information is nearly always free, including maps, and somebody invariably speaks English. Local offices can be found everywhere tourists are likely to go, and will often book hotel rooms. It's always worth asking about this if you haven't pre-booked somewhere – many offices don't charge to telephone around for personal callers. Some offices even book hotels in other towns too, though there's usually a commission for this (Sfr10). Tours and excursions are also often arranged. In German-speaking Switzerland offices are called *Verkehrsbüro*, or *Kurverein* in some resorts. In French they are *office du tourisme* and in Italian, *ufficio turistico*.

As if the combination of national and local tourist offices weren't already enough to meet the needs of visitors, the Swiss have made doubly sure that every angle is covered by dividing the country up into 12 tourist regions, each with its own regional tourist office. Each chapter in this book covers one tourist region, and the address of the regional office is given in the chapter introduction.

Computer terminals with tourist informa-

tion are springing up in many places in Switzerland. They're often located in train station entrance halls or outside tourist offices and are well worth perusing. They have databases (in English) for accommodation, restaurants, sport and sightseeing. Sometimes the information is limited to the resort; often it's cantonwide or even nationwide. Many terminals have a telephone hook-up for free reservations at local hotels; some have a free print-out facility.

Anglo-Telephone (☎ 157 5014) is a premium-rate English-language information service; it costs Sfr2.13 a minute throughout Switzerland.

Tourist Offices Abroad

The Switzerland Tourism headquarters is in Zürich (see the Zürich chapter for details). Offices outside Switzerland include:

Canada
> Switzerland Tourism, 926 The East Mall, Etobicoke, Toronto, Ontario M9B 6K1 (☎ 416-695 2090; fax 695 2774)

France
> Porte de la Suisse, 11 bis, rue Scribe, F-75009 (☎ 01 44 51 65 51; fax 47 42 43 88)

Japan
> CS Tower, 2nd floor, 1-11-30 Akasaka, Minato-ku, Toyko 107 (☎ 03-3589 5588; fax 3224 0888)

South Africa
> Switzerland Tourism c/o Swissair, Swiss Park, 10 Queens Road, Parktown, POB 3866, Johannesburg 2000, (☎ 011-484 19 86; fax 484 19 99)

UK
> Switzerland Tourism, Swiss Centre, Swiss Court, London W1V 8EE (☎ 0171-734 1921; fax 437 45 77)

USA
> Switzerland Tourism, Swiss Center, 608 Fifth Ave, New York, NY 10020 (☎ 212-757 59 44; fax 262 61 16)

Switzerland Tourism also has offices in California, Chicago, Tel Aviv and Cairo. Nearly half of all foreign visitors hail from Germany, as can be guessed from the distribution of the remaining European offices: Amsterdam, Berlin, Brussels, Düsseldorf, Frankfurt, Hamburg, Stockholm, Madrid, Milan, Munich and Vienna.

VISAS & DOCUMENTS

As a precaution against loss or theft, keep a separate record of document numbers, or a photocopy of key pages. Ensure your passport is valid until well after you plan to end your trip – six months is usually considered a safe minimum; if it's due to expire in that time, renew it before you depart. Once you start travelling, carry your passport at all times and guard it carefully. Swiss citizens are required to carry personal identification, so you also will need to be able to identify yourself. Citizens of many European countries don't need a valid passport to travel to Switzerland; a national identity card or expired passport may be sufficient. Be sure to check with your travel agent or the Swiss Embassy well before departure.

Allow plenty of time to arrange travel insurance, and make sure it covers winter sports if you plan to ski. An annual travel policy is probably the best deal for frequent travellers. Other useful documents are mentioned in the appropriate sections, eg student cards are discussed under the Student Travellers heading.

Visas

Visas are not required for passport holders of the UK, Ireland, the USA, Canada, Australia, New Zealand or South Africa, whether visiting as a tourist or on business. A maximum three-month stay applies although passports are rarely stamped. The few Third World and Arab nationals who require visas should have a passport valid for at least six months after their intended stay.

Enquire at a Swiss Embassy before departure if you're going to Switzerland to take up an employment offer, as you will need to acquire an 'Assurance of a Residence Permit'. Visa requirements can change, and regardless of the purpose of your trip, you should always check with the embassy or a reputable travel agent before travelling.

Being able to show a return ticket and 'sufficient means of support' are not an entry requirement, but if a border guard has cause to question the purpose of your trip you may have problems if you can't show either or both.

EMBASSIES

Swiss Embassies Abroad

These include:

Australia
  7 Melbourne Ave, Forrest, Canberra, ACT 2603 (☎ 06-273 3977; fax 273 3428)
Canada
  5 Marlborough Ave, Ottawa, Ontario KIN 8E6 (☎ 613-235 1837; fax 563 1394)
Ireland
  6 Ailesbury Rd, Ballsbridge, Dublin 4 (☎ 01-269 2515; fax 283 0344)
New Zealand
  22 Panama St, Wellington (☎ 04-472 1593; fax 499 6302)
South Africa
  818 George Ave, Arcadia 0083, PO Box 2289, 0001 Pretoria (☎ 012-436 707; fax 436 771)
UK
  16-18 Montague Place, London W1H 2BQ (☎ 0171-723 0701; fax 724 7001)
USA
  Cathedral Ave NW, Washington, DC 20008-3499 (☎ 202-745 7900; fax 387 2564)

Foreign Embassies in Switzerland

These are located in Bern (see the Bern Information section in the Bernese Mittelland chapter for details). Consulates can be found in many other towns (eg see the Zürich chapter). New Zealand doesn't have a full embassy in Switzerland, but there is a consulate and mission in Geneva (see the Geneva chapter).

CUSTOMS

Duty free limits are as follows: visitors arriving from Europe may import 200 cigarettes, 50 cigars or 250 grams of pipe tobacco. Visitors arriving from non-European countries may import twice as much. The allowance for alcoholic beverages is the same for everyone: one litre above 15% and two litres below 15%. Tobacco and alcohol may only be brought in by people aged 17 or over. Gifts up to the value of Sfr100 may also be imported, and food provisions for one day.

MONEY
Currency

Swiss francs are divided into 100 centimes (known as *Rappen* in German-speaking Switzerland). There are notes for 10, 20, 50, 100, 500 and 1000 francs, and coins for five, 10, 20 and 50 centimes, as well as for one, two and five francs. New counterfeit-proof notes are gradually replacing the older design.

If you're driving to Switzerland and intend to use the motorways, you'll have to pay a one-year motorway tax of Sfr40. Have this money ready, since there may not always be an exchange facility at the border.

Exchange Rates

Some exchange rates for the Swiss franc are:

Australia	A$1	=	Sfr0.93
Austria	ASch10	=	Sfr1.14
Canada	C$1	=	Sfr0.87
France	FF10	=	Sfr2.40
Germany	DM1	=	Sfr0.80
Italy	IL1000	=	Sfr0.76
Japan	¥100	=	Sfr1.12
New Zealand	NZ$1	=	Sfr0.81
UK	UK£1	=	Sfr1.81
USA	US$1	=	Sfr1.19

Costs

Switzerland, as you will quickly discover, is expensive. According to 1994 UBS survey, Zürich was then the fourth most expensive city in the world; compared to Zürich, prices were lower by 4% in Geneva, 17% in New York, 20% in London and 38% in Sydney. Since 1994 the Swiss franc has kept getting stronger, meaning prices for the tourist have kept getting higher. In 1996, a Visa Card survey revealed Switzerland to have the highest prices in Europe, 87% higher than those in the UK. To try to limit the inevitable dip in tourism levels, an effort has been made to freeze hotel prices, and in the second half of 1996 the franc did devalue slightly.

Despite the depressing prices, you needn't emerge from your trip as a pauper. The secret to low costs is cheap accommodation. Camping and staying at hostels are the cheapest

option and often great places to meet people. A student card can cut the cost of entrance fees (see the Student Travellers section) and rail and other transport passes almost invariably save money (see the Getting Around chapter). Don't forget to apply for the consumer tax rebate on large purchases (see the Consumer Taxes section). Hitchhiking, preparing your own meals and avoiding alcohol are other good ways of saving money.

Your budget depends on how you live and travel. If you're moving around fast, going to lots of places, spending time in the big cities, then your day-to-day living costs are going to be quite high; if you stay in one place and get to know your way around, they're likely to come down.

Daily Costs & Budgets Hotel prices are the biggest variable; expect to pay more than the average in Zürich, Geneva, Lucerne, Bern and plush ski resorts. Average costs are:

Youth hostel	Sfr25
Cheap hotel	Sfr45
Set lunch	Sfr14 to Sfr18
Two-course dinner (without drinks)	Sfr20 to Sfr30
Loaf of bread	Sfr3
Glass of draught beer	Sfr3.50 (0.3 litre)
Big Mac	Sfr5.90
Petrol	Sfr1.25 per litre (super)
100 km by train	Sfr31
City bus ride	Sfr1.50 to Sfr2.80
Local telephone call	Sfr0.60
Time magazine	Sfr5.90

Overall, around Sfr40 (US$33) per day is the *bare* minimum you can expect to spend if you limit yourself to camping, mostly self-catering, hitching, hiking and visiting inexpensive sights. After buying a railpass or allowing for car expenses, Sfr65 (US$54) a day will yield hostel accommodation, picnic lunch, admission to a tourist attraction, cheap dinner and the odd beer. Add about Sfr25 (US$21) a day if you want to stay in a cheap pension instead. You would still need to be very careful with your money at this level: at Sfr120 (US$65) a day you can relax a bit, albeit still staying in modest accommodation. If you have a larger budget available, you will have no trouble spending it! Always allow some extra cash for emergencies.

Admission prices are usually Sfr5 to Sfr10 or can even be free (some museums). An occasional expense that can blow any budget is trips in cable cars; these are rarely covered by travel passes (at best you can expect a 25-50% reduction). A short to medium ascent can cost Sfr10 to Sfr25. Return trips up Mt Titlis and Schilthorn exceed Sfr70. If you have the time and energy, walk up instead.

Changing Money

The Swiss make it as easy as they can for you to spend your money. Bank opening times vary depending on the bank, place and branch, but typical hours are Monday to Friday from 8.30 am to 4.30 pm (closed on public holidays). You can also change money at airports and nearly every train station every day until sometime in the evening. Exchange rates are virtually identical between these places. Rates for travellers' cheques are about 1% better than those for cash. Except in some airports, no commission is charged for changing cash or travellers' cheques (but ask anyway). Big hotels change money too, though at poor rates. All fully convertible currencies are equally acceptable, and as there's no commission, Switzerland is a good place to get rid of small sums of un-needed currencies.

Tourist Spending

In 1995, foreign visitors staying in hotels spent an average of Sfr151 per day on lodgings, Sfr65 on meals and Sfr77 on incidentals, giving a total of Sfr293. Those in holiday apartments spent respectively Sfr25, Sfr27 and Sfr23, in a daily total of Sfr75. Campers spent Sfr10, Sfr24 and Sfr20 (total Sfr54) and youth hostellers spent Sfr23, Sfr22 and Sfr9 (total Sfr54). Under 'incidentals', the greatest expenditure was on petrol, followed by tobacco, and sweets. Apparently only car-drivers were surveyed, as no expenditure was listed for train or bus travel. ■

Cash

Avoid carrying large amounts of cash, but taking some will allow more flexibility in changing upon arrival and departure. Secreting an emergency stash of cash (say around US$50), away from your main money and documents, is a good idea. Towards the end of your trip, you don't want to change more than you think you'll need as you will lose out if you have to reconvert the excess. Banks rarely accept coins in currencies other than their own, so spend your last coins on a cup of coffee or fuel if travelling by car.

Travellers' Cheques

All major travellers' cheques are equally acceptable, though you may want to stick to those from American Express, Visa or Thomas Cook because of their 'instant replacement' policies.

Keeping a record of the cheque numbers and the initial purchase details is vital when it comes to replacing lost cheques. Without this, you may well find that 'instant' is a very long time indeed. You should also keep a record of which cheques you have cashed. Keep these details separate from the cheques themselves. American Express has offices in Bern, Basel, Geneva, Lausanne, Lucerne and Zürich; addresses are listed in the appropriate city sections. Buy cheques in your home currency (as long as it's freely convertible and stable), as if you buy too many in Swiss francs you'll lose on the 'spread' of the exchange rate when cashing in the excess back home.

International Transfers

If you need to get money sent from home, nominate a large bank in a major city to receive the funds, instead of some out-of-the-way branch. There are always charges made by the sending bank – a telegraphic transfer would cost at least US$30. You sometimes need to allow up to two weeks to effect transfers. Using the 'Swift' system (electronic transfer of funds) within Europe can take a day or less, though charges are around US$65. The Union Bank of Switzerland (UBS) doesn't charge to accept transfers in Swiss francs; the Swiss Bank Corporation (SBC) charges about Sfr10; Credit Suisse also makes a charge.

A cheaper alternative (accruing charges of around US$12) is to get an International Money Order (IMO) sent. This is effectively a banker's cheque which you receive by post. But you will have a problem of where to cash it – Swiss banks won't let foreigners open a bank account unless they have a *huge* amount of money to deposit.

You can also transfer money through American Express or Thomas Cook. Americans can also use Western Union but there may not be a convenient collecting office. If you have an American Express card, you can cash up to US$1000 of personal cheques at American Express offices in a 21-day period. The easiest option if you have a credit card is to get a cash advance (see below) – get a friendly benefactor at home to feed the account.

Credit Cards & ATMs

Using a credit card can limit or even remove the need to carry travellers' cheques. Not only can you pay for many goods and services by card (eg Swiss train tickets worth over Sfr20), but you can also use them to get cash advances at most banks. Automated teller machines (ATMs), known as Bankomats, are extremely common and are accessible 24 hours a day.

ATMs are linked up internationally and have English instructions. Fees may work out lower than using travellers' cheques. There's no charge at the ATM end, but your credit card company will usually charge a 1% to 2% fee on the total withdrawn. You can avoid the monthly interest charged on your credit card account (due from the day of withdrawal) by leaving your account in credit at the start of your holiday. You may even earn interest on this credit balance. Not all cards are accepted by ATMs – Visa and MasterCard (also known as Eurocard or Access) are accepted in all ATMs at branches of SBC. UBS branches have EC-Bancomat machines which don't accept Visa, and if

your card has a PIN with over four digits you have to deal with a human teller instead.

Similarly, not all shops, hotels or restaurants will accept credit cards, but penetration is fairly widespread and Visa and Master-Card are the most popular. Charge cards like American Express and Diners Club are generally less widely acceptable than ordinary credit cards.

Guaranteed Cheques

Eurocheques are the most popular form of guaranteed personal cheque. Each cheque is guaranteed for up to Sfr300, and you get a Eurocheques card which is valid at banks for cash withdrawals and advances. But first you need a European bank account, and it can be an expensive system to use – there's a fee per annum and a fee per cheque cashed. Many hotels, restaurants and shops accept Eurocheques.

Post Office Accounts

Opening a postcheque account *(Postcheckkonto, compte de cheque postal)* is an efficient way to organise your money in Switzerland, especially if you plan a long or repeat trip to the country. There is no charge to open an account or make withdrawals (you even earn a small amount of interest), and post offices are open longer hours than banks. You can open one on arrival (the drawback is that you have to make your initial deposit in cash). You could also arrange it before departure through your national post office postgiro system (if there is one; it's mostly a European network), which can also transfer funds over for you. Don't ask for the paying bills facility as you would then have to lodge a large deposit as a guarantee. Enquire of your national system, as it may enable you to make cash withdrawals directly at Swiss post offices. (British Girobank postcheques allow you to do this.)

Tipping & Bargaining

Tipping is not really necessary or expected as hotels, restaurants and bars are required by law to include a 15% service charge in bills. Even taxis normally have a charge included. If you've been very happy with a meal or service you could round up the bill. Bargaining is virtually nonexistent, though you could try haggling on hotel prices in the low season.

Taxes & Refunds

On 1 January 1995, VAT (*MWST* in German, *TVA* in French) on goods and services replaced the old 'turnover' tax which applied only to goods. The rate is 6.5%, though it was later reduced to 3% for hotel bills. Nonresidents (including Europeans) can claim the tax back on purchases over Sfr500. Before making a purchase, ensure the shop has the required paperwork. Refunds are given at main border crossings and at Geneva and Zürich airports, or you can claim later by post. Note that you'll be able to buy most things cheaper in neighbouring countries, where you'll also be able to claim tax back, and at a higher rate.

If you're driving to Switzerland, see the Getting There & Away section for important information about paying the motorway tax.

POST & COMMUNICATIONS

As you might expect, the mail and telephone systems are very efficient, and have charges to match. Post office opening times vary but typically are Monday to Friday from 8 am to noon and 2 to 6.30 pm, and Saturday from 8 to 11 am. The larger post offices offer services at a 'Dringlichkeitsschalter' outside normal hours (eg lunch time, evening, Saturday afternoon, Sunday morning), but transactions are subject to a Sfr1 to Sfr2 surcharge. Information on main post offices is given in the city sections in this book.

Postal Rates

Within Switzerland, deliveries are either by A-Post (98% delivered next working day) or B-Post (takes two to three days). Letters and postcards by A-Post cost Sfr0.90, or Sfr1.60 if over 250 grams. By B-Post they cost Sfr0.70 or Sfr1.30.

For international deliveries, the categories are Priority/Prioritaire and Economy/

Economique. Priority deliveries to Europe take two to five days, and to elsewhere, four to 10 days. By Economy service, to Europe takes four to 10 days and to elsewhere takes six to thirty days.

Priority rates are:

Weight Not Over	Europe Sfr	Elsewhere Sfr
20g	1.10	1.80
50g	1.80	3.00
100g	2.80	4.30
150g	5.00	7.50

Economy rates are:

Weight Not Over	Europe Sfr	Elsewhere Sfr
20g	0.90	1.10
50g	1.20	1.40
100g	1.50	2.00
150g	2.20	3.00

Prices for countries bordering the Mediterranean are the same as for Europe. For sending parcels, you can buy special cardboard boxes in various sizes from the post office. Paketpost rates are cheaper for heavier items than Briefpost (letter post).

Receiving Mail

Mail can be sent to any town with a post office and is held for 30 days. Unless specified otherwise, it will go to the town's main post office and you need to show your passport to collect. There's no charge for this service. The international term for this system, *poste restante*, is widely understood although you might prefer to use the German term, *Postlagernde Briefe*. Ask people writing to you to print and/or underline your surname; if an expected letter isn't there, ask staff to check under your first name. The four digit postal code or other means of identifying a particular post office are given in this book for major destinations. If you use these in conjunction with the appropriate term for the post office, namely *Postamt* in German (or if it's the main post office, you can write *Hauptpost* instead), *PTT* in French, *Posta* in Italian, then a letter will get there even if you don't quote a street name. An example of a correctly addressed letter is:

William TELL
Poste Restante
Hauptpost
Luzern 1
CH-6000
Switzerland

American Express also holds mail (but not parcels) for one month for people who use its cheques or cards.

Telephone

Public telephone boxes are numerous, and there are invariably some outside post offices. The minimum charge is a massive 60c, which then increases by 10c increments. A few telephones take credit cards; many take the *Taxcard* telephone cards, which are available from post offices and other outlets for Sfr10 and Sfr20.

Some of the larger post offices have special telephone sections, usually open longer hours than the general post office counters. In these booths you pay the total charge at the counter after you've finished making your call. The call rates are the same as for normal telephones but there's an extra initial fee, giving a minimum charge of Sfr1.20. Hotels can charge as much as they like for telephone calls, so avoid using their telephones to make calls (even if they are direct dial). Telephone numbers starting with 155 are toll-free; an area code is not required. Numbers beginning with 156 or 157 are always premium-rate.

Calls within Switzerland are around 60% cheaper on weekdays between 5 pm and 7 pm and between 9 pm and 8 am, and throughout the weekend. The length of time you get depends upon the distance; zones are: local, up to 10 km, up to 100 km, and over 100 km. International calls to Europe are cheaper from 9 pm to 8 am on weekdays, and throughout the weekend. The cheap rate to USA and Canada is from 11 pm to 10 am and at weekends. There's no cheap rate to Australasia. You can direct dial to just about

anywhere worldwide. The normal/cheap tariff for one minute is: 75/60c to Europe (including Britain), Sfr1/75c to USA and Canada, Sfr1.60 to Australia, and Sfr1.92 to New Zealand. Reverse-charge (collect) calls are not possible to every country, so check with the operator.

To find a telephone number in Switzerland check the telephone book or dial ☎ 111 (minimum charge of Sfr2). For Germany dial ☎ 192, for France, ☎ 193, and for anywhere else, ☎ 191. All these enquiry numbers incur premium charges. There's no surcharge for calling the international operator (☎ 114).

Warning All Swiss telephone numbers now have seven digits, a change not completed till November 1996. This book quotes the new numbers, though it's possible a few individual numbers changed completely instead of adding extra digits in the normal way. If you have a problem getting through on a number, check the regional telephone book, contact the local tourist office, or dial ☎ 111.

International Dialling The country code for Switzerland is ☎ 41. When telephoning Switzerland from abroad you miss out the initial zero from the area code, hence to call Bern you dial ☎ 41 31 (*preceded* by the overseas access code of the country you're dialling from).

The overseas access code from Switzerland is ☎ 00. So to call Britain (country code 44), you would start dialling with ☎ 00 44. Other country codes are: Australia ☎ 61, Canada ☎ 1, Hong Kong ☎ 853, India ☎ 91, Ireland ☎ 353, Japan ☎ 81, New Zealand ☎ 64, Singapore ☎ 65, South Africa ☎ 27, USA ☎ 1.

Fax & Telex Services

Telephone offices in post offices also have fax and telex facilities. If you do it yourself, a fax costs Sfr2 plus the equivalent telephone call; if you get the counter staff to do it, it costs more. Telegrams and telexes can also be sent at the post office.

E-Mail

As you'd expect in such a technologically developed country, e-mail is in common use and cybercafés are opening up (eg in Zürich).

BOOKS

Most books are published in different editions by different publishers in different countries. As a result, a book might be a hardcover rarity in one country while it's readily available in paperback in another. Fortunately, bookshops and libraries search by title or author, so your local bookshop or library is best placed to advise you on the availability of the following recommendations.

English-language books are readily available in Switzerland, though for imported titles you always pay around Sfr2 to Sfr10 more than a straight conversion of the cover price. English-language books can be picked up cheaply second-hand in many cities.

Lonely Planet

Walking in Switzerland by Clem Lindenmayer is up to date, detailed, easy to follow and has lots of maps. Although it's also published by Lonely Planet, there's hardly any overlap with this book.

Guidebooks

Switzerland Tourism sells camping and hiking guides in English, and other books and maps on Switzerland. The TCS (Swiss Touring Club) and the SCCV (Swiss Camping & Caravanning Federation) both publish comprehensive guides to Swiss campsites. The TCS guide has more detail, but annoyingly for backpackers, it's printed on very heavy paper. *Off the Beaten Track – Switzerland* (various authors) concentrates, as the name suggests, on lesser known destinations, while missing out places like Geneva altogether.

Switzerland: A Phaidon Cultural Guide, edited by Niklaus Flüeler, gives a vast amount of detail on art and architecture. *Baedeker's Switzerland* has very extensive information on sightseeing in an A-Z format, but barely deals with accommodation, restaurants or transport details. Michelin's green *Tourist Guide to Switzerland* is similar.

Living and Working in Switzerland by David Hampshire, published by Survival Books, UK, (paperback) is an excellent practical guide for those doing what the title suggests, and covers every angle thoroughly. *Culture Shock! Switzerland* by Shirley Eu-Wong is a less comprehensive, more personal guide for foreign residents and visitors.

Nonfiction

The best book for people wanting to understand the historical, social and political side of Switzerland is *Why Switzerland?* by Jonathan Steinberg. His enthusiasm for Switzerland leaps off the page. *Switzerland – People, State, Economy, Culture* by Kümmerly + Frey (the map publishers) is a compact but very informative book that's updated annually.

The Xenophobe's Guide to the Swiss by Paul Bilton is an informative and sometimes amusing small volume. Bilton covers similar ground but from a personal point of view in his diary-style *The Perpetual Tourist*. The latter is published by Bergli Books (☎ 061-601 31 01), Aeuss Baselstrasse 204, CH-Riehen/BS, a Swiss publisher which offers a number of books that illuminate aspects of Switzerland. These include *Ticking Along With the Swiss* and *Ticking Along Too*, both edited by Dianne Dicks, which are crammed full of anecdotes and stories about the Swiss. *Switzerland for Beginners* is a collection of humorous essays by George Mikes. Although there is a common perception to the contrary, the Swiss do have a sense of humour, as the book *Tell me a Swiss Joke* by René Hildbrand indicates.

Two entertaining anecdotal travel books about Europe, where the author spent a fair amount of time in Switzerland, are Mark Twain's *A Tramp Abroad* and Bill Bryson's *Neither Here Nor There*. What's the best way to make a Swiss roll? Take him to a mountaintop and give him a push (Bryson's joke, not mine). The Swiss chapter in Mark

Lawson's *The Battle for Room Service* is also very amusing.

The Arts Council of Switzerland is called Pro Helvetia (☎ 01-267 71 71; fax 267 71 06) and it's at Hirschengraben 22, CH-8024, Zürich. Pro Helvetia promotes cultural activities and publishes a range of books covering specific interests such as music, dance, ballet, and languages. It can send books abroad.

Fiction

Graham Greene's *Dr Fischer of Geneva or The Bomb Party* is a short but entertaining novel about the doctor, a misanthropic control-freak, and his son-in-law. Anita Brookner won the Booker Prize in 1984 for *Hotel du Lac*, a novel set around Lake Geneva, which homes in on out-of-season hotel guests. Patricia Highsmith's *Small g: a summer Idyll* is a rather lightweight story about some gay people living in Zürich. Thomas Mann's *The Magic Mountain* is a weighty, reflective novel set in the Alps. The mountains also influenced the work of John Ruskin and Leslie Stephen. Mary Shelley wrote *Frankenstein* in Switzerland and set much of the action around Lake Geneva. This was when she was a neighbour of Lord Byron, who wrote the poem *The Prisoner of Chillon* about the unfortunate but true fate of Bonivard, chained to a pillar in the dank dungeon below the water level in Chillon Castle. Sherlock Holmes met his death in Switzerland, in a struggle with Moriarty at Reichenbach Falls. This episode is recounted by Sexton Blake in the short story *The Adventure of the Final Problem*.

Heidi, the famous story for children by Johanna Spyri, is set in the Maienfeld region, just north of the Graubünden capital of Chur. The *Chalet School* series by Brent-Dwyer is very popular with young girls, and many of the books are set in Switzerland.

ONLINE SERVICES

Switzerland Tourism has an internet web site: http://www.switzerlandtourism.ch. It includes SBB and Swissair timetables, and quotes pages for useful related organisations

(eg the Swiss Embassy). Some other local and regional tourist offices have web sites too.

NEWSPAPERS & MAGAZINES

English-language newspapers are widely available on the evening of the same day or a day late (depending on where you are) and cost around Sfr3.50 or more. All the main British and American titles are available; the *Guardian, Financial Times, Herald Tribune* and *USA Today* tend to hit the newstands the earliest. If you don't want to buy a newspaper, consider having a coffee in a plush hotel and reading the newspapers there. English-language newspapers are held in the larger libraries in main cities.

In the news-magazine category, *Time*, *Newsweek* and the *Economist* are widely available. A local English-language magazine worth looking at is *Swiss News* (Sfr7.50 monthly). It's fairly sober and dwells rather a lot on business news, but it still has good cultural features and illuminating news snippets, as well as a comprehensive *What's on in Switzerland* section.

RADIO & TV

The BBC World Service broadcasts on medium wave, 1296 and 648 kHz, and on short wave at 6195, 9410, 12095, 15070 and 15575 kHz , but not all at the same time. The American Forces Network is on the FM band (101.8 mHz) and The Voice of America (VOA) can usually be found on 1197 kHz.

Swiss Radio International broadcasts in English at 6 to 6.30 am, 8 to 8.30 am, and 1 to 1.30 pm. Pick it up on 3985 kHz, 6165 kHz or 9535 kHz. It also has a 24-hour telephone news service in English (☎ 157 300 30); calls cost Sfr1.50 per minute. World Radio Geneva (FM 88.4) is an English broadcasting music and news radio station that can be picked up throughout the Lake Geneva area.

Hotels with three or more stars invariably have radios in the room and these are usually automatically tuned into six subscriber channels of the Swiss Broadcasting Corporation.

Channel 1 is predominantly in English, with news, features and pop music.

If you have a TV in your hotel room it usually offers cable or satellite viewing, meaning you can pick up one or all of CNN (the American Cable News Network), MTV (music channel), Eurosport and Super Channel (a general entertainment channel with ITN world news at 10 pm and 8 am). The British Sky channel is less common. The Swiss complain their national TV is boring. It's highly information-oriented, designed to clue-in the populace on current affairs. The Swiss tune in to the networks of neighbouring countries for their entertainment.

VIDEO SYSTEMS

If you want to record or buy video tapes to play back home, you won't get a picture if the image registration systems are different. Switzerland uses PAL (as do Britain and Australia), which is incompatible with the North American and Japanese NTSC system.

PHOTOGRAPHY & VIDEO

Inter Discount is one of the cheapest places to buy film in Switzerland. For a 36-exposure roll it charges Sfr6.20 for Kodak Gold and Sfr16.50 for Kodachrome. Buy plenty – as soon as you hit the mountains you'll reel off a roll in no time. Photography in snow can be tricky. The whiteness of snow can dominate a picture and cause the subject to be under-exposed (dark and dull on the photograph). Some cameras will allow you to compensate for this.

TIME

Swiss time is GMT/UTC plus one hour. If it's noon in Bern it is 11 am in London, 6 am in New York and Toronto, 3 am in San Francisco, 9 pm in Sydney and 11 pm in Auckland. Daylight-saving time comes into effect at midnight on the last Saturday in March, when the clocks are moved forward one hour; they go back again on the last Saturday in September. The Swiss use the 24-hour clock for anything written down,

instead of dividing the day up into am and pm.

ELECTRICITY
Voltage & Cycle

The electric current in Switzerland is 220V, 50Hz. Most appliances that are set up for 240V will handle 220V quite happily without modifications (and vice versa). It's always preferable to adjust your appliance to the exact voltage if you can (some modern battery chargers and radios will do this automatically). Just don't mix 110/125 with 220V without a transformer, which will be built in if the appliance can be adjusted.

Several countries such as the USA and Canada have 60 Hz AC, which will affect the speed of electric motors even after the voltage has been adjusted to Swiss values, so record players and tape recorders (where motor speed is all-important) will be useless. But things like electric razors, hair dryers, irons and radios will be fine.

Plugs & Sockets

In a country where most things are well organised, plugs are a pain. Plugs and sockets vary, even sometimes inside the same building. Pins are round – three is usual, but two is not uncommon. The standard continental type, with two round pins, can be used in a three-pin socket, but it depends on the shape. Some are recessed, either circular, or more commonly, a six-sided shape, with the top and bottom sides being closer together. continental plugs are no good for these. Basically this means that you may be able to get by with the standard continental plug, but it may be easier to buy the six-sided shape once in Switzerland as this also fits into the three-pin round socket. To wire it up, getting the earth wire in the centre pin is crucial. It doesn't matter which way round the other wires go.

Using an adapter is an alternative to rewiring. Most hotels of the tourist class and above have adapters you can use, but they may not fit plugs from your home country. You can try and buy an adapter before you leave home, but then it may not fit the Swiss sockets (many so-called 'universal' adapters don't). There's generally no problem in finding a spare power point, even in hostels or camp grounds.

WEIGHTS & MEASURES

The metric system is used. Note that cheese and other foods may be priced per 100 grams rather than per kg (a futile attempt to cushion the shock of the high prices?). Like other continental Europeans, the Swiss indicate decimals with commas and thousands with points.

LAUNDRY

There is no shortage of coin-operated or service laundrettes *(Waschanstalt, laverie, lavanderia)* in cities – some are listed in this book. Expect to pay Sfr10 or more to wash and dry a five-kg load. Many youth hostels also have washing machines, and prices are usually slightly cheaper. Tourist class hotels always have a laundry service, but prices are high, and are charged per item.

HEALTH

No inoculations are required for entry into Switzerland, but you'll need an International Health Certificate entry requirement if you're coming from an infected area, such as Africa or South America, where cholera and yellow fever are prevalent. A tetanus jab is a good idea. There is no state health service in Switzerland and all treatment must be paid for. No reciprocal agreements exist for free treatment with any other country. Medication and consultations are expensive; costs vary, but you can expect the briefest consultation to cost a minimum of Sfr40, or Sfr80 at weekends. The local tourist office can tell you where to get treatment if no contact is given in this book.

Pre-departure Preparations

Health Insurance Good travel insurance is essential, and you should enquire about the claims procedure in the event medical treat-

ment is required. A few insurers require notification *before* treatment is sought in order to meet the claim – tricky in an emergency situation. Other things to look out for are whether the policy covers 'dangerous' sports (such as skiing and mountaineering) and if ambulances, helicopter rescue or emergency repatriation are included. Whatever your insurance, you will probably have to pay initial costs yourself (which you can claim back later) and the insurers will issue guarantees for subsequent charges.

Medical Kit A small, straightforward medical kit is a wise thing to carry. A possible kit list includes:

- Aspirin or Panadol – for pain or fever
- Antihistamine (such as Benadryl) – useful as a decongestant for colds and allergies, to ease the itch from insect bites or stings, and to help prevent motion sickness. Antihistamines may cause sedation and interact with alcohol so care should be taken when using them
- Kaolin preparation (Pepto-Bismol), Imodium or Lomotil – for stomach upsets
- Antiseptic such as Betadine, which comes as impregnated swabs or ointment, and an antibiotic powder or similar 'dry' spray – for cuts and grazes
- Calamine lotion – to ease irritation from bites or stings
- Bandages and Band-aids – for minor injuries
- Scissors, tweezers and a thermometer (note that mercury thermometers are prohibited by airlines)
- Insect repellent, sunscreen, suntan lotion, chap stick

You can buy all these things in Switzerland, but they will probably be more expensive than at home. A local product I've found excellent for clearing up blisters is *Hirschtalg* (Stag Fat). If you wear glasses, take a spare pair and your prescription. If you're taking medication, bring prescriptions with the generic rather than the brand name (which may not be locally available), as it will make getting replacements easier.

It's a wise idea to have a letter from your doctor to show you legally use the medication – you can't be sure that over-the-counter drugs in your home country won't be illegal in Switzerland, or without a prescription in Switzerland, or even banned altogether. Keep the medication in its original container. If you're carrying a syringe for some reason, have a note from your doctor to explain why you're doing so.

A Medic Alert tag is a good idea if your medical condition is not always easily recognisable (heart trouble, diabetes, asthma, allergic reactions to antibiotics etc).

Basic Rules

Switzerland is a healthy place, but it still pays to take care in what you eat and drink.

Tap water is safe to drink but always beware of natural water, even crystal clear Alpine streams. Take a water bottle with you if you're going on long walking trips. Drinking fountains are found along many well-transited hiking paths and are safe to drink from. In the unlikely event you need to resort to natural water, it should be boiled vigorously for five minutes; remember that at high altitude water boils at a lower temperature, so germs are less likely to be killed. Iodine is very effective in purifying water and is available in tablet form (such as Potable Aqua), but follow the directions carefully and remember that too much iodine can be harmful. Occasionally you will come across a tap or fountain labelled *Kein Trinkwasser* or *eau non potable* – that means it's *not* drinking quality.

Food should not really cause any health problem – salads, fruit and dairy products are all fine but try to vary your diet. Be careful with food that has been cooked and left to go cold, which might happen in some self-service places.

Potential Hazards

Sunburn On water, ice, snow or sand, and at high altitudes, you can get sunburnt surprisingly quickly, even through cloud. Use a sunscreen and take extra care to cover areas that don't normally see sun – eg your feet. A hat provides added protection, and it may be a good idea to use zinc cream or some other barrier cream for your nose and lips. Calamine lotion is good for mild sunburn.

Remember that too much sunlight can damage your eyes, whether it's direct or reflected (glare). If your plans include water, ice, snow or sand, then good sunglasses are doubly important. Make sure they're treated to absorb ultraviolet (UV) radiation – if not, they'll actually do more harm than good by dilating your pupils and making it easier for ultraviolet light to damage the retina.

Cold Too much cold is just as dangerous as too much heat, particularly if it leads to hypothermia. Cold combined with wind and moisture (ie soaking rain) is particularly risky. If you are trekking at high altitudes or in a cool, wet environment, be prepared (ie take wet-weather gear when hiking in the mountains, even if the weather looks fine).

Hypothermia occurs when the body loses heat faster than it can produce it and the core temperature of the body falls. It is surprisingly easy to progress from very cold to dangerously cold due to a combination of wind, wet clothing, fatigue and hunger, even if the air temperature is above freezing. It is best to dress in layers – silk, wool and some of the new artificial fibres are all good insulating materials. A hat is important, as a lot of heat is lost through the head. A strong, waterproof outer layer is essential, as keeping dry is vital. Carry basic supplies, including food that contains simple sugars to generate heat quickly, and lots of fluid to drink.

Symptoms of hypothermia are exhaustion, numb skin (particularly toes and fingers), shivering, slurred speech, irrational or violent behaviour, lethargy, stumbling, dizzy spells, muscle cramps and violent bursts of energy. Irrationality may take the form of sufferers claiming they are warm and trying to take off their clothes.

To treat mild hypothermia, first get the person out of the wind and/or rain, remove their clothing if it's wet and replace it with dry, warm clothing. Give them hot liquids – not alcohol – and some high-kilojoule, easily digestible food. Do not rub victims, instead allow them to slowly warm themselves. This should be enough to treat the early stages of hypothermia. The early recognition and treatment of mild hypothermia is the only way to prevent severe hypothermia, which is a critical condition.

Altitude Sickness The higher you go, the thinner the air and the easier you need to take things (and the quicker you get drunk!). Acute Mountain Sickness or AMS occurs at high altitude and can be fatal. There is no hard and fast rule as to how high is too high; AMS can strike at altitudes of 3000 metres, although 3500 to 4500 metres is the usual range. Older people and those with high blood pressure have an increased reaction to altitude. However, AMS is unlikely to be a problem in Switzerland, as few hikes ascend higher than 3000 metres.

Headaches, nausea, dizziness, a dry cough, insomnia, breathlessness and loss of appetite are all signs to heed. Mild altitude problems will generally abate after a day or so, but if the symptoms persist or become worse the only treatment is to descend – even 500 metres can help.

Motion Sickness Eating lightly before and during a trip will reduce the chances of motion sickness. If you are prone to motion sickness, try to find a place that minimises disturbance – near the wing on aircraft, close to midships on boats, near the centre on buses. Fresh air and a steady reference point like the horizon usually help, whereas reading and cigarette smoke don't. Commercial antimotion-sickness preparations, which can cause drowsiness, have to be taken before the trip commences – when you're feeling sick, it's too late. Ginger is a natural preventative and is available in capsule form.

Diarrhoea A change of water, food or climate can all cause the runs; diarrhoea caused by contaminated food or water is more serious, but unlikely in Switzerland. A few rushed toilet trips with no other symptoms is not indicative of a serious problem.

Moderate diarrhoea, involving half-a-dozen loose movements in a day, is more of a nuisance. Dehydration is the main danger with any diarrhoea, particularly for children, so fluid replenishment is the number one treatment. Weak black tea with a little sugar, soda water, or soft drinks allowed to go flat and diluted 50% with water are all good.

With a severe case of diarrhoea, seek medical help without delay. Stick to a bland diet as you recover.

Viral Gastroenteritis This is caused not by bacteria but, as the name suggests, by a virus. It is characterised by stomach cramps, diarrhoea, and sometimes by vomiting and/or a slight fever. All you can do is rest and drink lots of fluids.

Ticks Ticks are found throughout Switzerland up to an altitude of 1200 metres, and typically live in underbrush at the forest edge or beside walking tracks. A very small proportion are carriers of bacterial and viral encephalitis diseases, which may become serious if not detected early. Both types of encephalitis initially appear with influenza-like symptoms, and can affect the skin, nervous system, muscles or the heart, often causing headaches and sore joints. Treatment is usually with antibiotics, but inoculations are available for those particularly at risk. In rare instances, encephalitis can be fatal.

The tick embeds its head in the host's skin in order to suck its blood. While a good insect repellent will often stop ticks from biting, Swiss medical authorities now strongly discourage using oil, alcohol or the heat of a flame to persuade ticks to let go, as this may actually release encephalitis pathogens into the bloodstream. The recommended removal method is to grab the insect's head with a pair of tweezers (or ideally a special tick-removal instrument sold cheaply in local pharmacies) then pull the tick out slowly without 'levering' or twisting the hand.

Rabies Though rare in Europe, rabies occasionally crops up. There's actually been a slight resurgence in recent years. The only recently reported cases in Switzerland have been in the north-west. Dogs are a noted carrier, but cats, foxes and bats can also be affected. Any bite, scratch or even lick from a mammal should be cleaned immediately and thoroughly. Scrub with soap and running water, and then clean with an alcohol solution. If there is any possibility that the animal is infected, particularly if it froths at the mouth and behaves strangely, medical help should be sought immediately. Even if it is not rabid, all bites should be treated seriously as they can become infected or can result in tetanus.

Sexually Transmitted Diseases (STDs)
While abstinence is the only 100% preventative, using condoms is also effective. Gonorrhoea and syphilis are the most common of these diseases: sores, blisters or rashes around the genitals, discharges, or pain when urinating are common symptoms. Symptoms may be less marked or not observed at all in women. Syphilis symptoms eventually disappear completely but the disease continues and can cause severe problems in later years. The treatment of gonorrhoea and syphilis is by antibiotics.

The most dangerous STD is of course HIV (Human Immunodeficiency Virus), which may develop into AIDS (Acquired Immune Deficiency Syndrome). It can also be spread by dirty needles used for purposes of vaccinations, acupuncture, tattooing and ear or nose piercing or drug abuse.

Snakes Snakes tend to keep a very low profile, but to minimise your chances of being bitten, always wear boots, socks and long trousers when walking through undergrowth where snakes may be present. Tramp heavily and they'll usually slither away before you come near. Don't put your hands into holes and crevices, and be careful when collecting firewood.

Switzerland is home to several types of snakes, a couple of which can deliver a nasty although not fatal bite. They are more prevalent in the mountains. If the worst happens,

keep the victim calm and still, wrap the bitten limb tightly, as you would for a sprained ankle, and then attach a splint to immobilise it. Then seek medical help. Tourniquets and sucking out the poison are now comprehensively discredited.

TOILETS
Public toilets are invariably spick and span. Urinals are free but there's often a pay slot (around 20c) for cubicles. Toilet cubicles in self-service restaurants are generally free; they're supposed to be for customers only, but who will know?

WOMEN TRAVELLERS
Women travellers should experience no special problems. Some older Swiss men believe that a woman's place is in the home – under Swiss marriage laws, wives weren't granted equal rights until 1988! – but the independence of female travellers is respected. Sexual harassment (catcalls and the like) is much less common than in most other countries, though Ticino males tend to suffer from the same machismo leanings as their Italian counterparts. If it happens, it's best to ignore the perpetrator(s). Common sense is the best guide to dealing with potentially dangerous situations like hitchhiking, walking alone at night etc.

Some women experience irregular periods when travelling, due to the upset in routine. Don't forget to take time zones into account if you're on the pill; if you run into intestinal problems, the pill may not be absorbed. Ask your physician about these matters.

STUDENT TRAVELLERS
An International Student Identity Card (ISIC) can get the holder all sorts of discounts on admission prices, air and international train tickets, even some ski passes. If you're under 26 but not a student, you can apply for a Federation of International Youth Travel Organisations (FIYTO) card; this is not so useful, but may work for reductions in lieu of an ISIC. Both cards should be issued by both student unions and

by youth-oriented travel agents in your home country.

SSR-Reisen in German Switzerland or Voyages-SSR in French Switzerland (☎ 01-297 11 11; fax 297 11 12), Postfach, CH-8026, Zürich, is a budget travel agency specialising in student and budget fares. It is the only agency in Switzerland entitled to make changes to tickets issued by STA branches (Sfr40 fee) and to issue ISIC cards (Sfr15). It also issues USIT tickets (cheap tickets mainly oriented to student travellers) and is an agent for Eurotrain. SSR also sells activity packages for Switzerland. There are branches in Zürich, Geneva, Bern, Basel, Lausanne, Biel, St Gallen, Winterthur, Chur, Fribourg, Lucerne and Neuchâtel; these are listed in the appropriate chapters.

GAY & LESBIAN TRAVELLERS

Gays and lesbians should get in touch with their national organisation at home for more comprehensive information than space permits here. The *Spartacus International Gay Guide*, published by Bruno Gmünder (Berlin), is a good international directory of gay entertainment venues worldwide (mainly for men). The same publisher also puts out *Stuttgart & Zürich Von Hinten*, covering those cities and most of Switzerland. Lesbians can turn to *Places of Interest for Women* (Ferrari Publications).

Public attitudes to homosexuality in Switzerland are reasonably tolerant. The revision of the criminal code on sexual offences, granting equality of treatment under the law for homosexuals, was approved by referendum in May 1992. That means, among other things, that the age of consent for gay sex is the same as for heterosexuals: 16.

The Swiss gay scene, according to the Spartacus guide, is 'renowned for its high standards of service, cleanliness and friendliness'. There are a number of gay bars and saunas in all the main cities. Some bars are listed in this book, as well as contact addresses for gay and lesbian organisations in Basel, Bern, Geneva and Zürich. The *Cruiser* magazine (☎ 01-261 82 00), Postfach 599, CH-8025, Zürich, has exten-

sive listings of gay and lesbian organisations, places and events in Switzerland (Sfr4).

DISABLED TRAVELLERS

If you have a physical disability, get in touch with your national support organisation at home (preferably the travel officer if there is one). They often have complete libraries devoted to travel, and can put you in touch with travel agents who specialise in tours for the disabled, or provide useful advice on independent travel.

The British-based Royal Association for Disability and Rehabilitation (RADAR) publishes a useful guide titled *Holidays and Travel Abroad: A Guide for Disabled People*, which gives a good overview of facilities available to disabled travellers in Europe. Contact RADAR (☎ 0171-250 3222) at 12 City Forum, 250 City Road, London EC1V 8 AF.

Within Switzerland, many hotels have disabled access (though budget pensions tend not to have lifts), and 150 train stations have a mobile lift for train-boarding. Switzerland Tourism produces *Swiss Hotel Guide for the Disabled*, which categorises hotels according to ease of access for wheelchair users and those with walking difficulties. Criteria assessed include width of doorways and accessibility of toilets. The same booklet also lists which health spas and other resorts are suitable for a variety of medical complaints. The Swiss Invalid Association (☎ 062-212 12 62; fax 212 31 05), or Schweizerischer Invalidenverband, is at Froburgstrasse 4, CH-4600 Olten. It sells a booklet and map produced by Kümmerly + Frey about disabled travel in Switzerland (in four languages).

SENIOR TRAVELLERS

Senior citizens are entitled to many discounts in Europe on things like public transport (no longer on Swiss railways, but sometimes on cable cars), museum admission fees, and so on. Proof of age must be shown. The minimum qualifying age for Swiss men is 65; for Swiss women, the age is 62, rising to 63 in 2001. Tourists will *probably* be held to the same age limits within Switzerland. The abbreviation for senior citizens is *AHV* in German and *AVS* in French.

In your home country, a lower age may already entitle you to all sorts of interesting travel packages and discounts (on car hire, for instance) through organisations and travel agents that cater for senior travellers. Start hunting at your local senior citizens advice bureau. Hotels that offer special all-inclusive rates for seniors are listed in a booklet available from Switzerland Tourism and the Swiss Hotel Association.

TRAVEL WITH CHILDREN

Successful travel with young children can require some special effort. Don't try to overdo things; even for adults, packing too much into the time available can cause problems. And make sure the activities include the kids as well – balance that day seeing Lugano's churches with a day in the miniature fun park (Swissminiatur) at nearby Melide. Include children in the trip planning; if they have helped to work out where you will be going, they will be much more interested when they get there. See Lonely Planet's *Travel with Children* by Maureen Wheeler for much more information.

Places that might interest kids include Klagenfurt's Europa Park, the frogs in Estavayer's Regional Museum, the mirror maze in Lucerne's Glacier Garden, and the Knie Children's Zoo in Rapperswil. Look out also for the Knie travelling circus in summer.

Hotels that offer special facilities for families (eg supervised play rooms) are listed in a booklet available from Switzerland Tourism and the Swiss Hotel Association. Families should acquire the Family Card, good for free travel for children (see Passes in the Getting Around chapter).

DANGERS & ANNOYANCES

The average Swiss person's idea of living-on-the-edge law-breaking is to drop a sweet-wrapper on the pavement, or maybe if they're feeling really anarchic, a bit of jay-walking (for which a fine is theoretically possible, but unlikely). That's not to knock the Swiss – rather than the situation in places in the USA, where trading gunshots is a polite way to say hello. The Swiss are very rule-oriented, and some will have no qualms about pointing out to you any transgression you might make. Crime may be relatively uncommon but it's not unknown, so don't become too casual about security. The recent rise in unemployment and the growing drug problem among the young can only make matters worse. Based on the conviction rate, 44% of all crimes are committed by foreigners.

Emergency telephone numbers you can call are police, ☎ 117, fire brigade, ☎ 118, motoring assistance, ☎ 140, and ambulance, ☎ 144 (most areas). In call boxes you need to insert 60c, though it comes back at the end. (Too bad if you have an emergency and have no change!) For helicopter rescue by REGA, the airborne emergency service, call ☎ 383 11 11.

Theft

Even in 'safe' Switzerland, you should always be security-conscious – you're never more vulnerable to theft than when travelling. Be wary of leaving valuables in hotel rooms. Staff will look after expensive items if you ask them, even in hostels. Don't even leave valuables in cars – especially not overnight. Beware of pickpockets (who thrive in crowds) and snatch-thieves (a daypack is more secure than a shoulder bag). Carry your own padlock for hostel lockers. Use a moneybelt and keep some emergency money hidden away from your main stash.

Generally, keep your wits about you, and be suspicious of anything out of the ordinary, even unlikely offers of help. Sadly, other travellers are sometimes the people you most have to guard against.

In the event of theft or loss, get a police report – this will be necessary for you to claim on travel insurance. Your consulate should be able to help if you're left in a desperate situation.

Rules for Life

Switzerland is a very regulated society and rules are everywhere – some may seem laughably petty to outsiders, but the Swiss learn to live with them. Restrictions against working on Sunday even extend to prohibiting gardening or washing the car on this day of rest. As you might expect, there are strict regulations against making noise during anti-social hours, but the following are also genuine rules for some (or most) apartment dwellers:

No bathing or flushing the toilet is allowed between 10 pm and 7 am (if using the toilet between these hours, men must sit!)
Airing of bedding from windows is allowed only during specified times of the day
Use of the communal washing machine and laundry room is prohibited between certain hours
No footwear is to be left outside the door
Net curtains at windows are compulsory.

But controls and civil restrictions occur on a more serious level too. People can be imprisoned for months without charge or trial, purely on suspicion of having committed a crime. In 1990, the public was outraged when news broke that the federal police had kept 900,000 secret files on Swiss citizens and foreigners – that's over 13% of the population! ■

Drugs

Always treat drugs with a great deal of caution. Don't ever think about trying to carry drugs across the border. There is a fair bit of dope available, and young Swiss in places like Geneva aren't particularly shy about smoking it in public parks. It's illegal of course, but the police tend not to do much about it. If you're unlucky and get caught with a small amount of dope clearly for personal use, you might just get a small fine, say around Sfr100 to Sfr400. Possession of over about 30 grams and you may be looked upon as a dealer, and possibly liable for a large fine and jail or deportation. The police spend more time trying to solve the heroin problem, possession of which can get you in real trouble.

Local Laws

There are 26 different cantons, and each has its own cantonal laws. Generally the rules and regulations are the same, but there may be some variation in specifics. In Zürich, for example, women are not allowed to use or carry a pepper spray *(Pfefferspray)* to deter attackers, whereas in neighbouring Aargau they are. Similarly, busking (playing music in the streets) may be allowed in some places and not in others, or only between certain times. Very confusing for a visitor, but all you can do is ask the local police or tourist office if you're unsure about anything. Prostitution is legal, but not in residential areas.

BUSINESS HOURS

Most shops are open from 8 am to 6.30 pm, Monday to Friday, with a 90-minute or two-hour break for lunch at noon. Some are closed on Monday morning, and in towns, shops often stay open until 9 pm on Thursday. Closing times on Saturday are usually 4 or 5 pm.

Banks are open Monday to Friday from 8.30 am to 4.30 pm, with local variations.

PUBLIC HOLIDAYS

National holidays are:

1 January – New Year's Day
March or April – Good Friday, Easter Sunday and Monday
40th day after Easter – Ascension Day
7th week after Easter – Whit Sunday and Monday
1 August – National Day
25 December – Christmas Day
26 December – St Stephen's Day

Some cantons observe their own special holidays and extra religious days, eg 2 January, 1 May (Labour Day), 6 June (Corpus Christi) and 1 November (All Saints' Day). Ticino is the luckiest (laziest?) canton, enjoying 17 public holidays.

SPECIAL EVENTS

Numerous events take place at a local level throughout the year, so it's worth checking with the local tourist office. Most dates vary from year to year. Following is a brief selection of the main events; more information and further special events are mentioned in the relevant sections. Switzerland Tourism annually brings out a booklet giving an exhaustive list of local events, including cultural, social and sporting occasions.

January
 Costumed sleigh-rides in the Engadine, and the Lauberhorn ski race at Wengen.
February
 Carnival time *(Fasnacht)* in many towns, particularly in Catholic cantons, with parades, costumes and musicians. Basel's Fasnacht is best known, but it's also lively in Zürich, Lucerne and Fribourg.
March
 Engadine Skiing Marathon, Graubünden. Cow fighting (yes, the cows fight each other!) starts at the end of the month in lower Valais and continues for most of the summer.
April
 Meetings of the Landsgemeinde in Appenzell, Hundwil (or Trogen), Sarnen and Stans (last Sunday of the month).
May
 May Day celebrations, especially in St Gallen and Vaud.
June
 Geneva Rose Week. The annual performance of *William Tell* starts in Interlaken, and continues until early September. Open-air music festivals in Ticino (late June to August).
July
 Montreux Jazz Festival, Nyon Rock Festival.
August
 National Day (1 August) celebrations and fireworks, and Swiss wrestling in the Emmental. The middle of the month sees the start of the Geneva Festival and the International Festival of Music in Lucerne.
September
 Shooting contest *(Knabenschiessen)* in Zürich, and a religious festival in Einsiedeln.
October
 Vintage festivals in wine-growing regions such as Morges, Neuchâtel and Lugano.

November
 Open-air festivals on the fourth Monday in November including the onion market *(Zibelmärit)* in Bern.
December
 St Nicholas Day celebrations on 6 December and the Escalade festival in Geneva.

ACTIVITIES

The outdoor life is a bigger draw than the cities in Switzerland. The mountains and lakes make more than just a pretty picture; they're a natural playground for sporty types. Various activity programmes are offered by travel agents. If instead you prefer rest and recuperation, visit one of the Swiss health spas. The Swiss Spa Association (☎ 056-222 53 18; fax 222 53 20) is in Baden, Postfach, CH-5401.

Skiing

There are dozens of ski resorts throughout the Alps, the Pre-Alps and the Jura. Those resorts favoured by the package-holiday companies do not necessarily have better skiing facilities, but they do tend to have more diversions off the slopes, in terms of sightseeing and nightlife. Make sure your travel insurance covers you for winter sports.

On the Piste: Top Swiss Ski Resorts

Name & Region	Character	Skiing
Arosa, Graubünden	Family resort	Easy to medium
Crans Montana, Valais	Spread-out twin resorts, Sunny dry climate	All abilities; summer glacier skiing
Davos, Graubünden	Sporty ski town	Extensive and varied, all abilities
Grindelwald, Bernese Oberland	Chalet village Sunny dry climate	Suitable for all abilities; good off-piste
Klosters, Graubünden	Traditional chalet village	All abilities – linked to Davos
Saas Fee, Valais	Car-free chalet village	Something for everyone; summer glacier skiing
St Moritz, Graubünden	Exclusive and expensive	Varied; also famous for tobogganing
Verbier, Valais	Modern, lively, sophisticated chalet resort; pricey	Vast skiing area, mostly unsuitable for beginners. Challenging off-piste
Wengen, Bernese Oberland	Car-free family resort; a British favourite	Mostly easy and medium, also off-piste
Zermatt, Valais	Car-free chalet village; pricey and trendy	Mostly medium and difficult; summer glacier skiing. Challenging off-piste

The skiing season generally lasts from early December to late March, though at higher altitudes, skiing is possible until way into the summer, or even year-round on some glaciers. Snow conditions can vary greatly from one year to another, so telephone ahead to the tourist office to ask about the state of the runs. January can get cold on the slopes. Christmas and February tend to be the best (and busiest!) months, and most resorts are fairly dead in May and November.

Prices for ski passes are usually quoted in this book for one day (and sometimes one week to give an idea of the relative cost) but you can invariably specify the exact number of days you want, or even buy segments of one day. Expect to pay around Sfr40 to Sfr60 for a one-day pass, reducing over longer periods. Free use of ski buses is usually included. Beginners might consider buying ski coupons (where available) as a cheaper alternative if they only want to try a couple of experimental runs.

Equipment can always be hired at resorts; for one day you'll pay about Sfr43/20 for either downhill or cross-country gear. You can buy new equipment at reasonable prices, or try asking to buy ex-rental stock – affluent Swiss spurn such equipment so you might pick up real bargains.

Cross-country skiing (Langlauf, ski de fond) is nearly as popular as downhill skiing, and Switzerland's trails compare to the best in Scandinavia. It works out much cheaper than downhill skiing, as lift tickets are rarely required. Snowboarding, the snow-surfing phenomenon favoured by the young, has caught on in Switzerland as elsewhere.

Switzerland has some of the best downhill skiing in Europe, but it's no surprise to discover that it is also about the most expensive. If you're contemplating nipping across the border to look for cheaper skiing, France is almost as expensive, Austria and Germany a bit cheaper, and Italy cheaper still. But price isn't everything. There's not many places that can compare with Swiss resorts such as Zermatt and Verbier for the combination of great skiing, great scenery, and great nightlife.

There are also many schools where you can learn to ski in Switzerland. All the ski resorts listed in this book have at least one ski school (there are around 200 in total), and you can join a group class (fees around Sfr50 for half a day) or pay for individual tuition on a per lesson basis. It shouldn't be necessary to arrange these in advance, but if you want to, contact the Swiss Ski School Federation, SSSV (☎ 041-887 12 40; fax 887 13 69), Oberalpstrasse, CH-6490, Andermatt.

Hiking

There are 50,000 km of designated footpaths *(Wanderweg)* with regular refreshment stops en route. Bright yellow direction signs along the trail make it difficult to get lost; each usually gives an average walking time to the next destination. Yellow markers are often painted on trees alongside the path. At higher altitudes, signs and markers for mountain paths *(Bergweg)* are painted white-red-white. High Alpine routes are white-blue-white. Not surprisingly, the best trails are away from the towns and in the hills. If you can afford it, take a cable car to get you started. Always wear proper hiking boots and take rain gear and a waterbottle.

Try and go on one of the 'planetary paths', conceived as a scale version of the solar system with information boards and mini planets. The one in the Anniviers Valley in Valais has the best models of the planets and higher mountain peaks at which to gaze. See also Emmental, Doubs Basins and Zürich.

The Swiss Hiking Federation, SAW (☎ 061-601 15 35; fax 601 49 20), Im Hirshalm 49, CH-4125 Riehen, organises guided walking tours and produces good hiking maps. The Swiss Alpine Club (☎ 031-351 36 11; fax 352 60 63), or Schweizer Alpenclub (SAC), Helvetiaplatz 4, CH-3005 Bern, maintains huts for overnight stays at altitude – SAC members get a substantial discount. See under Accommodation later in this chapter.

Mountaineering

Mountaineering is not for the uninitiated and you should never climb on your own, or without being properly equipped/attired. There are well-established mountaineering schools in Pontresina and Meiringen, and in many other locations. Zermatt is perhaps the most famous destination for experienced

mountaineers, and has a Mountain Guides Office to help organise climbs in the region. Ski mountaineering is popular along the Haute Route in Valais. See Verbier, Zermatt and Saas Fee for more information. The Swiss Mountain Guide Federation, or Schweizerischer Bergführerverband (☎ 033-748 81 65; fax 748 81 69) is at c/o Tourismusverband Saanenland, CH-3792, Saanen. The Swiss Association of Mountaineering Schools, or Schweizer Verband der Bergsteigerschulen (☎ 041-887 1770; fax 887 17 37) is at Postfach 141 CH-6490, Andermatt. See also the Swiss Alpine Club (under Hiking above).

Aerial Sports

Mountains are made for paragliding and hang-gliding. Both are popular, especially paragliding, for which the equipment is more portable. Many resorts have places where you can hire the gear, get tuition, or simply go as a passenger on a flight. Ballooning is also taking off (sorry!), despite the high costs. Château d'Oex is one of the best-known locations.

Water Sports

The lakes are equally as developed for sports as the mountains. Water-skiing, sailing and windsurfing are common on most lakes, especially the latter two activities. Courses are usually available, especially in Graubünden and central Switzerland.

There are over 350 beaches in the country, most of which are private and require an entrance fee (around Sfr5 per day). Anglers should contact the local tourist office for a fishing permit valid for lakes and rivers.

The Rotsee, near Lucerne, is a favourite place for rowing regattas. Rafting is possible on many Alpine rivers including the Rhine (see the Graubünden chapter) and the Saane (see the Bernese Oberland chapter). Canoeing is mainly centred on the Muota in the Schwyz canton and on the Doubs River in the Jura. Paddleboats *(Pedalos)* are usually waiting for hire in lakeside resorts.

Cycling

For information on cycling in Switzerland, see the Getting There & Away and Getting Around chapters.

COURSES

Apart from learning new physical skills, you can enrich your mind in a variety of structured ways. Probably the best organisation for adult education courses in Switzerland is the Migros Klubschule *(école-club, scuola club)*. It has schools in all the large towns and cities, and offers a huge number of courses, including mainstream and marginal subjects such as astrology, astronomy, bonsai, cooking, dance, karate, photography, politics and music. It also has comprehensive coverage of languages, including Swiss-German.

Courses start at different times of the year and durations vary. Intensive language courses start regularly throughout the year: German for foreigners lasts four weeks (20 hours per week) and costs Sfr720. Write in advance for information to the schools mentioned in the sections on Bern, Zürich, Geneva and Lugano. The language school, Inlingua, also has many outlets in Switzerland.

WORK

It's not impossible to find legal work. Obviously your chances are vastly improved if you're fluent in at least one of the local languages. The trick is to start writing or asking around early. September is almost too late for the winter season and April the latest for the summer (many places close in May). If you do find a temporary job, the pay is likely to be less than that offered to locals, but the rates will still be good.

Work Permits

Officially, only foreigners with special skills can work legally and the job offer and paperwork should be sorted out before departure. Getting a work permit in this way can be tough, but in practice people manage to find work upon arrival just by asking around. Although it's beyond their brief, tourist offices can often be helpful. Employers sometimes have unallocated work permits that they can assign to you, or there's always the possibility of undeclared cash-in-hand work. If you get caught working illegally you can be fined and deported.

The seasonal 'A' permit *(Permis A, Saisonbewilligung)* is valid for up to nine months, and the elusive and much sought-after 'B' permit *(Permis B, Aufenthalts-bewilligung)* is renewable and valid for a year. Switzerland's bilateral negotiations with the EU will eventually affect employment prospects. Regulations for EU citizens should ease in the next few years, with talks planned for early next millenium about abolishing work permit quotas and giving freedom of movement.

Types of Work

Language skills are particularly crucial for any type of work in service industries. Wages are about the highest in Europe, even for casual workers. Generally, the ski resorts are the most likely places to find something. *Working in Ski Resorts – Europe* (paperback) by Victoria Pybus and Charles James provides specific information and case histories. Potentially all sorts of jobs are available during the season, ranging from snow clearing to washing dishes. Hotel work has the advantage of including meals and accommodation. Within Switzerland, check the ads for hotel and restaurant staff in the weekly newspaper, *hotel + touristik revue* (Sfr3.90).

In October, work is available in vineyards in Vaud and Valais. Rates are good and the quality of accommodation and food offered to grape-pickers is usually better than in other countries. WWOOF (Willing Workers on Organic Farms) will find volunteer work on small organic farms throughout Switzerland. You can travel about, working on a succession of farms, but you usually only get board and lodging, not wages. For information, send two international reply coupons to WWOOF Switzerland, Postfach 615, CH-9001, St Gallen.

Work Your Way Around the World by Susan Griffith (paperback) gives good, practical advice on a wide range of issues. The same publisher, Vacation Work, has a book entitled *The Au Pair and Nanny's Guide to Working Abroad* by Susan Griffith & Sharon Legg (paperback), which may also help. Busking (playing music in the street) is not uncommon in Switzerland and may make you a few francs if you have the required skills. Check with the local police if you plan to do this, as there are usually regulations on where and for how long you can play.

ACCOMMODATION

Accommodation is efficiently classified and graded according to the type of establishment and level of comfort provided. Tourist offices invariably have extensive lists of everything available, usually listing prices and facilities on-site. Often the office will find and book hotels and pensions for little or no commission; this service could save you a lot of time and effort, especially in somewhere like Zürich where finding a place to stay can be a problem. However, they may only try places affiliated to the national hotel network (cheaper places sometimes aren't). It's wise to book ahead where possible: sometimes a deposit is required, sometimes a telephone call is sufficient. Special deals are often available with advance bookings.

Hotels, pensions and hostels almost always include breakfast as standard – places mentioned in this book *do*, unless stated otherwise. In budget places, breakfast is basic, maybe only a beverage, bread rolls, butter, cheese spread and jam. As you pay more, breakfast gets better – usually it's a buffet (including cold meats and cereals) in places with two or three stars.

Except in some towns and cities, it is normal to have a low, middle and high season. The date of the changeover from low to high season prices varies not only from resort to resort but sometimes even from hotel to hotel in the same resort. This factor, together with possible special offers in slack times, makes it always worth phoning around to compare prices before you select somewhere. It also doesn't hurt to ask for a discount for cash, or for longer stays, or in low season.

Prices in budget hotels tend not to change very much between seasons, but the price difference in higher-rated hotels can be quite marked, especially in mountain resorts. In this book, prices are usually quoted as 'starting from...', meaning the price for the cheapest rooms during the *main* season. Off season prices may be 10% (towns) to 40% (Alpine resorts) lower, but you may have to pay more during specific events or festivals, such as at Christmas. Another consideration when budgeting is that the cheapest rooms may not always be available – some hotels offer a range of prices for rooms, depending on size, facilities and fittings. If you're a family, or a group of backpackers travelling together, ask about family rooms, which work out cheaper per person. These are commonly available, and usually have a double bed and one or two singles. All hotels have a fax number nowadays; this has only been quoted for top-end hotels in this book.

In many resorts (rarely cities) there's a visitor's card, sometimes called a Guest Card (Gästekarte) or Resort Card (Kurkarte), which provides various useful benefits such as reduced prices for museums, swimming pools or cable cars. The aim is to entice tourists to stay in the locality instead of just breezing in on a day trip. Cards are issued by your accommodation (even hostels and camp sites) though if you're in a holiday apartment you'll need to get one from the tourist office. They're well worth having, so ask if such a scheme exists if your hotel doesn't supply one spontaneously.

Camping

There are about 450 camp sites, which are classified from one to five stars depending upon their amenities and convenience of location. They are often scenically situated in an out-of-the-way place by a river or lake. Fine if you're exploring the countryside, but a bit of a pain if you want to sightsee in a town. For this reason, and because you have so much extra gear to carry, camping is more viable if you have your own transport.

Hostels, especially for solo travellers, don't work out much more expensive. Charges per night are around Sfr6 per person plus Sfr3 to Sfr8 for a tent, and from Sfr3 for a car. Camping Gaz replacement canisters are widely available. Telephone ahead: in high season, camps might be full; at the beginning or end of the season, camps may close down if demand is low or the weather is poor.

Many sites offer a slight discount if you have an International Camping Card (formerly Camping Carnet). This is basically a camping ground ID, obtainable from your local automobile association or camping federation. They incorporate third-party insurance for damage you may cause. The Swiss Camping & Caravanning Federation (☎ 041-210 48 22; fax 210 00 02), or Schweizerischer Camping und Caravanning-Verband (SCCV), is at Habsburgerstrasse 35, CH-6004 Lucerne. The Swiss Camping Association (☎ 033-823 35 23; fax 823 29 91), or Verband Schweizer Campings, is at Seestrasse 119, CH-3800 Interlaken.

Free camping *(Wildes camping)* is not strictly allowed and should be discreet, but it is perfectly viable in the wide open mountain spaces, and is fairly common in places like Ticino. If the police come across you, they may not do anything (especially if you've been responsible with your rubbish) or they may move you on. A fine is theoretically possible. Farmers might let you pitch on their land – but ask first.

Youth Hostels

Official youth hostels are no longer specifically aimed at youths, though most people who stay in them are young, and noisy school groups can sometimes disrupt the peace of such places. Facilities in hostels are improving: four to six-bed dorms with private shower/WC are common, and some places even have double rooms (with single or bunk beds) or family rooms. Having to do chores is a thing of the past, but the annoying habit of locking the doors during the day (usually from 9 am to 5 pm) and at night (any time

between 10 pm and midnight, though keys are sometimes available to avoid this) still persists in many places. Only rarely can you check in before 5 pm. Despite the hassles, they're easily the cheapest way to get a roof over your head.

Youth hostel is *Jugendherberge* in German, *auberge de jeunesse* in French, and *alloggio per giovanni* in Italian. There is a good network of hostels (over 70) spread throughout the country which are members of the Swiss Youth Hostel Association (SYHA). They are therefore automatically affiliated with Youth Hostelling International (HI). Membership cards must be shown. Nonmembers pay a Sfr5 'guest fee', but that's not as bad as it sounds, as six guest fees add up to a full international membership card. However, you'll find it cheaper and more convenient to become a member in your own country before you depart. Swiss membership would cost Sfr25.

Over half Swiss hostels have a kitchen, and most have TV and games rooms. Evening meals, where available, are usually three-course and cost Sfr11. Bed prices are mostly in the range of Sfr20 to Sfr27. Most hostels add an extra Sfr2.50 for the first night's stay only. It is the full *first night's charge* that is quoted in this book. Of those mentioned, the only hostels that *don't* have a first night's surcharge are Arosa, Bern, Bruson, Geneva, Lugano, Romanshorn and Vaduz. In busy times a three-day maximum stay may apply. Sheets are nearly always provided in hostels at no extra cost (or rather, there is a cost, but you must use theirs anyway) so you will only save money on the odd occasion by bringing your own.

Hostels do get full, and telephone reservations are not accepted. Write, or use the excellent telefax service (this is additional to the international booking network). Under this system, Swiss hostels will reserve ahead to the next hostel for you but you must give specific dates. The cost is only Sfr1 plus a Sfr9 refundable deposit, and you must claim your bed by 7 pm. A few hostels give out a worthwhile guide called *Downtown Switzerland*, containing recommendations for restaurants and bars in main towns. Nearly all hostels should be able to provide you with an excellent free map of Switzerland giving full details of all hostels on the reverse, including their fax numbers. Switzerland Tourism can usually supply this map too.

SYHA or Schweizer Jugendherbergen (☎ 01-360 14 14) is at Schaffhauserstrasse 14, Postfach, CH-8042, Zürich. It has a travel arm called Jugi Tours (☎ 01-360 14 00) in the same building. It offers a varied programme (especially in summer) of tours and activities in Switzerland, mainly staying in youth hostels or mountain huts. Write to the above address for brochures. One-week packages range from hiking in Grindelwald (Sfr435) to mountaineering near Adelboden (Sfr690).

Other Hostels & Dormitories

Private hostels of the 'backpacker' type are quite rare, but dormitory accommodation in ski resorts definitely isn't. Take care in studying accommodation lists, as the dormitory (*Touristenlager* or *Massenlager* in German, *dortoir* in French) may only take groups. It's not unusual for mattresses to be crammed side by side in massive bunks in these places; to compensate, there is usually no curfew restrictions or the hassle of the doors being locked during the day. They are usually run by an adjoining hotel or a restaurant.

Alpine huts tend to be dormitory-style, and prices are comparable to youth hostels. These are maintained by the Swiss Alpine Club, and there are around 150 of them at higher altitudes. Some are only accessible to experienced climbers. They're rarely full, or at worst you'll probably be offered a place on the floor rather than being turned away. If there's no warden about, payment depends on an honesty system, and there will be a book for signing in. Look out also for Naturfreundehaus (Friends of Nature) hostels. You may come across non-HI hostels that are not (or no longer) members because they simply haven't got enough facilities.

Hotels & Pensions

Swiss levels of service are renowned throughout the world. Accommodation is geared towards value for money rather than low cost, so even bottom-of-the-range rooms are fairly comfortable (and pricey). Rooms often have a sink *(Lavabo)*. Hotels and pensions are star rated according to an efficient and standardised system, and almost invariably, you get the level of comfort you're prepared to pay for. Prices start at around Sfr40/70 for a basic single/double room in a small town or village, or Sfr55/100 in top resorts. In these places, the showers and toilets will be down the corridor. Count on at least Sfr10 more per person for a room with a private shower. The shorthand used in this book to indicate this difference is 'with/without shower'. In low-budget accommodation, the private shower may be merely a shower cubicle rather than a proper en suite bathroom.

Pensions tend to be smaller than hotels, and usually provide a more personal service and less standardised fixtures and fittings. Pensions generally offer a better size and quality of room for the price than hotels. Where they usually can't compete is in back-up services (eg room service, laundry service) and on-site facilities (eg private car parking, bar and/or restaurant). If none of that matters to you, stick with the pensions. Mid-price places generally have a room telephone (direct-dial, but at inflated call rates), cable TV and mini-bar. With few exceptions, TVs can pick up a range of channels in different languages, sometimes even English-language channels.

A pension that has only breakfast available is a *Frühstückspension*; the hotel equivalent is *Hotel-Garni*. Other hotels and pensions will offer the option of paying for half or even full board. Small pensions with a restaurant often have a 'rest day', when check-in may not be possible, unless by prior arrangement (so telephone ahead).

The top hotels in Switzerland are among the top hotels in the world. Apart from meticulous service, in these places you can expect pristine fixtures and fittings, all the comforts of home, and facilities on site such as a swimming pool, sauna, fitness room (gym), nightclub, bars, elegant boutiques and a gourmet restaurant.

The Swiss Hotel Association (☎ 031-370 41 11; fax 370 44 44), or Schweizer Hotelier-Verein (SHV), is at Monbijoustrasse 130, CH-3001 Bern.

Other Accommodation

Private houses in rural areas sometimes offer inexpensive rooms; look out for signs saying *Zimmer frei*, (*Chambres libres*, *Camere libere*: 'room(s) vacant'). Some farms also take paying guests. Student rooms may be offered dubring holidays in university towns (such as in Geneva), which can be very good value.

Self-catering accommodation is available in holiday chalets, apartments or bungalows. These are often booked out well in advance – for peak times, reserve six to 12 months ahead of time. In low season, you can sometimes get apartments on demand. A minimum stay of one week (Saturday to Saturday) is common. Local tourist offices will send lists if requested. REKA (☎ 031-329 66 33; fax 329 66 01), Schweizer Reisekasse, Neuengasse 15, CH-3001 Bern, has '14 days for the price of 10' deals on some apartments in low season. Interhome has an office in the USA (☎ 201-882 6864), Australia (☎ 02-9976 21 55) and England (☎ 0181-891 1294), and gives one-third off bookings made in the week preceding the rental period. The head office (☎ 01-786 12 22; fax 497 27 23) is at Buckhauserstrasse, CH-8048, Zürich.

Another possible way to beat high Swiss prices is house swapping. Fair Tours, Postfach 615, CH-9001 St Gallen, is a home-exchange agency in Switzerland, and has links with similar agencies in Europe, USA and Australia. Send an international reply coupon for details (in English). To register, an initial fee of US$40 will be charged, plus US$130 once a match has been successfully made.

IAWA is not a home exchange, but rather a reciprocal network of women providing accommodation for women (men are only allowed with their female partners). Contact Barbara Amsler (☎ 031-331 54 97), Polygonstrasse 5, CH-3014, Bern.

FOOD

The Swiss emphasis on quality extends to meals. Basic restaurants provide simple but well-cooked food, and prices are generally high. Many budget travellers rely on picnic provisions from supermarkets, but even here prices can be a shock, with cheese costing over Sfr20 a kilo! The main supermarket chains are Migros and Coop. Aperto supermarkets are in some train stations; they're a little more expensive but are open daily, typically from 6 am to 9 pm.

In the larger Migros and Coop outlets, and in many department stores (especially the EPA chain) there are inexpensive self-service restaurants. Migros is generally not licensed for alcohol, Coop and EPA often are. These places are great value and the food is always fairly palatable, sometimes downright tasty. Usually they are open to around 6.30 pm on weekdays (sometimes with late opening on Thursday) and until 4 or 5 pm on Saturdays. In most towns they are the cheapest place for a hot meal, with dishes starting at around Sfr8.

University restaurants *(Mensas)* are a real bargain, even if the food tends to be fairly bland. Mensas mentioned are freely open to everyone. Other Mensas may be restricted to ISIC-carrying students or local students, but controls are rarely tight and you can usually get away with it if you're determined.

Buffet-style restaurant chains, like Manora and Inova, offer good, cheap food. Despite the low prices they are comfortable inside, the food is freshly cooked in front of you, and you can sometimes select the ingredients yourself. Draught beer in these places is only around Sfr2.60 for 3 decilitres (300 ml). Some wine bars *(Weinstübli)* and beer taverns *(Bierstübli)* serve meals.

The best value is a fixed-menu dish of the day *(Tagesteller*, *plat du jour*, or *piatto del giorno)*, frequently available at midday only. Fast food is available, particularly at train stations. Kiosks often sell cheap snacks that, like sausage and bread in St Gallen, are as much a regional speciality as the fancy dishes. McDonald's has long since moved into Switzerland. Its hamburgers are distressingly expensive but still cheaper than many alternatives. McDonald's restaurants aren't specifically mentioned in this book, though many outlets are on the city maps.

Main meals in Switzerland are eaten at noon. Cheaper restaurants tend to be fairly rigid about when they serve; lunch is noon to around 1.30 pm and dinner about 6.30 to 9 or 9.30 pm. Don't be fooled if some of the closing times given in this book are much later; the place may stay open several hours after the kitchen closes, catering for drinkers. Go to a hotel or more up-market restaurant for more flexible, later eating. Pizzerias are an inexpensive yet flexible option; it's not unusual for the ovens to be kept glowing straight through from around 11 am to 11 pm. The self-service places are normally flexible during the day, too.

If you have dietary restrictions, tourist offices should be able to help with lists of suitable restaurants. Dedicated vegetarian restaurants can be hard to come by, but it's common nowadays for restaurants to offer one or two non-meat choices. Information on vegetarian places is given in this book for all major towns. *Fitness Tellers* for the calorie counters are a growing phenomenon, especially in ski resorts. The *Jewish Travel Guide* published by Jewish Chronicle Publications details kosher restaurants, synagogues, and relevant institutions. There are seven pages on Switzerland in its worldwide listings.

The classier restaurants tend to have pretensions towards *nouvelle cuisine*, with beautifully presented but fairly insubstantial courses. Carbohydrates are anathema in these places, as if they're trying to distance themselves from the filling meat-and-potatoes fare of earthier joints.

Monday and Tuesday are the quietest nights in restaurants, and some places take the opportunity to have a rest day *(Ruhetag)*. These rest days may expand in off-season and be eliminated in high season. Weekends are the busiest times, yet some of the very top restaurants close on Saturday and/or Sunday, probably because they get a lot of their trade from expense-account business people.

The *Weltwoche* newspaper annually compiles a list of the 100 best restaurants in Switzerland. It draws on existing well-respected guides as well as local information from testers and regional media. Year after year, the No 1 restaurant on the list is *Girardet* (☎ 021-634 05 05), 1 Rue d'Yverdon, Crissier, near Lausanne, Vaud. It's the only restaurant in Switzerland with three Michelin stars. It closes on Monday and Tuesday. Many of the other restaurants in the top 100 are listed in the appropriate town sections.

Swiss Cuisine

Switzerland hasn't got a great indigenous gastronomic tradition – instead, Swiss dishes borrow from the best of German, French and (in Ticino) Italian cuisine. In addition, Zürich and particularly Geneva have loads of restaurants of all sorts of nationalities. You don't have to spend a fortune to enjoy a meal; a picnic lunch on a mountain top or by a lake can be one of the recurring highlights of any trip.

The typical breakfast is of the continental variety. *Müsli* (muesli) was invented in Switzerland at the end of the 19th century but few people seem to eat it here – *Birchermüsli* is the most common variety. Soups are popular and often very filling, and sometimes contain small dumplings *(Knöpfli)*.

Fondue is a hot concoction of melted cheeses and white wine, into which bread is dipped.

Müsli

It's a funny thing about müsli (muesli). It was invented in Switzerland at the end of the 19th century but few people seem to eat it in its country of origin. Go into any supermarket in Italy and half the shelves will be taken up with a thousand different varieties of pasta. In Swiss supermarkets you find maybe a couple of müsli packets tucked away in the corner and that's it. You're hardly force-fed the stuff as a visitor – it usually appears at lavish breakfast-buffets in the higher-class hotels, but the basic hotel breakfast is rolls, cheese, meat and jam, and that reflects national eating patterns.

So what's the story? Could it be an invidious modern invention that the Swiss created largely to inflict upon the rest of humanity, like life insurance sales people? (the Swiss developed the modern formula for life insurance); something that nobody really likes (Jilly Cooper once charmingly described it as 'rat droppings in sawdust') but feels compelled to put up with for reasons of health or security? The official tale is that Dr Bircher-Benner created it as a nutritious and healthy food to serve to patients in his private clinic in Zürich. But I think it could have been invented something like this:

Mr and Mrs Müsli, hard-up farm folk, awoke one morning at the crack of dawn to find no food in the house for breakfast – no bread, butter, meat, cheese or jam. The shops wouldn't be open for ages, so they searched the farm for stuff they normally spread on the fields, or gave to the farm animals.

'Here's some chicken feed,' cried Mrs Müsli triumphantly.

'And some bonemeal,' yelled Mr Müsli.

'And what about this old bag of oats?'

More leftovers were discovered, and everything they found was thrown into a big basin and mixed together. Unfortunately the whole thing looked like an unappetising stodge, so in desperation they turned to the fruit bowl. There was an old apple, shrivelled to the core, that was chopped up and chucked in.

'What about these old grapes?'

'But they're wizened and rock hard!'

'Never mind. In they go!'

They could find nothing else, and before they dared try the concoction, they drowned it in rich Alpine milk to try to disguise the taste. It didn't work.

'This is terrible,' said Mrs Müsli.

'I know,' said Mr Müsli, 'but we've got a whole vat full of the stuff now. I wonder if we can sell it?' ■

Cheeses form an important part of the Swiss diet. Emmental and Gruyère are combined with white wine to create *fondue*, which is served up in a vast pot and eaten with bread cubes. According to tradition, if your cube leaps off your fork and disappears in the pot, you have to buy a round of drinks. *Raclette* is another melted cheese dish, usually served with potatoes and small onions.

Rösti (crispy, fried, shredded potatoes), sometimes spelled *Röschti*, is German Switzerland's national dish. A wide variety of *Wurst* (sausage) is available. Veal is highly rated throughout Switzerland. In Zürich it is thinly sliced and served in a cream sauce (*Geschnetzeltes Kalbsfleisch*). *Bündnerfleisch* is air-dried beef, smoked and thinly sliced. Fresh fish from the numerous lakes frequently crop up on menus, especially perch and trout. Swiss chocolate, excellent by itself, is often used in desserts and cakes. Regional specialities are usually mentioned in the appropriate chapter.

Food Glossary These are some food terms you may come across in German (G), French (F) and Italian (I):

soup
    Suppe (G), potage or consommé (F), brodo (I)
shrimp cocktail
    Krevetten Cocktail (G), cocktail de crevettes (F), cocktail di gamberi (I)
butter-fried trout
    Forelle Müllerinart (G), truite à la meunière (F), trota fritata al burro (I)
whitefish fillets (with almonds)
    Felchenfilets (mit Mandeln) (G), filets de féra (aux amandes) (F), filetti di coregone (alla mandorle) (I)

grilled salmon
  Grillierter Salm (G), saumon grillé (F), trota salmonata alla griglia (I)
veal
  Kalb (G), veau (F), vitello (I)
fillet of beef
  Rindsfilet (G), filet de boeuf (F), filetto di manzo (I)
sirloin steak
  Zwischenrippenstück (G), entrecôte (F), costata di manzo (I)
pork
  Schwein (G), porc (F), maiale (I)
lamb cutlets
  Lammkoteletten (G), côte d'agneau (F), entrecôte d'agnello (I)
boiled potatoes
  Salzkartoffeln (G), pommes nature (F), patate bollite (I)
rice
  Reis (G), riz (F), riso bianco (I)
vegetables
  Gemüse (G), légumes (F), vedura (I)
pasta
  Teigwaren (G), pâtes (F), paste or pasta (I)
flat pasta/noodles
  Nudeln (G), nouilles (F), tagliatelle (I)
ice cream
  Rahmeis (G), glace (F), gelato (I)
fruit salad
  Fruchsalat (G), macédoine de fruits (F), macedonia di frutta

DRINKS

Mineral water is readily available but tap water is fine to drink. Coffee is more popular than tea – the latter will come without milk unless you ask specially for it. Hot chocolate is also popular. Note that milk from Alpine cows contains a high level of fat.

In bars, lager beer comes in 0.3 or 0.58-litre bottles, or on draught *(Bier vom Fass, bière à la pression, birra alla pressione)* with measures ranging from 0.2 to 0.5 litre. There isn't the tradition of beer-drinking as there is in neighbouring Germany, but the many small breweries dotted round the country testify to the popularity of the beverage. Beer and wine in basic beer halls or cafés aren't too pricey (comparatively speaking), but chic bars can be very expensive. Spirits are expensive everywhere. Happily, beer and wine prices in supermarkets are fairly low.

Wine is considered an important part of the meal even though it is rather expensive. For the cheapest choices, ask for decanted 'open' wines, sold by the dl (100 millilitres). Local wines are generally good but you may not have heard of them before, as output can not even meet domestic demand so they are rarely exported. The main growing region is the French-speaking part of the country, particularly in Valais and by Lake Neuchâtel and Lake Geneva. Both red and white wines are produced, and each region has its own speciality. Ticino is known for Merlot. See the boxed asides at the start of the Valais and Ticino chapters for more information. There is also a choice of locally produced fruit brandies, often served with or in coffee.

ENTERTAINMENT

The Swiss read more newspapers and watch less TV than any other European nationals. Jass is the national card game, played with 36 cards; it's so complicated that only native Swiss understand it. Listening to music is popular throughout the country, meaning that classical, folk, jazz and rock concerts can be found in many towns and cities. Two of Switzerland's best known orchestras are the Tonhalle in Zürich and the Suisse Romande in Geneva. Most headline rock bands eventually find their way to Switzerland. Bern has several good jazz venues.

In German Switzerland, cinemas nearly always show films in the original language. To confirm this, check the advertisements for the upper-case letter: E/f/g means that the film is in English with French and German subtitles. In French Switzerland, look for VO, which signifies 'original version'. Prices are lower on Mondays.

Nightlife is not all it could be in the cities, and where it does exist, it is expensive. Geneva is the best place for late nightclubs *(boîtes)*, but Zürich is also lively. Alternative arts flourish in many towns, usually centred in one main venue. Two of the best places are l'Usine in Geneva and Rote Fabrik in Zürich

– music, art, theatre, dance and cinema are featured. Zürich and Geneva are also the best places to catch up on English-language theatre.

Swiss folklore shows are standard tourist fare. If you want to investigate this strange phenomenon of alphorns, yodelling and flag throwing, there are a couple of places in Bern with free shows during summer.

Ski resorts have an atmosphere all their own. 'Après ski' entertainment seems to consist of drinking large amounts in bars and then dancing or falling over in clubs.

SPECTATOR SPORT

Football is a popular spectator sport, with most towns having their own professional team. Alpine festivals are common in the summer in rural villages, and may include some unique Swiss sports, such as *Schwingen* (Swiss wrestling), *Hornussen* (bat and ball game, played with strange curved bats), and *Unspunnenstein* (rock throwing). A listing of local events is invariably available from tourist offices.

THINGS TO BUY

Watches, penknives, textiles and embroidery are all popular buys. Swiss knives range from simple blades (Sfr10) to mini toolboxes (Sfr100 or more). A grotesquely tacky cuckoo clock with a girl bouncing on a spring will set you back at least Sfr25, a musical box anything upwards of Sfr35. Should you want a cowbell to warn people of your arrival, one with a decorative band will cost from Sfr8 to three figures, depending on the size.

Most of these goods are available in numerous souvenir shops in all tourist centres. Heimat or Heimatwerk shops tend to sell hand-made goods which can be pricey but are generally good quality. Department stores often sell similar products (eg Swiss knives) at more competitive prices. Video and cassette tapes, records and CDs, photographic film and tape recorders are all reasonably priced by European standards. A cheap outlet (especially for film) is Inter Discount, with branches all over Switzerland. EPA is an inexpensive department store.

Getting There & Away

Air travel is the quickest, easiest, and sometimes cheapest means of transcontinental travel. If you're visiting Switzerland from outside Europe, it may be cheaper to fly to a European 'gateway' city and travel on from there. Basel, for example, is only three hours and Sfr90 from Frankfurt by rail. Paris is Sfr78 and less than four hours from Geneva by the *train à grande vitesse* (TGV). There are some great fares available on certain routes thanks to severe competition between the airlines. Students, people aged under 26 and senior citizens often qualify for excellent deals.

Don't forget to arrange travel insurance. Paying for your ticket with a credit card often in itself provides limited travel accident insurance. For additional protection, limit your business dealings to travel agents who are bonded in some way (eg to ABTA in the UK), so you'll get reimbursed in the event of bankruptcy.

AIR

The main entry points for international flights are Zürich and Geneva. There are direct services to all main European destinations and to most major transport hubs worldwide. Both airports are linked directly to the Swiss rail network. Basel's airport, another busy centre for European flights, is on the French side of the border in Mulhouse. Bern and Lugano airports also have some international flights. See the respective city sections.

Swissair is the national carrier and has the most extensive services to/from Switzerland. Crossair, its subsidiary, also has a few international flights. Swissair has acquired a stake in Sabena and generally has combined reservations offices with Austrian Airlines. There are Swissair luggage check-in facilities at many Swiss train stations. Swissair offices are in all Swiss cities. For Crossair tickets and reservations, go to a Swissair office or dial ☎ 155 36 36, a toll-free number.

Remember always to reconfirm your onward or return bookings by the specified time – usually 72 hours before departure on international flights.

Airport Taxes

There is no departure tax to pay at the airport when flying out of Switzerland, as taxes must be paid when buying your ticket. Airport taxes are Sfr14 for Zürich, Sfr14.50 for Basel and Sfr15 for Geneva – ask if this is included in the initial price quoted by the travel agent. Travel agents may also quote prices exclusive of the departure tax levied by the country at the origination of the flight, even if (as in the UK) this sum must also be included in the final ticket price. The departure tax from the UK to Zürich or Basel is UK£10, yet it's only UK£5 to Geneva.

Buying Tickets

A plane ticket is a major expense, and it pays to spend some time researching the current state of the market. Start early: some of the cheapest tickets have to be bought months in advance (such as Apex tickets), and some popular flights sell out early. Alternatively, if your plans are flexible enough, you might risk waiting for last-minute bargains. Look for special offers that crop up from time to time.

Airlines release discounted tickets through selected travel agents, and they are often the cheapest deals going. Some Airlines now also sell discounted tickets direct, and it's worth contacting them for information on routes and timetables. Low-season, student, youth and senior citizens fares can be very competitive. Return tickets usually work out much cheaper than two one-way tickets. Open Jaw returns allow you to fly into one city and out of another.

Round-the-World (RTW) tickets are another possibility, and are comparable in price to an ordinary return ticket. RTW tickets start at about UK£850, A$1800 or

US$1300 depending on the season, and may be valid for up to a year. Special conditions might be attached to such tickets (eg you can't backtrack on a route). Also beware of cancellation penalties for these and other tickets.

Courier fares, where you get cheap passage in return for accompanying an urgent package through customs, offer low prices but there are usually special restrictions attached, and demand for couriers is decreasing in this electronic age.

If you are travelling from the USA, UK or South-East Asia, you will probably find that the cheapest flights are being advertised by obscure agencies. Most such firms are honest and solvent, but there are some rogue fly-by-night outfits around. If you feel suspicious about a firm, it's best to steer clear, or only pay a deposit before you get your ticket, then ring the airline to confirm that you are actually booked onto the flight before you pay the balance.

Established outfits, such as those mentioned in this book, offer more safety and are almost as competitive as you can get. The cheapest deals are only available at certain times of the year, or on weekdays, and fares are particularly subject to change. Always ask about the route: the cheapest tickets may involve an inconvenient stopover. Don't take schedules for granted, either: airlines usually change their schedules twice a year, on 26 March and 31 October.

Airlines can often make arrangements for travellers with special needs if they're warned early enough, eg arrangements for wheelchairs, vegetarian or kosher meals. Children aged under two travel for 10% of the standard fare (or free on some airlines) as long as they don't occupy a seat. They don't get a baggage allowance. 'Skycots', baby food and diapers should be provided by the airline if requested in advance. Children aged between two and 12 can usually occupy a seat for half to two-thirds of the full fare, and do get a baggage allowance.

Fly-Rail Programme
Most world airlines (except American carriers for outward flights from Switzerland) are part of this programme. It allows you to wave goodbye to your luggage when you check-in at your departure airport and pick it up again at your choice of any Swiss railway station. This saves you having to wait for your luggage at the arrival airport or accompany it through customs. Similarly, upon departure you can check-in your luggage at any of the 117 Swiss railway stations up to 24 hours before your flight and pick it up at your destination airport. The charge is Sfr20 per item of luggage.

The following Swiss railway stations provide a complete check-in service for Swissair, including issuing boarding passes: Aarau, Arosa, Basel SBB, Bern, Biel/Bienne, Davos Platz and Dorf, Fribourg, Geneva, Interlaken Ost and West, Lausanne, Locarno, Lugano, Lucerne, Montreux, Neuchâtel, St Gallen, St Moritz, Solothurn, Thun, Zug and Zürich.

The UK
London is one of the world's major centres for buying discounted air tickets. You should be able to find a scheduled return flight from about UK£120 (including taxes), which is less than the fare by rail (London to Zürich return is £137). For stays under 31 days, a charter flight may be cheaper than a scheduled fare. Try the Charter Flight Centre (☎ 0171-931 0504).

Check the cheap fares advertised in *Time Out*, the *Evening Standard* and *TNT* (a free magazine dispensed at tube stations). The Sunday national papers are also a good source of ads for cheap fares. British Airways (☎ 0345-222 111) has cheap fares called 'World Offers'.

Trailfinders (☎ 0171-938 3232), 194 Kensington High St, London W8, has decent fares, plus a travel library, bookshop, visa service and immunisation centre. Its Manchester branch (☎ 0161-839 6969), is at 58 Deansgate; other branches are in Bristol and Glasgow. Campus Travel (☎ 0171-730 3402), 52 Grosvenor Gardens, London SW1, has many interesting deals and very cheap travel insurance. Then there's Council Travel

MARK HONAN

TONY WHEELER

MARK HONAN

MARK HONAN

MARK HONAN

Top: The Aare River, Bern
Middle Left: Clocktower
(Zeitglockenturm), Bern
Middle Right: Fountain of Justice, Bern

Bottom Left: Tympanum of the main
doorway of the
Cathedral, Bern
Bottom Right: Ogre fountain, Bern

Lake Oeschinen, Kandersteg, Bernese Oberland

(0171-437 7767), 28A Poland St, London W1, the USA's largest student and budget travel agency. The London office of Swissair and Crossair (☎ 0171-434 7200) is at Swiss Court, W1.

STA Travel (☎ 0171-937 9921) is a world-wide agency for budget and student tickets, and has offices in London (117 Euston Rd, NW1, and 86 Old Brompton Rd, SW7) and other British cities, such as Manchester (☎ 0161-834 0668).

Continental Europe

Depending on your starting point, taking the train may be cheaper and just as convenient. Across Europe many travel agents have ties with STA Travel, where budget tickets can be purchased and STA-issued tickets can usually be altered free of charge, including at SSR branches in Switzerland. Outlets in major transport hubs include: CTS Voyages (☎ 1-43 25 00 76), 20 Rue des Carmes, Paris; SRID Reisen (☎ 069-43 01 91), Berger Strasse 118, Frankfurt; ISYTS (☎ 01-322 1267), 2nd floor, 11 Nikis St, Syntagma Square, Athens.

In continental Europe, Athens is a recognised centre for cheap flights: check the many travel agents in the backstreets between Syntagma and Omonia squares. In Athens, as well as ISYTS above, try Pioneer Tours (☎ 322 4321), also at 11 Nikis St.

Amsterdam also has a good reputation for cheap fares: try Budget Air (☎ 020-627 12 51), Rokin 34; ILC Reizen (☎ 020-620 51 21), NZ Voorburgwal 256; Malibu Travel (☎ 020-623 68 14), Damrak 30; or the student agency, NBBS (☎ 020-624 09 89), Rokin 38.

USA

The North Atlantic is the world's busiest long-haul air corridor: the *New York Times*, the *LA Times*, the *Chicago Tribune*, the *San Francisco Chronicle* and the *San Francisco Examiner* all produce weekly travel sections in which you'll find numerous travel agents' ads.

Using the budget agencies, you should be able to fly from New York to a European gateway city and return for US$350 to US$450 in the low season, or US$550 to US$650 in the high season. Swissair flies daily except Friday and Sunday from Los Angeles to Zürich; nonstop flights from New York are daily to both Zürich and Geneva. American Airlines, TWA and Delta also fly direct into Switzerland.

Council Travel (☎ 1-800-226 8624 toll free) and STA Travel (☎ 1-800-777 0112 toll free) sell discounted tickets from numerous outlets across the USA. One-way fares can be very cheap on a stand-by basis. Airhitch (☎ 212-864 2000) specialises in this sort of thing, and can get you from the USA to Europe one-way for US$160 from the east coast, US$269 from the west coast. Another interesting option is with Icelandair (☎ 800-223 5500), flying from New York to Luxembourg, via Reykjavík. This may prove to be one of the cheapest deals. For courier flights, contact Discount Travel International (☎ 212-362 36 36, fax 362 3236) in New York or Orbit Travel (☎ 213-466 72 48) in Los Angeles.

The *Travel Unlimited* newsletter, PO Box 1058, Allston, MA 02134, publishes details of the cheapest air fares and courier possibilities for destinations all over the world from the USA and other countries, including the UK. It's a treasure trove of information. A single monthly issue costs US$5, and a year's subscription, US$25 (US$35 abroad).

Canada

Check ads in the *Toronto Globe & Mail*, the *Toronto Star* and the *Vancouver Province*. Look for the budget agency, Travel Cuts. Its head office (☎ 416-979 2406) is at 187 College St, Toronto M5T 1P7, but it has offices in all major cities. Swissair flies from Montreal to Zürich four times a week for between about C$700 and C$1000. From Vancouver you can fly with Air Canada to Toronto then with Swissair to Zürich for around C$1000 in high season. Courier fares to London or Paris are much lower: contact FB On Board Courier Services on ☎ 514-631 7925 in Montreal or ☎ 604-278 1266 in Vancouver.

Air Travel Glossary

Apex Tickets Apex stands for Advance Purchase Excursion fare. These tickets are usually between 30 and 40% cheaper than the full economy fare, but there are restrictions. You must purchase the ticket at least 21 days in advance (sometimes more) and must be away for a minimum period (normally 14 days) and return within a maximum period (90 or 180 days). Stopovers are not allowed, and if you have to change your dates of travel or destination, there will be extra charges to pay. These tickets are not fully refundable – if you have to cancel your trip, the refund is often considerably less than what you paid for the ticket. Take out travel insurance to cover yourself in case you have to cancel your trip unexpectedly – for example, due to illness.

Baggage Allowance This will be written on your ticket; you are usually allowed one 20-kg item to go in the hold, plus one item of hand luggage. Some airlines which fly transpacific and transatlantic routes allow for two pieces of luggage (there are limits on their dimensions and weight).

Bucket Shops At certain times of the year and/or on certain routes, many airlines fly with empty seats. This isn't profitable and it's more cost-effective for them to fly full, even if that means having to sell a certain number of drastically discounted tickets. They do this by off-loading them onto bucket shops (UK) or consolidators (USA), travel agents who specialise in discounted fares. The agents, in turn, sell them to the public at reduced prices. These tickets are often the cheapest you'll find, but you can't purchase them directly from the airlines. Availability varies widely, so you'll not only have to be flexible in your travel plans, you'll also have to be quick off the mark as soon as an advertisement appears in the press.

Bucket-shop agents advertise in newspapers and magazines and there's a lot of competition – especially in places like Amsterdam and London which are crawling with them – so it's a good idea to telephone first to ascertain availability before rushing from shop to shop. Naturally, they'll advertise the cheapest available tickets, but by the time you get there, these may be sold out and you may be looking at something slightly more expensive.

Bumped Just because you have a confirmed seat doesn't mean you're going to get on the plane – see Overbooking.

Cancellation Penalties If you have to cancel or change an Apex or other discount ticket, there may be heavy penalties involved; insurance can sometimes be taken out against these penalties. Some airlines impose penalties on regular tickets as well, particularly against 'no show' passengers.

Check In Airlines ask you to check in a certain time ahead of the flight departure (usually two hours on international flights). If you fail to check in on time and the flight is overbooked, the airline can cancel your booking and give your seat to somebody else.

Confirmation Having a ticket written out with the flight and date on it doesn't mean you have a seat until the agent has confirmed with the airline that your status is 'OK'. Prior to this confirmation, your status is 'on request'.

Courier Fares Businesses often need to send their urgent documents or freight securely and quickly. They do it through courier companies. These companies hire people to accompany the package through customs and, in return, offer a discount ticket which is sometimes a phenomenal bargain. In effect, what the courier companies do is ship their freight as your luggage on the regular commercial flights. This is a legitimate operation – all freight is completely legal. There are two shortcomings, however: the short turnaround time of the ticket, usually not longer than a month; and the limitation on your luggage allowance. You may be required to surrender all your baggage allowance for the use of the courier company, and be only allowed to take carry-on luggage.

Discounted Tickets There are two types of discounted fares – officially discounted (such as Apex – see Promotional Fares) and unofficially discounted (see Bucket Shops). The latter can save you more than money – you may be able to pay Apex prices without the associated Apex advance booking and other requirements. The lowest prices often impose drawbacks, such as flying with unpopular airlines, inconvenient schedules, or unpleasant routes and connections.

Economy Class Tickets Economy-class tickets are usually not the cheapest way to go, though they do give you maximum flexibility and they are valid for 12 months. If you don't use them, most are fully refundable, as are unused sectors of a multiple ticket.

Full Fares Airlines traditionally offer first class (coded F), business class (coded J) and economy class (coded Y) tickets. These days there are so many promotional and discounted fares available that few passengers pay full fare.

Lost Tickets If you lose your airline ticket, an airline will usually treat it like a travellers' cheque and, after inquiries, issue you with a replacement. Legally, however, an airline is entitled to treat it like cash, so if you lose a ticket, it could be forever. Take good care of your tickets.

MCO An MCO (Miscellaneous Charges Order) is a voucher for a value of a given amount, which resembles an airline ticket and can be used to pay for a specific flight with any IATA (International Air Transport Association) airline. MCOs, which are more flexible than a regular ticket, may satisfy the irritating onward ticket requirement, but some countries are now reluctant to accept them. MCOs are fully refundable if unused.

No Shows No shows are passengers who fail to show up for their flight for whatever reason. Full-fare no shows are sometimes entitled to travel on a later flight. The rest of us are penalised (see Cancellation Penalties).

Open Jaw Tickets These are return tickets which allow you to fly to one place but return from another, and travel between the two 'jaws' by any means of transport at your own expense. If available, this c an save you backtracking to your arrival point.

Overbooking Airlines hate to fly with empty seats, and since every flight has some passengers who fail to show up (see No Shows), they often book more passengers than they have seats available. Usually the excess passengers balance those who fail to show up, but occasionally somebody gets bumped. If this happens, guess who it is most likely to be? The passengers who check in late.

Promotional Fares These are officially discounted fares, such as Apex fares, which are available from travel agents or direct from the airline.

Reconfirmation You must contact the airline at least 72 hours prior to departure to 'reconfirm' that you intend to be on the flight. If you don't do this, the airline can delete your name from the passenger list and you could lose your seat.

Restrictions Discounted tickets often have various restrictions on them, such as necessity of advance purchase, limitations on the minimum and maximum period you must be away, restrictions on breaking the journey or changing the booking or route etc.

Round-the-World Tickets These tickets have become very popular in the last few years; basically, there are two types – airline tickets and agent tickets. An airline RTW ticket is issued by two or more airlines that have joined together to market a ticket which takes you around the world on their combined routes as long as you don't backtrack, ie keep moving in approximately the same direction east or west. Other restrictions are that you (usually) must book the first sector in advance and cancellation penalties then apply. There may be restrictions on how many stopovers you are permitted. The RTW tickets are usually valid for 90 days up to a year.

The other type of RTW ticket, the agent ticket, is a combination of cheap fares strung together by an enterprising travel agent. These may be cheaper than airline RTW tickets, but the choice of routes will be limited.

Stand-by This is a discounted ticket where you only fly if there is a seat free at the last moment. Stand-by fares are usually only available directly at the airport, but sometimes may also be handled by an airline's city office. To give yourself the best possible chance of getting on the flight you want, get there early and have your name placed on the waiting list. It's first come, first served.

Student Discounts Some airlines offer student-card holders 15% to 25% discounts on their tickets. The same often applies to anyone under the age of 26. These discounts are generally only available on ordinary economy-class fares. You wouldn't get one, for instance, on an Apex or an RTW ticket, since these are already discounted.

Tickets Out An entry requirement for many countries is that you have an onward or return ticket, in other words, a ticket out of the country. If you're not sure what you intend to do next, the easiest solution is to buy the cheapest onward ticket to a neighbouring country or a ticket from a reliable airline which can later be refunded if you do not use it.

Transferred Tickets Airline tickets cannot be transferred from one person to another. Travellers sometimes try to sell the return half of their ticket, but officials can ask you to prove that you are the person named on the ticket. This may not be checked on domestic flights, but on international flights, tickets are usually compared with passports.

Travel Periods Some officially discounted fares, Apex fares in particular, vary with the time of year. There is often a low (off-peak) season and a high (peak) season. Sometimes there's an intermediate or shoulder season as well. At peak times, when everyone wants to fly, both officially and unofficially discounted fares will be higher, or there may simply be no discounted tickets available. Usually the fare depends on your outward flight – if you depart in the high season and return in the low season, you pay the high-season fare. ■

Australasia

STA Travel and Flight Centres International are major dealers in cheap airfares. Check the travel agents' ads in the Telecom Yellow Pages, and the Saturday travel sections of Sydney's *Sydney Morning Herald* and Melbourne's *Age* newspapers. STA has offices at 224 Faraday St, Carlton, Vic 3053 (☎ 03-9347 6911); 732 Harris St, Ultimo, NSW 2007 (☎ 02-9281 1530); and 10 High St, PO Box 4156, Auckland (☎ 09-309 0458).

Flight Centres International has offices at 19 Bourke St, Melbourne 3000 (☎ 03-650 2899) and 82 Elizabeth St, Sydney 2000 (☎ 02-235 3522). No airline flies direct into Switzerland from Australia – connections are usually via Singapore or Bangkok. Return fares to Europe on mainstream airlines through a reputable agent like the Flight Centre cost between A$1600 (low season) and A$2500 (high season). Flights to/from Perth are a couple of hundred dollars cheaper.

There are no direct flights to Switzerland from New Zealand, either, and the cheapest flights will usually be via the USA. An RTW ticket may be the best deal.

Africa

Nairobi is probably the best place in Africa to buy tickets to Europe, thanks to the many bucket shops and the strong competition between them. A typical one-way/return fare to London would be about US$550/800. Alternatively, a nonstop flight to Zürich (Monday, Wednesday and Saturday) on Swissair will start at around US$860 for a return 75-day excursion fare.

Swissair flies directly to Zürich from a number of other places in Africa, including Johannesburg (Tuesday, Friday, Saturday and Sunday). Several West African countries such as Burkina Faso and the Gambia offer cheap charter flights to France, and charter fares from Morocco can be incredibly cheap if you're lucky enough to find a seat. If you intend departing from Cairo, it's often cheaper to fly to Athens and to proceed with a budget bus or train from there.

Asia

Hong Kong is the discount airfare capital of Asia, and its bucket shops are at least as unreliable as those of other cities. Ask the advice of other travellers before buying a ticket. Many of the cheapest fares from South-East Asia to Europe are offered by Eastern European carriers. STA has branches in Hong Kong, Tokyo, Singapore, Bangkok and Kuala Lumpur.

To/from India, the cheapest flights tend to be with Eastern European carriers like LOT, or with Middle Eastern airlines such as Syrian Arab Airlines and Iran Air. Bombay is the air transport hub of Asia, with many transit options to/from South-East Asia, but tickets are slightly cheaper in Delhi. Try Delhi Student Travel Services in the Imperial Hotel, Janpath.

Swissair flies to/from Zürich to Karachi, Bombay, Delhi, Bangkok, Singapore, Hong Kong, Beijing, Seoul, Tokyo and Manila, with connecting flights to/from Geneva.

BUS

Buses are generally slower, cheaper and less comfortable than trains. Eurolines (☎ 0171-730 8235), 52 Grosvenor Gardens, Victoria, London SW1, is the main international carrier. Eurolines' European representatives include:

Budget Bus, Rokin 10, Amsterdam
   (☎ 020-627 51 51)
Xenagos Tourism, Stadiou, Syntagma Square, Athens
   (☎ 01-32 32 180)
Eurolines, 55 Rue Saint Jacques, 75005 Paris
   (☎ 1-43 54 11 99)
Deutsche Touring, Hauptbahnhof, Munich
   (☎ 089-54 58 70 15)
Lazzi Express, via Tagliamento 27R, Rome
   (☎ 06-88 40 840)

These may also be able to advise you on other bus companies and deals.

On ordinary return trips, youth fares are around 10% less than the ordinary full fare, eg a London-Zürich return ticket (via Basel; valid six months) costs £99 for adults or £89 for youths under 26 years old. There are up to three departures per week (only one in low season) from London's Victoria Coach Station. The London-Geneva return fare costs the same, and there are three departures per week year round. The journey time for each service is 20 hours. Geneva also has international bus routes heading to Rome, the south of France, and along the eastern coast of Spain (see the Geneva chapter). Eurolines' representative in Zürich is Marti Travel (☎ 01-221 04 72), Usteristrasse 10.

Eurobus has well-equipped buses which complete a figure of eight loop of Europe, taking in Amsterdam, Brussels, Paris, Zürich, Lucerne, Prague, Budapest and major cities in Germany and Italy. Unlimited travel fares are: under 26 years, UK£169 for two months and UK£219 for three months; and 26 and over, UK£219 for two months, UK£270 for three months. Tickets are available in many countries worldwide (eg from STA, or SSR within Switzerland), though you need to make your own way to a city on the loop to start off.

TRAIN

Trains are a popular, convenient and pollution-free way to travel. They are also good meeting places, comfortable and reasonably frequent.

Stories about train passengers being gassed or drugged and then robbed occasionally surface, though bag-snatching is more of a worry. Sensible security measures include not letting your bags out of your sight (or at least chaining them to the luggage rack) and locking compartment doors overnight.

Europe

European railpasses (see below) make train travel affordable, but unless you want to explore other countries in Europe as well, it will probably work out cheaper to pay the normal fare to Switzerland then use one of the Swiss railpasses to explore the country (see the Getting Around chapter). When weighing up options, bear in mind that within Switzerland, Swiss railpasses are valid on more private rail lines than the European passes, and you can get discounts on mountain transport (see the Getting Around

chapter), which the European passes tend not to include. Supplements and reservation costs are not covered by any railpasses, and pass holders must always carry their passport on the train for identification purposes.

If do you plan to travel extensively in Europe by train, it might be worth getting hold of the *Thomas Cook European Timetable*, which gives a complete listing of train schedules and indicates where supplements apply or where reservations are necessary. It is updated monthly and is available from Thomas Cook outlets in the UK and Australia, and in the USA from Forsyth Travel Library (☎ 800-367 7984), 9154 West 57th St, PO Box 2975, Shawnee Mission, KS 66201-1375.

Paris, Amsterdam, Munich, Milan and Vienna are all important hubs for international rail connections. Switzerland, located at the heart of Europe, has excellent services to/from these hubs and the rest of the continent. Zürich is the busiest international terminus. To Vienna it has two day trains (takes nine hours) and one night train, and to Munich it has four daily trains (takes four hours); from either city there are extensive onward connections to/from eastern Europe. There are several trains a day to both Geneva and Lausanne from Paris, and journey time is three to four hours by the super-fast TGV. Paris to Bern takes 4½ hours by TGV. Most connections from Germany pass through Zürich or Basel. Nearly all connections from Italy pass through Milan before branching off to Zürich, Lucerne, Bern or Lausanne.

Travellers aged under 26 can pick up Billet International de Jeunesse (BIJ) tickets which cut fares on international journeys by up to 50%. Unfortunately, you can't always bank on a substantial reduction; the youth return from London to Zürich costs UK£120, compared to the normal fare of £137. Various agents issue BIJ tickets in Europe, eg Campus Travel, already mentioned in the Air section, which sells Eurotrain tickets. British Rail International (0171-834 2345) and Wasteels (0171-834 7066) also sell BIJ tickets in London. They are also available from agents in all major European cities, such as Council Travel (☎ 0144 55 55 65) in Paris. See the previous Air travel section for details about other travel agents. Tickets combining several destinations on a circular tour, such as Eurotrain's 'Explorer' tickets, are also worth looking into.

For a small fee, European nationals aged over 60 can get a Rail Europe Senior Card as an add-on to their national rail senior pass. It entitles the holder to reduced European fares. Up to a third of the fare can be knocked off depending on the route, though the London-Zürich senior return of £121 saves only £16.

Express trains can be identified by the symbols EuroCity (EC, serving international routes) or InterCity (IC, serving national routes). The French TGV and the German Intercity Express (ICE) trains are even faster. Supplements can apply on fast trains, and it is a good idea (sometimes obligatory) to make seat reservations at peak times and on certain lines. Overnight trips usually offer a choice of couchette (around US$20) or a more expensive sleeper. Long-distance trains have a dining car or snacks available. Supplements sometimes apply on international trains. Reservations made in Switzerland are subject to a Sfr5 to Sfr22 surcharge depending upon the day and/or the service.

European Rail Passes These may not work out much more expensive than a straightforward return ticket, and are worth considering if you want to explore several destinations. Shop around, as pass prices can vary between different outlets. Once purchased, take care of your pass, as it can not be replaced or refunded if lost or stolen. European passes get reductions on Eurostar through the Channel Tunnel.

Eurail Pass This pass can only be bought by residents of non-European countries, and it will be easier and probably cheaper to buy before arriving in Europe. Eurailpasses are valid for unlimited travel on national railways and some private lines in Austria, Belgium, Denmark, Finland, France (including Monaco), Germany, Greece, Hungary,

Italy, Luxembourg, the Netherlands, Norway, Portugal, Ireland, Spain, Sweden and Switzerland (including Liechtenstein). Britain is not covered. The pass is valid for some international ferries and reductions are given on steamer services in various countries.

A standard Youthpass for travellers under 26 is valid for unlimited 2nd-class travel for 15 days (US$418), one month (US$598) or two months (US$798). The Youth Flexipass, also for 2nd-class travel, is valid for freely chosen days within a two-month period: 10 days for US$438 or 15 days for US$588.

The corresponding passes for those aged over 26 are available in 1st class only. The standard Eurailpass has five versions, costing from US$522 for 15 days unlimited travel up to US$1468 for three months. The Flexipass costs US$616 or US$812 for 10 or 15 freely chosen days in two months.

Two or more people travelling together (minimum three people between 1 April and 30 September) can get good discounts on a Saverpass, which works like the standard Eurailpass. Eurailpasses for children are also available.

Europass This is a cheaper, restricted version of Eurail, allowing travel in at least three countries out of a choice of France, Germany, Italy, Spain and Switzerland. The pass gives free unlimited travel on freely chosen days within a two-month period. Prices for adults/youths are: US$316/210 for five days in three countries (four countries for youths only), US$442/297 for eight days in four countries, or US$568/384 for 11 days in all five countries. Up to four additional free days cost US$42/29 each. A few other countries can be added on for a fee (eg Austria for US$45/32) but all chosen countries must be adjacent.

Inter-Rail Pass The Inter-Rail pass is available in Europe to people who have been resident there for at least six months. It can be purchased within all countries that are part of the scheme; terms and conditions vary, but you can expect to only get a discount of around 50% on normal fares in the country where you buy it (in other words, don't buy one in Switzerland if you want to travel around Switzerland).

The normal Inter-Rail pass is for travellers under 26 and has been split into zones. Zone A is Ireland (and Great Britain if the pass is bought outside Great Britain); B is Sweden, Norway and Finland; C is Denmark, Germany, Switzerland and Austria; D is the Czech Republic, Slovakia, Poland, Hungary, Bulgaria, Romania and Croatia; E is France, Belgium, Netherlands and Luxembourg; F is Spain, Portugal and Morocco; and G is Italy, Greece, Turkey and Slovenia. The price for any one zone is UK£185 for 15 days. Multizone passes are better value and are valid for one month: two zones is UK£220, three zones is UK£245, and all zones is UK£275. Depending on the zones purchased, many sea, river and lake services are covered for discounts or free travel.

There is a non-zonal Inter-Rail pass for travellers aged 26 and over, but this version is not valid for travel within Switzerland.

Euro-Domino Pass There is a Euro-Domino pass (called a Freedom pass in Britain) for each of the countries covered in the zonal Inter-Rail pass, except for Croatia and Romania. Adults (travelling 1st or 2nd class) and youths (under 26) can choose from three, five, or 10 days' validity within one month. Passes can be bought by European residents, but they can't buy a pass valid for their own country of residence. Discounts are given on transit routes from the country of purchase to the country paid for. The pass for Switzerland if purchased in Britain costs: adults, £109, £119, or £159 in 2nd class and £159, £189 or £229 in 1st class; youths, £79, £89 or £119 in 2nd class. See Swiss Travel Passes in the Getting Around chapter for more information.

Asia

It takes 50 hours on the direct train from Basel to Moscow (via Cologne) and costs Sfr346, plus Sfr62 for two nights in a compulsory sleeper. From there you can take four different trains for onwards eastern travel. Three of them (the trans-Siberian, trans-Mongolian and trans-Manchurian) follow the same route to/from Moscow across Siberia but have different eastern railheads. The fourth, the trans-Kazakstan, runs between Moscow and Ürümqi (northwestern China) across central Asia. Prices can vary enormously, depending on where you buy the ticket and what is included, but you won't save money compared to flying. If you have time (between six and nine days minimum) they are an interesting option, but only really worthwhile if you want to stop off and explore China and Russia on the way through. They could become more popular as tourism expands in the region.

CAR & MOTORCYCLE

Getting to Switzerland by road is simple, as there are fast, well-maintained motorways (freeways) through all surrounding countries. German motorways (*Autobahnen*) have no tolls or speed limits, whereas Austrian, French (*autoroute*) and Italian (*autostrada*) motorways have both. Austria has a flat charge of AS150 (nearly US$15) to use its motorways for two months, as well as having tolls for specific tunnels. To avoid a long drive to Switzerland, consider putting your car on a motorail service, which is run by the national railways: many head south from Calais and Paris.

The Alps present a natural hazard to entering Switzerland, but main highways tend to blast straight through such immovable objects. An important tunnel if approaching from the south is the Grand St Bernard between Aosta (Italy) and Bourg St Pierre (toll from Sfr27 for cars and Motorbikes). The minor roads are more fun and scenically more interesting but they can be time-consuming, and special care is needed when negotiating mountain passes. Some, such as the N5 (E21) route from Champagnole (in France) to Geneva are not recommended if you have not had previous experience of driving in the mountains.

Petrol is 10 to 15% cheaper in Switzerland than in all neighbouring countries, so aim to arrive with a nearly empty tank and fill up with fuel once you're inside the country.

Paperwork & Preparations

Proof of ownership of a private vehicle should always be carried (Vehicle Registration Document for British-registered cars) when touring Europe. An EU driving licence is acceptable for driving throughout Europe. If you have any other type of licence it is advisable or necessary to obtain an International Driving Permit (IDP) from an automobile association. If you're a member of one of these associations, ask for a letter of introduction, which will make it easier to enjoy reciprocal benefits offered by affiliated organisations in Europe.

Third-party motor insurance is a minimum requirement in Europe: get proof of this in the form of a Green Card, issued by your insurers. Also ask for a 'European Accident Statement' form. Taking out a European breakdown assistance policy, such as the AA Five Star Service or the RAC Eurocover Motoring Assistance, is a good investment.

Every vehicle travelling across an international border should display a nationality plate of its country of registration. A warning triangle, to be used in the event of breakdown, is compulsory almost everywhere in Europe, including Switzerland. Recommended accessories are a first-aid kit (compulsory in Austria, Slovenia, Croatia, Yugoslavia and Greece), a spare bulb kit, and a fire extinguisher. In the UK, contact the RAC (☎ 0181-686 0088) or the AA (☎ 0256-20123) for more information.

Driving is on the right throughout continental Europe, and priority is usually given to traffic approaching from the right. The RAC annually brings out its *European Motoring Guide*, which gives an excellent summary of regulations in each country, including parking rules. Motoring organisations in other countries have similar publications. Road signs are generally standard throughout Europe.

One thing to be aware of when driving through the continent is that Europeans are particularly strict on drink-driving laws. The blood-alcohol concentration (BAC) limit when driving is between 0.05% and 0.08%, but in some areas (Gibraltar, Eastern Europe, Scandinavia) it can be an extremely strict zero per cent.

Within Switzerland, you can drive a vehicle registered abroad for up to 12 months, and foreign driving licences are also valid for a period of one year. For more on Swiss motoring regulations, see the Getting Around chapter.

If you're from outside Europe and want to buy a vehicle to tour around, you'll find that most European countries have a restriction that only residents may buy and register a vehicle within their borders. This doesn't apply in Britain, and Britain is also one of the cheapest places for buying secondhand cars. However, a vehicle bought in Britain will be left-hand drive (ie the driver's seat will be on the 'wrong' side for driving on the right), and the headlights would need to be adjusted. An alternative to purchasing is to lease, eg the Renault Eurodrive Scheme.

Camper Van

Travelling in a camper van can be a surprisingly economical option for budget travellers, as it can take care of eating, sleeping and travelling in one convenient package. London is a good place to buy: look in *TNT* magazine, *Loot* newspaper and go to the Van Market in Market Rd, London N7. Expect to spend at least £1000 to £1500 (US$1600 to US$2400). The most common camper van is the VW based on the 1600 cc or 2000 cc Transporter, and spare parts are widely available in Europe. Discrete free camping is rarely a problem, and is certainly permitted in autobahn rest areas in Austria, Germany and Switzerland.

A drawback with camper vans is that they're expensive to buy in spring and hard to sell in autumn. A car and tent might do just as well instead.

Motorcycle Touring

Europe and Switzerland are ideal for motorcycle touring, with winding roads of good quality, stunning scenery to stimulate the senses, and an active motorcycling scene. The wearing of crash helmets for rider and passenger is compulsory everywhere in Europe nowadays. Austria, Belgium, France, Germany, Luxembourg and Spain require that motorcyclists use headlights during the day; in Switzerland it is recommended.

Motorway Tax

Upon entering Switzerland you will need to decide whether you wish to use the motorways and semi-motorways (identified by green signs). There is a one-off charge of Sfr40 if you do. Organise this money beforehand, since you might not always be able to change money at the border – or try to buy it in advance from a Switzerland Tourism office or a motoring organisation such as the AA. The tax is payable if using either the St Gotthard tunnel or the San Bernardino tunnel. Officials at some major crossings may insist you pay the charge even if you declare you only want to use minor roads, in which case backtrack and re-approach via a smaller road, where you should have no trouble getting in. The sticker (called a *vignette*) you receive upon paying the motorway tax must be displayed on the windscreen. It is valid for a calendar year with a month's leeway either side (ie if you visit on 1 December you can buy the following year's tax, or up to 31 January you can visit on the previous year's tax). If you're caught on the motorways without the vignette you pay a fine of Sfr100 plus the tax. A separate vignette is required for trailers and caravans, and motorcyclists are also charged the AS40.

BICYCLE

This is one of the best ways to travel in terms of your bank balance, your health, and the environment. But it does require a high level of commitment to see it through.

Starting from Britain, consider joining the Cyclists' Touring Club (☎ 01483-417 217), Cotterell House, 69 Meadrow, Godalming, Surrey GU7 3HS. It can supply information to members on cycling conditions in Europe as well as detailed routes, itineraries and cheap insurance. Membership costs £25 a year, or £12.50 for students and those under 18.

Good routes into the country from the north are through the German Black Forest or around Lake Constance. Access from the south is difficult because of the Alps. Coming from the west you need to negotiate the Jura Mountains chain to get into French Switzerland. The approach from Austria in the east is also mountainous but scenically rewarding.

If coming from farther afield, bikes can be carried by aeroplane, but check with the carrier in advance, preferably before buying your ticket. To take it as a normal piece of luggage, you may need to remove the pedals or turn the handlebars sideways, but beware of possible excess baggage costs.

A primary consideration on long cycling trips is to travel light, but you should take a few tools and spare parts including a puncture repair kit and a spare inner tube. Panniers are essential to balance your possessions on either side of the bike frame. A bike helmet is also a very good idea, as is a good bike lock. Seasoned cyclists can average 80 km a day but there's no point overdoing it. The slower you travel, the more locals you're likely to meet.

Bicycles are not allowed on European motorways – not that you would want to use those tedious bits of concrete anyway. Stick to small roads or dedicated bike tracks where possible. If you get weary of pedalling or simply want to skip a boring section, you can put your feet up on the train. On slower trains, bikes can usually be taken on board as luggage, subject to a small supplementary fee. Fast trains (IC, EC etc) can rarely accommodate bikes: they need to be sent as registered luggage and may end up on a different train from the one you take. British Rail is not part of the European luggage registration scheme, but Eurostar is: it charges UK£20 to send a bike as registered luggage on its routes. In Switzerland, it costs Sfr24 to send a bike as international luggage.

Europe by Bike written by Karen & Terry

Whitehall outlines some worthwhile European bike tours.

HITCHING

Hitching is never entirely safe in any country in the world, and we don't recommend it. Travellers who decide to hitch should understand they are taking a small but potentially serious risk. People who do choose to hitch will be safer if they travel in pairs and let someone know where they are going.

Throughout Europe, hitching is illegal on motorways – stand on the slip roads, or approach drivers at petrol stations, border posts and truck stops. *Autohof* usually indicates a parking spot able to accommodate trucks. You can increase your chances of getting a lift by looking presentable and cheerful and making a cardboard sign indicating your intended destination in the local language. Showing a flag or some other indication of your country of origin can also help. Never hitch where drivers can't stop in good time or without causing an obstruction. Once you find a good spot, stay put and hope for the best. When it starts getting dark – forget it!

Ferry tickets for a vehicle usually covers all passengers, so hitchers may be able to secure a free passage by hitching before cars board the boat.

A safer way to hitch is to arrange a lift through an organisation, such as Allostop-Provoya in France and Mitfahrzentrale in Germany. You could also scan university notice boards. Zürich has a Mitfahrzentrale – see the Zürich Canton chapter.

MOUNTAIN ESCAPES

The most dramatic way to arrive or leave Switzerland is over the Alps. This is straightforward by car, but there are more exciting ways to do it. By skis is one, on the Ventina route to Italy (see the Zermatt section in the Valais chapter for details). Ski mountaineers traverse the Valais Alps on the Haute Route to Chamonix in France.

There are also various hiking trails. A famous route is over the Great St Bernard Pass, via the historic hospice, towards Mont Blanc (see the Great St Bernard Pass section also in the Valais chapter). One route around Mont Blanc takes in three countries (see the Mont Blanc aside, also in the Valais chapter).

BOAT

Getting to Europe by boat is not the option it used to be. Nowadays you can all but forget about trying to work your passage. Travel agents can tell you about luxury cruise ships across the Atlantic, or consult the *OAG Cruise & Ferry Guide* published by OAG (☎ 01582-60 01 11), Church St, Dunstable, Bedfordshire, England, LU5 4 HB. This volume is also useful if you want to take the more adventurous option of travelling as a paying passenger on a freighter.

Once in Europe, you can use the river network to get about; it's slower, more expensive, but probably more enjoyable than getting about by land. It is possible to take a cruise down the Rhine all the way from Basel to Amsterdam but you'll need a boatload of money to do so. The main operator along the Rhine is the German K"ln-Düsseldorfer (KD) Line (☎ 0221-20 88 288), Its Frankenwerft, 50667 Cologne, Germany. Its agent in Britain is GA Clubb Rhine Cruise Agency Ltd (☎ 01372-742 033), 28 South St, Epsom, Surrey. The four-night trip costs upwards of UK£688 per person. A three-night cruise from Basel to Düsseldorf costs £408. Both services operate from late April to mid-October, and have discounts of 20% before June and 10% during July.

Boats sail from Basel to Budapest, making use of the Main-Danube Canal. The 15-day cruise costs at least Sfr2520. Contact Triton Reisen (☎ 061-271 94 30), Margarethenstrasse 60, Basel. Switzerland can also be reached by steamer from several lakes: from Germany via Lake Constance (Bodensee in German); from Italy via Lake Maggiore; and from France via Lake Geneva. (See the relevant sections.)

DEPARTURE TAXES

See Airport Taxes in the Air section at the start of this chapter.

ORGANISED TOURS

All-in skiing holidays are the most popular way to visit Switzerland using a tour operator. All the large companies, such as Thomson, Bladon and Kuoni, include Swiss ski resorts in their brochures. Enquire at travel agents or look in the national press for details of these and other special interest holidays.

Young revellers (age 18 to 35 or 38) can party on Europe-wide bus tours. Tracks offers budget coach/camping tours for under US$40 per day, plus food fund. It has a London office (☎ 0171-937 3028) and is represented in Australia and New Zealand by Adventure World; in North America, call ☎ 800-233 6046. Contiki (☎ 0181-290 6422) and Top Deck (☎ 0171-370 6487) offer camping or hotel-based bus tours. Both have offices or representatives in North America, Australasia and South Africa. All these operators converge on Lauterbrunnen, in the Jungfrau Region, for the Swiss leg of the European itinerary. Some of their routes also include Lucerne.

For people aged over 50, Saga Holidays (☎ 0800-300 500), Saga Building, Middelburg Square, Folkestone, Kent CT20 1AZ, Britain, offers good-value all-in holidays. Its brochure includes two tours of Switzerland.

Saga also operates in the USA as Saga International Holidays (☎ 0800-343 0273), 222 Berkeley St, Boston, MA 02116, and in Australia as Saga Holidays Australasia (☎ 02-99 57 56 60), Level One, 110 Pacific Highway, North Sydney, NSW 2060.

WARNING

The information in this chapter is particularly vulnerable to change: prices for international travel are volatile, routes are introduced and cancelled, schedules change, special deals come and go, and rules and visa requirements are amended. Airlines and governments seem to take a perverse pleasure in making price structures and regulations as complicated as possible. You should check directly with the airline or a travel agent to make sure you understand how a fare (and any ticket you buy) works. In addition, the travel industry is highly competitive and there are many lurks and perks.

The upshot of this is that you should get opinions, quotes and advice from as many airlines and travel agents as possible before you part with your hard-earned cash. The details given in this chapter should be regarded as pointers and are not a substitute for your own careful, up-to-date research.

Getting Around

Swiss public transport is a fully integrated and comprehensive system incorporating trains, buses, boats, funiculars and cable cars. It can claim to be one of the most efficient transport networks in the world. It is a rare luxury to travel on a system that works so well. The Swiss think nothing of co-ordinating schedules where there may be only a few minutes leeway between arrivals and departures. Missing a connection through a late arrival is rare. Various special tickets are available to the tourist to make the system even more attractive.

Information is readily available as and when you need it, but if you like to plan things down to the very last detail, pick up the complete timetable of trains, boats, buses and mountain transport that covers the whole country (Sfr16, in two volumes), and is sold at most Swiss train stations. Timetables often refer to *Werktags* (work days), which means Monday to Saturday, unless there is the qualification 'ausser Samstag' (except Saturday).

European railpasses (Inter-Rail and Eurail) will get you free travel to most places you might want to go (but not to Zermatt, for example), and rarely on mountain transport. Generally, where they are valid for boats or private railways, Inter-Rail gets a 50% discount and Eurail is good for free travel. Note that the Swiss travel passes mentioned below offer a wider choice of routes, including bus routes.

PASSES

The best deal for people planning to travel extensively is the Swiss Pass, entitling the holder to unlimited travel on Swiss Federal Railways, boats, most Alpine postbuses and also on trams and buses in 35 towns with reductions of 25% on funiculars and mountain railways. Passes are valid for four days (Sfr210), eight days (Sfr264), 15 days (Sfr306) and one month (Sfr420): these prices are for 2nd-class tickets – 1st class is about 50% higher.

The Swiss Card allows a free return journey from your arrival point to any destination in Switzerland, 50% off rail, boat and bus excursions, and 25 to 50% reductions on mountain railways. The cost is Sfr140 (2nd class) or Sfr170 (1st class) and it is valid for a month. The Half-Fare Card is a similar deal minus the free return trip. The cost is Sfr90 for one month or Sfr150 for one year. If you plan to use many cable cars, it may pay to get the Half-Fare Card rather than the Swiss Pass, as the reduction is greater (50% as against 25%). This pass would certainly be worth considering for car drivers – it would pay for itself after only three or four mountain trips. The Swiss Flexi Pass allows free, unlimited trips for three days out of 15. The cost for 2nd class is Sfr210.

All these cards are best purchased before arrival in Switzerland from Switzerland Tourism or travel agents, as they are only available from a few major transport centres once within the country (such as at Zürich's Hauptbahnhof). The Family Card can save families a lot of money. It's good for free travel (on trains, buses and boats – even on some cable cars) for children aged under 16 accompanied by at least one parent. Additionally, unmarried children aged 16 to under 25 accompanied by at least one parent pay 50%. Most vendors of the various Swiss travel passes will supply a Family Card free to pass purchasers; if not, they can be bought from major Swiss railway stations for Sfr20.

Regional passes are available for free travel on certain days and for half-price travel on other days within a seven or 15-day period, but they are only valid within that particular region. Details are given at the beginning of the relevant chapters. Buy these passes in the region or at some major stations before you get there.

Another option worth considering is a Euro-Domino Pass (see European Rail Passes in the Getting There & Away chapter). The pass for Switzerland is sold by European national railways *outside* Switzerland and can be bought by non-Swiss Europeans. For getting around Switzerland, the Euro Domino is far superior to Inter-Rail, as it covers many private railways for free travel (where Inter-Rail only gives 50% off) as well as including postbuses and city transport in many towns. However, unlike the Swiss national passes, it gives no discounts on cable cars.

AIR

Internal flights are not of great interest to the visitor, owing to Switzerland's excellent ground transport. Swissair has flights between Zürich and Geneva, but it is Crossair, a subsidiary of Swissair, that is the major carrier. It has several flights daily between Zürich, Geneva, Basel (Mulhouse), Bern and Lugano. The fare from Zürich to Geneva is Sfr325 return or Sfr225 one-way. Swissair is a sales agent for Crossair. See the Getting There & Away chapter for information on the Fly-Rail programme.

Some mountain resorts have helicopter operators which offer hugely enjoyable but highly expensive cruises around the Alps.

BUS

Yellow postbuses are a supplement to the rail network, following postal routes and linking towns to the more inaccessible regions in the mountains. In all, routes cover some 8000 km of terrain. They are extremely regular, and departures tie in with train arrivals. Postbus stations are almost invariably next to train stations. Tickets are usually purchased from the driver, although on some routes over the Alps (for example, the Lugano-St Moritz service) it is necessary to reserve a place in advance. Details are given in the relevant chapters. For a flat fee of Sfr12 unaccompanied luggage can be sent ahead to a post office and picked up later – an especially useful service for hikers relying on the postbus network.

TRAIN

The Swiss rail network covers 5000 km and is a combination of state-run and private lines. The train is a great way to see the country and classic scenic rail routes abound. The Glacier Express route is the most famous (see Zermatt), but there are many other trips to enjoy, such as the Panorama Express from Montreux to Zweisimmen.

The Swiss Federal Railway is abbreviated to SBB in German, CFF in French and FFS in Italian. All major stations are connected to each other by hourly departures, and the normal operating time is between 6 am and midnight. Trains are clean, reliable, frequent and as fast as the terrain will allow. A rack and pinion (cogwheel) system is utilised on railtracks with severe gradients. An example is the line to Zermatt. Carriages are always divided into smoking and non-smoking sections and long-distance trains usually have a dining car.

In fact, Switzerland is the first country in the world to have a McDonald's restaurant on board. There are two of them (McDonald's paid around US$5 million for them in 1992) and they are on the Basel-Geneva and Geneva-Brig service. Prices are the same as in a normal McDonald's restaurant.

Information & Tickets

Larger stations have separate information offices that can help you plan your route and give you a computerised print-out of your itinerary. Even small stations can usually give advice in English and itineraries. Free timetable booklets are invariably available. A Switzerland-wide number for train information is ☎ 157 22 22; calls are charged at Sfr1.19 per minute.

Single train tickets for journeys over 80 km are valid for two days and it is possible to break the journey on the same ticket, but tell the conductor of your intentions before your ticket is punched. Train schedules are revised yearly, so you should double-check all fares and frequencies quoted. Ordinary fares are expensive, meaning that one of the special passes mentioned will almost certainly save you money. If you have a specific itinerary and don't require flexibility, then a *Rundfarht* (*Billet Circulaire* in French) ticket

Major Swiss Rail Routes

might do the job instead. This is a return ticket that allows you to take a circuitous route, with stops along the way. Like all return tickets over 160 km, it is valid for one month. Unfortunately, these tickets are now priced according to a different system, and aren't the bargain they once were.

All fares quoted are for 2nd class unless stated otherwise, and fares for 1st class average about 65% higher. Return fares are cheaper than two singles only on longer trips. Look out for special deals offered by SBB, such as cheap day passes in low season, or off-peak tickets.

Some rural, smaller rail lines have a 'self-control' ticketing system – look out for the yellow eye pictogram. On these services, be sure to buy a ticket before boarding, or risk a fine.

Luggage
Train stations invariably offer luggage storage, either at a special counter (usually Sfr5 per piece) or in 24-hour lockers (Sfr2 or Sfr3 small, Sfr3 or Sfr5 large). Nearly every station allows you the option to send your luggage ahead by train where you can pick it up at your destination station in the eve-

ning. This is especially useful if you're on a tight schedule and are visiting several different locations in the course of the day before your overnight stop. The charge is Sfr10 per piece (Sfr8 for skis, Sfr12 for bikes).

Platforms & Trains
Station announcements state on which track (*Gleis* in German, *voie* in French) the train is due. Station platforms are long and are divided into sections, A to D. Take care – a small rural train may already be waiting at one end while you're vainly waiting for it to arrive at the other end.

In SBB trains, first class seats are comfortable and spacious, usually a single and a pair across the width of the carriage. A few private lines are less generous with space, or may not have 1st class at all. It is rare for 1st class to be full; often it's virtually empty. The placement of 1st-class sections is usually announced over the loudspeaker in stations, or shown in a diagram on the platform. As the train approaches, look for the easy-to-see horizontal yellow stripe along the carriage. But second class is perfectly comfortable, with two seats either side of the aisle. These carriages are sometimes fairly full, espe-

MARK HONAN

The St Bernard Express at Martigny, Valais.

cially when the army is on the move, but it is rare that you'll have to stand.

CAR & MOTORCYCLE

Driving is an enjoyable experience in Switzerland. Roads are well maintained, well signposted and generally not too congested. You may find it frustrating to have to concentrate on the road while magnificent scenery unfolds all around, but at least you can stop at frequent parking bays to take it all in.

Travelling in your own vehicle gives you the most flexibility, and compared to most other countries, it is not necessary to spend very long on the road between places of interest. Unfortunately, the independence you enjoy does tend to isolate you to some extent from the local people. You should also consider the effect your exhaust emissions have on the Alpine environment. Cars are usually inconvenient in city centres, where it's probably worth ditching your trusty chariot and relying on public transport.

You generally have a choice when driving in mountainous areas. Principal routes are as direct as the terrain will allow, often ploughing through mountains via long tunnels. Smaller roads go over the mountains. They take much longer to negotiate and add miles to your journey, but are scenically much more rewarding. Some of these minor passes are closed from November to May (see the Alpine Passes section later in this chapter) and you should stay in low gear on steep stretches. Carrying snow chains is recommended in winter.

The Swiss Touring Club (☎ 022-737 12 12; fax 737 12 12), or Touring Club der Schweiz (TCS), is at 9 Rue Pierre Fatio, CH-1211, Geneva 3. It is the largest motoring organisation in Switzerland, and is affiliated with the RAC (Britain), AAA (USA) and AAA (Australia). The Swiss Automobile Club (☎ 031-311 77 22; 311 03 10), or Automobil-Club der Schweiz (ACS), at Wasserwerkgasse 39, CH-3000 Bern 13, also has with affiliations round the world. TCS operates the national 24-hour emergency breakdown service (☎ 140). It can be used free by members of the Swiss motoring clubs or their affiliates; anybody else has to pay, and charges can be high. The TCS or the ACS can provide detailed information about motoring in Switzerland. Call ☎ 163 for traffic conditions (recorded information).

Petrol prices per litre are around Sfr1.25 for leaded (Super), Sfr1.15 for unleaded (*Bleifrei, sans plomb*), and Sfr1.20 for diesel.

Road Rules & Signs

A handbook on Swiss traffic regulations (in English) is available for Sfr5 from cantonal registration offices and at some customs posts. The minimum driving age for car and motorcycles is 18; it's 14 for mopeds.

The Swiss drive on the right, and if in doubt, always give priority to traffic approaching from the right. Vehicles on roundabouts have priority over those about to enter it. On mountain roads, the ascending vehicle has priority, unless a postbus is involved, which always has right of way. Postbus drivers let rip a multi-tone bugle that sounds like a call to a cavalry charge when approaching blind corners. In towns, allow trams plenty of respect, and give way to disembarking passengers.

Many driving infringements incur an on-the-spot fine, and you should always ask for a receipt. Speed limits are 50 km/h in towns, 120 km/h on motorways, 100 km/h on semi-motorways and 80 km/h on other roads. Car occupants are required to wear a seat belt (even in the back seat, if they're fitted), and vehicles must carry a breakdown warning triangle which must be readily accessible (ie not in the boot). Dipped headlights must be used in all tunnels, and are recommended for motorcyclists during the day. Motorcyclists must not overtake a line of vehicles . Both motorcyclists and their passengers must wear crash helmets.

Switzerland is tough on drink-driving, so don't risk it; the BAC limit is 0.08%, and if caught exceeding this limit, you may face a heavy fine, a ban from driving in Switzerland for two months, or even imprisonment.

Road signs are straightforward, easy to follow, and adopt internationally recognised conventions. Triangular signs with a red border warn of dangers and circular signs with a red border illustrate prohibitions. Signs you may not have come across before are: a criss-crossed white tyre on a blue circular background means snow chains are compulsory, and a yellow bugle on a square blue background means it is a mountain postal road and you must obey indications given by postbus drivers.

As in most other European countries, motorways and principal routes are designated by two different numbering systems: the national one (N) and the pan-European one (E). Both versions are usually listed in the text. A motorway is identified by the sign showing a white dual-carriageway on a rectangular green background, and a semi-motorway by one showing a white car on a rectangular green background. This is important if you don't want to stray onto a motorway without a vignette (See Motorway Tax in the Getting There & Away chapter).

Urban Parking It is difficult to park in many city centres (especially Zürich). Street parking in surburban white zones is unrestricted, but in the centre (assuming traffic isn't banned altogether, as it often is), street parking will be controlled by parking meters during working hours (Monday to Saturday from 8 am to 6 or 7 pm). These cost around Sfr1 per hour with a maximum of one or two hours. Central streets outside metered areas will probably be marked as blue zones, allowing 1½ hours stay during working hours, or as red zones, with a 15 hour-maximum. In either case parking is free but you need to display a parking disc in your window, indicating the time you first parked. Discs are obtainable free from offices of the Swiss motoring organisations (TCS and ACS), and sometimes from tourist offices or banks.

Alpine Passes

Some minor Alpine passes are closed from November to the end of May. Most of the major ones are negotiable year-round, depending on the weather. Where they aren't (eg the St Bernard, St Gotthard, San Bernardino), there's usually a tunnel to take instead. Other passes that are open only from June to October are Albula, Furka, Grimsel, Klausen, Lukmanier (open from May), Nufenen, Oberalp, Susten, Splügen and

Umbrail. Passes that are open year-round are Bernina, Brünig, Flüela, Forclaz, Il Fuorn (Ofen) Julier, Maloja, Mosses, Pillon and Simplon.

More information on important passes is given throughout the book. A motoring organisation should be able to supply greater detail (gradients, altitudes etc), and a decent road map will also have that information. The local tourist office can tell you if passes are open, or signs on approach roads will state if passes are open and if snow chains are required.

Trains can sometimes carry cars, such as through the Lötschberg tunnel south of Kandersteg.

Car Rental

For the lowest prices, organise car rental before departure. Holiday Autos has good rates for Europe. Its office in England (☎ 0990-300 400) has a lowest price guarantee, and charges UK£173 all-inclusive per week for the lowest-category car in Switzerland. Rates are lower for rental in Germany (from UK£157 per week), and you can drive the car across the border into Switzerland. But this wouldn't be worth the effort unless you wanted to see Germany too; contact the Munich office (☎ 089-17 91 92 93). Holiday Autos has an office in the USA (☎ 909-949 1737).

Fly/drive combinations and other deals are worth looking into. Rail Europe (☎ 800-438 7245) in the USA has 'Rail 'n' Drive' packages, combining car rental and Swiss travel passes. It also offers car rental through Hertz and Avis from US$158 inclusive per week.

Prices are much higher for on-the-spot rates in Switzerland. Local firms are the cheapest operators, though with the multinationals you usually get the option of one-way drop-off (usually no charge within Switzerland). Weekend rates (noon Friday to 9 am Monday) for Budget and Europcar are Sfr190; this is cheaper than for Hertz (Sfr199) and Avis (Sfr214), though all charge from about Sfr185 for the normal daily unlimited rate. The day/km rates are also almost identical between the four – the cheapest category of car costs about Sfr64 per day and Sfr0.90 per km. However, Avis gives a lower rate on the third day, Budget only on the seventh. Collision Damage Waiver (if required) is extra and costs around Sfr26 per day. Theft protection is Sfr9 per day (Sfr5 for Budget). Compare time-spans on weekend deals for other operators – they're not always the same. Toll-free numbers for use within Switzerland are: ☎ 155 05 05 for Europcar and ☎ 155 12 34 for Hertz.

No matter where you rent, make sure you understand what is included in the price (unlimited km, tax, insurance, collision damage waiver etc) and what your liabilities are. The minimum rental age varies from 20 to 25 depending upon the company and category of vehicle, and you'll probably need a credit card (life will certainly be easier with one). Be wary of signing anything in a language you can't read and if you're dealing with a local, cut-price operator it might be worth looking over the car before you agree to the terms.

Motorcycle and moped rental is not very common in Switzerland, but there are a few places that do this (see the Geneva chapter).

Car Purchase

The price of new and used cars in Switzerland is not bad compared to the rest of Europe; unfortunately you must be a Swiss resident to buy one. The TCS publishes a monthly guide to used car prices. All Swiss-registered cars must undergo an emission test every two years (annually for older cars) and a serviceability control test every three years. Car registration plates are issued to the owner, so whether you buy new or second-hand the vehicle will come without plates (though the vending garage can apply for the plates on your behalf). Likewise, if you sell a vehicle, you remove the plates and return them to the cantonal motor registration office (or transfer them to your new car, unless you move canton).

Importing a vehicle into Switzerland is a long and tediously bureaucratic process, and all newly registered cars must be fitted with a catalytic converter. You can drive for one year in a vehicle registered abroad.

BICYCLE

Despite the hilly countryside, cycling is popular in Switzerland. Cycles can be hired from most train stations and returned to any other station with a rental counter, though there is a Sfr6 surcharge if you don't return it to the same station (declare your intentions at the outset). The rental charge for ordinary bikes (seven-speed) is Sfr18 for half a day, Sfr22 for a full day or Sfr88 per week. Counters are open daily, usually from the crack of dawn until some time in the evening. The larger stations also rent mountain bikes (Sfr25/30 for a half/full day, Sfr120 for one week). Bikes can be transported on normal trains but not on IC or EC trains. On slow trains a bike can go in the luggage carriage for Sfr6 – this is a per day fee and you can make more than one journey. On express trains it needs to go as unaccompanied luggage (Sfr12), and may end up on a different train to the one you take. Switzerland Tourism issues three free, useful booklets on cycling holidays, concentrating on the Pre-Alps, the Midlands, and from the Rhine to Ticino.

The Swiss Bike Pass, new in 1996, is valid for two, three or five days and costs Sfr180, Sfr220 or Sfr290. It includes bicycle rental and provides free travel on trains, buses and boats. It can be bought from Swiss train stations.

HITCHING

Although illegal on motorways, hitching is allowed on other roads and can be fairly easy. At other times it can be quite slow. Indigenous Swiss are not all that sympathetic towards hitchers, and you'll find that most of your lifts will come from foreigners. A sign is helpful. Make sure you stand in a place where vehicles can stop. This in itself can be a problem, as rural roads are rarely wide enough to allow stopping (except for passing bays), and there's often no pedestrian walkway beside the road. In other words,

you can't really walk between lifts; find a good spot and stay there. To try to get a ride on a truck, ask around the customs post at border towns (also see the Hitching section in the Getting There & Away chapter).

WALKING

Many city centres are compact enough to enable major tourist sights to be seen on a walking tour, but walking really comes into its own in rural areas. Hikes are an excellent way to leave behind the wail of car horns and the opaque logic of train schedules. (For more information, see the Activities section in the Facts for the Visitor chapter, as well as the individual regional chapters.) Lonely Planet's *Walking in Switzerland* is a detailed and extensively mapped guidebook. Switzerland Tourism also shows the way with its *Switzerland Step by Step* booklets detailing 100 walks to mountain lakes, over mountain passes, and from town to town.

BOAT

All the larger lakes are serviced by steamers operated by Swiss Federal Railway (SBB), or allied private companies for which national travel passes are valid. Lakes covered include Geneva, Constance, Lucerne, Lugano, Neuchâtel, Biel, Murten, Thun, Brienz and Zug, but not Lake Maggiore. Rail passes are not valid for cruises offered by smaller companies on these lakes. A Swiss Navigation Boat Pass costs Sfr35 and entitles the bearer to 50% off fares of all services operated by SBB and major lake carriers (like CGN on Lake Geneva). It is valid for a calendar year, but only a few services operate in winter. The pass is well worth buying for those who aren't covered by a railpass (eg car drivers).

MOUNTAIN TRANSPORT

There are five main modes of transport used in steep Alpine regions. A funicular (*Standseilbahn, funiculaire, funicolare*) is a pair of counter-balancing cars drawn by cables along an inclined track. A cable car (*Luftseilbahn, téléphérique, funivia*) is a cabin dramatically suspended from a cable

MARK HONAN

Revolving cable car at Mt Titlis, Engleberg.

the same ticketing system, so you can change lines on the same ticket. You should buy tickets before boarding from ticket dispensers by stops (beware – some machines don't give change). In some towns, single tickets may give a time limit (eg one-hour) for travel within a particular zone. This means you can break the journey within the time limit but you can't double-back to complete a return trip. Multi-strip tickets are often available at a discount (validate it in the on-board machine at the outset of the journey), and one-day passes are even better value. There are regular checks for people travelling without tickets; those found wanting pay an on-the-spot fine of Sfr40 to Sfr60.

high over a valley, also with a twin that goes down when it goes up. A gondola *(Gondelbahn, télécabine)* is a smaller version of a cable car except that the gondola is hitched onto a continuously running cable once the passengers are inside. Nowadays the terms gondola and cable car are interchangeable and I haven't been pedantic about the distinction. A cable chair or chair lift *(Sesselbahn, télésiège, seggiovia)* is likewise hitched onto a cable but is unenclosed. A ski lift *(Schlepplift, téléski, sciovia)* is a T-bar hanging from a cable, which the skiers hold or sit onto while their ski-clad feet slide along the snow. T-bars aren't as safe as modern cable cars (as they are vulnerable to careless skiers letting go) and are being gradually phased out.

LOCAL TRANSPORT
Public Transport
All local city transport is linked together on

Taxi
Good bus, rail and underground railway networks make the taking of taxis all but unnecessary, but if you need one in a hurry they can usually be found idling like a gang of street urchins by train stations, or you can telephone for one. They are always metered and work on the basis of a starting flat fee plus a charge per km. Prices are high.

ORGANISED TOURS
Tours are booked through local tourist offices. The country is so compact that excursions to the major national attractions are offered from most towns. A trip up to Jungfraujoch, for example, is available from Zürich, Geneva, Bern, Lucerne and Interlaken. Most tours represent reasonable value. They work out more expensively than going it alone, but can be the best option if you are pressed for time. A short city tour will give you a quick overview of the place and can be a good way to begin your visit.

Bernese Mittelland

The main focus of the Bernese Mittelland (Berner Mittelland, Le Plateau Bernois) region is the Swiss capital, Bern, an enticing city with a provincial feel that belies its status. The Bernese Mittelland is also known as the home of the famous cheese, Emmental.

History

In the 12th century the Dukes of Zähringen were the most powerful family in the locality, and in 1191, founded the fortified town of Bern. Shortly after it became established, Bern independently concluded alliances with lesser nobles and gradually extended its own sovereignty in the region. In 1218 it managed to win the status of an imperial city under the direct responsibility of the Habsburgs. Meanwhile, it continued with its territorial ambitions and entered into a series of alliances known as the Burgundian Confederation.

Bern joined the Swiss Confederation in 1353, as it was concerned with protecting itself in the east while it expanded in other directions. In 1415 Bern gained control of Aargau in the north, and in the 16th century, most of the territory around Lake Geneva fell under Bernese rule, largely at the expense of the House of Savoy. At this stage, Bern had reached the peak of its power and influence, a situation that continued until 1798.

In 1798, the French invaded Switzerland and completely destroyed Bern's power base. Under the ensuing Helvetic Republic, Bern was chopped down to size and lost control of the Oberland. In 1803, Bern was reunited with the Oberland but, in the new Switzerland that emerged from the Congress of Vienna (1814-15), it was stripped of Aargau and Vaud, which became separate cantons. Although it was chosen as the capital of Switzerland in 1848, more land was lost when the canton of Jura was created in 1979.

Orientation & Information

The Bernese Mittelland is the fertile plain in the northern part of the canton of Bern. Bern itself is slightly south-west of the geographical centre of the region.

The countryside is characterised by small villages and rolling, green hills. German is the principal language spoken, except for a small area round Biel where French is on an equal footing.

The tourist office for Bern handles tourist enquiries for the whole of the Bernese Mittelland. Direct postal enquiries to: Verkehrsverein Bern, Postfach, CH-3001 Bern.

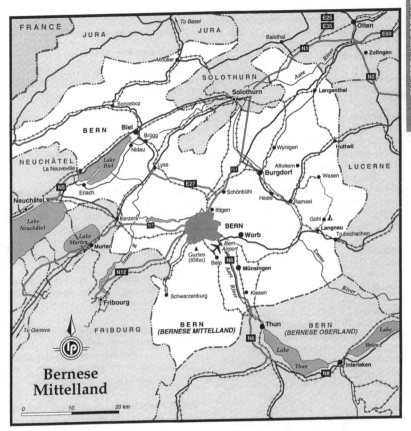

**Bernese
Mittelland**

0   10   20 km

Bern

• *pop 133,000* • *540m* • ☎ *(031)*
Founded in 1191 by Berthold V, Bern (Berne
in French, and, usually, English) is Switzerland's capital and fourth-largest city. Its
name, so the story goes, is in honour of the
bear (*Bär* in German, and *Bärn* in local
dialect) that was Berthold's first kill when
hunting in the area. Even today the bear
remains the heraldic mascot of the city.

In 1405 the predominantly wood-built town
was all but destroyed by a devastating fire. It

was rebuilt using sandstone, and although
most of the houses were replaced in the 16th
and 17th centuries, the structure of the centre
remains largely unaltered from that period.
Bern was elected as the seat of federal
authority upon the adoption of the new Swiss
Constitution in 1848. The other main candi-
date at the time was Zürich, but French-
speakers swayed the vote in Bern's favour as
they considered Zürich too Germanic.

Despite playing host to the nation's politicians, Bern retains a relaxed, small-town
charm. Except, that is, in the train station
during rush hour, where you feel like a cork

bobbing in a sea of surging humanity; mere flotsam in a tide of purposeful commuters. Its picturesque old town contains six km of covered arcades and 11 historic fountains, as well as the descendants of the city's first casualty (the bear) who perform tricks for tourists.

Orientation

The compact centre of town is contained within a sharp U-bend of the Aare River, and access to some of the main streets in this part is restricted to pedestrians and public transport. The main train station is in the mouth of this 'U' and is within easy reach of all the main sights. The station has luggage lockers (Sfr4), bicycle rental (daily from 6.10 am to 11.45 pm) and Swissair check-in.

Information

Tourist Office The Offizielles Verkehrsbüro Bern (☎ 311 66 11; fax 312 12 33) is in the train station and is open daily from 9 am to 8.30 pm. From 1 October to 31 May it shuts two hours earlier and Sunday hours are reduced to 10 am to 5 pm. Services include hotel reservations (Sfr3 commission, so use the free phone outside instead) and excursions. Its free booklet, *Bern aktuell*, contains much practical and recreational information in three languages. The tourist office map is fine for the centre, but if you need to go into the suburbs, pick up a free map with a street index from one of the many branches of the Swiss Bank Corporation. The train information office is opposite the tourist office, open Monday to Friday from 8 am to 7 pm and Saturday from 8 am to 5 pm.

Foreign Embassies Most embassies can be found south-east of the Kirchenfeldbrücke.

Australia
Alpenstrasse 29 (☎ 351 01 43)
Canada
Kirchenfeldstrasse 88 (☎ 352 63 81)
Eire
Kirchenfeldstrasse 68 (☎ 352 14 42)
France
Schosshaldenstrasse 46, south-east of the Nydeggbrücke (☎ 351 24 24)
Germany
farther south at Willadingweg 83 (☎ 359 41 11)
Italy
Elfenstrasse 14 (☎ 352 41 51)
South Africa
Jungfraustrasse 1 (☎ 352 20 11)
UK
Thunstrasse 50 (☎ 352 50 21)
USA
Jubiläumsstrasse 93 (☎ 357 70 11)

As Bern is Switzerland's capital, dozens of other embassies are also located here. The tourist office has a full list.

Money Exchange facilities, including cash advances with Visa, Eurocard, American Express and Diners Card, are in the SBB office in the lower level of the train station. It is open daily from 6.15 am to 9.45 pm (8.45 pm from mid-October to May).

Business Hours Some shops are shut on Monday morning, and most have extended hours on Thursday evening until 9 pm.

Post & Communications The main post office (Schanzenpost 3001) is at Schanzenstrasse; it is open Monday to Friday from 7.30 am to 6.30 pm and on Saturday from 7.30 to 11 am.

Travel Agencies Kehrli & Oeler Reisebüro (☎ 311 00 22), Bubenbergplatz 9, is the American Express travel service representative; it is open Monday to Friday from 8.30 am to 12.30 pm and 1.30 to 6 pm and Saturday from 9 am to noon. The Swiss budget travel agency SSR (☎ 302 03 12) has two branches, at Falkenplatz 9 and Rathausgasse 64. Both are open weekdays from 9.30 am to 6 pm, with late opening on Thursday to 7 or 8 pm respectively.

Bookshops Stauffacher (☎ 311 24 11), Neuengasse 25, has many books in English and French, both fiction and nonfiction. Atlas (☎ 311 90 44), Schauplatzgasse 31, specialises in travel books and backpacking accessories. Check Postgasse, Rathausgasse or Kramgasse for places selling second-hand books.

Library The Municipal and University Library, Müstergasse 61, has a reading room with English-language newspapers, and is open weekdays from 8 am to 9 pm and Saturday to noon. The book collection is open 10 am to 6 pm weekdays and 10 am to noon Saturday.

Laundry Jet Wash, Philosophenweg 3, is south-west of the train station. Five kg self-service machines cost Sfr4 to wash and the same for 60 minutes drying. It's open Monday to Saturday from 7 am to 9 pm.

Medical & Emergency Services There is a police station (☎ 321 21 21) and a chemist in the train station. For a doctor, dentist or chemist out-of-hours, call ☎ 311 22 11. The national emergency numbers can also be used:

police ☎ 117
fire brigade ☎ 118
ambulance ☎ 144
car breakdown service ☎ 140

The university hospital (☎ 632 21 11), with a casualty department, is on Fribourgstrasse.

Gay & Lesbian Information HAB (☎ 311 63 53), Mühleplatz 11, is a gay counselling and information centre. There's a women's centre in the Reithalle.

Dangers & Annoyances There are quite a few young hard-drug users in town, who tend to congregate at the back of the parliament.

Walking Tour
The city map from the tourist office details a picturesque walk through the old town. The core of the walk is Marktgasse and Kramgasse with their covered arcades and colourful fountains. The statues appear every 150m and were constructed in approximately 1545. The **Ogre Fountain** on Kornhausplatz, dividing the two streets,

depicts the unusual subject matter of an ogre devouring small children.

Nearby is the **Zeitglockenturm**, a clock tower on which revolving figures herald the chiming hour. Congregate on the Kramgasse side at least four minutes before the hour on the east side to see them twirl. Originally a city gate, the clock was installed in 1530. The next fountain along shows a bear holding a shield bearing the Zähringen coat of arms – this appears in many a postcard.

Just over the Aare River to the east are the **bear pits** *(Bärengraben)*, open daily to 6 pm (4 pm October to March). Bears have been at this site since 1857, although records show that as far back as 1441 the city council bought acorns to feed the ancestors of these overgrown pets. Up the hill is the **Rose Garden**, which has 200 varieties of roses and an excellent view of the city. Another good place to wander is the **Botanical Gardens** (free entry), on the north side of the Lorrainebrücke.

Cathedral
The unmistakably Gothic, 15th century cathedral *(Münster)* stands tall with the highest spire (100m) in Switzerland. The tower gives a fine view extending to the Bernese Alps, with the reddish rooftops of Bern itself scattered below. The best feature of the church is the **main portal**, with an elaborate tympanum depicting the Last Judgement – notice one pope ascending to

For over 500 years the brown bear has been associated with Bern. It has become both mascot and symbol of the city.

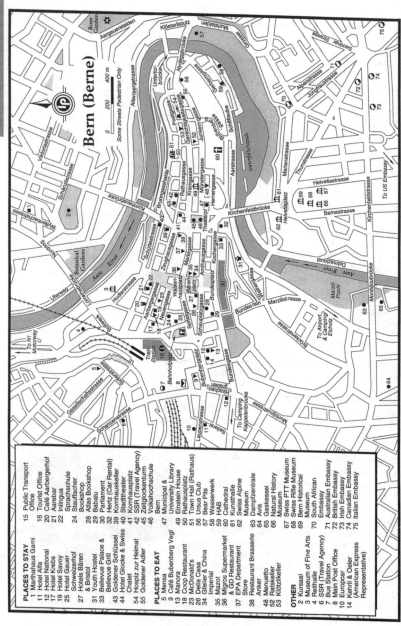

Bern (Berne)

0   200   400 m

Some Streets Pedestrian Only

PLACES TO STAY
1   Marthahaus Garni
11 Hotel Alfa
12 Hotel National
17 Hotel Krebs
19 Hotel Savoy
25 Hotel Gauer
    Schweizerhof
27 Hotel Bären
    & Bristol
31 Youth Hostel
33 Bellevue Palace &
    Bellevue Grill
43 Goldener Schlüssel
44 Hotel Glocke & Swiss
    Chalet
54 Hospiz zur Heimat
55 Goldener Adler

PLACES TO EAT
5   Mensa
9   Café Bubenberg Vegi
13 Manora
18 Coop Restaurant
23 McDonald's
26 Della Casa
34 Gfeller & China
    Imperial
35 Mazot
36 Migros Supermarket
    & GD Restaurant
37 EPA Department
    Store
38 Restaurant Brasserie
    Anker
48 Menuetto
52 Ratskeller
53 Klötzlikeller

OTHER
2   Kursaal
3   Museum of Fine Arts
4   Reithalle
6   SSR (Travel Agency)
7   Bus Station
8   Main Post Office
10 Europcar
14 Kehrli & Oeler
    (American Express
    Representative)

15 Public Transport
    Office
16 Tourist Office
20 Café Aarbergerhof
21 Aarebar
22 Inlingua
24 Sprachschule
    Stauffacher
    Bookshop
28 Atlas Bookshop
29 Babalu
30 Parliament
32 Hertz (Car Rental)
39 Kornhauskeller
40 Stadttheater
41 Kornhausplatz
42 SSR (Travel Agency)
46 Zeitglockenturm
    Volkshochschule
47 Municipal &
    University Library
49 Einstein House
50 Rathausplatz
51 Town Hall (Rathaus)
56 Ursus Club
57 Bear Pits
58 Wasserwerk
59 HAB
60 Cathedral
61 Kunsthalle
62 Swiss Alpine
    Museum
63 Dampfzentrale
64 Avis
65 Gaskessel
66 Natural History
    Museum
67 Swiss PTT Museum
68 Swiss Rifle Museum
69 Bern Historical
    Museum
70 South African
    Embassy
71 Australian Embassy
72 British Embassy
73 Irish Embassy
74 Canadian Embassy
75 Italian Embassy

heaven and another cast into the fires of hell. The cathedral was Catholic until the Reformation, at which point many of the statues were thrown out (hence the empty recesses in the chancel), but the Catholic saints on the ceiling remain as they were too high to get at.

Other features to notice are the stained-glass windows (mostly built between 1421 and 1450) and the carved choir stalls (1523). The cathedral is open daily except Monday from 10 am (11 am Sunday) to 5 pm, except from November to Easter Sunday when hours are 10 am to noon and 2 to 4 pm (5 pm Saturday; Sunday hours are 11 am to 2 pm). The tower always closes half an hour earlier than the rest of the cathedral, and costs Sfr3 or Sfr1 for children.

Parliament

Well worth a visit is the Bundeshäuser, on Bunderplatz, home of the Swiss Federal Assembly. There are free daily tours (45 minutes) when the parliament is not in session. Arrive early and reserve a place for later in the day. A multilingual guide takes you through the impressive chambers. This grand, domed building was built in 1902, and on the glass of the dome are displayed the coats of arms of 22 cantons (the canton of Jura wasn't yet inaugurated). Inside are other plaques, pictures and statues that reflect important events in Swiss history. There are two main chambers, the National Council and the Council of States; the latter has a huge chandelier, a tangled mess of wrought iron weighing 1½ tonnes and sprouting 214 bulbs. During parliamentary sessions, watch from the public gallery.

Museums

There is no shortage of museums. Many are grouped together on the south side of the Kirchenfeldbrücke; for these museums there is a general day pass for Sfr7 (Sfr4 students and seniors), which is good value though it doesn't cover special exhibitions.

Museum of Fine Arts The Kunstmuseum, Hodlerstrasse 8-12, holds a huge Paul Klee collection, a total of over 2000 works (mostly drawings), although it is not possible to show all of them at once. The museum also displays canvasses by Italian masters from the 14th, 15th and 16th centuries, such as Fra Angelico *(Madonna and Child)* and Duccio. Swiss artists since the 15th century are well represented, particularly Ferdinand Hodler. More modern schools of art are not overlooked, either, with paintings by Cézanne, Matisse and Picasso, and works by contemporary artists. It is open Tuesday from 10 am to 9 pm, and Wednesday to Sunday from 10 am to 5 pm; entry costs Sfr6 (students Sfr4, children free).

Bern Historical Museum This interesting museum (Bernisches Historisches Museum) is on Helvetiaplatz, and is open Tuesday to Sunday from 10 am to 5 pm (admission Sfr5, or Sfr3 for students and senior citizens; free on Saturday). Highlights include the original sculptures from the Münster doorway depicting the Last Judgement, Niklaus Manuel's macabre *Dance of Death* panels, and the ridiculous codpiece on the William Tell statue upstairs. Elsewhere, the museum contains Habsburg Church treasures (from the Königsfelden Abbey), and tapestries captured from the Burgundian troops of Charles the Bold. Various rooms show how life was lived in the canton of Bern in the last two centuries, and, somewhat tangentially, there is the Islamic collection of Henri Moser-Charlottenfels.

Natural History Museum This museum (Naturhistorisches Museum) on Bernastrasse, has eye-catching and extensive displays of animals depicted in realistic dioramas. Near the entrance are the stuffed remains of Barry, the most famous of the 40 St Bernard dogs who between them rescued an estimated 2000 travellers stranded in the Alps. Such moth-eaten preservation is a dubious reward for sterling service. It is open Monday from 2 pm to 5 pm, Tuesday to Saturday from 9 am to 5 pm, and Sunday from 10 am to 5 pm. Entry is Sfr3, or Sfr1.50 for students and senior citizens.

Other Museums The **Einstein House**, Kramgasse 49, is where the physicist developed his special theory of relativity in 1905, while working as a clerk in the patents office. There's not a vast amount to see, but it's relatively interesting (Sfr2; closed Sunday, Monday, December and January). The **Swiss**

Doing Time in the Bern Patent Office

There is hope for all daydreaming clerks. Albert Einstein, gazing into space instead of attending to his tedious job at the patent office, had in 1907 what he later described as 'the happiest thought of my life.' It was the realisation that a person in freefall would not feel their own weight. This apparently trivial insight impelled him to a new theory of gravitation, the General Theory of Relativity. Einstein postulated that gravity was caused by the curvature of space-time, a hypothesis subsequently supported by scientific tests.

Einstein worked at the patent office from 1902 to 1907. During that time he also came up with his Special Theory of Relativity (1905). This explained the puzzling fact that the speed of light is always the same, irrespective of the relative motion of observers, by stating that time itself must be relative.

Einstein was born of Jewish ancestry in Germany in 1879. He did not excel at school, but was admitted to Zürich Polytechnic on the strength of his mathematics test alone. Upon graduating, his failure to find a teaching post led him to the patent office in Bern and a place in history. He won the Nobel Prize for Physics in 1932, and later emigrated to the USA where he died in 1955. ∎

Alpine Museum, Helvetiaplatz 4, will whet your appetite for the mountains if you haven't yet headed into the Alps (closed Monday morning). It details the history of Alpine mountaineering and cartography and has an impressively comprehensive collection of relief maps (Sfr5, concessions Sfr2.50). Across the square is the **Kunsthalle**, an exhibition space for contemporary artists (Sfr6, concessions Sfr3; closed Monday, with late opening on Tuesday).

Philatelists will stamp their feet with joy at the **Swiss PTT Museum**, Helvetiastrasse 16, where countless postage stamps are displayed on endless panels (Sfr2). Afterwards, shoot over to the **Swiss Rifle Museum**, Bernastrasse 5, for a collection of firearms made since 1817 (free). Both are closed on Monday.

Markets

An open-air vegetable, fruit and flower market can be found at Bundesplatz on Tuesday and Saturday. On the first Saturday of the month there's a craft market in front of the cathedral.

Activities

Near the town is the hilltop, **Gurten**, where you can hike and enjoy the fine views. Get there by tram No 9 to Gurtenbahn then the funicular (Sfr6). Alternatively, do the whole trip on the Sfr7.50 version of the city pass.

Something the Bernese enjoy on a sunny summer's day is floating down the **Aare River**. They take the plunge in the Sandrain district and float downstream in the swift current to where they left their possessions at the open-air swimming pools at Marzili or Lorraine (both pools are free and open May to September).

Courses

Inlingua Sprachschule (☎ 311 24 13) is at Waisenhausplatz 28. Volkshochschule Bern (☎ 311 41 92), Kornhausplatz 7, has adult education courses (usually of 10 weeks minimum) for all sorts of disciplines ranging from languages to gymnastics. The administration for the Migrosschule (Migros school; ☎ 311 44 33) is on the 1st floor at Marktgasse 46.

Organised Tours

There is a daily (Saturday only in winter) two-hour city tour by coach, which costs Sfr22 and departs from outside the tourist office. The multilingual commentary is informative. Departures are at 10 am (except winter) and 2 pm. The guided walking tour of the centre costs Sfr12 and leaves daily at 11 am, May to October. Tours also depart daily to all the main attractions in the Bernese Oberland, central Switzerland and to some lesser-known local destinations. Prices are from Sfr23 to Sfr164; the tours are worth considering if you're on a lightning visit.

Special Events

On the 4th Monday in November, Bern hosts its famous **onion market** *(Zibelemärit)*, where traders take over the whole of the centre of town. According to tradition, the origin of the market dates back to 1405 and the great fire. The farmers of the canton of Fribourg helped the Bernese to recover from the resulting devastation and were allowed to sell their produce in Bern as a reward. But it's more than just a market – people walk around throwing confetti and hitting each other on the head with plastic hammers, and many street performers (particularly South

American bands) add to the carnival atmosphere.

Bern also has an important **jazz festival** in early May. Prices for evening events are between Sfr50 and Sfr90 and tickets are available in advance from the Ticket Corner, Schweizerischer Bankverein (☎ 336 25 39), Bärenplatz 8, Bern. The **Altstadtsommer** comprises concerts and other events (some are free) in the old town during July and August. Look out for the Gurten Rock Festival in late July.

Places to Stay – bottom end

Camping To get to *Camping Kappelen-brücke* (☎ 901 10 07), take postbus No 3 or 4 from the train station to Eymatt. The site is open year-round except for the first two weeks in February; reception is shut from 1 to 4 pm and the gates close at 11 pm. Overnight charges are Sfr6 per adult and Sfr6 for a car and tent. Near the river but to the south of town is *Camping Eichholz* (☎ 961 26 02), Strandweg 49. Take tram No 9 from the station to Wabern. The site is open from 1 May to 30 September, and charges are Sfr5.50 per person, from Sfr4 for a tent and Sfr2 for parking. It also has two-bed rooms for Sfr14 plus Sfr5.50 per person.

Hostel The SYHA *hostel* (☎ 311 63 16), Weihergasse 4, is in a good location below Parliament (the paths down are signposted). It is usually full in summer, when a three-day maximum stay applies. Reception is shut from 9.30 am to 3 pm (summer) or to 5 pm (winter), but bags can be left in the common room during the day. Dorm beds are Sfr17, breakfast is Sfr6 and lunch and dinner are Sfr11 each. There are lockers, a midnight curfew, and washing machines at Sfr4 to wash and Sfr1 per 15 minutes of drying.

Hotels There's a limited choice of budget rooms in Bern. *Bahnhof-Süd* (☎ 992 51 11), Bümplizstrasse 189, to the west of town beyond the autobahn, has singles/doubles using hall shower for Sfr50/80 without breakfast. Doubles with shower are Sfr100.

To get there, take bus No 13 from the city centre.

Take bus No 20 from Bahnhofplatz for *Marthahaus Garni* (☎ 332 41 35), Wyttenbachstrasse 22A. It's a friendly place with comfortable rooms and two TV lounges. Singles/doubles are Sfr60/95 and triples/quads are Sfr120/140. Prices for singles/doubles/triples with private shower/WC and TV are Sfr85/120/150.

Conveniently close to the train station is *Hotel National* (☎ 381 19 88), Hirschengraben 24. It has good-for-the-price singles/doubles from Sfr60/100, or Sfr85/120 with private shower and toilet. Family rooms (up to five people) are Sfr170 to Sfr260.

Within the old town in an 18th century building is *Hospiz zur Heimat* (☎ 311 04 36), Gerechtigkeitsgasse 50. Features include clean, spacious rooms and an unpredictable proprietor. Singles/doubles for Sfr64/96, and triples/quads for Sfr126/168, all with hall showers. Rooms with private shower/WC are around Sfr30 extra, and next-door is a cheap restaurant. *Goldener Schlüssel* (☎ 311 02 16), Rathausgasse 72, charges a little more for its rooms – they are of a similar standard except they do have TV and radio.

Also ideally situated is *Hotel Glocke* (☎ 311 37 71), Rathausgasse 75. Singles/doubles are Sfr90/136 with private shower/WC or Sfr70/116 without.

Places to Stay – middle
Hotel Goldener Adler (☎ 311 17 25), Gerechtigkeitsgasse 7, offers comfortable rooms for the price, with TV: Sfr105/140 with private shower/WC or Sfr75/130 without. Another good choice for mid-price accommodation is *Hotel Krebs* (☎ 311 49 42), Genfergasse 8, near the train station. Singles with shower, toilet, TV and breakfast buffet are expensive at Sfr128, but the corresponding doubles are a much better deal at Sfr158; the family room for four costs Sfr245. There are a few singles/doubles with showers in the hall for Sfr90/130.

Hotel Alfa (☎ 381 38 66), Laupenstrasse 15, has perfectly adequate rooms for Sfr140/195 with all the requisite amenities.

But it hasn't much character, and the bare concrete in the hallways hardly adds to the ambience.

Places to Stay – top end
Hotel Bären (☎ 311 33 67; fax 311 69 83), Schauplatzgasse 4, and the adjoining *Hotel Bristol* (☎ 311 01 01; 311 94 79), at No 10, are effectively the same hotel. They're part of the Best Western chain and have comfortable if uninspiring rooms from Sfr150/210. The best place to stay without jumping to the luxury class is the *Hotel Savoy* (☎ 311 44 05; fax 312 19 78), Neuengasse 26, where prices start at Sfr160/230. The rooms are bigger, better furnished, and have an overall more welcoming feel than those of its rivals.

There are two five-star hotels in town, both suitably sumptuous: the *Bellevue Palace* (☎ 320 45 45; fax 311 47 43) at Kochergasse 3-5 and the *Hotel Gauer Schweizerhof* (☎ 311 45 01; 312 21 79) at Bahnhofplatz 11. The latter is slightly the cheaper, starting at Sfr260/360.

Places to Eat
Self-Service There are several snack and take-away places in the lower level of the train station. *Migros* supermarket at Marktgasse 46 has a cheap self-service restaurant on the 1st floor. On the same floor is *GD Restaurant* with regional dishes from Sfr10; both are open normal shop hours, with late opening to 9 pm on Thursday, though Migros is closed Monday morning and lunchtime.

Also good value is the university *Mensa*, Gesellschaftsstrasse 2, on the 1st floor. Menus cost around Sfr8 to Sfr12, and there's a Sfr1.70 reduction for students. It is open Monday to Friday from 11.30 am to 1.45 pm and (not on Friday) 5.45 to 7.30 pm. The café downstairs keeps longer hours for drinks and snacks. Both parts close from mid-July to early August.

The *EPA* department store, straddling Zeughausgasse and Marktgasse, has a restaurant on the 1st floor where meals cost between Sfr7 and Sfr12 (closes 9 pm on Thursday). A *Coop* restaurant, open the same hours, is in the Ryfflihof department store on

Neuengasse and Aarbergergasse. *Manora*, Bubenbergplatz 5a, is a busy and sometimes hectic restaurant, but usually has the tastiest food of the self-service bunch. Meals are Sfr9 to Sfr16, and the pile-it-on-yourself salad is Sfr4.20 to Sfr9.40 per plate. It is open daily from 6.45 am (8.45 am on Sunday and holidays) until 10.45 pm.

Cheap Restaurants *Café Bubenberg Vegi* (☎ 311 75 76), Bubenbergplatz 8, has terrace seating and good vegetarian food for Sfr15 to Sfr20. There are weekly buffets of Thai or Indian food, and it is open Monday to Saturday from 7.30 am to 10.30 pm. *Menuetto* (☎ 311 14 48), Münstergasse 47, is generally slightly more expensive for vegetarian food, though it does have a daily special for Sfr13. It is open daily except Sunday from 11 am to 10 pm.

Several pleasant restaurants with outside seating line Bärenplatz, though there's little to choose between them. *Gfeller* has a reasonable range of food. On the 1st floor above is *China Imperial*, offering an extensive buffet of Chinese food, freshly cooked. The Tellerservice is the best deal: for Sfr17.50 you can select a plateful, and take a bowl of rice with sauces. It's available daily, lunchtime and after 10 pm. The three-course evening buffet costs Sfr39.50. Go to *Mazot* at No 5 to try Swiss specialities such as Rösti (Sfr12.50) and fondue (Sfr19).

Restaurant Brasserie Anker, Zeughausgasse 1, has standard Swiss food for a similar price. Its earthier front section is popular with drinkers – beer is only Sfr3.80 for half a litre. It is open until midnight except on Sunday when it shuts at 6 pm.

Mid-Price & Expensive Restaurants The dingy exterior of *Della Casa* (☎ 311 21 42), Schauplatzgasse 16, hides a good-quality restaurant within. The local speciality, Bernerplatte (a selection of meats with sauerkraut and beans) costs Sfr39, but perhaps you can find it on the excellent three-course daily menu for Sfr21 (different menu for lunch and dinner). The menu is available on the ground floor only, from 11.30 am to 2 pm and 6 to 9 pm. The upstairs section is plusher and meals there cost about Sfr2 more. Della Casa is open Monday to Friday from 8.30 am to 11.30 pm and Saturday from 8.30 am to 3 pm.

For good-quality fish and meat dishes (Sfr17.50 to Sfr45) in a calm setting, try *Ratskeller* (☎ 311 17 71), Gerechtigkeitsgasse 81 (open daily). *Klötzlikeller* (☎ 311 74 56) is a lively and atmospheric wine cellar at Gerechtigkeitsgasse 62, with live music every second Wednesday in winter. Menus (cheapish to mid-price) feature food and wine from different regions and are changed every two months. Tripe (Kulten; Sfr18.50) and Rösti are permanent fixtures. It is open Tuesday to Saturday from 4 pm till after midnight.

Bellevue-Grill in the Bellevue Palace Hotel (see Places to Stay) is considered the best restaurant in Bern. Reserve ahead, as despite the high prices, it is often full. Main courses start at Sfr44 but most people go for the creative menu for Sfr114. The food is presented with a flourish here; the servers troop out in file, each bearing the main course for each guest around the table. When all the plates are carefully placed before the appropriate diner, they simultaneously whip off the metal cover to reveal the feast beneath. They then stand reverently in a circle, covers held aloft, as the head server recites a short spiel describing each dish. It's almost a religious ceremony and has to be seen to be believed.

Entertainment

On Mondays, cinemas cost Sfr10 instead of the usual Sfr14 to Sfr15. There are a couple of cinemas on Laupenstrasse. Bärenplatz is a great place to linger on a sunny day. There's always something happening, whether it be street music, giant chess games, or demonstrations outside the parliament building.

The *Kursaal* (☎ 33 10 10), Schänzlistrasse 71-77 (take tram No 9 from Kornhausplatz), has gambling and a night club. A few late venues in the city centre run until around 3 am (except Sunday) but entry and drinks can be expensive. *Babalu*, Gurtengasse 3, is a nightclub with a DJ or live music and different themes each night. Cover charge is around Sfr15.

Bars, Clubs & Arts Venues Young people with fewer francs go to places like *Wasserwerk*, Wasserwerkgasse 5. There's a not too expensive bar with pool tables (open 8 pm) and a disco (Sfr5 to Sfr15; open from 10 pm). About 10 times a month there's live music (Sfr10 to Sfr35). Also try *Aarebar*, Speichergasse 13, where a DJ features anything from Reggae to Oldies to House, depending on the night (open around 10 pm). For food and drink there's the bright bar/café *Café Aarbergerhof*, Ursus Club, Junkerngasse 1, is a gay bar (Thursday from 8 pm) and disco (Friday and Saturday from 9 pm).

Reithalle (☎ 302 63 17), Schützenmattstrasse, a former riding school, is a fascinating place to spend time. It's a semi-legal centre for alternative arts housed in several graffiti-splattered, derelict-looking buildings under the railway line. On site there is a music venue, theatre, library, café and cheap restaurant. There's also a women's-only disco on the first Friday of the month. Entry fees for events are reasonable. The place looks a bit seedy, and there have been safety problems in the past, but nowadays it is pretty safe and almost respectable, though there's still something of a drug culture in the bar.

Gaskessel (☎ 372 49 00), Sandrainstrasse 25, in two domed buildings in Marzili, has concerts, theatre, cinema, live music and discos. It attracts a very young crowd and entry fees are Sfr8 to Sfr12. It sells no alcohol but you can bring in your own wine and beer. Near to the Marzili pools is *Dampfzentrale* (☎ 311 63 37), Marzilistrasse 47, a venue for jazz, soul, funk, avant-garde and art exhibitions, either in the main hall or the Musikkeller bar. Jazz is also on the agenda at *Marian's Jazzroom* (☎ 309 61 11), Engestrasse 54, a slightly more expensive and exclusive venue.

If your tastes lean more toward the traditional, go to the *Swiss Chalet* at the Hotel Glocke (see Places to Stay). A folklore show starts at 8.30 pm from June to October (closed Sunday). Inevitably these places are a bit touristy but it's free (you pay for it in the drink prices) and the music goes on until at least 1 am. *Kornhauskeller* (☎ 311 11 33), Kornhausplatz 17, is an atmospheric, traditional beer hall which is worth at least glancing inside. It has live piano music nightly, and a summer folklore show on Monday (free entry). Food is standard fare mostly above Sfr16, though there is Rösti from Sfr10. It is open Monday to Saturday from 11.30 am to around midnight. On Sunday it has a jazz matinee from 11 am to 1 pm (Sfr15).

Theatre & Concerts The *Stadttheater* has productions almost every day and tickets are available from the Theaterkasse (☎ 311 07 77), Kornhausplatz 18. There is also a number of small theatre groups (including a puppet theatre) which perform in the cellars along Kramgasse and Gerechtigkeitsgasse; plays are in local dialect or High German. Bern has a symphony orchestra, and there's always something going on in the classical music field. Concerts are often held in the large hall of the Casino, Herrengasse 25. Check the free Information booklet, *Bern aktuell*, for events listings.

Spectator Sport

North of the centre is the Wankdorf football and athletics stadium. Nearby is a famous ice-hockey stadium (Allmend Eisstadion); it's one of the biggest in Europe and Bern has one of the best teams in the country.

Things to Buy

Bern's covered arcades make shopping a weather-proof experience. There's no better place to buy Toblerone chocolate, as it's made in Bern. The Swiss Craft Centre (Heimatwerk) on Kramgasse 61 offers handmade but expensive souvenirs, such as wood-carvings, jewellery and Bernese pottery. There are many other souvenir shops on Kramgasse and Gerechtigkeitsgasse. Klözli, Rathausgasse 84, boasts a huge selection of Swiss army knives.

Getting There & Away

Air There are daily direct flights by Crossair (☎ 960 21 21) to/from Paris, Lugano, Frankfurt, Munich, Vienna and Brussels. Air Engiadina (☎ 960 12 00) flies daily to London Stansted. The Swissair check-in counter in the train station will take your luggage and get it on your flight from Zürich or Geneva. See the Getting There & Away chapter for details.

Bus Postbuses depart from the west side of the train station, although the train service should meet the needs of most visitors.

Train Bern has excellent train connections. Departures are at least hourly to most destinations, including Geneva (Sfr48, takes 1¾ hours), Basel (Sfr34, 70 minutes), Interlaken (Sfr24, 50 minutes) and Zürich (Sfr42, 1½ hours).

Car & Motorcycle There are three motorways which intersect at the northern part of the city. The N1 (E25) is the route from Neuchâtel in the west and Basel and Zürich in the north-east. The N6 connects Bern with Thun and the Interlaken region in the southeast. The N12 (E27) is the route from Geneva and Lausanne in the south-west.

There are several underground parking spots in the city centre, including one at the train station (Sfr2.50 per hour). The tourist office map lists locations. 'Park & Ride' parking is free at Guisanplatz, Wankdorf in the north and Gangloff, Bümpliz in the south-west.

Car Rental Hertz (☎ 318 21 60) is in the old town at Kasinoplatz, and Avis (☎ 372 13 13) is at Wabernstrasse 41. Both have an office at the airport. Europcar (☎ 318 75 55) is at Laupenstrasse 22.

Getting Around

The Airport The small Bern-Belp airport is nine km south-east of the city centre. A small white shuttle bus links the airport to the train station (Sfr14). It takes 20 minutes and is coordinated with flight arrivals and departures. There's no easy cheaper alternative – the train to Belp (Sfr6) leaves you 30 minutes' walk from the airport.

Bus & Tram Getting around on foot is easy enough if you're staying in the city centre. Bus and tram tickets cost Sfr1.50 (under seven stops) or Sfr2.40. A day pass for the city and regional network is Sfr7.50. Buy single-journey tickets at stops and daily cards from the tourist office or the public transport office (☎ 321 86 31) at Bubenbergplatz 5. Special night buses depart from Bahnhofplatz at 12.45 am and 2 am; the fare is Sfr5 and passes are not valid.

Taxi Many taxis wait by the station. The cost is Sfr6.50 plus Sfr2.70 (Sfr3 on Sunday and at night) per km.

Biel

- *pop 51,800* • *429m* • ☎ *(032)*

Biel (or Bienne in French), is one of those Swiss towns nonchalantly spanning the linguistic divide. The town has expanded greatly since the end of the 19th century, thanks in part to cashing in on the burgeoning watch and clock-making industry. This expansion has recently reversed (the town has high unemployment), but still some of the biggest names, such as Omega and Rolex, are based in Biel. Its lake and old town centre are the main attractions.

Orientation & Information

Biel is at the northern end of Lake Biel (Bielersee, Lac de Bienne). It's a bilingual city and all street names are shown in both languages. The Biel-Bienne train station is between the lake and the old town and has bike-rental and money-exchange counters open daily. The tourist office (☎ 322 75 75)

BERNESE MITTELLAND

Biel (Bienne)

0   150   300 m

PLACES TO STAY
5   Hotel Dufour
8   Hotel Bären
12 Heilsarmee
16 Hotel de la Poste
17 Hotel Elite

PLACES TO EAT
2   Restaurant
    Au Vieux Valais
4   Migros Supermarket
    & Restaurant
6   Asia Food
7   EPA Department Store
11 McDonald's
14 Trattoria Alfredo
21 Coop Supermarket
    & Restaurant

OTHER
1   The Ring
3   Theatre & Town Hall
9   Art & History Museum
10 Schwab Museum
13 Villa Wahnsinn
15 Congress Centre
    (Kongresshaus)
18 SSR (Travel Agency)
19 Tourist Office
20 Main Post Office
22 BSG Boat Landing
    Stage

and bus information are in the car and bicycle park in front of the station. Opening hours are weekdays from 8 am to 12.30 pm and 1.30 to 6 pm, and (May to October) Saturday from 9 am to noon and 2 to 5 pm. Another tourist office is in the Congress Centre, Zentralstrasse 60. The main post office (2500 Biel 1) is by the train station. The old town is a partially pedestrian-only knot of streets around Burggasse and the Ring, 12 minutes' walk north of the station (or take bus No 1).

SSR (☎ 322 58 88), the budget travel agency, is at Hans Hugi Strasse 3.

Things to See & Do

The old town has as its centrepiece the **Ring**, a picturesque square with a 16th century fountain. The name harks back to bygone days when justice was dispensed in the square. The community big-wigs would sit in an intimidatory semicircle to pass judgement upon unfortunate miscreants who were brought before them.

Adjoining the Ring on Obergasse (Rue Haute) is another 16th century fountain, depicting an angel with a leering devil at her shoulder. Leading from the opposite side of the Ring is Burggasse (Rue de Bourg), where there's the step-gabled town hall and theatre, the Fountain of Justice (1744), and attractive shuttered houses. The centre doesn't take long to explore. If you have some time to kill, drop into a café and indulge in some eavesdropping, but only to admire the ability of the locals to switch between French and German with barely a break in the rhythm of their conversations.

The **Schwab Museum**, Seevorstadt 50 (Faubourg du Lac 50), is a museum of pre-history and archaeology, named after the 19th century colonel who was instrumental in unearthing the secrets of the ancient lake-dwellers of the region. Many of the more interesting finds from around the lakes of Biel, Murten and Neuchâtel are on display. The 6000-year-old settlements were revealed when the level of the lakes fell by some two metres following measures intro-duced to control the water flow in the Jura. The museum is open from Tuesday to Sunday from 10 am to noon and 2 to 5 pm, and entry costs Sfr4.

The **Omega Museum** (☎ 344 92 11), Stämpflistrasse 96, gives a free glimpse of the company's watch-making activities, past and present (open on request). There's also an **Art & History Museum** at Schüssprom-enade 26 (closed Monday).

Special Event
The town puts on a weekend carnival starting the Friday after Ash Wednesday.

Places to Stay – bottom end
Camping There are four camp sites clus-tered round the southern end of Lake Biel. Much nearer Biel and also by the lake is *Sutz-Lattrigen* (☎ 397 13 45). The train to Sutz runs every 30 minutes (Sfr3.50) and brings you to within one km of the site. It's open from Easter to mid-October and costs Sfr6 per person and from Sfr4 per tent.

Hotels & Pensions With the closure of the SYHA hostel, budget travellers have to turn to the *Heilsarmee* (Salvation Army; ☎ 322

68 38), 2nd floor, Oberer Quai 12. It's neither rough nor gloomy, and if there's space they're happy to take travellers. It has 18 singles and three doubles at Sfr32 per person or Sfr47 with half-board. There are hall showers and a Sfr3 surcharge for a single night. Reception shuts at 11 pm. South of the centre is *Zum Weissen Rössli* (☎ 365 60 55), Madretschstrasse 74, with singles/doubles for Sfr45/80 with own shower, and private parking. Take bus No 51 from the station. *Hotel de la Poste* (☎ 322 25 44), Güter-strasse 3, is poorer value (Sfr60/110 using hall showers) but more central.

Places to Stay – middle & top end
Hotel Bären (☎ 322 45 73), Nidaugasse 22, near the old town, has singles/doubles for Sfr95/140 and triples for Sfr225, all with shower or bath, toilet, radio and telephone. Rooms are a bit plain but reasonably large, and there's a lift. Reception is at a small counter in the busy pizza restaurant. Rooms are comparable in the *Hotel Dufour* (☎ 342 22 61) on Neumarktplatz (Place du Marché), except each room has a TV. Prices start at Sfr110/170.

At the four star *Hotel Elite* (☎ 322 54 41; fax 322 13 83), Bahnhofstrasse 14, you'll pay at least Sfr160/240, but the attentive service makes it worthwhile.

Places to Eat
Self-Service There's a large *Coop* with a restaurant round the back of the station on Salzhausstrasse. More convenient for the centre is *EPA* on Nidaugasse, or the *Migros* on Neumarktplatz. All offer similar quality and prices (meals for under Sfr10) and are open until 6.30 pm on weekdays (except Thursday, with late closing at 9 pm) and to 4 pm on Saturday. *Asia Food*, Neumarkt-strasse, has Chinese and Thai takeaway dishes for Sfr6.50 to Sfr10. It's open from 10.30 am to 7 pm (9 pm Thursday, 4 pm Saturday; closed Monday).

Restaurants For authentic ambience, explore the typical and fairly inexpensive places in the old centre. Look for the *Restaurant Au Vieux Valais* (☎ 322 34 55), off the Ring at Untergässli 9, which has lunches with soup from Sfr14, fondue for Sfr16.50 and meat dishes from Sfr18 (closed Monday). *Hotel Dufour* (see Places to Stay) has a café with plenty of vegetarian options from Sfr12, plus menus with soup from Sfr14. It's closed on Saturday evening. *Trattoria Alfredo*, Zentralstrasse 56, has cheery décor and pizzas from Sfr11.80 (closed Sunday).

Gourmet's heaven is at the restaurant of the *Hotel Elite* (see Places to Stay). The food is mainly French style although it periodically has festivals featuring different culinary themes. Main dishes top Sfr35 and multi-course menus are around the Sfr80 mark. It is closed on Sunday. The attention to presentation is meticulous, even down to the waiters or chefs carefully constructing patterns from the dessert sauces.

Entertainment

Villa Wahnsinn, Zentralstrasse 54, is a lively, young bar with dancing, games and competitions. Entry costs Sfr5 and includes the first drink, and it's open from 8 pm to beyond midnight. Nearby is the *Kongresshaus* (☎ 323 33 11) where concerts and cultural events are held. Biel has its own orchestra and municipal theatre; productions are usually in German.

Getting There & Away

Biel is under 30 minutes from Bern by train (Sfr10.40). Solothurn (Sfr8.40, 20 minutes), Neuchâtel (Sfr9.60, 20 minutes), and Murten (Sfr11.40, 40 minutes) are also close by train, but a more enjoyable way to get to these towns is by boat. They sail in summer; to both Murten (Sfr27 one-way or Sfr46 return) and Neuchâtel (Sfr22 one-way or Sfr38 return) takes around 2½ hours. Solothurn can be reached by BSG boat along the Aare River; there are five departures a day (except on Monday) and it takes less than 2½ hours (Sfr25 one-way, Sfr43 return). See also the following Around Biel section.

AROUND BIEL

Flora and fauna abound in **St Peter's Island** (St Peterinsel, Île de St Pierre), at the south-west end of Lake Biel. Because of the quality of the environment, especially for birdlife, the whole island was declared a nature reserve. Rousseau spent, in his own words, the happiest time of his life here. The carefully preserved 11 century monastery where he stayed can be visited.

The island became connected to the shore when the level of the lake dropped, exposing a natural causeway. It's a relaxing 1½-hour stroll to the island along this causeway from the town of Erlach on the shore. From Biel, a train runs to La Neuveville and an infrequent bus continues to Erlach. But the easiest way to get to the island is by boat from Biel (Sfr8.40, takes 50 minutes), which calls at several lakeside villages en route.

The southern shore of **Lake Biel** offers the best swimming spots. The northern shore is noted for a string of wine-growing villages. The tourist office has a leaflet (German or French) showing a walking path connecting these villages, including information on several wine cellars *(caveaux)* where produce can be sampled and purchased.

The neighbouring lakes of Neuchâtel and Murten are connected to Lake Biel by canal, and day-long tours of all three lakes are offered in summer. Boats are run by two boat companies: BSG (☎ 322 33 22), based in Biel, and LNM (☎ 032-725 40 12), based in Neuchâtel. BSG's tour departs Biel daily at 9.50 am (Sfr46). LNM's tour departs Murten daily except Monday at 10 am, with the return Biel-Murten leg by rail (Sfr38.40 inclusive). Other services between and around the lakes are regular only in summer, though there are special cruises (eg fondue evenings) during other seasons. Both companies share the same prices on scheduled services that overlap, though only LNM has a day pass for Sfr40.

About a 30-minute walk on the road to Solothurn (or take bus No 1) is the **Taubenloch Gorge**. A path runs along its two-km length (no entry charge, but there's a donation box).

Emmental Region

Emmental is the region to the east of a line drawn between the towns of Langenthal, Bern and Thun. The core of the area is the valley of the Emme River, from which the name is derived (valley in German is *Tal*). A tour along the banks of the river yields picturesque towns and villages, and many buildings display architecture typical of the area. The angled roof is the most distinctive feature; it hangs very low over the sides of the house and usually has a section over the front façade, forming a triangular covering. Below this triangle there is often a semicircular trim framing the upper windows.

Things to See & Do
The local tourist offices promote hiking, and an interesting path is the **Plantenenweg** from Burgdorf to Wynigen, on which tiny models of the planets allow you to pretend you're marching through the universe on a scale of one to 1000 million. It takes about three hours to walk from the sun to Pluto. Afterwards, you can get the train back to **Burgdorf** which has a castle bearing a large representation of the emblem of the canton. There is a historical museum inside the castle (open daily from April to October).

The town of **Langnau** is known for its ornamental crockery; the production process may be viewed at a pottery demonstration *(Schautöpferei)* in the Heimat Museum (☎ 495 60 38), in nearby **Trubschachen**, reached by rail. For more details contact the tourist office for the Emmental (☎ 402 42 52), Schlossstrasse 3, in Langnau. Ask the office about dates of local markets *(Märit)* and traditional fairs *(Chilbi)*.

The best known product of the area is **Emmental cheese**. The Emmental Dairy

Show (Emmentaler Schaukäserei) gives you the chance to see the stuff being made into huge wheels (60 to 130 kg – a bit bulky to take on a picnic). It is at **Affoltern**, six km east of Burgdorf. From Burgdorf, take the train to Hasle, then catch the postbus. The dairy is open from 8.30 am to 6.30 pm every day, but it's better to get there between 9 and 11 am or 2 and 4 pm when the various production stages are being instigated (free entry). **Kiesen**, on the rail route running south-east of Bern (Sfr7.20), has a museum of dairy products that can provide more background information (open between 1 April and 31 October, daily except Sunday from 2 to 5 pm).

Places to Stay
There are only a few camp sites in the area. There's a TCS (Touring Club Schweiz) site, *Waldegg* (☎ 422 79 43), by the river in Burgdorf, (open 1 April to 1 October) and another site, *Mettlen* (402 36 58), at Gohl, near Langnau (open year-round).

Langnau has an SYHA *hostel* (☎ 402 45 26), 10 minutes' walk from the station at Mooseggstrasse 32. Beds cost just Sfr13 without breakfast and the hostel is closed for a few weeks in early February and late September.

Tourist offices can help you find somewhere to stay. Accommodation is mostly in small-scale country inns and pensions which are very reasonably priced (around Sfr35 to Sfr75 per person).

Getting There & Away
Every hour from Bern to Burgdorf there's a fast train (takes 15 minutes) and a local train, and the fare is Sfr7.20. Langnau can be reached by direct train from Bern (Sfr12.20) or Burgdorf.

Bernese Oberland

The Bernese Oberland (Berner Oberland) is where the scenic wonders of Switzerland come into their own. People often end up staying longer than they planned, such are the toe-twitching hikes and eye-spinning sights on offer. Good weather is essential to fully enjoy the stunning landscape, so if the sun shines, flee the cities and head for here. From Bern, a train will get you to Interlaken in less than an hour.

Orientation & Information

The Bernese Oberland tourist region covers the southern part of the canton of Bern, stretching from Gstaad in the west to the Susten Pass (2224m) in the east. The regional tourist office for the whole area is the Berner Oberland Tourismus (☎ 033-822 26 21; fax 822 57 16), Jungfraustrasse 38, CH-3800, Interlaken. It's on the 1st floor without a recognisable office front, and the opening hours are Monday to Friday from 7.30 am to noon and 1 to 5.30 pm, and Saturday from 7.30 am to noon. Pick up the detailed *Summer Info* or *Winter Info* brochures covering sights and sports in the whole region. The annual *Budget Accommodation* brochure is also useful. See the Bernese Mittelland chapter for information on the history of the canton.

Getting Around

The Berner Oberland Regional travel pass is one of the most useful regional passes available. It is also one of the most expensive, costing Sfr190 for 15 days or Sfr150 for one week, with reductions for holders of Swiss travel passes (around 20% off). It gives free travel on five days (three days in the case of the Sfr150 pass) on certain routes, such as cruises on Lake Brienz and Lake Thun, and trains as far as Gstaad, Kleine Scheidegg, Thun and Meiringen. On the other days there is a 50% reduction. Many other routes (including to Bern, Zermatt, Mt Titlis, and

HIGHLIGHTS

- Hiking and skiing in the Jungfrau region
- Jungfraujoch – Europe's highest railway
- The hike from Schynige Platte to Grindelwald-First
- Mountain panoramas seen from Schilthorn and Männlichen
- Boat trips on Lakes Thun and Brienz
- Tour of the Alpine passes, south of Meiringen

Bern

the three-pass bus tour) are 50% off on all days, and mountain transport (Jungfraujoch, Schilthorn, Gornergrat, etc) is 25% off. The pass is available from 1 May to 31 October.

Interlaken

• *pop 15,000*   • *570m*   • ☎ *(033)*

Interlaken, flanked by Lake Thun and Lake Brienz and within striking distance of the mighty peaks of the Jungfrau, Mönch and Eiger, is an ideal centre from which to

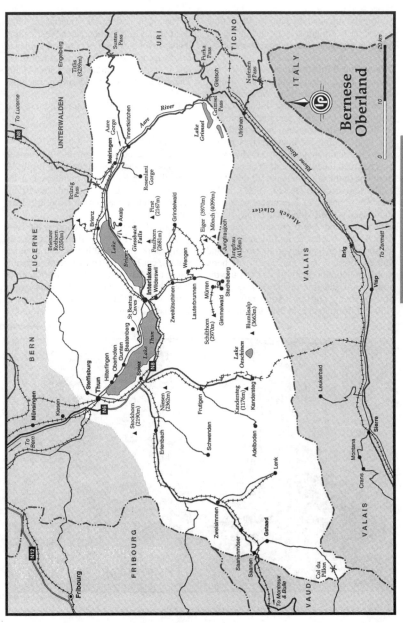

BERNESE OBERLAND

explore the surrounding delights. But if time allows, an overnight stay farther inside the Jungfrau region is even more rewarding.

Orientation & Information

Most of Interlaken is coupled between its two train stations: Interlaken West and Interlaken Ost. Each station offers bike rental and daily money-exchange facilities (including credit card cash advances), and behind each is a boat landing for boat services on the lakes. The main shopping street, Höheweg, runs between the two stations. You can walk from one to the other in under 20 minutes.

The tourist office (☎ 822 21 21), Höheweg 37, is nearer to Interlaken West train station and is open Monday to Friday from 8 am to noon and 2 to 6 pm, and Satur- day from 8 am to noon. During July and August, it's also open on Saturday from 2 to 4 pm and Sunday from 5 to 7 pm. Staff will book rooms (no commission), or you can use the hotel board and free phone outside and at both railway stations. Jungfrau region railway information is in the same office.

The main post office (Interlaken 3800, Postplatz) is near the Interlaken West station. It is open for postal services from Monday to Friday from 7.45 am to noon and from 1.30 to 6.15 pm, and Saturday from 8.30 to 11 am. There are telephones and stamp machines outside.

Call ☎ 823 23 23 if you have a medical emergency.

Things to See & Do

Most of the points of interest are around Interlaken rather than in the town itself. All the following attractions mentioned in the Jungfrau region, Lake Thun and Lake Brienz sections can be reached on a day trip from Interlaken.

A good circular orientation walk is to wander down Höheweg, glancing at the souvenir shops and grand hotels, and at either station, cut back to the tree-lined footpaths along the Aare River. The prettiest area of Interlaken is around the **Stadthaus** dating from 1471, on the north side of the Aare in Unterseen. There's a large cobbled square

GLENN VAN DER KNIJFF

An Interlaken street

bordered by attractive old buildings with a church tower at two opposite corners. One of the old buildings is the **Tourist Museum**, Obere Gasse 26. It gives a rundown of the development of tourism and transport in the region, displaying models, old posters and photos, skis and chair lifts. Explanations are in German but you can pick up a summary in English, and it's worth spending up to an hour in here. Entry costs Sfr3 (Sfr2 with Guest Card, Sfr1 for children), and it's open May to mid-October, Tuesday to Sunday from 2 to 5 pm.

If you're a train enthusiast, or travelling with children, the **Model Railway Exhibition** (Modelleisenbahn-Treff) by Interlaken West train station on Rugenparkstrasse, could take up another hour of your time. There are model trains whizzing all over the place on perimeter tracks (you can even get a train to serve you coffee) and elaborate representations of famous railway routes. Not to suggest that they're biased or anything, but it's funny that, while the trains chug along freely, most of the cars shown are either held up by roadworks or passing cows, or being towed out of a ditch. It's open from 30 April to mid-October, daily from 10 am to noon and 1.30 to 6 pm. Entry costs Sfr6 or Sfr3 for children.

Although expensive for what it is, it's still better value than the 15-minute model railway show at **Heimwehfluh** that costs Sfr6 (children Sfr4). Heimwehfluh does at least have a play area outside that's quite fun (free, or Sfr4.50 for the Bob-Run) and a good view of the town and lakes from the tower by the pricey restaurant. Don't bother taking the expensive funicular (Sfr8 return, children Sfr6) as the signposted walk up takes only 20 minutes, and leads to further walking trails. There's an even shorter route up (unsignposted) that starts 10m to the right of the base funicular station as you face it.

Chäsdorfli, a summer demonstration dairy off Höheweg, accepts groups only.

The village of Wilderswil can be reached in eight minutes by bus No 5 from Interlaken West (see the Jungfrau Region map). It's a good deal quieter than Interlaken, and many of the wooden houses here retain a traditional, rural ambience. Wilderswil is also the starting point for a cog-wheel train (Sfr28, closed late October to late May) that runs up **Schynige Platte** to 2001m. The views are terrific from here and there is also an Alpine garden (Sfr3) with 500 types of flora. At this altitude, many flowers are just beginning to bloom in June or July. There is a great hike from here to Faulhorn (2681m), Lake Bach (featured in many tourist brochures) and on to First, Grindel and Grindelwald. The whole thing takes about six hours one-way and treats hikers to excellent unfolding panoramas of the Jungfrau massif.

Numerous hiking trails dot the area surrounding Interlaken, all with signposts giving average walking times. The funicular up to **Harder Kulm** (Sfr12.40 up, Sfr12 return, closed late October to late April) yields a memorable panorama and further prepared paths. While you're waiting for the funicular, wander around the enclosures containing ibexes and marmots (free). The restaurant up at Harder Kulm with the pointed roof is another regular in tourist brochures. To walk up from Interlaken takes about 2¼ hours. Below and to the right of the pointed roof, when viewed from the town, is an illusory moustached face in the tree-free section of the cliffs, known as the Harder Mann.

Places to Stay

All types of accommodation provide the useful Guest Card (refer to Accommodation in the Facts for the Visitor chapter). Except in the hostels, winter prices are usually slightly lower. Call ahead in off-season, as some places close.

Places to Stay – bottom end
Camping There are five camp sites close together north-west of Interlaken West. *Camp Alpenblick* (☎ 822 77 57), on Seestrasse by the Lombach River, costs Sfr5.80 per person, from Sfr9 per tent and Sfr4 for a car. Just along the road by the lake is *Manor Farm* (☎ 822 22 64), which is more

BERNESE OBERLAND

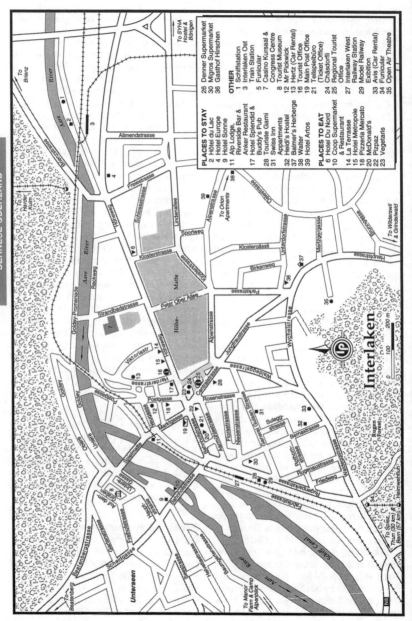

PLACES TO STAY
2   Hotel du Lac
4   Hotel Europe
9   Hotel Sonne
11 Alp Lodge,
    Riverside Bar &
    Anker Restaurant
17 Hotel Splendid &
    Buddy's Pub
28 Touriste Garni
31 Swiss Inn
    Apartments
32 Heidi's Hostel
37 Balmer's Herberge
38 Walter
39 Hotel Artos

PLACES TO EAT
6   Hotel Du Nord
10 Coop Supermarket
    & Restaurant
14 La Terrasse
15 Hotel Metropole
18 Pizzeria Mercato
20 McDonald's
22 Pizpaz
23 Vegetaris

26 Denner Supermarket
30 Migros Supermarket
36 Gasthof Hirschen

OTHER
1   Schiffstation
3   Interlaken Ost
    Train Station
5   Funicular
7   Casino Kursaal &
    Congress Centre
8   Tourist Museum
12 Mr Pickwick
13 Hertz (Car Rental)
16 Tourist Office
19 Main Post Office
21 Telispelbüro
    (Ticket Office)
24 Chasodorfli
25 Regional Tourist
    Office
27 Interlaken West
    Railway Station
29 Model Railway
    Exbition
33 Avis (Car Rental)
34 Funicular
35 Open Air Theatre

expensive in the high season, but has more facilities. Both sites are open all year.

Hostels The SYHA *hostel* (☎ 822 43 53), Aareweg 21, am See, Bönigen, is a 20-minute walk around the lake from Interlaken Ost, or take bus No 1. It has an excellent location by the lake, with swimming facilities and a kitchen. Beds in large dorms are Sfr17, breakfast is Sfr7 and dinner is Sfr11 The reception shuts between 9 am and 4 pm, but the communal areas stay open. There is a 1 am curfew, and the hostel is closed from mid-December to mid-March.

Balmer's Herberge (☎ 822 19 61), Hauptstrasse 23, is a 15-minute walk (signposted) from either station. Excellent communal facilities include a kitchen, reading room, games room, music room, videos every night, store and book-exchange (Sfr1 to Sfr5 to buy, free to swap). Balmer's also organises excursions, rents bikes and gets discounts on adventure activity packages. There is a great atmosphere and it's a refreshing change of style from SYHA hostels. Somebody even escorts you to your dorm in quiet periods. During the high season, however, the American summer-camp atmosphere and queuing for showers and breakfast can get a bit too much for some people. It can be noisy, too, especially since the opening of the cellar bar.

Beds are Sfr17 in dorms, Sfr27 in doubles and Sfr22 in triples and quads. Showers are Sfr1, optional sheet rental is Sfr4, and evening meals are Sfr5 to Sfr10. Sign for a bed during the day (facilities are open) and check in at 5 pm (or before noon in summer). If it's full, get a mattress on the floor for Sfr11. It is open all year, and in summer they open *Balmer's Tent*, 800m south, to take care of excess demand (showers and reception in the Herberge).

Rooms & Apartments There are some cheap private rooms, mostly requiring a three-day minimum stay. Shorter stays are OK at *Walter* (☎ 822 76 88), Oelestrasse 35. This friendly host has four doubles (hall shower) for Sfr20 per person, and you can make lunchtime sandwiches from the huge Sfr7 breakfast. Apartments are normally for a minimum seven days, but shorter stays are also possible at *Orion Appartments* (☎ 822 92 25), Bühlstrasse 40. Singles/doubles with a kitchenette (no breakfast) and fold-down beds are Sfr60/80. Both places have off-street parking.

Hotels & Pensions Basic but cheap is *Heidi's Hostel* (☎ 822 90 30), Bernastrasse 37, sometimes called Beyeler Garni. Doubles/triples/quads with private shower are Sfr70/85/100; breakfast costs Sfr7 per person. Check the rooms first – they vary in quality and some have a strange smell about them. There's a quaint breakfast room and TV area in this family-run place.

The *Alp Lodge* (☎ 822 47 48), at Marktgasse 59, is a low-budget annex of the Bellevue, a comfortable mid-price hotel. Creatively-decorated rooms for one to six people are Sfr39 per person with shower/WC or Sfr29 without. Singles aren't available in summer. There's 24-hour access though check-in is from around 3 pm.

By Interlaken West train station is *Touriste Garni* (☎ 822 28 31), with a few parking spaces. Good-value singles/doubles are Sfr55/110 with shower or Sfr48/90 without. Another good choice is *Hotel Sonne* (☎ 822 88 35), Bahnhofstrasse 9. The furnishings are a bit old, but the rooms are more spacious than in a modern place, and there is a shower and toilet on every floor. Singles/doubles are Sfr50 per person, and the simple restaurant serves meals from around Sfr14. It closes in November.

Places to Stay – middle & top end
Swiss Inn Appartments (☎ 822 36 26), General Guisan Strasse 23, is small, central and friendly, with parking and a garden. Singles/doubles with shower/WC and cable TV are Sfr100/140. Apartments are also available. For stays of five days or more at special rates, consider *Hotel Artos* (☎ 828 88 44), Alpenstrasse 45, with new-looking singles/doubles at Sfr105/160 with shower

and half-board. This quiet place is linked with an old people's home.

Hotel Splendid (☎ 822 76 12), Höheweg 33, offers three-star comfort and a central location. Well-presented singles and doubles are Sfr110/182 with private shower/toilet or Sfr80/117 without; all rooms have a TV, telephone, and tea and coffee-making facilities. Less central but convenient if you're taking the Jungfrau train is *Hotel Europe* (☎ 822 71 41) at Höheweg 94. Renovated rooms with all facilities are Sfr150/220, and there is ample free parking.

The plush choice without spending vast sums of money is *Hôtel du Lac* (☎ 822 29 22; fax 822 29 15), Höheweg 225, overlooking the Lake Brienz boat-landing stage. Singles/doubles start at Sfr90/150 with private bath/toilet and cable TV. Riverside and balcony rooms cost slightly more. The restaurant serves a range of meals.

Places to Eat

The *Migros* supermarket opposite Interlaken West has a self-service restaurant, with late opening till 9 pm on Thursday. Meals are around Sfr10. Similarly-priced is the *Coop* supermarket, by the river on Bahnhofstrasse; its restaurant has late opening on Friday until 9.30 pm, and is also open Sunday from 9 am to 5.30 pm. There are a number of *Denner* supermarkets around town, providing picnic fare and alcohol.

Anker Restaurant, Marktgasse 57, has a varied menu with dishes costing from Sfr11 to Sfr33, and substantial portions. There is a games area at the back, but the restaurant section is fairly civilised. On Saturday night, except in summer, there's live music, usually with an entry fee. It's closed on Thursday. Opposite is *Ristorante Arcobaleno*, good for Italian food from Sfr11 (closed Tuesday).

There are several decent pizzerias around town, where smallish pizzas start at around Sfr10.50. Try *Pizzeria Mercato* on Postgasse, open daily, and *Pizpaz* on Centralstrasse (closed Monday). Vegetarians can head to the *Vegetaris* section in the restaurant of the Weisses Kreuz Hotel, Höheweg.

Meals are Sfr13 to Sfr25 and it's closed on Wednesday in winter.

The *Hotel Europe* (see the previous Places to Stay section) has a tasty two-course menu for Sfr13.50 or Sfr14.50. Other dishes start at Sfr15 and there's always a vegetarian choice. There's a wider selection of both food and wines in summer. Ambience and quality exceeds expectations given the low prices and it represents one of the best eating deals in Interlaken (open daily). Beer is Sfr4.20 for half a litre, and the kitchen closes around 9 pm. A good place for traditional food in rustic yet comfortable surroundings is *Gasthof Hirschen*, on the corner of Hauptstrasse and Parkstrasse. Main courses start from around Sfr30 and it's closed for Wednesday lunch and on Tuesday.

The *Il Bellini* restaurant in the Hotel Metropole (☎ 828 66 66), by the tourist office on Höheweg, is an expensive place for quality Italian fare, but has a Sfr17 lunch menu from Monday to Saturday. The hotel also has the *Panoramic Bar/Café* on the 15th floor – it's worth going up for a beer or a coffee to admire the view and to walk around the balcony.

The restaurant in the *Hotel Du Nord* (☎ 822 26 31), on Höheweg , offers Swiss food, seafood and vegetarian dishes, mostly in the range of Sfr20 to Sfr40. There's also a five-course 'degustation' menu for Sfr54. It's open daily. For splendid surroundings and attentive service you can't beat *La Terrasse* in the Victoria-Jungfrau Hotel (☎ 828 28 28), Höheweg 41. Soothing piano music helps you digest excellent French cuisine from around Sfr40, with full menus starting at Sfr70. Lunchtime dining is less expensive (open daily).

Entertainment

For a traditional Swiss folklore show, go to the *Casino Kursaal*. The Spycher restaurant serves up Swiss food to complement the entertainment. Three-course menus including the show start at around Sfr40, or it's Sfr16 just for the show and late dancing. Shows are mostly in the summer; check with

the tourist office for schedules, or phone
☎ 827 61 00.

Balmer's Bar (see Places to Stay) is open
daily in summer and only weekends in
winter. Prices are low (Sfr3.50 for half a litre
of beer), making it popular with young
English-speakers. Other places are *Buddy's
Pub* in the Hotel Splendid, Höheweg 33, and
the *Riverside Bar* (closed Sunday and
Monday), Marktgasse 59. *Mr Pickwick*,
Postgasse 3, is a British-style pub with a free
disco or live music on weekends. There's
also *Johnny's Dancing Bar* in the Hotel
Carlton, Höheweg 92 (cover charge).

Between mid-June and mid-September
there are at least weekly performances of
Schiller's *Wilhelm Tell* in the *open-air
theatre* in the Rugen forest. The first performance was in 1912 and it's now an annual
event. Over 200 amateur actors take part in
the production, not to mention the many
horses, cows and goats who wander around
and add sound effects as appropriate. It is
staged in German but an English synopsis is
available. Get tickets (Sfr12 to Sfr32) from
Tellspielbüro (☎ 822 37 23), Bahnhofstrasse 5.

The biggest local event, with over 2500
participants, is the Unspunnen Festival.
Unfortunately it's only every 12 years, and
the next one isn't until 2005.

Things to Buy
There are plenty of souvenir shops along
Höheweg, many with a good selection of
Swiss army knives. If you're interested in
wood carvings, it's better to buy directly in
Brienz.

Getting There & Away
Trains to Lucerne depart hourly from Interlaken Ost train station. Trains to Brig (via
Spiez and Lötschberg) and to Montreux (via
Bern or Zweisimmen) depart from Interlaken West or Ost. Main roads head east to
Lucerne and west to Bern, but the only way
south for vehicles without a big detour round
the mountains is to take the car-carrying train
from Kandersteg, south of Spiez.

Car Rental Reasonably central are both
Avis (☎ 822 12 14), Waldeggstrasse 34a,
near a 24-hour petrol station, and Hertz
(☎ 822 61 72), Harderstrasse 44.

Getting Around
Interlaken taxis cost Sfr5 plus around
Sfr3.20 per km, depending upon the number
of passengers. There are usually some
waiting by the railway stations, or call ☎ 822
80 80. Bus fares start at Sfr2.20

Jungfrau Region

Some of the best scenery in the whole of
Switzerland can be found in the Jungfrau
region. Magnificent views and hikes
compete for attention from various vantage
points, usually accessible by railway or cable
car. Attention is wrested by the towering
triplets: the Jungfrau (4158m), Mönch
(4099m) and Eiger (3970m), which head a
series of mountains over 3000m that undu-
late to the south. But the shimmering peaks
of these snow-topped giants are only half the
story; the white and grey of their rugged
flanks are made all the more beautiful by the
green, gold and brown of the nearer hills and
valleys. It's a hard place to leave.

Cast member from *Wilhelm Tell*

BERNESE OBERLAND

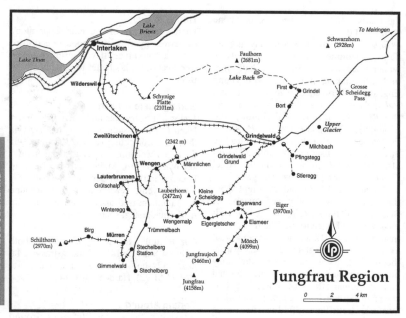

Jungfrau Region

0   2   4 km

Orientation & Information

There are two valleys branching southwards from Interlaken. The valley that curves to the east is dominated by Grindelwald, a well-established skiing and hiking centre. The valley that runs more directly south leads first to Lauterbrunnen, a leaping-off point for the car-free resorts nestled on the hills above. Above Lauterbrunnen (via funicular) on the western ridge is Grütschalp. Walking or taking the train along the ridge yields tremendous views across the valley to the Jungfrau, Mönch and Eiger peaks, and brings you to the ski resort of Mürren (fare from Lauterbrunnen Sfr8.40). A 40-minute walk down the hill from Mürren is tiny Gimmelwald, relatively undisturbed by tourists.

Gimmelwald and Mürren can also be reached from the valley floor by the Stechelberg cable car, which runs all the way up to Schilthorn at 2970m (Sfr83 return). Wengen perches on the eastern ridge of the Lauterbrunnen Valley.

Save mountain-top excursions for clear days. There are revolving cameras on Jungfraujoch, Schilthorn, Kleine Scheidegg, Männlichen and Grindelwald-First, and live pictures are shown on the local cable TV information channel. However, weather conditions are volatile in mountain areas, and the outlook might have changed by the time you get up there.

Staying in resorts earns a Guest Card (Gästekarte), which is good for a number of discounts throughout the Jungfrau region. Benefits are listed in the informative (free) Jungfrau *Top Magazine*, or tourist offices and hotels can provide details. Grindelwald and Mürren even have two types of Guest Card – the superior version (called 'A' or 'Passepartout' respectively) gives extra benefits at the local sports centre (eg free swimming). Holiday chalets or apartments are ubiquitous in this area. They sleep from one to eight people or more and can work out as little as Sfr20 per day per person. In the off season these may be available on demand, but for peak season contact the local tourist office around six months in advance. Chalets are generally available for one week minimum, Saturday to Saturday.

Beware of exchanging money at train stations in the Jungfrau region. Rates are generally around 4% lower than those offered at banks. The telephone code for the whole area is ☎ 033.

Activities

Skiing is a major activity in the winter months, with a good variety of intermediate runs plus the demanding run down from the Schilthorn. In all there are 200 km of prepared runs and 49 ski lifts. A one-day ski pass for either Grindelwald-First or Mürren/Schilthorn costs Sfr50 (Sfr25 for children, or Sfr40 for ages 16 to 20). For Kleine Scheidegg/Männlichen it's a couple of francs more. Ski passes for the whole Jungfrau Top Ski Region cost Sfr100/50/80 for a minimum two days, or Sfr750/375/550 for the whole season.

Adventure World (☎ 826 77 11; fax 826 77 15), Wilderswil, offers many daredevil-type activities such as river rafting, rock climbing and canyoning. You can even bungy jump off the Stechelberg-Mürren cable car – the 100m jump is Sfr129 and the 180m jump, claimed to be the world's largest fixed-point jump, is Sfr259. If you stay in Balmer's (see Places to Stay in Interlaken) you can get around 10% off most prices.

Scenic helicopter flights of the Jungfrau region are conducted by Bohag (☎ 822 92 30). There are several departure points, such as Männlichen (daily in winter), Jungfraujoch (in fine weather) and Gsteigwiler, near Interlaken. Prices for a short, eight-minute trip start at Sfr60 per person, but the views are incredible, and it's worth doing if your budget can handle it. One-way trips are possible by arrangement (minimum three people), so it's viable to take the helicopter up to Jungfraujoch and not pay hugely more than the equivalent expensive train fare.

Getting There & Around

One or two trains depart for the region per hour from Interlaken Ost train station; sit in the front half of the train for Lauterbrunnen or the back half for Grindelwald. The two sections of the train split up where the two valleys diverge at Zweilütschinen. The railtracks loop around and meet up again at Kleine Scheidegg, at the foot of the Eiger. Many cable cars close briefly for servicing at the end of April and at the end of November. On transport in the region, usual reductions are 25% with Eurail and Europass, and 50% with Inter-Rail (not on buses).

GRINDELWALD

• *pop 36001* • *1090m* ☎ *(033)*

Grindelwald is the largest ski village in the Jungfrau, and occupies an enviable position under the north face of the Eiger. It is also a great base for hiking, especially in the First region where there are 90 km of paths above 1200m. Of these, 48 km stay open in winter.

Orientation & Information

The main village is to the east of the train station. At either end of the village, Terrassenweg loops north off the main street and takes a scenic, elevated east-west course. Below and south of the main street is the Schwarze Lütschine River. The tourist office (☎ 854 12 12) is in the centre at the Sportzentrum; it's open daily from July to mid-October, and weekdays to 6 pm and Saturday to noon (in low season) or 5 pm the rest of the year. It is 200m up from the train station – only follow the more visible 'i' sign down the hill to the Regina Hotel if you want information in Japanese.

Postbuses and local buses depart from near the train station, and a post office (3818) is close by. Local buses are free with the Guest Card in winter. There are several open-air car parks scattered around. The one by the bus station costs Sfr8 for a maximum 12 hours stay from 7 am to 7 pm; it's free at night. Many sports shops down the main street rent ski equipment.

Winter Sports

The gondola from Grindelwald to First is in three sections and takes 20 minutes (Sfr27 up, Sfr43 return). This is the main **skiing** area, with a variety of runs (mostly intermediate or difficult) stretching from Oberjoch at 2486m, right down to the village at 1050m. From Kleine Scheidegg or Männlichen there are long, easy runs back to Grindelwald. The ski school (☎ 853 52 00), open daily on the main street, has had good reports for its instruction to children. Grindelwald is also a good base for cross-country skiing (33 km of trails). For **tobogganing**, routes include the 12-km run down from Faulhorn, starting at 2543m.

Hiking

From First, you can hike to Schwarzhorn (2 hours 50 minutes), Grosse Scheidegg (1½ hours) the Upper Glacier (1½ hours), Grindelwald (2½ hours), Lake Bach (1

Thomas Cook: the First Conducted Tour of Switzerland

Thomas Cook, the excursionist who spawned the world-wide travel company, was instrumental in opening up Switzerland to mass tourism in the 19th century. He embarked on his first conducted tour of Switzerland in 1863. Previously Mr Cook had concentrated on Scotland for excursions into lake and highland scenery, but in frustration at the refusal of the English and Scottish Railway to renew a cheap excursion ticket to that country (20th century British Rail travellers know how he felt), he decided to look further afield. Switzerland seemed the ideal substitute. Various notices subsequently appeared about his plans in the regular newsletter written and produced by Mr Cook, *Cook's Excursionist and Advertiser*.

Public interest was immediate and extensive. Cook initially wanted a party of 25, but ultimately in excess of 130 people set off from London on 26 June 1863. They travelled by ferry to Dieppe and then took the train to Paris. The original party was whittled down to 62 who were scheduled to continue the whole way to Switzerland, and included in that number were many independently-minded Victorian ladies. One of these, Miss Jemima Morrell, wrote a book about their experiences *(Miss Jemima's Swiss Journal* – now out of print but still available in some libraries). Various locations in Switzerland were included in the tour, with the main focus of the trip being the Jungfrau region. This was in the days before the mountains had been tamed by funiculars and cable cars, yet these hardy ladies were undaunted as they negotiated steep mountain passes. Some trails, Miss Jemima wrote, were 'a mere groove cut in the face of (a) huge cliff, just wide enough for a mule to pass'.

The trip proved to be a great success, even though not everything about foreign countries appealed to the tourists (French tea, Miss Jemima considered, was 'truly peculiar'). It's worth noting, in our current climate of supposedly free movement between European nations, that these Victorian British travellers did not need a passport to enter France and Switzerland. Mr Cook followed up his success with regular subsequent trips, but not everybody appreciated the influx of masses: the English gentry, who had previously made the Swiss Alps their private playground, were particularly miffed.

In those days, Switzerland was relatively cheap. The exchange rate was around £1 = Sfr24. Mr Cook's personal bill for tea, bed and attendance in the Hotel Clerc, Martigny where the treatment was 'kind and liberal' was Sfr4.50. Costs for mules and guides over the mountain passes were less than Sfr8 per person. Mr Cook reckoned that with careful spending, all-in costs for a 14-day jaunt to Switzerland could be as little as £10 to £12, or £20 for a month. Nevertheless, £20 was still a substantial amount of money for the average Victorian. But not, apparently, for Mr Cook, because he wrote in his *Excursionist* (21 July 1863) that £20 was 'a sum often spent at home, in fashion and folly, in a single night, leaving little for the disbursement but aching heads, wearied limbs and restless ennui'. Mr Cook himself was teetotal, but it seems, was in the habit of indulging in wild nights out in the company of dissolute spendthrifts! ■

hour), Faulhorn (2 hours 20 minutes) and Schynige Platte (5½ hours). The scenery from up here is breathtaking.

The **Upper Glacier** (Oberegletscher) is well worth a visit. It's a 1½ hour hike from the village, or a postbus goes to the Hotel-Restaurant Wetterhorn, from where it's just 15 minutes. It costs Sfr5 (with Guest Card Sfr4, children Sfr2.50) to get in to see the ice grottoes, open June to October. The sculptures themselves are pretty pathetic, but notice the air bubbles and stones trapped in the ice that create kaleidoscopic patterns.

From here it's a few minutes' walk up to the Restaurant Milchbach where a further track, incorporating wooden ladders, climbs up alongside the ice. It's a good route but it's annoying to have to pay to use it (Sfr3, allow around 1½ hours return). There's a viewpoint up there looking over the sea of ice (Eismeer), but if you carry on along a less well-defined path to where there's a 'skull and crossbones' glacier avalanche warning, there's an even better perspective looking up to the top.

A cable car glides up to **Pfingstegg** (Sfr9.20 or Sfr14 return) from May to October. Apart from enjoying the view, you can take short hiking trails to Stieregg, near the Lower Glacier, or to the Restaurant Milchbach. Along the latter route you pass the **Breitlouwina**, a sloping terrace of rock billed as a geologist's paradise. You can see pot-holes, scratches on the rock caused by stones inside moving ice, and places where two different types of rock (40 million years and 120 million years old) have fused together.

The **Glacier Gorge** (Gletscherschlucht) is a 30-minute walk from the village centre. It's open from May to October between 9 am and 6 pm and entry costs Sfr5 (reductions as for ice grottoes). It's not a bad spectacle, but you can get a good idea of what it looks like from the entrance and it doesn't really get any better further in.

Organised Activities

The Bergsteigerzentrum (☎ 853 52 00), based in the ski school, has a programme of guided activities in summer and winter, taking place in the Jungfrau region and beyond. Options include ski touring, mountaineering and hiking.

Special Events

The **World Snow Festival** in mid-January sees international teams create inventive sculptures from blocks of ice (free to spectate). In July, Grindelwald has a yodelling festival and later in the month there's Swiss wrestling at nearby Grosse Scheidegg.

Places to Stay

There are hundreds of holiday chalets, especially on Terrassenweg and near the Glacier gorge. The tourist office has prices and availability logged on its computer, and some are listed in the hotel information hut (free telephone) at the bus station.

There are also various hotels (many with dorms) outside the village, such as the *Wetterhorn* (☎ 853 12 18) at the bottom of the Upper Glacier, the *Glecksteinhütte SAC* (☎ 853 25 00) high up on the mountain overlooking the glacier (experienced climbers only), the *Berggasthaus* (☎ 853 12 84) on First, and the *Berghaus Bort* (☎ 853 17 62), half-way up by the Bort station.

Camping Grindelwald has several camp sites. The most convenient is *Gletscherdorf* (☎ 853 14 29), near the Pfingstegg cable car, open May to late October for tents or year-round for caravans. *Aspen* (☎ 853 11 24), is on the lower slopes of the Männlichen, open year-round.

Hostels The SYHA *hostel* (☎ 853 10 09), is at Terrassenweg, 20 minutes' climb from the train station, taking the road that follows the tracks on the north side. If you're walking, don't miss the small sign on the brown and white house indicating the steep short-cut footpath up to the right. Beds in six-bed dorms (including local tax) are Sfr29.50. These (and reception) are in the typical wood chalet which must have accounted for a couple of forests' worth of wood all by itself. The view is fantastic and there is an open fire and musical instruments. The house is always open (no curfew) but reception and check-in is from 3 pm (5 pm on Sunday). The wood building next door, newly opened in 1996, houses doubles or four-bed rooms with sink (Sfr34.50 per person) and doubles with shower/WC for Sfr45 per person. The hostel is closed in the off season.

A 10-minute walk from the youth hostel along Terrassenweg is the *Naturfreundehaus* (☎ 853 13 33), which has dorms for Sfr32 (Sfr28 with ISIC card or HI membership). In the high season you must take a half-pension for Sfr47 (Sfr43). Child rates are around 25% lower, and it closes in off-season.

If you don't fancy the walk to these hostels, bus No 4 departs the bus station every 30 minutes and completes a circuit of Terrassenweg. *Mountain Hostel* (☎ 853 39 00) is a new place by the Grund cable car, with dorm beds from Sfr29 (Sfr20 for children). There's 24-hour access and a TV and games room. Take bus No 1 or 3.

Hotels & Pensions *Lehmann's Herberge* (☎ 853 31 41) has good-value rooms for one to six people with shower. The price is Sfr40 per person, except for the doubles with shower/WC for Sfr90. There's a surcharge of Sfr5 for single-night stays in this family-run place. It's in the centre of the village just off the main road (signposted). At the same turning on the main street, with private parking, is *Hotel Tschuggen* (☎ 853 17 81). Attractive singles/doubles are Sfr77/120 with private shower/WC and TV. There are also some rooms for Sfr57/100 with a radio only, and use of a hall shower.

At the eastern end of the village is *Mounty* (☎ 853 11 05), with a young atmosphere. Basic but pleasant singles/doubles are for Sfr55/90, using a hall shower. Prices are lower in the off season and from Sunday to Friday. There's a dormitory, and breakfast buffet is Sfr10. *Gydisorf* (☎ 853 13 03), by the bottom First cable station, is a small, staid place with a nice flower garden. It's often booked ahead by regulars: singles/doubles with own shower start at Sfr77/144.

Moving upmarket a bit, try *Fiescherblick*

(☎ 853 44 53; fax 853 44 57), in a flower-strewn chalet towards the east of the village on the main street. Rooms start at Sfr192 or Sfr120 for single occupancy. *Sunstar-Hotel* (☎ 854 77 77; fax 854 77 70) charges Sfr140 per person and has good facilities including a swimming pool, sauna and tennis court.

Places to Eat
For eating, just follow your nose. Most hotels have reasonable restaurants but they can be a bit pricey. There's a *Coop* supermarket opposite the tourist office.

On the main street is *Ristorante Mercado*, about the cheapest place to eat. Small but tasty pizzas start at Sfr11, and there's an outside terrace. Along the road, *Restaurant Rendez-vous* also has a panoramic terrace, and meals from around Sfr13, including simple vegetarian food. Fondue costs Sfr39 for two (closed Tuesday).

Hotel Derby, by the train station, has Italian and Swiss food from Sfr13, and cheap beer. *Hirschen Restaurant*, on the main street, has a good selection of meals from Sfr16, or Sfr13 at lunchtime. The lunch and evening menu du jour is Sfr35 for four-courses (closed Thursday in low season).

Fiescherblick (see the previous Places to Stay section) has two restaurants. The main restaurant is gourmet-quality, with main dishes from Sfr36. The Swiss Bistro has typical Swiss food from Sfr15. Both are closed Wednesday lunch time and Tuesday.

Entertainment
A popular watering-hole in the centre is the small *Espresso Bar*. In the same hotel complex is *Mescalero*, a Mexican restaurant open evenings, with live music in winter and a disco after 11 pm (free entry but pricey drinks; closed Sunday).

Mounty (see Places to Stay) has another popular bar, with two pool tables. The downstairs section of the *Hotel Derby* (see Places to Eat), serves inexpensive Italian food and has live music nightly in winter (free entry, but drink prices double when the music starts).

CLEM LINDENMAYER

MARK HONAN

MARK HONAN

CLEM LINDENMAYER

Top Left: Architecture in Bernese Oberland
Top Right: Cable car, Lake Lucerne, Central Switzerland
Middle: Leading herd through village, Interlaken, Bernese Oberland
Bottom: View of the Aletsch Glacier from Jungfraujoch, Bernese Oberland

MARK HONAN

MARK HONAN

MARK HONAN

Top: The city of Zürich from Utoquai, Zürich Canton
Bottom Left: Window by Chagall, Fraumünster, Zürich, Zürich Canton
Bottom Right: Town Hall (Rathaus), Basel, North-West Switzerland

Getting There & Away

Grindelwald is only 40 minutes by train from Interlaken Ost (Sfr9 each way). It can also be reached by a good road from Interlaken. A smaller road continues from the village over the Grosse Scheidegg Pass (1960m). This is a great way to get to Meiringen – the hillside is very desolate-looking with many rocks half-overgrown with grass and shrubs, and the views are excellent. The army performs manoeuvres here twice a year. I've been assured that this has no relevance to the fact that private traffic is banned from using the road. Postbuses use this route from the end of May to mid-October to get to Meiringen (takes two hours). It's possible to make a round trip, including bus to Meiringen, a train to Brienz, a boat to Interlaken and a train back to Grindelwald, with stops en route allowed. The validity is two days and the adult fare is around Sfr57, including supplements.

LAUTERBRUNNEN
• *pop 1000* • *806m* ☎ *(033)*
This village can be reached by car or rail. It's a suitable base for a number of excursions, although many people simply use it as a car park before visiting the nearby car-free resorts. There is a multi-storey car park by the station with space for 900 cars; summer rates are Sfr9 for a day and Sfr59 for a week. Winter rates are slightly higher. There is also an open-air car park by the Stechelberg cable-car station, costing Sfr5 for a day.

The tourist office (☎ 855 19 55) is on the main street above the train station. Its opening hours are Monday to Friday from 8 am to noon and 2 to 6 pm. In Summer it is also open on Saturday depending upon demand, and even on Sunday in July and August. The post office, bank and nearly all the shops and hotels are along this same street. Crystal Sport (☎ 855 20 80) rents mountain bikes, ski equipment and mountaineering gear. The valley floor is good for cross-country skiing in the winter.

Spare a glance for the **Staubbach Falls** just outside the village, where wispy threads of spray cascade down the sheer face of the western ridge. It's just one of many waterfalls in the valley. Lauterbrunnen has the small **Heimat Museum** featuring historical exhibits and mountain-related stuff. It's open from 2 to 5.30 pm, on Tuesday, Thursday, Saturday and Sunday, and costs Sfr2.50 (Sfr2 with Guest Card, Sfr0.60 for children).

Trümmelbach Falls

A short bus ride (Sfr2.80) or a 50-minute walk down the valley is the Trümmelbachfälle, which drains the detritus from 24 sq km of Alpine glaciers and snow deposits. It's viewed mainly from inside the mountain (illuminated), and as you get quite damp anyway, it's something to do if the weather is poor. The water generates incredible power – up to 20,000l of water is propelled down per second, and the noise is unceasing. The fissures of rock have been sculptured into dramatic shapes by the swirling waters over the 10 stages of the falls. It's worth seeing, but Sfr8 (Sfr3 for children) is a lot to charge to view a natural phenomenon, even if they did build a few staircases and install a lift. An hour is ample time to see the whole thing. The falls are open from April to November, daily between 9 am and 5 pm (8 am to 6 pm June to September).

Places to Stay

Lauterbrunnen is well fixed for self-catering dormitory accommodation. *Camping Schützenbach* (☎ 855 12 68) and *Camping Jungfrau* (☎ 856 20 10) both offer kitchen facilities, rooms and dorms from only around Sfr15 per person. The sites are on either side of the river a few minutes' walk to the south of the village. Camping Jungfrau is used by Contiki tour buses, although their parties in the 'Bombshelter' don't disrupt the rest of the site too much. Schützenbach is used by Top Deck tours. Prices for campers are around Sfr8 per person and from Sfr6 for a tent.

The best budget place to bed down is *Matratzenlager Stocki* (☎ 855 17 54). To get there from the station, follow the white signs that take you around the right side of the multi-storey car park and over the river. It's

BERNESE OBERLAND

about 200m down the road on the right; see Frau Graf in the next house along for check-in by 8 pm. She's a trusting soul and runs free-and-easy lodgings for Sfr12 a night (no breakfast; closed November). Mattresses in the dorms are side-by-side and there's only one shower, but there are good kitchen facilities (no meters) and the open communal area generates a sociable atmosphere.

Chalet im Rohr (☎ 855 21 82), by the church, has one to four-bed rooms for Sfr26 per person in a creaky old wood chalet. There are hall showers, a kitchen (Sfr1 per day) but no breakfast. Nearby *Hotel Horner* (☎ 855 16 73), another wood chalet, has singles/doubles using hall shower for Sfr45/85, and doubles with a shower cubicle in the room for Sfr95. *Hotel Jungfrau* (☎ 855 34 34; fax 855 25 23) is the mid-price choice. Comfortable singles/doubles with private shower/toilet are Sfr65/120, rising in high season. The hotel has a swimming pool and a solarium on the premises.

In Stechelberg at the end of the valley there are various private rooms and apartments, as well as *Camping Breithorn* (☎ 855 12 25). Stechelberg has its own *Coop* supermarket.

Places to Eat

There is less choice when it comes to cheap eating in Lauterbrunnen. The *Coop* supermarket provides microwave-heated burgers and pasties. The *Metzg-hus* meat store, between the Coop and the tourist office, offers hot sausage snacks, and usually has spit-roast chickens cooking outside (Sfr8, or Sfr4.50 for a half). It closes for a half-day on Wednesday in winter.

Hotel Horner (see Places to Stay), serves pizza and pasta from Sfr11 (closed Monday). It also has a bar-disco open till late, but drinks prices rise after midnight. Go to the *Hotel Jungfrau* (see Places to Stay) for a variety of meals, including vegetarian dishes, starting at Sfr14.50. The restaurant in the *Hotel Oberland* has as similar range and prices. The *Hotel Silberhorn* is another good choice for food. It's generally a little more

expensive, but has senior and child plates, and serves fondue for Sfr16.

GIMMELWALD

• *pop 140* • *1370m* • ☎ *(033)*

There's nothing to do in car-free Gimmelwald except relax, enjoy the view and keep away from the crowds. Various hiking trails lead up and around the mountains from the village. In winter, it's perfectly viable to enjoy the ski runs around Mürren and to retreat back down here for the night. It's cheaper to stay here than in Mürren, and you still get the normal Jungfrau Guest Card.

The steep hike down from Gimmelwald to Stechelberg takes around two hours, taking the trail to the right of the cable car as you're facing the valley.

Places to Stay & Eat

The *Mountain Hostel* (☎ 855 17 04), close to the cable-car station and with a great view, was renovated in 1996. Dorms without breakfast cost Sfr18 and there are new showers and kitchen facilities. There's daytime check-in and no curfew. Next door is *Restaurant-Pension Gimmelwald* (☎ 855 17 30), with simple accommodation (including dormitory beds for Sfr12) and hot meals from Sfr11. It adjoins a shop that's open just a few mornings a week.

Five minutes up the hill, along a tarmac then cinder path, is *Mittaghorn* (☎ 855 16 58), sometimes known as Walter's. Singles/doubles are Sfr55/60, triples/quads are Sfr85/105, and dormitory beds in the loft are Sfr25. Beds are available from May to mid-November only, as it's pre-booked by a ski group in winter. Beer in the small café costs Sfr4 for an 0.58-l bottle, but the tasty meals are only for guests who must pre-order. There are a few holiday apartments in the village.

MÜRREN

• *pop 320* • *1650m* • ☎ *(033)*

This car-free resort hosted the first ever Alpine ski race in 1922, and has had a long association with British skiers. The tourist office (☎ 856 86 86) is in the sports centre, open in off-season from Monday to Friday, 9 am to noon and 2 to 5 pm. Hours lengthen with demand; in the high season, Sunday morning is the only time it's shut during the day.

The village is long on views and pretty chalets and short on nightlife. Hiking and skiing are the main seasonal pursuits. There are 50 km of prepared ski-runs in the vicinity, mostly suited to intermediates. The ski school (☎ 855 12 47) charges Sfr27 for half a day. Other activities on offer include swimming, ice-skating and curling. There's a yodelling festival every year in late July at Allmendhubel, above Mürren.

Places to Stay & Eat

Mürren is more touristy and therefore more expensive than either Lauterbrunnen or Gimmelwald. The only budget places are two pensions about 30 minutes' walk up the hill, or you can save your legs by taking the Allmendhubel funicular from the village. *Pension Suppenalp* (☎ 855 17 26) and *Pension Sonnenberg* (☎ 855 11 27) each charges Sfr37 in dorms and around Sfr100 for double rooms.

Believe it or not, *Hotel Edelweiss* (☎ 855 13 12), with singles/doubles for Sfr95/190 with own shower/WC, is one of the cheaper places in the village. It also has reasonable food from Sfr12, and good views from the south-facing terrace. The restaurant is closed on Tuesday in low season.

The small *Stägerstübli*, a few paces from the Coop supermarket, has filling meals from Sfr13.50, including fondue for Sfr18. It's open daily.

SCHILTHORN

This 2970-m peak provides a perfect viewing platform from which to gaze at the mountains across the valley. It's easily (if expensively) reached from the Stechelberg cable car, via Gimmelwald and Mürren. From the top there's a fantastic 360° panorama, and the film shows in the **Touristorama** will remind you that James Bond performed several stunts here in *On Her Majesty's Secret Service*. The view is

more spectacular than that from Jungfraujoch in some ways, as you see a broader expanse of peaks, and you get a real sense of the height of the mountains across the valley. The view from Birg (2677m), the station after Mürren, is well worth stopping off for; the 'big three' are closer than from the summit and you get a great perspective of the dark ridge of the Männlichen.

The high cost of the trip by cable car can sometimes be reduced by special offers. There are usually lower prices in the spring, autumn, or for the first/last ascent of the day (Sfr64 return instead of Sfr83). European railcards, the Swiss Half-Fare Card and the Swiss Pass are also good for reductions.

The **hike** up is a strength-sapping four hours from Mürren, often very steep, and you're likely to encounter snow above Birg. The walk down is more manageable, and you're facing the mountains across the valley, rather than climbing with your back to them. About halfway between Mürren and Birg there's a grassy knoll to the valley-side of the path which is an ideal place to break for a picnic. At the top, refreshment is provided by the *Piz Gloria* revolving restaurant (meals from Sfr18); the bar has a snack section.

Ever since 1928, Schilthorn has welcomed amateur skiers eager to take on the difficult course down to Mürren, known as the **inferno run**. It takes place in mid-January and attracts well over 1000 participants, making it the largest event of its kind in the world.

WENGEN
• *pop 1050* • *1350m* • ☎ *(033)*

This car-free, chalet-style ski resort is slightly more developed than Mürren, across the valley, and is popular with British skiers. As with most places in this region, the views are breathtaking.

From the train station, take a left at Hotel Silberhorn and walk 100m to get to the tourist office (☎ 855 14 14). Opening hours in the low season are Monday to Friday from 8 am to noon and 2 to 6 pm, and Saturday from 8.30 am to 11.30 pm. In the high season it is also open from 4 to 6 pm on both Saturday and Sunday. Next door is the post office.

The high point in Wengen's calendar is when it hosts the international **Lauberhorn downhill ski race** in late January: it costs Sfr20 to watch the race or Sfr10 to watch just the training. Expect price hikes and accommodation problems at this time. Wengen has a ski school (☎ 855 20 22) where half-day classes cost Sfr37 each or Sfr186 for six. The ski runs are reached by gondola to Männlichen, or by railway to Allmend, Wengernalp or Kleine Scheidegg. The same areas are also excellent for hiking in the summer, and 20 km of paths stay open in winter, too. The hike down to Lauterbrunnen takes about an hour, or the frequent train does it in 15 minutes (Sfr5.40). Other attractions include a natural and an artificial ice rink, and tennis courts. There's also a cinema, with a pool hall next door.

Places to Stay & Eat

Several mid-price hotels in the village offer a dormitory annex. Prices generally exclude breakfast, which can be taken in the main hotel if desired. The best deal is at the *Bergheim YMCA* (☎ 855 27 55) where a place in the mixed six-bed dorm costs Sfr22 in summer and Sfr25 in winter. It's run by the plush Hotel Jungfraublick, five minutes away, where you check-in. Rooms in the comfortable main *Bergheim* average around Sfr100 but dorm-users can use the TV room there, or even the library in the Jungfraublick.

En route you pass *Bernerhof* (☎ 855 27 21) where dorm beds are a couple of francs cheaper, but guests are generally excluded from hotel amenities. The dorm is a large room, partitioned into unappealing two-person boxes. The hotel also has quite acceptable 'tourist rooms' for Sfr95/178, and better-quality rooms for Sfr104/198 (all rooms priced at half-board). The best thing about its restaurant is the salad bar, which costs Sfr6.50, Sfr9.80, or Sfr14.50 for a plate the size of a wok. The restaurant also has a wide choice of Swiss dishes from Sfr13.50.

Half-board rates at *Garni Hotel Bären* (☎ 855 14 19) are Sfr55 for dorms, Sfr85/150 for singles/doubles with hall shower, and Sfr180 for doubles with private shower/WC. The restaurant serves affordable Swiss food. Around the back of this place, the *Hotel Edelweiss* (☎ 855 23 88) has reasonable rooms and the best prices for stays of three days or more: from Sfr60/120 with shower/WC and Sfr42/80 without. To get to both these hotels, take the road passing under the railtracks and look for the signs.

Few food options are open apart from eating in the hotel restaurants. The large *Coop* across from the station provides budget provisions. *Da Sina*, by the cinema, is comfortable and has good pizza/pasta from Sfr13 (open daily in season). Part of the same building is *Sina's Pub*, which usually has live music for après-ski and on summer evenings.

MÄNNLICHEN

Männlichen (2230m) is up on the ridge dividing the two valleys. Take the gondola (Sfr19.60 up, Sfr32 return) from Wengen or make the pleasant three-hour hike up through the trees.

From the top station, walk 10 minutes up to the crown of the hill for a magnificent panorama. At the southern end of the ridge are the dark conical shapes of Tschuggen (2520m) and Lauberhorn (2472m), with the snow-capped giants looming impressively in the background. These are flanked by the two valleys, and their different characteristics are particularly evident from here; the broad expanse of the Grindelwald Valley to the left, and the glacier-formed Lauterbrunnen Valley to the right with its severe square sides. This valley is the deepest hanging or 'u' valley in the world. To the north you can see gentler green hills and a stretch of Lake Thun. The hike from here to Kleine Scheidegg is an extremely rewarding gradual descent on the Grindelwald side, and takes a little over an hour. By foot, Grindelwald itself can be reached in three hours, or you can take the thirty-minute cable car to Grindelwald-Grund (Sfr27 one-way,

Sfr43 return). It is the longest gondola cableway in Europe, traversing 6.2 km.

KLEINE SCHEIDEGG

This small place is little more than a few buildings grouped around the train station, yet it occupies such an enviable position at the base of the Eiger that it's surprising that it is not more developed than it is. It looks like a toy village against the backdrop of soaring peaks. Most people only linger a few minutes while changing trains for Jungfraujoch (see the following section), but Kleine Scheidegg (2061m) is a good base for a longer exploration of this scenic area. There are short (one hour apiece), undemanding hiking trails to Eigergletscher, down to Wengernalp, and up the Lauberhorn (green in summer, red-brown in autumn) behind the village. These areas become intermediate ski runs from early December to April.

Find out local information and change money in the train station. The small post office is also in the train station. The *Röstizzeria Bahnhof Restaurant* (☎ 855 11 51) offers dormitory accommodation year-round for Sfr38 with breakfast or Sfr55 with half-pension. *Restaurant Grindelwaldblick* (☎ 853 13 73) has slightly cheaper dorms but it closes in the off-season. There's only one hotel in Kleine Scheidegg (☎ 855 12 12). It's in two buildings by the station, and singles/doubles with private shower and half-pension start at Sfr160/280.

Eat in one of the restaurants mentioned already or pick up cheap snacks at the outside kiosk by the station.

JUNGFRAUJOCH

The trip to Jungfraujoch by railway (the highest in Europe) is excellent. Unfortunately, the price is as steep as the track and is hardly worth it unless you have good weather – call ☎ 855 10 22 for forecasts in German, French and English. From Interlaken Ost, trains go via Grindelwald or Lauterbrunnen to Kleine Scheidegg. From here, the line is less than 10-km long but took 16 years to build. Opened in 1912, the track powers through both the Eiger and the Mönch with majestic views from windows cut into the mountain side, before terminating at 3454m at Jungfraujoch.

On the summit there is the **ice palace**, a gallery cut in the glacier featuring disparate sculptures carved in ice, such as Sherlock Holmes and a sumo wrestler. From the terrace of the Sphinx Research Institute (a weather station) the panorama of peaks is unforgettable, including the Aletsch Glacier to the south, and mountains as distant as the Jura and the Black Forest in Germany. Expect to queue up to an hour for the terrace in the peak of summer. There's also a small exhibition in the complex giving an erudite rundown of the work of the weather station, including various facts about the atmosphere (there's one-third less oxygen in the air at Jungfrau compared to at sea-level, for example). Entry to the above places is free.

You can walk across the glacier behind the Mönch on a marked path, but remember to keep a leisurely pace because of the high altitude. The views keep getting better. On the glacier there's a very tame ski lift (skis provided in the modest charge). A sled ride courtesy of a team of husky dogs is another attraction.

Take warm clothing any time of the year, and sunglasses if you're going to walk on the glacier. Bringing your own food will help to cut costs, although the self-service restaurant in the complex is quite reasonably priced. There is another, more expensive, restaurant upstairs. If you walk the full way across the glacier along the prepared path (50 minutes) you reach the *Möchsjochhutte* (☎ 971 34 72) at 3650m. This mountain hut offers dormitory accommodation for Sfr25.50 and a great view across the mountains fringing the glacier. Breakfast is Sfr8.50, dinner is Sfr17, and other meals and snacks are also available. It closes in off-season (including June), and in winter no meals are available.

Getting There & Away

From Interlaken Ost, journey time is 2½ hours each way and the return fare is Sfr158

BERNESE OBERLAND

(Eurail Sfr116, Inter-Rail Sfr76.60, Swiss Pass Sfr105). Allow at least three hours at the site. The last train back is 6.10 pm in the summer and 4 pm in the winter. It is not possible to walk up much beyond Kleine Scheidegg. There's a cheaper (or more accurately, less exorbitant) 'good morning ticket' of Sfr120 (Eurail Sfr101, Inter-Rail Sfr76.60, Swiss Pass Sfr90) if you take the first train (6.35 am from Interlaken) and leave the summit by noon. From 1 November to 30 April the reduction is valid for the 6.35 and 7.38 am trains, and the noon restriction doesn't apply.

Getting these early trains is not such an effort if you start from farther down the track. If you stay overnight at Kleine Scheidegg, you can pick up the excursion-fare train at 8.02 am in the summer and at 8.02 or 9.02 am in the winter. From here, the full return is Sfr94 and the excursion return is Sfr56. Ordinary return fares are valid for one month.

The Lakes

A boat tour of Lake Thun (Thunersee) or Lake Brienz (Brienzersee) is a popular and enjoyable excursion. Lake Thun has the greater number of resorts and villages clustered around it, and has more facilities to offer water sports enthusiasts. Lake Brienz, in contrast, has a more rugged shoreline and fewer diversions. It claims to be the cleanest lake in Switzerland, ideal for angling. No fishing permit is needed for the shore of the lakes; if you go out on a boat or fish in a river you need to get a permit from the tourist office (Sfr35 for one day or Sfr95 for one week, valid for the whole canton). At one time the lakes were one great waterway, but deposits from the Lütschine in the south and the Lombach in the north gradually formed a plain (the Bödeli, upon which Interlaken now stands) that divided it in two. The lakes are still linked by the Aare River, but boats can't navigate this stretch.

Steamers are most frequent from the end of May to late September. Both lakes also have services in spring and autumn, and Lake Thun even has a daily boat sailing up till early December. A day pass valid for both lakes costs Sfr32 (Sfr49 in 1st class) or Sfr42 (Sfr62) in July and August. Children travel half price and people with a Half-Fare Card pay Sfr21 (Sfr31 in 1st class) any time of the year. Passes are also available for seven and 15 days, or even longer. Eurailpasses are valid on all boats and Inter-Rail and the Swiss Half-Fare Card are good for 50% off the fare of individual rides. The Regional Pass and the Swiss Pass are valid on all boat rides.

The most famous ferry on Lake Thun is the *Blümlisalp*, a paddle-steamer built in 1906. It started operating again in 1992 after plans to scrap it were overturned in a public referendum. A 'steam supplement' of Sfr5 is payable on top of the normal ferry ticket if you travel on this boat, and it sails daily in summer.

THUN
• *pop 38,700* • *563m* • ☎ *(033)*
Evidence of habitation in Thun dates back to 2500 BC. Its name is derived from the Latin, *Dunum* (meaning fortified hill), and its castle remains its most dominant feature today. The town was acquired by the canton of Bern in 1384.

Orientation & Information
Thun (pronounced Toohn) is the largest town on the lake. The Aare River separates the train station (which has bike rental and money-exchange counters) from the medieval centre around the castle. The river itself is split by a sliver of land which has Bälliz, a partly pedestrian-only street, running along its length. This island is laced to the mainland by several roads and footpaths. The central area can easily be covered on foot.

The tourist office (☎ 222 23 40) is in the train station, open Monday to Friday from 9 am to noon and 1 to 6 pm, and Saturday from 9 am to noon. Hours are extended in July and August. If it's shut, the train information counter usually has a hotel list. The main

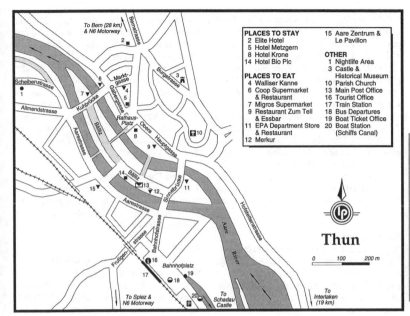

PLACES TO STAY
2 Elite Hotel
5 Hotel Metzgern
8 Hotel Krone
14 Hotel Bio Pic

PLACES TO EAT
4 Walliser Kanne
6 Coop Supermarket
& Restaurant
7 Migros Supermarket
9 Restaurant Zum Tell
& Essbar
11 EPA Department Store
& Restaurant
12 Merkur

15 Aare Zentrum &
Le Pavillon

OTHER
1 Nightlife Area
3 Castle &
Historical Museum
10 Parish Church
13 Main Post Office
16 Tourist Office
17 Train Station
18 Bus Departures
19 Boat Ticket Office
20 Boat Station
(Schiffs Canal)

Thun

post office is on Bälliz, open Monday to
Friday from 7.30 am to noon and 1.30 to 6.15
pm, and Saturday from 7.30 to 11 am,
although there's also an out-of-hours counter
(surcharge applies).

Things to See & Do
Roaming around the river and the old town,
enjoying the views, is an attraction in itself.
Obere Hauptgasse, leading off the harmonious Rathausplatz, is a two-tier street,
where the roofs of the shops on the lower
level provide the walkways for the upper
level. Wherever you are in the town, attention is drawn to the 12th century **castle**
(Schloss Thun), up on the hill. It contains the
Historical Museum for which entry costs
Sfr5 (students Sfr2, children Sfr1). It's open
from April to October from 10 am to 5 pm (9
am to 6 pm from June to September). The
museum contains several interesting exhibits, encompassing weapons, toys, ancient
coins, and pottery-making. It also provides

access to the Romanesque tower with its four
corner turrets, yielding fine views. The
parish church, which shares the skyline with
the castle, is fairly nondescript inside.

In July, Thun has its International Barrel
Organ Festival (every odd-numbered year)
and an annual yodelling festival. For
nightlife, explore the former industrial
quarter round Scheibenstrasse, where
several lively bars, clubs and concert venues
have spawned.

Places to Stay
The best deal in the centre is at *Hotel Bio
Pic* (☎ 222 99 52), Bälliz 54. It has singles/
doubles/triples for Sfr36/64/100 on the fifth
floor, which is dominated by huge pot plants.
The hall showers are on the lower floors
where rooms are from Sfr46/82. For rooms
with private shower/toilet the charge is
Sfr62/102/130. Not surprisingly, it's nearly
always full, so reserve ahead. A lift goes as
far as the 4th floor.

BERNESE OBERLAND

Rathausplatz is an attractive cobbled square in the medieval part of town, below the castle. At one side of it is *Hotel Metzgern* (☎ 222 21 41), with simple singles/doubles for Sfr55/110. On the other side of the square, with its own pointed tower, is *Hotel Krone* (☎ 222 82 82), with spacious but not-particularly-plush-for-the-price rooms with radio, telephone, mini-bar, and private shower/toilet. Singles/doubles start at Sfr105/170. The Hotel Krone has several restaurants, catering for a range of preferences and budgets. The *Elite Hotel* (☎ 223 28 23), Bernstrasse 1, is not so comely as the Krone from the outside, but has similar standard rooms (with cable TV) for the same price.

Places to Eat
Thun is a great place to eat well and cheaply. There are dozens of restaurants clustered around the old town, offering all types of cuisine. Pizzerias are particularly numerous, with pizzas starting at Sfr11.

Self-Service The old favourites are here, offering daily specials from around Sfr7.50. They're open shop hours; most have late-closing on Thursday. A *Migros* restaurant and supermarket is on the island by Kuhbrücke. Across the river from it is a *Coop* supermarket and restaurant. On the other side of the island by Sinnebrücke is an *EPA* department store and restaurant. But perhaps the best place to go is *Le Pavillon*, 1st floor, in the Aare Zentrum shopping centre on Aarestrasse. You can browse among the different counters offering Italian food (from Sfr9.50), Asian food (from Sfr8.50), a salad buffet (Sfr7.50 or Sfr10.50 per bowl), or coffee and confectionery.

Restaurants A small place with friendly service is *Restaurant Zum Tell* on Obere Hauptgasse 28. It has tasty two-course menus for around Sfr14 and the usual selection of meats and grills. It's closed Sunday. Downstairs is the *Essbar*, open to 1.30 am except Sunday, with Spanish and Mexican bar snacks. Another small and cosy restaurant is *Walliser Kanne*, Marktgasse 3, with a good selection of fondues (from Sfr18) and Röstis (from Sfr15.50). This traditional-style place is closed on Sunday and Monday.

The *Merkur* restaurant at Bälliz 62 also has a reasonable selection of affordable daily and weekly specials. Vegetarians can eat here, or feast in the restaurant at *Bio Pic* (see Places to Stay), which is open from 7 am to 8 pm on weekdays and 7 am to 4 pm on Saturday. Meals start at around Sfr9.50, and there's a salad buffet.

Getting There & Away
Thun is on the main north-south rail route from Frankfurt to Milan and beyond. From Interlaken, Thun is Sfr15.60 each way by steamer, Sfr14 by train.

SPIEZ
• *pop 11,000* • *628m* • ☎ *(033)*
Spiez (pronounced 'Schpee-its') is a pretty little town hunched around a horseshoe-shaped bay. Its medieval castle and lakeside views are the main attractions.

Orientation & Information
The tower of the castle makes orientation easy. The train station is about a 10-minute walk uphill from the bay and 15 minutes from the castle. They're connected by Seestrasse, the main street. The tourist office (☎ 654 21 38) is outside the train station, open Monday to Friday from 8 am to noon and 2 to 5 pm. In the summer season it's open on Saturday and weekday hours are extended.

Things to See & Do
The castle, **Schloss Spiez**, was the home of the influential von Bubenburg and von Erlach families. Many of the portraits hang on the walls. It's amusing to note how the children have no childlike quality at all; they all look like midget adults, especially the dour grandchildren of Franz Ludwig von Erlach (painted in 1645). The castle tower was constructed in the 16th to 17th centuries and provides a fetching view of the town and the bay. Elsewhere, the castle contains

weapons, period furniture, and impressive wooden doorway surrounds and stucco ceilings. The Romanesque **church** by the castle dates from the 10th century. It is open daily from April to October, 10 am to 5 pm (2 to 5 pm on Monday); entry costs Sfr4, or Sfr1 for children.

Near the castle is the small **Heimat and Rebbaumuseum** with exhibits on wine cultivation; it's free and open Wednesday, Saturday and Sunday from 2 to 5 pm.

Spiez has a heated swimming pool at Schachenstrasse 19, and a well-known **sailing school** (☎ 654 56 42). In October there's a Vintage Wine Festival, the Läsetsunntig, with a fair, parades and music.

Places to Stay & Eat

It is viable to use Faulensee youth hostel as a base for Spiez (see Around Lake Thun), or you could ask the tourist office about cheap private rooms.

The only budget central hotel is *Krone* (☎ 654 41 31), near the station on Seestrasse, with singles/doubles for Sfr50/95 using hall shower. Reception is closed on Sunday afternoon and Monday.

Nearby on Seestrasse is *Bellevue* (☎ 654 84 64), (Sfr40/70), charging Sfr65/120 with shower/WC. Its restaurant has a good selection of vegetarian dishes for under Sfr13. Next door, *Des Alpes* (☎ 654 34 34), has rooms with shower/WC from Sfr70/130. The restaurant terrace (and some rooms) have a good view over the harbour; daily menus are around Sfr17.

Other places for affordable eating are the tea rooms along Seestrasse, or *Pizzeria al Porto* by the harbour on Schachenstrasse 3. A *Coop* (without restaurant) is on Oberlandstrasse, with late closing on Friday.

There's a good view from the four-star *Strandhotel Belvédère* (☎ 654 33 33; fax 654 66 33), on Schbachenstrasse. Well-equipped rooms start from Sfr155/230, and there's a large garden for lakeside strolls. It also has a renowned restaurant with a sumptuous dining area. À-la-carte main courses nudge the Sfr45 mark (closed Sunday evening and Monday in low season).

Getting There & Away

From Interlaken, Spiez is Sfr11.60 each way by steamer, Sfr6.60 by train. Spiez is also the rail junction for the car-carrying train to Brig (see Brig in the Valais chapter for more details) and the MOB line south-west to the Vaud Alps and Montreux.

AROUND LAKE THUN

A short, Sfr6 boat ride from Interlaken are the **St Beatus Caves** (St Beatus Höhlen), with some impressive stalagmite and stalactite formations, and a small museum. Combined entry is Sfr12, or Sfr11 for students. The department store dummies in a 'realistic reconstruction of a prehistoric settlement' are a laugh. Photography is prohibited in the caves as it holds up the guided tour – not that this stops anybody. The caves can also be reached from Interlaken by bus or a 90-minute walk, and are open from Palm Sunday to October, daily from 9.30 am to 5 pm.

The loudest sound in quiet **Faulensee** is the wind rustling in the sails of the windsurfers. Get on board by calling Maluco Sportferien (☎ 654 54 68), which rents various sports equipment and organises outings. Contact the tourist office (☎ 654 32 64) for more information on the resort; it's by the harbour and closed in winter. Faulensee has an SYHA *hostel* (☎ 654 19 88), Quellenhofweg, a 35-minute walk from Spiez train station. The hostel is closed from late October to 31 March and costs Sfr23.50.

Därligen, towards Interlaken, is another water sports centre. It has windsurfing, water-skiing and diving, all arranged at the Hôtel du Lac (☎ 821 61 51). The same activities are offered at **Gunten**, on the north shore. Its tourist office (☎ 251 11 46) has details. On the hill above Gunten is **Sigriswil**, where there are two folklore-related festivals in July.

Castles

One of the best castles around the lake is **Schloss Oberhofen**. It looms over Oberhofen boat-landing stage and dates from the 13th century. It was held by the Habsburgs

BERNESE OBERLAND

for a while before Bernese troops wrested control after the Battle of Sempach (1386). The castle contains a good collection of grand furniture, portraits, weapons, children's toys, and even a Turkish smoking room. The gardens were landscaped in the 19th century and are a fine place for a stroll. The castle and grounds are open from mid-May to mid-October, and combined entry costs Sfr4 (Sfr1 children) or Sfr1 just for the garden. Opening hours for the garden are from 9.30 am to 6 pm, and for the castle are 10 am to noon and 2 to 5 pm every day. The resort also has a new museum, displaying clocks and music boxes.

In Oberhofen, compile a picnic at the *Coop* on the main street (half-day Wednesday), or chomp cheap meals in the *Berger Tea-Room* (open till 6.30 pm; closed Thursday). *Hotel Restaurant Kreuz* (☎ 243 16 76) by the castle has fair-sized rooms from Sfr45 per person (closed in January).

Another interesting castle is **Schloss Hünegg**, one boat-stop down the lake at Hilterfingen. The interior illustrates the comfortable lifestyle of the 19th century elite. Particularly evocative is the main bedroom with adjoining Lady's Dressing Room, Master's Dressing Room, and split-level bathroom complete with a gleaming nickel-plated bathtub and complicated taps. It was built in the 1860s and renovated in 1900, and provides a fascinating mix of Neo-Renaissance and art nouveau (Jugendstil) styles. It's open from early May to mid-October, daily from 2 to 5 pm, plus Sunday morning from 10 am to noon. Entry costs Sfr5 (children Sfr1.50). Hilterfingen also has a free concrete-and-grass 'beach', the **Strandbad Hünegg**, open daily from 9 am to 7 pm.

There's time enough to fit in a visit to all the castles at Spiez, Thun, Oberhofen and Hilterfingen in a single day trip by boat. They're all worth seeing, but that's probably a bit of overkill, especially as the first three collections cover similar ground. Keep your sanity by skipping an interior, probably Spiez or Thun, as they contain fewer and less diverse exhibits. On the other hand, if your appetite is insatiable, you can also digest the

Swiss Museum of Gastronomy. It's in the castle at Schadau, on the outskirts of Thun, where the Aare River meets the lake. On display are 4000 cookery books dating from the 16th century, plus crockery and pottery. It is open from the end of March to mid-October, daily except Monday; hours are 1 to 5 pm except from June to August when they are 10 am to 6 pm. Only a few boats stop here, though you can walk from Thun centre in 20 minutes. Entry costs Sfr5 (children Sfr2). All the castles offer a discount with the Guest Card. In the Schloss Schadau grounds there's usually a rock festival in July.

GIESSBACH FALLS

These falls by Lake Brienz are a popular excursion, one hour from Interlaken Ost by boat (Sfr10.60 each way). The water spills down over several stages and makes an attractive rather than a spectacular sight. A funicular runs up from the boat station (Sfr3.50) but the walk doesn't take long. The sun is at a better angle for photography in the afternoon. Various footpaths traverse the surrounding hillside. It takes a little over an hour to walk around the lake to Brienz; unfortunately the route is along the road rather than on a separate footpath.

BRIENZ
• *pop 3075* • *566m* • ☎ *(033)*
Brienz is the centre of the Swiss wood-carving industry and the main town on the shores of Lake Brienz. It is a convenient base for visiting the Ballenberg museum.

Orientation & Information
Orientation in Brienz is easy. The train station, boat station, Rothorn Bahn lower terminal, post office (Postamt 3855) and a Coop supermarket are all within a stone's throw of each other in the centre of town. The tourist office (☎ 951 32 42) is also here; opening hours are Monday to Friday from 8 am to noon and 2 to 6 pm, and, from April to June, also Saturday from 8 am to noon. In July and August, hours are extended to Monday to Friday from 8 am to 6.30 pm and Saturday from 8 am to noon and 4 to 6 pm.

The local Guest Card gives excellent benefits, including free water-skiing (Monday at 5 pm) and free entry to the beach.

Things to See & Do

There are many touristy shops and boutiques along Hauptstrasse, selling locally-carved statues and mementoes. Linden is a popular wood to use for sculpting as it is so soft; a 20cm high statue of a bear would take about 18 hours to carve. Some shops have factories attached where you can take a quick tour and see the crafts people at work; one such is **Jobin** which has been in business since 1835. Its most elaborate piece is a music box for Sfr24,800. **Walter Stähli** at No 41 also gives workshop tours.

The **Woodcarving School** (Schnitzlerschule) is open for free visits on weekday mornings during term time (check dates with the tourist office), and has an exhibition room packed with finished work. The tourist office books courses with a local crafts person: five days including materials, private room and full board costs around Sfr800.

The **Rothorn Bahn** is the only cog-wheel steam train still operating in Switzerland. It hauls passengers up to 2350m for excellent views and hikes. Departures are hourly; check with the station as a standard diesel train is sometimes used (usually the first ascent/decent of the day). The fare is Sfr40 single or Sfr62 return (25% discount with Swiss Pass, no reductions Eurail or Inter-Rail). As always, there's a hotel and restaurant at the summit. Walking to the top from Brienz takes around five hours.

Brienz gives access to Axalp, where **skiing** is neither extensive nor expensive: a one-day pass costs Sfr32 (Sfr20 for children).

Places to Stay

Camping Aaregg (☎ 951 18 42) is by the lake, 15 minutes' walk east of the centre, and is open from 1 April to 31 October. The SYHA *hostel* (☎ 951 11 52), Strandweg 10 is nearby, in a brown and white house by the railway tracks. Per person costs are: dorms Sfr25.10, family rooms Sfr27.10 and doubles Sfr30.10. It is closed from 1 December to the end of February and has a kitchen. The reception is closed from 9 am to 5 pm, but the doors stay open.

The cheapest hotel is *Sternen am See* (☎ 951 24 12), Hauptstrasse, costing from Sfr50/80 for singles/doubles, or Sfr120 for doubles with private shower. A few minutes east of the station on Hauptstrasse is *Schültzen am See* (☎ 951 16 91), an oldish house with rooms for Sfr60/120 with shower/WC or Sfr55/110 with shower only. Prices don't go up in the summer, but there's no single occupancy in July and August.

Places to Eat & Drink

All the restaurants are ranged along Hauptstrasse, and there are some reasonable places with seating overlooking the lake. One of these is *Walz* at No 102. It has a Tagesmenu for Sfr14.50, weekly specials, and pizza/pasta from Sfr11.50. It's open daily from 8 am to 10.30 pm (6.30 pm in winter). Double rooms with private shower start at Sfr97 (Sfr127 in summer). *See-restaurant Löwen* at No 8 also overlooks the water; fish specialities are Sfr26 to Sfr37 (closed Monday).

Restaurant Steinbock (☎ 951 40 55) at No 123 has meticulously arranged pink tablecloths and ruffled napkins. Similar care is devoted to the food – locals consider it one of the best places to eat. Dishes cost from Sfr11 to Sfr38.50, and include fish, steaks, regional specialities and vegetarian choices (closed Tuesday).

A youngish environment for a drink is *Helvetia Pub*, which also serves pizzas (from Sfr11) and fast food. It's open daily from 8 am to 12.30 am.

Getting There & Away

From Interlaken, Brienz is Sfr12.40 by steamer, or Sfr6 by train. The scenic Brünig Pass (1008m) is the road route to Lucerne.

FREILICHTMUSEUM BALLENBERG

This open-air park is east of Brienz, and displays traditional Swiss crafts and houses from all over the country. The wide diversity of architectural styles between different regions is clearly shown. It's too big to absorb the whole thing in one visit so don't even try. Instead, pick up a plan at the entrance (Sfr2), check the times of special demonstrations on the board, and work out an itinerary. According to the plan, the park is four km across; by my calculations that scale is exaggerated, but it still takes a lot of walking to get round. It's set in parkland and there are often big gaps between groups of buildings.

Most of the properties were slated for demolition before they were moved brick-by-brick to the park. The Geneva Farmhouse (No 551) contains an exhibition outlining its own history; it took eight months and Sfr1,880,000 to move it in 1984. Statistics like that, I suppose, justify the admission price of Sfr12 (students Sfr10, children Sfr6). The park is open daily from mid-April to 31 October, from 10 am to 5 pm (6 pm in fine weather from July to September), and entry is half-price after 4 pm. There are restaurants on site or you can buy sausages and cheese and make use of the barbecue areas (free firewood).

Getting There & Away
From Brienz, take the hourly bus (Sfr2.80) or walk for one hour. There are car parks at each of the two entrances; take the east entrance if coming from Lucerne or Meiringen. The nearest train station is Brienzwiler, east of Brienz.

East Bernese Oberland

East of the Jungfrau region is the Hasli Valley (Haslital), with its main town of Meiringen.

MEIRINGEN
• *pop 4600* • *595m* • ☎ *(033)*
Meiringen is a suitable base for exploration of the Hasli Valley.

Orientation & Information
The town is on the north bank of the Aare River. The train station (where bike rental is available) is in the centre, with postbuses and the main post office opposite. Three minutes' walk away is the tourist office (☎ 971 43 22) on the main thoroughfare, Bahnhofstrasse. It's open Monday to Friday from 8 am to noon and 2 to 6 pm, and Saturday from 8 am to noon. In July and August, it stays open weekday lunchtimes and Saturday from 4 to 6 pm. There's a Hotel Reservation Board at Rudenz.

Things to See & Do
The **Reichenbach Falls** achieved notoriety when Arthur Conan Doyle allowed his famous hero, Sherlock Holmes, to tumble down from them to his death in a struggle with the evil Moriarty. Eccentric fans of the fictional detective still make an annual pilgrimage to the site in the summer (his 'death' was on 4 May). A funicular makes the journey up from Willigen, south of the Aare River, from mid-May to late September, and the fare is Sfr4.40, or Sfr6.50 return (children half-price). In winter the Reichenbach Falls are a mere trickle, as most of the water upstream is diverted for hydro-electricity production. It takes nearly an hour to walk back down to Meiringen from the top.

The **Reichenbach Valley**, the route to Grindelwald, is certainly worthy of exploration. The views of the mountains (particularly the Welhorn and the Wetterhorn) and the glacier are tremendous, and a path leads to the Rosenlaui glacier gorge (Gletscherschlucht), which is open from around May to October (Sfr5, Sfr3.50 for students). Buses somehow negotiate the dramatically winding road along the valley from the end of May to mid-October, and the walk back to Meiringen takes two hours or more.

Less than two km from the town in the direction of Innertkirchen is the **Aare Gorge** (Aareschlucht). The sides are precipitous, narrow (as little as one metre apart in places) and worn smooth by thousands of years of erosion. The gorge is open from April to

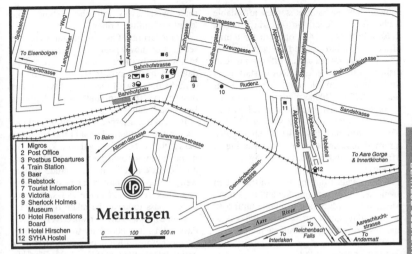

1 Migros
2 Post Office
3 Postbus Departures
4 Train Station
5 Baer
6 Rebstock
7 Tourist Information
8 Victoria
9 Sherlock Holmes Museum
10 Hotel Reservations Board
11 Hotel Hirschen
12 SYHA Hostel

Meiringen

0   100   200 m

BERNESE OBERLAND

October; and buses make the trip regularly in summer (takes 12 minutes). Entry to the gorge costs Sfr5 (students Sfr3.50).

Meiringen really milks its tenuous Sherlock Holmes connection; a statue of the detective reclines in Conan Doyle Place, and the Sherlock Pub is in 'Baker St' (the real Baker St in London was never like this!). There's also the **Sherlock Holmes Museum**, featuring a replica of the study at 221b Baker St. It's nicely done but they need to extend the theme somehow to make it worthwhile – a visit doesn't take more than 10 or 15 minutes. It's open daily from 10 am to 6 pm between 1 May and 30 September, and Wednesday to Sunday from 3 to 6 pm for the rest of the year. Entry costs Sfr3.80 or Sfr2.80 for children.

Meiringen has a famous mountaineering school, the *Bergsteigerschule Rosenlaui* (☎ 971 35 37), CH-3860 Meiringen. Write for its special programme.

Places to Stay & Eat

Camp at *Aareschlucht* (☎ 971 19 66), near the Aare Gorge. It's open year-round and costs Sfr4.90 for an adult and from Sfr6 for a tent.

The SYHA *hostel* (☎ 971 17 15) is a signposted 10-minute walk east of the station near the tracks. Dorms cost Sfr24.90 in communal bunks and there are too few showers. The hostel closes from early April to early May and from late October to before Christmas. Reception is closed from 9 am to 5 pm although you can gain access to the building during this time.

Prices are reasonably low for hotel rooms – telephone ahead on restaurant rest days (see below). The *Victoria* (☎ 971 10 33) on Bahnhofplatz is a good place to stay, despite the strange wooden phallic shapes in the garden. It has a choice of old-style or more modern rooms. Singles/doubles/triples start from Sfr50/90/150 using hall shower; doubles/triples with private shower are from Sfr100/160. It also has one of the best restaurants in town. Pasta and vegetarian dishes start at only Sfr10, yet it also has meat dishes above Sfr17 and multi-course gourmet menus.

The *Hotel Hirschen* (☎ 971 18 12) also has some old rooms, with huge cast-iron radiators and sturdy sinks. It's along the main road towards the hostel, and singles/doubles start at Sfr50/90, or Sfr60/110 with own shower. The restaurant serves affordable Swiss food (closed on Tuesday). *Hotel Rebstock* (☎ 971 17 41), opposite the tourist office, is similarly priced for accommodation. Its pleasant restaurant offers a range of dishes, with pizzas and Röstis starting at Sfr12 (closed on Monday). The three-star *Baer* (☎ 971 46 46) has modern, comfortable rooms bang in the centre of town. Singles/doubles with own shower/WC and TV cost around Sfr80/140. It has a good, informal restaurant with meals starting at Sfr9.50 (closed Sunday evening in low season).

A 50m walk from the front of the station awaits a *Migros* supermarket and restaurant. Meals from Sfr8.50 are available until 6.30 pm weekdays and 4 pm Saturday. It has salad and dessert buffets, and outside tables.

Getting There & Away

Meiringen has frequent trains to Lucerne (one hour 20 minutes, a scenic ride over the Brünig Pass) and Interlaken Ost (30 minutes, via Brienz). In summer, buses and cars can take the pass road south-east (Andermatt) but the road south-west over Grosse Scheidegg (to Grindelwald) is closed to private vehicles.

ALPINE PASS TOURS

The Three Alpine Pass Tour is a wonderful all-day excursion if the weather is clear. Starting from Meiringen, you can make a circular trip crossing the Susten, Furka and Grimsel passes before returning to Meiringen in late afternoon. The views are excellent all the way round, with the mountain ranges showing huge variations in colour and profile. From the Susten Pass there's a great view over the Stein Glacier and lake. The Furka Pass has the Rhône Glacier, which looks stupendous between rocky shoulders of brown and green. There's an ice grotto (Sfr4.50), and if you take the Panoramaweg and cut down over the rocks you'll enter the closed-off area without realising you were supposed to pay. On the south-west side of the pass the landscape looks browner and more parched, and the

road twists away into the distance like lengths of unfurled ribbon.

At the Grimsel Pass, to the south you can see tufts of snowy peaks above the lake, and to the north there are two more lakes, dammed by the power station that barely disturbs the view of the valley beyond. The pass marks the cantonal border between Bern and Valais.

By making a larger loop south, you can take in the Gotthard Pass and the Nurfenen Pass at the cost of missing the Furka Pass (or if you have your own car you can detour and double-back at Gletsch to include that as well). If you don't have a car, or simply want your eyes free to take in the views, the three or four-pass tour can be taken by postbus, costing Sfr68 and Sfr84 respectively (Swiss Pass valid). It is necessary to reserve a seat the day before, either in person in Meiringen or by telephoning ☎ 971 32 05. The bus departs from Meiringen post office on Bahnhofplatz. As the road constantly winds back on itself, it doesn't really matter which side of the bus you sit, except for the stretch between Susten and Furka, where the left side is better. On the three-pass tour, there's a break at Andermatt (see the Central Switzerland chapter) for lunch. Both tours can be completed the same day using different starting points along the route, for example Andermatt. You don't have to start at Meiringen.

The tours only operate from mid-June to late September as the passes are closed for most of the rest of the year.

West Bernese Oberland

At the western side of the Jungfrau are Simmental and Frutigland, dominated by two river valleys, the Simme and the Kander. In the extreme west of the Bernese Oberland is Saanenland, known mainly for the ski resort of Gstaad.

STOCKHORN

This summit (2190m) offers a heart-

Traditional house of the Bernese Oberland region.

pumping view of mountains and lakes. Mont Blanc is visible on a clear day, and you can watch the hang-gliders leaping off into space. There are 70 km of mountain and hiking trails; you can walk to/from the summit but the path is fairly steep. The cable car to the top operates from June to mid-April and costs Sfr36 return. The lower station is 15 minutes' walk from Erlenbach train station, easily reached from Spiez (Sfr5.40, takes 15 minutes).

Erlenbach is the starting point for **white-water rafting** on the Simme River. There are several companies that arrange this – see the listings in the Berner Oberland summer brochure.

NIESEN
This ascent is from the Mülenen station in the Kander Valley. Niesen (2362m) offers views nearly as good as those from better-known peaks. The cable car up this conical peak runs from early May to the end of autumn and costs Sfr36 return. There's a guesthouse (☎ 033-76 11 12) at the top, charging Sfr38 per person for rooms.

KANDERSTEG
• *pop 960* • *1176m* • ☎ *(033)*
Kandersteg is a good base for **hiking** excursions. The trip to the **Blue Lake** (Blausee) and the **Klus Gorge** are well worth considering. Contact the tourist office (☎ 675 22

33) for advice. Its office is in the village centre, ahead from the train station then left on the main street. Opening times are Monday to Friday from 8 am to noon and 2 to 6 pm; in high season they're weekdays from 8 am to 6 pm, and Saturday from 8 am to 11.30 am and 2.30 to 6 pm.

The Blue Lake is open from late April to late October and entry costs Sfr4.30 (families Sfr10). The best outing is to the **Lake Oeschinen** (Oeschinensee). This is superbly situated with sturdy mountains crowding its shores. In summer, its waters are sparkling blue; in winter, it's an iced-over cross-country ski trail. The ancient chair lift up costs Sfr10.60, or Sfr15 return, and it leaves you about a 20-minute walk away from the lake. Once at the lake, it only takes an hour to walk directly back to Kandersteg.

In winter there are 75 km of cross-country skiing trails, and 20 km of hiking tracks stay open. The downhill skiing is suited to beginners and passes cost only Sfr32 for one day.

Places to Stay & Eat
The *Rendez-vous Camp Site* (☎ 675 15 34), by the chair lift, is open year-round. It costs Sfr5 per adult and from Sfr6 for a tent. Reception is in the hut next to the *Restaurant Rendez-vous* (☎ 675 13 54). The restaurant has Swiss food from Sfr11 and closes on Tuesday during low season. It also offers dorms for Sfr15; showers are Sfr1 and breakfast, if required, is Sfr10. Like many other places in the resort, it closes between seasons. *National* (☎ 675 10 85) has dorms for Sfr22, plus Sfr5 if you need sheets. Singles/doubles are Sfr55/90. Breakfast is an extra Sfr8 per person. To get there from the station, take a right once you're on the main street. A few minutes farther south is the *International Scout Centre* (☎ 675 11 39), providing camping (Sfr8) and dorms (Sfr14, with kitchen, without breakfast) for scouts and non-scouts alike.

In the centre, *Hotel zur Post* (☎ 675 12 58) offers compact rooms for Sfr42 per person using hall showers, or Sfr52 with private shower. Swiss food in the restaurant costs Sfr12 to Sfr30 (closed Monday and

Tuesday). Nearby is *Chalet-Hotel Adler* (☎ 675 11 21), where good rooms with shower and TV are Sfr105/170. The restaurant is mostly mid-price (open daily) but has many cheaper options for vegetarians.

The *Bahnhof* restaurant in the train station has food from Sfr12, including decent vegetarian options. In front of the station is a *Coop* supermarket.

Getting There & Away

Kandersteg is at the north end of the Lötschberg tunnel, through which car-carrying trains trundle south to Brig (see Brig for details). The traditional way to head south is to hike; it takes a little over five hours to get to the Gemmi Pass and a further one hour and 40 minutes to reach Leukerbad.

GSTAAD

• *2500 pop* • *1100m* • ☎ *(033)*

This resort is an understudy for St Moritz in that it aspires to the same aura of affluence. It's smaller and not quite so elitist, but still attracts many fur-lined celebrities who come to pose on the slopes and in the chic bars. The pronunciation of the name is tricky to get right, and sounds half-way between spitting and stifling a sneeze; try saying *Hchstaadt*.

Orientation & Information

The train station is in the centre, on a parallel street to the main street, Hauptstrasse. It has bike rental, luggage storage and money-exchange counters; the post office is next door. Turn right on Hauptstrasse and walk 200m to the tourist office (☎ 748 81 81). Opening hours are Monday to Friday from 8.30 am to noon and 2 to 6 pm, and Saturday from 8.30 am to noon. In the season it's also open Saturday from 9 am to 4 pm.

Activities

There's reasonable **skiing** for intermediates but little for experts, and the fact that the lifts around the village only go up around 2000m is also limiting. To enjoy more varied skiing you need to take the train or bus to neighbouring resorts such as Saanen, Saanenmöser, Zweisimmen and St Stephan.

These are only some of the places that are included in the Gstaad Super Ski Region, totalling 250 km of ski runs. In all, 69 lifts are covered, some as far afield as Château d'Oex and the Diablerets Glacier (see the Lake Geneva Region chapter). A one day pass costs Sfr46. There are reductions for youths under 21 and children, and ski coupons are available.

Four main valleys radiate out from Gstaad, allowing a good variety of **hikes**. The tourist office sells two versions of hiking maps. Take the cable car up to Wispile (Sfr19.70 up, Sfr25.10 return) and walk down to the valley on either side. From Lauenen or Feutersoey a bus runs back to Gstaad. A long but undemanding excursion is to walk to Turbach, over the Reulisenpass, and down to St Stephan or Lenk in the adjoining Simmen Valley (around 4½ hours total). From either resort, a train runs back to Gstaad (change at Zweisimmen).

Various other **sports** are on offer, such as swimming, tennis (from Sfr21 per hour) and horse-riding Just to the left of the station on Hauptstrasse is a curling hall *(Eislauf)* where games in winter cost Sfr14 per person per hour. **River-rafting** on the Saane River happens between the end of April and August. A half-day excursion with Swissraft (☎ 744 50 80) costs Sfr99, transport to the river included. If you have your own transport to and from the river, Eurotrek's version costs Sfr80; call ☎ 01-462 02 03.

Every year at the beginning of July, Gstaad hosts the **Swiss Open** tennis tournament. Nearby Saanen is a pretty little village which is the location for the **Yehudi Menuhin Festival** of classical music in August. It's held in Saanen's 15th century Mauritius church and in a marquee in Gstaad.

The après-ski scene can get expensive (so what's new!).

Places to Stay & Eat

There is year-round camping in the west of the village at *Bellerive* (☎ 744 63 30), by the river. The SYHA *hostel* (☎ 744 13 43) is at Chalet Rüblihorn in nearby Saanen, just four minutes away by train. It is closed in the off season and costs Sfr25.50.

Saanen also has the cheapest hotels, such as *Bahnhof* (☎ 744 14 22), costing from Sfr70 per person (closed in June). Gstaad itself is bristling with hotels sporting three or more stars. On Hauptstrasse by the station is the *Sporthotel Victoria* (☎ 744 14 31). Rooms with rustic wooden furniture and private shower/toilet start at Sfr145/260 per person (Sfr85/140 in low season). The restaurant has pizzas from Sfr12, weekly specials from Sfr13 and other meat and fish dishes above Sfr15 (open daily).

Fairly similar is the *Sporthotel Rütti* (☎ 744 29 21), near the Wispile cable car, with singles/doubles starting at Sfr105/185. Pizzas and Swiss dishes are from Sfr12.50 in the restaurant. There's also a nightclub with live music or (in low season) a disco.

Right outside the station stands *Bernerhof* (☎ 748 88 44). Good rooms start at Sfr126/212, and the hotel swimming pool and sauna are free for guests. The busy restaurant is closed Tuesday and offers a lunch special for around Sfr17, fondue for Sfr23 and has a section for Chinese food. The cheapest eating is at the *Coop* supermarket and restaurant, where menus are about Sfr10. It is on Hauptstrasse to the left of the station, and the restaurant section is open until 6.30 pm Sunday to Friday, 4 pm on Saturday.

The top of the pile, literally and figuratively, is the *Gstaad Palace* (☎ 748 50 00; fax 748 50 01), which despite its hefty price tag of at least Sfr360/600 still gives good value for money. You can't miss its turrets up on the hill. Of comparable quality for dining is *Chesery* (☎ 744 24 51), near the tourist office on Lauenenstrasse. Expect to pay over Sfr50 for a main course or Sfr120 for a multi-course menu. It's small and cosy, so reserve ahead in season (closed Monday and Tuesday). There's a piano bar downstairs.

Getting There & Away

Gstaad is on the Panoramic Express rail link between Montreux (Sfr19.40, takes 1½ hours) and Spiez (Sfr23, takes one hour 20 minutes; change at Zweisimmen). There is also a regular postbus to Les Diablerets (Sfr10.60, 50 minutes). It runs during the summer and winter seasons; in off-season it goes only as far as Reusch. The principal road is highway 11 connecting Aigle and Spiez, which passes close to Gstaad at Saanen.

BERNESE OBERLAND

Central Switzerland

This region sums up what many visitors believe to be the 'true' Switzerland. Not only is it rich in typical Swiss features – mountains, lakes, tinkling cowbells, and Alpine villages – but it is also where Switzerland began as a nation 700 years ago, with the signing of a pact in 1291 by the communities of Uri, Schwyz and Nidwalden. The focus for tourism in the region is Lucerne (which annually receives five million visitors), and the convoluted contours of its namesake lake that links the founding cantons.

Orientation & Information

The tourist region that is central Switzerland has at its heart Lake Lucerne (Vierwaldstättersee in German). The German name translated literally means 'lake of the four forest cantons'. The four cantons in descending order of size are Lucerne, Uri, Schwyz and Unterwalden. Unterwalden is subdivided into two half-cantons, Nidwalden and Obwalden. Also included in this region is Zug: at just 239 sq km it's the smallest rural canton in Switzerland.

In the north and west, central Switzerland is fairly flat, but a southern tongue of territory reaches deep into the Alps, as far as the St Gotthard Pass. Lake Lucerne is ringed by other large lakes, notably Lake Zug (Zugersee) to the north. There are also several mountains thrusting up from its irregular shoreline, providing good hiking and excellent views.

The regional tourist office is: Verkehrsverband Zentralschweiz (☎ 041-410 18 91; fax 410 72 60), Alpenstrasse 1, CH-6002 Lucerne. It's on the 5th floor and opening times are Monday to Friday from 8 am to noon and 2 to 5 pm. For hotel reservations throughout Central Switzerland, telephone ☎ 637 04 04; no commission is charged.

The half-canton of Obwalden (including Engelberg) has a religious holiday on 25 September.

HIGHLIGHTS

- The historic heartland of Switzerland
- Lucerne's medieval centre and covered bridges
- Switzerland's best technology museum – the Transport Museum in Lucerne
- Boat trips on Lake Lucerne
- Splendid vistas from mountain viewpoints – Pilatus, Rigi, Stanserhorn and Titlis
- Einsiedeln, Switzerland's prime pilgrimage site

Lucerne   Nidwalden   Obwalden

Schwyz   Uri   Zug

Getting There & Away

The nearest airport is at Zürich. Road and rail connections are excellent in all directions. An interesting way to leave the region is by the William Tell Express, which runs from mid-May to late October. Departing from

130

Lucerne, it includes 1st-class passage on a paddlesteamer to Flüelen, with multilingual commentary and a gourmet meal along the way, then a train ride through the St Gotthard Tunnel to either Lugano or Locarno. The fare is Sfr127, or Sfr86 with the Swiss Half-Fare Pass. Reservations are advised; contact the Lake Lucerne Navigation Company SGV, Werftestrasse 5, PO Box 4265, CH-6002, Lucerne (☎ 041-367 67 67; fax 367 68 68).

Getting Around

The Central Switzerland Regional Pass is a good buy if you want to spend a lot of time exploring Lake Lucerne (unless you have a Eurailpass or a Swiss Pass, both of which get free passage on paddlesteamers). It is valid for seven or 15 days, and gives half-price fares on public transport for the whole period, and unlimited free travel for two or five days on selected routes, including Lake Lucerne steamers, the different routes up Mts Pilatus and Rigi, and most of the way up Mt Titlis. The seven-day pass costs Sfr124, and the 15-day pass costs Sfr170 (Sfr136 with Swiss travel passes). Prices are slightly higher if you want 1st-class boat travel, and it is available from 1 April to 31 October. Get

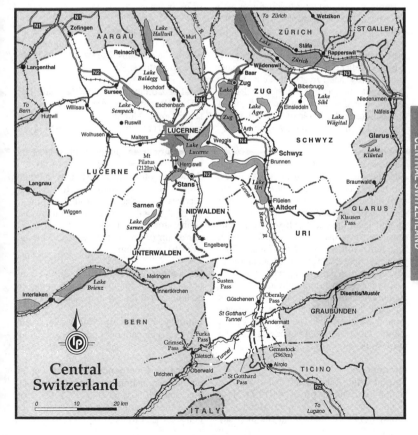

Central Switzerland

free travel for children with a Family Card (see the Getting Around chapter).

Lucerne

• *pop 62,500* • *435m* • ☎ *(041)*

Lucerne (Luzern in German), once a small fishing village, increased in size and importance when the St Gotthard Pass became a trade route around 1220. As late as the 19th century, merchandise had to be sent to Lucerne before being transported by barge to Flüelen, and thence over the pass. In 1332, Lucerne was the first town to join forces with the original three forest cantons, and was one of the few Swiss cities to remain Catholic during the Reformation. Ideally situated in the historic and scenic heart of Switzerland, it is an excellent base for a variety of excursions, yet also has a great deal of charm in its own right, particularly the medieval town centre. Indeed, it is one of the main tourist destinations in the whole of Switzerland, as indicated by the myriad of souvenir shops.

Orientation

Lucerne is on the western edge of Lake Lucerne, on both sides of the Reuss River. The train station is on the south bank within walking distance of the medieval town centre. Extensive station facilities below the ground level include a self-service restaurant, train information (daily to 7.45 pm), bike rental (office hours from 7 am to 7.45 pm daily; bike returns till 9 pm) and money-exchange (open daily to 6 pm or later).

City buses leave from in front of the train station at Bahnhofplatz. Boats for excursions on Lake Lucerne depart from the quays around Bahnhofplatz. The old part of town and the city towers and ramparts are on the north bank.

Information

Tourist Office Take the left exit of the train station for the tourist office (☎ 410 71 71) at Frankenstrasse 1. It is open Monday to Friday from 8.30 am to 6 pm and Saturday

from 9 am to 5 pm. Between 1 November and 31 March it shuts from noon to 2 pm on weekdays and at 1 pm on Saturday. Pick up a copy of the useful *Official Guide*. The office has a room-booking service, charging for Sfr5 per reservation. Staff also sell tickets for mountain excursions: the specially reduced winter return price of Sfr73.40 to Mt Titlis by rail and cable car is cheaper than travelling independently (further reductions with travel passes). Guided tours by coach to Mt Titlis and Mt Pilatus are Sfr85 each and two-hour guided tours of the old town cost Sfr15 (drink included). Many other excursions are available, all detailed in the tourist office brochure.

Foreign Consulates The Austrian Consulate (☎ 210 62 26) is at Hirschengraben 13 and the Italian Consulate (☎ 310 40 57) is at Obergrundstrasse 92.

Post & Communications The main post office (Hauptpost, Luzern 1, 6000) is by the station, open Monday to Friday from 7.30 am to 6.30 pm and Saturday from 8 to 11 am.

Travel Agencies On the north side of the river is American Express (☎ 410 00 77), Schweizerhofquai 4, open Monday to Friday from 8.30 am to 6 pm (5 pm for financial services), and Saturday from 8.30 am to noon. SSR (☎ 410 86 56), in the old town at Grabenstrasse 8, is open weekdays from 10 am to 6 pm (9 pm on Thursday) and Saturday from 10 am to 4 pm.

Bookshops Robert Räber, Schweizerhofquai 2, sells English-language books, as do branches of Raeber in the old town.

Laundry Jet Wasch, Bruchstrasse 28, is self-service, if comparatively pricey (closed Sunday).

Medical & Emergency Services For an out-of-hours pharmacy or doctor, dial ☎ 111. The cantonal hospital (☎ 205 11 11) is on Spitalstrasse, north of the old town. Call the police on ☎ 117.

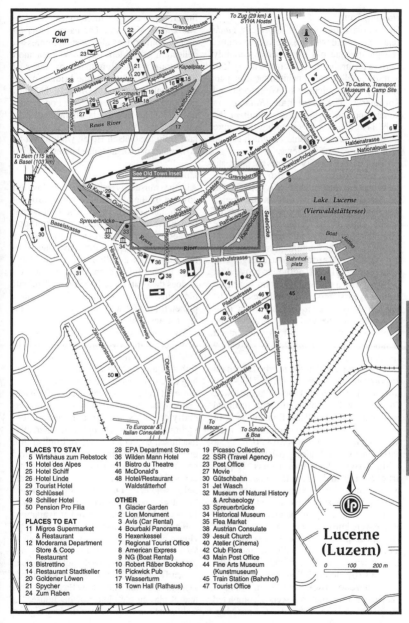

PLACES TO STAY
5 Wirtshaus zum Rebstock
15 Hotel des Alpes
25 Hotel Schiff
26 Hotel Linde
29 Tourist Hotel
37 Schlüssel
49 Schiller Hotel
50 Pension Pro Filia

PLACES TO EAT
11 Migros Supermarket
& Restaurant
12 Moderama Department
Store & Coop
Restaurant
13 Bistrettino
14 Restaurant Stadtkeller
20 Goldener Löwen
21 Spycher
24 Zum Raben

28 EPA Department Store
36 Wilden Mann Hotel
41 Bistro du Theatre
46 McDonald's
48 Hotel/Restaurant
Waldstätterhof

OTHER
1 Glacier Garden
2 Lion Monument
3 Avis (Car Rental)
4 Bourbaki Panorama
6 Hexenkessel
7 Regional Tourist Office
8 American Express
9 NG (Boat Rental)
10 Robert Räber Bookshop
16 Pickwick Pub
17 Wasserturm
18 Town Hall (Rathaus)

19 Picasso Collection
22 SSR (Travel Agency)
23 Post Office
27 Movie
30 Gütschbahn
31 Jet Wasch
32 Museum of Natural History
& Archaeology
33 Spreuerbrücke
34 Historical Museum
35 Flea Market
38 Austrian Consulate
39 Jesuit Church
42 Club Flora
43 Main Post Office
44 Fine Arts Museum
(Kunstmuseum)
45 Train Station (Bahnhof)
47 Tourist Office

**Lucerne
(Luzern)**

0   100   200 m

Walking Tour

The tourist office sells *A short city guide* detailing several walking tours of the centre. The picturesque old town centre certainly merits a leisurely stroll. There are many 15th century buildings with painted façades, particularly in the vicinity of Weinmarkt and Kornmarkt. The **town hall** *(Rathaus)* is Renaissance in style and was built in the early 17th century. Overlooking the centre are the **city towers**, some of which can be climbed for extensive views.

North-east of the city walls is the poignant **Lion Monument**, Denkmalstrasse, carved out of natural rock in 1820. It is dedicated to the Swiss soldiers who died in the French Revolution in 1792. They were slaughtered on the steps of the Tuileries Palace while defending Louis XVI and the French royal family. Next to the monument is the fascinating **Glacier Garden** (Gletschergarten), where giant glacial potholes prove that Lucerne was a subtropical palm beach 20 million years ago. The potholes can be perused daily (except Monday from mid-November to the end of February), and admission costs Sfr7, or Sfr5 for students. It includes a mirror maze that is incredibly disorientating.

Also worth a look is the nearby **Bourbaki Panorama**, Löwenstrasse 18, an 1100-sq m circular painting of the Franco-Prussian war. The scene is brought to life with recorded commentary (in English). Entry is Sfr3, or half price for students. A combination ticket with the Glacier Garden is Sfr8.50.

Be sure to walk along the two covered bridges over the River Reuss. **Kapell-brücke**, built in 1333, is the most famous, and together with its octagonal water tower appears in just about every photograph of Lucerne. The sides and gabled roof of the bridge were burnt away when a tethered boat caught fire in 1993. Under the replacement roof are scenes from national and local history, which are photo reproductions of the originals (by Heinrich Wägmann in 1614).

The **Spreuerbrücke** dates from 1408 and likewise features pictorial scenes, completed from 1625 to 1635. The artist, Caspar Meg-

linger, chose a rather more macabre theme, *The Dance of Death*. The eaves under the roof of both bridges also host an impressive collection of spiders that look even more enormous when illuminated by the strip lights at night. Between the bridges on the south bank is the **Jesuit Church**, the oldest Baroque church in Switzerland, consecrated in 1677. The interior is characteristically ornate. There's a fine **view** of the town and lake from the Gütsch Hotel; walk uphill for 20 minutes or take the Gütschbahn (Sfr2.50).

Museums

All the museums mentioned below are covered by the Museum Pass, valid for one month and costing Sfr25. The biggest and best museum in Lucerne is the **Transport Museum** (Verkehrshaus), Lidostrasse 5, receiving more visitors than any other Swiss museum – half a million a year. Bus No 2 from Bahnhofplatz drops you right outside, as does the boat. It has large halls filled with old trains, cars, aeroplanes and boats, plus a planetarium and a gallery devoted to the artist, Hans Erni.

There are several hourly shows, the best of which is the Swissorama, a 20-minute, 360° film which whizzes you around the sights of Switzerland as if you were travelling by air, sea, road and foot. You get a real sense of motion as your 'aircraft' banks between the mountains. Also great fun, especially for kids, is the communications section, with lots of toys and interactive machines. Explanations are in English. It is open daily from 9 am to 6 pm (10 am to 5 pm from 1 November to 31 March). Entry costs Sfr16, or Sfr11 for students and railpass-holders. On site is IMAX, a new high-tech cinema, showing transport-related films (Sfr12; combination ticket available).

The **Picasso Collection** in the Ann Rhyn House on Furrengasse demands an hour of your time. There are some paintings and graphics by the man himself, but the best part is nearly 200 photographs taken by David Douglas Duncan. They show Picasso at work and at play in the clutter of his house, 'La Californie', in Cannes, over the last 17 years of his life. Admission costs Sfr6 (Sfr3 for students and senior citizens), and it is open daily: from 10 am to 6 pm in the summer and 11 am to 1 pm and 2 to 4 pm from November to March.

The **Historical Museum**, with its exhibits and short film (in English), successfully places the city and region in their historical context. The **Fine Arts Museum** (Kunstmuseum) by the train station mainly displays local art, from the Middle Ages to the present. Natural history and archaeology are combined in the **Museum of Natural History** (Naturmuseum). Interesting for music lovers is the **Richard Wagner Museum**, Wagnerweg 27, in Tribschen, on the southern shore of the lake. All four museums are closed on Monday, except that the Fine Arts Museum is open daily in summer.

Markets

Fruit and vegetable stalls spring forth along the river quays on Tuesday and Saturday mornings. There's a flea market at Unter Burgerstrasse/Reusssteg every Saturday from May to October.

Activities

Water pursuits are important in the summer. In summer, international rowing regattas take place on the Rotsee. SNG (☎ 368 08 09), at the north side of Seebrücke, rents rowing boats (one hour costs Sfr28 for three people and Sfr34 for four people), motorboats (up to five people, Sfr40 for one hour), and pedalboats (for three people, Sfr19 for one hour). You can try kayaking on the lake through Eurotrek (☎ 01-462 02 03), a travel company based in Zürich, at Malzstrasse 17-21. It also organises river-rafting on the Reuss River. There is swimming in the confines of the Lidostrandbad (☎ 370 38 06), near the camp site, for which entry costs Sfr6. Save money by swimming for free on the other bank of the lake by Seepark, off Alpenquai.

If you like the idea of para-gliding off Pilatus, telephone ☎ 820 54 31. Ballooning

GLENN VAN DER KNIJFF

Street theatre, Lucerne

excursions are organised by the Ballonclub Pilatus (☎ 918 08 88).

Special Events

Six days of **Fasnacht** celebrations begin on the Thursday before Ash Wednesday. There's music and folklore in the **city festival** (Altstadtfest) on the 4th Saturday in June. Lucerne hosts the annual **International Festival of Music** from mid-August to mid-September, one of the most important classical music events in Switzerland. Details are available from the Internationale Musikfestwochen (☎ 210 35 62), Hirschmattstrasse 13, CH-6002 Luzern. Prices for concerts are anything between Sfr10 and Sfr180. Individual ticket applications are processed from late March; the booking office is on ☎ 210 30 80.

Places to Stay

Get your accommodation to stamp your *Official Guide*; this entitles you to discounts on entry fees to most attractions.

CENTRAL SWITZERLAND

Places to Stay – bottom end
Camping *Camp Lido* (☎ 370 21 46), Lidostrasse 8, is on the north shore of the lake and east of the town. It is open from March to October and charges Sfr7.20 per person, from Sfr3 per tent and Sfr5 per car. It also has six-bed dorms for Sfr13 per person (no breakfast, sleeping bag required). To get there take bus No 2 from Bahnhofplatz.

Backpackers Lucerne (☎ 360 04 20), Alpenquai 42, is a new private hostel charging from Sfr21.50 per person, without breakfast and excluding sheets. Reception is closed from 10am to 4pm.

Hostel The modern SYHA *hostel* (☎ 420 88 00) is at Sedelstrasse 12, north of the centre. Bus No 18 from the train station gets you closest (stop: Goplismoos) but after 7.40 pm you'll have to take bus No 1 (stop: Schlossberg). The hostel is actually less than a 15-minute walk from the city walls, but you'll need a detailed map to pick out the footpaths and avoid the long walk by road. Dorm beds with lockers are Sfr28.50; doubles are Sfr83 with shower/WC or Sfr71 without, either way reducing Sfr5 after the first night. Dinners are Sfr11. Reception is shut from 10 am to 4 pm (2 pm in summer) when the doors are also locked. Curfew is at 12.30 am.

Pensions & Hotels The small *Hotel Linde* (☎ 410 31 93), Metzgerrainle 3, off Weinmarkt, has fairly spartan singles/doubles without breakfast for Sfr44/88 with use of shared hall showers. The walls are paper-thin and the streets outside can be noisy, but it has an excellent central location and it's the best place for those with low budgets. Rooms are available from 1 April to 31 October, and check-in is not possible on Sunday as the restaurant is closed.

Tourist Hotel (☎ 410 24 74), St Karli Quai 12, has large, pricey dorms for Sfr33, and doubles for Sfr134 with private shower/WC, Sfr108 without, or Sfr98 in bunk beds. If there's space, single occupancy is possible for Sfr81, Sfr69 and Sfr64 respectively.

Families and students get a 10% discount on prices. There are also triples and quads as well as laundry facilities. From 1 November to 31 March, prices reduce by about 20% and breakfast is not included, but there is free tea and coffee during this time to compensate.

Schlüssel (☎ 210 10 61), Franziskanerplatz 12, is central and small-scale. It has singles/doubles from Sfr74/113 with shower or Sfr51/85 without. Reception shuts early, so phone ahead for an evening check-in. *Pension Pro Filia* (☎ 240 42 80), Zäringerstrasse 24, is slightly more expensive, though it does have good-value family rooms.

Places to Stay – middle
Out of the centre towards the transport museum is *Pension Villa Maria* (☎ 370 21 19), at Haldenstrasse 36, in a residential part of town. Doubles are from Sfr118 with private shower or Sfr97 using hall facilities. There are a few triples but no singles. Telephone ahead to make a reservation.

Overlooking the river is the comfortable *Hotel des Alpes* (☎ 410 58 25; see the Central Lucerne map), Rathausquai 5. It has decent-sized rooms, all with shower, toilet, and a TV, and includes a buffet breakfast. Singles/doubles start at Sfr110/175, reducing about 20% in winter.

Hotel Schiff (☎ 418 52 52), Unter der Egg 8, is similar in price, situation and standard, except in addition it has rooms from Sfr70/115 with use of shared hall showers.

Places to Stay – top end
Wirtshaus zum Rebstock (☎ 410 35 81; fax 410 39 17), St Leodegar-Strasse 3, has rooms from Sfr140/240 (Sfr130/210 in winter) decorated with flair and more than a touch of modern art. All have shower/bath, toilet, TV, radio and telephone.

Schiller Hotel (☎ 210 51 55; fax 210 34 04), Pilatusstrasse 15, starts at Sfr190/210 (Sfr140/170 in winter) and has similar facilities. The cheaper rooms have modern fittings and stuccowork around the ceilings. Pay a bit more and you'll get a larger room with elaborate stylised decor, ranging from Thai to nautical.

Places to Eat

Lucerne is bursting with restaurants of all types. Eating can get pricey but there are still plenty of places with a Tagesmenu in the range of Sfr13 to Sfr15. Local speciality is the Kügelipastetli, a vol-au-vent stuffed with meat and mushrooms and served with a rich sauce.

For the cheapest chomping, look to the self-service places, which have late opening till 9 pm on Thursday. *Migros* supermarket and restaurant is at Hertensteinstrasse 44. Next door is the Moderama department store with a *Coop* restaurant on the first floor. *EPA* department store, Mühlenplatz, has an excellent self-service restaurant with unbeatable prices for Switzerland: meals from Sfr8, soup from Sfr1.50, salad buffet at Sfr1.80 per 100 grams, and tea or coffee for Sfr1.80.

Wirtshaus zum Rebstock (see Places to Stay), has several eating areas, including a sociable café and a potato-speciality place upstairs. Meals cost Sfr13 to Sfr35, and there are always vegetarian dishes, not least in the linked *Hofgarten* vegetarian restaurant beyond the garden. A mainly young hang-out is *Bistro du Theatre*, Theaterstrasse 5. It is a French-style bar and restaurant which manages to be both elegant and informal. Midday menus with soup are Sfr14 and Sfr16; evening dining is mostly above Sfr17, though the chicken wings (Knusperli) for Sfr12 are popular.

Goldener Löwen, Eisengasse 1, has a typical local ambience, despite the tourist-tat signs outside. Swiss specialities start at around Sfr15 in this small restaurant; try the chocolate fondue (you dip fruit in the mix) at Sfr29 for two.

Around the corner is *Spycher* (☎ 410 43 53), a rustic restaurant with Swiss and cheese specialities, including Raclette and fondue (Sfr19.50).

The widest choice for vegetarian food is *Hotel-Restaurant Waldstätterhof* (☎ 210 54 93), Zentralstrasse 4, next to the tourist office. It has a daily menu with soup for Sfr16.60 and serves meat dishes too. *Bistrettino*, Theilinggasse 4, has adequate if unspectacular pizza and pasta from around Sfr12. Plates from the salad bar cost between Sfr4.30 and Sfr9.80.

The restaurant in the *Hotel Schiff* (see Places to Stay) has lunch specials with soup from Sfr15, and it's also a good place to shed some francs and gain some pounds on quality evening dining (starting from Sfr17). Cuisine from different nationalities is featured in winter festivals. A giant version of the local speciality, here called Aechti Lozärner Chögelipastete, costs Sfr25.50. The nearby *Zum Raben* (☎ 370 51 35), Kornmarkt 5, is also good, and has meals for Sfr17 to Sfr40.

The *Wilden Mann Hotel* (☎ 210 16 66), Bahnhofstrasse 30, serves quality dishes from Sfr30 in the French-style Wilden Mann Stube. Its Burgerstube has more of a Swiss atmosphere and some cheaper choices. Both are open daily.

Entertainment

Restaurant Stadtkeller (☎ 410 47 33), Sternenplatz 3, has two folklore shows a day to allow you to yodel with your mouth full. Dishes cost from Sfr20 at lunch and Sfr30 in the evening, plus it's Sfr10 for the show (there's a bar – you don't have to eat). Reservations are usually necessary for meals. The show is professionally done, and most guests eagerly participate in the party mood. Although lunch is cheaper, there tends to be less atmosphere. From November to mid-March, the show is replaced by live music (evening only).

Sedel (☎ 420 63 10), near the hostel, behind Rotsee at Emmenbrücke, is a former women's prison which holds rock concerts and/or discos at the weekend. Local bands practice in the cells during the week, so it can be fun to just walk around the corridors, absorbing the clashing sounds and the vivid colours of the graffiti-covered walls. Other good, slightly alternative venues are *Schüür* (☎ 360 44 12), Tribschenstrasse 1, for live

CENTRAL SWITZERLAND

music and *Boa* (☎ 360 45 88), Geissenstein-ring 41, for music, theatre and dance.

There are several decent bars in the centre and most close around midnight or just after. The Schiller Hotel (see Places to Stay) shelters the small *Casablanca* bar, the *Grand Café* which has huge Greek-style statues, and *Cucaracha*, a Mexican bar and restaurant.

On the north side of the river is the *Pickwick Pub* near the Kapellbrücke, a pseudo-English bar where the punters overflow onto the quayside. On Weinmarkt is *Movie*, a bar with film star pics and movie promos on the walls. If you go through the section around the side where they serve food, the premises open out into a terrace overlooking the river.

Hexenkessel, Haldenstrasse 21, is a large and busy young person's bar with loud music, games and dancing. The décor is halfway between a beach party and a junk shop (open 5 pm to 2.30 am). There's no entry charge as such – you pay for your first drink (from Sfr6) as you go in. Drinks are cheaper up to 10 pm.

The *Club Flora*, on Seidenhofstrasse, is a disco with occasional 'theme' evenings. Women usually get in free; men pay Sfr10 but from Sunday to Thursday can get this back in a drinks-credit, with a stamped *Official Guide* (this'll buy one drink). Dress standards are fairly casual. The *Casino* on Haldenstrasse caters for gamblers, dancers, and has a summer folklore show.

There are many cinemas in town. *Atelier* (☎ 210 12 30) on Theaterstrasse has some interesting non-mainstream offerings (Sfr14, students Sfr10).

Things to Buy

A few shops are shut on Monday morning but most stay open until 9 pm on Thursday. Gift stalls at the boat quays and some other souvenir shops even open up on Sunday in summer (from 11 am). You can buy anything you could possibly want (and lots of things you couldn't), such as Swiss knives, cuckoo clocks, beer tankards and pug-faced dolls. More practical goods can be bought in the many department stores.

Getting There & Away

Hourly trains connect Lucerne to Interlaken (Sfr23, via the scenic Brünig Pass), Bern (Sfr31), Zürich (Sfr19.40), Lugano (Sfr55) and Geneva (Sfr65, via Olten or Langnau). The N2 (E9) motorway connecting Basel and Lugano passes by Lucerne, and the N14 provides the road link to Zürich.

Car Rental Europcar (☎ 310 14 33) has a rental office at Garage Epper, Horwerstrasse 81. Hertz (☎ 420 02 77) is at Maihofstrasse 101 and Avis (☎ 410 32 51) is at Zürichstrasse 35. Local firm Miecar (☎ 210 00 44), at Neuweg 4, has weekend (Friday 8 am to Monday 6 pm) prices starting at just Sfr139, including 1000 km.

Boat For information on boat transport see the following Lake Lucerne section. You can either take round trips with smaller operators, or use the scheduled services from Bahnhofplatz.

Getting Around

Walking is the best way to explore the centre where many of the streets are pedestrian-only anyway. Bus tickets cost Sfr1.50 for one zone, Sfr2 for two and Sfr2.50 for three. Ticket dispensers state the number of zones to each destination. The expensive 24-hour pass for Sfr10 covers all zones. The underground parking garage at the train station costs Sfr3 for one hour, Sfr19 for 12 hours and Sfr25 for 24 hours.

Lake Lucerne

You could spend several days exploring the historic locations and the scenic mountains around this lake (Vierwaldstättersee in German). The views are constantly changing around its twisting coastline and there are many typical villages and attractive resorts to enjoy along the way.

Always ask if there is a guest card if you stay anywhere around the lake, as not all hotels and pensions provide these spontane-

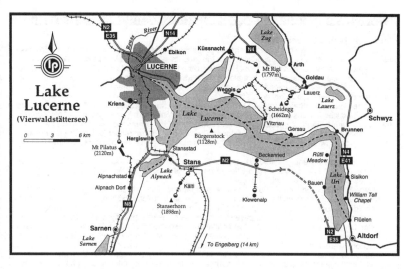

ously. It is definitely worth having. The Gästekarte Schwyzerland in Brunnen, for example, entitles the bearer to various discounts on sporting facilities in Brunnen, 20 to 25% off certain cable cars, and reductions on some admission prices in Lucerne and elsewhere.

If contemplating ascending Mt Pilatus or Rigi, inquire about weather conditions from the Lucerne tourist office. In winter, also ask about special low-season prices.

The telephone code of all places round the lake is ☎ 041.

Getting Around

Old-fashioned paddlesteamers operate at certain times of the day, more frequently in summer, although any of the boats provide a fun day out. Boats sail daily year round, though for the Lake Uri section they operate in winter only on Sunday. Longer trips are relatively much cheaper than short ones, and you can alight from the boat as often as you want. Swiss Pass and Eurailpass are valid on all scheduled boat trips and Inter-Rail gets you half price. All passes are valid or get discounts only on selected mountain railways and cable cars.

Examples of return boat fares from Lucerne are: Alpnachstad Sfr26, Weggis Sfr20, Vitznau Sfr26, Brunnen Sfr35, and Flüelen Sfr39. Return fares are about 60% more than singles, and 1st-class prices (less crowded, but otherwise not particularly more comfortable) is about 50% more than 2nd-class prices. Some single fares from Flüelen are: Brunnen Sfr11.20, Weggis Sfr23 and Lucerne Sfr26. There are also special dinner/dancing cruises. Lake Lucerne attracts more boat passengers than any other lake – over two million per year. (Next in order come the lakes of Geneva, Zürich and Thun.)

Driving around the lake is perfectly viable. Roads run close to the shoreline all the way around, with the exception of the stretch from Flüelen to Stansstad. Here there is a motorway (N2) that ploughs a fairly straight line, sometimes underground, usually away from the water.

Mt Pilatus

The rugged contours of Mt Pilatus (2120m) overlook Lucerne from the south. According to tradition it was named after Pontius Pilate, who apparently haunted its heights; any

Mountain Myths & Legends

On a dark evening, when the brooding shapes of giant peaks blot out half the night's stars, it's easy to believe the ancient legends associated with the mountains. One tall tale tells of a cooper who fell down a mountain crevice and into a cave. He survived the fall as he landed on the backs of two peaceful dragons. Although the dragons left him alone, there was no escape and he lived through the winter by licking the salty water seeping from the cave walls. In the spring the dragons ventured out, and one gave the cooper a ride to safety on his tail.

A rather less amiable dragon lived in a cave above Oedwil. It preyed on the local villagers and livestock and was finally slain by the knight Struthan von Winkelried. The knight tossed his sword in the air in triumph, but three specks of the wicked beast's blood fell from the sword onto his head, and he died instantly. In 1420 a farmer saw a dragon fly between Mt Pilatus and Mt Rigi, and simultaneously stumbled across what has become known as the 'dragon stone' (on display in Lucerne's Natural History Museum).

The souls of evil tyrants are said to haunt the Enziloch on the Napf massif. Pontius Pilate rises out of the lake on Mt Pilatus every Good Friday (the day he condemned Jesus Christ). Anybody who witnesses this event will die within the year.

Tiny 'wild folk' called Chlyni Lüüt once inhabited Mt Rigi. Their children always had their spleen removed at birth, giving them the ability to leap around mountain slopes with the agility of the chamois. They held other powers, but disappeared from view in the face of constant mockery by humans.

A foolhardy shepherd boy once baptised a favoured lamb, which instantly changed into a fearsome monster. It was given the name 'Griess' and preyed on the populace. A special bull was reared to take on the monster. It was led by a white-clad maiden to the alpine meadow where the Griess lived. Her hair ribbons were tied to the bull's nose ring. Although the monster was defeated, the bull also died. The maiden was never seen or heard of again, but the bull is remembered in the Uri coat of arms.

Suitably desperate bachelors may be tempted to seek the enchanted virgin who inhabits the Schibenloch cave on the Schrattenfluh. After rejecting an honest but poor suitor the virgin had been buried alive with her money. Every year, on the Thursday before Easter, she appears at the cave entrance to count her money. Only at this time can a young man enter the cave to seek her hand. To be successful, he must meet three challenges. First he must pass under a huge millstone held only by a thread. It the man already has a girlfriend, the thread will break. Next he must overcome a monstrous giant cat which dwells in the deeper recesses of the cave. Finally, upon reaching the virgin, he must answer three riddles to free her. If he fails to solve all the riddles he will be lost in the cave forever. The virgin still awaits – no one has yet completed these three challenges. ∎

who apparently haunted its heights; any climber with the temerity to approach the summit would cause his spirit to unleash storms onto the populace below. Foolhardy tourists ignore this ancient wisdom and regularly ascend for panoramic views of the lake and the Alpine range. The inspiring vistas make it worth risking Pilate's wrath. However, there is a more prosaic and probably more accurate derivation of the name – *pileatus* in Latin means covered in clouds.

A popular route from Lucerne is to take the lakesteamer to Alpnachstad, the cog railway up Mt Pilatus, the cable car down to Kriens and bus No 1 back to Lucerne. The total cost for this jaunt is Sfr76.20. Kriens-Pilatus return or Alpnachstad-Pilatus return is Sfr58. The Swiss Pass gets 25% off, Eurail gets 35% off and there's no reduction with Inter-Rail. Children (six to 16) can go half-price.

This cog railway is the steepest of its kind in the world, reaching a gradient of 48%; it's closed from late November to mid-May. The cable car is closed for maintenance from mid-October to mid-November.

The cog railway is an all-or-nothing trip but the cable car is in several stages, allowing you to ride some of the way and walk the rest. The last stage to the summit is the steepest. Walking up from Alpnachstad takes around four hours and from Kriens about five hours. From the summit, it's three hours down to Alpnachstad, 3½ hours to Kriens or three hours down to Hergiswil boat station. The cable station of Fräkmüntegg is about halfway up in walking terms, so you could ride Alpnachstad-Mt Pilatus-Fräkmüntegg for Sfr43 and take the easy walk down from there.

At the top of Mt Pilatus are two hotels, *Pilatus Kulm* and *Hotel Bellevue*. They share the same reception (☎ 610 12 55) in the circular building. Singles/doubles cost from Sfr94/188 with private shower and breakfast or Sfr60/120 without either. Prices in the self-service restaurant are reasonable, with hot meals starting from Sfr14.

If you want to stay in Alpnachstad, look for the private B&B run by Frau Schnider (☎ 670 19 32) at Brünigstrasse 23. Singles/doubles are Sfr40/75. There is a better selection of restaurants a couple of km down the road in Alpnach Dorf than in Alpnachstad itself.

Mt Rigi

From the top there is a great view of tiers of mountain peaks to the south and east; on a clear day Mt Titlis and the Jungfrau region giants are visible. The view to the north and west is also good, with an aeroplane-eye view of Arth-Goldau below, and Lake Zug (Zugersee in German) curving around until it almost joins Küssnacht and an arm of Lake Lucerne. The green slopes of Mt Rigi itself, the swathes of conifers and the constantly tinkling cowbells all add to the scene. Seeing the sunrise from the summit is a popular activity with a long precedent.

The mountain can be ascended in a number of ways. Hiking is of course the cheapest, but it's at least a four-hour slog from Weggis. Walking can be made more manageable by taking the cable car from Küssnacht up to Seeboldenalp (Sfr12.50 up, Sfr9 down, Sfr17 return). There are two paths from there, the shortest takes a little over two hours, and the last section is quite steep. The lazy, rushed or infirm can take the rack railway to within 200m of the summit in 40 minutes. Two rival tracks were built in the 1870s: one from Arth-Goldau and the other from Vitznau. Either route costs Sfr37

Mt Rigi & 19th Century Tourism

Everything works so well in Switzerland. The people are affluent, well-dressed, courteous, unflappable...and above all, in command. It's not hard as a tourist to get the feeling that you're the poor relation from an underdeveloped country visiting a successful cousin. The balance of power is definitely with the Swiss.

But it wasn't always like that. The picture that emerges from 19th century texts is that tourists were like visiting royalty, with the Swiss scurrying around attending their needs and desperately hoping to make a few coins to eke out a meagre lifestyle. Many locals – men and boys bearing mules and eager grins – would offer their services as guides for tourists walking in the hills. Always there would be people determinedly trying to sell snacks and trinkets. Mark Twain in his travel reminiscences reported being plagued by Alp horn players at Mt Rigi. He paid them generously to get rid of them, only to find their number had doubled at the next village, hoping for a similar pay-off. Such scenes ring bells with any traveller to the Third World.

Jemima Morrell, writing in 1863 *(Miss Jemima's Swiss Journal)*, describes being surrounded by dozens of would-be guides at Weggis: 'We were literally infested by, dogged and danced around by these importunates. Our efforts to evade them were numerous and varied.' They ignored the throng and proceeded to walk up Mt Rigi. Unaccompanied – but not for long: 'Again, we are reminded that tourists are the staple commodity in the twenty-two cantons of Switzerland as another band of parasites would feed upon us, or rather feed us, as they dangled branches of cherries in our faces with the cry "Vingt centimes, vingt centimes!" These cherry vendors regarded us as their legitimate prey – they industriously reap a good harvest in their Rigi farms as they try every art and device to make us purchasers.'

The party of British tourists eventually left behind even the most persistent vendors, and continued climbing towards the summit. They attained a promontory and were standing around admiring the view towards Uri, when: ' "Vingt centimes! Vingt centimes!" again rings in our ears, putting to flight our dreams of history, or valour, of poetry and beauty.'

The cherry vendors may have been unlucky with Miss Morrell's party, but they had plenty of other tourists to pester instead. Morrell reported that there were as many as 150 early risers congregated at the summit of Mt Rigi the next morning, all there to enjoy the view at sunrise. ■

up or Sfr52 return. The Arth-Goldau service closes for two weeks in late May but Vitznau operates year round.

The Vitznau track gives the further option of diverting at Rigi Kaltbad and taking instead the cable car to/from Weggis. The whole thing can be done from Lucerne for Sfr78 (reductions with railpasses).

Being at the top for the sunrise is made easier by the presence of the *Rigi Kulm Hotel* (☎ 855 03 03), just five minutes' walk from the summit. South-facing singles/doubles with private shower and toilet cost Sfr90/160, and with a bath, Sfr100/180. North-facing rooms cost Sfr60/100 with use of hall shower, and rooms in the annex cost Sfr35/70. There are even dorms for Sfr25 per person. The restaurant is OK considering it has a captive market; light meals start at Sfr12 but most dishes are around Sfr20. A half litre bottle of beer is Sfr4.50. An outside kiosk is open during the day.

Weggis

• *pop 2400*   • *440m*   • ☎ *(041)*

This south-facing, lakeside resort enjoys plenty of sunshine, meaning that the quay-side parades a palette of colours from its flowerbeds, magnolias, palm trees and fig trees. Musicians play in the Kurplatz on summer mornings (except Monday), and there's a couple of churches worth peeking into, plus a monument to Mark Twain, who stayed here. It's also the base for the cable car up to Rigi Kaltbad (Sfr32 return). There is swimming in the lake and in an indoor pool at Lido-Hallenbad (Sfr6; open 1 April to 30 September) to the west of the centre, and bikes can be hired through the tourist office. Don't expect much nightlife – it's a quiet resort favoured mainly by older visitors.

The tourist office (☎ 390 11 55) is next to the boat station, open in winter Monday to Friday from 8 am to noon and 1 to 5 pm, and in summer Monday to Friday from 8 am to noon and 1.30 to 6.30 pm, and Saturday from 9 am to noon and 2 to 4 pm. Klemenz Reisen (☎ 390 21 21), a travel agent, sells good-value tours to regional attractions.

Places to Stay & Eat The best deal is at the *Hotel-Restaurant Viktoria* (☎ 390 11 28), overlooking the lake promenade. Reason-ably spacious rooms, some with balconies, are Sfr42 per person, with use of hall shower. The restaurant (closed Wednesday in winter) has daily menus including soup, salad and main course for Sfr17.50 to Sfr20. Fish dishes are around Sfr25. The place is closed from mid-December to mid-January.

Just 100m to the east along the promenade is *Hotel Gotthard am See* (☎ 390 21 14). The room aren't really that much better than the Viktoria's, except they do have private shower/toilet. Singles/doubles start at Sfr90/160. Guests can use the private pool of the *Beau Rivage* (☎ 390 14 22), opposite, which sports four stars and has rooms from Sfr125/220 (closed in winter). The Gotthard's restaurant has a shaded, open-air section overlooking the lake where pizzas start at Sfr12. The hotel and restaurant are closed mid-October to mid-December.

Stans

The capital of Nidwalden, Stans is notewor-thy as one of only four Swiss communities to still hold the show-of-hands vote, the *Landsgemeinde* (open-air parliament). It takes place on the last Sunday in April, and is worth watching if you're in the area. Stans is also the starting point for the excellent excursion up the **Stanserhorn** mountain (1898m). It is not as popular as the trip up to Mt Rigi, which faces it across the lake, but it provides at least as good a view. The big ranges to the south (including Mt Titlis and the Jungfrau Massif) are closer and seem to surround you more, yet you still have the panorama of the lakes and hills to the north, including a wide expanse of Lake Lucerne and Lake Zug, and also Lake Sarnen, squeezed between the mountains in the south-west. There are plenty of viewing boards at the top so you can identify what you're seeing. From the cable station it's just 10 minutes' hike to the summit, and you can return by a different route. As always, a restaurant awaits by the top cable station; this one has outside seating.

The journey up – by funicular to Kälti then a cable car – costs Sfr22 each way or Sfr40 return, and the base station is five minutes' walk (signposted) from the train station. It operates from mid-April to mid-November. The hike up from the town takes around 4½ hours to ascend the grassy slopes, or if you have a car you can save almost an hour by driving up to Kälti and parking there.

In the main town, the central Dorfplatz is worth a stroll. It has a fountain and attractive 18th century buildings, as well as essentials such as hotels (around Sfr50 per person), supermarkets, restaurants and a pharmacy. Its centrepiece is the early Baroque **Parish Church**, tastefully decorated inside in white and black, rather than the usual overdose of gold gilding. Adjoining the church is a Romanesque belltower with a 16th century spire.

Stans is on the Lucerne-Engelberg railway, or it can be reached by hourly bus from Buochs boat station.

Beckenried

Beckenried, on the southern shore, is a bus ride from Stans. A few minutes' walk from the boat station will bring you to a cable car which makes the 10-minute ascent to **Klewenalp** (Sfr17 single or Sfr27 return). The views across the lake are good, and there are a number of hiking trails heading into the hills and valleys beyond. A map up there outlines the options.

Gersau

Remarkably, this tiny place (population 1700) was an independent republic, the world's smallest, between 1390 and 1817 before joining the canton of Schwyz. There is a SYHA *hostel* (☎ 828 12 77) between Vitznau and Gersau at Rotschuo. It's open from early March to early December and costs Sfr21. The reception is closed from 10 am to 4.30 pm, and there's a kitchen.

Brunnen

• *pop 6300* • *443 m* • ☎ *(041)*
This resort is at the dog-leg where Lake Uri (Urnersee) and Lake Lucerne meet. It's worth visiting if only for the view, with the two stretches of the lake shimmering either side of the spit of land on the opposite shore: the green patch to the left of that promontory is the famous Rütli meadow where the 1291 pact was signed. It's one of the livelier resorts on the lake (which, to be honest, isn't saying very much), and it's a good base for exploring in either direction, or for visiting Schwyz. Brunnen offers sailing, water-skiing and windsurfing, and there are schools for each of these activities. There's also swimming in the lake (at the Lido) or in the adjoining heated indoor pool *(Hallenbad)*; a day ticket for the whole complex is Sfr5.50. Contact the Outdoor sports centre (☎ 820 54 31), Gersauerstrasse 25, for river rafting and kayaking. The sports centre is also the place for surfing, roller-skating and mountain biking.

Farmer from the Uri Canton.

The tourist office (☎ 825 00 40), Bahnhofstrasse 32, is open Monday to Friday from 8.30 am to noon and 1.30 to 6 pm and Saturday for a half or full day. Don't forget to ask about the guest card; discounts are listed in the *Gäste Information* booklet.

Places to Stay & Eat There are two campsites overlooking the lake in west Brunnen: *Camping Urmiberg* (☎ 820 33 27) and *Camping Hopfreben* (☎ 820 18 73). Both have similar facilities and are open for the summer season. Urmiberg is the cheaper of the two and costs Sfr6.20 per person, Sfr3 to Sfr5 per tent and Sfr2.50 per car.

In Brunnen you must pay at least Sfr60 per person for any hotel overlooking the water. *National* (☎ 820 18 78), at Bahnhofstrasse 47, is more affordable, starting at Sfr45/85 for singles doubles using hall facilities, or Sfr55/100 with private shower/toilet. It has an inexpensive restaurant with outside seating, is family-friendly, and has adequate parking. The restaurant is shut on weekends in winter. National is convenient for the train station which has money-exchange counters and bike rental available daily.

Nearer the lakefront is *Brunnerhof* (☎ 820 17 57), at Kapellplatz, with singles/doubles starting at Sfr70/100. Some slightly more expensive rooms have TV and/or balcony. Brunnerhof has a restaurant offering several non-meat choices. It is open daily in season but closes down from around December to February. Not far away is the busy *Pizzeria Bacco* at Gersauerstrasse 21. Great pizzas start from Sfr12 and there's a wide range of more expensive fish and meat dishes (closed Tuesday).

Entertainment Opposite Pizzeria Bacco on Gersauerstrasse is the *Kingfish Pub*, a popular British-style drinking place (open daily from 4 pm to midnight). *Bierhalle Kleinstadt*, Kleinstadt 8, is a more traditional drinking den where prices are lower. *Hotel Eden*, on the waterfront, houses the casino, with gambling from 10 pm (casual dress

OK), a piano bar, and the Weinkeller bar where there's often dancing (open from 8 pm).

Lake Uri
There are several historic sights on this section. If you take the ferry from Brunnen towards Flüelen, the first sight you pass is a natural obelisk protruding from the water to a height of nearly 26m. The gold lettering inscribed thereon is a dedication to Schiller, the author of the play *Wilhelm Tell* (1859), who was so instrumental in creating the Tell legend.

Next stop is the **Rütli Meadow**, where the Oath of Eternal Alliance was signed by the three cantons of Uri, Schwyz and Nidwalden. You can see it well enough from the boat, but if you want to alight, all you will find is a flagpole, a grassy field, and (inevitably) a souvenir shop which doubles as a café and post office.

To commemorate the 700th anniversary of the 1291 pact, the **Swiss Path** was built, which runs all the way round Lake Uri from Rütli to Brunnen. It is in 26 sections, each representing one of the 26 cantons, starting with the first three to sign up and concluding with Jura (1979). Right at the end in Brunnen is a square dedicated to the Swiss living abroad, featuring a surprisingly ugly metal structure. The length of each section of the path is determined by the population of the canton, with every five mm representing one person. Surprisingly, the Swiss haven't been so meticulous as to inscribe the name of every individual person along the path, but they have marked off each section with a stone plaque. It would require some determination to walk the whole 36 km, but one or two sections (for example between boat stops) are easily manageable and worth undertaking. The hilliest stretches are from Rütli to Bauen and from Sisikon to Brunnen. Bauen to Flüelen (around 270 minutes in total) is almost flat and Flüelen to Sisikon (145 minutes) isn't too up-and-down either.

One of the boat stops on the lake is the **William Tell Chapel** (Tellskapell). The walls

MARK HONAN

MARK HONAN

MARK HONAN

Top Left: Castle Garden, Gruyères, Fribourg Canton
Top Right: Gruyères Church, Fribourg Canton
Bottom: Castle and Collegiate church, Neuchâtel, Neuchâtel Canton

Top Left: Russian Church, Geneva
Top Right: Reformation Monument, Geneva
Bottom: Grand Theatre, Geneva

Tell: a Tale from the Dawn of the Confederation

Hermann Gessler, the newly installed Austrian bailiff of Uri and Schwyz, placed his hat on a pole in Altdorf town square. Everyone was compelled to bow in respect to this symbol of Habsburg rule. But William Tell from Bürglen was unaware of the requirement, and failed to do this when passing through the square. Gessler, who knew of Tell's reputation as a crossbow marksman, decreed he would forfeit his life and that of his son, unless he shot an apple off his son's head. To Gessler's disappointment, Tell succeeded. Yet Gessler

noticed Tell had secreted a second arrow about his person. Tell was forced to admit that the second arrow was intended for Gessler himself, had his aim not been true and his son hurt. Gessler arrested Tell and took him on his boat, intending to imprison him for life in his fortress above Küssnacht. As they crossed the lake, Föhn winds whipped up and threatened to capsize the boat. Tell, who was also a master helmsman, was untied in order that he could steer the boat to safety. Tell took the opportunity to steer close to the shore. He leapt on to a rock (at the site of the Tellskapell), at the same time pushing the boat back into the stormy waves. Realising his family would never be safe from Gessler, Tell rushed over to Küssnacht to ambush the tyrant. He hid by the Hohle Gasse, a sunken lane. The bailiff and his entourage soon approached, and Tell shot an arrow into his heart. Gessler died instantly. ■

are covered in murals depicting four episodes in the Tell legend, including the one that's supposed to have occurred on this spot, involving his escape from Gessler's boat (see boxed aside).

The last port of call on the lake is Flüelen. Its main importance is that it's on the main road and rail route through the St Gotthard Pass, and historically it was a staging post for the mule trains making this crossing. Near the town is **Altdorf**, where William Tell is reputed to have performed his apple-shooting stunt. A statue of the man himself stands in the main square, and Schiller's play is sometimes performed in the Tellspielhaus in Altdorf.

Engelberg

• *pop 3500* • *1050m* • ☎ *(041)*

This sunny resort at the foot of Mt Titlis is an ideal day trip from Lucerne, or a base for a longer stay. In summer, the hills above Engelberg sing with the melodic yet insistent sound of cowbells – it sounds like there's a never-ending procession of Hare Krishna devotees up there.

Orientation & Information

Engelberg, in the canton of Unterwalden, is visited summer and winter. The main street is Dorfstrasse (partially pedestrian-only). Most of the shops and restaurants are ranged either side of this road, or on the intersecting Bahnhofstrasse.

The tourist office (☎ 637 37 37) is five minutes' walk from the train station, in the Tourist Center at Klosterstrasse 3. Opening hours are Monday to Friday from 8 am to 12.15 pm and 2 to 6.30 pm, and Saturday from 8 am to 6.30 pm. During the summer and winter high season there's no lunch break and it also opens on Sunday. Hotel prices vary according to the season: peak times are late January to early March, and early July to mid-September. In November most of Engelberg closes down. The tourist office has a free room-booking service for hotels and has list of holiday chalets, private rooms and cheap mountain lodgings.

The guest card is good for various discounts, including 20% off the Mt Titlis cable car in summer and 10% off winter ski passes exceeding four days. The benefits are off-set by the resort Kurtaxe (Sfr3.20 per night) which is *excluded* from accommodation prices. Ski buses are free for everyone in winter.

Banks are open till 5.30 pm on weekdays; several have a Bankomat.

Engelberg Monastery

This is one of only five such Benedictine monasteries in Switzerland. The original building dated from 1120 but was burnt down three times before finally being rebuilt in stone. There is a guided tour from Monday to Saturday at 10 am and 4 pm. It costs Sfr2.50 and lasts around 45 minutes. You're taken around several rooms decorated with incredibly detailed wood inlays – all done by one of the monks who continued this task until he was well into his seventies. A typical panel measuring around 50 cm by 20 cm contains 300 pieces of wood, and he spent years on each room. The Baroque monastery church is also impressive (free entry), having numerous side-altars. It even has a one-handed clock above the main altar so parishioners can time the sermon.

Tal Museum

This small museum at Dorfstrasse 6 is merely of passing interest. One floor is a representation of a typical late 18th century dwelling. It is open most afternoons and costs Sfr6 (Sfr5 with guest card).

Mt Titlis

The trip to the top cable station at 3020m is the most spectacular excursion in Engelberg. First there is the ascent to Gerschnialp (1300m), then there's a horizontal passage over cow pastures, before rising again to Trübsee (1800m). From here you transfer to a gondola which goes to Stand (2450m) and provides a sweeping view back down to the lake and the valley below. Finally you board the world's first revolving gondola (completed in December 1992) for the passage over the Titlis Glacier, a dazzling expanse of ice with ridges, hollows and hints of blue. From Mt Titlis station to the 3239m summit it's about a 45-minute hike (wear sturdy shoes) in the summer – it doesn't look so far but at this altitude you need to take it slow. The station complex provides a sun terrace, restaurant, and the highest laser karaoke bar in Europe. There are also south-facing windows reached through a tunnel in the ice, and an ice grotto.

The whole journey is rather expensive, and if you go up in cloud you've wasted your money. Single/return prices from Engelberg are: Gerschnialp (Sfr6/8), Trübsee (Sfr17/24), Stand (Sfr34/48), and Titlis (Sfr52/73). Reductions are: Swiss Half-Fare Card and Regional Pass 50%, Swiss Pass 25%, Eurail and Inter-Rail 20%. From Engelberg to the Mt Titlis station takes around 45 minutes. The cableway closes for maintenance for a few days in late November. See the Lucerne Tourist Office section for winter reductions.

As ever, you can save on the cost and walk some sections. Between Stand and Trübsee the *panoramaweg* is open from July to September; it takes about 1¾ hours up and 1¼ hours down. From Trübsee up to Jochpass takes about 1½ hours (or there's a chairlift beyond the lake), and down to Engelberg takes around the same time.

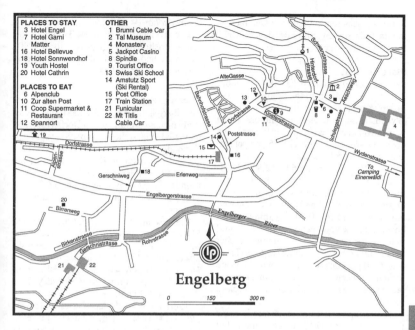

Engelberg

0   150   300 m

Brunni

The Brunni cable car, on the opposite side of the valley, goes up 1600m and provides access to a number of hiking trails. A traveller complained to me that the 5½-hour Benediktusweg went up and down too many hills – but I suppose that's what happens when you go hiking in the mountains! The Brunni cable car costs Sfr10 or Sfr16 return (half-price for kids), or you can make the steep hike up in little over an hour.

Skiing

Engelberg is well known as a skiing centre. Most of the runs are intermediate although there are a few easy ones, mainly around Brunni and the lifts branching from Gerschnialp. The main season is from mid-December to mid-April and a one-day pass costs Sfr47 for adults or Sfr28 for children. Part-day passes are available and rates are slightly higher on the weekends and holidays. Limited validity day passes cost Sfr18 (kids Sfr14) for Gerschnialp and Sfr32 (Sfr18) for Brunni.

There are lots of places which hire out skiing equipment. One of the cheapest is Amstutz Sport (☎ 637 12 68), Dorfstrasse 39. Skis, poles and ski boots for Alpine skiing cost Sfr37 for the first day, reducing with each subsequent day. Cross-country equipment is Sfr22 for one day. The Swiss ski school (☎ 637 10 74) is at Dorfstrasse 34, or there is another school in the tourist office.

Bungy Jumping

The seriously insane can contemplate bungy jumping off Mt Titlis. The 120m jump (from a cable car) costs Sfr169, or the trifling 70m jump, Sfr119. For information and reservations contact Adventure World (☎ 033-826 77 11), Wilderswil, Interlaken.

Mountain Biking

There are routes up both sides of the valley.

Various places rent mountain bikes, including the train station (Sfr33 per day, or Sfr21 for a 'country' bike).

Places to Stay

Camping Einenwäldli (☎ 637 19 49) is about a 25-minute walk from the train station. Go down Klosterstrasse until it becomes Wydenstrasse, then take the right fork. In the winter you can take the ski bus instead. It's open year-round and costs Sfr6 per person, and around Sfr5 for a car.

The SYHA *hostel* (☎ 637 12 92), Dorfstrasse 80, is 10 minutes back down the railway line on the north side of the tracks. Dorm beds are Sfr25 and the dinners are well worth the extra Sfr10.50 – if things aren't chock-a-block you keep getting refills until you beg for mercy. It is closed mid-October to late November and for most of May. There is a 10.30 pm curfew and the main doors are locked between 9 am and 5 pm (you can leave your bags in the ski room and check-in later).

The cheapest place in the centre is *Hotel Garni Matter* (☎ 637 15 56), Dorfstrasse, but it only has one single and four doubles with dim lighting for Sfr50/90. Reception is in the 1st floor café (from 8 am; not Monday) or downstairs in Peter's Pub (from 5 pm daily). *Hotel Engel* (☎ 637 11 82), in front of the monastery church, has old-style singles/doubles with private shower/WC from Sfr75/150.

Hotel Bellevue (☎ 637 12 13), overlooking the station, has a surprisingly majestic lobby, with pseudo-marble pillars and a grand piano. The rooms are newly renovated, but vary in size from very spacious to difficult-to-swing-a-cat-in (Sfr100/170 with private shower/WC). It closes in November, May and June, and is mostly filled with young students in winter.

A good choice for personal service is *Hotel Cathrin* (☎ 637 44 66), Birrenweg, near the Mt Titlis cable car. Singles/doubles with private shower start at Sfr90/160 and great four-course dinners are an extra Sfr26. Book ahead as this place is used by the Kuoni tour group (closed in off-season). *Hotel*

Sonnwendhof (☎ 637 45 75), Gerschniweg 1, is convenient for both Mt Titlis and the centre. Pristine rooms (it was built in 1990) are neatly laid-out with all required amenities, and cost Sfr140/200.

Places to Eat

Engelberg is not cheap for food, but if you study menus carefully down Dorfstrasse you may find Tagestellers from around Sfr15. The budget place to go is the *Coop* supermarket and restaurant on Klosterstrasse. Meals start at Sfr10; it has a salad bar and it's open Monday to Saturday from 8 am to 6.30 pm. There are restaurants at all the cable car stations.

The restaurant in the *Hotel Bellevue* (see Places to Stay) is not too expensive for Mexican food, and it's a popular après-ski place. The café-restaurant *Zur alten Post,* Dorfstrasse, has Asian and Swiss dishes from Sfr13. It is open Friday to Wednesday from 7.15 am to 6.30 pm.

There are several places to eat at *Alpenclub* on Dorfstrasse. Downstairs is a pizzeria, open from 5 pm, with pizzas starting at Sfr14. Also open from the afternoon onwards are the ground floor restaurant serving Swiss food from Sfr30, and the first-floor section serving fondue from Sfr19. All are closed Tuesday and Wednesday in the low season. *Spannort* (☎ 637 26 26), Dorfstrasse 28, is a gourmet restaurant serving Swiss and French food (above Sfr30). It is closed on Monday.

Entertainment

Behind the Hotel Engel (see Places to Stay) is a pool and snooker hall. In front is the *Angel Pub*, an English-style pub with darts and pool. An un-English touch is the tree trunk in the corner of the bar. This is used in a German game where you try to hammer in a nail using the thin end of the hammer head. The last person to succeed buys the drinks. It is open daily from 9 am to 12.30 am, and beer is Sfr4.50 per half-litre. The *Jackpot Casino* on Dorfstrasse has a bar (live music in winter) as well as gambling (noon to 3 am in winter) as well as gambling (noon to 3 am daily). Close by, *Spindle* has dancing from 10 pm to 3 am (closed Sunday to Tuesday).

Getting There & Away
By train, Engelberg is at the terminus of the line an hour or less from Lucerne (Sfr14.20 each way; change usually required at Hergiswil). Seeing Engelberg and Mt Titlis in a day trip from Lucerne is easily viable; the first train leaves Lucerne at 6.32 am (6.19 am on Sunday) and the last one back leaves Engelberg at 9.50 pm. The Lucerne tourist office sells special excursion tickets. (See the Getting Around section at the beginning of this chapter for details.)

Hiking Unless travelling by road from Lucerne or Stans, the only other way to leave or reach Engelberg is by foot, but the passes are only accessible in the summer. The Surenen Pass (2291m) is the route to Attinghausen, and from there a bus can take you to Altdorf and the southern end of the Urnersee. It takes around seven hours to get to Attinghausen; taking a cable car along the route can save two hours. From Jochpass a path goes to Meiringen via Engstenalp and Tannalp. The highest point you reach is 2245m. From Meiringen it is easy to get to Lake Brienz. Acquire a decent map and check on snow conditions before you try one of these routes.

Schwyz Canton

The fame of Schwyz rests upon the fact that it gave Switzerland both its name and flag. Together with the communities of Uri and Nidwalden, it was signatory to the Oath of Eternal Alliance of 1291. This charter is considered as the birth of the Swiss Confederation and can be viewed in Schwyz town. Some destinations in Schwyz canton are covered in the earlier Lake Lucerne section.

Cherries are grown locally, and different towns are grouped under an itinerary called the Kirschstrasse (Cherry Road). One destination along the way is the Fabio-Fassbind distillery (☎ 041-855 40 42) in Oberarth, between Arth and Goldau. Reserve ahead for a guided tour of the distillery in English (Sfr8), including a tasting of the cherry spirit made there.

SCHWYZ
• *pop 12,000*   • *517m*   • ☎ *(041)*
Schwyz, the capital of its canton, cowers beneath the twin peaks of the Mythen (1898m and 1811m).

Orientation & Information
The train station is two km away from the town centre in Seewen. For the centre, take any bus outside the station marked Schwyz Post, and get off at Postplatz (Sfr2.40; Swiss Pass not valid). The tourist office (☎ 811 27 10) is a counter inside the post office at Steisteg-Märcht, 100m down the hill. It is open Monday to Friday from 9 am to noon and from 1.30 to 5 pm. Pick up the *Gäste Information* booklet which also covers Brunnen and Morscharch, and ask about the guest card. Other than this, there's little information available, but staff will telephone free of charge for rooms.

Federal Archives
Historic charters and other agreements are collected in the Bundesbriefarchiv building on Bahnhofstrasse in the town centre. Entry is free and it is open daily from 9.30 to 11.30 am and from 2 to 5 pm. The federal charters are in the circular cabinet in the centre of the room. The inaugural 1291 charter displayed here is the only copy in existence. It is written in Latin and bears only the seals of Uri and Nidwalden – Schwyz's own seal has been lost. In the document, the partners agreed to work for mutual defence and security and formulated their own legal system. They successfully defended this pact in 1315 by defeating the Habsburg force at Morgarten. The second charter marks this victory by restating the original agreement (in German) and making provision for a common foreign policy.

CENTRAL SWITZERLAND

The other charters mark the acceptance of further cantons to the Confederation, with a corresponding increase in the number of heavy seals attached to each document. The last charter proclaims the entry of Appenzell in 1513 and resolves not to admit any other members to its elite circle. The Confederates kept this resolution intact until the French marched onto the scene in 1798.

Also on display round the outside of the room are charters relating to privileges won by Schwyz through the years, and flags and banners carried in important battles.

Other Things to See & Do

The **Forum of Swiss History**, in the old granary, enlivens its subject matter with interactive displays (closed Monday; Sfr5, children free). In Hauptplatz there is the 17th century **Town hall**, complete with 19th century murals depicting famous events in Swiss history, particularly the Battle of Morgarten. On the other side of the square is

St Martin's Church, with Baroque fixtures and a marble pulpit. Schwyz was the home of many of the 16th and 17th century mercenaries who fought in foreign armies. Those who returned with body and fortune intact built some of the grand houses that can still be seen round the town today. At the rear of Seewen train station is a building that looks like a block of cheese. This is the **Schaukäserie Schwyzerland** (☎ 811 61 61), where the different stages in making cheese are shown and explained. Entry costs Sfr1 and it's open Tuesday to Saturday from 9 am to 6 pm.

Hiking and skiing are possible on the surrounding mountains, accessible by cable car or funicular. For information on the Mythen ski region, ask the tourist office. There is also skiing at Stoos (1300m), a car-free resort. From Schwyz, take bus No 3 to Schlattli then the funicular (Sfr11 up, Sfr20 return). A cable car goes up from Stoos to Frontalpstock (1922m). A good, if steep, circular hike

The Swiss Flag

Soldiers from the canton of Schwyz went to the aid of the excommunicated Emperor Frederick II in 1240, during his campaign in Italy. As a reward Schwyz was granted freedom from sovereign overlords and the right to use a red flag, the blood banner of the Holy Roman Empire, complete with heraldic cross. But a subsequent Diet in Nuremberg declared Frederick's dispensation invalid, so Schwyz pitched in behind Rudolf I of Habsburg in a battle against the Burgundians in 1289, and was rewarded by having its privileges confirmed.

The different Swiss cantons all had their own flags, yet they soon accepted the use of the white cross as a common emblem for Swiss mercenary soldiers. When Napoleon created the Helvetic Republic in 1798 he gave the country its first official national flag, a green, red and yellow tricolour. This flag was ditched in 1803, but it wasn't until 1841 that the cantons agreed to accept the free-standing white cross on the red field as a federal flag. Tireless campaigning by General Henri Dufour was instrumental in getting the flag accepted.

But the matter did not end there. People got very excited about whether the cross should consist of four equal squares arranged around a central square, or whether the bars of the cross should be one-sixth longer than their width. The federal constitutions of 1848 and 1874 neglected to settle this burning issue, and it wasn't till 1889 that the Federal parliament voted for the latter cross. Even so, debate raged on this crucial matter for years to come.

The federal decision was vindicated when in 1906 the international community honoured the Swiss flag by choosing to reverse its colours (to make a red cross on white) as a universal emblem for army medical corps. Nowadays the Swiss seem to have forgotten the passions aroused by the extra one-sixth, and seem content in the knowledge that they have the only square national flag in the world. ∎

from Stoos around the Frontalpstock area takes three to four hours.

Schwyz is near to Lake Lauerz and to Brunnen (see the Lake Lucerne section for details). From Brunnen, you can get to Stoos via bus No 4 to Morscharch, then a cable car (Sfr11 up, Sfr20 return).

Places to Stay & Eat

Some pension receptions are closed on Monday. For budget private rooms, ask the tourist office. Otherwise, the cheaper places are up the mountains, such as the *Berggasthaus* (☎ 811 17 74) on Haggenegg (Sfr30 per person in a dorm, Sfr40 in a room).

Drei Königen (☎ 811 24 10) is by St Martin's Church on Schulgasse. Rooms are Sfr50 per person, or Sfr60 with private shower/WC, though it's often filled by the military. The food is not bad value (from Sfr14; closed Sunday evening and Monday). *Hotel Engel* (☎ 811 12 42) is opposite and similarly priced.

Hirschen Garni (☎ 811 12 76), Hinterdorf strasse 9, is typically Swiss, with comfortable singles/doubles starting at Sfr62/104 (less 10% if three nights or more). *Restaurant Löwen* is opposite and not expensive (closed Tuesday evening and Wednesday).

The *supermarket* by the tourist office has a deli counter with hot food. *Sternen*, Zeughausstrasse 6, up behind the Postplatz bus stop, has decent pizzas from Sfr9.50 to Sfr16.50 (closed Monday). The best restaurant in Schwyz is *Ratskeller* (☎ 811 10 87) at Strehlgasse 3. Main courses are above Sfr25, though there's a plainer area where you can eat from Sfr17. It is closed Sunday evening, Monday, and for two weeks from mid-February (no credit cards accepted).

Getting There & Away

Schwyz station is 30 minutes away from Zug on the main north-south rail route; Lucerne is 40 minutes away (direct, or change at Goldau). Schwyz centre is only a few kms detour off the N4 which passes through Brunnen. (See the Zug and Einsiedeln Getting There & Away sections for more information.)

EINSIEDELN

• *pop 7000* • *900m* • ☎ *(055)*

Einsiedeln is the most important pilgrimage destination in Switzerland, and its church is worth visiting simply for its sumptuous interior. Einsiedeln's reputation stems from 964, when the Bishop of Constance attempted to consecrate the original monastery. He was halted in his tracks by a heavenly voice declaring, 'Desist – God Himself has consecrated this building'. Presumably somebody checked the premises for ventriloquists, because a papal bull subsequently acknowledged the miracle as genuine.

Orientation & Information

Einsiedeln is south of Lake Zürich and by the western shore of Lake Sihl. The train station and the post office (8840) are together in the centre of town. In front of them is Dorfplatz, from which leads the main street, Hauptstrasse. The church is at the end of this street, overlooking Klosterplatz (10 minutes' walk from the station). The tourist office (☎ 418 44 88), near the church at Hauptstrasse 85, is open Monday to Friday from 9 am to noon and 2 to 5.30 pm and Saturday from 9 am to noon and 2 to 4 pm.

Things to See & Do

The main focus of activity is the **Abbey Church**. This majestic Baroque edifice was built from 1719 to 1735 by the architect Caspar Moosbrugger. Much of the interior of the church is the work of the Asam brothers from Bavaria. The frescoes and stucco embellishments are exceptional, even if the newly restored colours are a bit overpowering. (Which misguided soul chose that salmon pink?) The church influenced the design of the similarly lavish St Gallen Cathedral; conversely, the original monastery here was based on the original monastery in St Gallen.

The main prize for pilgrims is the **Black Madonna**, housed in a chapel by the

CENTRAL SWITZERLAND

entrance to the church; it is to this that most of the prayers are directed. It's only a small statue, but one that has somehow survived three fires. The chapel is built on the spot where St Meinrad was murdered in 861.

In front of the church is a large square (plenty of parking) where stalls sell kitsch religious souvenirs. Continuing the religious theme, there's a **diorama** of Bethlehem, featuring 450 figures, and a **panorama** painting of Calvary. These are in Benzigerstrasse; entry for each costs Sfr3.50 (children Sfr1.50) and they are open from Easter to the end of October and on Sundays during December.

Every year on the 14 September there is the **Festival of the Miraculous Dedication** involving a torchlit procession. Every five to seven years is the formidable production of *The Great Theatre of the World*, a religious drama by Calderón de la Barca. Over 600 villagers act in the event. It runs from around mid-June to mid-September and the next one is in 1998.

Activities in the surrounding area include winter cross-country skiing, hiking, and boating and bathing in nearby **Lake Sihl**. Fishing permits for the lake cost Sfr14 per day and Sfr40 per week (buy from lakeside restaurants). There are suggestions for hikes in the free *Gäste Information* booklet from the tourist office. Walk beside the church through the monastery buildings (pausing to pat the horses in the paddock) and continue along the path for 15 minutes for a good viewpoint of the church, green hills, the lake and the adjoining mountains.

Places to Stay & Eat

There's *camping* (☎ 412 17 37) on the far shore of Lake Sihl at Willerzell. *Meinradsberg* (☎ 412 28 36), in front of the church at Igenweidstrasse 3, has homely singles/doubles for Sfr39/73 but no shower is available in winter. Two doors along at No 2 is *St Josef Garni* (☎ 412 21 51) where rooms start at Sfr58/90 with private shower or Sfr45/80 using one in the hall. *Storchen* (☎ 412 37 60), Hauptstrasse 79, has largish singles/doubles

with shower/toilet and TV from Sfr85/130, and a mid-price restaurant.

There's a *Coop* supermarket off Dorfplatz and a *Migros* supermarket and restaurant (late opening till 8 pm on Friday) 200m away by the railway line. *Pizzeria zia Teresa* (closed Monday and Tuesday) and the small café-restaurant *Central* (closed Monday), both on Dorfplatz, are reasonable choices for an inexpensive meal. *Restaurant Sihlsee*, Hauptstrasse 28, has cheap lunch menus, or try the speciality of the house – half chicken in a basket for Sfr13.50 (closed Wednesday). *Landgasthof Heidenbühl*, Zürichstrasse, has good meals from Sfr12 (closed Wednesday evening and Thursday).

Getting There & Away

Einsiedeln is in a rail cul-de-sac so getting here usually involves changing at Biberbrugg, but this is rarely a problem as arrivals/departures coincide. It is also within range of the canton of Zürich's S-Bahn trains. Zürich itself (Sfr15) is less than one hour away (via Wädenswil). There are direct trains to Lucerne (Sfr21, Sfr36 return; takes one hour), or you may need to change at Goldau (70 minutes). From Einsiedeln to Schwyz, you can take the scenic 'back route' in the summer: postbus to Oberiberg, then private bus (Swiss Pass not valid) from there.

By car, Einsiedeln is five km off highway 8 between Schwyz and Rapperswil.

Zug

• *pop 21,640* • *426m* • ☎ *(041)*

Many multinational companies are registered in affluent Zug, thanks to the canton's status as a tax haven. The canton is easily the richest in Switzerland, earning an incredible Sfr74,300 per inhabitant in 1993, over 65% higher than the national average. Tourists, however, will be attracted more by its delightful medieval town centre and the nearby lake. Maybe the lake is a little too nearby – parts of the town sank into it in 1435, 1594 and 1887.

Orientation & Information

Zug (pronounced Tzoogk) hugs the north-east shore of Lake Zug (Zugersee). The train station is one km north of the old town centre, and has bike rental and money-exchange counters. The tourist office (☎ 711 00 78), Alpenstrasse 16, is at the train station, and is open Monday to Friday from 9.30 am to 6.30 pm, and Saturday from 9.30 am to 4 pm. For the old town *(Altstadt)*, exit the station on the east side of the tracks and walk 800m south along the main road, passing the main post office (6301) along the way.

Things to See & Do

The medieval town centre can easily be explored on foot. Start with the **clocktower** (Zytturm) in Kolinplatz. It's the symbol of the town and its distinctive tiled roof is painted in the blue and white of the cantonal colours. The shields below the 1557 clockface are those of the first eight cantons to join the Confederation (Zug was the seventh in 1352). The fountain in Kolinplatz was built in honour of Wolfgang Kolin, the flag bearer of the Swiss army that was defeated in the Battle of Arbedo (1422) by a vastly superior force led by the Duke of Milan.

Leading off from Kolinplatz are the pedestrian-only medieval streets of Fischmarkt, Oberaltstadt and Unteraltstadt. The old step-gabled houses are notable for their overhanging balconies. Nearby is Landsgemeindeplatz, where there's an aviary (free) containing a number of feathered inmates, such as owls, peacocks, ibises and parakeets.

Off Kolinplatz to the other side is Kirchenstrasse, which leads to the 13th century castle, now containing the **Museum in der Burg**. It shows temporary exhibitions of a historical or archaeological nature (entry fee varies). Opening hours are Saturday and Sunday from 10 am to noon, and daily except Monday from 2 to 5 pm. Almost opposite is **St Oswald's Church**, built in late-Gothic style from the 15th and 16th centuries. It has a number of interesting features including a trio of carved wooden altars.

There are paddleboats available by Landsgemeindeplatz for trips on the lake (Sfr17 per hour). There are also various beaches: free ones are near the camp site and just south of Landsgemeindeplatz. The funicular from Schönegg will take you up the Zugerberg (988m), where there are hiking trails and an unobstructed view.

A good excursion from Zug is to the **Stalactite Grottoes** (Höllgrotten) near Baar, about eight km to the north-east. These limestone caves are open 1 April to 31 October, every day from 9 am to noon and 1 to 5.30 pm. Entry costs Sfr7 (Sfr3.50 for students and children) and they take about an hour to get around. To get there by public transport, take the Menzingen bus and get off at Tobelbrücke-Höllgrotten.

Places to Stay

There is *camping* (☎ 741 84 22) on the shore of the lake, two km west of the centre, along Chamer Fussweg. Charges are Sfr5.40 per person and Sfr5 per tent. The modern SYHA *hostel* (☎ 711 53 54) is at Allmendstrasse 8, a 10-minute walk west of the station along Gubel Strasse. Dorm beds cost Sfr27, and there are kitchen facilities and evening dinners. The hostel is closed from late January to early March.

Other accommodation is on the expensive side. The only cheap place is two km south of Zug at *Adler* (☎ 711 16 94), Artherstrasse 119, Oberwil. Singles/doubles from Sfr46/80 are only available in the summer. Take bus No 3 heading south down Bahnhofstrasse (which becomes Artherstrasse). The best value in the centre is *Hotel Löwen* (☎ 711 77 22) at Lands-gemeindeplatz, a good location near the lake. Smallish singles/doubles with private shower/WC and TV are Sfr96/150 or Sfr66/125 using hall facilities. All rooms have a radio.

People with more money to spend should head for *City-Hotel Ochsen* (☎ 729 32 32; fax 729 30 32) at Kolinplatz. This quiet place has well-equipped singles/doubles from Sfr157/255. Dating from 1480, it's the oldest inn in central Switzerland; Goethe once stayed here.

Places to Eat

Cherry trees are grown locally, so look out for the speciality, Zug cherry cake (Zuger Kirschtorte). It's a diet-busting combination of pastry, biscuit, almond paste, and butter cream with cherry brandy.

Several self-service places in town provide budget eats. Across Baarstrasse from the train station there's a *Migros* supermarket and restaurant in the huge Metalli shopping mall. Just down the street there's a large *Coop* supermarket and restaurant in the arcade opposite Bundesplatz. On Bundesplatz itself there's an *EPA* department store restaurant with even cheaper meals. All have late opening till 9 pm on Thursday.

On Landsgemeindeplatz there's *Café Platzmühle*, with pizzas and other meals from Sfr14 (closed Wednesday), or you could try the Hotel Löwen's restaurant.

There are two top restaurants in this small town, opposite each other in Oberaltstadt, by the clocktower. The *Rathauskeller* (☎ 711 00 58) has the best reputation. Also highly regarded is *Aklin* (☎ 711 18 66), where French-style gourmet menus are above Sfr70. Both have a cheaper bistro restaurant, of which Aklin's is considered superior, and both are closed Sunday and Monday.

Getting There & Away

Train connections are good. Zug is on the main north-south rail route from Zürich to Lugano, and it is also the station at which trains from Zürich branch off to Lucerne and the Bernese Oberland.

By road, the north-south N4 (E31) runs from Zürich, sweeps round the western shore of Lake Zug and joins the N2 (E35), which continues through the St Gotthard Pass and on to Lugano and Italy. Highway 25 peels off the N4 north of Zug at Sihlbrugg, completes the corset round the eastern shore of the lake, then rejoins the N4 at Goldau.

Boats depart from Zug's Schiffsstation Bahnhof and chug south to Arth (Swiss Pass and Half-Fare Card valid) in the summer, and to many other destinations round the lake. Some outings include meals and music on board. Reserve on ☎ 726 24 26.

CENTRAL SWITZERLAND

Andermatt

• *pop 1600* • *1447m* • ☎ *(041)*

Andermatt is a skiing resort at the crossroads of four major Alpine passes: Susten, Oberalp, St Gotthard and Grimsel. The views from the town itself are surprisingly unspectacular given the mountain ranges all around – but that changes as soon as you gain some altitude.

Orientation & Information

Andermatt is at the southern end of the canton of Uri, and was formerly an important staging-post on the north-south St Gotthard route. Nowadays the town has been bypassed by the St Gotthard tunnel, but it still remains an important transport junction. The train station is 400m north of the core of the village, and has hotel brochures. The tourist office (☎ 887 14 54), 200m to the left of the station, shares the same hut as the postbus ticket office. Its opening hours are Monday to Friday from 9 am to noon and 2 to 6 pm, and Saturday from 9 am to noon. From mid-June to late September and early December to mid-May it is also open on Saturday from 2 to 6 pm.

The post office (6490) is on the main street, Gotthardstrasse, the site of most of the hotels and restaurants. Andermatt has a useful Guest Card.

Things to See & Do

The **skiing** is between 1438 and 2963m, with runs mostly for experts and intermediates. A one-day general ski pass costs Sfr55 (Sfr37 for children). There is cross-country skiing along the broad, flat valley towards Realp. Realp also has a small ski lift where beginners can hone their skills (Sfr24 for one day, children Sfr13).

From Realp, steam trains run to Tiefenbach on weekends between 1 June and early October, except from mid-July to late August when they're daily. The return fare for this 20-minute ride is Sfr20 for adults and Sfr10 for children.

The high passes on all four sides make for excellent driving tours. A circular tour by postbus, visiting the passes of St Gotthard, Nufenen and Furka departs Andermatt twice a day in summer (see Alpine Pass Tours in the Bernese Oberland chapter for more on this route). It's also fun to watch the trains winding their way backwards and forwards over the mountains. The **St Gotthard Museum** (☎ 091-869 15 25), on the St Gotthard Pass (2109m), is open from 9 am to 6 pm daily (Sfr8, senior citizens Sfr4), but only between June and October when the pass itself is open. The museum uses reliefs, models, documents and weapons to tell the history of the pass, highlighting mule drivers, stagecoaches, and the new tunnel (there's English text). The St Gotthard tunnel now takes the brunt of most Alp crossings.

The tourist office has information on walking tours to/from the passes and other points of interest, taking one to six hours. From **Gemsstock** (2963m), there's a panorama of 600 Alpine peaks. The journey to the top by cable car from Andermatt is in two sections and costs Sfr17.40 up or Sfr34.80 return (children half-price, reductions with Swiss railpasses).

Places to Stay & Eat
Beware of places closing in off-season. *Lager Zgraggen* (☎ 887 16 58), Boden-strasse, offers dorm beds, with kitchen facilities, for groups in winter (Sfr20), and individuals in summer (Sfr18). It's 200m from the station: go right and cross over the river.

Other accommodation in the village is quite expensive. *Löwen* (☎ 887 12 23), Gotthardstrasse 51, has singles/doubles using

hall shower for Sfr44/88. Pizza and pasta starts from Sfr13 in its restaurant. *Bergidyll* (☎ 887 14 55), at No 39, offers pleasant, reasonably spacious rooms for Sfr75/150 with private shower or Sfr60/120 without. There's also a lounge with easy chairs and an open fire. Between the two, the *Hotel Monopol* (☎ 887 15 75) has better-appointed rooms from Sfr95 per person with private shower, and a small swimming pool.

Bonetti Haus (☎ 887 19 60), near the gondola station, looks like business premises but has doubles for around Sfr60 per person with shower and toilet. The public self-service restaurant upstairs has three-course meals for around Sfr15 (open 7.30 am to noon and from 4 pm 'until it's empty').

For eating, check the hotel restaurants for daily specials, or try *Badus*, close to the station on Gotthardstrasse. It has meals from Sfr13, including vegetarian dishes. There is a *Coop* supermarket on Gotthardstrasse.

Getting There & Away
Andermatt is a stop on the Glacier Express from Zermatt to St Moritz. For north-south destinations, change at Göschenen, 15 minutes away. Andermatt train station (☎ 887 12 20) can supply details on the car-carrying trains over the Oberalp Pass (direction: Graubünden) and through the Furka tunnel (the route to Valais). Postbuses stop by the train station. The St Gotthard tunnel (N2/E35) is one of the busiest north-south routes across the Alps. The 17-km tunnel opened in 1980. It extends from Göschenen to close to Airolo, bypassing Andermatt. Each weekend *30 tonnes* of nitrogen is emitted into the atmosphere by traffic on the St Gotthard route.

CENTRAL SWITZERLAND

Zürich Canton

The canton of Zürich is the most populous in Switzerland with 1,168,000 inhabitants. It is also one of the most affluent – in Küsnacht (which has low taxes) millionaires are commonplace. The canton is a hub of industry and the financial centre of the country. Heavy industry (metals and machines) are particularly important for a number of towns. As a tourist centre it is not so pre-eminent. Zürich itself welcomes many visitors – tourists and business people – who can enjoy the old centre, museums and galleries, and lakeside setting. Otherwise, there's little in the canton to detain the visitor, except perhaps a visit to Winterthur, or a tour on Lake Zürich.

Information

The tourist office in Zürich city handles enquiries for the whole Zürich tourist region, and has racks of brochures on many towns throughout Switzerland. The headquarters of Switzerland Tourism is also in Zürich (see the Zürich Information section for details). Zürich's train station has a computer terminal with canton-wide information (on the mid-lower level).

HIGHLIGHTS

- Elegant shops and diverse museums in Zürich
- Switzerland's largest zoo
- Zürich's varied cycle of festivals
- Art collections in Winterthur

Zürich

Zürich

- *pop 363,000* • *409m* • ☎ *(01)*

The city of Zürich started life as a Roman customs post with the name of Turicum. Expansion thereafter was slow, but merchants trading in textiles gradually increased the financial clout of the town, and in 1218 it graduated to the status of a free city under the Holy Roman Empire. In 1336 the increasingly powerful merchants and artisans formed guilds which took over the governing of the city.

Zürich's reputation as a cultural and intellectual centre began after it joined the Swiss Confederation in 1351. Zwingli helped things along with his teachings during the Reformation, from 1519, and became a key figure in the running of the city. Zürich's intellectual and artistic tradition continued during WWI with the influx of luminaries such as Lenin, Trotsky, Tristan Tzara, Hans Arp and James Joyce. The Dada art movement was born in Zürich in 1916. Around the same time, Carl Jung was honing his psychoanalytical theories in the city. Johann Heinrich Pestalozzi (1746-1827), seminal educationalist, was also a citizen of Zürich, and his statue stands on Bahnhofstrasse.

On the financial side, Zürich's international status as an industrial and business centre is thanks in no small part to the efforts of the energetic administrator and railway magnate, Alfred Escher, in the 19th century.

The Birth of Dada

Dada was a phenomenon that delighted in contradictions. It was an art movement that was anti-art. It had an intellectual dimension, yielding countless erudite polemics, yet was also fun, rebellious, and often plain strange. It used manufactured objects and re-defined them as art; it delighted in chance outcomes. Dada was short-lived but very influential, and paved the way for Surrealism.

The birth of the movement is accepted to be the creation of the Cabaret Voltaire in February 1916 by Hugo Ball. Raucous artistic events (including poetry, singing and dancing) were held at a room in a pub at Spiegelgasse 1, in the heart of the old town. The Alsatian artist, Hans or Jean Arp, and especially the Romanian poet, Tristan Tzara, were key figures in these early days. Diagonally opposite the pub, at No 12, lived Lenin. This studious Russian, although planning a world revolution, was viewed with much less suspicion by the Swiss authorities than were the breed of new artists. ■

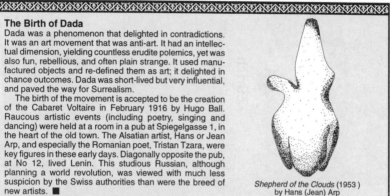

Shepherd of the Clouds (1953)
by Hans (Jean) Arp

His statute is in front of the station. Zürich's stock exchange was founded in 1877 and is the most important in the country.

Switzerland's most populous city offers an ambience of affluence and plenty of cultural diversions. In recent years, the Social Democrats have been at the helm of Zürich's administration, but the guilds retain a powerful, if behind-closed-doors, voice in the running of the city.

Orientation

Zürich is at the northern end of Lake Zürich (Zürichsee), with the city centre split by the Limmat River. Like many Swiss cities, it is compact and conveniently laid out. The main train station (Hauptbahnhof) is on the west or left bank of the river, close to the old centre.

Information

Tourist Offices The main tourist office (☎ 211 40 00; fax 212 01 41) is at the Hauptbahnhof, Bahnhofplatz 15, and arranges hotel reservations (Sfr5 commission; ☎ 211 11 31), car rentals and excursions. Opening hours from 1 April to 31 October are Monday to Friday from 8.30 am to 9.30 pm, and Saturday and Sunday from

8.30 am to 8.30 pm. The rest of the year it closes two hours earlier each day. Staff charge for city maps – the one they sell for Sfr3 is available free from the Swiss Bank Corporation. Other banks in the city have free maps, too. There's also an airport tourist office in Terminal B arrivals (☎ 816 40 81), open daily from 10 am to 7 pm.

The Switzerland Tourism headquarters (☎ 288 11 11; fax 288 12 05) is at Bellariastrasse 38, and has information on the whole of Switzerland. It's open Monday to Friday from 8 to 11.45 am and 1 to 5 pm.

Foreign Consulates Consulates in town include the following:

Austria
    Minervastrasse 116 (☎ 383 72 00)
Britain
    Dufourstrasse 56 (☎ 261 15 20)
France
    Mühlebachstrasse 7 (☎ 251 85 44)
Germany
    Kirchgasse 48 (☎ 265 65 65)
Italy
    Tödistrasse 67 (☎ 286 61 11)
South Africa
    Basteiplatz 7 (☎ 221 11 88)
USA
    Zollikerstrasse 141 (☎ 422 25 66)

ZÜRICH CANTON

ZÜRICH CANTON

Zürich

Zürichberg

Some Minor Streets Not Depicted

0   250   500 m

To Dolder Grand Hotel

Bergstrasse

Kraftstrasse

Zürichbergstrasse

Plattenstrasse

Freiestrasse

Gloriastrasse

Freudenbergstrasse

Susenbergstrasse

Toblerstrasse

Gladbachstrasse

Germaniastrasse

Gemsenstrasse (G)

Rigiplatz

Universitätstrasse

Rämistrasse

Künstlergasse

Hirschengraben

Seilergraben

Mühlegasse

Niederdorf

Central

strasse

Limmatquai

Bahnhofquai

Rennweg

Bahnhofstrasse

Oetenbachgasse

See Central Zürich Map

Augustiner Gasse

Winterthurer Strasse

Riedstrasse

To Airport

Scheuchzer strasse

Sonneggstrasse

Weinbergstrasse

Leonhardstrasse

Schaffhauser Strasse

Nordstrasse

Platz-promenade

Museumstrasse

Bahnhofplatz

Uraniastrasse

Gessnerallee

Löwenstrasse

Limmat River

Sihlquai

Hans Strasse

Train Station (Hauptbahnhof)

Sihlquai

Wasserwerkstrasse

Kornhausstrasse

Josef Strasse

Gasometerstrasse

Neugasse

Limmatstrasse

Neugasse

Röntgenstrasse

To Basel (113 km) & Bern (125 km)

Brauerstrasse

Lagerstrasse

Militärstrasse

Kinoanstrasse

Zeughausstrasse

Müllerstrasse

Backerstrasse

Stauffacherstrasse

Kanzlei-strasse

Lang Strasse

Badener Strasse

Zweier Strasse

Gartenhofstrasse

Molkenstrasse

Staufflacher Quai

Sihl River

Sihlporte

Morgartenstrasse

1 •
2 ■
8 ●
9
10 ■
11
12 ■
13 ●
14 ■
15 ✚
16 ●
17 ●
18 ■
19 ●
20
21 ▶
22
23 ▶
24 ▶
25 ■
26 ■
27 ■
28 ▶
29 ▶
30 ▶
31 ■
32 ■

PLACES TO STAY
2 Justinusheim
10 Hotel Zürich
12 Hotel Poly
26 Hotel Regina
27 Salvation Army
33 Hotel St Georges
43 Hotel Ambassador
47 Foyer Hottingen
48 OASE Evangelisches
   Haus
55 Hotel Dufour

PLACES TO EAT
3 Restaurant JOSEF
7 Silberkugel
16 University Mensa
20 Mr Wong
21 Migros City
23 Clipper Restaurant
24 Bernerhof
29 Silberkugel

30 EPA Department Store
36 Silberkugel
44 Spaghetti Factory
54 Riesbächli

OTHER
1 SYHA Head Office
4 Speed-Wash Laundry
5 Frauenzentrum
   (Women's Centre)
6 Europcar (Car Rental)
8 Haz (Gay & Lesbian Centre)
9 Swiss National Museum
11 Limmat Boat Terminus
13 Mittlahrzentrale
   (Hitching Agency)
14 SSR (Travel Agency)
15 Cantonal Hospital
17 Archaeological Collection
18 Tourist Office
19 Swissair
22 Post Office

25 SSR (Travel Agency)
28 Kansiei (Cinema & Disco)
31 Hertz (Car Rental)
32 Avis (Car Rental)
34 Italian Consulate
35 South African Consulate
37 Sixt-Econo (Car Rental)
38 Arboretum
39 Open Air Swimming Pool
40 Lonthalle
41 Lake Steamers Landing
   Stage
42 Opera House (Opernhaus)
45 Museum of Fine Arts
   (Kunsthaus)
46 French Consulate
49 Austrian Consulate
50 Open Air Swimming Pool
51 British Consulate
52 Johann Jacobs Coffee
   Museum
53 USA Consulate

Jung Ideas

Carl Gustav Jung founded the analytical school of psychology. He was born on 26 July 1875 in Kesswil, Thurgau, and graduated in medicine in 1902 from Basel and Zürich universities. Initially an ally of Freud, he soon rejected the Viennese psychoanalyst's purely sexual interpretation of subconscious drives. Jung identified the distinct personalities, extrovert and introvert, in *Psychological Types*, published in 1921. He later proposed the existence of the collective unconscious (inherited feelings, thoughts, and memories shared by all humanity), which individuals have to integrate with their own personal unconscious in order to achieve wholeness of self. Jung died in Küsnacht, Zürich, on 6 June 1961.

Money

There's no shortage of choice in this banking city for exchanging money or seeking credit card cash advances. Most banks are open Monday to Friday from 8.15 am to 4.30 pm (6 pm Thursday), though a few branches keep later hours. The exchange office by platform 16 in the Hauptbahnhof is open daily from 6.15 am to 10.45 pm. In the airport, don't change banknotes at the UBS bank in Terminal B (Sfr5 commission) – use the commission-free Credit Suisse in Terminal A (open daily).

Post & Communications The main post office is Sihlpost (☎ 296 21 11), Kasernenstrasse 95-97, 8021. It is open Monday to Friday from 7.30 am to 6.30 pm, and Saturday from 7.30 to 11 am. Like many other large Swiss post offices, there's a counter open daily (to 8 pm Saturday, 10.30 pm other days), but with a Sfr1 surcharge outside normal hours for many transactions (not payable when collecting poste restante).

The post office in the Hauptbahnhof has a fax and telegram service; it's open normal hours.

American Express The office (☎ 219 61 11) at Bahnhofstrasse 20 has financial and travel services; it's open Monday to Friday from 8.30 am to 5.30 pm and Saturday from 9 am to noon.

Travel Agencies SSR is a specialist in student, youth and budget fares. Branches are at Leonhardstrasse 10 (open Monday to Friday) and Bäckerstrasse 40 (open Monday afternoon to Saturday morning), or call ☎ 297 11 11 for telephone sales. Globetrotter (☎ 211 77 80), Rennweg 35, also has worldwide budget fares, and a travel noticeboard and magazine. It's open weekdays only. Reisebüro Intravex (☎ 462 05 80), Kalkbreitestrasse 40, has low prices and good knowledge of short-term special offers for flights and holidays.

Bookshops Stäheli English Bookshop (☎ 201 33 02; see the Central Zürich map), Bahnhofstrasse 70, has a wealth of English-language books covering fiction, nonfiction and travel. It is open Monday to Friday from 9 am to 6.30 pm and Saturday from 9 am to 4 pm.

English and French-language books are also available at Librairie Payot, Bahnhofstrasse 9 (closed Monday morning). The Travel Book Shop (☎ 252 38 83; see the Central Zürich map), Rindermarkt 20, has a huge selection of English-language travel books and can order anything you want. It also runs the map shop next door. It's open Monday from 1 pm, otherwise hours are as above.

There is a very large general bookshop called Orell Füssli at Füsslistrasse 4.

Libraries The Pestalozzi Library, Zäringerstrasse 17, has magazines and newspapers in English. The reading room is open weekdays from 9 am to 8 pm and Saturday until 5 pm. The nearby Central Library (Zentralbibliothek) Zähringerplatz, has English books.

Laundry Speed-Wash, at the corner of Mattengasse and Josef Strasse, is self-service. Machines cost from Sfr5 to wash and Sfr1.50 per 10 minutes for drying. It's open daily until 10 pm. The Waschsalon in the Hauptbahnhof costs from Sfr7.50.

Medical Services For medical and dental help, ring ☎ 261 61 00. The Cantonal University Hospital (☎ 255 11 11), Ramistrasse 100, has a casualty department. There is a 24-hour chemist at Bellevue Apotheke (☎ 252 56 00), Theaterstrasse 14.

Emergency The police (☎ 216 71 11) are at Bahnhofquai 3. The national emergency numbers are: ☎ 117 for police, ☎ 118 for the fire brigade, ☎ 144 for an ambulance and ☎ 140 for the car breakdown service.

Gay & Lesbian Haz (☎ 271 22 50), 3rd floor, Sihlquai 67, is a gay and lesbian centre, open Tuesday to Friday from 7.30 pm to 11 pm, and Sunday from 11 am to 2 pm. It has a library, café (open Friday), distributes the gay newspaper *Cruiser*, and has a list of Zürich's gay venues. Helplines are: gays (☎ 271 70 11), open Tuesday from 8 to 10 pm; lesbians (☎ 272 73 71), open Thursday from 6 to 8 pm. The Frauenzentrum (see next heading) organises lesbian events.

Women Travellers Frauenzentrum (☎ 272 85 03), Mattengasse 27, is a women's centre which has a health centre (☎ 272 77 50) and a bar on the premises.

Dangers & Annoyances Zürich has a large contingent of hard drug users, who tend to congregate in specific (variable) locations. You may be hassled if you come across them.

Crime & Drugs

Switzerland may not have a high crime rate, but it doesn't pay to be too blasé about security. In the city of Zürich alone there were 636 armed robberies in 1995. Admittedly, crime is more of a problem in Zürich than anywhere else in Switzerland. There would seem to be a correlation between the rising crime figures and the rise in drug addicts in the city. Dealers and users (all drugs) known to the police numbered 9464 in 1995. Zürich is in danger of becoming an international drugs market: the products dirty the streets and the proceeds get laundered in the banks.

Switzerland hasn't yet worked out how to combat the drug problem. The drug culture was slow in catching up with the country, but now seems fully entrenched. Switzerland as a whole has the highest number of drug deaths in Europe per capita – in 1995 there were 87 drug deaths in the canton of Zürich alone.

In the 1970s and 1980s the authorities took a hard line on drug abuse, imposing sentences for dealing of up to 20 years imprisonment and a fine of up to Sfr1 million. The heavy-handed policy didn't work. In 1989 a narcotics commission recommended a soft approach, advocating legalisation of consumption. Drugs remain illegal, though some cantons now have 'fixer rooms' where addicts can inject themselves safely. But a liberal policy is not necessarily the answer either. Crime in Zürich peaked in 1991 during the operation of the infamous, now defunct 'Needle Park' (behind the National Museum) where heroin addicts were supplied with sterilised needles.

One thing is certain. The pushers won't go away – not when, to quote the narcotics commission, prices for heroin, cocaine and cannabis in Switzerland are 'among the highest in the world'. ∎

A different sort of annoyance is the cost of lockers in the train station – Sfr4!

Walking Tour

The pedestrian streets of the old town on either side of the Limmat River contain most of the major sights. Features to notice are winding alleyways, 16th and 17th-century houses and guildhalls, courtyards and fountains. Zürich has 1030 fountains and the locals insist the water is drinkable in them all. Don't be surprised if a waiter heads for the nearest fountain if you ask for tap water in a restaurant!

Lindenhof, a raised terrace on the west bank, has trees, gravel and giant chess games. This is the spot where the Romans founded their customs post in 15 BC. The elegant **Bahnhofstrasse** was built on the site of the city walls which were torn down 150 years ago. Underfoot are bank vaults crammed full of gold and silver. Zürich is one of the world's premier precious metals markets but the vaults (for some reason) aren't open to the public. The 13th century tower of **St Peter's Church**, St Peter-hofstatt, has the largest clock face in Europe (8.7m in diameter). The **Fraumünster Church** nearby is noted for the distinctive stained-glass windows in the choir, created by Marc Chagall in 1970, AND completed when he was 83. The building itself dates from the 13th century (closed lunchtime). Augusto Giacometti also made a window here, as well as in the **Grossmünster Cathedral** across the river, where Zwingli preached his message of 'pray and work' in the 16th century. The figure glowering from the south tower of the Grossmünster is Charlemagne, who founded the church that was originally at this location. This part of Zürich was once an island, said to be the burial site of the town's patron saints, Felix and Regula, who carried their heads here after they were decapitated by the Romans.

Museums

Museum of Fine Arts This is one of the most important of Zürich's many museums. Known as the Kunsthaus (☎ 251 67 65), it's

at Heimplatz 1. The large permanent collection ranges from 15th century religious art to the various schools of modern art. Most big names have works on display, such as Dali, Arp, Man Ray, Hockney, Bacon, Cézanne, Renoir, Manet, Monet and Gauguin. There's a fair sprinkling of Picassos, a whole room devoted to Marc Chagall and the largest Edvard Munch collection outside Scandinavia. Franz Gertsch's *Franz und Luciano* (1973) is a remarkable image in the photorealism genre, capturing seventies fashion.

Swiss artists are well represented, too. Johan Heinrich Füssli (1741-1825) favours waif-like, pale figures against dark backgrounds. Ferdinand Hodler's *Einmutigkeit* depicts a show-of-hands vote and dominates the stairway. On the 1st floor are many sculptures by Alberto Giacometti (pin-headed, lumpy, skinny figures with seven-league boots) and some of his paintings. The gallery is open Tuesday to Thursday from 10 am to 9 pm, and Friday to Sunday from 10 am to 5 pm. Entry costs Sfr5 (students and seniors Sfr3) except on Sunday when it's free. Temporary exhibitions always cost extra.

Swiss National Museum This museum (Schweizerisches Landesmuseum), is at Museumstrasse 2, housed in a pseudo-castle built in 1898. It gives the ultimate rundown on Swiss life and times from the prehistoric to the present. It exhibits a good selection of church art, plus weapons, coins, room interiors, costumes and utensils. The fresco in the Hall of Arms, the *Retreat of the Swiss Confederates at Marignano* is by Ferdinand Hodler. In the basement there's an interesting section on book-inscribing in the Middle Ages (the colour purple was extracted from snails), with some fine facsimiles of 14th-century books to leaf through. Opening hours are Tuesday to Sunday from 10 am to 5 pm and entry is free. Some signs are in English.

Other Museums The tourist office has information on many other museums, covering a range of interests. The **Zur Meisen** guildhall (see the Central Zürich map),

Münsterhof 20, was built in the 18th century and houses a collection of ceramics. Admission is free and it's closed on Monday. Also free is the **Zürich Toy Museum** (Züricher Spielzeugmuseum) at Fortunagasse 15 (closed mornings and Sunday). The measurement of time is the theme in the **Beyer Museum** at Bahnhofstrasse 31, open Monday to Friday from 10 am to noon and 2 to 4 pm (free entry). In the university on Rämistrasse 73, is an **Archaeological Collection**, mainly from southern Europe and the Middle East. It is open Tuesday to Friday from 1 to 6 pm and weekends from 11 am to 5 pm and entry is free. Look out also for the numerous private art galleries around the city.

The **Lindt & Sprüngli chocolate factory** is to the south at Seestrasse 204 (take bus No 165 from Bürkliplatz to Schooren). It has a free museum (ask for the extensive English notes) and a rather self-congratulatory film, but it's well worth visiting, not least for the very generous free gift of chocolate at the end. It's open Monday to Thursday from 9 am to noon and 1.30 to 4 pm, but phone ahead on ☎ 716 22 33. Coffee-lovers might want to make it to the free **Johann Jacobs Coffee Museum** (☎ 388 61 51), Seefeldquai 17. Or there's the **Hürlimann Brewery** (☎ 288 26 26), Brandschenke Strasse 150, which has free guided tours for groups, usually in German. Phone well in advance to request to join an existing group.

Zoo

Zoo Dolder, Zürichbergstrasse 221, vies with the zoo in Basel for the status of being the most important in the country. Whereas Basel's is in the city centre, this one is on the Zürichberg, allowing it to spread out more. It has 250 animal species from all around the world, in all about 2500 animals. It's open daily from 8 am to 6 pm (to 5 pm November to February). Entry costs Sfr12 (students Sfr6) and you can get there by tram No 5 or 6 from the town centre. The zoo backs on to Zürichberg, a large wood ideal for walks away from the noise of the city.

Activities

Don't neglect a stroll round the shores of Lake Zürich (Zürichsee). The concrete walkways give way to trees and lawns in the Arboretum on the west bank. Look out for the flower clockface at nearby Bürkliplatz. On the east bank, the Zurichhorn park has sculptures (eg by Jean Tinguely) and a Chinese Garden (Sfr7, open daily). The garden received plenty of publicity when it opened in 1994, but there's not much to it.

Locations for outdoor swimming and sunbathing are open from May to September, and entry costs around Sfr5. Well-known places are Utoquai, Utoquai 49, on the west shore of the lake and Mythenquai, Mythenquai 95, on the east shore. Other sports are listed in the *Sport in Zürich* booklet available from the tourist office.

Courses

Perhaps the best organisation for education courses, including language courses, is the Migros Klubschule (☎ 277 27 44; fax 277 28 97), Limmatstrasse 152.

Organised Tours

Informative if expensive guided walks around the old town, organised by the tourist office from June to September, last around 2½ hours and cost Sfr18 (Sfr14 for students, Sfr9 for children). The tourist office books tours ranging from a two-hour coach tour of Zürich (Sfr29) to day trips to Mt Titlis (Sfr110) and Lucerne (Sfr45). These are available year-round.

Special Events

Most shops are shut in the afternoon on the third Monday in April when Zürich's spring festival, **Sechseläuten**, is held. Guild members parade down the streets in historical costume and later complete a tour of the guildhalls, playing music. A fireworks-filled 'snowman' (the *Böögg*), is ignited at 6 pm to celebrate the end of winter. Another local holiday is **Knabenschiessen**, held during the second weekend of September. Events revolve around a shooting competition for 12 to 16-year-old youths. In November's

ZÜRICH CANTON

Central Zürich

0   100   200 m

PLACES TO STAY		29	Café Zähringer	22	Globetrotter Travel
3	Hotel Limmathof	37	Cafeteria zur Münz		Agency
5	Du Théâtre	40	Zeughauskeller	23	Zürich Toy
6	Hotel Martahaus	44	Mère Catherine		Museum
8	Hotel Scheuble	46	Bodega Española	28	Barfüsser
10	Alexander	47	Café Schlauch	30	Central Library
	Guesthouse	50	EPA Department	31	The Travel
20	Hotel Glockenhof		Store		Bookshop
25	Hotel Splendid	51	Kronenhalle	32	Oliver Twist
27	City Backpacker	52	Bauschänzli	34	Casa Bar
33	Hotel Goldenes			36	St Peter's Church
	Schwert	**OTHER**		38	Beyer Museum
35	Hotel Rothus	2	Coop Supermarket	39	Sprüngli
		7	Rheinfelder	41	American Express
PLACES TO EAT			Bierhalle	42	Fraumünster Church
1	McDonald's	9	Pestalozzi Library	43	Zur Meisen
4	Mensa Polyterrace	11	Heimatwerk		Guildhall
14	Brasserie Lipp	12	Police Station	45	Grossmünster
17	Manora	13	Billettzentrale		Cathedral
18	McDonald's		Ticket Office	48	German
19	Hilti Vegi	15	Buchhandlung Stäheli		Consulate
21	Coop Restaurant &		Bookshop	49	Bellevue Apotheke
	Supermarket	16	Swiss Bank	53	Bürkliplatz
24	Stadtküche		Corporation	54	Librairie Poyot
26	Königstuhl				

Expovina, wines from around the world can be sampled on the boats on Bürkliplatz (there's an entry fee).

Fasnacht brings lively musicians and a large, costumed procession. The carnival commences with typical Swiss precision at 11.11 am on 11 November, but the big parades and the liveliest atmosphere is saved until late February. A huge fairground takes over central Zürich during the **Züri Fäscht**, from Friday to Sunday at the start of July. It's only held once every three years; the next is in 1997. The **International June Festival** concentrates on music and the arts, and the **International Jazz Festival** takes place at the end of October.

Places to Stay

Accommodation can be a problem, particularly from August to October. Cheaper hotels fill early. Book ahead if you can, or use the information board and free phone in the train station. The tourist office accommodation service can sometimes get lower rates than those published. Private rooms are virtually nonexistent. Central hotels, although more convenient, are noisier, and parking can be a problem.

Places to Stay – bottom end

Camping *Camping Seebucht* (☎ 482 16 12) is on the west shore of the lake, four km from the city centre, at Seestrasse 559. It is well signposted and can be reached by bus No 161 or 165 from Bürkliplatz. It has good facilities including a shop and café, but it is only open from 1 May to 30 September. Prices are Sfr5.50 per person (10% discount with the International Camping Card), Sfr8 for a tent or Sfr10 for a camper van.

Hostels Some of the places mentioned are not strictly hostels, but they appear here because they offer dorm beds as well as comfortable private rooms.

The SYHA *hostel* (☎ 482 35 44) is at Mutschellenstrasse 114, Wollishofen, and has 24-hour service. To get there, take tram No 6 or 7 to Morgental, or the S-Bahn to Wollishofen. Four or six-bed dorms (with lockers) are Sfr29, and doubles are Sfr80. There's a restaurant, laundry facilities (Sfr8 to wash and dry), TV room (with CNN) and games.

More convenient is *City Backpacker* (☎ 251 90 15), Schweizerhofgasse 5, otherwise known as Hotel Biber and newly opened in 1994. Small dorms are Sfr30, reducing for multiple nights; singles/doubles are Sfr65/85 and triples/quads are Sfr115/140. Prices are without breakfast but there are kitchens, and showers are in the hall. Reception is closed from 11 am to 3 pm.

Hotel Martahaus (☎ 251 45 50; see the Central Zürich map), Zähringerstrasse 36, is in an excellent location in the old town. Singles/doubles/triples cost Sfr66/98/117, and Sfr32 gets you a place in a six-bed dorm which is separated into individual cubicles by partitions and curtains. There is a comfortable lounge and breakfast room, and a shower on each floor. Book ahead (telephone reservations OK), particularly for single rooms.

Foyer Hottingen (☎ 261 93 15), Hottingerstrasse 31, is run by nuns. Women, couples (married, ideally) and families are welcome, but the sisters of the cloth are wary of carousing young men, so single males are only accepted in an emergency. Singles/doubles are Sfr55/90 and triples/quads are Sfr105/120. Dorms (with lockers) for women only are Sfr25 or Sfr30. Showers cost Sfr1.50 each. Reception hours are from 8 am to midnight, and there's a midnight curfew. Telephone reservations are accepted.

OASE Evangelisches Haus (☎ 267 35 35), Freiestrasse 38, is a student residence, with kitchen facilities, available to tourists from July to October. Singles/doubles are Sfr80/130 with shower or Sfr65/110 without. Dorms with canvas beds are Sfr35. At weekends there's no breakfast and prices reduce by Sfr5 per person. Check-in by noon or from 5 to 7 pm.

Justinusheim (☎ 361 38 06), Freudenbergstrasse 146, is another student home. Most beds are available during student holidays (particularly from mid-July to mid-October), though it usually has a few vacancies in term time too. Singles/doubles are Sfr60/90 with shower or Sfr50/80 without.

Triples (using hall shower) are Sfr120. It's just a few paces away from the woods of Zürichberg, in an attractive old building with balconies, a terrace and good views of Zürich and the lake. Take tram No 10 from the Hauptbahnhof to Rigiplatz and then the Seilbahn to the top (it runs every few minutes and city network tickets are valid).

If you're really stuck consider staying at the *Salvation Army (Heilsarmee)* (☎ 298 90 00), Molkenstrasse 6. Four-bed rooms are Sfr31 per person and dinner is Sfr10, but it's a depressing atmosphere, with more than a hint of down-and-out territory.

Hotels *Hotel Splendid* (☎ 252 58 50), Rosengasse 5, offers a choice of old-style or newer rooms in the old town. Either type is good value, with singles/doubles/triples for Sfr58/96/127 (hall showers). The optional breakfast is Sfr10 and there's live piano music nightly in the bar downstairs.

Hotel Dufour (☎ 422 36 55), Seefeldstrasse 188, has acceptable if slightly dowdy rooms with double beds for Sfr65/75. Showers are in the hall and there's no breakfast. Reception in the bar downstairs is open daily from 9 am to midnight. Get there by tram No 2 or 4.

Hotel Poly (☎ 362 94 40), Universitätsstrasse 63, has fresh singles/doubles for Sfr55/80 using hall showers. Rooms from Sfr75/110 are bigger and have a TV and private shower. Rooms for Sfr110/170 also have a toilet.

Hotel St Georges (☎ 241 11 44), Weberstrasse 11, on the west bank of the Sihl river, is quiet and comfortable and has a lift; singles/doubles are Sfr69/98, using hall showers.

Places to Stay – middle
In the city centre, *Hotel Limmathof* (☎ 261 42 20; see the Central Zürich map), Limmatquai 142, has modern fittings but you may experience slight noise from the adjoining funicular and tram stops. Singles/doubles with bath or shower and WC are from Sfr100/125, and triples are Sfr180. The nearby *Alexander Guesthouse* (☎ 251

ZÜRICH CANTON

82 03), Niederdorfstrasse 40, offers shower/WC and TV as standard. Rooms cost from Sfr95/140 in the guesthouse section, or Sfr140/195 in the main hotel, where most rooms have air-conditioning.

Hotel Goldenes Schwert (☎ 252 59 40; see the Central Zürich map), Marktgasse 14, has singles/doubles for Sfr150/190, with bath and toilet. The staff thoughtfully (and significantly) lay out ear plugs in each room. Reception is opposite in the *Hotel Rothus*, which is quieter and has rooms using hall shower for Sfr75/95, as well a few rooms with private shower.

The following three-star places all have singles/doubles with shower/WC, cable TV and telephone. The *Hotel Scheuble* (☎ 251 87 95; see the Central Zürich map), is in the old town at Mühlegasse 17, and has sizeable singles/doubles starting at Sfr95/135 in winter and Sfr110/140 in summer. Also good is the *Du Théâtre* (☎ 252 60 62), nearby at Seilergraben 69, with rooms for Sfr130/180. The singles for Sfr80 have their own toilet but no access to a shower. Prices are around 30% lower in winter.

Regina (☎ 298 55 55), Hohlstrasse 18, is a recently refurbished hotel within a small red-light district. The reception is open 24 hours. Compact singles/doubles start from Sfr110/160 (lower in winter).

Places to Stay – top end

All rooms mentioned in this section have private shower or bath, toilet, TV, and other luxuries. The four-star *Hotel Glockenhof* (☎ 211 56 50; fax 211 56 60), Sihlstrasse 31, has singles/doubles from Sfr170/250, and a pleasant garden restaurant and terrace. The rooms are quiet and there is good disabled access. *Hotel Ambassador* (☎ 261 76 00; fax 251 23 94), Falkenstrasse 6, is near the lake but without lake views. Standard four-star rooms are Sfr220/320, or Sfr180/260 at weekends.

The top hotels in Zürich are very nearly the top hotels in the world. The pick of them all is perhaps the *Dolder Grand Hotel* (☎ 251 62 31; fax 251 88 29), Kurhausstrasse 65. This architecturally interesting place occupies a quiet and panoramic position on the edge of the Zürichberg. It has a whole heap of facilities including a nine-hole golf course, tennis courts, swimming pool, and ice rink (in winter), all of which are free to guests. Its restaurant is also highly rated, especially for its French cuisine. There is garage parking, or to get there by public transport take tram No 3, 8 or 15 to Römerhof and the Dolderbahn from there. Rooms cost upwards from Sfr370/490 for singles/doubles.

Slightly more affordable luxury comes from the modern high-rise *Hotel Zürich* (☎ 363 63 63; fax 363 60 15), Neumühlequai 42, overlooking the Limmat River. Extensive facilities include an indoor swimming pool, a sauna and a bowling alley. Singles/doubles start at Sfr280/330.

Places to Eat

Zürich has hundreds of restaurants serving all types of local and international cuisine. The Zürich speciality, Geschnetzeltes Kalbsfleisch (thinly sliced veal in a cream sauce), generally costs above Sfr20. Fastfood stands offer Bratwurst and bread from around Sfr4.50. There is a large *Coop* opposite the Hauptbahnhof (see the Central Zürich map), with late opening on Thursday. The *Migros* under the station in Bahnhofpassage is open every day till 8 pm (9 pm on Thursday). Beer halls (see the Entertainment section) are often good places for an inexpensive meal. From the tourist office, *Zürich News* lists a variety of restaurants, or there's the more detailed *Züricher Gastro-Spezialitätehführer*.

Places to Eat – bottom end

Self-Service *Mensa Polyterrace*, Leonhardstrasse 34 (see the Central Zürich map), is next to the Polybahn Seilbahn (funicular) exit, overlooking the city. It has good meals for Sfr10.50 (Sfr8.10 for ISIC holders) including vegetarian options. The self-service counters are open Monday to Friday from 11.15 am to 1.30 pm and 5.30 to 7 pm, and every second Saturday from 11.30 am to 1 pm. From mid-July to around mid-October it's open for lunch only. There is a café upstairs which is open longer hours and also popular. Just along the road, there is another *Mensa* in the university building, Rämistrasse 71, open Monday to Friday from 7.30 am to 8 pm, and alternate Saturdays to the Polyterrace.

The *Stadtküche* are state-subsidised kitchens, offering a limited choice of meals from around Sfr8.50. There are 19 of these dotted round the city, but the most convenient is the one at Schipfe 16, overlooking the Limmat and adjoining the Limmat-Club Zürich. It is open Monday to Friday from 11.30 am to 1.30 pm.

The underground area by the station is called Shop Ville, and it's a good place to find cheap food. *Silberkugel* is a basic café and takeaway with very low prices, open daily until 10 pm (7.30 pm Sunday). At the western end is *Restaurant Marché Mövenpick*, where well-presented buffet-style food costs around Sfr10 to Sfr18. Salad or vegetable plates are Sfr4.10 to Sfr10.80, and it's open daily from 6.30 am to 11 pm. Other branches of Silberkugel are at Löwenstrasse, Dreikönigstrasse and Limmatstrasse.

The *EPA* department stores on Sihlporte and at Stadelhoferstrasse each has a very cheap self-service restaurant. The Manor department store on Bahnhofstrasse has a good *Manora* buffet-style restaurant, and there is a *Migros* restaurant in the Migros City shopping centre at Löwenstrasse 35. A *Coop* restaurant and supermarket is in the Annahof department store on Bahnhofstrasse. All these places have late opening on Thursday until 9 pm. *Mr Wong*, opposite the train station, serves big portions of Asian food from Sfr11, and has a salad buffet. It's open daily from 11 am to 11.30 pm.

East Bank In the centre, explore the smaller streets off the main thoroughfares for the best value. *Café Schlauch*, Münstergasse 20, offers an unusual combination of pocket-less pool tables and food encompassing free-range meat and vegetarian dishes (from Sfr11). It's closed on Monday and Tuesday.

An 'alternative' café, run by a collective, is *Café Zähringer* on Spitalgasse (see the Central Zürich map). It serves up mostly organic, vegetarian food (from Sfr15), and is a good place for a coffee and a game of chess. Most Wednesday nights there's live music (usually free, with a collection for the band). It's open from 6.30 pm (5 pm on weekends) to midnight, and it's closed Mondays.

The *Spaghetti Factory*, Theater Strasse 10, has pizza and pasta for Sfr10 to Sfr20 (Sfr2 surcharge after 11.30 pm). Spaghetti Factory branches are of interest to late-night revellers as they keep late hours – this one is open daily from 11 am to 2 am (4 am on Friday and Saturday nights).

Mère Catherine (☎ 262 22 50; see the Central Zürich map), Nägelhof 3 near Schoffelgasse, is a popular French restaurant in a small courtyard, open daily from 11 am to midnight. The food is mostly mid-price (Sfr19.50 to Sfr36), unless you choose the lunchtime menus for Sfr14.50 or Sfr16.50 (not on Sunday).

West Bank *Clipper Restaurant*, Lagerstrasse 1, is basic and busy with good-value if simple meals for around Sfr12 to Sfr16. The 1st floor part is more expensive. Seating opens on to the pavement making it nice and cool in the summer and the cheap beer (Sfr4 for half a litre) attracts many local drinkers. It is open daily from 10 am to 11.30 pm.

Bernerhof (☎ 241 73 06), Zeughausstrasse 1, has satisfying, filling food in an unpretentious environment. Several daily menus from Sfr11.80 (including soup) are available midday and evening. It's open daily from 8 am (weekdays), 10 am (Sunday) or 3 pm (Saturday), up until midnight, though the kitchen closes at 9 pm. In the evening, locals come to drink and play board and card games.

Zürich is well-known for its cafés where you can linger over a coffee, soak up the atmosphere and maybe take a light meal. Try the entertaining *Cafeteria zur Münz* (see the Central Zürich map), Münzplatz 3, where Jean Tinguely mobiles hang from the ceiling. It is open Monday to Friday from 6.30 am to

7 pm (9 pm on Thursday), and Saturday from 8 am to 5 pm.

Places to Eat – middle

Vegetarians will have a field day in the meat-free environment of *Hiltl Vegi* (☎ 221 38 71; see the Central Zürich map), Sihlstrasse 28, on two floors. Varied lunches cost from Sfr16 and the salad buffet is very extensive but quite expensive (100 grams for Sfr3.50, or Sfr2.80 takeaway). Every evening at 6 pm there's an Indian buffet which costs Sfr4 per 100 grams, or it's Sfr36 for all you can eat.

Splurge on French food amid the mirrors and gleaming metal of *Brasserie Lipp Restaurant* (☎ 211 11 55; see the Central Zürich map), Uraniastrasse 9. The décor reflects the Parisien Belle Epoque period. A clientele of all ages is attracted by the wide choice of sumptuous dishes in the Sfr20 to Sfr40 range (open daily). Servings are generous and there are English menus.

Restaurant JOSEF (☎ 271 65 95), Gasometerstrasse 24, was re-modelled in 1996, and now has a bar area that stays open all day. Mainly youngish diners enjoy meals for around Sfr24 to Sfr34. Dishes change daily, encompassing varied styles, but often with an Italian emphasis. It's closed Saturday and Sunday lunchtime.

To sample quality Spanish fare (Sfr17 to Sfr45) go to *Bodega Española* (☎ 251 23 10; see the Central Zürich map), on the 1st floor at Münstergasse 15. The paella (Sfr37 per person) is a popular choice here, and rightly so. There is a good selection of Spanish wines from Sfr33.50 a bottle. Reserve ahead. The café-bar downstairs also does food.

Housed in a former armoury, *Zeughauskeller*, Paradeplatz, is an atmospheric, busy restaurant serving decent portions of Swiss food for around Sfr18 to Sfr30 (open daily). *Bauschänzli*, Stadthausquai, is worth visiting on a sunny summer's day. It is open-air and often has live music (middle-of-the-road). Meals are around Sfr15 to Sfr40.

Places to Eat – top end

As you might expect, there are plenty of these. *Königstuhl* (☎ 261 76 18; see the Central Zürich map) Stüssihofstatt 3, changed ownership in 1995 but still serves up excellent food (main courses from Sfr30). The bistro downstairs is cheaper (different menu, same kitchen), less formal, and open daily.

Kronenhalle (☎ 251 66 69), Rämistrasse, is a long-established restaurant attracting the artistic elite. Many original artworks (especially by Chagall) hang on the walls. Swiss/French dishes are Sfr25 to Sfr58 and it's open daily.

Flühgass (☎ 381 12 15), Zollikerstrasse 214, two km from the centre on the east bank, is the gourmet's choice for French food. *Riesbächli* (☎ 422 23 24), is another top restaurant; it's a little out of the way at Zollikerstrasse 157. Both places are closed on Saturday and Sunday.

Entertainment

Pick up from the tourist office the free events magazines, *Züritip* and *Zürich Next*. Tickets for most events in the city can be obtained from the *Billettzentrale* (☎ 221 22 83), Werdmühleplatz, off Bahnhofstrasse; it's open Monday to Friday from 10 am to 6.30 pm, Saturday to 2 pm. This government agency has minimal commission charges, and closes in July and August when activity in the arts die down. Zürich has a famous orchestra, the *Tonhalle*, which performs in the venue of the same name (☎ 206 34 34) at Claridenstrasse 7, as does the Zürich Chamber Orchestra. Prices are anything from Sfr10 to Sfr120, depending on the seat and the event. The *Opernhaus* (Opera House; ☎ 268 66 66), Falkenstrasse 1, also has a world-wide reputation.

The *Comedy Club* performs plays in English. Venues vary, so check the events magazines. Cinema prices are reduced to Sfr11 every Monday from their normal price of around Sfr15. Films are usually in the original language.

Many late-night pubs, clubs and discos are in Niederdorfstrasse and adjoining streets in the old town. This area is also a red-light district. If you're making a night of it in Niederdorfstrasse, kick off with a few cheap beers (Sfr4.10 for half a litre) at *Rheinfelder Bierhalle* at No 76 (see the Central Zürich map). The food is tasty and good-value, with all-day menus including soup starting from Sfr12.80. Opening hours are 9 am to midnight daily. There are many other beer halls in this part of town.

Down the road is the *Casa Bar*, Münstergasse 30 (see the Central Zürich map), a claustrophobic, crowded pub with live jazz from 8 pm daily (free entry but pricey drinks).

Around the corner is *Oliver Twist*, Rindermarkt, a magnet for English speakers, with draught Guiness and Irish and British sports on satellite TV. Happy hour is 4 to 8 pm daily.

Rote Fabrik (☎ 481 98 11 for music, ☎ 482 42 12 for theatre), Seestrasse 395, is a venue for alternative arts, though it's getting more mainstream nowadays. It has concerts most nights ranging from rock and jazz to avant-garde (Sfr15 to Sfr25), original-language films (Sfr10), theatre, dance, and a bar and restaurant. It's all closed on Monday. Take Bus No 161 or 165 from Bürkliplatz. *Kanslei,* Kansleistrasse, is another fairly alternative venue, and has a cinema (the Xenix Filmclub: ☎ 242 73 10), bar and disco. Zürich is also known for its rave/techno parties.

Barfüsser (☎ 251 40 64), Spitalgasse 14, is Switzerland's oldest gay bar, open daily from 5 pm to midnight.

Spectator Sport
Zürich has two football teams, which means there's a match in the city every weekend during the season. Ice hockey is played at the Hallenstadion in the district of Oerlikon.

In early August, Zürich hosts an important international athletics meeting at the Letzigrund stadium (take tram No 2).

Things to Buy
Bahnhofstrasse is a famous shopping street, and has large department stores, such as Manor, and specialist shops. Sprüngli (see Central Zürich map) is the place to go for quality confectionery. Many places have late

opening on Thursday. Heimatwerk is where you can get hand-made Swiss souvenirs, and the good quality is reflected in the prices. There's a large store on the west side of the Rudolf Brun bridge, and branches in the train station and airport.

At Rosenhof, in the old town on the east bank, there's a crafts market on Thursday and Saturday.

Getting There & Away
Air The major gateway of Kloten Airport is 10 km north of the city centre and has several daily flights to/from all important destinations. Swissair and Austrian Airlines share an office in the Hauptbahnhof (☎ 258 33 11) which is open Monday to Friday from 8 am to 6 pm and Saturday from 8.30 am to 1 pm. For Swissair reservations around the clock, ring ☎ 258 34 34. The airport has two terminals: terminal A is for flights by Swissair, Crossair, Austrian, Singapore, Sabena and Delta; all other airlines use terminal B. Parking is available and costs Sfr4 for one hour and Sfr36 for 24 hours.

Train The busy Hauptbahnhof has direct trains to Stuttgart (Sfr63), Munich (Sfr90), Innsbruck (Sfr66) and Milan (Sfr68) as well as to many other international destinations. There are also hourly departures to most Swiss towns, eg Lucerne (50 minutes, Sfr19.40), Bern (70 minutes, Sfr42) and Basel (65 minutes, Sfr30). Winterthur (Sfr10.20) is only 20 minutes away by train and there are four to five departures an hour.

Car & Motorcycle The N3 approaches Zürich from the south along the shore of Lake Zürich. The N1 is the fastest route from Bern and Basel and the main entry point from the west. The N1 also services routes to the north and east of Zürich.

Car Rental The agencies Europcar (☎ 271 56 56), Josef-Strasse 53, Hertz (☎ 242 84 84), Mortgarten strasse 5 and Avis (☎ 242 20 40), Gartenhofstrasse 17, all also have an airport branch. See the introductory Getting Around chapter for rates.

Of the local firms, V-Rent (☎ 321 33 69), Roswiesenstrasse 185, charges only Sfr100 per day (one to four days) including insurance and unlimited km. Sixt-Econo (☎ 201 13 13), Tödistrasse 9, is cheaper for longer-term rentals and has good weekend deals.

Hitching Zürich's Mitfahrzentrale (☎ 632 56 17) is at Leonhardstrasse 15. This agency links drivers and hitchers, but only for international journeys. It charges a commission of Sfr10 to Sfr20 and is only open Monday to Friday from noon to 1 pm.

Getting Around

The Airport You're unlikely to need a taxi (around Sfr40). On average, five trains an hour go to/from the Hauptbahnhof between around 6 am and midnight, and the journey takes 10 minutes. Don't board without first buying a ticket from the machine (Sfr5.40; press 8000), as tickets from the conductor cost Sfr12. Various cantonal buses also go to/from the airport.

Bus, Tram & Train There is a comprehensive and unified bus, tram and S-Bahn service in the city, which includes boats on the Limmat River. Operating times are approximately 5.30 am to midnight, and tickets must

---

Zürich's Transport System

In the 1970s Zürich's citizens voted against constructing an underground system, thereby forcing a re-introduction of the old city trams. Environmental concerns were paramount in this decision. It was backed up by the introduction of a non-profit ticket in the late 80s for use on the city's public transport network. Zürich was anxious to avoid the situation in cities like Los Angeles where an unbelievable 70% of ground space is devoted to the motor car – in the form of roads, car parks, driveways and petrol stations. In contrast, thanks to Zürich's forward-looking transport policy, car-parking spaces have been gradually converted over to pedestrian areas with seating and planted shrubs. Motorists have been enticed and persuaded to use public transport for commuting. The city's environmentally-sound transport policy even extends to providing free use of bicycles.

For the most part, ex-motorists are happy to use the tram network. The Swiss have studied the problem of how to make public transport an acceptable option, and they have concluded that what is psychologically crucial is not how long the journey takes, but how long one expects it to take. Reliability is therefore the key. The progress of trams in Zürich is monitored by a series of ultra-sound beacons at the roadside (those inconspicuous little boxes at junctions) which are triggered by passing trams but are unaffected by normal traffic. The signals are relayed back to transport headquarters which then passes instructions to the appropriate driver to either speed up or slow down. If a rogue tram route is shown to be consistently behind time, the schedule is adjusted accordingly. Zürich trams, therefore, should always be on time.

But reliability isn't the only criterion: waiting time is important too. Studies also showed that the average limit of acceptability for waiting is 10 minutes. Most Zürich trams run to six-minute intervals.

It is a pity that more cities worldwide don't follow Zürich's lead. Zürich's streets have always been clean, but now the air is cleaner too – trams are much more environmentally friendly than cars. Road junctions are safer as well – everybody knows who has the right of way as trams *always* have priority over cars. And the greening of the city is another positive effect – I'd rather spend time in a tree-lined pedestrian cul-de-sac than in a concrete car park. ■

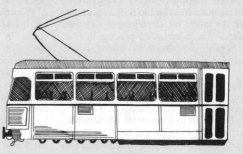

be bought in advance from dispensers at stops. The variety of tickets and zones available can be confusing. Short trips of five stops or less are Sfr2.10. The city of Zürich counts as zones one and two, for which a one-hour pass costs Sfr3.60. It's worth getting a 24-hour city pass for Sfr7.20 (press the blue key and return symbol). The range of this ticket is sufficient for most purposes, including very short trips on the lake. Seek advice from the counter staff in the train station if you want to take longer lake trips. Getting to the airport involves travel in an extra zone (Sfr10.80 for a 24-hour pass, including Zürich city).

A 24-hour pass valid for unlimited travel within the whole canton of Zürich costs Sfr28.40, including access to virtually all the lake. Zürich's suburban trains (S-Bahn) reach Baden, Schaffhausen, Stein am Rhein, Zug and Einsiedeln, but these places are just beyond the validity area of the cantonal ticket.

Nightbuses (Sfr5, passes not valid) depart from Bellevue at 1, 1.30 and 2 am for suburban destinations.

Taxi Taxis in Zürich are expensive even by Swiss standards, at Sfr6 plus Sfr3.20 per km.

Car & Motorcycle The tourist office has a list of car-parking garages in Zürich (eg there's one opposite the main post office). Parking on the street in the centre is a bit of a problem; streets with meters usually have a one hour maximum (Sfr2). Parking garages cost anything from Sfr1 to Sfr3.50 per hour, with the lowest rates applying to suburban garages. For unrestricted parking in blue zones, buy a day pass for Sfr10 from a police station.

Bicycle Rental in the Hauptbahnhof is open from 6 am to 11.30 pm. City bikes may be borrowed free of charge from early May to late October at four locations: Werdemühleplatz near the main station, Tessinerplatz by Enge station, Theaterplatz near Stadelhofen station and Marktplatz near Oerlikon station. There are 50 available at each depot and

they're open weekdays only from 7.30 am to 9.30 pm. A passport or identity card must be left as a deposit.

Boat Lake steamers leave from Bürkliplatz, departing every 30 to 60 minutes from early April to late October (Swiss Pass and Eurail valid, Inter-Rail 50% discount). For boat information, phone ☎ 482 10 33.

AROUND ZÜRICH
Uetliberg
One of the best short excursions to take from Zürich starts off with the train (line S10) to Uetliberg at 813m (takes 23 minutes, departures every 30 minutes). From here, there is a panoramic two-hour **Planetary Path** (Planetenweg) running along the mountain ridge overlooking the lake to Felsenegg. En route you pass models of the planets in the solar system: these and the distances between them are on a scale of one to 1000 million. At Felsenegg, a cable car descends every 10 minutes to Adliswill, from where frequent trains return to Zürich (line S4, takes 16 minutes).

Maur
The village of Maur is close to Lake Greifensee where swimming, boating and hiking are possible.

A good possibility for accommodation is in the farming village of Maur, 10 km southeast of the city. Reinhard Lüder (☎ 01-980 22 48), Kehlhofstrasse 518, Maur, offers bed and breakfast in his 200-year old country house. In this friendly, health-conscious place there are vegetarian meals (Sfr6), a kitchen, bike rental for only Sfr1 per day, and a washing machine for Sfr3 per load. Smoking is not allowed in the house. Singles/doubles/triples are Sfr34/56/75, and every 7th night is free (telephone ahead).

Get to Maur from Zürich by taking tram No 3, 8 or 15 to Klusplatz, then a 20-minute bus ride on No 747 to Maur Dorf. The whole journey can be undertaken on a Sfr6.80 ticket (Sfr13.60 for a 24-hour pass).

Winterthur

• *pop 89,000* • *447m* • *☎ (052)*

Although a mechanical engineering and textiles centre, Winterthur attracts visitors with its impressive museums and art galleries – 15 in all.

Orientation & Information

Winterthur is in the north-east of Zürich canton and has a compact old town centre. Exit the train station on the platform 1 side for the tourist office (☎ 212 00 88), Bahnhofplatz 12. Opening hours are Monday to Friday from 8 am to noon and 2 pm to 6 pm, and Saturday from 9 am to noon and 2 to 4 pm.

Budget travel agency, SSR (☎ 213 81 25), is at Neustadtgasse 1a, with late opening on Thursday (closed weekends and Monday morning).

The main post office (Hauptpost, 8401) is opposite the train station.

Things to See & Do

Winterthur owes much of its eminence as an art centre to Oskar Reinhart, who turned his back on the banking and insurance enterprises of his powerful family and collected art instead. Upon his death in 1965, the whole collection was bequeathed to the nation and entrusted to his home town. The **Sammlung Oskar Reinhart am Römerholz** is sited in his former home at Haldenstrasse 95, a 20-minute walk or short bus ride (No 3 to Spital) from the centre. The extensive impressionist section includes works by Van Gogh, Renoir, Manet, Monet and Cézanne, plus there are notable paintings by Rubens, Rembrandt, Greco and Goya.

Less well-known but conveniently central is the collection of Swiss, German and Austrian art at the **Museum Oskar Reinhart am Stadtgarten**, which he established during

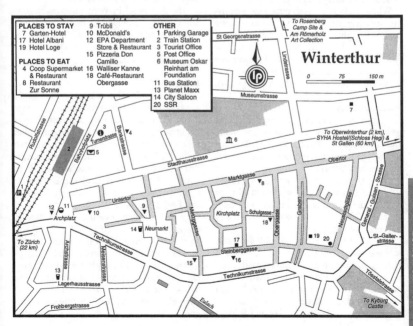

his lifetime. Entry for each gallery costs Sfr6 (Sfr4 for students) and they are open daily except Monday from 10 am to 5 pm. The Stadtgarten is a relaxing park graced by several naked ladies (in statue form only).

The **Swiss Technorama**, Technorama-strasse 1 in Oberwinterthur, has hands-on exhibits and creative displays that demystify science and technology. It's open from Tuesday to Sunday from 10 am to 5 pm and costs Sfr13 (Sfr7 for children). To get there, take bus No 5 from the bus station to its terminus.

Winterthur also has four castles, including one that houses the hostel. The best is the **Kyburg Castle**, six km south of town over the Töss River. Dating from the 10th century, it was occupied by the Habsburgs for several centuries until possession was won by the city of Zürich in 1452. It has an interesting Romanesque chapel and makes a good starting place for a number of hikes. Admission costs Sfr4 (students and children Sfr3); it's closed on Monday and in December.

When walking around, notice the surprising number of specialist shops selling designer lights. The ridiculous prices – Sfr100 to Sfr1200 or more – makes one speculate with envy at the size of the average Swiss disposable income (or cringe with horror at Swiss concepts of interior design).

Places to Stay
Finding accommodation can be difficult in spring and autumn when there are many trade conventions, but the tourist office can help with its room-booking service for personal callers (Sfr3).

The camping site *Rosenberg* (☎ 212 52 60), open year-round, is on the outskirts of Winterthur by an area of woodland. Get there by taking bus No 3 to Seuzacherstrasse and walking five minutes north.

The SYHA *hostel* (☎ 242 38 40) is at Schloss Hegi, Hegifeldstrasse 125. It's a friendly place in a 15th century castle, and has large dorms and a kitchen (Sfr2). Beds are just Sfr16 (Sfr14 after the first night) without breakfast. Reception is closed from 10 am to 2 pm (5 pm Monday and Friday)

and the hostel is open from 1 March until 31 October. Take bus No 1 or the train to Oberwinterthur and then it's 10 to 15 minutes' walk to the castle.

Hotel prices are sky high in the centre. The cheapest place is *Albani* (☎ 212 69 96), Steinberggasse 16, with singles/doubles/triples without breakfast for Sfr70/90/110. It's only good value if you like music (see the following Entertainment section) – guests get free entry to see bands, though the bands themselves often occupy all the rooms. Light, sparsely-furnished rooms with shower/WC and cable TV are at *Hotel Loge* (☎ 213 91 21), Graben 6, and cost Sfr140/170. There's a cinema and theatre downstairs.

You get better value to the east of the town centre: *Grüntal* (☎ 232 25 52), Im Grüntal 1, Oberseen (take bus No 6), offers singles/doubles with private shower from Sfr75/120, and some showerless singles for Sfr60; *Hotel Römertor* (☎ 242 69 21), Guggenbühlstrasse 6 (take bus No 1), has three-star rooms from Sfr115/160 with private shower.

The best hotel in Winterthur is the four-star *Garten-Hotel* (☎ 212 19 19; fax 213 68 70), Stadthausstrasse 4, with convenient parking and good facilities. Singles/doubles start at Sfr140/200.

Places to Eat
There is a *Coop* supermarket and restaurant near the tourist office at Bankstrasse, open to 9 pm Thursday. An *EPA* department store beckons by the bus station on Bahnhofplatz (open to 8 pm Thursday). Hot food costs from Sfr7 to Sfr15, including vegetarian dishes, and the salad buffet is cheaper (if smaller) than at Coop. Look out also for the open-air markets in the centre on Tuesday and Friday morning.

Elsewhere, cheap eating can be hard to come by. *Pizzeria Don Camillo*, Steinberggasse 51, is popular but the quality is only average. Pasta/pizza starts at Sfr12 (closed Sunday and Monday). *Café-Restaurant Obergasse*, on the corner of Obergasse and Schulgasse is a lively place with a young clientele. It serves good-sized plates of spaghetti and various salads, with most dishes in the range of Sfr12 to Sfr25. The beer is inexpensive (closed Monday and during the day at weekends).

Restaurant Zur Sonne, Marktgasse 15, offers many varieties of Rösti from Sfr14, and lunch and evening specials (with soup) start at Sfr16.50. There is a 1st floor terrace and it is open daily.

More staid but quite cosy is the *Walliser Kanne* (☎ 212 81 71), Steinberggasse 25, which specialises in fondues from Sfr22.50. Other dishes start at Sfr25, though there are cheaper two-course lunch menus (from Sfr13.50). It is closed on Saturday and Sunday in summer.

For top quality dining go to *Trübli* (☎ 212 55 36) on Bosshardengässchen 5, just near Untertor. Main dishes start at Sfr35 or you can go for the three to six-course menus for Sfr66 to Sfr105 (closed Sunday and Monday).

Entertainment

A good area for a lively time is Neumarkt, off Untertor in the old town. There are several music bars grouped together, including *City Saloon* at No 5, and it's fairly chaotic with people spilling out into the street. Live music can be heard most nights (except in summer) at the *Albani Bar*, Steinberggasse 16 (entry Sfr15 to Sfr30). *Planet Maxx*, Archstrasse 8, is an evening entertainment complex containing various bars, clubs and discos (entry free or up to Sfr18) – most are closed Monday and Tuesday.

Getting There & Away

There are several trains an hour to Zürich airport (takes 15 minutes, Sfr6.80) and Zürich itself (Sfr10.20). Many trains also run to Schaffhausen and Lake Constance. By road, the N1 (E60) motorway goes from Zürich, skirts Winterthur and continues to St Gallen and Austria. Main roads also go to Constance and Schaffhausen.

Getting Around

All buses go to/from the bus station by the train station. Single bus journeys in the town cost Sfr2.10, though it's Sfr3.60 to Oberwinterthur (get a 24-hour pass for Sfr7.20 instead). Rent bicycles from the train station. There's a cheap parking garage behind the station.

North-West Switzerland

The north-west is a densely populated area, where affluent towns fill the landscape rather than the scenic vistas found elsewhere. Coincidentally, four out of Switzerland's five nuclear power stations are in this region. To enjoy the countryside you need to nip over to Germany and the Black Forest, easily accessible from Basel.

The relative dearth of scenic attractions does not mean that the region is not worth a visit. There are some fine old town centres and some particularly diverting museums and art galleries. In any case, Basel is such an important transport hub that you're quite likely to spend some time here, one way or another.

The north-west comprises the cantons of Basel (split into two half-cantons, City and District, in 1833), Aargau, and Solothurn. Although the Basel tourist office is nominally the regional office, and has information on the whole area, administrative functions have largely been devolved to the local tourist offices.

Basel

• *pop 190,000* • *273m* • ☎ *(061)*

Basel (Bâle in French, sometimes Basle in English) is Switzerland's second largest city. It is a major centre for commerce, particularly the chemical and pharmaceutical industry, yet retains an attractive old town and offers many interesting museums. Influences from neighbouring France and Germany and a large student population make Basel a vibrant and creative city. It is also the home of the liveliest carnival in Switzerland. Don't miss it if you're in the country on the Monday after Ash Wednesday.

Basel had its origins as a Roman settlement founded in 44 BC, and was successively occupied by the Alemanni, Franks and

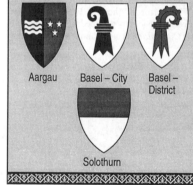

HIGHLIGHTS

- Museums and nightlife in Basel, a town where three countries meet
- Basel's famous Fasnacht, a festival starting at 4 am
- Churches, fountains and weaponry in Solothurn
- Baden – health spa dating from Roman times

Aargau   Basel – City   Basel – District

Solothurn

Burgundians until it became part of the Germanic Empire in 1032. By this time the Bishop of Basel has already been granted secular authority over the town by the Emperor Henry II. The town hosted the Council of Basel (1431-48), which attempted (unsuccessfully) to avoid a schism in the Catholic church. In 1460, under the patronage of Pope Pius II, the University of

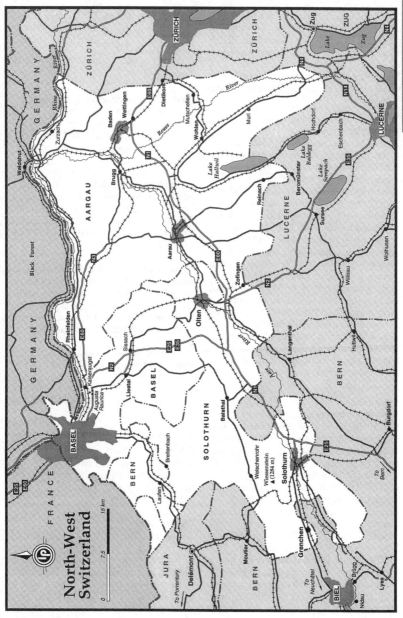

North-West Switzerland

Basel was opened, the oldest in Switzerland. Basel joined the Swiss Confederation in 1501 and 28 years later adopted the Reformation. The famous Renaissance humanist, Erasmus of Rotterdam, was associated with the city and his tomb rests in the cathedral. Basel reached the peak of its influence in the 18th century.

Orientation

Basel's strategic position on the Rhine River at the dual border with France and Germany has been instrumental in its development as a commercial and cultural centre. On the north bank of the Rhine is Kleinbasel (Little Basel), surrounded by German territory. The pedestrian-only old town and most of the sights are on the south bank in Grossbasel (Greater Basel). Historically, the 'Klein' tag was partially a denigrating term as it was a working-class locality. The statue of *Lälle Keenig*, or 'Tongue King' (at the crossroads at the southern end of the Mittlere Brücke) sticking his tongue out at the northern section, just about sums up the old attitude.

Grossbasel has the SBB Bahnhof, the train station for travel in Switzerland. Tram Nos 1 and 8 go from here to the old town centre. In Kleinbasel is the BBF Bahnhof, the station for travel to Germany.

Information

Tourist Offices The main tourist office (☎ 261 50 50; fax 261 59 44) and a train information counter are by the Mittlere Brücke (bridge) at Schifflände 5. Opening hours are Monday to Friday from 8.30 am to 6 pm, and Saturday from 10 am to 4 pm. Less than two km south is the main SBB Bahnhof which has bike rental (7 am to 9 pm daily), money exchange (6 am to 9 pm daily) and another tourist office (☎ 271 36 84), open Monday to Friday from 8.30 am to 6 pm, and Saturday from 8.30 am to 12.30 pm. This tourist office is open additional hours between April and September: up to 7 pm weekdays and from 1.30 to 6 pm Saturdays; from 1 June it is also open on Sunday from 10 am to 2 pm.

Foreign Consulates The German Consulate (☎ 693 33 03) is at Schwarzwaldallee 200, on a long road parallel to the BBF station. The French Consulate (☎ 272 63 18) is at Elisabethenstrasse 33, not far from the SBB station.

Post & Communications The main post office (4001 Basel 1, Freie Strasse) is in the centre, though by the SBB train station there's a large post office (4002 Basel 2, Post Passage 9) with a daily emergency counter (surcharge payable).

Travel Agencies SSR (☎ 284 90 60) has an office at Steinenberg 19, open Monday to Friday from 10 am to 6 pm and Saturday from 10 am to 1 pm. The American Express travel representative is Reise Müller (☎ 281 33 80), Steinenvorstadt 33.

Bookshops Jäggi Buchhandlung, Freie Strasse 32, is a large store with English and travel books. Specialising mainly in English texts is Tanner, Streitgasse 5. For travel books and maps the best place is Buchhandlung Bider, Steinenvorstadt 79, ☎ 061 281 99 94.

Medical & Emergency Services The Cantonal Hospital (☎ 265 25 25), Petersgraben 2, has a casualty department. telephone ☎ 117 for the police and ☎ 144 for an ambulance.

Gay & Lesbian A gay and lesbian centre, Schlez (☎ 631 55 88), is at Gärtnerstrasse 55, in northern Kleinbasel. Arcados (☎ 681 31 32), Rheingasse 69, is a gay bookshop with an information service, open Tuesday to Saturday in the afternoon.

Walking Tour

The tourist office hands out free do-it-yourself guides to walks through the old town, taking in cobbled streets, colourful fountains and 16th century buildings. The **Fischmarkt** is the core of the old town, and is graced by a Gothic fountain. The **Spalentor** gate tower is 700 years old, a remnant from the time when the city was encircled by a protective wall. The **town hall** *(Rathaus)* was built in the 16th century and has been impressively restored. It looks very patrician with its vivid red façade, embellished with shields, painted figures and a golden spire. Don't omit to peek into the frescoed courtyard; the statue here depicts Munatius Plancus, the founder of the town.

The 12th century **cathedral** *(Münster)* is an unmistakable landmark, with Gothic spires built in red sandstone. Take in the view of the Rhine from the rear. Also noteworthy is its Romanesque St Gallus doorway, fringed by a scene showing the Judgement of the Dead.

Be sure to take a look at the **Tinguely Fountain** on Theaterplatz. It's a typical display by the Swiss sculptor, Jean Tinguely, with madcap machinery playing water games with hoses – art with a juvenile heart. By the tourist office in the SBB train station is another example of his work, a massive mobile incorporating steel girders, wheels, coloured lights and animal heads. He died shortly after finishing it, before it was even officially opened in late 1991.

Museums

Depending upon taste and inclination, you could spend days in Basel's 35 museums. Contemporary arts, history, ethnography, natural history, musical instruments, cinema and pharmaceuticals are just some of the fields explored. Ask for the museums booklet in English from the tourist office. Most museums are closed on Monday (but not all); a few are free, and many of the others (cantonal museums) are free on the first Sunday of the month. Consider buying the museum pass, valid for three days for most museums. It costs Sfr23 (Sfr16 senior citizens, Sfr46 families).

The **Museum of Fine Arts** (Kunstmuseum), St Albangraben 16, is the largest art collection in Switzerland, and covers religious, Swiss and modern art. Important German artists represented include Konrad Witz and Holbein the Younger. Rodin's *The Burghers of Calais* stands in the courtyard.

The museum is open Tuesday to Sunday from 10 am to 5 pm, and costs Sfr7 (students Sfr5; free to all on the first Sunday in the month). It has an excellent collection of Picasso's work. The artist was so gratified when the people of Basel paid a large sum for two of his paintings that he donated a further four from his own collection.

The Paper Mill (Papiermühle), St Alban Tal 37, won an award as the best museum in Europe. You can make your own paper and watch the experts at work (Sfr8, students Sfr5; open Tuesday to Sunday from 2 to 5 pm).

Zoo

Basel's zoo rivals Zürich's in importance. It's laid out in a large rectangular park near the SBB station, and has a varied collection from around the world. Some of the rare and highly prized species on display include Indian rhinos, pygmy hippos, golden lion tamarins and king penguins. Feeding times *(Fütterungen)* are displayed by the entrance and are fun to watch. The big cats devour bloody slabs of meat at 4 pm daily. It is open daily from 8 am to 6.30 pm (5.30 pm winter, 6 pm March, April, September and October) and costs Sfr10 for adults, Sfr8 for students and senior citizens, Sfr4 for children, and Sfr24 for families.

Markets

There's a daily fruit and vegetable market in Marktplatz. Barfüsserplatz is the venue for the flea market (every 2nd and 4th Wednesday in the month from January to mid-October), the Christmas Market, and the Autumn Fair (starting the Saturday preceding 30 October, and continuing for over two weeks).

Organised Tours

Contact the main tourist office for details. Most tours are from mid-May to mid-October. Options include city tours by foot (Sfr12) or bus (Sfr20), or a tour of Germany's Black Forest (Sfr45).

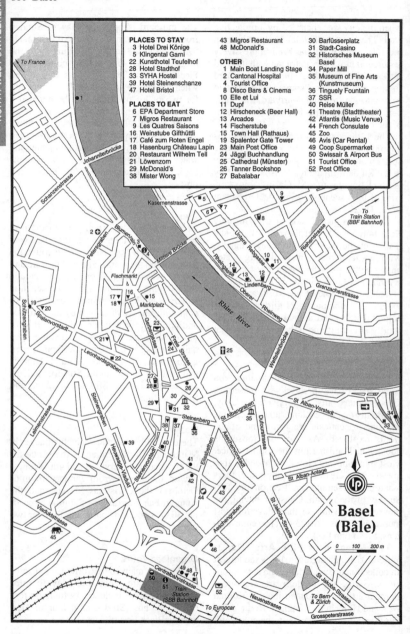

PLACES TO STAY
3 Hotel Drei Könige
5 Klingental Garni
22 Kunsthotel Teufelhof
28 Hotel Stadthof
33 SYHA Hostel
39 Hotel Steinenschanze
47 Hotel Bristol

PLACES TO EAT
6 EPA Department Store
7 Migros Restaurant
9 Les Quatres Saisons
16 Weinstube Gifthüttli
17 Café zum Roten Engel
18 Hasenburg Château Lapin
20 Restaurant Wilhelm Tell
21 Löwenzorn
29 McDonald's
38 Mister Wong

43 Migros Restaurant
48 McDonald's

OTHER
1 Main Boat Landing Stage
2 Cantonal Hospital
4 Tourist Office
8 Disco Bars & Cinema
10 Elle et Lui
11 Dupf
12 Hirscheneck (Beer Hall)
13 Arcados
14 Fischerstube
15 Town Hall (Rathaus)
19 Spalentor Gate Tower
23 Main Post Office
24 Jäggi Buchhandlung
25 Cathedral (Münster)
26 Tanner Bookshop
27 Babalabar

30 Barfüsserplatz
31 Stadt-Casino
32 Historsches Museum Basel
34 Paper Mill
35 Museum of Fine Arts (Kunstmuseum)
36 Tinguely Fountain
37 SSR
40 Reise Müller
41 Theatre (Stadttheater)
42 Atlantis (Music Venue)
44 French Consulate
45 Zoo
46 Avis (Car Rental)
49 Coop Supermarket
50 Swissair & Airport Bus
51 Tourist Office
52 Post Office

Basel
(Bâle)

0   100   200 m

Special Events

Basel is a carnival town. At the end of January, **Vogel Gryff** is when winter is chased away from Kleinbasel. Three key figures are the griffin *(Vogel Gryff)*, the savage *(Wilde Mann)* and the lion *(Leu)*.

On the Monday after Ash Wednesday, Basel commences a three-day celebration, the **Fasnacht** spring carnival. It kicks off exactly at 4 am with the **Morgestraich**, when the street lights are suddenly extinguished and the procession starts to wend its way through the central district. All the participants wear elaborate costumes and masks. Some carry large painted lanterns, others have lights dangling from their heads, and in between the marchers are musicians in alternating sections playing flutes or drums. Bars and cafés stay open all night to ensure the celebrations don't flag. SBB puts on special night trains from other towns for this event. The main parades are on the Monday and Wednesday afternoon, when the large floats get wheeled out and fruit, flowers, confetti and candies are thrown into the crowd. On Tuesday afternoon is the children's parade. Speciality food for the carnival is *Zibelewaaire*, an onion flan.

Trade fairs play an important part in the Basel calendar, and have done so ever since the city was granted its licence to stage such events in 1471. The **Autumn Fair** at the end of October and the **Swiss Industries Fair** (MUBA), held every spring, are the most important ones.

Places to Stay

Hotels are expensive and liable to be full during the numerous trade fairs and conventions (when prices rise). Be sure to book ahead. There are no trade fairs in July and August, which helps during these months. The tourist office in the SBB Bahnhof reserves rooms for Sfr10 commission. The same service is undertaken in the Schifflände office for Sfr5. Check the tourist office hotel list for cheaper, out-of-town places.

Places to Stay – bottom end

Camping Six km south of the SBB train station is *Camp Waldhort* (☎ 711 64 29) at Heideweg 16, Reinach. To get there, take tram No 11 to Landhof. It's open from March to October.

Hostel The SYHA *hostel* (☎ 272 05 72) is fairly near the centre of town at St Alban Kirchrain 10. Dorm beds are Sfr26.80 and double rooms are Sfr37.80 per person. Reception is shut from 11 am to 2 pm, when the doors are also locked. Curfew is at midnight.

The flamboyant Basel Carnival sees a parade of wonderful masks and eccentric costumes, accompanied by the music of drums and pipes.

The First Hippie

The first man ever to take an LSD 'trip' was Swiss. In 1943 Albert Hofmann was a chemist working for the Sandoz drug company in Basel. While conducting tests during a search for a migraine cure he synthesised lysergic acid diethylamide (LSD), and the chemical was accidentally absorbed through his fingertips. Shortly afterwards the mind-bending sensations began, and he experienced a powerful series of psychedelic pictures and a dreamlike state.

Hofmann's next excursion with the drug, a deliberate experiment, produced the first 'bad trip', in which he thought a demon had invaded him and his neighbour was a witch. Heavy, man!

The drug was soon taken up by writers and artists, such as Aldous Huxley, who saw it as a creative and elevating force. It was later crucial in the evolution of the 60s flower generation, who believed it could be an instrument for world peace. From 1953 the CIA conducted extensive tests, lasting many years, to establish its usefulness as a truth drug. Tests on whether LSD had any clinical value were curtailed when the drug was outlawed in 1966.

Fifty years after his discovery, Mr Hofmann (then 87) defended the drug in an interview with a British newspaper *(The Independent)*, saying medical tests should be carried out to establish its potential. He went on to express the hope that LSD may one day become part of our mainstream culture, with the same acceptability as alcohol.

In the meantime, mine's a pint. ■

Budget Hotels Unfortunately, there aren't really any of these. In the old town, *Hotel Stadthof* (☎ 261 87 11), Gerbergasse 84, has standard singles/doubles for Sfr80/160 (less in low season), but without breakfast. Reception is in the restaurant on the 1st floor. In Kleinbasel, try *Klingental Garni* (☎ 681 62 48), Kasernenstrasse 20. This hotel/restaurant also charges around Sfr80 per person (with breakfast), though extensive renovations in 1996 may raise prices. In both places the shower and toilet are off the corridor.

Near the pedestrian zone is *Hotel Steinenschanze* (☎ 272 53 53), Steinengraben 69, which has uncluttered white singles/doubles from Sfr100/140 with private shower and toilet. The price for students is reduced to Sfr50 per person for the first three nights, except during trade fairs.

Hotel Bristol (☎ 271 38 22), Centralbahnstrasse 15, is right outside the SBB station. Rooms are fair-sized and reasonably comfortable, though you may experience some noise from the long-term building works outside. Singles/doubles are Sfr95/140, reduced to Sfr85/110 in the off season. Doubles with own bathroom are Sfr140 and triples (hall showers) are Sfr180. There are some small singles (so-called 'B Zimmer') for Sfr75 or Sfr65 but these can be hard to get.

Places to Stay – middle

The most interesting hotel in Basel is the *Kunsthotel Teufelhof* (☎ 261 10 10; fax 261 10 04), Leonhardsgraben 47. Each of the rooms was assigned to a different artist to create a piece of environmental art. All rooms will stay intact for about two years before being reassigned to a new artist. The shock of waking up in a piece of art is quite something. The rooms have private bath or shower and toilet, and prices start at Sfr215/280 for single/double occupancy. Some rooms are more elaborately kitted out than others, but all are a welcome respite from standard hotel fixtures. Prices are Sfr145/260 in the newly opened Galeriehotel annex. Its expensive 1st floor restaurant has an excellent reputation, and there is also a bar, Weinstube and two theatres on site.

Places to Stay – top end

If you can afford to really splash out on accommodation, make for the *Drei Könige* (☎ 261 52 52; fax 261 21 53), Blumenrain 8. It has welcomed luminaries through its portals since 1026 – royals such as Princess (later Queen) Victoria, and the likes of Napoleon, Voltaire and Dickens. You can join them, but only if you can afford the king's ransom of at least Sfr255/420 for a single/double. Breakfast buffet is Sfr29 extra. The three kings referred to in the hotel's name were Emperor Conrad II, his son, the future Henry III, and the last king of Burgundy, Rudolf III, who met in the inn in the year it was founded. As a result of their meeting the territory that became Switzerland was incorporated into the Germanic Empire. The present building dates from 1844, and the three kings on the façade are now the three wise men.

Places to Eat

Eating is generally a better deal in Basel than accommodation. The train station has an *Aperto* supermarket (open daily from 7 am to 11.30 pm), though prices are lower across the road at *Coop*, open daily from 6 am (9 am on Sunday and holidays) to 10 pm.

Self-Service Cross the bridge over the tracks by the SBB post office to get to Güterstrasse. Here you will find *Migros* at No 180 and *Coop* at No 190. Both have a restaurant with meals from Sfr8, a salad bar, and late opening until 8 pm on Thursday. The *EPA* department store, Untere Rebgasse, Kleinbasel, is equally cheap, and also open till 8 pm on Thursday. Other *Migros* restaurants are on Untere Rebgasse (opposite EPA) and on Sternengasse.

Mister Wong, Steinenvorstadt 1a, offers a reasonable choice of Asian dishes. Heaped portions on smallish plates cost from Sfr10, and there's a salad bar. It is open daily to 10.30 pm except on Friday and Saturday when it closes at 11.30 pm.

Other Restaurants *Restaurant Wilhelm Tell*, Spalenvorstadt 38, by the Spalentor city gate, is very small, simple and busy, but it's still worth paying a visit for tasty Swiss dishes from Sfr14.50. It's open daily, with Röstis available evening only. For Italian and Tunisian food, call in at *Restaurant Salmen* next door (closed Sunday).

For Basel specialities in a typical ambience, try *Weinstube Gifthüttli* (☎ 261 16 56), Schneidergasse 11. Meals start at Sfr14.50, with more expensive choices available in the smarter section upstairs. Menus are written in incomprehensible Swiss-German dialect, with English and German translations. Opposite is the slightly more down-to-earth *Hasenburg Château Lapin*, with snacks and meals from Sfr6.50 to Sfr36. Drinkers mostly fill the tables in the evening. Both places are closed Sunday. Vegetarians should check the environmentally sound *Café Zum Roten Engel* in the adjoining courtyard, with outside tables. There's a limited choice of organic vegetarian food and fish dishes for around Sfr12.50 to Sfr15, plus breakfasts. Many types of tea are available, though it's also well known for huge cups of milky coffee (Sfr3.90). It's open daily until 8 pm (9 pm on Thursday). *Löwenzorn* (☎ 261 42 13), Gemsberg 2, is something of a local secret, serving typical Swiss fare. This 16th century house offers a choice of four dining areas and a courtyard garden. There are small dishes from Sfr9.50 and lunch menus with soup from Sfr13.80, though most meals are in the range Sfr17 to Sfr40 (closed Sunday).

Stucki (☎ 361 82 22), Bruderholzallee 42, in the suburbs south of the SBB station, is rated in the top three restaurants in all Switzerland (closed Sunday and Monday). You have to pay for the reputation, of course, with à la carte main courses costing Sfr40 to Sfr75 and menus above Sfr100, but its creative concoctions merit a taste. Duck (*le canard* in French) is a speciality at Sfr130 for two (closed Sunday and Monday). Duck (Sfr62) is also a favoured choice at *Les Quatre Saisons* (☎ 691 80 44) in the Hotel Europe, Clarastrasse 43. This popular gourmet French restaurant is closed Sunday.

Entertainment

Basel has a busy cultural scene, with many theatre groups and two symphony orchestras. *Basel Live*, free from the tourist office, comes out every two weeks and contains full listings.

For more basic evening entertainment, explore the beer halls, especially in Kleinbasel. *Fischerstube*, Rheingasse 45, brews its own beer. There are four varieties, starting at Sfr4.50 per half litre. A good place that attracts an 'alternative' crowd is

Hirscheneck (☎ 692 73 33), Lindenberg 23. Beer is Sfr5.10 for a 0.58-litre bottle. It serves food and has live music downstairs (entry around Sfr10) at 9 pm on Saturday (not in summer). On Friday there's a year-round disco (entry from Sfr5). Gay bars nearby are *Dupf* at Rebgasse 43, and *Elle et Lui* at Rebgrasse 39 (both open daily from 4 or 5 pm). At Claraplatz there's are stairs leading down to several disco bars and a cinema.

On the Grossbasel side, try the late-night bars in the *Stadt-Casino* complex on Barfüsserplatz. *Atlantis* (☎ 272 20 38), Klosterbergstrasse 13, is one of the best venues in town. It has live music nightly (mainly rock, R & B and jazz), and entry costs anything up to Sfr35. Sometimes it's free, but with a drinks surcharge. Another good place is *Babalabar*, Gerbergasse 76. It has a disco section with different musical themes nightly, where entry costs Sfr5 during the week (closes midnight) or Sfr10 on Friday and Saturday (closes 2 am). Entry is free after 11.30 pm and beer is Sfr5 for 0.30 litre.

Getting There & Away

Air The airport serving Basel is five km away in Mulhouse, France. Telephone the Basel number (☎ 325 31 11) for information. There are several flights daily to main European destinations. There's a Swissair/ Austrian Airlines office at the SBB station; the number for reservations is ☎ 284 55 55.

Train Basel is a major European rail hub. For most international trains you pass the border controls in the station, so allow extra time to make your connection. All trains to France go from SBB Bahnhof. There are four to five trains a day to Paris (Sfr68) and connections to Brussels and Strasbourg. Trains to Germany stop at BBF Bahnhof on the north bank; local trains to the Black Forest stop only at BBF, though fast IC and EC services stop at SBB too. Main destinations via BBF are Frankfurt (Sfr79, plus around Sfr11 German rail supplement), Cologne, Hamburg and Amsterdam. Two to three

trains an hour run to Freiburg (takes 40 minutes). Services within Switzerland go from SBB: there are two fast trains an hour to both Geneva (Sfr67; via Bern or Biel/ Bienne) and Zürich (Sfr30).

Car & Motorcycle By motorway, the E25/ E60 heads down from Strasbourg and passes by Mulhouse Airport, and the E35/A5 hugs the German side of the Rhine.

Car Rental Various offices are near the SBB station, such as Hertz (☎ 205 92 22), Nauen-strasse 33, Avis (☎ 271 22 62), in the Hilton Hotel, Aeschengraben 31, and Europcar (☎ 361 66 60), Hochstrasse 48. All three have a branch at the airport.

Boat An enjoyable if expensive way to travel north is to take a boat down the Rhine. The landing stage is between Johanniterbrücke and Dreirosenbrücke. A major operator is KD (☎ 322 58 09), Margarethenstrasse 60. See the Getting There & Away chapter for more on long-distance routes. Circular tours by Basler Personenschiffahrt (☎ 639 95 00) depart from near the tourist office. Prices start at Sfr16, and tours are more frequent in the summer.

Getting Around

Buses run every 20 to 30 minutes from 5 am to around 11.30 pm between the airport and the SBB station. It's the yellow bus that goes from outside the Swissair office (Sfr2.60, takes 15 minutes) at the station. The trip by taxi costs around Sfr25.

In the city, buses and trams run every six to 10 minutes. Tickets cost Sfr1.80 for up to and including four stops, or Sfr2.60 for the whole central zone. A day pass costs Sfr7.40. The tourist office sells three-day passes (Sfr20) and multi-journey cards.

Parking garages are dotted around – there are several between the SBB station and the pedestrian zone. Expect to pay at least Sfr1.50 an hour. Small ferries cross the Rhine at various points in the centre (Sfr1.20; day passes not valid), a pleasant alternative to using the bridges.

If you need a taxi, look outside the train stations or ring ☎ 691 77 88 or ☎ 271 22 22.

Around Basel

AUGUSTA RAURICA

These Roman ruins by the Rhine are the largest in Switzerland, and an easy excursion from Basel. The Roman colony was founded in 43 BC and swelled to a population of 20,000 in the 2nd century. Restored remnants include an open-air theatre and several temples. The **Roman Museum** (Römermuseum) has an authentic Roman house amongst its exhibits (Sfr5, Basel museum pass valid; closed Monday). There's no charge to walk around the rest of the site.

Getting There & Away

The trip by local train from Basel to Kaiseraugst takes 15 minutes (Sfr4.60 each way); it's then a 10-minute walk to the site. In summer, taking the boat is another option from Basel.

THE BLACK FOREST

The Black Forest (Schwarzwald), named for its dark canopy of evergreens, is an ideal excursion from any of the northern border towns between Basel and Schaffhausen. This hiking region is actually the home of the cuckoo clock, for so long associated with Switzerland itself. Hansel and Gretel of childhood fiction encountered their wicked witch here, but 20th century hazards are rather more ominous – acid rain, ozone pollution and insect plagues are all leaving their mark. Enjoy the area while you can.

Orientation & Information

The Black Forest lies east of the Rhine between Basel and Karlsruhe. It's roughly triangular in shape, about 160 km long and 50 km wide. Freiburg is the unofficial capital of the southern Black Forest, although many other small towns in the area have excellent tourist information offices – all can give information about accommodation and res-

taurants. Freiburg's tourist office (☎ 0761-388 1880) is at Rotteckring 14.

Money exchange is available in Germany at banks, train stations and post offices, but commission is charged so you'd do best to change money before you leave Switzerland. Some shops and restaurants will accept Swiss francs directly.

The country telephone code for Germany is ☎ 49.

Things to See

Though taking advantage of the countryside will be the main focus, there's still lots of history and culture to explore in the region.

Freiburg's main tourist sight is the **cathedral** (Münster), a classic example of high and late-Gothic architecture. Its red pinnacles loom over Münsterplatz. Of particular interest are the stone and wood carvings, stained-glass windows, the west porch and the pierced spire. The pedestrian area of the town is great for walking tours, and the many resident students make this place both relaxed and lively.

The area between Freudenstadt and Freiburg is cuckoo clock country, and a few popular stops are **Triberg, Schramberg** and **Furtwangen**. Prices for cuckoo clocks are generally lower than in Switzerland. The history and traditional lifestyle of the region are well documented in the **Deutsches Uhrenmuseum** (German Clock Museum) in Furtwagen and the **Schwarzwald Museum** (Black Forest Museum) in Triberg. Triberg also has a famous **Wasserfall** (waterfall), which hurtles down 162m over seven stages (admission charge).

The Danube

The Donau (Danube) rises in the Black Forest and flows all the way to the Black Sea. It's ideal for hiking, biking and motoring tours. Donaueschingen is recognised as being the source of the river, and this town is the start of the cycle track (Donauradweg) that runs most of the way along the river right into and through Austria. The two tributary rivers that rise even deeper in the Black

Forest, the Brigach and the Breg, are also worth exploring.

Activities

There are 7000 km of marked **hiking** trails to explore. Three long-distance routes running north from the Swiss border are: the 280 km Westweg from Basel, the 230 km Mittelweg from Waldhut-Tiengen, and the 240 km Ostweg from Schaffhausen. In the southern Black Forest, the Feldberg area provides great hikes; consider using Todtmoos or Bonndorf as a base. The 10 km gorge, the Wutachschlucht, near Bonndorf, is justifiably famous. If you haven't time to explore the Black Forest thoroughly, take the Schauinslandbahn, on the outskirts of Freiburg, up to the 1284m Schauinsland peak (DM18 return – about Sfr15). It's a good setting for one-day and half-day hikes.

In winter, there is some downhill **skiing** around Feldberg (DM36 for a day pass – about Sfr30), but cross-country skiing is more widespread.

Getting There & Away

Trains run hourly between Basel and Karlsruhe, calling at Freiburg en route. There is also a scenic rail line between Freiburg and Constance. By road, the A5 skirts the western side of the forest (linking Basel and Frankfurt) and the A81 the eastern side.

Getting Around

Rail lines run north and east from Freiburg. The prettiest stretch (called the Höllental route) runs from Freiburg to the lake Titisee. The Germans rave about this but it's nothing compared to most Swiss train journeys. Where the rail fails to go, the bus system usually provides the way, although services can be slow and sometimes infrequent. Ask at transport information centres about special bus and railpasses for the region.

The main tourist road, the Schwarzwald-Hochstrasse (B500), runs from Baden-Baden to Freudenstadt and Triberg to Waldshut. Cycling is a good way to get about, despite the hills (look for rental in Baden-Baden and Freiburg train stations).

Solothurn

• *pop 15,900* • *440m* • ☎ *(032)*

Solothurn, originally a Celtic settlement, grew in importance when the Romans built a fort here in 370 AD. In 1481 it was the 11th canton to join the Swiss Confederation. The people of Solothurn took this number to their hearts: the town features 11 towers, 11 churches and chapels, 11 guilds and 11 historic fountains. Despite this evident strong allegiance to the Confederation, the town maintained close links with France, and sent many mercenaries to fight for French kings. It rejected the Reformation, choosing to remain Catholic, thereby placing itself in opposition to nearby Bern and Basel and strengthening the affinity with France. The town was the residence of French ambassadors from 1530 to 1792.

Orientation & Information

Solothurn is a cantonal capital. The train station is south of the Aare River and has an information office, money-exchange counters and bike rental, all open daily. There's also left luggage and 24-hour lockers. The main post office (4501 Solothurn 1) is just to the left of the station as you exit.

Across the river lies the old town, less than a 10-minute walk away. The core of the centre is Kronenplatz, dominated by the cathedral. The tourist office (☎ 622 19 24) is on this square, open Monday to Friday from 8.30 am to noon and 1.30 to 6 pm, and Saturday from 9 am to noon. Staff will phone for hotel rooms without charging and also conduct informative guided walking tours of the centre (Saturday 2.30 pm from June to September, lasting one to two hours; Sfr5 per person).

Things to See & Do

Despite the French influences in its history, the centre of town is dominated by an Italianate church, the 18th century **Cathedral of St Ursus**. It was designed and overseen by the Ticino architect, Gaetano Matteo Pisoni, with help from his nephew. The cathedral is dedicated to the two patron saints of Solothurn, Ursus and Victor, who were beheaded in the town during Roman times for refusing to worship the Roman gods. Inside it features a fine pink marble pulpit. A stone's throw down Hauptgasse is the **Jesuit Church**. It's unprepossessing on the outside yet inside it displays magnificent Baroque embellishments and stucco work. The coats of arms of the families who funded the building can be seen at the back of the church. Incidentally, all the 'marble' in here is fake, just spruced up wood and plaster. It's a common deception in Baroque churches.

A little further down Hauptgasse you reach the **Zeitglockenturm**, a 12th century astronomical clock where the figures do a little turn on the hour. Don't be confused by the clock hands – the smaller one shows the minutes. It was added centuries later than the large hour hand; it only became necessary when modern life dictated that people become yoked to the tyranny of timetables.

The rest of the old centre merits an exploration. There are a couple of city gates to see and several old fountains. Especially note the **Justice Fountain** (1561) in Hauptgasse. It shows a blindfolded representation of Justice, holding aloft a pair of scales, and at her feet are the four most important figures in Europe at that time. Firstly, the Holy

Roman Emperor (in red and white robes, by Justice's right foot), then proceeding anti-clockwise: the Pope, the Turkish Sultan, and...the mayor of Solothurn!

Museums The **Old Arsenal** is essential viewing in Solothurn. It efficiently illustrates the town's past status as a centre for mercenaries, and contains armour for 400 men, plus canons, guns and uniforms. The only exhibit you can touch is the small suit of armour near the entrance: lift up the visor and the dwarf inside will 'spit' on you. Not, thankfully, a typical Solothurn welcome. The Arsenal is open Tuesday to Sunday from 10 am to noon and 2 to 5 pm. From November to April it stays closed on weekday mornings (adults Sfr6, families Sfr10, students and seniors Sfr4).

For a provincial museum, the **Museum of Fine Arts** (Kunstmuseum), Werkhofstrasse 30, holds some impressive works. The *Madonna of Solothurn* (1522) by Holbein the Younger is the most striking, along with *Virgin in the Strawberries* (1425) by the Master of the Garden of Paradise. Swiss artists are strongly represented, especially Ferdinand Hodler, whose famous portrait of William Tell is here. It is open Tuesday to Saturday from 10 am to noon and 2 to 5 pm (9 pm Thursday) and Sunday from 10 am to 5 pm (free entry).

Ferdinand Hodler

Ferdinand Hodler is perhaps the most important turn-of-the-century Swiss painter. He was born in Bern in 1853 and was influenced early on by the landscape works of Sommer and Calame. He produced many landscapes of his own, right up to the end of his life, with Lake Thun and Alpine scenes cropping up frequently. Hodler embraced the art nouveau style and particularly explored the use of allegory and symbolism. He spent most of his working life in Geneva, despite the fact that its climate of Calvinistic rectitude was often hostile towards him. He died in Geneva in 1918. Historical themes were also important in his paintings. Some Hodler works hark back to the early days of the Swiss Confederation, when ill-equipped rural villages pitted themselves against the might of the Habsburgs. His famous picture of William Tell is in the Kunstmuseum in Solothurn. Hodler re-worked the scene of the show-of-hand vote several times (eg the *Einmütigkeit* in Zürich's Fine Arts Museum), where villagers stand in a cohesive group listening to an orator. All are rugged he-man types with physiques carved out of granite – the sort who cut their razors when shaving. The lack of three dimensional perspective makes them seem like a solid wall. All the men are about the same height and all have a hand raised in seamless unison. The line of heads and the line of hands create two intimidating tiers of defiance that make it seem plausible that such men could take on the Habsburgs – and win. ■

NORTH-WEST SWITZERLAND

Places to Stay & Eat

The new SYHA *hostel* (☎ 623 17 06), Landhausquai 23, is in the centre by the river. A range of beds and prices are available, starting at Sfr25.50 for the largest dorms. Reception is open all day and the place shuts from early November to mid-December.

Hotel Kreuz (☎ 622 20 20), Kreuzgasse 4, is near the hostel. Uncluttered and spacious singles/doubles/triples (with hall showers) start at Sfr42/70/85, without breakfast; deduct Sfr5 if staying more than one night. It is a cooperative and has a restaurant with inexpensive organic and vegetarian food (closed Sunday lunch and Monday evening). Ring the bell for reception when the restaurant is shut.

Hotel Nelson (☎ 622 04 22), Rossmarktplatz 2, by the north side of the Wengibrücke, is a British hotel. Singles/doubles with shower/WC are Sfr70/90, without breakfast. It also has singles using hall shower for Sfr55, but these cost the same, except with breakfast, at *Schlüssel Pub* (☎ 622 22 82), Kreuzgasse 3.

Baseltor (☎ 622 34 22), Hauptgasse 79, near the tourist office, has modern rooms with private shower, toilet and telephone for Sfr90/150. The restaurant has an interestingly diverse if not extensive menu, with meals costing about Sfr10 to Sfr25 (closed Sunday and holidays; hotel open daily).

Hotel Krone (☎ 622 44 12), Hauptgasse 64, opposite the tourist office, is a Best Western hotel with prices starting at Sfr140/170. Rooms are decked out in Baroque style and its pricey restaurant is open daily.

The impecunious can find fodder at the *Coop* supermarket and restaurant, Dornacherplatz, 200m left of the station and opposite a large car park. Meals are around Sfr10 and it's open to 6.30 pm weekdays (9 pm Thursday) and to 5 pm Saturday. Self-service restaurants in the old town are in the *Migros* supermarket on Wengistrasse and the *Manor* department store on Gurzelngasse. *Rebstock*, Kronengasse 9, is a simple café with daily menus for Sfr13.50 and Sfr15.50 and other meals from Sfr12 (closed Sunday and Monday).

Getting There & Away

Solothurn has two trains an hour to Bern on the private RBS line (Sfr13, takes 40 minutes, railpasses valid). Regular trains also run to Basel (Sfr24, takes one hour or more, change at Olten), and Biel (Sfr8.40, 20 minutes). A more enjoyable way to get to and from Biel is to take the boat along the Aare River (see Biel for details). By road, the Weissenstein mountain impedes access directly north, but the N1/E25 motorway passes a few km east of town, providing a fast route to Bern, Basel and Zürich. Take highway 5 for Biel.

AROUND SOLOTHURN

The grand **Castle Waldegg**, a few km north of town, was built in the 17th century and displays period furniture and paintings. The design betrays French and Italian influences. It is open mid-April to the end of October, daily except Monday and Friday, and from November to mid-December on weekends only (entry fee as for Solothurn Arsenal). Take bus No 4 from the station to St Niklaus. The nearby **Weissenstein** (1284m) to the north, is a hiking and cross-country skiing centre (see Jura Canton in the Fribourg, Neuchâtel and Jura chapter for information on scenic driving routes). A few km north-west of Solothurn is **Lommiswil**, where dinosaur footprints have recently been discovered in the forest. A viewing platform has been built (free access).

Aargau Canton

This industrial and residential canton is rather lacking in tourist attractions, though some towns retain well-preserved old centres. That includes the cantonal capital, **Aargau**, which was formerly the seat of the mighty Habsburg family. Mid-way between Aargau and Baden are the ruins of the Habsburg castle, offering excellent views from its tower.

BADEN

• *pop 16,000* • *388m* • *☎ (056)*

Baden has a dual reputation, as an electro-mechanical engineering centre and as a leading spa town.

Orientation & Information

Baden is split into two localities about 15 minutes' walk apart: the Altstadt (old town centre) to the south and the spa centre to the north, with the train station positioned conveniently between the two. By the station is the main post office (5400 Baden 1) and the postbus departure point. A few metres further on down Bahnhofstrasse at No 50 is the tourist office (☎ 222 53 18), open Monday to Friday from 8.30 am to noon and 2 to 6 pm and Saturday from 10 am to noon.

Things to See & Do

Baden's status as a health spa is thanks to the presence of 19 hot **sulphur springs**, with the highest mineral content of any Swiss spa. Their curative properties have been known for 2000 years and are believed to be effective in the treatment of rheumatism, respiratory and cardiovascular complaints, and even some neurological disorders. Alternatively, the springs may be of interest if you simply like wallowing in a 35°C bath. Pools are open to everyone in all the major hotels. Depending on the place, entry costs between Sfr7 and Sfr14, or much more if you want special treatments such as mudpacks or a massage. The only pool large enough for swimming is the Thermalbad in the Hotel Verenahof.

The old town centre has some interesting features, including a **covered bridge** (*Holzbrücke*), step-gabled houses and the city tower. The **Bailiff's Castle** (Landvogteischloss) is on the east side of the Limmat River. Inside is a historical museum (Sfr5; closed Monday). Take the stairs near the city tower for a bird's-eye view of the town. Between the Altstadt and the station is the **Swiss Children's Museum** (Schweizer Kindermuseum), Ölrainstrasse 29, featuring all sorts of games (ancient and modern) that can be viewed and played. It is only open on

Wednesday and Saturday from 2 to 5 pm and Sunday from 10 am to 5 pm; entry costs Sfr5 for adults, Sfr4 for students and Sfr3 for children. West of the spa centre is **Stiftung Langmatt**, Römerstrasse 30, a stately home with a good collection of French Impressionist art (open 1 April to 31 October, every afternoon except Monday, plus Sunday morning; Sfr10, students Sfr5). Baden also has a casino and a theatre.

Places to Stay

Campingplatz Aue (☎ 221 63 00) is a 15 minute walk from the station: turn right for the Altstadt, cross the Limmat River at Hochbrücke, then take the first right into Kanalstrasse. It's overlooking the river and is open from 1 April to 31 October.

The SYHA *hostel* (☎ 221 67 96) is nearby at Kanalstrasse 7. It is closed from Christmas to mid-March, costs Sfr23, and the reception is closed from 9.30 am to 5 pm.

Hirschen (☎ 222 69 66), Badstrasse, on the opposite side of the Limmat River from the spa, is the cheapest hotel. Singles/doubles using hall showers are Sfr46/92 but they are unrenovated. If you can afford it, stay at *Atrium-Hotel Blume* (☎ 222 55 69), Am Kurplatz 4, in the spa centre. It's a cheery place featuring an excellent Romanesque inner courtyard with a fountain and plenty of foliage. Singles/doubles with private shower/toilet start at Sfr122/230, or Sfr78/148 using hall facilities. Breakfast is buffet-style and the hotel has its own (small) thermal pool.

Places to Eat

Below ground level in the station are market stalls and takeaway shops, as well as an *EPA* department store with a self-service restaurant. It has meals for Sfr8 to Sfr12, a cheap salad buffet, and late opening till 8 pm on Wednesday. Nearby, opposite the post office, is a *Migros* supermarket and restaurant, with late opening (8 pm) on Wednesday and Friday. Open the same hours is the *Manora* restaurant in the Manor department store on Schlossbergplatz.

In the old town, try *Chen Lay*, Untere

Halde 2, for Chinese food; it has special midday menus from Sfr12.50 (closed Monday). *Rebstock*, down the road at No 21, is more traditional and more expensive (closed Sunday and Monday).

Getting There & Away

Baden is just 15 minutes away from Zürich by rail (Sfr6.80). It is also within Zürich's S-Bahn network (lines S6 and S12, takes 30 minutes). By road, it is simple to get to Zürich (N1/E60 motorway) and the German Black Forest town of Waldshut (highway 5).

ZOFINGEN

• *pop 10,000* • *440m* • ☎ *(062)*

This town has an attractive old centre, with historic fountains, remnants of ancient fortifications, and gabled houses with overhanging roofs. It's worth a stop-off but not a big detour (Zofingen is on the rail route between Basel and Lucerne). It has a tourist office (☎ 751 65 22), Vordere Hauptgasse 33 (closed weekends and Monday morning), and a SYHA *hostel* (☎ 752 23 03), General Guisan Strasse 10 (closed mid-December to the end of February).

Fribourg, Neuchâtel & Jura

This region includes the cantons of Fribourg (population 185,900), Neuchâtel (population 165,500) and Jura (population 64,000) as well as the north-west tip of the canton of Bern.

The canton of Fribourg is tacked on to a tourist region that is otherwise dominated by the long chain of the Jura Mountains. It is this canton that provides many of the highlights: the historic town of Murten, the delightful cheese-making centre of Gruyères, and Fribourg itself. On the other hand, don't neglect a visit to the watch-making towns, merrily ticking away in the Jura mountains. The most important of these are Neuchâtel and La Chaux-de-Fonds in the canton of Neuchâtel.

The Neuchâtel canton produces both red and white wine, and a well-known rosé (oeil-de-perdrix). The first vineyard in Neuchâtel was planted by monks in the 10th century, under the auspices of providing communion wine. Locally-produced brandies include Marc, Prune and Kirsch.

Most towns in the canton of Jura have a street named after the 23 June. It was on this day in 1974 that a popular vote supported its creation as a separate canton. Previously it had been part of the canton of Bern, despite tensions and grievances dating back to the 19th century. The Federal Constitution was accordingly amended and, on 1 January 1979, the new canton came into being. It is ironic, therefore, that the Jura region should still be lumped within the same tourist region as part of its former ruler.

Orientation & Information

This region is within French-speaking Switzerland, except for the eastward edge of Fribourg canton where German is spoken. The area north and west of Lake Neuchâtel includes the relatively gentle slopes of the Jura Mountain range, a range which extends all the way along the French border almost to Geneva (see also the Lake Geneva Region

HIGHLIGHTS

* Picturesque town centres: Fribourg, Murten and Gruyères
* Cheese-making tour in Gruyères
* Clocks and automata in museums in Neuchâtel, La Chaux-de-Fonds and Le Locle
* 'Restaurants de nuit' in Neuchâtel canton
* Cross-country skiing and horse-riding in the Jura Mountains

Fribourg   Jura   Neuchâtel

chapter). In contrast, the Fribourg area south-east of the lake is mostly in the Mittelland plain. Four regional tourist offices serve the region, each covering its respective canton:

Union Fribourgeoise du Tourisme
Route de la Glâne 107, Case postale 921 CH-1701 Fribourg (☎ 026-424 56 44; fax 424 31 19). Contact by telephone or post preferred, rather than visit in person
Tourisme neuchâtelois
6 Rue du Trésor (Place des Halles), CH-2001 Neuchâtel (☎ 032-725 17 89; fax 724 49 40). Personal callers welcome (weekdays 8 am to noon

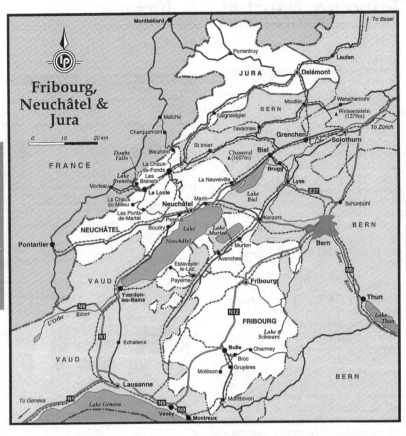

Fribourg, Neuchâtel & Jura

and 2 to 6 pm); gives out leaflets and *passeport loisers* for entry-fee reductions

Jura Tourisme
Rue de la Gare 18, CH-2726 Saignelégier (☎ 032-951 26 26; fax 951 25 55). Open Monday to Friday from 7.30 am to noon and 1.30 to 5 pm

Office du tourisme du Jura bernois
Ave de la Liberté 26, Case postale 759, CH-2740, Moutier (☎ 032-493 64 66; fax 493 61 56)

Some of the information is available only in French or German.

Getting Around

There is a special 'carte 2 jours' ticket for postbus travel on two consecutive days. It covers selected routes in the area between Neuchâtel, Le Locle and Yverdon, plus the train between Noiraigue and Couvet. It's a good deal if you want to explore the lesser-known destinations in the region. The price is Sfr33 or Sfr25 for children or those with a Half-Fare Card. *Arc Jurassien* is a day card (Sfr22) covering selected buses and trains between Le Locle and Porrentruy. Onde Verte is a zonal pass for Neuchâtel canton, valid for one week (also available for one month/year). Three zones, such as Neuchâtel to La Chaux-de-Fonds, costs

Sfr29; five zones (Sfr48) covers the whole canton.

The Neuchâtel regional office sells a booklet (Sfr5, in French and German) describing different cycling routes within the canton, including altitude variations. It also sells a detailed walking map. There are no motorways in the Jura region, but other main roads make getting around by car easy, even in winter.

Fribourg Canton

In the 15th and 16th centuries Fribourg was protected from Bern's expansionist policies by a treaty of association signed in 1403. This alliance held firm despite Fribourg remaining Catholic in the face of the Reformation. The town even managed to extend its own territory during this period, and gobbled up several regions to the south and west, such as Gruyère and Broye.

FRIBOURG
• *pop 36,500* • *630m* • *☎ (026)*
Built on the hilly banks of a river bend and with a skyline dominated by a cathedral, Fribourg (Freiburg in German) is a little reminiscent of Bern. This is not too surprising as it was founded in 1157 by Duke Berchtold IV of Zähringen, father of the bear hunter who founded Bern, Berchtold V. It became a free imperial city in 1478 at the end of the Burgundy Wars. Three years later it joined the Swiss Confederation, the first French-speaking town to do so. Fribourg's prosperity in the Middle Ages was based on manufacturing; affluent artisans were drawn to the city and many of their Gothic houses still survive in the medieval town centre. Other main attractions are its churches and art galleries. The entrepreneur Georges Python was the founder of the Catholic university in 1889.

Orientation
Fribourg is a bilingual cantonal capital. The Sarine River (Saane in German) marks the linguistic divide: inhabitants on the west bank mostly speak French, and those on the east bank, German. Street names may differ dependent upon the language used; 4 Rue de Morat and Murtengasse 4, for example, are two versions of the same address. Both street names usually appear on street signs.

Much of the old town is on the west bank of the river, with the main focal point being the Cathedral of St Nicholas. The train station (Gare CFF) is conveniently central. Leading from it is the shopping street, Ave de la Gare; this becomes Rue de Romont (pedestrian-only) and opens out into the hub of the town, Place Georges-Python.

Information
The tourist information office (☎ 321 31 75) is by the station at Ave de la Gare 1. The opening hours are Monday to Friday from 8 am to noon and 2 to 6 pm, and Saturday from 9 am to noon (and 2 to 4 pm from May to September). It can help with room reservations (Sfr3 deposit), or visitors can make use of the information screens and free telephone in the station. The station also has money-exchange facilities daily from 6 am to 8.30 pm, plus storage lockers (Sfr3) and bike rental.

The main post office (1700 Fribourg 1) is close to the station on Ave de Tivoli.

SSR Voyages (☎ 322 61 61), the budget travel agency, is at Rue de Lausanne 35, open Monday afternoon to Saturday morning.

Things to See
A walking tour of the old town centre is enlivened by several historic fountains, mostly constructed in the 16th century. They depict figures as varied as St George (outside the Town hall), Samson (Place de Notre-Dame) and Christ with the Samaritan woman (Rue de la Samaritane). These are copies; the originals are in the Museum of Art and History. There are a number of good spots for panoramic views of the town, particularly Grand-Places, Route des Alpes, Chemin de Loret on the south of the river, and the two bridges, Pont de Zaehringen and Pont du Milieu. The latter yields the classic view of

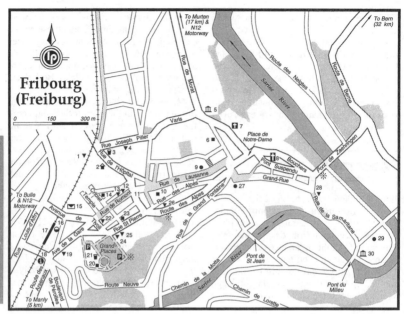

Fribourg (Freiburg)

the town that appears on many tourist posters. Consider taking a guided tour of the centre by mini train (Sfr8.50; Sfr5 for children), departing from Place Georges-Python, daily except Monday.

Town Hall The 16th century town hall *(hôtel de ville)* features a clock tower and a fine double staircase. In front of the building is the **Morat Linden Tree**. In 1476 the Swiss defeated Charles the Bold at Murten (Morat). The messenger who conveyed the good news to the people of Fribourg promptly died of exhaustion immediately after uttering his announcement. As even the Swiss hadn't sorted out proper compensation for death or injury at work in those days, by way of scant recompense they planted the linden twig decorating his hat. The present tree is said to be a descendent from this twig. The messenger's journey from Murten is retraced in a popular race on the first Sunday in October.

Cathedral of St Nicholas Construction of this Gothic cathedral was started in 1283. Around the main portal is a representation of heaven and hell and the Last Judgement. Inside, notice the distinctive organ that took six years to build in the 19th century. The stained glass windows (by Joseph Mehoffer) are bright and lively, except those in the **Chapel of the Holy Sepulchre** near the entrance, where the blue and purple tones put together by Alfred Manessier in 1977 create a suitably sombre mood in which to view the sculptural group, *The Entombment* (1433). The 74m **tower** (completed in 1490) affords a great view but it's only open from mid-June to the end of September (Sfr3, students and children Sfr1). Hours are 10 am to 5.30 pm daily, except lunchtimes and Sunday morning.

Franciscan Church This church (Église des Cordeliers) on Rue de Morat dates from the 13th century but was much modified 500

PLACES TO STAY
2	SYHA Hostel
6	Hotel Musée
10	Hotel Faucon
14	Hotel Elite
20	Golden Tulip
23	Hotel Central

PLACES TO EAT
1	Mensa
4	Pension Beau-Sejour
12	Le Frascati
13	McDonald's
19	EPA Department Store
22	Placette Department Store
24	Migros Supermarket
25	Coop Supermarket & Restaurant
26	A l'Aigle-Noir
28	Auberge de Zaehringen

OTHER
3	Willi's
5	Museum of Art & History
7	Franciscan Church
8	Cathedral of St Nicholas
9	SSR Voyages (Travel Agency)
11	Place Georges-Python
15	Post Office
16	GFM Bus Departures
17	Train Station
18	Tourist Office
21	Café des Grand Places
27	Town Hall
29	La Spirale
30	Swiss Puppet Museum

combine animal skulls with rusted-metal machine components. These mobiles were constructed by Jean Tinguely (1925-91), who was born in Fribourg. Tinguely is also responsible for the mobile fountain in Grand-Places, but it's not as impressive as his similar effort in Basel.

Also look out for the wooden relief panels that were carved around 1600. These show biblical scenes in fantastic detail, especially the *Flight in Egypt* panel. The museum is open Tuesday to Sunday from 10 am to 5 pm, Thursday evening from 8 to 10 pm, and entry is free (Sfr8 during temporary exhibitions).

Other Museums The **Swiss Puppet Museum** (Musée Suisse de la Marionnette), is at Derrière-les Jardins 2, and entry costs Sfr5 (students Sfr4, children Sfr3; limited opening times). There is also a **Beer Museum** in the large brewery just south of the station entrance in Passage du Cardinal. Appointments must be made on ☎ 429 22 11.

Places to Stay

Camping The nearest site is *La Follaz* (☎ 436 30 60), five km south of town in the village of Marly, overlooking a river. It is open from early April to the end of September. *Camping Schiffenen* (☎ 493 19 17) is north of Fribourg by Lake Schiffenen, at Düdingen. This one is open year round.

Hostel The SYHA *hostel* (☎ 323 19 16) is at 2 Rue de l'Hôpital, in a hospital wing. Beds in the mostly six-bed dorms cost Sfr23, or it's Sfr30 each for double occupancy of a dorm. Curfew is at 10 pm (keys available) and there's a kitchen. The hostel is closed from 9 am to 5 pm (6 pm on weekends) and from late November to late January.

Hotels The cheapest hotel in the centre is *Hôtel Faucon* (☎ 322 13 17), 76 Rue de Lausanne. It's functional and has a cheap restaurant. Prices vary depending upon the length of the stay. Prices are Sfr60/100 for singles/doubles with private shower or Sfr50/80 without; triples are Sfr140. Knock off Sfr5/10 for stays exceeding three nights.

years later. On the right upon entering is an impressive wooden triptych which was carved and gilded around 1513. Yet what really grabs the attention is the large triptych above the high altar. It was painted in 1480 by two different anonymous artists, who signed their work by drawing carnations. The triptych depicts a crucifixion and other religious scenes.

Museum of Art & History The Musée d'Art et d'Histoire, Rue de Morat, has an excellent collection of late-Gothic sculpture and painting. It is housed in the Renaissance Hôtel Ratzé, with annexes in the former slaughterhouse and armoury. The underground corridors and rooms are atmospherically lit. Particularly effective is the cavernous chamber where religious statues are juxtaposed with moving sculptures that eerily

FRIBOURG, NEUCHÂTEL & JURA

The rooms are nicer and larger in the *Hôtel Musée* (☎ 322 32 09), Rue Pierre-Aeby 11; reception is closed Sunday. It has singles/doubles using hall shower for Sfr50/90; doubles with private shower/WC are Sfr120. *Hôtel Central* (☎ 322 21 19), Rue St Pierre 3, has good-value rooms for Sfr60/90, all with private shower/WC and TV. These are often snapped up so telephone ahead.

Hôtel Elite (☎ 322 38 36) at 7 Rue du Criblet, near Place Georges-Python, offers better-appointed rooms and two bars. Singles/doubles with private shower/WC and TV start at Sfr90/130. *Golden Tulip* (☎ 321 31 31; fax 323 29 42) is the soaring block at Grand-Places 14. Charges start at Sfr135/215 for large, smart rooms with four-star facilities, and it has a reasonably-priced restaurant. Parking costs Sfr16.

Places to Eat

There are plenty of good choices in town. See Entertainment below for other suggestions.

Self-Service Eat for below Sfr10 in the *EPA* department store opposite the station (stand-up tables only) or at the *Coop*, Rue St Pierre. The *Migros* supermarket next door has no restaurant. The best deal is at the university *Mensa*, providing meals with soup from just Sfr6 (open Monday to Friday from 11 am to 1.30 pm and 5.30 to 7.30 pm). *Pension Beau-Sejour*, Rue Joseph Piller 4, is open similar hours; it's less hectic and nearly as cheap. The Placette department store, Rue de Romont, has a *Manora* restaurant on the 5th floor, with good help-yourself buffets. The train station has fast food and an *Aperto* supermarket, open daily from 6 am to 9 pm.

Other Restaurants The restaurant in the *Hotel Musée* (see Places to Stay), has excellent Chinese food. Stick to the barer café side for a four-course meal for Sfr16; dishes on the other side are above Sfr25 (closed Sunday).

Hôtel Central (see Places to Stay) is also good, and has great prices. Meals, including Thai food, are Sfr10 to Sfr17. The less formal eating area is a popular drinking spot for young people. For pizzas from Sfr12, try out

Le Frascati in Rue de Romont (closed Monday).

The *Buffet de la Gare* (☎ 322 28 16) on the 1st floor of the train station has quality food with prices to match (closed on Sunday and mid-July to mid-August); downstairs is cheaper (open daily). *A l'Aigle-Noir* (☎ 322 49 77), Rue des Alpes 10, has good French dishes from Sfr30.

The best restaurant in Fribourg is reckoned to be the *Auberge de Zaehringen* (☎ 322 42 36), Rue de Zaehringen 13 (closed Sunday evening and Monday). Its Brasserie has meals from Sfr26, though lunch menus are cheaper; the Gallerie has gourmet menus and is closed from 1 July to mid-August.

Entertainment

Willi's, Rue de l'Hôpital, is a young, sociable bar with theme nights (open from 8 pm, or 2 pm on weekends). Food is great value (eg spaghetti bolognese for Sfr5.90). *Café des Grand Places*, Grand-Places 12, has a café on the ground floor with weekday lunch menus (Sfr11.50 vegetarian, Sfr13.50 meat course). Upstairs is a bar with live music or a DJ (open from 8 pm, closed Monday; usually no cover charge).

Fri-son (☎ 424 36 25), Route de la Fonderie 13, south of the station, has rap, reggae, soul and house music. *La Spirale* (☎ 322 66 39), Place du Petit St Jean 39, welcomes jazz and blues musicians. Entry for either place costs around Sfr15.

Getting There & Away

Fribourg is on the north/south N12 (E27) which connects Lake Geneva to Bern and beyond. Trains run hourly to Neuchâtel (Sfr18.20 via Murten; takes one hour), and even more frequently to Geneva (Sfr38, around 90 minutes) and Bern (Sfr10.40, 30 minutes). Interlaken Ost (takes two hours) is reached via Bern or Bulle. GFM Buses (green with an orange stripe; Swiss Pass valid) depart from the train station and go to nearby destinations such as Avenches and Bulle (Sfr13.20). A side trip to consider by GFM bus is to Lake Schwarz (Sfr13.20 each way).

A local car rental firm is Garage Lehmann (☎ 424 26 26), Ave Beauregard 16. Hertz (☎ 436 56 25) is at Route de Fribourg 13, Marly.

Getting Around
Walking is fine in the centre, although those hills can get a bit wearing. Bus tickets are Sfr1.50 to Sfr2 or it costs Sfr5 for a day pass (Sfr10 for three days). All the city bus lines stop by the station and Place Georges-Python. There is parking at Grand-Places, or underground at Place Georges-Python.

ESTAVAYER-LE-LAC
• *pop 4100* • *455m* • *☎ (026)*
Frogs are the unique attraction of this lakeside resort. They're all 130 years old and inside glass cases in the museum. Much of the medieval town centre looks like it has been preserved under glass too, because this is another of those Swiss towns that the ravages of time seems to have all but ignored.

Orientation & Information
The small train station has bike rental and luggage storage. It's 400m from the old centre; orientate yourself using the map outside. The tourist office (☎ 663 12 37) is in a travel agent, Inter Voyages SA, by the Swiss Bank on Place du Midi. It's open Monday to Friday from 9 am to noon and 2 to 6 pm, and (summer only) Saturday from 10 to noon and 2 to 4 pm.

Things to See & Do
François Perrier, an eccentric 19th century military man, spent much of his leisure hours killing frogs, preserving their skins, and filling them with sand. He would then arrange them in parodies of human situations, complete with props. The **Regional Museum** displays 108 of his stuffed frogs engaged in courting, studying, playing games and much more. The result is halfway between the bizarre and the cute. Kids are fascinated by it. Less unusual museum exhibits include weapons and kitchen utensils, and a surprisingly extensive collection

of railway lanterns and signs. Also notice the novel three-faces-in-one portraits on the right wall just before you go downstairs. It is open 1 March to 31 October from 9 to 11 am and 2 to 5 pm (closed Sunday and Monday except in July and August). The rest of the year it's only open Saturday and Sunday from 2 to 5 pm. Entry costs Sfr3 for adults, Sfr2 for senior citizens and students, and Sfr1 for children.

When you tire of amphibians you can be aquatic yourself in the pleasure boat harbour, or try water-skiing (get towed around the lake by a special cable-way), windsurfing and sailing. The old Gothic centre is well worth a wander. The 13th century **castle** is well preserved and is now the home of the cantonal police. Also peek into the **St Laurent Church** for a look at the fresh stained-glass and the heavily barred altar.

Places to Stay & Eat
Camp at *Nouvelle Plage* (☎ 663 16 93), by the lake to the right of the harbour. It's open from 1 April to 30 September and costs Sfr4.40 per person and Sfr6 per tent; rates are slightly higher in July and August.

My Lady's Manor (☎ 663 23 16), Route de la Gare, between the station and the centre, is an excellent deal. It's a genuine stately home, with ornamental furnishings, converted in piecemeal fashion to hotel rooms (Sfr38 per person, using hall showers). There's extensive gardens and off-street parking.

Hôtel de Ville (☎ 663 12 62), Rue de l'Hôtel de Ville 16, has rooms using hall showers for Sfr40 per person in winter and Sfr45 in summer. There's a good quality French restaurant on the 1st floor. Nearby at No 5 is the *Tea Room Carmen* where you can consume cheap snacks and pizzas. It closes on Monday and at 7.30 pm (11 pm in summer) during the week and 6 pm on Sunday.

Café-Restaurant du Cerf, 1st floor, Grand-Rue 11, has pizzas and other dishes (closed Monday). Also good is the *Gerbe d'Or*, Rue du Camus, opposite the Denner supermarket. This café-restaurant has lunches with soup for Sfr14.50, plus fondue and other dishes (closed Sunday).

For comfortable rooms by the lake (from Sfr60 per person), try *Hôtel du Lac* (☎ 663 13 43; fax 663 53 43). It has a restaurant.

Getting There & Away
Estavayer-le-Lac is on the direct road and rail route between Fribourg and Yverdon, or it's a short detour off the northbound highway 1 (E4) from Lausanne. Estavayer is also a stop on boat services on Lake Neuchâtel; it's 1½ hours to Neuchâtel and 1¼ hours to Yverdon, with around three departures a day from late May to late September except on Monday. Enquire at the tourist office or telephone LNM (☎ 032-725 40 12) in Neuchâtel for more information.

MURTEN
• *pop 5000* • *450m* • ☎ *(026)*
In May 1476, Charles the Bold (the Duke of Burgundy), still smarting from his recent defeat by the Swiss Confederates at Grandson, set off from Lausanne to lay siege on Murten. Two weeks after his arrival in the town the Swiss army arrived in force and trapped the Burgundians on the shore of the lake. The Duke fled with his life, but 8000 of his men were butchered or drowned.

Picturesque Murten retains a strong sense of history and has much of its medieval fortifications still intact. The lake provides added attractions.

Orientation & Information
French speakers call this place Morat; German speakers call it Murten. You can take your pick as it's right on the linguistic divide, though most of the inhabitants speak German. It is on the eastern shore of Lake Murten (Lac de Morat, Murtensee) and Bern is 28 km to the east. The train station is 300m outside the city walls and has money-exchange daily to midnight and bike rental. There's a map outside so you can orientate yourself. The post office is opposite. The tourist office (☎ 670 51 12) is in the centre at Französische Kirchgasse 6 near the Bern Tower. In the winter (approximately October to March) it's open Monday to Friday from 9 am to noon and 2 to 5.30 pm. In the summer it's open to at least 6 pm plus Saturday morning. It has a useful booklet giving information on activities, excursions, and biking and hiking tours. Most hotels and restaurants close for part of the winter; the tourist office compiles a list.

Things to See & Do
Spend an hour or so roaming around the cobbled streets of the walled centre, admiring the arcaded houses displaying window boxes and shutters. Dwellings in the centre were rebuilt in stone after being destroyed in a fire in 1416. There's a free guided tour on Friday in July and August. The **castle** dates from the 13th century and offers a view of the lake from the courtyard. At the north-east end of Hauptgasse is the distinctive **Bern Tower**, also 13th century. The best view of the centre is from the city walls themselves. Ascend at the tower behind the German church on Deutsche Kirchgasse and walk around to the tower at Pfisterplatz, where you get the best view. The rows of brown-tiled roofs form an attractive arrangement from this elevated perspective. You could also stroll around Stadtgraben, a path circling the outside of the walls, where you might see locals toiling in their garden allotments beside the ancient fortifications.

Outside the walls near the castle is the **Historical Museum**, housed in the old water mill. In 1829 the dredging of the Broye canal and the drawing of the marshes caused a lowering of the lakes at the foot of the Jura. This uncovered evidence of ancient dwellings dating from 4000 BC, and these archaeological finds were just lying there for any wanderer to pick up. Fortunately, many found their way to this museum. In addition to these relics, there are various other oddities: a huge bullet that killed an elephant, dated and decorated leather fire buckets – a compulsory household utensil after the 1416 fire, and some surprisingly suggestive pewter council flagons (with an arm caressing the spout). Opening hours from 1 May to 30 September are Tuesday to Sunday from

10 am to noon and 2 to 5 pm. In the winter it's closed mornings (and weekdays in January and February). Admission costs Sfr4 for adults, Sfr2 for students and senior citizens, and Sfr1 for children. Ask at the desk for the informative notes in English.

Lake Murten provides numerous recreational possibilities. The harbour is by the walled centre. Circular tours of the lake depart from late May to late September (tickets on the boat). Contact the tourist office, the harbour (☎ 670 26 03) or the train station (☎ 670 26 46) for details. Fishing permits can be obtained from the Préfecture (☎ 670 22 57) in the castle. The beach (and a swimming pool) are near the Historical Museum. For the sailing school and boat hire contact Pierre Tschachtli (☎ 670 48 17). The Surfcenter Murten (☎ 670 23 17) is the windsurfing school.

At the beginning of March, Murten celebrates its **carnival**, comprising three days of fun and parades. On the first Sunday in October there's the Murten-Fribourg race; up to 8,000 participants retrace the 17 km route of the messenger who relayed news of the Battle of Murten. Participants are not expected to re-enact the journey too faithfully – the man died upon arrival!

Avenches This village is eight km south of Murten along highway 1 (E4) and within canton Vaud. It was built on the site of the old capital of the Helvetii, a Celtic tribe who were the first inhabitants of the region. Later it became a flourishing Roman town and reached the peak of its influence in the 1st and 2nd centuries. At this time its population was around 10 times greater than its present total of 2000. The town's defences – a high wall and ring of fortified observation towers – were not sufficient to prevent it being destroyed in 259 by the Germanic Alemanni tribe. Little remains of its former glory except a large amphitheatre (seating 12,000), a Roman Museum (closed Monday) and the occasional turret. Ask the tourist office (☎ 675 11 59), in the town centre at Place de l'Église 3, for directions to outlying ruins.

Payerne If you're driving along the Lausanne-Murten highway 1, it's worth stopping off for a brief look at the former abbey in this small town in Vaud, 10 km south of Avenches. The abbey has become a museum and its 11th century Romanesque church has been extensively restored (open daily; entry Sfr7, or Sfr5 for students and seniors).

Places to Stay

There's a SYHA *hostel* (☎ 675 26 66) in Avenches at Rue du Lavoir 5. Dorms cost Sfr22 and the hostel closes from mid-November to the end of February. It's situated about a 15-minute walk from Avenches train station; take Ave General Guisan and walk to the far south-west corner of the old centre (or take the bus to 'Restaurant Croix Blanc').

Opposite Murten station, *Hotel-Restaurant Bahnhof* (☎ 670 22 56) has plenty of parking. Standard singles/doubles using hall shower are Sfr60/100; doubles for Sfr110 have private facilities.

The other hotels are in Murten's old centre, where the best budget choice is the small and welcoming *Hotel Ringmauer* (☎ 670 11 01), Deutsche Kirchgasse 2. Singles/doubles are Sfr60/105 with hall showers. *Hotel Krone* (☎ 670 52 52), Rathausgasse 5, has rooms from Sfr90/130 with private shower, toilet and TV. Next door is the *Hotel Murtenhof* (☎ 670 56 56), offering the same standard and prices, but with the advantage of private parking. Most rooms have interesting décor with patches of old brickwork showing through the modern plaster (intentionally!). Both places have more expensive rooms overlooking the lake.

Places to Eat

There's a *Coop* supermarket with a restaurant on Bahnhofstrasse near the castle. It has menus for around Sfr9 and is open Monday morning and Tuesday to Thursday until 6.30 pm, Friday until 8 pm, and Saturday to 4 pm.

Other than that, it's probably best to stick to the hotels already mentioned. *Hotel Krone* is the best place to eat, if all the gastronomic plaques outside are to be believed; there's a gourmet restaurant on the 1st floor and a cheaper downstairs section. *Hotel Ringmauer* has a fairly limited but tempting choice of hot food from Sfr15. *Hotel Murtenhof* has a good salad buffet (Sfr7.50 for a smallish plate) and views of the lake. There are special menus from around Sfr14 and other dishes starting at Sfr19 (closed Monday).

Try *Weisses Kreuz*, Rathausgasse, for expensive fish specialities (closed Sunday evening in low season).

Getting There & Away

There are hourly trains to/from Fribourg (Sfr9.60; 30 minutes) and Bern (via Kerzers, Sfr11.40; 35 minutes). Avenches (Sfr2.80) is just two stops and eight minutes away on the hourly train to Payerne, which is also on the route to Lausanne (Sfr24). Neuchâtel is 30 minutes away (Sfr10.40).

Murten is on highway 1, which runs from Lausanne in the south and links with the motorway to Bern. Neuchâtel and Biel can be reached by boat on the 'three lake tour' in the summer; contact the harbour or the tourist office for details (see also the Around Biel section in the Bernese Mittelland chapter).

Getting Around

Walking is best. Parking is limited within the town walls (maximum 90 minutes from 8 am to 6 pm daily: Sfr1.50 per hour). There's a new parking garage by the Coop.

GRUYÈRES

• *pop 1500* • *830m* • ☎ *(026)*

This picturesque town attracts busloads of tourists with its fine 15th and 17th century houses and commanding castle. Visitors can catch the odd scent of cheese in the air, too.

Orientation & Information

Gruyères is on the western edge of the Pre-Alps in the canton of Fribourg. The small train station will hold baggage behind the counter but opening hours are limited. The main village is a 10-minute walk up the hill.

Buses and cars must be left in the free car park at the entrance to the village.

The tourist office (☎ 921 10 30) is at the start of the main street. It is open Monday to Friday from 8 am to noon and 1.30 to 5 pm, and (mid-July to mid-September) from 10.30 am to 4.30 pm on Saturday and Sunday. It changes money (marginally poor rates, 2% commission), a useful service as there's no bank. There are no street names in this tiny place.

Things to See

If you can avoid the tour buses, Gruyères is a great place to linger and enjoy the harmonious setting and relaxed atmosphere. The main street is extremely photogenic. The impact is immediate upon entering the village; you see the road dipping down to a central fountain, flanked on either side with quaint old buildings with hanging signs, and all dominated in the distance by the rising turrets of the castle.

Castle The Château de Gruyères offers an expansive view from its 13th century ramparts. The dungeon is also 13th century but much of the rest of the castle dates from after the fire in 1493. It was the home of the Counts of Gruyères who held sway over the whole Sarine Valley from the 11th to the 16th century. Inside there are various items on display, such as ecclesiastical vestments (booty from the battle of Murten), tapestries, and period furniture. Look out for representations of the crane (*grue* in French), the heraldic emblem of the Counts of Gruyères. Allow an hour to get around, or more if there's a good temporary exhibition on the ground floor. The castle is open daily: 1 June to 30 September from 9 am to 6 pm, and the rest of the year from 9 am to noon and 1 pm to 4.30 pm (5 pm during March, April, May and October). Admission costs Sfr5 or Sfr2 for students and children.

Cheese-Making Gruyère cheese is one of the best known of Swiss cheeses, and it's one of the main cheeses used in fondue. It takes nearly 12l of full cream milk to make one kg of Gruyère and there are 12 different stages in the three-month production process. Two local dairies allow you to see cheese-making in action (free entry) and try to buy the finished product. The most convenient is in Pringy (☎ 921 14 10), opposite Gruyères train station, where the cheese is made into 'wheels' weighing 35 kg. It is open daily from 8 am to 7 pm but the best time to go is when the cheese is actually in production, from 9 to 11.30 am and 1 to 3.30 pm (shorter hours on Sunday, and not Monday afternoon). The most active phase is when the cheese is pumped from the vat to the moulds, about 1½ hours after the start. This modern dairy gets through 13,000l of milk per day. There's a slide show and commentary in English that's informative but rather over-stresses the 'harmony with nature' aspect (this has more to do with 'bull' than 'cow', despite the many references to the latter).

There's another dairy in a 17th century chalet in Moléson, five km south-west of Gruyères. It is open 15 May to 15 October, every day from 9.30 am to 6.30 pm, but again you should try and visit during cheese production hours. This one uses old-fashioned production methods. Contact the Moléson tourist office (☎ 921 24 34) for information and reservations.

Wax Museum The Musée de Cire is in Moléson, and recreates influential figures from Swiss history such as Henri Dunant, creator of the Red Cross. It is open daily except Tuesday and entry costs Sfr3 (Sfr2 for children and students).

Activities

The Gruyère region offers winter cross-country skiing, plus a few medium and easy downhill runs, particularly at Charmey and Moléson. The 2002m Moléson peak also yields a good panorama of the taller peaks further south. Signposted walking trails can be found everywhere, including on Moléson and on neighbouring Vudalla (1668m).

Places to Stay & Eat

There are only four small hotels in the centre of Gruyères so it's a good idea to book ahead. Don't even think of staying overnight if you're on a tight budget, though you could camp at *Haute Gruyère* (☎ 921 22 60), five km south of Gruyères at Enney. In Moléson, *Hotel-Restaurant Plan Francey* (☎ 921 10 42) has rooms (Sfr40 per person) and dormitory beds (Sfr25).

The cheapest place in Gruyères village is *Hôtel de Ville* (☎ 921 24 24) where all rooms have private shower/toilet and TV; singles/doubles cost Sfr90/130 and triples/quads Sfr160/180 (closed Wednesday and Thursday in winter). Also in the main street, *Hostellerie St Georges* (☎ 921 22 46) costs at least Sfr110/150. *Hostellerie des Chevaliers* (☎ 921 19 33; fax 921 33 13), by the car park, is the biggest and classiest hotel and has a quality restaurant. Singles/ doubles start at Sfr140/160.

Inevitably, cheesy creations figure strongly when contemplating a bite to eat. As well as looking at the hotel restaurants, try *Auberge de la Halle* which has its filling Soupe de Chalet (mushrooms, pasta, cheese etc) for Sfr16. *Café-Restaurant des Remparts*, on the other side of the main road, is reasonably priced and offers a range of meals (eg fondue for Sfr20). *Restaurant Le Relais de Gruyères*, by the station, is cheaper, with dishes from Sfr11.

Getting There & Away

From Fribourg, Gruyères can be reached by taking the hourly bus (Sfr13.20) to Bulle (see below) and the train (Sfr2.80) from there. Coming from the south, change trains at Montbovon. Buses depart from the train station in Fribourg, Bulle and Gruyères. A two-hourly GFM bus links Bulle, Gruyères station, Gruyères village and Moléson.

The main road route is the north-south N12 (E27) motorway from Vevey to Fribourg and Bern, which passes by Bulle. There are also good roads heading south and east through the mountains from Gruyères and Broc.

FRIBOURG, NEUCHÂTEL & JURA

BULLE

• *pop 9700* • *770m* • ☎ *(026)*

Five km north-west of Gruyères is Bulle, with a 13th century castle (now administrative offices). Behind the castle is the **Gruyère Region Museum** (Musée Gruérien), with a reasonable collection including paintings, furniture, costumes, room interiors and religious artefacts. It is open Tuesday to Saturday from 10 am to noon and 2 to 5 pm, and Sunday and holidays in the afternoon only. Entry costs Sfr4 (students Sfr3).

Between the train station and the castle is a tourist office (☎ 921 16 36). At the same junction is *Café de la Gare* (the best place for fondue) and *Café-Restaurant Au Fribourg-eois* (good lunch menus, and an antique orchestral machine in the corner). *Hôtel du Tonnelier* (☎ 912 77 45),

31 Grand-Rue, has singles/doubles from Sfr45/90.

Getting There & Away

Bulle is the main transport hub for the Gruyère region, accessible by train and bus.

BROC

• *pop 2000* • ☎ *(026)*

Broc, a few km north of Gruyères, is known mainly for the **Nestlé-Caillers Chocolate factory** (☎ 921 51 51). Full factory tours have been stopped for reasons of hygiene, but you can still see a 20 minute film about chocolate-making (free; English commentary), help yourself to some free samples and buy the products. Visits are permitted on weekdays from early May to late October (except July), but telephone ahead.

The Making of Chocolate

Cocoa plantations had already been important in Central America for over 1000 years before Hernando Cortez first transported cocoa back to Europe in 1528. Europeans initially consumed chocolate only in liquid form, often with wine, beer or pepper added. Eating chocolate in solid form did not become popular until the 19th century, when tea and coffee replaced drinking chocolate as the beverage of choice. But still ingredients were added to the chocolate that we would consider strange today, such as barley, rice, oatmeal and even meat extracts.

Swiss chocolate built its reputation in the 19th century, thanks to pioneering spirits such as François-Louis Cailler (1796-1852), Philippe Suchard (1797-1884), Henri Nestlé (1814-90), Jean Tobler (1830-1905), Daniel Peter (1836-1919) and Rodolphe Lindt (1855-1909). Cailler established the first Swiss chocolate factory in 1819, near Vevey, after he learned the chocolate trade in Italy. Daniel Peter was the first person to add milk to chocolate (1875). Lindt invented the production method called conching, a rotary aeration process that gives chocolate its smooth, melt-in-the-mouth quality.

The cocoa bean is very bitter – even dark chocolate is two-fifths sugar. It is grown in equatorial countries, particularly Brazil, the Ivory Coast, Ghana and Nigeria. Harvest times are May and October to November. The beans, after being extracted from the cocoa fruit, are left to ferment for two to six days. They're then dried and shipped to the chocolate manufacturing countries. The USA is the biggest chocolate manufacturer. Switzerland is only 10th biggest, but the Swiss by far consume more chocolate than anybody else – 11.3 kg per person per year, 43% more than their nearest rivals, the Norwegians.

At the factory, the cocoa beans are cleaned, roasted (to develop the aroma) and crushed. The husks are extracted and used in the chemical industry. Different types of beans are blended according to the recipe and ground into a fine paste. Part of the cocoa paste is then processed to extract cocoa butter, a yellowish fat comprising about 50% of the original bean. The powder that is left after extracting the cocoa butter is used for various purposes, including making instant chocolate drinks. The cocoa butter itself is used to make white chocolate, or is re-combined with the original cocoa paste to make plain or milk chocolate.

The cocoa paste, cocoa butter, sugar and milk (if making milk chocolate) is kneaded, rolled and conched until it is a completely smooth, homogeneous liquid. After tempering (a heating and cooling process) it is finally ready to be shaped into chocolate sweets or bars. As centuries ago, the use of additives and fillings is common, even though the ingredients have changed. Common fillings nowadays are praline (crushed and caramelised almonds and hazelnuts, said to have been discovered after a kitchen accident in 1671), nougat, truffles and marzipan. Adding meat extracts, as was the case with the 'Royal Prussian Patented Chocolate Product' in late 19th century Berlin, is no longer done. Perhaps a niche market exists for some meat-oriented entrepreneur? ■

Around the back is **Electrobroc**, a power station and energy information centre. Free tours (in French or German) are conducted on Saturday between March and December, and take two hours. For information, telephone ☎ 921 27 74. It is by Lake Gruyère, where there's swimming (free access).

Broc can be reached from Bulle by a small train: for the above sights, get off after the village at Broc Fabrique (Sfr2.80).

Neuchâtel Canton

The first inhabitants of this region were lake dwellers who settled as early as 3000 BC. The 2nd Iron Age in Europe is referred to as the 'La Tène Period', after the settlement on the eastern end of Lake Neuchâtel where a store of weapons and utensils were discovered. Modern industries include watchmaking, precision engineering and printing and publishing. The observatory in Neuchâtel town gives the official time-check for the whole of Switzerland.

NEUCHÂTEL
• *pop 34,000* • *430m* • ☎ *(032)*
Neuchâtel is the capital of its canton. It's a relaxing town, on the north-west shore of the largest lake totally within Swiss territory, Lake Neuchâtel.

The descendants of Ulrich II became known as the Counts of Neuchâtel from the early 12th century. The territory was elevated to a principality at the beginning of the 17th century, with Henry II of Orléans-Longueville as its head. The title of Prince ultimately devolved to Frederick-William III of Prussia, who allowed it to join the Swiss Confederation in 1815. Yet, curiously and incompatibly, the canton remained a principality under Prussia until 1848, when a bloodless revolution won it the status of a republic.

The French spoken in Neuchâtel is the purest in Switzerland.

Orientation & Information
The train station (Gare CFF) changes money daily from 5.45 am (6.30 am on Sunday) to 9.10 pm and rents bikes. It also has lockers (Sfr2 and Sfr5), luggage storage, restaurants and a train information office (open weekdays and Saturday morning).

From the station, take bus No 6 (or walk for 10 minutes) to get to the hub of the town, Place Pury, on the edge of the central pedestrian zone. The tourist office (☎ 725 42 42) is close by at Rue de la Place d'Armes 7, and is open Monday to Friday from 9 am to noon and 1.30 to 5.30 pm, and Saturday from 9 am to noon (open daily in summer). Pick up a copy of its walking tour of the town centre. The cantonal office is nearby (see this chapter's introduction).

The main post office (Poste Principal, 2001) is at Place du Port, overlooking the harbour. Post counters are open weekdays from 7.30 am to 12.15 pm and 1.15 to 6.30 pm and Saturday from 8 to 11 am. There's another post office just opposite the train station (2002 Neuchâtel 2), which has an out-of-hours counter open daily (Sfr1 surcharge).

Do laundry at Salon Lavoir Lavmatic, Rue des Moulins 37 (closes 8 pm).

Central Sights
The centrepiece of the old town is the **castle** (with free guided tours in summer) and the adjoining **Collegiate Church**. The castle dates from the 12th century and now houses cantonal offices. Walk along the ramparts for a view over the town. The church combines Gothic and Romanesque elements. Its most striking feature is a cenotaph of 15 statues dating from 1372. This depicts medieval knights and ladies (most of whom have been identified) standing in suitably pious postures. Nearby, the **Prison Tower** (entry Sfr0.50) offers a good view of the area and has interesting models showing the town as it was in the 15th and 18th centuries. While roaming around the centre, look out for the six historic fountains which were built around the turn of the 16th century. They were all the work of Laurent Perroud and

have recently been restored. The fountain at the north end of Rue du Trésor is particularly attractively situated.

Museums

The best museum, and an essential visit, is the **Museum of Art and History** (Musée d'Art et d'Histoire), Quai Léopold Robert 2, which is especially noted for three 18th century clockwork figures. They were built between 1764 and 1774 by Jaquet Droz who was formerly a watchmaker based in La Chaux-de-Fonds. The technical achievement in constructing these automata was incredible for the time, and they were performed before admiring crowds in the fairs and royal courts of Europe.

The most elaborate is the **Writer**, who can be programmed to dip his pen in an inkpot and write up to 40 characters. This is achieved via 120 internal revolving discs; the adjustment of these is so fine – to within 0.1 mm – that if the room gets too hot the expansion of the metal can cause him to make spelling mistakes! The **Musician** can play up to five tunes; it's a real organ she plays, not a disguised musical box, and she breathes and moves her eyes as her fingers strike the keys. The **Draughtsman** is technically the simplest, but he still has a repertoire of six drawings. They were purchased for the museum in 1909 for Sfr75,000, and it is so protective of them that they are only activated on the first Sunday of each month. On other days you can see them at rest and watch a film (in English) explaining their history and functions. Elsewhere in the museum are clocks, coins, decorative arts, and works by Swiss painters. Entry is Sfr7 (Sfr4 for students and children), except on Thursday when it's free. The museum is open on Tuesday to Sunday from 10 am to 5 pm.

Also interesting is the **Museum of Ethnography** (Musée d'ethnographie), Rue St Nicolas 4, which concentrates mainly on exhibits from Africa, Bhutan and Oceania (closed Monday; Sfr7 or Sfr4 for students and children). It's on the westward continuation of Rue du Château. The **Natural History Museum** (Musée d'histoire naturelle), 14 Rue des Terreaux (Sfr6, students Sfr3, children free; free for everyone on Wednesday) and the **Archaeological Museum** (Musée cantonal d'archéologie), 7 Ave du Peyrou (free) are also closed on Monday.

Lake Neuchâtel

Cruises on the lake are well worth considering in the summer. All places of interest around Lake Neuchâtel can be reached, and the neighbouring lakes of Biel and Murten are also accessible via a canal. Trips can be a relaxing day out with meals on board or simply a means to continue onward travel. For more information contact the boat company LNM (☎ 725 40 12) at the harbour. See also the Around Biel section in the Bernese Mittelland chapter. A one-day pass for free travel on the lake costs Sfr40, or Sfr28 with a Half-Fare Card. It costs Sfr7 to transport bikes.

Fishing is allowed on the shores of the lake without a permit, but to fish on a boat you need to get a permit from the cantonal police (☎ 724 24 24), Poudrières 14.

Special Events

Neuchâtel hosts the **Grape Harvest Festival** (Fête des Vendanges) on the last weekend in September. It includes parades and costumes, and a fair amount of drunken revelling. At the end of June, **Festi-Jazz** provides free live music in the pedestrian zone. In August, the **Festival Hors Gabarit** is three days of free 'alternative' music in the hills above Neuchâtel. Expect special events in 1998, when Neuchâtel canton celebrates its 150th birthday as a republic.

Places to Stay

Camping There are camp sites a few km away either side of Neuchâtel. *La Tène Plage* (☎ 753 73 40) in Marin is open from April to September and costs Sfr4.30 per person, Sfr5 for a tent and Sfr2.20 for parking. It's by the lake, a short walk from Marin Epagnier train station. *Paradis Plage* (☎ 841 24 46), by the lake in Colombier, has loads of facilities but

FRIBOURG, NEUCHÂTEL & JURA

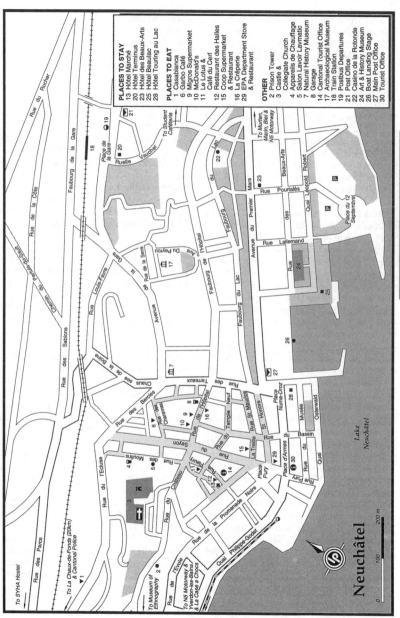

PLACES TO STAY
13 Hôtel Marché
20 Hôtel Terminus
23 Hôtel des Beaux-Arts
25 Hôtel Beaulac
28 Hôtel Touring au Lac

PLACES TO EAT
1 Casablanca
6 Garbo Café
9 Migros Supermarket
11 McDonald's
11 Le Lotus &
12 Café du Cerf
15 Restaurant des Halles
15 Coop Supermarket
& Restaurant
16 La Crêperie
29 EPA Department Store
& Restaurant

OTHER
2 Prison Tower
3 Castle &
3 Collegiate Church
4 Appareils de Chauffage
5 Salon Lavoir Lavmatic
7 Natural History Museum
8 Garage
14 Cantonal Tourist Office
17 Archaeological Museum
18 Train Station
19 Postbus Departures
21 Post Office
22 Casino de la Rotonde
24 Art & History Museum
26 Boat Landing Stage
27 Main Post Office
30 Tourist Office

Neuchâtel

To Museum of Ethnography

To N5 Motorway & Yverdon-les-Bains & La Case a Chocs

To La Chaux-de-Fonds (20km) & Cantonal Police

To SYHA Hostel

To Student Cafétéria

To Murten, Marin, Biel & N5 Motorway

Lake Neuchâtel

0   100   200 m

it's more expensive (open March to October). Bus No 5 goes to Colombier from Place Pury in Neuchâtel. By car, you can take either the N5 or Quai Philippe-Godet.

Hostel The SYHA *hostel* (☎ 731 31 90), Rue du Suchiez 35, is over two km from the town centre. It's a long, dull walk so take bus No 1 from Place Pury to Vauseyon then follow the signs. It is a small, pleasant, family-run place with good evening meals and a laundry service. Beds are Sfr22 per night; reception is closed from 9 am to 5 pm and the hostel closes from early November to early April. Get a key to avoid the curfew.

Hotels *Hôtel du Poisson* (☎ 753 30 31), Ave Bachelin 7, Marin, has singles/doubles for Sfr41/76 with private shower. In Neuchâtel, the ageing *Hôtel Terminus* (☎ 725 20 21), opposite the station, has the cheapest rooms: Sfr90/120 with shower or Sfr50/90 without.

Hôtel Marché (☎ 724 58 00) is ideally central at Place des Halles 4, with rooms overlooking the square (you may find these noisy if you're a light sleeper). Singles/doubles vary in size, each has a TV but showers are in the hall. Prices are Sfr70/100, and an extra bed in the room costs Sfr35. *Hôtel des Beaux-Arts* (☎ 724 01 51), Rue Pourtalès 3, is friendly and reasonably central. Rooms with private shower/toilet start at Sfr96/150, and there are some rooms using hall shower for Sfr64/118. The inexpensive restaurant is open daily.

Hôtel Touring au Lac (☎ 725 55 01; fax 725 82 43), Place Numa-Droz 1, is by the harbour. It has good rooms from Sfr130/175 with bath/toilet, TV, radio, mini bar and telephone. There are a few cheaper rooms in a less salubrious section of the building. The airy restaurant is a good place to sit and watch the boats, and consume mid-price food. Top of the range in Neuchâtel is *Hôtel Beaulac* (☎ 723 11 11; fax 725 60 35), Quai Léopold Robert 2, overlooking the harbour. Large rooms from Sfr145/205 have all the expected amenities. The cable TV picks up 26 channels and there are two restaurants on site.

Places to Eat
Local specialities include tripe, and tomme Neuchâteloise chaude, a baked cheese starter. Fish from the lake, especially trout (truite), is another treat.

Self-Service Opposite the tourist office is an *EPA* department store with a restaurant offering menus for as low as Sfr7. It's open to 6.30 pm weekdays and 5 pm on Saturday. Nearby is a *Coop* with a self-service restaurant at Rue de la Treille 4. There is also a *Migros* supermarket on Rue de l'Hôpital, with a snack counter. Meals for around Sfr8 are available in the *student cafétéria*, Cité Universitaire, Ave de Clos-Brochet. It's open weekdays from 11.30 am to 1.30 pm and 5.30 to 7.30 pm, and for Saturday lunch.

Other Restaurants *La Crêperie*, Rue de l'Hôpital 7, is popular with mainly youngish locals. There is no name sign outside. If you don't like thin pancakes you'll think this place is a load of crêpe, because that's all it serves. The price is between Sfr2.50 and Sfr10, depending on the filling, of which there's a wide choice ranging from the exotic to the mundane. A savoury one followed by a sweet one is just about enough for a meal. Have one as a dessert if nothing else.

Le Lotus (☎ 724 27 44), 1st floor, Rue de l'Ancien 4, is near Rue du Château. It serves excellent oriental food (mainly Thai) for around Sfr30. For lunch, there are assiettes du jour and two or three-course menus (Sfr19 to Sfr25). At ground level is the *Café du Cerf* where the same daily specials are available for lunch and dinner, but it's mainly used as a drinking venue. It attracts a young crowd with its beer on draught (bier pression, Sfr4.50 for half a litre) and in bottles from around the world (about Sfr6 for 0.3 litre).

The gourmet's choice is *Restaurant des Halles*, (☎ 724 31 41) in the historic 16th century building with a turret on Place des Halles. The cooking is French in style with main courses starting at Sfr35 and multi-course menus at Sfr70 or more. It's on the 1st floor and closes on Sunday and Monday. Downstairs, the Brasserie serves good-sized tasty pizzas costing Sfr13 to Sfr18 (open daily).

Restaurants de Nuit Neuchâtel canton is unique in allowing restaurants to stay open all night, and there are usually plenty of people eager to take advantage of this fact. Another name for these places is *Cercle*. The emphasis is often more on drinking than eating; usually there's a large bar (beer around Sfr4) and loud music, with the restaurant section (meals from Sfr15) in a side room. These places are typically open from 9 pm to 6 am, and can actually stay open later than nightclubs that don't serve food. *Garbo Café*, Rue des Chavannes 7, is in the old town (closed Monday); *Casablanca*, Rue de l'Ecluse 56, is a little less central (closed Tuesday).

Entertainment
Casino de la Rotonde, Faubourg du Lac, has a range of attractions: cabaret with dancing girls (nightly except Sunday from 10 pm), restaurant (weekdays only, with lunch specials), games room, and disco (Friday and Saturday night; Sfr14 entry, or Sfr10 with flyer). In the same building is *Club Cave aux Moines*, a student-type bar/café (open from 4 pm, closed Sunday). Another bar favoured by students is *Appareils de Chauffage*, Rue des Moulins 37. *Garage*, Rue de l'Hôpital 4, is a bar and disco with free entry (open from 8.30 pm; closed Wednesday). *La Case a Chocs* (☎ 721 20 56), Quai Philippe Godet 16, in a former brewery, is an 'alternative' venue where there is live music most weekends and occasional cinema and art shows.

Getting There & Away
There are hourly fast trains to Geneva (70 minutes, Sfr41), Bern via Kerzers (35 minutes, Sfr16.60), Basel (95 minutes, Sfr35), Biel (20 minutes, Sfr9.60), and many other destinations. Around two an hour run to Yverdon (20 minutes, Sfr11.40). Neuchâtel is also the hub for buses and trains into the Neuchâtel Jura. Postbuses leave from outside the station. The bus to Le Locle (Sfr15.80) via La Chaux du Milieu departs

every two hours and takes one hour. The bus information office is on Place Pury and train information is at the *Hôtel Touring au Lac*; both are open weekdays and Saturday morning.

Avis car rental (☎ 725 99 91), is at Rue de la Pierre-à-Mazel 51, and Hertz (☎ 730 32 32) is less central at Rue de Bourgogne 12.

Boat Boat services on the lake are most frequent from the end of May to late September. There are several departures a day (except Monday) to Murten (takes 1½ hours, Sfr15), Estavayer-le-Lac (1½ hours, Sfr14) and Yverdon (3 hours, Sfr22).

Getting Around
Local buses cost Sfr1.60 to Sfr2.60, depending upon the length of the journey (colour-coding on dispensers tell you what you need). Sfr6 gets you a 24-hour ticket. All local buses hit the main transport hub, Place Pury. The free timetable booklet shows the different departure points from the square. Street parking in blue zones (90-minute limit) are free in town, as is car parking at Place du 12 Septembre by the lake (though charges may be introduced).

AROUND NEUCHÂTEL
Vineyards clothe the hills on the northern shore of Lake Neuchâtel. Families have been making wines here for many generations, and most producers are still small-scale concerns. The tourist office has a list of cellars where the output can be sampled. Red wines come from the Pinot Noir grape and white wines from the Chasselas. The white wine, by the way, must be poured from a height of at least six inches above the glass for the best results. A bit of a problem if you're just swigging it from the bottle.

Marin is six km north-east of Neuchâtel, where you'll find **Papiliorama**, a hot and humid tropical garden within a large dome. Inside are over 1000 butterflies of all sizes and hues, and a hatchery where, if you're lucky, you'll see chrysalises breaking out of their cocoons. There's also numerous colourful and exotic birds flying around, plus tropical plants, fish, tortoises and an insectarium. Next-door is **Nocturama**, a dome for night creatures from Latin America. A combined ticket costs Sfr11 (Sfr5 for children) and they're open daily from 9 am (10 am for Nocturama) to 6 pm, reducing to 10 am to 5 pm daily in winter. The domes are near the Marin Centre, a huge shopping complex with a *Migros* supermarket and restaurant. Take bus No 1 from Place Pury and get off after Marin village at Bellevue, or take the local train to Marin Epagnier. If driving, go north-east along Ave du Premier Mars.

The best view of the Alps and the lakes can be achieved from **Chaumont** (1087m). It's just 20 minutes by car (heading northeast) from the centre of Neuchâtel, or take bus No 7 to La Coudre (direction: Hauterive) then a short funicular ride (Sfr5.80 up or Sfr9.20 return; half-price with city day pass).

LA CHAUX-DE-FONDS

• *pop 37,300* • *1000m* • ☎ *(032)*

This is the largest town in the region and the highest in Switzerland. It's an important centre for watch and clock-making and the impressive horology museum is the main reason for a visit. The architect Le Corbusier was born in the town in 1887 and various examples of his innovative work can be seen.

Orientation & Information

The tourist office (☎ 914 20 10) is at Espacité 1, in the ground floor of the tall tower (with a viewing terrace) 10 minutes' walk from the train station. Opening hours are weekdays from 8 am to 5.30 pm and Saturday from 10 am to 2 pm. From 1 November to 30 April it closes from noon to 1.30 pm on weekdays and Saturday hours change to 9 am to noon. There's touch-screen information outside.

Warning: some street names and numbers changed at the end of 1996, but it shouldn't affect places mentioned in this book.

Museums

International Museum of Horology It was the technical expertise of Huguenot refu-

gees, settlers in Geneva at the end of the 16th century, which started Switzerland on the way to its current annual production of over 100 million watches. The craft soon spread throughout the Jura which quickly established itself as the centre of the industry. This Musée International d'Horlogerie, Rue des Musées 29, tells you everything you need to know about time-keeping. Many signs are in English. It displays clocks and watches from the earliest constructed to the latest; some are extremely elaborate and beautiful. Sections explain and illustrate all aspects of watchmaking, including construction, engraving and enamelling. There's plenty to amuse kids, eg a machine that tests reaction times. In the car park is a 15-tonne carillon that chimes every 15 minutes. Allow one to two hours to get around. Admission costs Sfr8 (Sfr7 for senior citizens, Sfr4 for children and students, Sfr18 for families) and it is open Tuesday to Sunday from 10 am to noon and 2 to 5 pm (no lunch-break in summer).

Next door to the Horology museum is the **Museum of Fine Arts** (Musée des Beaux-Arts). It has an interesting contemporary art section plus many works by Swiss painters. Local boys Léopold Robert, Le Corbusier and Edouard Kaiser are well represented. It's open Tuesday to Sunday from 10 am to noon and 2 to 5 pm, and costs Sfr6 for adults, Sfr3 for children, seniors and students, and Sfr14 for families. The **Museum of Natural History** (Musée d'histoire naturelle) is above the main post office; it's free and closed on Monday.

Other Sights

Thirteen buildings that relate to Le Corbusier's early life or work are described in an itinerary available from the tourist office. The interior of the Turkish Villa (Villa Schwob) can be viewed by telephoning in advance on ☎ 912 31 23.

Blondeau SA (☎ 968 39 43), Rue de l'Hôtel de Ville 26-28, is a small **cowbell foundry**. Each bell cast is handmade from Parisien burnt sand, and every third day the molten metal (80% copper and 20% zinc) is poured into the prepared casts. The metal takes only

Top: Le Château de Chillon, Lake Geneva Region
Bottom: Statue of former resident, Charlie Chaplin, Vevey, Lake Geneva Region

MARK HONAN

MARK HONAN

Top: Parade participants of the International Balloon Week in Château d'Oex,
Lake Geneva Region
Bottom: Parade participants, Brig, Valais

Le Corbusier

Le Corbusier was born Charles Edouard Jeanneret on 6 October 1887 at Rue de la Serre 38. His adopted name was derived from that of his maternal grandfather. In 1917 he moved to Paris where his career began in earnest. Le Corbusier was one of the key innovators behind the development of the International Style of architecture which achieved dominance in the 20th century, and especially since the 1950's. Characteristic features of this style are the use of modern materials (particularly reinforced concrete and steel) to create functional buildings with pure, straight lines. Aesthetic considerations weren't overlooked, although today's boring office complexes and blocks of flats are clear descendants of this genre. Some of Le Corbusier's own creations, however, explore spatial relations in a much more dynamic way. He died in 1965. ■

Le Corbusier was the architect of the Chapel of Notre Dame du Haut (1951-53) in Ronchamp.

10 minutes to one hour to cool and is then removed from the cast and smoothed. Visitors may watch the artisans at work (free). Pouring the metal is the most interesting stage, and happens around 8.30 am (telephone ahead).

In the **Bois du Petit Château** is a zoological garden and a vivarium. Entry is free; walk to the north-west end of Rue Docteur Coullery or take bus No 4.

Places to Stay

Camping *Bois du Couvent* (☎ 913 25 55) is on the edge of a wood two km behind the main station, off Boulevard de la Liberté. It's open from May to September.

The SYHA *hostel* (☎ 968 43 15), Rue de Doubs 34, has beds for Sfr23. Reception is closed from 9 am to 5 pm (6 pm on Sunday) but there's daytime access. The hostel closes in November and December. To avoid the 15-minute walk from the station, take bus No 4 (or No 22 after 7 pm).

Croix d'Or (☎ 968 43 53), Rue de la Balance 15, has simple rooms sharing one hall shower for Sfr32/64. Breakfast is Sfr7.50 per person. By the station is *Garni de France* (☎ 913 11 16). It has singles/doubles ranging from simple (Sfr45/76) to comfortable (Sfr88/146) but it has something of a sleazy reputation. Breakfast costs Sfr8 per person. *Griffin's* (☎ 913 40 31), Ave Léopold Robert 11, is a lively pub offering rooms with shower for Sfr55/85.

Hôtel du Moulin (☎ 926 42 26), Rue de la Sere 130, has comfortable, nicely decorated rooms with TV and shower for Sfr80/110. Some cheaper rooms are available using the hall showers. The hotel has a car park and even a 10-pin bowling alley.

Places to Eat

There's a *Migros* supermarket and self-service restaurant (on the 3rd floor) in the Métropole shopping centre, 200m to the right of the station. Nearby is a *Coop*, Rue

La Chaux-de-Fonds

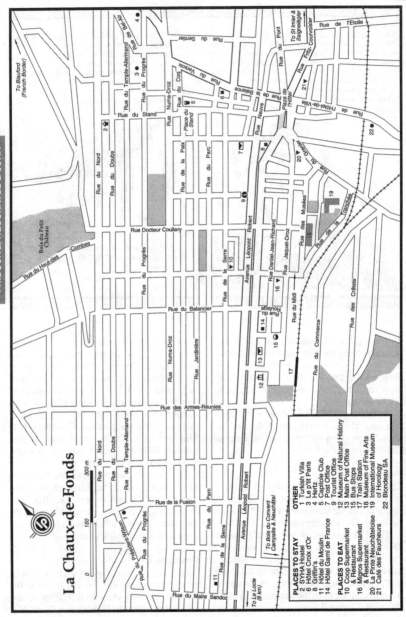

PLACES TO STAY
2 SYHA Hostel
6 Hôtel Croix d'Or
8 Griffin's
11 Hôtel du Moulin
14 Hôtel Garni de France

PLACES TO EAT
10 Coop Supermarket
& Restaurant
16 Migros Supermarket
& Restaurant
20 La Pinte Neuchâteloise
21 Café des Faucheurs

OTHER
1 Turkish Villa
3 Le p'tit Paris
4 Hertz
5 Capitole Club
7 Post Office
9 Tourist Office
12 Museum of Natural History
13 Main Post Office
15 Bus Stops
17 Train Station
18 Museum of Fine Arts
19 International Museum
of Horology
22 Blondeau SA

0   150   300 m

FRIBOURG, NEUCHÂTEL & JURA

de la Serre 37. It's not self-service but it's as cheap as those that are (open to 7 pm weekdays and 5 pm Saturday). In a big shopping complex to the south-west of town is *Manora*, Blvd des Eplatures 20, with good buffet-style food for around Sfr11. It's open daily to 10 pm. Take bus No 2 (or No 44 after 7 pm) and get off at Eplatures.

An excellent choice is *Café des Faucheurs* on Rue des Granges. It's unobtrusive, small, very cheap and frequented by locals. There's no written menu, so ask the server about the six or so dishes on offer (eg fondue for just Sfr13). The service is friendly but very slow – sample the beers or open wines and be prepared to settle down for the evening (closed weekends).

Croix d'Or, already recommended under Places to Stay, has an Italian restaurant called *Il Caminetto*. There are filets de perch for Sfr18.80 and good pizzas for Sfr10.10 to Sfr13.90. It's open daily to midnight.

Restaurant *La Pinte Neuchâteloise* (☎ 913 38 64), at Rue du Grenier 8, has a lunch menu for Sfr13.50 including soup or salad (closed Tuesday). There's also fondue from Sfr15 – sometimes the atmosphere is so thick with bubbling cheese that people on a diet can dine on the smell alone. Meat and fish dishes are Sfr20 or more, and there's a room where a well-dressed clientele can consume the menu degustation: Sfr68 for five courses. The chef and the staff are moving to a new location in 1997, so check the new address with the tourist office.

Entertainment
Le p'tit Paris (☎ 968 65 33) is at Rue du Progrès 4. It serves mid-price food and has a cellar called *La Cave* where there's live music (usually jazz-rock) every Friday and Saturday. Entry is free or up to Sfr12 and beers are not expensive. Nearby is *Capitole Club*, Place du Strand 6, one of several restaurants de nuit (see Neuchâtel); it's closed Sunday night.

Bikini Test (☎ 968 06 66), Joux Perret 3, is a venue that has live music (entry around Sfr20)and occasional dance and alternative films. It's on the edge of town to the northeast: take bus No 2 or 22.

Getting There & Away
Trains run to Neuchâtel every hour (Sfr9.60, takes 30 minutes). Local trains run to Basel via Saignelégier and Delémont, but this is a slow journey: travelling via Biel is quicker. Postbuses connect the smaller places; schedules are available from the tourist office. To Neuchâtel by car, a new road and tunnel (highway 20) means you can get there in 20 minutes. A slower route is via Vue des Alpes (1283m), giving an expansive view of the Alps. From here, detour a couple of km to the Tête de Ran Hotel, then climb a steep path for 15 minutes. The panorama at this belvedere (1422m) is even better.

There is a postbus service running northwards into France to Charquemont, crossing the border at Biaufond. The road is in good condition, if rather winding.

Hertz (☎ 968 52 28) has a car rental office at Charrière 15.

Getting Around
Buses become less frequent at around 7 pm when some routes combine to form a new route under a new number. Rides cost Sfr2 for adults and 'juniors' (age 16 to 25) or Sfr1.20 for 'enfants' (age six to 16). A five strip ticket costs Sfr8 (Sfr5 for enfants and juniors) and a day pass is Sfr5 (Sfr3 for enfants and juniors). There's a major bus hub just to the right of the train station.

NEUCHÂTEL MONTAGNES
Less rugged than the Alps, these mountains make fewer demands on hikers (1500 km of maintained and marked footpaths, some accessible in winter) and cyclists(1760 km of bike paths). In winter, there is some downhill skiing (30 ski lifts), but of greater importance is cross-country skiing. In all there are 400 km of cross-country trails; some of these are groomed regularly and a few are even lit. For equipment rental, try

Calame Sports (☎ 032-968 24 40), Neuve 3, La Chaux-de-Fonds. Ice skating on frozen lakes is also popular, particularly on the Lake of Taillères.

In addition to watch-making, agriculture and milk production are important to the local economy. A network of postbuses connects the smaller towns and villages in the region, although departures can be infrequent.

Le Locle

Le Locle is an important watch-making centre. It was in the late 18th century that Daniel Jean-Richard introduced this skill to the Neuchâtel Jura, practising his craft in Le Locle. The town's **Museum of Horology** is located in 18th century Château des Monts. There are some grand period rooms as well as numerous timepieces that span the centuries from the earliest devices to the latest technological innovations. Experience an aural earthquake as dozens of clocks simultaneously chime the hour. An unusual automation in the Maurice Sandoz room depicts an old woman with a stooped gait supporting herself on two walking sticks. The museum is open Tuesday to Sunday from 10 am to noon and from 2 to 5 pm (afternoons only between November and April). Admission costs Sfr6 adults, Sfr5 senior citizens, Sfr4 students, Sfr3 children, and Sfr15 families.

Two km from the town are the **Col-des-Roches Underground Mills**. These mills exploit the underwater flow of the Bied River on its way to join the Doubs River. It was Jonas Sandoz who started the work of widening existing fissures in the rock and creating waterfalls and wells, until by the end of the 17th century the underground complex included a thresher, two flour mills, an oil mill and a saw mill. The building on the surface dates from 1844. The mills were gradually allowed to fall into disuse and for much of the 20th century were used as a slaughterhouse. Renovations to turn the mills into a tourist attraction started in 1973. There's an exhibition in the entrance hall and large pieces of machinery in the underground caves. The site is open 1 May to 31 October from 10 am to noon and 2 to 5.30 pm every day; entry costs Sfr7 for adults, Sfr6 for senior citizens, Sfr4 for students and children, and Sfr15 for families.

For more information, contact the Le Locle tourist office (☎ 032-931 43 30), Daniel Jean-Richard 31.

Getting There & Away From La Chaux-de-Fonds, Le Locle is only seven minutes and eight km (Sfr2.80) by the hourly train that originates at Neuchâtel; the bus is the same price. Trains also run into France to Morteau and beyond. The Col-des-Roches Underground Mills can be reached by postbus on the more-or-less hourly Le Locle-La Brévine service (Sfr2.40 each way; if coming from La Chaux-de-Fonds, it's cheaper to buy a straight-through ticket). For postbus information ring ☎ 032-931 32 31.

Doubs Basins

The Doubs Basins is the area on the French border where the River Doubs broadens into Lake Brenets (Lac des Brenets, or Lac de Chaillexon on the French side of the border). Along part of its length, the shapes of the limestone cliffs are reputed to resemble famous historical figures such as Louis-Philippe (hardly flattering – gives a new significance to the description 'craggy features'). There's also the **Doubs Falls** (Saut du Doubs) which hurtle down from a height of 27m. Contact the boat operator, NLB (☎ 032-932 14 14), for short cruises of the lake in the summer. Boats sail between the village of Les Brenets and the waterfall; to walk between these two points takes an hour. The **Chemin des Planètes** between Le Locle and Saut du Doubs is a path modelled on scaled-down distances between the planets in the solar system.

Getting There & Away Les Brenets is five km from Le Locle. Trains run frequently and cost Sfr2.80 each way.

Jura Canton

FRANCHES MONTAGNES

This is the part of the Jura mountain chain that is within the canton of Jura. It is usually overlooked by foreign visitors, which means that relatively inexpensive accommodation can be found. It's an area of pastures and woodlands where there are 1500 km of hiking trails and 200 km of prepared cross-country ski trails. Horse-riding is another popular activity; the horses in the area are known for their gentleness and calm disposition. There are equestrian centres in over 30 towns and villages offering all-in weeks, weekends, or simple hourly rides. Chez Cindy (☎ 032-951 16 85), La Theurre 1, Saignelégier, charges Sfr25 per hour and Sfr35 for an overnight stay. The weekend rate including rides, meals and accommodation is Sfr190 for adults and Sfr80 for kids.

The main town in the region is **Saignelégier,** where the annual national horse show is held in August. Get more information from Jura Tourisme (see the introduction to this chapter). The number for accommodation reservations throughout the Jura canton is ☎ 032-951 28 12.

Getting There & Away

Saignelégier is on the rail line between La Chaux-de-Fonds (takes 40 minutes, Sfr12.20) and Basel (2½ hours, Sfr26). By

An example of Jura architecture.

car, there are two famous viewpoints you can detour to on the way to this part of the Jura. The northernmost one is at **Weissenstein** (make for the Kurhaus Weissenstein at 1284m), 10 km from Solothurn. The road continues to Moutier where it branches to either Delémont or Tavannes. The more southern of the two routes starts at La Neuveville, on the shore of Lake Biel. A minor road winds up from here to St Imier (33 km). This road is usually impassable in winter and spring and ascends the **Chasseral** (1607m) peak. Stop off at the Hôtel du Chasseral, where there is a viewing table, then walk 30 minutes to the telecommunications tower for a 360° panorama. From either Weissenstein or Chasseral you can see the broad expanse of the Alps spread out before you.

Geneva

• *pop 175,630* • *375m* • ☎ *(022)*

Geneva (Genève in French) is Switzerland's third-largest city, comfortably encamped on the shores of Lake Geneva (Lac Léman). But Geneva belongs not so much to French-speaking Switzerland as to the whole world. Whether the issue is world climactic changes or peace in the Balkans, the mediators rush to the neutral territory of Geneva to seek common ground. It is truly an international city. One in three residents are non-Swiss and over 200 international organisations are based here. Among the most important are the European headquarters of the United Nations, the International Red Cross and the World Health Organisation.

For the administrators, secondment to Geneva must seem more like a holiday than hard work. The city enjoys a fine location. Strolls around the lake on a sunny day are hugely enjoyable, as are boat excursions. The cuisine is excellent and varied, and the same applies to the cultural diversions. Geneva is a city in pristine condition: it is clean, efficient and safe. Some say it is too successful in these respects, and complain the city is sterile. Some people wouldn't recognise a good thing if it waved a dozen flags and shouted in their ear.

HIGHLIGHTS

• Jet d'Eau – the world's tallest fountain
• Extensive museum collections
• Unique opportunity to explore CERN, a leading physics research centre with the world's biggest machine
• Varied international cuisine
• Thriving alternative arts scene

Geneva

History

Geneva was occupied successively by Romans and Burgundians and became a powerful bishopric from the 5th century. It was partially subservient to the Imperial Emperor, but that did not prevent the House of Savoy from making repeated attempts to gain control of the city, which was becoming increasingly affluent through its fairs and markets.

Under pressure from the Swiss Confederation, the Duke of Savoy agreed in 1530 to leave Geneva alone. A couple of years later the Reformation was introduced to the city by Guillaume Farel, who was followed and superseded by John Calvin. Calvin's teachings were so effective in Geneva that it became known as the 'Protestant Rome'; there ensued a time of austerity in which fun became frowned upon. Corrupting habits like dancing and wearing jewels were actually forbidden (yet interestingly, around the same time the taking of interest on a loan was legalised). Such a repressive environment might be expected to deter visitors, but over the ensuing centuries, Geneva earned a reputation as an intellectual centre and attracted many free thinkers.

In the meantime Geneva had to put up with another incursion from Savoy. Led by the duke, Charles Emmanuel, an attempt was made to take the city on the night of 11 December 1602. An advance guard scaled the city walls with the intention of opening the gates and letting in the main force. The Savoyards were spotted by a sentry just in time, and the whole force was routed with the loss of only 18 Genevan lives. An event from this victory is commemorated in the annual Escalade festival (see Special Events later in this chapter).

After this success in 1602, Geneva had no further trouble with Savoy, but in 1798 the French annexed the city and held it for nearly 16 years. During this period it was the capital of the French Léman Department. Geneva was freed on 1 June 1814 and within a year it was admitted to the Swiss Confederation.

Orientation

Geneva and the small enclave of Swiss territory around the south-west lip of Lake Geneva constitute both a separate canton and a distinct tourist region. The canton is home to 395,600 people. The centre of the city hugs the shore of the lake and is split through the middle by the westward progress of the Rhône. Conveniently in the centre of town on the north side of the river is the main train station, Gare de Cornavin. To the south of the river lies the old part of town *(vieille ville)*, with the pedestrian-only Grand-Rue at its core. Most of the museums skirt the old section. East of the old town is Gare des Eaux-Vives, the French Railways station for trains running south-east into France.

The two parts of the city are often known as *rive droit* (right bank, ie north of the Rhône) and *rive gauche* (left bank, ie the south). Geneva's most visible landmark in summer is the 140m Jet d'Eau, a giant fountain spouting water into the lake from a pier on the southern shore.

International organisations are mostly north of the station, and the main shopping area is around Rue du Rhône, on the south bank.

Information

Tourist Offices The busy tourist office (☎ 738 52 00, fax 731 90 56; see the Geneva Station Area map) is in the railway station, and is open Monday to Saturday from 9 am to 6 pm. From mid-June to 31 August hours extend to Monday to Friday from 8 am to 8 pm and Saturday and Sunday from 8 am to 6 pm. Pick up the free weekly *Geneva Agenda* booklet, covering art events, exhibitions, nightclubs, sights and restaurants. Either side of the office are information offices for trains (closed Sunday) and city public transport.

The Centre d'Accueil et de Reseignements (CAR) (☎ 731 46 47; see the Geneva Station Area map) has tourist and accommodation information, and runs a hitching/car-sharing agency. It is based in a yellow bus at the station end of Rue du Mont Blanc and is open mid-June to 31 August, daily from 8 am to 11 pm.

Detailed information on the city is also dispensed in the old town at Information de la Ville de Genève (☎ 311 98 27; see the Geneva Old Town map), 4 Place du Molard. It is open weekdays from 9 am (12.30 pm Monday) to 6.30 pm and Saturday from 10.30 am to 4.30 pm. Counselling and information for young people is at Centre d'Information pour Jeunes (☎ 311 44 22), 13 Rue Verdaine, daily from 10 am (2 pm on weekends) to 10 pm.

The best free map of the city (with a street index) is the one given by the Swiss Bank Corporation (Société de Banque Suisse). There's a branch opposite the station.

Foreign Consulates Among the consulates in Geneva are:

Australia
    56-58 Rue de Moillebeau (☎ 918 29 00)
Canada
    1 Pré de la Bichette (☎ 919 92 00)
France
    11 Rue J Imbert Galloix (☎ 311 34 41)
Italy
    14 Rue Charles Galland (☎ 346 47 44)
New Zealand
    28A Chemin du Petit-Saconnex(☎ 734 95 30); there is no full embassy in Switzerland
UK
    37-39 Rue de Vermont (☎ 734 38 00)
USA
    1-3 Ave de la Paix (☎ 738 76 13)

GENEVA

GENEVA

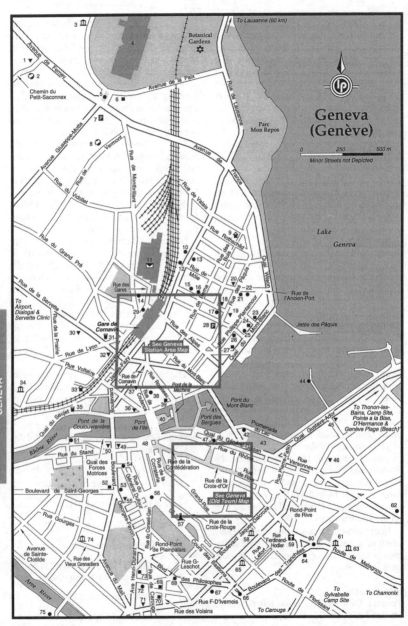

Geneva
(Genève)

0   250   500 m
Minor Streets not Depicted

Lake Geneva

To Lausanne (60 km)

Botanical Gardens

Avenue de Ferney

Chemin du Petit-Saconnex

Avenue de la Paix

Parc Mon Repos

Avenue Giuseppe-Motta

Rue de Vermont

Rue de Montbrillant

Avenue de France

Rue de Valais

Rue du Grand Pré

Rue de la Servette

Rue de Lausanne

Rue Rothschild

Rue du Môle

Rue de Berne

Rue des Gares

Quai Wilson

Quai du Mont-Blanc

Rue de l'Ancien-Port

Jetée des Pâquis

To Airport, Dialogai & Servette Clinic

Rue de la Prairie

Gare de Cornavin

See Geneva Station Area Map

Rue Philippe-Plantamour

Rue des Alpes

Rue de Lyon

Rue Voltaire

Boulevard James-Fazy

Rue de Cornavin

Rue du Mont-Blanc

Pont de la Machine

Pont du Mont-Blanc

Rue de la Rôtisserie

Rue des Pâquis

Pont des Bergues

Pont de l'Île

Promenade du Lac

Quai Gustave-Ador

To Thonon-les-Bains, Camp Site, Pointe à la Bise, D'Hermance & Genève Plage (Beach)

Quai du Général-Guisan

Rue du Rhône

Rue de Rive

Rue Versonnex

Quai des Seujet

Rhône River

Quai de la Poste

Pont de la Coulouvrenière

Rue du Stand

Quai des Forces Motrices

Boulevard de Saint-Georges

Rue de la Confédération

Rue de la Croix-d'Or

See Geneva (Old Town) Map

Grand-Rue

Rue de la Croix-Rouge

Rond-Point de Rive

Rue Pierre-Fatio

Rue du Diday

Rue du Général-Dufour

Boulevard Georges-Favon

Rue Gourgas

Rue des Vieux Grenadiers

Avenue de Sainte-Clotilde

Rue du Mail

Rond-Point de Plainpalais

Rue G-Leschot

Boulevard des Philosophes

Boulevard Jacques-Dalcroze

Rue Ferdinand-Hodler

Rue Lefort

Rue de Carouge

Avenue Henri-Dunant

Cours des Bastions

Route de Malagnou

Arve River

Rue F-D'Ivernois

Rue des Voisins

To Carouge

To Sylvabelle Camp Site

Route de Florissant

To Chamonix

PLACES TO STAY

6	Centre Masaryk
9	SYHA Hostel
23	Hôtel de la Cloche
24	Noga Hilton Hôtel & Le Cygne Restaurant
27	Hôtel Beau Rivage
33	Armée du Salut Hostel
39	Hôtel Ambassador
52	Hôtel Beau-Site
64	Hôtel Kaufmann
69	Centre Universitaire Zofingien
70	Hôtel le Prince
73	Hôtel Aïda

PLACES TO EAT

1	Les Continents
18	Le Blason
19	Auberge de Savièse
20	Migros Supermarket & Restaurant
30	Kong Restaurant
32	La Trattoria
36	Le Neptune
37	Auberge de Coutance
45	L'Amiral
46	Dent de Lion
49	Café Huissard
50	Le Béarn
55	Cave Valaisanne et Chalet Suisse
71	Café Universal

OTHER

2	New Zealand Consulate
3	International Red Cross & Red Crescent Museum
4	Palais des Nations
5	Place des Nations
7	Varembé Parking Garage
8	UK Consulate
10	Horizon Motos (Motorcycles)
11	Post Office (Genève 2)
12	Budget (Car Rental)
13	Avis (Car Rental)
14	Ilot 13
15	Europcar (Car Rental)
16	Bureau de Change
17	Laveblanc (Laundrette)
21	Sixt-Alsa (Car Rental)
22	Edelweiss Manotel
25	Casino
26	American Library
28	Parking
29	Place du Reculet
31	Casting Café
34	Voltaire Museum
35	l'Inderdit & Le Loft
38	Fruit & Vegetable Market
40	Tour d'Île

41	Île Rousseau
42	CGN Ticket Booth
43	Jardin Anglais
44	Jet d'Eau
47	Place du Lac
48	Place Bell Air
51	l'Usine
53	Victoria Hall
54	Place de la Synagogue
56	Place Neuve
57	Promenade des Bastions & Reformation Monument
58	Museum of Art & History
59	Russian Church
60	Place Emile Guyénot
61	Museum of Natural History
62	Gare des Eaux Vives
63	Horology Museum
65	Petit Palais
66	Place Edouard Claparéde
67	Cave 12
68	Place des Philosophes
72	SSR (Travel Agency)
74	Museum of Modern & Contemporary Art
75	Centre Sportif des Vernets

Money The exchange office in Gare de Cornavin is open daily from 6.45 am to 9.30 pm. The best rates seen while researching this edition were in the Bureau de Change at 32 Rue de Zürich, open weekdays from 9 am to 6.30 pm and Saturday from 9 am to 1 pm. In the airport, banks are open daily and charge Sfr5 commission to change cash (so change commission-free in the adjoining train station); they make no charge to redeem travellers' cheques.

Post & Communications The main post office (1211 Genève 1) is at 18 Rue du Mont Blanc. It is open Monday to Friday from 7.30 am to 6 pm, and Saturday from 7.30 to 11 am. The large post office (1211 Genève 2) behind the station has emergency counters (Sfr1 surcharge) open daily till late (closed Sunday morning).

Travel Agencies American Express (☎ 731 76 00; see the Geneva Station Area map) is at 7 Rue du Mont Blanc, open Monday to Friday from 8.30 am to 5.30 pm and Saturday from 9 am to noon. The student and budget travel agency SSR (☎ 329 97 33 or 34), 3 Rue Vignier, is open Monday to Friday from 9 am to 12.30 pm and 1.30 to 6 pm. Many other travel agents and airline offices are concentrated along Rue Chantepoulet and Rue du Mont Blanc.

Bookshops Elm Book Shop (☎ 736 09 45), 5 Rue Versonnex, sells English-language books, as do the rest of the places mentioned here. Good shops for second-hand books from around Sfr3 are Librairie des Amateurs, 15 Grand-Rue (see the Geneva Old Town map), and Book Worm (☎ 731 87 65), 5 Rue Sismondi. Artou (☎ 818 02 40), 8 Rue de

26 Countries in One

Switzerland is viewed as being a single country since the Rütli meadow oath in 1291. Yet up to 1848 the cantons were more-or-less independent states with separate armies, currencies and customs duties between each border. Even now they have their own constitution, government, police force, laws, courts and schools. Some cantons even describe themselves as a republic to emphasise their independence (eg Jura, Neuchâtel). Income tax levels vary between the cantons, and the fees charged for obtaining Swiss citizenship varies enormously too (Sfr75,000 for some communes in Geneva, down to purely administrative costs in Glarus).

Four categories of control have been identified in the sharing of power between country and canton. In the first category, the federal government has absolute authority: customs, currency, post and telecommunications, railways and navigation. In the second, the cantons are in charge: police, social services, housing and religion. In the third, the legislative powers belong to the Confederation, but the cantons are responsible for implementation: weights and measures, road traffic, military affairs, unemployment, social insurance, and civil and criminal courts. In the fourth category, powers are shared: taxation, road construction, hunting and fishing, health insurance, education and training. An example of the difference between the cantons can be seen in medical policy regarding organ donations. Most cantons (such as Basel City) will allow doctors to presume consent for taking organs for transplant. Some (like Basel District) say there must be explicit consent before this is done. Others (like Solothurn) have no overall legislation on the matter. ■

Representatives from the cantons of Uri, Schwyz and Unterwalden take the oath for unity at Rütli meadow (1291).

Rive, is a good place for travel books, and sells air tickets.

Cultural Centres Numerous social and cultural organisations are listed in the free English-language newspaper, *What's On In Geneva*, and the detailed *Guide to English-speaking Geneva*, available in the tourist office. The American Library (☎ 732 80 97), 3 Rue de Monthoux, is a place to browse among stacks of English-language books

(closed Monday). Radio 74 (88.8 MHz FM) broadcasts news from the BBC.

Laundry Laveblanc, 29 Rue de Monthoux, is self-service and open daily from 6 am to midnight.

Medical Services Ring ☎ 111 (premium rate) for information on medical services on call. The Cantonal Hospital (☎ 382 33 11), 24 Rue Micheli du Crest, has an emergency department.

Permanence Médico Chirurgicale (☎ 731 21 20), 21 Rue de Chantepoulet, is a private clinic, open 24 hours a day. Emergency dental treatment is at the Servette Clinic (☎ 733 98 00), 60 Ave Wendt, from 7.30 am and 8 pm weekdays, and every second weekend to 6 pm. Rosa Canina (☎ 738 66 66), 4 Rue de Môle, is a health centre for women.

Emergency The national emergency numbers apply: ☎ 117 for police, ☎ 118 for the fire brigade, ☎ 144 for an ambulance and ☎ 140 for the car breakdown service. There's a rape hotline on ☎ 733 63 63.

Gay & Lesbian Dialogai (☎ 340 00 00), 57 Ave Wendt, provides information, publishes a guide to the gay scene in Switzerland, and runs a bar on the premises that's open Wednesday from 8 pm and Sunday from 11 am to 2 pm.

Dangers & Annoyances On sunny days youngsters smoke dope in the Jardin Anglais and along the pier of the Jet d'Eau (some may consider this an opportunity rather than an annoyance). Like in most other Swiss cities, there's a growing problem with hard drug users; they tend to congregate between the Jardin Anglais and Place du Molard. It might be wise to exercise caution around this area at night.

Walking Tour
Take advantage of the recorded commentary available from the tourist office (Sfr10 plus Sfr50 deposit) that details 26 points of interest in the old town (duration around 2½ hours). There are also guided walks in summer.

A good starting point for a scenic walk is the **Île Rousseau**, spanning the Rhône. It is noted for a statue in honour of the celebrated free thinker, who formulated his seminal thoughts on democracy while, in his own words, a 'citizen of Geneva'.

Turn right and walk along the south side of the Rhône until you reach the 13th century **Tour d'Île**, once part of the medieval city

fortifications. Walk south down the narrow, cobbled Rue de la Cité until it becomes Grand-Rue. Here, at No 40, is Rousseau's birthplace. Grand-Rue terminates at **Place du Bourg-de-Four**, the oldest square in Geneva. It was once a Roman forum, evolved into a medieval marketplace, and now has a fountain and touristy shops.

Take Rue de la Fontaine to reach the lakeside. Anti-clockwise round the shore is the **Jet d'Eau**. Calling this a fountain is something of an understatement. The water shoots up with incredible force (200 km/h, 1360 horsepower) to create a 140m plume. At any one time, seven tonnes of water is in the air, and much of it, depending on the whims of the wind, falls on spectators who venture out on the pier. It's not activated in winter.

St Peter's Cathedral
The centre of town is dominated by the imposing, partially Romanesque, partially Gothic, Cathédrale de St Pierre. John Calvin preached here from 1536 to 1564; his seat outlasted him and can be seen in the north aisle. The body of the church still matches the austerity of Calvin's teaching in its lack of ostentation. This is in contrast to the small side chapel, first on the right after entering, with its ornate walls, windows and hanging light. Back in the main church, notice the aisle ceilings and the stained glass windows. There is a good view from the tower, which is open daily to 5.30 pm (entry Sfr2.50).

The cathedral rests upon a significant if unspectacular archaeological site (entry Sfr5, students Sfr3, closed Monday), though there are some fine 4th century mosaics amid the crumbling foundations.

Parks & Gardens
South of Grand-Rue, the **Promenade des Bastions** is a pleasant park which contains a massive monument to the Reformation. The giant figures of Bèze, Calvin, Farel and Knox are flanked by smaller statues of other important figures and carved depictions of events instrumental in the spread of the movement. It was created in 1917. The scale is deceptively large; Calvin and his chums

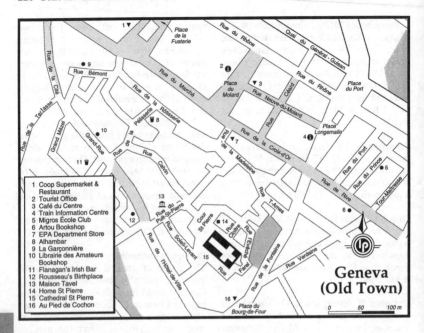

1 Coop Supermarket &
   Restaurant
2 Tourist Office
3 Café du Centre
4 Train Information Centre
5 Migros École Club
6 Artou Bookshop
7 EPA Department Store
8 Alhambar
9 La Garçonnière
10 Librairie des Amateurs
    Bookshop
11 Flanagan's Irish Bar
12 Rousseau's Birthplace
13 Maison Tavel
14 Home St Pierre
15 Cathedral St Pierre
16 Au Pied de Cochon

**Geneva
(Old Town)**

0   50   100 m

stand 4.5 metres tall, and it is over 100m long.

On the lakefront near the old town, the **Jardin Anglais** features a large clock composed of flowers. Colourful flower gardens and the occasional statue line the promenade on the north shore of the lake, and lead to two relaxing parks. One of these, the **Botanical Gardens** (Jardin Botanique), features exotic plants, llamas and an aviary. Entry is free and it is open daily from 7 am to 7.30 pm.

Museums & Galleries

Geneva is not a bad place to get stuck on a rainy day as there are plenty of museums, many of which are free. Two new museums are the large **International Motor Car Museum**, Palexpo, 40 Voie-des-Traz, near the airport (Sfr10, students and seniors Sfr6), and the **Museum of Modern & Contemporary Art**, 10 Rue des Vieux Grenadiers (Sfr9, students and seniors Sfr6); both are closed Monday.

Museum of Art & History The Musée d'Art et d'Histoire, 2 Rue Charles Galland is one of the most important museums. The vast and varied collection comprises some 500,000 items, including paintings, sculpture, room interiors, weapons and archaeology.

A highly-prized exhibit is *La Pêche Miraculeuse* by Konrad Witz. It was painted as an altarpiece for the cathedral and shows fishermen distracted from tending their catch, looking on in awe and astonishment as Christ walks on the water. What is remarkable about the composition is that Witz transposed the scene onto Lake Geneva, and in the background you can see Genevan houses, Mont Blanc and the foothills of Mt Salève.

Elsewhere there is a room of paintings by Ferdinand Hodler, particularly showing Alpine scenes, and several important works by Quentin de la Tour. The museum is open Tuesday to Sunday from 10 am to 5 pm and entry is free.

International Red Cross & Red Crescent Museum The Musée International de la Croix-Rouge et du Croissant-Rouge, 17 Ave de la Paix, is a compelling multi-media trawl through atrocities perpetuated by humanity in recent history. The message is supposed to be one of hope (as proclaimed by the banner above the reception counter, 'Each person has a shared responsibility to humanity'), but the horrors etch deeper in the mind than the palliative. Witnessing the carnage of the Battle of Solferino (1859) caused business-man Henri Dunant to agitate for an international body to care for wounded sol-diers. In 1863 the precursor organisation to the Red Cross was formed, with Dunant as secretary and Henri Dufour as the first pres-ident.

The subsequent achievements of the Red Cross (and the Moslem adjunct, the Red Crescent) are well documented; but people keep fighting, as the films, photos, sculptures and soundtracks vividly illustrate. The scale of the problem is bought home by the *seven million* index cards compiled by the Red Cross during WWII to keep track of prison-ers. Allow around 1½ hours to see the 11 areas of the museum, arranged in chronolog-ical order. Admission costs Sfr8 (Sfr4 for students and senior citizens, free for children under 12) and it is open Wednesday to Monday from 10 am to 5 pm. Buses 8 and F from Place de Cornavin drop you outside.

Petit Palais This compact gallery at 2 Terrace Saint Victor is expertly presented. The art sometimes encompasses the room décor in which the paintings and sculptures are displayed, creating a powerful effect. The gallery covers modern art, including Impressionist, Surrealist and Abstract works, and among the famous names represented are Picasso, Chagall, Renoir, Cézanne and Monet. The section on the Paris School is particularly good. It is a privately-owned gallery so unfortunately admission prices are high: Sfr10 for adults and Sfr5 for senior citizens and students (up to 25 years). It is open weekdays from 10 am to noon and 2 to 6 pm, and weekends from 10 am to 1 pm and 2 to 5 pm.

While you're in the area, wander down Rue Lefort to look at the **Russian church**, with gold domes that shimmer from afar on a sunny day. The small interior is a clutter of marble and religious images (Sfr1).

Museum of Natural History The Musée d'Histoire Naturelle, 1 Route de Malagnou, has dioramas, minerals and anthropological displays. Living species are displayed in the aquarium and vivarium sections, but the dinosaurs, shown in their natural environ-ment, are not alive. Entry is free, and it's open Tuesday to Sunday from 10 am to 5 pm.

Horology Museum The Musée de l'Horlogerie et de l'Emaillerie, 15 Route de Malagnou, hints at the importance of clocks and watches to the Genevan economy, and shows expert work in enamel on timepieces and other objects. It's free and open Wednes-day to Monday from 10 am to 5 pm.

Maison Tavel The oldest private house in the old town is Maison Tavel, 6 Rue du Puits St-Pierre. It is notable for a very detailed relief map of Geneva as it was in 1850. It covers 35 sq m and took the architect, August

GENEVA

Gold coin from Geneva displaying the Geneva coat of arms.

Magnin, 18 years to construct. The museum also gives a good account of Geneva's life and times from the 14th to the 19th century (detailed English notes available). Once again, entry is free, and it is open Tuesday to Sunday from 10 am to 5 pm.

Voltaire Museum Voltaire's residency in Geneva is celebrated in the Voltaire Museum at 25 Rue des Délices (admission free; open Monday to Friday from 2 to 5 pm).

United Nations

The Palais des Nations was once the headquarters of the defunct League of Nations. It is now the European home of the offspring of that organisation, the United Nations (UN), and the focal point for a resident population of 3000 international civil servants. The hour-long tour of the interior is only moderately interesting, and comparatively expensive at Sfr8.50 (students Sfr6.50). There is no charge to walk around the gardens, where there's a towering grey monument coated with heat-resistant titanium, donated by the USSR to commemorate the conquest of space.

The gardens are open Monday to Friday from November to March and daily from April to October. Guided tours are from 10 am to noon and 2 to 4 pm, and from 9 am to noon and 2 to 6 pm during July and August. You need to show your passport to gain admittance.

CERN

CERN, near Meyrin, is a research laboratory into particle physics funded by 19 nations. It accelerates electrons and positrons down a 27-km circular tube (the world's biggest machine) and the resulting collisions create new forms of matter – it achieved world headlines in 1996 by creating anti-matter for the first time. The Microcosm multi-media exhibition explains it all (free; English text), and is open Monday to Saturday from 10 am to 5 pm. Take bus No 15 from the station. Three-hour guided tours of the site are on Saturday only (free; reserve ahead on ☎ 767 84 84). You pass into France on the

tour but as it's not an official crossing you won't need a visa (take your passport anyway).

Mountain Views

Lake Geneva is often clouded over in winter, but if you gain some height you can attain good views of peaks poking above the cloud layer. Genevans often make for viewpoints in the Jura mountains to enjoy the winter sun, which make equally good summer excursions. Another possibility is Mont Salève (1100m) to the south-east. Take bus No 8 to Veyrier and walk across the border into France to reach the cable car (Sfr15 return, Sfr9.20 for students). It operates daily from May to September, Tuesday to Sunday during April and October, and only weekends and holidays during winter (closed 1 November to 25 December). A trip to Mont Blanc is also viable – see the Valais chapter.

Activities

There are several sports centres in the city. Centre Sportif des Vernets (☎ 343 88 50), 4 Rue Hans Wilsdorf, has swimming (Sfr4.50; students Sfr1.50) and ice skating (same price) and is open daily except Monday from 9 am. At weekends in the summer Lake Geneva is alive with the bobbing white sails of sailing boats. Swim in the lake at Genève Plage (Sfr5, including entry to a large pool with waterslide) on the south shore and at Jetée des Pâquis (Sfr1) on the north shore.

Courses

The Migros École Club (☎ 310 65 55; see the Geneva Old Town map), 5 Rue du Prince, has all sorts of adult-education courses, including French language classes. From mid-July to early October the University of Geneva (☎ 705 71 11) has French language classes lasting three weeks. Call ☎ 738 88 12 for information on private schools.

Organised Tours

Many excursions are organised by Key Tours (☎ 731 41 40), 7 Rue des Alpes, ranging from a two-hour bus tour of the city centre for Sfr27 (in English; departs daily from the

Routière bus station) to a day trip up Mont Blanc for Sfr188. Pick up the Excursions brochure from the tourist office or Key Tours.

Special Events

The celebration of l'Escalade on 11 December is Geneva's best known festival. In 1602, during Savoy's unsuccessful attempt to take Geneva, one of the Savoyard soldiers on the wall was repelled by a housewife, who poured her boiling soup over him, and proceeded to smash the cauldron over his head. This event has been adapted and is commemorated in the annual Escalade festival. In many Genevan homes, as part of the traditional celebrations, a chocolate cauldron is filled with marzipan which represents the vegetables of the soup. The cauldron is smashed by the youngest member of the family, then it and its contents are quickly consumed with un-Calvinistic eagerness.

As well as the ritual of the soup pot, there are torch-lit processions in historic costumes and a huge bonfire in the cathedral square. On the second weekend in August the **Fêtes de Genève** is a time of jollity, parades, open-air concerts and fireworks.

Places to Stay

As befits an international city that receives many important visitors on unlimited expense accounts, there is no lack of high-class, high-cost hotels. Happily, the city also has an excellent selection of places offering dormitory accommodation, and various religious and university institutions have youth-oriented singles/doubles at low rates. These are listed in the *Young People Info* leaflet issued by the tourist office, which also has *Hotels* and *Budget Hotels* brochures. Hotel reservations made by the tourist office cost Sfr5, or use the accommodation boards with free telephone outside. Ask the tourist office about 'Welcome to Geneva' vouchers if you plan to stay two nights or more.

Places to Stay – bottom end

Camping The most central camping ground, *Sylvabelle* (☎ 347 06 03), 10 Chemin de Conches, is reached by bus No 8 from Gare de Cornavin or Rond-Point de Rive. Four-person bungalows are available and camping is Sfr6 per person, Sfr5 per tent and Sfr3 per car (closed winter).

Seven km north-east of the city centre on the southern lakeshore is *Camping Pointe a la Bise* (☎ 752 12 96), Vesenaz. It's open from 1 April to 30 September, and costs Sfr6 per person and from Sfr7 for a tent. Take bus E from Rond-Point de Rive. Reception shuts at 10 pm. Seven km farther north and a five-minute walk from the last stop on bus E is *Camping D'Hermance* (☎ 751 14 83), Chemin des Glerrets. It's cheaper and has free beach access. Reception shuts at midnight. Both sites are open from around April to October and include car parking.

Hostels This is only a small selection of the places listed in *Young People Info*. In particular, there are seven places that take women only – of these, *Home St Pierre* (☎ 310 37 07), 4 Cour St Pierre, is a favourite among young female travellers.

North of the Rhône The SYHA *hostel* (☎ 732 62 60), 28-30 Rue Rothschild, is big, modern and busy, with helpful and knowledgeable staff. Dorms are Sfr23 (without a first night's surcharge) and there are a few family rooms and doubles (Sfr60 with shower). Dinners are reasonable value (Sfr11.50), and a TV room, laundry and kitchen facilities (Sfr1) are all available. The hostel is closed from 10 am to 5 pm (to 4 pm in summer) and there is a flexible midnight curfew. If you tire of eating at the hostel, try the cheap university café next door on the other side of Rue des Buis (closed weekends).

Centre Masaryk (☎ 733 07 72), 11 Ave de la Paix, has dorms for Sfr25 with an 11 pm curfew. Singles/doubles/triples cost Sfr38/64/90 and you can get a key for late access. Take bus No 5 or 8 from Gare de Cornavin.

Although intended for the socially disadvantaged, the *Armée du Salut hostel* (☎ 344 91 21), Chemin Galiffe 4, will give beds to

GENEVA

travellers. At just Sfr10 per person in very simple double rooms it's a bargain, but expect insalubrious co-habitees (closed from 9 am to 6 pm in winter, 8 am to 7 pm in summer; two nights' maximum stay for foreigners).

South of the Rhône *Cité Universitaire* (☎ 346 23 55), 46 Ave Miremont, has 500 beds available. Take bus No 3 from Cornavin to the terminus at Champel, south of the city centre. Dorm beds in July and August cost Sfr15 (they're restricted to groups the rest of the year). Rooms are subject to a two-night minimum stay: singles/doubles cost Sfr40/55 or Sfr34/50 for students. A double studio with kitchen, toilet and shower costs Sfr61. Prices exclude breakfast (from Sfr5). Reception is open from 8 am to noon (9 to 11 am on Sunday) and 2 pm (6 pm on weekends) to 10 pm.

Centre Universitaire Zofingien (☎ 329 11 40), 6 Rue des Voisins, has well-equipped rooms which are excellent value even if they are slightly cramped. Singles/doubles/triples with toilet, shower and sink are Sfr48/72/90.

Budget Hotels Choice in this category is limited, and at busy times you may be forced to move up or down-market.

North of the Rhône *Hôtel de la Cloche* (☎ 732 94 81), 6 Rue de la Cloche, is small, old-fashioned, friendly, and liable to be full unless you call ahead. Big singles/doubles using hall shower are Sfr50/75; doubles with shower cubicle in the room are Sfr85. Breakfast costs Sfr5.

Hôtel Lido (☎ 731 55 30; see the Geneva Station Area map) 8 Rue de Chantepoulet, has decent-sized rooms compared to the Geneva average; genial staff, too. Singles/doubles with private shower, toilet, TV and radio start at Sfr75/120, and there are a couple of rooms for Sfr65/110 using hall shower.

South of the Rhône *Hôtel Aïda* (☎ 320 12 66), 6 Ave Henri-Dunant, has renovated singles/doubles using hall shower for Sfr55/75. Rooms with shower/WC (Sfr75/100) also have a TV.

Hôtel Beau-Site (☎ 328 10 08), 3 Place du Cirque, has good-sized old-fashioned rooms with high ceiling and creaky wood floors. Singles/doubles/triples are Sfr59/80/96 (hall shower), Sfr64/85/110 (own shower cubicle) or Sfr75/102/120 (private bathroom).

Hôtel Kaufmann (☎ 346 29 33), 48 Blvd des Tranchées, has a new owner who is gradually renovating. It has a similar choice of rooms to Beau-Site but prices are a little higher. However, young people get a discount, rooms have TV, and there are a couple of tiny, cheaper rooms.

Hôtel le Prince (☎ 329 84 44/5), 16 Rue des Voisins, has comfortable if smallish rooms with shower/WC, TV and telephone. Singles/doubles are Sfr80/102, or Sfr60/80 using hall shower.

Places to Stay – middle

There's not much to choose between the tourist-class hotels clustered around the train station. The three-star *International & Terminus* (☎ 732 80 95) is at 20 Rue des Alpes (see the Geneva Station map). Singles/doubles cost from Sfr92/128 with shower/WC or Sfr57/78 without. There's an inexpensive restaurant on site. *Bernina* (☎ 731 49 50), 22 Place de Cornavin, is ren-ovating rooms (all with TV and telephone) and charges Sfr105/145 with shower and Sfr80/105 without.

Astoria (☎ 732 10 25), 6 Place de Cornavin, and *Excelsior* (☎ 732 09 45), 32 Rue Rousseau, both have reasonably comfortable singles/doubles with shower and toilet for around Sfr110/150. *Hotel Suisse* (☎ 732 66 30), 10 Place de Cornavin, is slightly nicer, with a swirling staircase and better appointed rooms, but it's also more expensive, starting at Sfr135/180.

Places to Stay – top end

Dozens of four and five-star hotels will allow you to spend a fortune on accommodation if you wish. For a standard room, count on anything between Sfr100 to Sfr340 per person in four star and Sfr150 to Sfr450 in

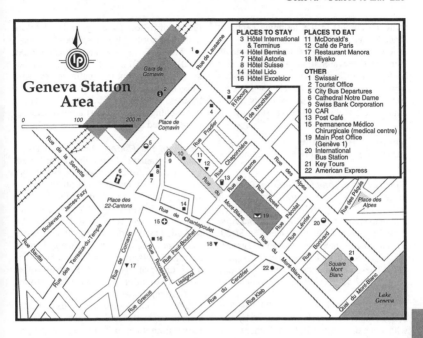

Geneva Station Area

PLACES TO STAY
3 Hôtel International & Terminus
4 Hôtel Bernina
7 Hôtel Astoria
8 Hôtel Suisse
14 Hôtel Lido
16 Hôtel Excelsior

PLACES TO EAT
11 McDonald's
12 Café de Paris
17 Restaurant Manora
18 Miyako

OTHER
1 Swissair
2 Tourist Office
5 City Bus Departures
6 Cathedral Notre Dame
9 Swiss Bank Corporation
10 CAR
13 Post Café
15 Permanence Médico Chirurgicale (medical centre)
19 Main Post Office (Genève 1)
20 International Bus Station
21 Key Tours
22 American Express

five star. The lobbies of some of these places are so plush that you feel practically naked if you're not wearing formal dress. One such place is the *Hôtel Beau-Rivage* (☎ 731 02 21; fax 738 98 47), 13 Quai du Mont Blanc, an atmospheric 19th century hotel dripping with the opulence of the era. More modern but similarly lavish is the *Noga Hilton* (☎ 908 90 81; fax 908 90 90), 19 Quai du Mont Blanc. It's slightly cheaper (singles/doubles from Sfr310/410) and has its own swimming pool (free for guests). Both places have top-notch restaurants (see Places to Eat).

At the more affordable end of the scale and conveniently located is *Hotel Ambassador* (☎ 731 72 00; fax 738 90 80), 21 Rive Droite. Prices start at Sfr155/220; the rooms are well fitted-out but not exactly overflowing with space. Breakfast is Sfr14 extra and parking costs Sfr16 for 24 hours.

Places to Eat

Geneva is the cuisine capital of Switzerland.

There is a staggering choice in styles and regional specialities. All price ranges are catered for, but as with hotels, getting what you want is easier if you have more money to spend. Eating is generally cheaper around Gare de Cornavin, or south of the old town in the vicinity of the university.

Fondue and Raclette are widely available. Also popular is locally-caught perch, which typically costs well over Sfr20 unless you can find it as a plat du jour. There is a small fruit-and-vegetable market, open daily except Sunday, on Rue de Coutance. *Aperto*, a supermarket in the train station, is open daily from 6 am to 9 pm.

Self-Service The *Migros* supermarket on Rue des Pâquis has a cheap self-service restaurant. For budget eating in the old town, make for the restaurant in the *EPA* department store on Rue de la Croix d'Or, with late opening (8 pm) on Thursday. Meals are Sfr8 to Sfr14. There's also a *Coop* supermarket

GENEVA

(with restaurant) in the shopping centre at Place Fusterie.

Restaurant Manora, 4 Rue de Cornavin (see the Geneva Station Area Map), is a buffet-style restaurant with tasty daily dishes from Sfr10 and extensive salad and dessert bars. Always popular, it is open daily from 7 am to 9.30 pm (9 am to 9 pm on Sunday).

Mid-Price Restaurants Geneva has a variety of reasonably priced restaurants.

North of the Rhône *La Trattoria*, 1 Rue de la Servette, near the station, has excellent Italian food from Sfr14 (closed Sunday). Along the road at No 31 is *Kong Restaurant*, providing tasty Chinese dishes for Sfr20. Visit at lunch, when every weekday there are meals for Sfr12 including rice and starter, and (Tuesday, Wednesday and Thursday only) Sfr17.50 secures an all-you-can-eat buffet.

Le Blason (☎ 731 91 73), 23 Rue des Pâquis, looks a typical bar/restaurant by day, with a plat du jour for Sfr14 and other meals from Sfr14. Yet it also courts late night clubbers by opening daily from 4 am to 2 am (4 am to midnight on weekends) – prices rise slightly for the insomniacs. *Auberge de Savièse* (☎ 732 83 30), nearby at No 20 has lunch-time plats du jour from Sfr13, and Swiss specialities such as fondue from Sfr18.90 (closed Saturday lunchtime and Sunday).

Auberge de Coutance (☎ 732 79 19) is recommended for exquisite specialities from Sfr26, including duck delicacies. It's an atmospheric below-ground restaurant at 25 Rue de Coutance (closed Saturday evening and Sunday).

Café de Paris (☎ 732 84 50; see the Geneva Station Area Map), 26 Rue du Mont Blanc, serves up one dish only – succulent entrecôte steak with a special herb and butter sauce, chips and salad (Sfr35.50). It's well-established and very busy, and the harassed table servers can be a bit abrupt at times (open daily from 11 am to 11 pm).

Take advantage of the international flavour of Geneva to vary your diet. Explore the streets north of Rue des Alpes for cheapish Mexican, Chinese and Oriental food. *Miyako* (☎ 738 01 20), 11 Rue de Chantepoulet, is expensive but the quality is excellent. This Japanese restaurant has three-course business lunches for Sfr29 to Sfr39, and a full evening meal will cost around Sfr50 or more (closed Sunday).

South of the Rhône The very cheap *Le Zofage* restaurant, downstairs in the Centre Universitaire Zofingien (see Places to Stay), has a plat du jour for Sfr11.50 (Sfr10 for students) and is open daily from 7 am to midnight. *Café du Centre* (☎ 311 85 86; see the Geneva Old Town map), 5 Place du Molard, has outside seating in a pleasant square near the old town. Office staff relax here after work over a coffee or a beer. The lunch-time plat du jour costs Sfr15 and other meals are Sfr12 or more (open daily from 7 am to 2 am).

Dent de Lion, 14 Rue des Eaux-Vives, is a small vegetarian place, open Monday to Friday from 9 am to 3 pm and 6 to 10 pm. Three-course lunches are Sfr15, and crêpes start from Sfr5.50.

Au Pied de Cochon (☎ 310 47 97; see the Geneva Old Town map), 4 Place du Bourg-de-Four, specialises, as the name suggests, in pig's trotters. These appear in several styles and sauces (from Sfr23), and there are various other porcine products to choose. The weekday lunch menu costs Sfr15, and it is open daily.

The large and popular *Cave Valaisanne et Chalet Suisse* (☎ 328 12 36) is at 23 Blvd Georges-Favon. It's an excellent place to try many varieties of fondue (starting at Sfr19.80); the scent of bubbling cheese inside could give a mouse palpitations at 20 paces. It's open from 8 am to 1 am daily. *Café Huissard*, 51 Rue Strand, is an authentic, no-frills place, frequented by wine-drinking locals. Fondue novices can try a half portion for Sfr12 (closed Saturday lunch).

Café Universal (☎ 781 18 81), 26 Blvd du Pont d'Arve, is atmospheric, French and smoky (closed Sunday and Monday in summer). The mirrors and camp chandeliers attract theatrical patrons. Plats du jour are from Sfr15 and dinners are mostly above Sfr20. *L'Amiral* (☎ 735 18 08), 24 Quai Gustave Ador, is a good place for fish dishes from Sfr25. The 'menu du touriste' is fillet of perch with the salad and dessert for Sfr32 (open daily).

Expensive Restaurants Reserve ahead for all these places. *Le Béarn* (☎ 321 00 28), 4 Quai de la Poste, is one of the best restaurants in Geneva. It serves sumptuous fish specialities and creative cuisine (dishes around Sfr50, menus from Sfr100). The restaurant is closed weekends (except Saturday evening in winter) and from mid-July to late August. Of comparable quality is *Le Cygne* (☎ 908 92 20) in the Noga Hilton hotel, 19 Quai du Mont Blanc. The cooking is French-style; main course are in the Sfr35 to Sfr60 price range and there are over 400 different wines on the wine list. It is open daily.

Also very highly rated are *Le Chat Botté* (☎ 731 65 32) in Hôtel Beau-Rivage, 13 Quai du Mont-Blanc, *Le Neptune* (☎ 731 98 31), Hôtel du Rhône, 1 Quai Turrettini, and *Les Continents* (734 60 91) in Hôtel Intercontinental, 7-9 Chemin du Petit Saconnex. All three are closed weekends.

Auberge de Pinchat (☎ 342 30 77), 33 Chemin Pinchat, is another top-notch place. It's in the southern suburb of Carouge, reached by tram No 12 from Place Bell Air.

Entertainment

Different genres of music are covered in various festivals through the year. Geneva is the home of the Orchestra of the Swiss Romande; it and other orchestras often perform at the Victoria Hall, 14 Rue du Général Dufour. English-speaking theatre thrives in Geneva on an amateur level. Contact Theatre in English (☎ 301 06 08) for information and tickets. In cinemas, films usually retain their original soundtrack: look for VO (version original) to make sure.

Geneva has a flourishing alternative arts scene. A well-established venue is *l'Usine* (☎ 781 34 90), 4 Place de Volontaires. A con-

verted old factory, it is now a centre for cinema, cabaret, theatre, concerts and homeless art objects (closed Monday). It has a good restaurant (inexpensive food) and a bar (Sfr4.50 for half a litre of beer), though these are closed Saturday to Monday. Look out also for the semi-legal squats in the city. *Cave 12* (☎ 320 97 90), 12 Blvd de la Tour, puts on experimental music concerts twice a month, and a five-day festival in May. *Ilot 13*, 12 Rue de Montbrillant, is a collection of squats offering art shows, organic food, drinks, music and theatre.

Au Chat Noir (☎ 343 49 98), 13 Rue Vautier, Carouge, is a jazz and rock club with interesting murals and live music. Also good for drinks, food and live music is *Alhambar* (☎ 312 30 11; see the Geneva Old Town map), on the 1st floor of the Alhambra cinema, 10 Rue de la Rôtisserie. It's open from Tuesday to Sunday until midnight or later.

A good British/Irish meeting place is *Post Café*, 7 Rue de Berne. It's open daily (Sunday only from 5 pm) and has cider and Guiness on draught. There's British sports (via Sky TV) and limited, inexpensive food. A similar if larger place in the old town is *Flanagan's Irish Bar*, Rue du Cheval-Blanc. *Casting Café*, 6 Rue de la Servette, is a multi-sectional bar and restaurant with creative décor exploring cinematic and US themes (open 11 am to 2 am weekdays, 2 pm to 2 am weekends).

Geneva has plenty of plush nightclubs but they are expensive. *Gos Club*, 7 Route de St Julien, is multi-cultural and more reasonably priced (Sfr10 entry on Saturday night includes a drink). *La Garçonnière* (☎ 310 21 61; see the Geneva Old Town map), 22 Place Bémont, 15 Rue de la Cité, is a mainly gay bar and disco, although many heterosexuals turn up for the transvestite shows on Friday and Saturday. It's open daily from 10 pm to 4 am. Two other bar/discos that attract both gays and straights are *l'Inderdit*, Quai du Seujet 18, and the next-door *Le Loft*.

The *Casino* at 19 Quai du Mont-Blanc is open daily from noon. Go there to play Boule (the tame Swiss version of roulette), slot

GENEVA

machines, and to dance after 9 pm. Folklore shows are not to everybody's taste, but *Edelweiss Manotel* (☎ 731 36 58), 2 Place de la Navigation, believes it has a 'genuine Alpine village in downtown Geneva'. Students of kitsch may want to see for themselves; the nightly show is free with dinner (dishes from Sfr30).

Things to Buy
Geneva is well known as a place to buy watches, jewellery and enamel work. Less expensively, there are several places on Rue Mont Blanc with a good selection of Swiss knives. Various shops, such as the one opposite the Jardin Anglais, sell folklorish things. A flea market occupies Plaine de Plainpalais every Wednesday and Saturday.

Getting There & Away
Air Geneva airport is an important transport hub and has frequent connections to every major European city and many cities worldwide – see the Getting There & Away chapter for more. Enquire at the Swissair office (☎ 799 59 99; see the Geneva Station Area map) about youth fares (for under 25s) and one-off offers; the office is by the station on Rue de Lausanne, open Monday to Friday from 8.30 am to 6 pm.

Swissair is the booking agent for Crossair, which flies daily at least six times to Lugano, twice to Basel and a dozen times to Zürich. Internal flights are expensive: Geneva-Zürich one-way is Sfr212, though ask about special deals.

Bus International buses depart from the Gare Routière (☎ 732 02 30; see the Geneva Station Area map) on Place Dorcière off Rue des Alpes. There are three buses a week to both London (Sfr150) and Barcelona (Sfr90) – advance reservations are advisable. There are several buses a day to Chamonix (Sfr47 one way, Sfr81 return).

Train TGV depart five or six times a day to Paris-Lyon (Sfr78), and the journey takes 3½ hours. Reservations are essential and cost Sfr5 to Sfr17 (Sfr5 to Sfr22 in 1st class)

depending upon the time and day of travel. There are also regular international trains to Hamburg (Sfr261), Milan (Sfr71) and Barcelona (Sfr99) – ask about special reduced fares.

There are more-or-less hourly connections to most Swiss towns. Zürich takes three hours (Sfr74), as does Interlaken Ost (Sfr60), both via Bern. Gare des Eaux-Vives is the station for Annecy and Chamonix. To get there from Gare de Cornavin, take bus No 8 or 1 to Rond-Point de Rive and then tram No 12.

Car & Motorcycle An autoroute bypass skirts Geneva, with major routes intersecting south-west of the city: the N1 from Lausanne joins with the E62 to Lyon (130 km) and the E25 heading south-east towards Chamonix. Toll-free main roads follow the course of these motorways.

Rental Sixt-Alsa (☎ 732 90 90), 1 Place de la Navigation, has the best day-by-day rates (from Sfr115 per day, unlimited km) and offers one-way drop-offs to Zürich airport. Its weekend deals (Sfr205) are for 72 hours. Europcar (☎ 731 51 50), is at 35 Rue de Zurich, and has a branch (☎ 798 11 10) in the airport arrivals hall. Hertz (☎ 343 79 20), 21 Rue Eugène Marziano, Avis (☎ 731 90 00), 44 Rue de Lausanne, and Budget (☎ 732 52 52), 37 Rue de Lausanne, also all have an airport branch. See the Getting Around chapter for rates.

Horizon Motos (☎ 731 23 39), 51 Rue de Lausanne, rents motorcycles (including helmets) ranging from 125 cc to 1100 cc; weekend rates (2½ days, unlimited mileage) are Sfr117 to Sfr492. Monthly rates are very reasonable: a 650 cc machine would cost Sfr1750 with unlimited mileage.

Boat Compagnie Générale de Navigation (CGN) (☎ 311 25 21) by the Jardin Anglais operates a steamer service to all towns and major villages bordering Lake Geneva, including those in France. Most boats only operate between May and September, such as those to Lausanne-Ouchy (3½ hours,

Sfr27) and Montreux (4½ hours, Sfr34). Both Eurail and Swiss railpasses are valid on CGN boats. Special circular tours and dancing cruises are detailed in the CGN timetable.

A CGN one-day pass costs Sfr47 (Sfr63 in 1st class). Another option is the Swiss Boat Pass (see the Getting Around chapter).

Getting Around

The Airport Getting to/from Cointrin Airport is easy. It's five km from the city centre and there are 200 trains a day into Gare de Cornavin (Sfr4.80; takes six minutes) Alternatively, take bus No 10 to Gare de Cornavin for Sfr2.20 (every 10 minutes). A metered taxi would cost Sfr25 to Sfr35.

Bus A combination of buses, trolley buses and trams makes getting around just as easy. There are ticket dispensers at bus stops. A ticket for multiple rides within one hour costs Sfr2.20, a book of six such tickets costs Sfr12, and a book of 12 tickets costs Sfr22. One, two or three-day passes for the whole canton cost Sfr8.50, Sfr15 or Sfr19, though most people will only need a city day pass (Sfr5, or Sfr27 for six passes). The city day pass for Sfr7 includes Lausanne. Passes and multi-tickets are available from the tourist office bus section, from Transports Publics Genevois at the lower level of Gare de Cornavin (by the yellow escalators), or at Rond-Point de Rive.

Car & Motorcycle See the Getting There & Away section for information about rentals.

Most streets in or near the centre have restricted parking on Monday to Saturday from 8 am to 7 pm (meters with one or two-hour maximum stay), and hotels rarely have private parking. Parking garages are clearly signposted. The one at Jardin Anglais has typical prices for the centre (Sfr1 for 45 minutes); the Varembé garage near the United Nations is the cheapest (Sfr1 per hour, half-price at night).

Taxi The cost for taxis is Sfr6.30 plus Sfr2.70 per km within the city and Sfr3.50 outside. However, as fares aren't regulated some operators charge higher prices. Get a taxi by the station or ring ☎ 141.

Bicycle The bike rental office at Gare de Cornavin is open daily from 7 am to 6.45 pm (7.45 pm weekends). It has a leaflet showing cycle routes in and around the city.

Boat In addition to CGN (see the previous Getting There & Away section) smaller companies operate excursions on the lake between April and October but no passes are valid. Ticket offices and departures are along Quai du Mont Blanc and by Jardin Anglais. Trips range from half an hour (Sfr10, several departures a day) to two hours (Sfr25), with commentary in English. Small boats, called *mouettes*, cross between Geneva's two shores (city passes valid).

Lake Geneva Region

The tourist area known as the Lake Geneva Region comprises the canton of Vaud (pronounced Voh; Waadt in German). In the 1980s the tourist authorities decided they wanted to establish a separate identity for the region, instead of simply being viewed as a mere adjunct to Geneva and the lake. Consequently, they renamed the tourist region after the canton. But then they had a new problem. Previously the territory was easily located on the mental map of most visitors to Switzerland, but few people confronted with the name 'Vaud' had any idea where or what it was. Finally in 1993 those responsible for Vaud tourism marketing accepted the inevitable, and the area again became known as the Lake Geneva Region, or Région du Léman in French.

The canton of Vaud covers the area south of the cantons of Neuchâtel and Fribourg; in fact, not to overstress the point, the region around Lake Geneva (Lac Léman in French, though sometimes also known, much to Lausanne's chagrin, as Lac de Genève). It is the towns on the shores of Lake Geneva that provide the most compelling reasons to visit the canton.

Vaud is well-known for its wines. A tour of wine-growers' cellars *(caveaux des vignerons)* is easy if you have your own transport. The communities bordering the lake to the west and the east produce wines with their own distinctive flavours, and these are discussed in the vineyard guide from the tourist office. A different tourist office booklet details the opening times of the cellars.

History

In 1229 Vaud became a vassal territory of Savoy. In 1536 Bern declared war on Savoy and successfully took over the region. As Bern had an existing treaty of fellowship signed with Lausanne, the people of Vaud naturally thought this might result in them

HIGHLIGHTS

- Unique art collection – l'Art Brut in Lausanne
- Tours of Vaud vineyards
- Château de Chillon in Montreux
- Music festivals – Jazz in Montreux and Rock in Nyon
- Music boxes and automata in Sainte Croix
- Alpine sports, including hot air ballooning in Château d'Oex

LIBERTÉ ET PATRIE

Vaud

gaining more autonomy. But Bern thought differently; it installed a bailiff in the bishop's castle in Lausanne and proceeded to siphon off the city's wealth.

The situation was endured until January 1798 when Fréderic César de la Harpe, leader of the Liberal Party, declared Lausanne and Vaud independent under the title of the Lemanic Republic. Not surprisingly, Bern did not wholly go along with this assertion but the matter was settled in 1803 by Napoleon in his Act of Mediation, in which Vaud became an independent canton within the Swiss Confederation, and Lausanne was installed as the capital.

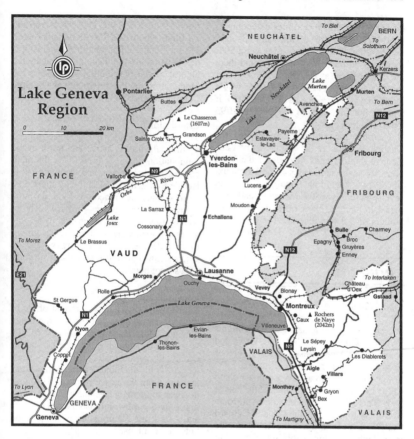

Lake Geneva Region

0   10   20 km

Orientation & Information

Vaud is almost exclusively French-speaking, and encompasses the three main geographical regions of Switzerland: the Jura Mountains in the west, the relatively flat plain of the Mittelland, and a section of the Alps in the south-east.

The regional tourist office (☎ 021-617 72 02; 617 30 80) is at 60 Ave d'Ouchy, CH-1006, Ouchy, Lausanne. Opening times are Monday to Friday from 8 am to noon and 1.30 to 5.30 pm. It gives out the detailed *Guide Touristique Canton de Vaud* (partially in English), and a good map of the canton showing different walking routes accompanied by a brief description (in French). It also has a couple of guides to vineyards in Vaud.

For information on Avenches and Payerne see Murten in the Fribourg, Neuchâtel & Jura chapter.

Getting Around

There are two regional transport passes that cover part of the canton and overlap to a small degree. The Region Montreux/Vevey pass gives free travel on three days in seven around the eastern half of Lake Geneva (including boat rides to French resorts) and on buses and trains on routes extending to Gruyères, Château d'Oex, and Gstaad, among other places. These trips get a 50% reduction on the other four days, and there are other routes (as far apart as Geneva and Interlaken) that get 50% off on the whole seven days. The price is Sfr80 (Sfr64 if already holding a Swiss railpass) or Sfr95 (Sfr76) in first class.

The other pass covers a smaller area, the Chablais Region to the south-east of Lake Geneva, and extends to parts of the Vaud Alps. It has the same rules as the Montreux/Vevey pass regarding three days travel in seven days at 50% reduction, and costs Sfr54 in second class only, or Sfr43 for holders of a Swiss railpass. The passes are only issued from 1 April to 31 October.

Lausanne

• *pop 128,000* • *495m* • ☎ *(021)*
This hilly city is Switzerland's fifth-largest, and enjoys a thriving arts scene. Highlights include a Gothic cathedral, lake views and water sports. Don't miss l'Art Brut, one of Europe's most unusual art collections.

The Romans used to have a military camp called Lousonna, on the shores of the lake at Vidy. This was an important stop on the route from Italy to Gaul, via the Great St Bernard Pass. With the invasion of the Alemanni, the inhabitants abandoned this settlement and joined the people who had settled on the site of the present old city. The commercial and religious importance of Lausanne began to develop hand-in-hand, helped by its first bishop, St Marius, who was previously based in Aventicum and came to live in the city in the 6th century. The Reformation arrived in 1529, thanks to the preaching of Guillaume Farel, a cohort of Calvin. But the conversion wasn't underlined until the invading forces from Bern took over the city in 1536 and proceeded to ransack the Catholic churches.

Lausanne flourished in the following centuries despite its period of subservience to Bern, and welcomed important literary figures such as Voltaire, Dickens, Byron and TS Eliot (who wrote *The Waste Land* here). The city retains a fair measure of status; it is the location of the Federal Tribunal, the highest court in the country, and has been the headquarters of the International Olympic Committee since 1915.

Orientation
The old town and its winding streets, topped by the cathedral, is above and north of the train station. Place St François is the main hub for local transport, and leading off it is Rue de Bourg, the main shopping street. Just west of Place St François is Flon, an intriguing older area where formerly derelict warehouses have been taken over by art galleries and trendy shops. The city has grown to include the former fishing village of Ouchy, now a picturesque harbour sporting a cluster of hotels.

Information
Tourist Offices There is a tourist office in the train station, open daily (closed mornings in winter). The main tourist office (☎ 617 14 27), 2 Ave de Rhodanie, is by the harbour in Ouchy. It's open Monday to Saturday from 8 am to 7 pm, and Sunday from 9 am to noon and 1 to 6 pm. From 1 October to 31 March it's open to 6 pm on weekdays and weekend hours are Saturday only from 8 am to noon and 1 to 5 pm. Commission is charged for hotel reservations.

The tourist office for the canton de Vaud is also in Ouchy: see the introduction to this chapter.

Foreign Consulates The French Consulate (☎ 311 41 91), 30 Ave Ruchonnet, is open on weekdays and the Italian Consulate (☎ 320 12 91), 12-14 Rue Centrale, is open from Tuesday to Saturday morning.

Train Station The main station (Gare CFF) has luggage lockers (Sfr3 and Sfr5), and a train information office open daily except Sunday from 8 am to 7 pm. Money-exchange counters are open daily to at least 7.30 pm, and bicycle rental in the summer is daily from 6.40 am to 7.50 pm.

Post & Communications The large post office (1002) at 15 Place St François is open Monday to Friday from 7.30 am to 6.30 pm and Saturday from 8 to 11 am. The main post office (Poste Principale 1001), by the station at 43 Ave de la Gare, has an emergency counter open daily.

Travel Agencies SSR (☎ 614 60 30), the student and budget travel agency, is at 20 Blvd de Grancy, open Monday to Friday from 9.30 am to 5.30 pm. American Express (☎ 320 74 25), is at 14 Ave Mon Repos. Swissair (☎ 343 22 22) has an office at 4 Rue du Grand Chêne.

Bookshop The Librairie Payot, 4 Place Pépinet, (☎ 021 341 33 31), is the biggest bookshop in French-speaking Switzerland, and has English books too.

Medical Services The Vaudois University Hospital (☎ 314 11 11), Rue du Bugnon 46, provides emergency cover.

Cathedral

This is considered one of the finest medieval Gothic churches in Switzerland. It was built in the 12th and 13th centuries, and was consecrated by Pope Gregory X in 1275, in the presence of Rudolph of Habsburg, Emperor of the Holy Roman Empire. Its most striking decoration is the acclaimed **rose window** from the 13th century in the south transept (unfortunately, hidden by restoration work until 1999). Also worthy of study are the main portals with their tiers of adorning statues, and the 16th century stalls in the north aisle (ask the tower cashier to turn on the lights). The cathedral is open daily until 7 pm (5.30 pm in winter) – don't try to visit during Sunday morning services. Ascend the tower for a view worthy of a deity (Sfr2); it's open Monday to Saturday from 9 to 11 am and 1.30 to 5.30 pm (4.30 pm in winter) and Sunday from 2 to 5.30 pm (4.30 pm in winter).

The tradition of the nightwatch is still maintained in Lausanne; the hour is called from the cathedral tower between 10 pm and 2 am every night.

Old Town

Place St François has a **church** (Église St François) that was once part of a 13th century monastery. From the north-east corner, Rue St François becomes Rue du Pont and leads into Place de la Palud, which has a **Fountain of Justice**. This square is taken over by a market every Wednesday and Saturday morning. The 17th century building with the clock tower and the protruding winged dragons is the **town hall**, which sometimes has exhibitions in the foyer. The covered stairway leading up from the fountain climbs to the cathedral. Two hundred metres north of the cathedral is the Castle St Marie (Château St Marie). This 15th century building was once the residence of the bishops of Lausanne, and is now the seat of government of the Vaud canton. There's little to see except the view from the terrace.

Musée de l'Art Brut

This is a fantastic (in both the literal and colloquial meaning of the word) collection at 11 Ave de Bergières. It was put together by the French artist, Jean Dubuffet, and was opened in Lausanne in 1976. 'Brut' means raw, crude, or rough, and that's exactly what you get.

None of the artists featured is properly trained or part of any artistic circle. On the contrary, many can't even take their place in normal society. Some are criminally insane, others are simply eccentric; most have spent at least some time in a mental institution. Some were so impaired that drawing was just about the only thing they could do; Philipp Schöpke was discharged from the army 'unable to even lace his shoes' (according to the military doctor) and went on to draw figures with the raw impact of primitive tribal icons. Often the people exhibiting started creating art only late in their lives,

LAKE GENEVA REGION

To Neuchâtel (75 km)
& N1 Motorway

Avenue Bergières

Avenue de Beaulieu

Avenue de France

To Morges

Avenue de d'Echallens

Avenue de Morges

Rue de Genève

Avenue Vinet

Rue du Tunnel

Rue des Terreaux

Rue Neuve

Rue St-Laurent

Rue Curtat

Rue St-Martin

Rue Dr César-Roux

To Place
de l'Ours,
Hospital,
Murten &
Bern

To Ada-Logements

Pont Chauderon

Rue des Côtes de Montbenon

Rue de Genève

Avenue de Tivoli

Avenue de Tivoli

Avenue Jules Gonin

Le Grand-Pont

Rue

Rue Cheneau
de Bourg

Rue St
François

Place Bel-Air

Centrale

Rue de Bourg

Place Benjamin

Mon-Repos

Avenue Marc-Dufour

Avenue Louis-Ruchonnet

Rue du Grand-Chêne

Rue du Petit-Chêne

Avenue Sainte-Luce

Avenue du Théâtre

Place
de la Gare

Avenue de la Gare

To
SYHA Hostel
& Jeunotel

Avenue Mont d'Or

Ave Fraisse

Avenue

Boulevard

de Grancy

Dapples

Avenue Juste-Olivier

Botanical
Gardens

Avenue de Cour

Avenue de la Harpe

Avenue d'Ouchy

Chemin de Bellevue

Avenue de l'Elysée

Avenue

de Montchoisi

To
Camping
de Vidy &
Geneva (62 km)

Avenue de Rhodanie

Avenue d'Ouchy

Avenue de l'Elysée

To
Montreux
(31 km)

Quay d'Ouchy

Port d'Ouchy

LAKE GENEVA REGION

Lausanne

0   200   400 m

Some Minor Streets not Depicted

Lake Geneva

PLACES TO STAY			26	Paradiso		12	Cathedral
16	Des Voyageurs		27	Calèche		13	Dolce Vita
28	Elite		29	McDonald's		15	Place de la Palud
30	Continental Hotel		37	Mövenpick Radisson		17	l'Aterlier Volant
41	Hôtel du Port			Hotel		20	Place St François
43	Hôtel d'Angleterre		40	Boccalino		21	St François
45	Le Château d'Ouchy		42	Crêperie Ouchy			Church
						24	Post Office
PLACES TO EAT			OTHER			31	Avis
8	Migros Supermarket &		1	Palais de		32	Main Post Office
	Restaurant			Beaulieu		33	Main Train
9	Coop Supermarket &		2	Musée de			Station
	Restaurant			l'Art Brut		34	Musée de l'Elysée
11	Placette Department		3	Les Négociants		35	Regional Tourist
	Store		4	Castle St Marie			Office
14	Café de l'Everche		5	Palais de Rumine &		36	CGN Head Office
18	Ma-jong			Museum of Fine		38	Main Tourist
19	Manora			Arts			Office
22	La Grappe d'Or		6	Place de la		39	Ouchy Metro
23	Restaurant Au			Riponne		44	Olympic Museum
	Couscous		7	Europcar		46	CGN Boat Departure
25	Pizza Italia		10	MAD			Point

perhaps led to it following a crisis, after which they would draw or paint obsessively.

The work they produce breaks all the rules. It is vivid, startling, or just plain strange. There are sculptures made out of broken plates and discarded rags, faces made out of shells. Some insisted their drawings originated directly from the spirit world. One woman who believed she was a medium drew on long scrolls of paper in near darkness. As she unrolled fresh areas of paper she rolled up the sections she had completed, and therefore never had any idea what her work looked like in its entirety. A wooden wall shown upstairs was taken from an asylum; it's from a bare cell where Clément Fraisse was incarcerated for two years. The carved designs were done using a broken spoon, and after that was confiscated, the handle of his chamberpot.

Edmund Monseil found it hard to communicate with other people, especially women, and he spent most of WWII hiding from the Germans in an attic. His drawings are cramped, claustrophobic creations on small bits of paper, filled with glaring eyes surrounding the central figure or figures.

A potted biography of each artist (in English) is displayed alongside the work. This greatly adds to the fascination, but also runs the risk of undermining the art on display; the viewer is sucked into becoming an amateur psychoanalyst and starts looking for specific themes or symbols in the work – phallic shapes in the output of the sexual obsessive, internal conflict in the schizophrenic, or portents of doom in the manic depressive. There is the danger of forgetting that art is a work of imagination, and can perhaps provide an escape from a tormented life rather than merely reflecting it. But sometimes the comparison between the life and the work is inevitable. Read the biographies, but be careful not to close your mind to the unexpected.

The gallery is open Tuesday to Sunday from 11 am to 1 pm and 2 to 6 pm. The collection is not huge, but if you see and read everything you could easily be there for three to four hours. Entry costs Sfr6 for adults, Sfr4 for students, and it's free for children. It's near the Jomini stop on the route of bus Nos 2 and 3.

Palais de Rumine

This grand building overlooking the Place de la Riponne holds several museums. The main one is the **Museum of Fine Arts** (Musée cantonal des Beaux-Arts) with many works by Swiss and foreign artists. Only a fraction of the works in the collection may be displayed, however, depending upon the frequent temporary exhibitions (admission fee varies, though it's free from 2 to 6 pm Wednesday).

It's open daily except Monday from 11 am until 5 pm (Friday to Sunday), 6 pm (Tuesday and Wednesday) or 8 pm (Thursday). The other museum collections in the building are all free and open daily from 10 am to noon and 2 pm to 5 pm. Subjects covered include natural history, anatomy, zoology, mineralogy, archaeology and history.

Other Things to See & Do

Given that Lausanne is the base for the International Olympic Committee, it is perhaps inevitable that there's a museum devoted to the games. The **Olympic Museum** (Musée Olympique) is sited in a lavish new building in the Petit Ouchy park, 1 Quai d'Ouchy. It tells the Olympic story using videos, archive film, interactive computers and memorabilia. It's open daily from 10 am to 6 pm (7 pm summer, 9.30 pm Thursday) and entry costs Sfr14 (students and seniors Sfr9, families Sfr34).

Other museums in the city cover topics as diverse as photography (Musée de l'Elysée), pipes and tobacco, archive films and contemporary art. Opening times and entry fees are listed in the *Mosaïque* booklet from the tourist office. The three-day **museum pass**, valid for all museums, costs Sfr26 (Sfr20 for students and seniors) and includes public transport.

Lake Geneva provides plenty of sporting opportunities. Vidy Sailing School (☎ 617 90 00) offers courses on windsurfing, water-skiing and sailing, and equipment rental for these activities. Various boat tours are organised by CGN (see the Getting There & Away section). The boat for the night cruise has an orchestra and restaurant on board (Sfr22). Lausanne's **Botanical Garden** (free, open daily) is south-west of the station at Ave de Cour 14 (closed winter), and there are large areas of woodsland to the north and east of the city.

Places to Stay – bottom end

Camping Year-round camping is possible at *Camping de Vidy* (☎ 624 20 31), 3 Chemin du Camping, just to the west of the Vidy sports complex. It has a lakeside location, stacks of facilities, and costs Sfr6.50 per person and Sfr6.50 to Sfr11 for a tent. Bungalows are also available. To get there, take bus No 2 from Place St François. Get off at Bois de Vaux and walk under the Autoroute towards the lake.

Hostel The SYHA *hostel* (☎ 616 57 82), 1 Chemin du Muguet, Ouchy, can be reached from the train station by bus No 1 (direction: Maladière, stop: Batelière) or a 20-minute walk. Dorms cost Sfr24 per night and dinners are Sfr11.50. Reception is closed from 9 am to 5 pm and curfew is at 11.30 pm. There's a lounge, and washing machines cost Sfr5.

Hotels & Pensions *Jeunotel* (☎ 626 02 22), 36 Chemin du Bois de Vaud, offers no-frills accommodation in dorms (Sfr21), singles/doubles (Sfr64/74 with shower or Sfr54/58 without), and triples/quads (Sfr69/92 without). The self-service restaurant serves cheap meals; if you want breakfast add Sfr7. Studio apartments are available on a monthly basis (Sfr750/950 for one/two people). By bus, get off at the same stop as for Camping de Vidy.

Villa Cherokee (☎ 647 57 20), 4 Chemin des Charmilles, is a family-run pension with good-sized, clean (if slightly shabby) rooms – telephone ahead as there aren't many. Singles/doubles from Sfr35/50 include use of a hall shower and breakfast is Sfr5 extra if required. To get there, take bus No 2 (direction: Désert), get off at Presbytère, backtrack a few steps and walk up Chemin du Presbytére, take the second left then first right (five minutes). *Ada-Logements* (☎ 625 71 34), 60 Ave de Tivoli, is student oriented but takes tourists if there's space (phone ahead). Singles/doubles are Sfr40/65, or Sfr45/75 with breakfast.

Hôtel du Port (☎ 616 49 30), 5 Place du Port in Ouchy, has rooms above a restaurant (closed Tuesday except in July and August).

Singles (hall shower) are Sfr42 and doubles (own shower/WC) are Sfr106; add Sfr8 per person for breakfast.

Places to Stay – middle
The best mid-price deal is *Hôtel d'Angleterre* (☎ 617 41 45) on the Quai d'Ouchy in Ouchy, by Hôtel du Port. It's a stately old building (no lift) and has large, comfortable rooms with TV and views of the lake (closed Christmas to 31 January). Singles/doubles start at Sfr100/140 with shower or Sfr65/110 without. Byron wrote the *Prisoner of Chillon* here in 1816.

Des Voyageurs (☎ 323 19 02), 19 Grand St-Jean, is a convenient, comfortable hotel in the pedestrian zone. Rooms with shower/WC and TV start at Sfr126/174. *Elite* (☎ 320 23 61), 1 Ave Ste Luce, is a similar standard (from Sfr125/170) but has its own grounds and easier parking.

Places to Stay – top end
The *Hotel Continental* ☎ 320 15 51; fax 323 76 79), has stylish rooms and is right opposite the station at 2 Place de la Gare. Prices start at Sfr140/190; breakfast-buffet, if required, costs Sfr20.

Enjoy the luxurious setting of *Le Château d'Ouchy* (☎ 616 74 51; 617 51 37), a castle dating from the 12th century in Ouchy. Rooms are nicely furnished in Louis XIII style, and all have TV, toilet and bath or shower. Prices start at Sfr175/275 and rooms differ markedly in size. The hotel also has a good-quality restaurant and private parking.

Places to Eat
Self-Service There is a *Migros* restaurant at Rue Neuve, open weekdays to 7 pm and Saturday to 5 pm. A better bet is probably the buffet-style *Manora*, 17 Place St François, open daily from 8 am (9 am Sunday) to 10.30 pm. Main dishes are around Sfr10, and there's an excellent choice at the salad buffet (Sfr4.20 to Sfr9.40 per plate), which usually includes meat and fish offerings. Round the back is *Ma-jong*, Escaliers du Grand-Pont 3, a near-equivalent serving Asian food for Sfr14 (closed Sunday). Inexpensive self-service restaurants are also in two department stores on Rue St Laurent: *Coop* and *Placette*.

Other Restaurants *Restaurant Au Couscous* (☎ 312 20 17), 2 Rue Enning, on the 1st floor, has a wide menu including Tunisian, vegetarian and macrobiotic food. Meals start at Sfr12 and it's open daily to 1 am.

Café de l'Everche, 4 Rue Louis Curtat, by the cathedral, has a lunch and evening two-course menu for Sfr14.50 and a pleasant garden around the back. It is a small place, open daily from 7 am to midnight. *Calèche* (☎ 323 01 31), in the Hotel Alpha, Petit-Chêne 34, is a little lacking in atmosphere but has reasonable food. Plats du jour are from Sfr14.50 and a three-course menu is Sfr23 (all available lunch and evening). Fondues and grills are Sfr20 to Sfr37 (open daily). Just up the road is *Paradiso*, with Italian food (from Sfr11) and occasional live music. It is closed on Sunday and has a sunny terrace on the roof which is open in summer. A few doors up the hill is *Pizza Italia,* with take-away pizzas from Sfr8 (closed early evening).

La Grappe d'Or (☎ 323 07 60), Cheneau de Bourg 3, is excellent if very expensive. The cooking is mainly French, but with additional oriental flavours. Expect to pay upwards of Sfr30 for a starter and between Sfr50 and Sfr65 for a main course. The service is very attentive in this small restaurant. Advance reservations are usually necessary (closed Saturday noon and Sunday).

In Ouchy, there are many restaurants around the port, most with good fish specialities. Cheaper options on Quai d'Ouchy are *Crêperie Ouchy*, with crêpes from Sfr4, and *Boccalino*, an Italian place where weekday lunches are Sfr13 and include a starter and coffee. Both places are open daily.

Along the road is the *Mövenpick Radisson Hotel* (☎ 617 21 21) which has several restaurants on the ground floor, where meals start from Sfr18. The Brasserie has the same menu but higher prices than the adjoining section; the Pêcherie has pricey fish and meat dishes in more leisurely environs.

Entertainment

Concerts, operas and ballets are staged at the *Palais de Beaulieu* (☎ 643 21 11), 10 Ave des Bergières. Lausanne has its own chamber orchestra, and a famous ballet troupe directed by Maurice Béjart, called the Rudra Béjart Ballet. Reservations for these and other performances can be made at the Ouchy tourist office. The theatre scene flourishes at several venues in town – the tourist office has events listings. Every year at the beginning of July is the City Festival, a week long celebration of music, dance and theatre.

Dolce Vita (☎ 323 09 43), 30 Rue Dr César Roux, is a fairly alternative, jam-packed bar and live music venue serving up anything from rock to blues to rap, and beers are reasonably priced. Entry to see bands is around Sfr20 and it's usually closed Monday and Tuesday. *MAD* (☎ 312 11 22), 23 Rue de Genève, is an interesting venue where events include live music, theatre, cinema, and art shows. On Friday and Saturday there's a disco from 11 pm to 4 am; non-members pay Sfr24 on these nights, but as members can bring two guests free, people just wait outside until they can get someone to sign them in. The nearby *l'Aterlier Volant* (☎ 311 52 80), Côtes de Montbenon 12, is another venue offering diverse events.

Les Négociants (☎ 312 97 66), 10 Place du Tunnel, is a gay bar and disco (closed Monday).

Getting There & Away

Train Lausanne is on the direct TGV route to/from Paris (Sfr77, four departures a day). Advance reservations are compulsory, and cost Sfr13. Vallorbe (where you can also pick up the Paris-bound TGV) is serviced by hourly regional trains.

There are three trains an hour to/from Geneva (Sfr19.40; takes 40 to 50 minutes), and one or two an hour to Bern. Trains to Interlaken Ost cost Sfr50 either via Bern or the scenic route via Montreux. Fast trains run

every hour to Yverdon-les-Bains (Sfr12.20, 25 minutes).

Car & Motorcycle There are motorways linking Lausanne to Geneva and Yverdon (N1), Martigny (N9/E62), and Bern (N9 then N12).

Car Rental There are a dozen different car rental companies in the city, including Avis (☎ 320 66 81), 50 Ave de la Gare, Hertz (☎ 312 53 11), 17 Place du Tunnel, and Europcar (☎ 323 71 42), 12 Place de la Riponne.

Boat Boats depart from Ouchy. Contact the head office of CGN (☎ 617 06 66), 17 Ave de Rhodanie, for information. The summer season is from the end of May to late September, when there are many departures a day and boats take in all resorts around the lake, including the French side. Bicycles can be taken on board the larger boats, but there are no car ferries. Lausanne has direct crossings to France, to Thonon-les-Bains and Evian-les-Bains with departures every one to three hours. If you want to do a lot of boat cruising buy a day pass for Sfr47 (Sfr63 in 1st class). The boat fare to Montreux is Sfr17.

Winter Services Nine ferries a day cross over to Evian-les-Bains; it takes 35 minutes and costs Sfr13. A boat goes around the coast of the Swiss Riviera (stopping at Vevey, Montreux and the Château de Chillon) all the way to St Gingolph on the French border, before turning around again. It departs daily in autumn and spring, and on Sunday only from November to March.

Getting Around

Buses and trolley buses service most destinations, but there are also metro lines from Ouchy up to the main station (every seven minutes or so to midnight) and an almost non-stop service (to 8 pm) between the station and the Flon area. Another metro line goes from Flon to the western suburbs. Short trips on city transport of up to three stops cost

Sfr1.30, and tickets are valid for 30 minutes. Unlimited journeys for one hour cost Sfr2.20 or Sfr1.30 for children. Travel passes for 24 hours cost Sfr6.50 (half-price for children).

Parking garages can get expensive; the largest is at Place de la Riponne. Street parking in blue zones (1½ hours maximum) and red zones (15 hours) is free, but you need to display a time indicator (see the Getting Around chapter).

AROUND LAUSANNE
The shoreline west of Lausanne is called La Côte. **Morges** is a wine-growing centre with its own castle, built in 1286 by Louis of Savoy. Inside is a military museum containing weapons, uniforms, and 8000 toy soldiers (Sfr5, students Sfr3, children free; open daily from February to mid-December). The town hosts a tulip festival from April to May. **Rolle** also has a castle built by the Savoy dynasty in the 13th century. Like the one at Morges, it is right by the lake.

The town of **Nyon** is of Roman origin. It has several museums and (surprise, surprise) a castle that was home to the dukes of Savoy. The quintuple-towered château was started in the 12th century and extensively modified in the 16th century; its elevated perspective allows a fine view from the terrace. One of the town's museums recalls the Roman era, another collects pieces of porcelain, and a third evokes life as it was and is lived around the lake. One ticket (Sfr5) gains entry to all three. The Porcelain Museum is open daily from April to October; the Roman and Lake Geneva museums are likewise open daily from April to October, and also the rest of the year except Monday.

Nyon's **Paléo Festival** is a well-known rock festival lasting several days in late July. There's a great atmosphere in the massive camp site that springs up by the four music stages. The 1995 event attracted 200,000 people and tickets are available on the day.

Coppet is halfway between Nyon and Geneva. It too has a castle, which can be visited by guided tour between April and October (Sfr7, or Sfr5 for students and senior citizens; closed Monday except in July and

August). The interior contains furniture in the Louis XVI and Directoire styles. It became the home of Madame de Staël after she was exiled from Paris by Napoleon. She soon presided over a court that was visited by some of the literary élite of the day – Edward Gibbon and Byron among them.

Getting There & Away
All the towns mentioned are on the rail route between Lausanne and Geneva, although only the local trains stop at Coppet and Rolle. All of them can be reached by boat on Lake Geneva steamers run by CGN (☎ 021-617 06 66). Fares from Lausanne are: Morges Sfr9, Rolle Sfr16, and Nyon Sfr22.

Swiss Riviera

The Swiss Riviera rivals its French counterpart in its ability to attract rich and famous residents. The name describes the stretch of Lake Geneva roughly between Lausanne and Villeneuve. A mild climate allows sub-tropical flora to flourish along the lake promenade.

The main resorts of the Riviera, Vevey and Montreux, work closely together. Either tourist office can supply the leaflet *On the Trail of Hemingway*, a walking tour that picks out locations associated with famous past visitors. The museum pass (Passeport Musées) is excellent value (Sfr15, valid for two months), giving free entry to all museums mentioned below, including the Château de Chillon. There are several free **swimming spots** on the lake between Vevey and Montreux. Sailing, water-skiing, windsurfing, rowing and boat rental are all available.

The Montreux-Vevey Holiday Card, given to overnight guests, provides excellent benefits, such as free swimming pool and cinema entry, free lessons (in summer) in water-skiing and windsurfing, a free 24-hour pass for bus No 1, and various reductions (including Sfr5 off the museum pass).

LAKE GENEVA REGION

VEVEY
• *pop 15,400* • *385m* • ☎ *(021)*
Like neighbouring Montreux, Vevey exudes a swanky ambience. The town has welcomed numerous celebrities in the past; a famous recent resident was Charlie Chaplin, who spent 25 years here until his death in 1977, and is buried in the Corsier cemetery.

Orientation & Information
The hub of the town is Grande Place (with lots of parking spaces), 200m ahead and to the left from the train station. The tourist office (☎ 922 20 20) is on this large square in the La Grenette building. Opening times are Monday to Friday from 8 am to noon and 1.30 to 6 pm and Saturday from 8 am to noon. The main post office (1800 Vevey 1) is 100m to the right of the station.

Things to See & Do
Vevey has a 15th century church, St Martin's, up the hill behind the station. The old streets east of Grande Place and the lakeside promenades are worth exploring – a tourist office brochure details points of interest. Apart from that, the main entertainment comes from several museums, *all* of which are closed on Monday.

The **Swiss Museum of Games** (Musée Suisse du Jeu) is certainly the most fun. The games are arranged according to various themes – educational, strategic, simulation, skill and chance, and there are many that you can play (explanations are in French). Admission costs Sfr6 (senior citizens and students Sfr3, children free) and it's open from 2 to 6 pm. The museum is in the Château de la Tour de Peilz: take trolley bus No 1 and get off at Place du Temple.

The head office of the huge Nestlé food company is in Vevey. It is responsible for the **Food Museum** (Musée de l'Alimentation), Rue du Léman, open from 10 am to noon and 2 to 5 pm. It looks at food and nutrition in historical, scientific and sociological terms in such a didactic way that you almost expect to have to pass a written exam before you're allowed to leave. Ask for the English text. The interactive computer games are enjoy-able, though. Entry costs Sfr5, or Sfr3 for students, senior citizens and children.

The **Jenisch Museum**, Ave de la Gare 2, exhibits Swiss art from the 19th and 20th centuries and has a special section on Oskar Kokoschka, the Viennese expressionist. Admission depends on exhibitions (at least Sfr8), and it's closed mornings in winter. The **Swiss Camera Museum**, 6 Ruelle des Anciens Fossés, near Grande Place, concentrates on the instruments rather than the images they produce. Admission costs Sfr5 for adults, Sfr4 for students and seniors, and it's free for children (closed winter mornings). Other museums in Vevey cover wine-growing and the history of the town.

Vevey is the capital of the Lavaux wine-growing region, and every 25 years the growers congregate on the town for an elaborate and exuberant summer festival that is years in the planning. The next one occurs in 1999. Film-makers arrive every July for the annual International Comedy Film Festival. There's a folklore market every Saturday morning in July and August.

Places to Stay
Camp by the lake at *La Pichette* (☎ 921 09 97), west of the centre towards St Saphorin. The site is open from 1 April to 30 September.

A brand new *Auberge* for youths and families is opening in late 1996 on Grande Place. Beds in rooms or dorms are Sfr25 to Sfr35 per person – check with the tourist office. Otherwise, the best budget central option is *Pension Bürgle* (☎ 921 40 23), 16 Rue Louis Meyer. It's an ageing building with large rooms and hall showers. The price is Sfr35 per person and it's open year-round. It's often full in summer with long-term guests, so check for vacancies by telephone (reservations not accepted).

Just off Grande Place in the old town is *Des Négociants* (☎ 922 70 11), 27 Rue du Conseil, providing rooms from Sfr75/110 with private facilities. *Hotel De Famille* (☎ 921 39 31; fax 921 43 47), 20 Rue des Communaux, by the station to the left, has an indoor swimming pool, sauna, and private

Top: Matterhorn from the Grindjisee, Valais
Bottom Left: Leysin ski area, Lake Geneva Region
Bottom Right: Homes and barns, Hinterdorf, Zermatt, Valais

CLEM LINDENMAYER

MARK HONAN

Top: Kühmad Church in Lötschental, Valais
Bottom: Chalet homes at Leukerbad, Valais

parking (all free for guests). Singles/doubles start at Sfr85/150, although there are a few cheaper rooms without private shower.

Places to Eat

The train station has an *Aperto* supermarket, open daily from 6 am to 9 pm. Opposite the post office is the Centre Commercial, containing a supermarket, *McDonald's*, and a *Manora* buffet restaurant, open until 6.30 pm weekdays (8 pm Thursday) and 5 pm on Saturday. It has a salad bar (Sfr4.20 to Sfr10.50), dessert bar, and main meals for Sfr9 to Sfr17.

A *Migros* supermarket and restaurant has entrances on both Ave Paul Cérésole and Rue de Lausanne (open same hours as Manora). Cheap self-service food is also available at *EPA* department store at Place Ste Claire.

For traditional local fare, explore the centre of town east of Grande Place. *Le Mazot*, 7 Rue du Conseil, is a typical place, offering perch (Sfr21), fondue (Sfr19) and horse steaks (Sfr26); it's closed Sunday lunch and Wednesday. *Des Négociants* (see Places to Stay), has a lunch and evening assiette du jour with soup for Sfr15.

Café-Restaurant du Raisin (☎ 921 10 28), Grande Place, has a café on the ground floor where meals start at Sfr15. In its plush gourmet restaurant upstairs, main dishes cost from Sfr35 and multi-course menus from Sfr55.It is closed on Sunday evening and Monday, except in summer when it's open daily.

Getting There & Away

Two or more trains an hour travel around the lake: Vevey is 15 minutes from Lausanne (Sfr6) and five minutes from Montreux (Sfr2.80). Trolley bus No 1 runs from Vevey to Montreux (Sfr2.40) and Villeneuve (Sfr3).

By boat, the fare to Lausanne is Sfr13 and to Montreux, Sfr6. Boats depart from the Débarcadère by Grande Place; also see Getting There & Away for Lausanne.

AROUND VEVEY

Ask the tourist office about the wine train that runs in the summer to Puidoux (Sfr9.60 return). A steam train chugs along the three-

km track from Blonay to Chamby, where a railway museum houses some steam engines and machinery. Sfr11 (children Sfr5.50) gets entry and the return trip, but it only operates from early May to late October, on Saturday afternoon and Sunday. Spots near to Vevey for good views and walks are Les Pléiades (1397m; accessible by train) and Mont Pèlerin (1080m; accessible by funicular, and with a new panoramic tower on Plein Ciel).

MONTREUX

• *pop 19,700* • *385m* • ☎ *(021)*

Centrepiece of the Swiss Riviera, Montreux offers marvellous lakeside walks and access to the ever-popular Château de Chillon (pronounced Sheeyoh). The town's reputation grew in the 19th century as many artists, writers and musicians discovered the beauties of the area. Lord Byron, Peter Shelley and Mary Shelley (who wrote *Frankenstein* by the lake) were among the first of the literary influx – themselves following in the earlier footsteps of Jean Jacques Rousseau.

Montreux retains a strong musical tradition. It has hosted a major jazz festival annually since 1967 and a classical music festival since WWII. Montreux was also the site of a famous event in rock history. On 4 December 1971 the Casino Theatre in Montreux caught fire during a gig by Frank Zappa. The fire raged all night, casting a great pall of smoke over the placid waters of Lake Geneva. The burning building was watched by the band, Deep Purple, from across the lake, and inspired their classic track *Smoke on the Water*.

Orientation & Information

The train station (with bike rental, money-exchange counters, and Sfr2 luggage lockers) and the main post office (1820 Montreux 1) are on Ave des Alpes. The quickest way from here to the tourist office (☎ 962 84 84), in the Pavillon on the lake shore, is to take the lift down from round the back of Restaurant City (see Places to Eat). The office is open Monday to Friday from 8.30 am to noon and 1.30 to 6 pm, and on Saturday from 9 am to noon. Hours are

Montreux

0   100   200 m

Lake
Leman

PLACES TO STAY
8 Pension Wilhelm
12 Hôtel-Restaurant
   Du Pont
16 Hostellerie du Lac
17 Eden au Lac
19 Hôtel Helvetie

PLACES TO EAT
2 Restaurant City
7 Brasserie des Alpes
9 Tea-Room Les Arcades
10 Caveau des Vignerons
14 Pizzeria de la Place
15 Palais Hoggar
18 Migros Supermarket

OTHER
1 Boat Landing Stage
3 Train Station
4 Post Office
5 Tourist Office
6 SSR (Travel Agency)
11 Old Montreux Museum
13 Salon-Lavoir (laundry)
20 Casino

extended in summer, when the place is open daily. Staff make free hotel bookings – ask well in advance if your visit coincides with one of the festivals. Don't buy their city map (Sfr1), get it for free in one of the banks.

The budget travel agency, SSR (☎ 961 23 00), is at 25 Ave des Alpes. The Salon-Lavoir self-service laundry, Rue Industrielle, costs only Sfr3.50 to wash and Sfr0.20 per 7½ minutes in the dryers (open Monday to Saturday from 7 am to 6.45 pm).

Things to See & Do
Château de Chillon Chillon Castle receives

more visitors than any other historical building in Switzerland. Occupying a stunning position right on Lake Geneva, the fortress caught the public imagination when Lord Byron wrote about the fate of François de Bonivard, who was chained to the fifth pillar in the dungeons for four years in the 16th century. Byron is credited with scratching his own name on the third pillar, though it could equally well be the work of a more recent vandal.

Bonivard's crime was to preach about the Reformation, despite the vehement opposition of the Duke of Savoy who was then resident in the castle. Eschewing intellectual debate, the duke imprisoned Bonivard in his dungeon. Bonivard was only freed when Bernese troops, themselves followers of the Reformation, took over the region in 1536.

The castle is still in excellent condition, and dates from the 11th century. It has undergone much modification and enlargement since then. Allow at least two hours to view the tower, courtyards, dungeons and numerous rooms containing weapons, utensils, frescoes and furniture. Notice particularly the designs on the carved wooden chests and the ceiling in the **Great Hall**. Four models in the museum show how the castle has been altered over the years.

Entry costs Sfr6.50 for adults, Sfr5.50 for students and Sfr3 for children, and the castle opens daily at 10 am (9 am from April to September). The closing time varies through the year: it is 4.45 pm from November to February; 5.30 pm in March and October; 6.30 pm in April, May, June and September; and 7 pm in July and August. The castle is a pleasant 45-minute walk along the lakefront from Montreux (15 minutes from the youth hostel), or it's also accessible by train or trolley bus No 1 (Sfr1.70).

In the old town is a small museum, the **Museum of Old Montreux** (Musée du Vieux Montreux), recounting the history of the town and locality (Sfr6, students Sfr3). It's open daily from mid-April to mid-October, at 40 Rue de la Gare.

Montreux's **casino** (☎ 963 53 31) has gambling and a small cinema, plus several bars and nightclubs, including the Western Saloon where there's live country music.

Organised Tours
The MOB Railways counter in the tourist office books various excursions such as trips to Mont Blanc and Gruyères, and tours of local vineyards.

Special Events
Montreux's major festivals are in the summer. The best known is the **Montreux Jazz Festival**, lasting for two weeks in early July. The programme is announced in May

and tickets are available shortly afterwards from the Montreux tourist office or from the ticket corner in branches of the Swiss Bank Corporation throughout Switzerland. You could also write in advance to Montreux Jazz Festival, Service de Location, Case postale 1451, CH-1820, Montreux, or call the festival hot line (from May) on ☎ 623 45 67. There are sometimes free events during the day, but count on around Sfr50 for one of the big evening gigs.

The week-long **Golden Rose Television Festival** (Rose d'Or) is in late April, and hordes of the industry's professionals hit town.

The **Montreux-Vevey Music Festival** is an extravaganza of classical music lasting from late August to the end of September. Tickets for performances can cost anything from Sfr20 to Sfr140. Write in advance to Festival de Musique, 5 Rue de Théâtre, Case postale 162, CH-1820, Montreux.

Places to Stay
Camping The nearest camping is at the optimistically named *Les Horizons Bleus* (☎ 960 15 47) at Villeneuve. It's by the lake and the harbour, and is open from 1 April to 30 September. Take trolley bus No 1 from Montreux (Sfr2.40).

Hostel The SYHA *hostel* (☎ 963 49 34) is at 8 Passage de l'Auberge, Territet, a 30-minute walk along the lake clockwise from the tourist office (or take the train or bus No 1). It's near the waterfront and under the railway line, open year-round, and has new facilities throughout. Dorms are Sfr27.40 and doubles (bunk beds) are Sfr72.80. Check-in is from 4 pm (5 pm in winter).

Hotels & Pensions Most hotels raise their prices for the summer season. An exception is *Villa Germaine* (☎ 963 15 28), 3 Ave de Collonge, not far from the station in Territet. Singles/doubles are Sfr65/100 with shower or Sfr50/85 without. It is also open year-round, whereas most of Montreux's hotels close for at least part of the winter.

Pension Wilhelm (☎ 963 14 31), 13 Rue de

Marché, charges Sfr60/90 for singles/doubles in an old-fashioned, family-run hotel. Rooms with own shower are given out first. *Hostellerie du Lac* (☎ 963 32 71), 12 Rue du Quai, has rooms with high ceilings, big balconies and views of the lake. Doubles start at Sfr70 using hall shower or Sfr110 with private facilities, and all rooms have TV and radio. Subtract Sfr10/20 for single occupancy (closed mid-December to late February).

Hôtel-Restaurant du Pont (☎ 963 22 49), is in the old town at 12 Rue du Pont. The rooms are fairly average and cost around Sfr90/150 with private shower/toilet and TV. It's right by the river.

Hôtel Helvetie (☎ 963 25 51; fax 963 81 66), 32 Ave du Casino, is a great place to stay. The large rooms, high ceilings, wide corridors give a wonderful feeling of space, as does the huge lobby with several different sections. There's also a rooftop terrace and chunky period radiators. All rooms have bath or shower, toilet, TV, mini-bar and telephone; prices start at Sfr110/170. Parking across the road costs Sfr12 for 24 hours, and there's a quality restaurant.

Eden au Lac (☎ 963 55 51; fax 636 18 13), 11 Rue du Théâtre, occupies a fine site by the lake. The restaurant and lobby areas are very grand but this opulence isn't present to the expected degree in the cheaper rooms. Prices start at Sfr190/240.

Places to Eat

Migros supermarket at 49 Ave du Casino has a self-service restaurant, open Monday to Wednesday until 6.30 pm, Thursday and Friday until 7.45 pm, and Saturday until 5 pm. It sometimes has very cheap special offers. *Restaurant City*, 37 Ave des Alpes, is also self-service with meals for under Sfr12. The main advantage of this place is the sunny terrace overlooking the lake; it's open daily from 7 am to midnight (9 pm from October to mid-May). It also gives a 10% discount to students.

Brasserie des Alpes, 23 Ave des Alpes, has a lunchtime menu du jour, and tasty pizza and pasta from Sfr14. It's a typical French café environment, open daily to around midnight.

Pizzeria de la Place, 4 Place du Marché, is, despite the name, long on pasta and short on pizza (from Sfr12). There are also expensive multicourse menus (closed Wednesday). Around the corner along Rue de Quai, check *Palais Hoggar*, decked out in ceramic inlays like a low-budget version of the Taj Mahal. It's fairly pricey, with Oriental and vegetarian food for around Sfr25 to Sfr35, but the ambience and lakeside location make up for the expense (closed Monday in winter).

Caveau des Vignerons, at 30 Rue Industrielle in the old part of town, is the place to go for fondue (from Sfr20). It also serves fillets of perch (Sfr24.50) and Raclette, and is closed on Sunday. Opposite, *Tea-Room Les Arcades*, offers fantastic value for a weekday lunch (to 2 pm): soup, main course, dessert and drink is only Sfr13. The vegetarian plate is Sfr9. It closes at 6 pm and on Sunday.

Hostellerie du Lac (see Places to Stay) has a mid-price restaurant that is especially good for fish specialities (closed Tuesday). One of Switzerland's top gourmet restaurants is *Pont de Brent* (☎ 964 52 30), north-west of Montreux in the nearby village of Brent, accessible by train. It has a terrace and is closed on Sunday and Monday.

Getting There & Away

Hourly trains depart to/from Geneva and take one hour 10 minutes to cover the lakeside route (Sfr27). From Lausanne, there are three trains an hour (Sfr8.40) which take 19 to 35 minutes. Slow local trains continue eastwards from Montreux to stop at Territet for the youth hostel and Chillon for the castle. Interlaken can be reached via a scenic rail route, with changeovers at Zweisimmen and Spiez (railpasses valid, though there is a Sfr6 supplement for 'Panorama Express' trains only). The track winds its way up the hill for an excellent view over Lake Geneva. For boat services, see Getting There & Away in the Geneva and Lausanne sections.

AROUND MONTREUX

Rochers de Naye There is a magnificent panorama of the lake and the Alps from this viewing point at 2042m. Two restaurants at the top allow you to enjoy the view in comfort, or you can stroll around the grassy plateau and visit the Alpine garden. It's a winding, scenic, 55-minute train journey from Montreux. Trains are run by MOB: the Half-Fare Card is valid and the Swiss Pass is free only up to Caux, and thereafter gets a discount of 25% (you pay Sfr31.60). Inter-Rail gets 50% off but Eurail is about as useful as a clown costume at a funeral. Discounts apply to the *full* return fare of Sfr56.60, which actually is never charged. The normal return deal from Montreux is Sfr47, and there are sometimes further reductions, eg the winter return fare of Sfr32 includes a ski pass. Cars can get as far as Caux, and the return fare from there is Sfr38. The walk up from Montreux takes about 3½ hours.

North-West Vaud

This part of the canton of Vaud is dominated by the Jura mountain chain and Lake Neuchâtel.

YVERDON-LES-BAINS

• *pop 22,000* • *437m* • ☎ *(024)*

Yverdon (pronounced Ee-verdon) has been a health centre since Roman times. It's an enjoyable lakeside resort and Vaud's second-largest town after Lausanne.

Orientation & Information

Yverdon is on the southern shore of Lake Neuchâtel. The train station has money-exchange facilities daily from at least 5.45 am to 8.40 pm, and Sfr3 or Sfr5 luggage lockers. Close by is the post office (1400 Yverdon 1). The tourist office (☎ 423 62 90) is on Place Pestalozzi, at the start of the pedestrian-only zone of the old town. It is open Monday to Friday from 9 am to noon and 1.30 to 6 pm, and (between June and September only) on Saturday from 9 am to noon.

Things to See & Do

The centre of town is clustered round the 13th century **castle**, built by Peter II of Savoy. Inside is a **museum** containing local prehistoric artefacts, arms, clothing, and a Ptolemaic Egyptian mummy. The Guard's Tower is devoted to the champion of primary education, Heinrich Pestalozzi (1746-1827), whose educational institution was actually based in the castle for 20 years from 1805. It is open Tuesday to Sunday from 10 am to noon (June to September) and 2 to 5 pm (year round). Admission costs Sfr4.

Next to the castle at Place Pestalozzi 14 is the **House of Elsewhere** (la Maison d'Ailleurs). This science fiction museum has temporary exhibitions, as well as permanent features: a mock-up of a spaceship, film stills, a room devoted to artist HR Giger (of *Alien* fame) and a library of books and magazines. It is open Tuesday to Sunday from 2 to 6 pm and entry costs Sfr8, or Sfr5 for students, children and senior citizens – ask about the combination ticket with the castle.

An interesting feature of Yverdon are the **trotting races** *(trot attelé)* in the hippodrome between the train station and the lake. These mainly take place at weekends

Heinrich Pestalozzi (1746-1827), educational reformer

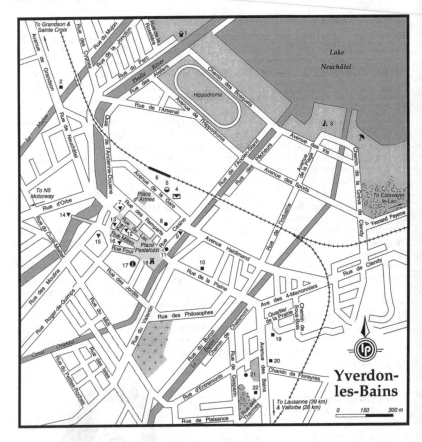

between June and November; entry costs around Sfr5 and you can bet anything from Sfr1 up to the shirt off your back.

The lake offers the opportunity for various boat rides (see Getting There & Away) and the usual water sports, including windsurfing, water-skiing and sailing. There are five km of sandy beaches by the town.

Health Spa The water from the 14,000-year-old mineral springs starts off 500m below ground. By the time it hits the surface it has picked up all sorts of salubrious properties from the layers of rock, and is particularly good for sufferers of rheumatism and respiratory ailments. It has even spawned a bottled mineral water under the name of *Arkina* which is claimed to be effective in combating obesity.

The **Centre Thermal** (☎ 425 44 56), the health complex to the east of the centre off Ave des Bains, offers a range of treatments. Even if you feel fine you can enjoy bathing in indoor and outdoor pools (temperature 28 to 34°C, entry Sfr13), take a sauna (Sfr30) or have a massage (Sfr55). It is open Monday to Friday from 8 am to 10 pm, and weekends and holidays from 9 am to 8 pm.

PLACES TO STAY
1 Youth Hostel
2 Hôtel Industriel
3 Camping des Iris
10 l'Ecusson Vaudois
19 Hôtel La Prairie
20 Motel des Bains
22 Grand Hôtel
   des Bains

PLACES TO EAT
7 Manora
9 La Fourchette
12 Placette Supermarket
13 Don Camillo
14 McDonald's & Coop
   Restaurant
15 Restaurant des Sports
16 La Couronne

OTHER
4 Post Office
5 Bus Stop
6 Train Station
8 Casino
11 House of Elsewhere
17 Tourist Information
18 Castle & Museum
21 Health Spa & Centre
   Thermal

Places to Stay

Camping des Iris (☎ 425 10 89) is by the lake to the north-east of the station (well signposted). It is open from 1 April to late September and costs Sfr5.50 per person, Sfr5.50 per tent and Sfr2.50 for a car.

The SYHA *hostel* (☎ 425 12 33), Rue du Parc 14, is a 10-minute walk from the station, near the lake. Dorms cost Sfr19, reception is closed from 9 am to 5 pm and the hostel is closed from mid-December to late February.

Yverdon has surprisingly few hotels. Less than 15 minutes' walk west of the old town is *Hôtel Industriel* (☎ 445 20 06), Ave de Grandson 8, with basic rooms for Sfr40/80. The only central place is *l'Ecusson Vaudois* (☎ 425 40 15), Rue de la Plaine 29, with a ground floor café. Fresh, newly renovated rooms are Sfr55/90 using hall showers or Sfr75/110 with private shower/WC. Daytime parking is a problem.

The top-quality hotels are on Ave des Bains, near the Centre Thermal. *Motel des*

Bains (☎ 426 92 81) at No 21 starts at Sfr110/145, *Hôtel La Prairie* (☎ 425 19 19), No 9, at Sfr130/190, and *Grand Hôtel des Bains* (☎ 425 70 21; fax 425 21 90), No 22, at Sfr180/260.

Places to Eat

The Bel-Air shopping centre has a *McDonald's* and a *Coop Restaurant* (both open daily) and a large supermarket. A *Placette Supermarket* is on Rue du Lac. *Manora*, the buffet-style restaurant chain, is on Rue de l'Ancienne Poste, open daily from 7 am to 10 pm.

Don Camillo (☎ 425 42 82), Rue du Pré 10, is the place to go for Italian food (pizza/pasta from Sfr12; closed Sunday). *La Couronne*, Rue du Milieu, has Swiss food for around Sfr15, including salad and dessert (closed Monday lunch and Sunday).

La Fourchette, Rue de Casino 8, is a new French restaurant with meals for Sfr15 to Sfr35. The place for those with a discerning palate is *Restaurant des Sports* (☎ 425 27 63), Rue du Milieu 47, where main courses are around Sfr30, though it also has a ground floor café where meals start at Sfr14 (closed on Sunday evening and Monday).

Getting There & Away

Yverdon has direct trains to Lausanne (Sfr12.20, takes 25 minutes), Neuchâtel (Sfr11.40, 20 minutes) and Estavayer-le-Lac (Sfr6, 15 minutes). The train to Vallorbe (Sfr14) is awkward (via Cossonay) and takes two hours. By road is much easier as the N9 goes directly there; postbuses depart from in front of the train station three to five times daily (Sfr15.80, 40 minutes).

Several times a day in summer (except Monday), boats sail to Neuchâtel (Sfr22, three hours). Stops en route include Grandson and Estavayer-le-Lac. You can even get as far as Solothurn by boat, by way of the Zihl canal to Lake Biel then on the Aare River. Call the boat company in Neuchâtel (☎ 032-725 40 12) for information.

LAKE GENEVA REGION

Getting Around

All local buses (Sfr1.50 per trip) leave from in front of the train station, bordering a large car park. There are parking meters on some streets (two hour daytime maximum).

GRANDSON

The present **castle** at Grandson dates from the 13th century. Early in 1476 it was taken by Charles the Bold and his Burgundian troops, but they didn't hold it for long. On 2 March the same year the Swiss Confederates returned and easily defeated the Duke's forces. The vengeful Swiss strung up some of his men from the apple trees in the castle orchard. The rest scattered in disarray and left behind much artillery and treasure.

The castle has two museums. The **Historical Museum** tells the story of 1476 and other battles with dioramas and displays of weapons. The **Automobile Museum** has as its prize exhibit a white Rolls Royce formerly owned by Greta Garbo. From 1 March to 31 October it is open daily from 9 am to 6 pm; in winter hours are reduced to Saturday from 1 to 5 pm and Sunday from 10 am to 5 pm. Admission costs Sfr8 (senior citizens and students Sfr6). There is a tourist office in the castle (☎ 024-445 29 26).

Getting There & Away

Only the slow trains between Yverdon and Neuchâtel stop at Grandson (one every one to two hours). From Yverdon it costs Sfr2.40 and takes a few minutes. Bus departures from outside Yverdon station are more frequent. Better still, get there by enjoying the five-km stroll around the lake.

SAINTE CROIX

- *pop 4500* • *1066m* • ☎ *(024)*

This town has been famous for its music boxes since the mid 19th century. The art of making these expensive items is well documented in the **CIMA Museum** (Centre International de la Méchanique d'Art), Rue de l'Industrie 2.

Music boxes contain a rotating spiked cylinder that bends and releases metal prongs, causing them to vibrate and hum melodiously. Some of the larger, more elaborate boxes also incorporate mini drums, bells, and accordions. The best exhibits are the musical automata, such as the acrobats, a tiny Mozart, and Pierrot the writer. These and many other ingenious machines are activated by the guide on the 70-minute tour (in French, but English notes are available). There are some good examples of early radios and phonographs, which the town started producing once music boxes became largely superseded by the new technology. Music boxes are still made, however, as the shop on the ground floor demonstrates.

The museum is open Tuesday to Sunday from 1.30 to 6 pm, and entry costs Sfr9 for adults, Sfr8 for senior citizens, Sfr7 for students, Sfr6 for children and Sfr23 for families. The tourist office (☎ 454 27 02) is in the same building. In nearby l'Auberson is the **Musée Baud**, Grand-Rue, displaying mainly older music boxes. It's open every afternoon from 1 July to 15 September (Sfr7; students Sfr6, children Sfr4), but only Saturday afternoon and Sunday for the rest of the year.

The highest point in the area is **Le Chasseron** (1607m). The summit provides a marvellous 360° panorama of the Alps, Lake Neuchâtel and the Jura. There is a car park which is a 45-minute walk from the top. Starting from Sainte Croix it takes under two hours to walk to the summit.

Downhill skiing in the winter is centred on Le Chasseron and the adjoining summits. The one-day pass covers 10 lifts and costs Sfr28 (Sfr20 for children). The local ski school (☎ 454 10 61) can give group lessons (Sfr18 per person for two hours) or individual tuition. There are also 80 km of cross-country trails.

Places to Stay & Eat

Sainte Croix has an SYHA *hostel* (☎ 454 61 18 10), Rue Centrale 16, behind the Coop supermarket on Rue Nueve. It costs Sfr23 and is closed from late October to mid-December, and for two weeks before Easter. The town only has a few hotels. The renovated *Hôtel des Fleurettes* (☎ 454 22 94),

Chemin des Fleurettes, off Rue Nueve, has singles/doubles for Sfr40/80, or Sfr50/100 with private shower. It also has dormitory beds (Sfr20 without breakfast).

Rue Nueve is the main shopping street and has several restaurants. *Buffet de la Gare*, by the station, is a simple place but with decent food (open daily).

Getting There & Away

The only way to get there by train is on the hourly narrow-gauge line from Yverdon (Sfr11.40, takes 35 minutes). There is a fine view of the Alps and Lake Neuchâtel from the hill just outside Sainte Croix. Hourly postbuses run north from Sainte Croix to Buttes, which is connected by rail and bus to the northern Jura. A major road links Sainte Croix to Yverdon and Pontarlier in France.

VALLORBE

• *pop 3200* • *750m* • ☎ *(021)*

This small industrial town has only recently developed its tourist attractions (as yet, tourists fail to arrive in droves). In 1974 the caves of the Orbe were first open to the public; 1980 saw the opening of the Iron Museum and 1990 the opening of its twin, the Railway Museum. A nearby military fort has been revealing its secrets only since 1988.

Orientation & Information

Vallorbe is a couple of km from the French border and English is not widely spoken. The train station (money-exchange counters, bike rental, Sfr2 lockers) is a 10-minute walk from the central street, Grand-Rue. A map outside shows the way. The tourist office (☎ 843 25 83) is just beyond Grand-Rue, in the Musée du Fer et du Chemin de Fer, open daily from 8.30 am to noon and 1.30 to 6 pm. From 1 November to 1 April it's only open Monday to Friday (closes 5 pm).

Military Fort

The Jourgne Pass near Vallorbe acquired strategic importance as war began to threaten in the late 1930s. An underground fort was constructed at Pré-Giroud in 1937 to guard this pass and the route along the Vallée de Joux. From the outside it looks like an unremarkable mountain chalet, yet below ground it can accommodate 130 men. There are dormitories, canteens, a kitchen, a telephone exchange, even an infirmary with an operating room. Tunnels connect the living area with the combat zone. As it turned out, the fortress was never used in direct conflict and, following a period as a training centre, it was allowed to fall into disuse.

The commune of Vallorbe purchased the fort from the federal authorities for the princely sum of one franc. Plastic dummies have now replaced flesh and blood personnel, but it still provides a fascinating hint of the myriad military installations that remain hidden away in the Swiss countryside. Despite the nominal purchase price it costs a hefty Sfr9 (Sfr8 students, Sfr5 children) to get in. It is open from 1 May and 31 October, 10 am to 5 pm on weekends and holidays (daily in July and August). The guided tour takes around 75 minutes (notes in English). Parking is available nearby. It takes 70 minutes to walk there from Vallorbe or 40 minutes from Le Day train station, the next station in the direction of Lausanne. There is no bus service.

Caves

Less than three km south-west of Vallorbe are stalactite and stalagmite caves, caused by the underground course of the Orbe River on its way to Lake Brenet. To get there, follow the signs for 'Source Grottos' (free parking outside). The guided tour of the caves takes one hour and costs Sfr12 (children Sfr6). In the entrance hall are displays of rare rocks and minerals, included in the tour price. The caves are open from Palm Sunday to All Saint's Day (November 1st). It's shut Monday until the end of May, otherwise it's open daily from 9 am to 5 pm (6 pm July and August).

A farther two km towards the Joux Valley is **Mont d'Orzeires**, where there is a reservation with grazing North American buffaloes (free entry). Some of these beasts graduate in style to the dinner plate in the reservation's restaurant (☎ 843 17 35) during spring and autumn.

Iron & Railway Museum

Iron production and tool manufacturing have been important in Vallorbe since the 13th century. The main attraction is the traditional forge where a blacksmith can be seen diligently working away. Power for the furnace is derived from four large paddlewheels turning outside in the Orbe River. The railway section includes models, memorabilia, and a slide show. The museum is open the same days as the caves, but from 9.30 am to noon and 1.30 to 6 pm. Enter via the tourist office; prices are as for the fort. The Clover Card (Sfr24, children Sfr12) allows entry to the museum, caves and fort, and is valid for the whole season.

Activities

Mont d'Or (across the French border) and the Joux Valley provide opportunities for summer hiking and winter downhill and cross-country skiing. Sailing and windsurfing are just two of the water sports that are popular on Lake Joux. The fishing season (trout) is from March to October. Contact the local tourist office (☎ 021-845 62 57) for more information.

Places to Stay

Camp at *Pré Sous Ville* (☎ 843 23 09), five minutes from the station by the Orbe River and alongside an open-air swimming pool. It is open from 1 May to early October.

The SYHA *hostel* (☎ 843 13 49), Rue du Simplon 11, is 10 minutes' walk from Vallorbe train station. Beds cost Sfr22 and reception is closed from 9 am to 5 pm. The hostel is closed from late October to mid-December.

There are only two hotels in town, though the tourist office can supply lists of cheap private rooms. *Hôtel Restaurant l'Orbe* (☎ 843 12 41), Rue de Lausanne 41, has nine beds in five rooms for Sfr40 per person using hall shower. Breakfast costs Sfr8. *Hôtel des Jurats* (☎ 843 19 91), Rue des Eterpaz, 1.5 km east of the centre, has singles/doubles from Sfr85/120 with private shower or bath.

Places to Eat

There's more choice when eating out. Fish is a speciality of Vallorbe restaurants, especially local trout.

The main street, Grand-Rue, has three supermarkets and several places to eat. *Le Rio*, Grand-Rue 20, has a smoky bar area with a restaurant beyond (closed Sunday). Lunches for Sfr14.50 include starter or desert. Opposite, at No 20, is *Le France* with good pizzas from Sfr11.50 and trout for Sfr19 (open daily). Towards the train station is *Mont d'Or*, a tiny place with low prices, including pizza from Sfr10 and perch for Sfr16 (closed Sunday).

Hôtel Restaurant l'Orbe (see Places to Stay) has meals in the café for about Sfr20. It also has a gourmet restaurant where main courses start at Sfr30 and multi-course menus are above Sfr40. It is closed on Monday evening and Sunday.

Getting There & Away

The high-speed TGV service from Paris to Lausanne stops at Vallorbe. Border checks are on the train. One regional train an hour goes to Lausanne; it takes 45 minutes and costs Sfr15. By road, the quickest route is the eastwards N9 followed by the southwards N1, but it would be more fun to take the smaller roads across the Jura.

Trains also run along the western shore of Lake Joux and the Orbe River as far as Le Brassus. Roads go either side of the lake, with the quickest route along the eastern shore. A direct bus goes north-east to Yverdon several times a day; the journey takes 40 minutes and costs Sfr15.80.

Vaud Alps

Only the south-east corner of Vaud extends into the Alps, but it still boasts several interesting resorts and year-round skiing. A regional ski pass for the Vaud Alps (Alpes

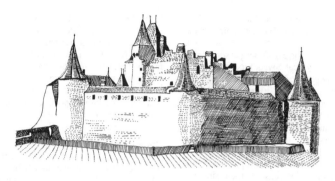

Aigle Castle, an important medieval stronghold in the Rhône Valley, now houses a wine museum. It was once home to the Counts of Savoy. The town bought the property in 1804.

Vaudoises) costs Sfr49 for one day and Sfr263 for seven days, with reductions for people under age 20. You can also ski at Vaud resorts using the Gstaad Super Ski Region (see the Gstaad section in the Bernese Oberland chapter).

Hiking is a popular pastime in the summer, and all the resorts mentioned offer possibilities for circular hikes lasting from two to five hours. Tourist offices can give details.

For holiday chalets, write to the local tourist office well in advance, listing requirements. Upon arrival, ask the tourist office about discounts that apply with the local Guest Card.

Aigle, a transport junction for Alpine resorts, has a wine museum based in its 12th century château (open 1 April to 31 October, except Monday). Wine-tastings are offered. Express trains on the Lausanne-Brig route stop at Aigle.

CHÂTEAU D'OEX
• *pop 2900* • *970m* • ☎ *(026)*
This attractive family resort (pronounced Shato Day) has quaint chalets and limited night life. There's an excellent blue (easy) ski run that goes all the way from Tête du Grin to Gerignoz, though there's also a good range of more difficult slopes. The ski school (☎ 924 68 48) charges Sfr22 for a half-day

lesson. A one-day ski pass for the resort (50 km of runs) costs Sfr37.

A speciality of Château d'Oex is **hot air ballooning**, and (expensive) passenger flights are available winter and summer (☎ 924 61 74). In late January it hosts the International Hot Air Ballooning Week where every day there's a special event or competition. The group take-off is truly spectacular. **River-rafting** is another possibility. There's also a **museum** highlighting traditional crafts and dwellings of the local Enhaut district. It's closed Monday, Wednesday and for most of October (Sfr4). **Le Chalet** (☎ 924 66 77) is a touristy centre where there's cheese-making (daily except Monday), a model railway (Sfr2), a cheese and crafts shop, and a restaurant specialising in fondues.

The tourist office (☎ 924 77 88) is in the centre and can book rooms by telephone.

Places to Stay & Eat
Accommodation prices are reasonable, even in high season. Camp year-round by the Sarine River at *Au Berceau* (☎ 924 62 34). The SYHA *hostel* (☎ 924 64 04) is a 10-minute walk downhill (signposted) from the train station. Beds cost Sfr23 and there's daytime access; it's closed from late October to mid-December.

Buffet de la Gare (☎ 924 77 17), by the

station, has singles/doubles for Sfr43/75 using hall showers. By the cable car base station is *La Poste* (☎ 924 63 88), with simple rooms for Sfr40 per person. Its restaurant has typical Swiss food and is good value (closed Sunday in low season). *Motel Bouquetins* (☎ 924 57 04), is on the Bulle-Gstaad main road but is still central. Rooms are Sfr45 per person or Sfr50 with private shower, and there's a restaurant and plenty of parking.

A new, large *Coop* supermarket is in the centre, and its deli counter (open lunch time) has hot and cold snacks. On the main street, near the tourist office, is *Le Relais*, serving decent pizza from Sfr12 (closed Wednesday).

Getting There & Away

The resort is on the scenic rail route (the Panoramic Express) run by the private railroad, MOB, that connects Montreux to the Bernese Oberland. Departures are at least hourly (railpasses are valid). From Montreux it takes one hour and costs Sfr15. National roads run to Château d'Oex from Bulle, Aigle and Gstaad.

LEYSIN

- *pop 2000* • *1350 m* • ☎ *(024)*

Leysin started life as a tuberculosis centre but it's now a well established skiing area with 60 km of marked runs. A one-day local ski pass costs Sfr38, and there are plenty of other sports on offer. Take in the scenery (views of the Rhône Valley and the Dents de Midi) from the revolving restaurant at the top of **Mt Berneuse** (2048m). The cable car costs Sfr13.50 one way or Sfr18 return. Leysin's annual rock festival ran into trouble a few years back, and has now re-emerged as an **Alpes Festival**, comprising three days of music and other events in late August. Get details from the tourist office (☎ 494 22 44), based in the New Sporting Centre (open daily).

There's year-round camping at *Semiramis* (☎ 494 18 29). *Club Vagabond* (☎ 494 13 21), above the Feydey station, is a young person's haunt. There are beds for Sfr25 to Sfr36 per person in two to six-bed rooms (singles will be expected to share), plus good-value food, a bar and regular special events. *Les Orchidées* (☎ 494 14 21) is a family hotel by Vermont station, with Alp views and private parking. Singles/doubles cost from Sfr55/104 with shower or Sfr45/90 without. The New Sporting Centre has a cheap restaurant.

Getting There & Away

This spread-out resort is reached from Aigle by an hourly cog-wheel train (Sfr9 each way, 30 minutes; railpasses valid). Leysin tourist office is a 10-minute walk down from the Vermont stop (free buses in winter). The road route (16 km) is indirect: take highway 11 from Aigle (the road to Château d'Oex) then take a minor road at Le Sépey that doubles back to Leysin.

LES DIABLERETS

- *1150m* • ☎ *(024)*

This village is dominated by the mountain of the same name (3210m). The **glacier** at 3000m offers the opportunity to ski virtually year-round, as well as offering fantastic views. There are two different cable cars running up to the glacier from the valley floor, and both are linked to the village by bus: starting from either Reusch or Col du Pillon you get to Cabane des Diablerets, where a further cable car whisks you almost to the summit at Scex Rouge. To ski from here all the way back down to Reusch is an exhilarating 2000m descent over 14 km.

A one-day summer ski pass costs Sfr49, which although expensive, compares favourably to a simple return fare to the glacier of Sfr45. For winter skiing, use the regional pass or get the Diablerets-Villars pass costing Sfr42 for one day (reduced prices for students and families), which is not valid for the glacier. To explore the glacier by snow bus costs Sfr9. Les Diablerets hosts the **International Alpine Film Festival** at the end of September.

Get more information from the tourist office (☎ 492 33 58), which is open daily.

There's year-round camping at *La Murée* (☎ 021-653 49 29) in the adjoining village of Vers l'Eglise. Places to stay in the centre include *Les Lilas* (☎ 492 31 34), just left of the station, with singles/doubles from Sfr65/108 and *Hostellerie les Sources* (☎ 492 21 26), near the mini-golf course, starting at Sfr88/136 for rooms with private shower and TV. *Auberge de la Poste* (☎ 492 31 24), near the tourist office, costs Sfr54/108. All three places have a restaurant. *Potinière* has a three-course lunch menu for Sfr15.

Getting There & Away
By rail, Les Diablerets is also reached from Aigle: take the hourly train that goes via Le Sépey (Sfr9.60, 50 minutes). Alternatively, there's the postbus from Gstaad (Sfr11, takes one hour) which departs in season every one to two hours. A good road runs from either direction.

VILLARS
• *pop 1400* • *1350 m* • ☎ *(024)*
Villars shares the same local ski pass as Les Diablerets, yielding 96 km of runs. It's a not-too-lively, family resort, and the ski school (☎ 495 22 10) is particularly good for kids. This shares the same office as the tourist office (☎ 495 32 32), near the post office and train station, which is open daily in season. The views across the Rhône Valley are inspiring, encompassing the Dents de Midi, Mont Blanc and the Trient Glacier. On the slopes, experts have few possibilities as most runs are geared towards beginners and intermediates. Ski lifts are not too crowded and the highest skiing is **Chamossaire** at 2113m.

Places to Stay & Eat
Hôtel St Louis (☎ 495 82 71) has beds (Sfr30) for groups and individuals in the west of the resort. The cheapest central accommodation is at Hôtel Suisse (☎ 495 24 25), with compact, wood-walled rooms for Sfr50 per person (doubles with own shower, singles using hall shower). It has a typical café-restaurant where meals start at Sfr13. *Alpe Fleurie* (☎ 495 13 17), by the post office, has rooms with shower/WC and TV for Sfr135/230. Next door, *Hôtel du Golf* (☎ 495 24 77; fax 495 39 78), provides large, well-equipped rooms from Sfr255/330, and good hotel facilities. *La Chaumiere*, by the tourist office, is a tea room open daily to 7 pm, serving pizzas (from Sfr12), crêpes (from Sfr5) and cakes.

Gryon This quiet, untouristed village at 1130m has several cheap places to stay – check with the tourist office (☎ 498 14 22). *Swiss Alp Retreat* (☎ 498 33 21), based in the Chalet Martin, is five minutes' walk from Gryon train station (go past the post office and the Coop and look for the place on your left). It's a real backpackers' retreat, with a relaxed atmosphere and traveller-orientated Swiss/Australian owners. They rent full ski gear (slight seconds from the ski shops) for only Sfr15 per day, bikes for Sfr10, and organise excursions. Dorms cost Sfr15 in summer (Sfr18 in winter) and doubles or family rooms are Sfr20 (Sfr25) per person, plus Sfr1 or Sfr2 for sheets. There's a kitchen (no breakfast) and check-in is from 9 am to 9 pm. Telephone ahead. The train from Gryon to Villars is free with the ski pass.

Getting There & Away
From Bex to Villars, take the small, red hourly train (Sfr7.20 each way, 45 minutes; railpasses valid). Gryon is reached after 30 minutes. An hourly bus runs between Villars and Aigle (Sfr7.20, 30 minutes). The road from Villars to Les Diablerets is only open in the summer (bus service).

BEX
The town of Bex (pronounced Bay), on the Lausanne-Sion rail route, has the only operational salt mine in Switzerland, producing 150 tons of salt every year. It can be visited daily from 1 April to 15 November by guided tour (Sfr14), but you must telephone in advance on ☎ 024-463 24 62. The mines are north-east of town and are not easily accessible by public transport.

Valais

The dramatic Alpine scenery of Valais (Wallis in German) once made it one of the most inaccessible regions of Switzerland. The 10 highest mountains in the country – all of them over 4000m – are within this canton. Nowadays the mountains and valleys have been opened up by an efficient network of roads, railways and cable cars. It is an area of great natural beauty, and naturally enough, each impressive panorama has spawned its own resort.

The ski resorts in Valais are world-renowned. Zermatt is one of the oldest, and thrives on stupendous views of the Matterhorn. Verbier has a shorter history but is equally famous and gives access to a vast area of exciting and varied skiing. Less-known resorts such as Leukerbad can offer perfectly satisfying skiing yet be much cheaper for ski-lift passes.

In all there are 47 listed ski centres. If that is not enough, just across the border in France is the magnificent Mont Blanc Massif, and equally close across the border in Italy is the Monte Rosa Plateau – both large centres known for their excellent skiing.

In the summer, the mountains yield their treasures to hikers and mountaineers rather than skiers, but many resorts offer a whole host of additional sports, including angling, swimming, mountaineering, tennis and golf.

The extreme mountain terrain has meant that the Swiss have been forced to establish and maintain an incredibly extensive network of pipes and canals, to supply water for homes and irrigation in this remote canton. It has been estimated that this network, if laid end-to-end, could wrap completely around the equator once, although the likelihood of anybody actually wanting to do this is very small. Some of these pipes feed the hydro-electric power installations, including the Grande Dixence Dam – a fantastic engineering feat and a great day excursion from Sion. Much of the irrigation system is now very

HIGHLIGHTS

- The highest mountains in Switzerland, including the Matterhorn
- Scenic resorts with varied summer and winter sports
- Traditional Alpine culture and unique cow fights
- Home of the traveller-rescuing St Bernard dogs
- Centre for Swiss wine production

Valais

sophisticated, but in some parts the old *bisses* (*Suonen* in German dialect), narrow wooden aqueducts, are still in place.

History

Sion's pre-eminence in Valaisan history started after the Bishop of Valais left Martigny in 580 AD in order to settle in Sion. After 999 AD the Bishop of Sion received the patronage of the Emperor Rudolph III of Burgundy; Sion became an Imperial city and the bishop was able to rule the territory of Valais from Martigny to the Furka Pass. A

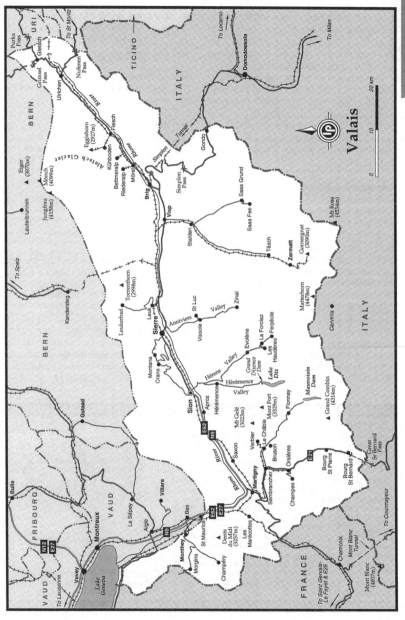

Valais

VALAIS

consistent thorn in the sides of successive bishops was the Dukes of Savoy, and in 1475 an army of Savoyards besieged the city. Sion was freed at the battle of the Planta with the help of the Swiss Confederation.

The invasion of the French in 1798 saw Valais become the Department of the Simplon. Napoleon was determined to control routes into Italy and he instigated the building of the Simplon Pass road which was opened in 1805. With the exit of Napoleon, Valais was able to join the Swiss Confederation in 1815.

Orientation & Information

The canton and tourist region of Valais covers an area of approximately 5220 km, stretching from Lake Geneva to Ticino and bordering France and Italy. The Rhône Valley, particularly from Sion to Sierre, is known for its hot, dry climate. The French/German language divide cuts right through the middle of the canton. The western part of the canton is the Lower Valais (Bas Valais, Unterwallis) and the eastern part the Upper Valais (Haut Valais, Oberwallis). The Germanisation of the Upper Valais dates from the migration of communities from the north in the 6th century.

The regional tourist office, known as the Union Valaisanne du Tourism (☎ 027-322 31 61), is at 6 Rue de Pré-Fleuri, Sion. Information is available on the first floor; opening hours are Monday to Friday from 8 am to noon and 2 to 6 pm.

Getting There & Away

The chains of mountains strung across the region make north-south progress extremely difficult. See Martigny for routes into France and Italy from west Valais, and Brig for transport routes in east Valais. Brig and Martigny are linked by the east-west N9 which follows the course of the Rhône, turning north from Martigny to Lake Geneva. In winter, the 'Snow TGV' from Paris, for international travel only, runs along the Rhône valley as far as Brig.

Lower Valais

SION

- *pop 26,000* • *490m* • *☎ (027)*

From afar, Sion (Sitten in German) looks fantastic within its cusp of Valaisan peaks. It sits on the mostly flat ribbon of the Rhône Valley, yet rising from the town are two hills, looking (it must be said, though guidebooks tend not to) like a pair of breasts, each topped by its own 'nipple', a medieval fortification.

Valais Wine

Valais is also Switzerland's main region for wine-producing, and accounts for 37% of the total land area devoted to this industry. Two-thirds of the wine produced is white wine. Fendant is the name reserved exclusively for Valais white wine. It is dry and fruity, and goes well with cheese dishes, fish, and Valais dried meats. Johannisberg is another well-known Valais white, and comes from the Sylvaner grape. Drink it to accompany fish, shellfish and asparagus. Like Fendant, it is ideal in fondue. Other whites you may come across are Muscat (good with fish) and Ermitage (good with cheese and poached fish). Amigne and Malvoise are dessert wines.

The principal red wine is Dôle, a product of the Pinot Noir and Gamay grapes. It is full-bodied and fruity, and is considered best with red meats, game and cheese, as is the robust red wine, Humagne. Goron is best with white meat and pork.

There are numerous vineyards and wine-growing villages bordering the Rhône between Martigny and Sierre. The regional or local tourist offices can give information about driving itineraries through this area. ■

They lend a sense of history to the town, which is accentuated by the cobbled streets and warren of side-alleys in the centre. Thanks to its status as the cantonal capital, it is the location of several provincial museums.

The bishops of Sion, enjoying the powers of temporal princes, had the habit of dispensing justice with an unecclesiastical ruthlessness and indulging in all sorts of worldly intrigues. The most famous Cardinal-Bishop was Mathieu Schiner who dispatched troops in the early 16th century to aid the papal throne. The political power of the bishops gradually waned until it was removed completely under the 1848 constitution.

Orientation & Information
French-speaking Sion lies predominantly on the north bank of the Rhône River. The train station is conveniently central and has bike rental and money-exchange counters open daily. The post office (1950, Sion 1) is nearby. The old town lies 400m to the north. The tourist office (☎ 322 85 86), Place de la Planta, is open Monday to Friday from 8.30 am to noon and 2 to 5.30 pm, and Saturday from 9 am to noon. In summer, hours are weekdays from 8.30 am to 6 pm and Saturday from 10 am to 4 pm. Staff will book hotels without charging commission. The free city map (also available from the Swiss Bank Corporation on the corner) is small-scale but has an index and useful postbus timetables.

Things to See & Do
The **Tourbillon Castle** (Château de Tourbillon) is open daily (except Monday) from 10 am to 6 pm. Little remains to see except the exterior walls, but the view from the top is worth the climb and there's a good picnic area. The grassy hill buzzes with cicadas on the walk up.

The other hill is crowned by the fortress-like **Basilique de Valère**. It dates from the 12th century and has faded frescoes and elaborately carved wooden stalls. Bursting out of the interior back wall, looking like the hull of a ship, is the oldest playable organ in

the world, constructed in the 15th century. Next to the church is a museum dealing with history and ethnography, as well as temporary exhibitions. Entry to the church costs Sfr3, or Sfr6 including the museum (reduced rates for students, seniors and families).

On the way up to the castle and the church, spare five minutes for the town hall (hôtel de ville), which has some fine wooden doors inside on the first floor. Also take a look in the **cathedral** in the old town. It has a wooden triptych above the high altar and a Romanesque belfry dating from the 11th century.

Between Rue de Conthey and Rue de Lausanne is a tiny covered shopping arcade, and leading from this is the **Maison Supersaxo**, built in 1505 by Georges Supersaxo (1450-1529). The father of 23 children, his history is tied in with that of the powerful bishop, Mathieu Schiner, a worldly cleric who courted European leaders to an unprecedented degree during his period in power. Between them they plotted the downfall of an earlier bishop, Josse de Silenen, and forced him into exile. But they later fell out, and Supersaxo built this ostentatious dwelling partly as an exercise in one-upmanship over his erstwhile ally. The most impressive remnant is the Gothic rosette on the ceiling in the 2nd floor room (free entry, and there are notes in English). It's open daily from 8 am to noon and (except on Saturday and Sunday afternoon) 2 to 6 pm. Ultimately, Schiner proved the dominant force, as he instigated the arrest of Supersaxo in Rome in 1512. Supersaxo was jailed for two years and eventually exiled to Vevey.

Museums All the museums in the town are closed on Monday. The **Valais Museum of Fine Arts** (Musée Cantonal des Beaux-Arts) is in two sections of the old episcopal residences at the foot of the castle. It concentrates on Valaisan artists, both ancient and modern, and costs Sfr5 (students, children and senior citizens Sfr2.50, families Sfr10) for admission. The **Valais Archaeological Museum** (Musée Cantonal d'Archéologie), on Rue des Châteaux, has

VALAIS

wordy displays but no English translations, which limits its appeal to the linguistically challenged (Sfr4, students Sfr2). Both are open from 10 am to noon and 2 to 6 pm. The **Valais Museum of Natural History** (Musée Cantonal d'Histoire Naturelle), Ave de la Gare 42, is comparatively small, and has cases full of stuffed animals (Sfr2, students Sfr1, families Sfr4; open 2 to 6 pm).

Places to Stay

The nearest camping is four km west of Sion, at *Les Îles* (☎ 346 43 47), by the Rhône river, off the Route d'Aproz. It has excellent facil-

ities and is closed in November and for most of December. Take the Condémines postbus from the station and get off at Les Îles.

The SYHA *hostel* (☎ 323 74 70), Rue de l'Industrie 2 is behind the station (exit left and turn left under the tracks). It's in a modern building with a lift, TV room, kitchen (Sfr2 fee) and easy-going management. Beds in four-bed dorms are Sfr25.80 and doubles are Sfr65.60. Reception is closed from 10 am to 5 pm (9 am to 6 pm in winter) and the hostel closes from mid-October to mid-December. Get a key to avoid the curfew.

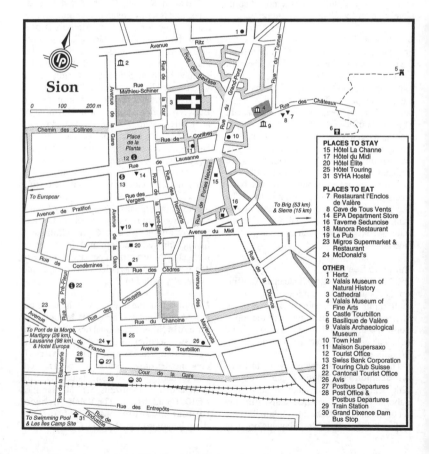

If you have your own transport it is easily viable to stay in Pont de la Morge, two km west of Sion, where *Relais du Simplon* (☎ 346 20 30) has rooms for Sfr34 per person and *Inn des Collines* (☎ 346 20 80) for Sfr40 per person. Both are close to each other on the main road, Rue de Savoie. Postbuses to Aven and Ardon leaving from Sion station stop at the Pont de la Morge post office.

Sion itself has no cheap hotels. One of the most affordable is *Hôtel Élite* (☎ 322 03 27), Avenue du Midi 6, which was extensively renovated in 1996. Singles/doubles with own shower are Sfr70/120 and there is parking round the back.

Hôtel La Channe (☎ 322 32 71), Rue des Portes Neuves 9, is in a central pedestrian street so parking can be a problem. Fairly smart singles/doubles above a quaint restaurant are Sfr75/110 with shower or Sfr60/90 without. Close parking can also be difficult at *Hotêl du Midi* (☎ 323 13 31), Place du Midi, which has a pricey restaurant and corridors painted an unsettling pink/orange colour. Singles/doubles start at Sfr80/110 with private shower.

Conveniently close to the station is the three-star *Hôtel Touring* (☎ 223 15 51), Avenue de la Gare 6, with free private parking. Singles/doubles are Sfr100/170 for rooms with private bath or shower, toilet, TV, mini bar, radio and telephone. The most central four-star place, *Europa* (☎ 322 24 23; fax 322 25 35), Rue de l'Envoi 19, is a bit out of the way in the west of Sion. Rooms have all amenities and start at only Sfr100/160. It has a bar, sauna and restaurants on site, and there is good disabled access.

Places to Eat
There is a huge *Migros* shopping complex a five-minute walk from the station at Avenue de France. There's a self-service restaurant on the ground floor with a wide choice of food (closed Monday morning; open till 8 pm on Tuesday). An *EPA* department store is opposite the tourist office on Rue de Lausanne, open to 6.30 pm weekdays and 5 pm on Saturday. Its restaurant has meals for under Sfr10. Attached to the Placette department store is a buffet-style *Manora* restaurant, Avenue du Midi, with good, inexpensive food but no alcohol. It is open until 10 pm daily. The salad buffet costs between Sfr4.20 and Sfr10.50 depending upon plate size; the dessert buffet is also good.

Le Pub, on Avenue de la Gare, offers dining for all price ranges, either in the bar or in the restaurant section downstairs. Pizza and pasta starts at Sfr11 and there is a two-course lunch menu for Sfr15.50. It is open until 1 am daily. For more authentic eating, explore the small bistros and brasseries in the central pedestrian district. *Taverne Sedunoise*, Rue de Rhône, is typical and inexpensive (closed Sunday evening).

A good mid-price choice is *Restaurant l'Enclos de Valère*, (☎ 23 32 30), Rue de Château 18, a small and quiet French restaurant with meat and fish dishes above Sfr28 and multicourse menus from Sfr58 (closed Monday and Sunday in winter). Valais wines start at Sfr28 a bottle and lunch plate is Sfr15. On a sunny day take to the outside tables in the garden. Almost next door at No 16 is the *Cave de Tous Vents*, an atmospheric cellar offering fondue from Sfr36 for two. It's open daily from 5 pm to midnight.

Getting There & Away
The airport (☎ 322 24 80) is two km west of the train station; bus No 1 goes there (Sfr2, or Sfr1 if under 25), or you can take a taxi for around Sfr12. Crossair has one or two daily non-stop flights to Zürich which take 50 minutes.

Sion is a major postbus centre (☎ 322 22 09 for information), with 29 different routes leaving from outside the train station. A regional pass, valid for seven days within two weeks, costs Sfr66, or Sfr44 for children and those with the Half-Fare Card.

All trains on the Lausanne-Brig express route stop at Sion. To Lausanne takes 70 minutes and costs Sfr27, and to Brig takes 40 minutes and costs Sfr16.60.

The N9 motorway passes through the south of Sion, with exits on both the west and

VALAIS

east side of the city. There's free parking by the swimming pool, five minutes' walk west of the youth hostel.

Europcar (☎ 323 86 86) is at Garage Delta, Rue de Lausanne 148. Hertz (☎ 322 37 42) is at Garage du Nord, Ave Ritz 33, and Avis (322 20 77) is at the garage at 23 Ave de Tourbillon.

AROUND SION
Grande Dixence Dam
This dam is hugely impressive because of its sheer size. Almost six million cubic metres of concrete went into building it, and it's twice the volume and twice the height (284m) of the Great Pyramid of Egypt. It retains 400 cubic metres of water and produces annually 1600 kWh of hydro-electricity. To appreciate the beauty of the surroundings you need to gain some height, and footpaths and a cable car (from Le Chargeur to the lake) allow you to do this. It's at the end of the Hérémence Valley and is circled by towering peaks.

Getting There & Away The road from Sion to the dam is closed in winter and spring. A private bus service runs between the two places two to four times a day from early June to mid-October. The journey takes an hour and costs Sfr28 return. Take the blue bus from directly outside the train station in Sion (Swiss Pass valid).

Hérens Valley
This is the other valley heading south from Sion. It promotes itself as the 'true' Valais, where villagers in traditional costumes carry out their traditional lifestyle. Exactly how much of this is tourism-inspired tradition is difficult to gauge. What isn't open to doubt are the many hiking possibilities and the copious wildlife – look out for the Black Woodpecker, the largest in Europe, which has a red marking on its head. The main resorts are south of Evolène. Buses run from Sion several times a day year-round to La

Forclaz (change in Les Haudrères), and beyond to Ferpècle in summer only.

MARTIGNY
• *pop 14,000* • *476m* • ☎ *(027)*
Martigny is the oldest town in Valais. It was seized by the Roman Empire in 15 BC, and in the reign of Emperor Claudius was given the snappy name of Forum Claudii Vallensium.

Orientation & Information
French-speaking Martigny is an important junction at the 'L' bend of the Rhône River. The hub of the town is Place Centrale, where you will find the tourist office (☎ 721 22 20), open Monday to Friday from 9 am to noon and 2 to 6 pm, and Saturday from 9 am to noon. In Summer it's also open on Saturday from 2 to 6 pm, and in July and August on Sunday from 10 am to noon and 4 to 6 pm. The train station (with bike rental and money exchange) is one km to the north-east of Place Centrale, and most of the Roman remains are to the south.

Things to See & Do
After visiting the tourist office, exit by the

Bronze head of the three-horned bull, found during excavations at the Roman settlement of Octodurus (Martigny).

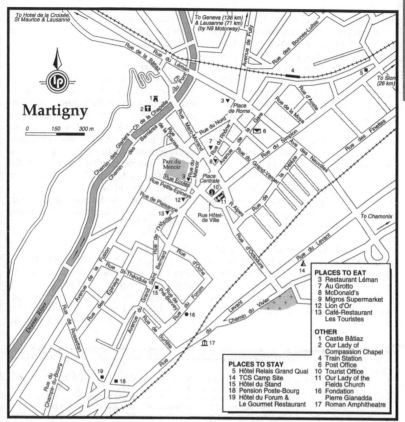

Martigny

PLACES TO EAT
3 Restaurant Léman
7 Au Grotto
8 McDonald's
9 Migros Supermarket
12 Lion d'Or
13 Café-Restaurant
Les Touristes

OTHER
1 Castle Bâtiaz
2 Our Lady of
Compassion Chapel
4 Train Station
6 Post Office
10 Tourist Office
11 Our Lady of the
Fields Church
16 Fondation
Pierre Gianadda
17 Roman Amphitheatre

PLACES TO STAY
5 Hôtel Relais Grand Quai
14 TCS Camp Site
15 Hôtel du Stand
18 Pension Poste-Bourg
19 Hôtel du Forum &
Le Gourmet Restaurant

interior door leading directly to the stairway of the town hall. There's an impressive stained glass window over three floors (55 sq metres) created by Edmond Bille. Nearby is the 17th century church of **Our Lady of the Fields** (Notre Dame des Champs), with a Rococo altar and a belfry combining Romanesque and Gothic elements. Also take a look at the chapel of **Our Lady of Compassion Church** (Notre Dame de Compassion), by the Dranse River, noted especially for its ex-voto paintings. Above the chapel is the 13th-century **Bâtiaz Castle** (Château de la Bâtiaz), thrusting up from the hill. It is

seldom open, but provides a good view of the valley. In this direction are two vineyards within a 50-minute walk (follow signs for Chemin du Vignoble).

Pick up the leaflet from the tourist office which shows a **walking tour** (*Promenade archéologique*) of the main Roman ruins. The **Roman Amphitheatre** can seat 6000 people and is the site for the annual Combat de Reines (see the Special Events section).

The main cultural attraction in the town is the **Fondation Pierre Gianadda**. Not only does it have a Gallo-Roman Museum (the best exhibit is a bronze three-horned

VALAIS

bull's head – a Gallic divinity), but it also has a busy programme of classical music concerts, and an art exhibition periodically reviewing major artists. In the garden are more archaeological excavations, interestingly juxtaposed with modern art sculptures (by Miró, Moore, Arp, Segal, etc) on the green lawns.

In the automobile museum there's an impressive collection of historic cars, spanning the spectrum from a 1897 Benz (maximum speed 25 kmh) to a 1929 Mercedes (maximum speed 200 kmh). A few of the early Swiss cars (like the 1910 and 1911 Turicum) have a horn by the steering wheel, connected by a metal tube to a serpent's head on the front mudguard. When you blow the horn the serpent emits a goose-like honk – who said the Swiss haven't got a sense of humour!

The Fondation is open daily from 9 am to 7 pm (10 am to 6 pm from late October to early May, and with a lunch break in winter). Entry costs Sfr12 for adults, Sfr5 for children (to 10 years) and students, and Sfr25 for families. Ask for the English notes at the ticket desk.

Within 10 km of Martigny are three picturesque **gorges**: Trient, Durnand, and Triège, all accessible by train.

Special Events

The town hosts the **Valais Regional Fair** in early October. Later that month is the traditional event, **Combat de Reines**, the climax of a series of cow-fights conducted in spring and autumn. It's not distasteful (unlike Spanish bullfighting) and the combatants rarely get hurt. See the boxed aside for background information. Tickets to view the proceedings in the amphitheatre are around Sfr16 for seats and Sfr10 to stand.

In December, the **Bacon Fair** (Foire du Lard), takes place, an annual event dating back to the Middle Ages.

Places to Stay

The TCS *camp site* (☎ 722 45 44), Rue de Levant 68, is reasonably convenient for the centre. It's open year round and reception is open daily from 7 am to 10 pm. Price per person including tax is Sfr7.20 (Sfr6.70 in winter), and Sfr7.50 each for a tent and car.

Cow Fights

A peculiarity of Valais is the Combats de Reines (Kuhkämpfe in German), cow fights which are organised in villages to determine which beast is most suited to lead the herd up to the summer pastures. The cows that take part in these combats are from the Hérens breed, renowned for their fighting instincts. The events have outgrown the traditional *raison d'être*. Breeding is big business: a winner, acclaimed to be the 'queen' of the herd, can be worth up to Sfr20,000, and much more in terms of prestige. Techniques such as genetic selection and embryo freezing are used to breed the most effective contenders for the field of combat. Once selected, they are fed oats concentrate (believed to act as a stimulant), and sometimes even wine.

Contests usually take place on selected Sundays through the summer from the end of March, accompanied by much celebration and consumption of Valaisan wine. The combatants rarely get hurt. There is a grand final in Aproz in May on Ascension Day and the last meeting of the season is held at the Martigny Fair in October. Aproz is only a 10-minute postbus ride from Sion. ■

De la Croisée (☎ 722 23 59), west of the Dranse River at Rue du Léman 51, has singles/doubles with shower for Sfr49/98. Basic rooms using hall shower cost Sfr37/60 at *Pension Poste-Bourg* (☎ 722 25 17), Ave du Grand St Bernard 81. Opposite at No 74 is the rather plusher *Hôtel du Forum* (☎ 722 18 41), with rooms from Sfr85/138 with private shower/toilet and TV. On the same road towards town, at No 41, is *Hôtel du Strand* (☎ 722 15 06), with maze-like, velvety-green corridors and modern rooms with shower/toilet for Sfr65/94.

A five-minute walk from the station by the tracks is *Hôtel Relais Grand Quai* (☎ 722 20 50), Rue du Simplon 33, offering plenty of parking and decent-sized rooms with own bathroom and TV for Sfr64/97. Prices are a little lower in winter; this also applies for most of the more expensive places in town.

Places to Eat

There is a large *Migros* supermarket with groceries and general goods at Rue du Manoir. The restaurant has meals for around Sfr10 and a comprehensive salad buffet (closed Monday morning).

Hôtel Relais Grand Quai (see Places to Stay) has quite a smart restaurant but low prices. There's a lunch special for Sfr14 including soup and dessert, and snacks and meals for Sfr6 to Sfr27 (closed Sunday).

Café-restaurant Les Touristes, Place Plaisance, is not particularly touristy, despite its name, and has pizza/pasta from Sfr10.50 and regional food from Sfr13 (closed Monday). Pizzas are better in *Au Grotto*, Rue de Rhône 3. Italian food is also good and cheap at *Lion d'Or*, Ave du Grand St Bernard 1 (closed Sunday and Monday).

Restaurant Léman, Rue du Léman 19, is a large place specialising in French cuisine, including fish and game for around Sfr30 (closed Monday evening and Sunday). The best restaurant in Martigny, albeit pricey, is *Le Gourmet* at the *Hôtel du Forum* (see Places to Stay). It offers seasonal specialities and three different set menus (closed Sunday evening and Monday).

Getting There & Away

Martigny is on the main rail route running from Lausanne (Sfr21, takes one hour) to Brig (Sfr24, takes 55 minutes). There is also a train departing every one to two hours to Chamonix in France (see the Mont Blanc section for more details). The fare is Sfr31 (Sfr61 return) and the journey takes two hours or less, depending upon connections at the border.

Martigny is also the departure point for the St Bernard Express, which goes to Le Châble (Sfr9; bus connection for Verbier) and Orsières. Buses go from Martigny via Orsières and the St Bernard Tunnel to Aosta in Italy (Sfr30, at least two departures a day).

AROUND MARTIGNY
Les Marécottes

Not far from Martigny to the west, this small chalet village has a zoo exhibiting Alpine species in their natural habitat (open May to October). From Martigny, take the Chamonix train (Sfr7.20; see Mont Blanc section).

St Maurice

This small town is named after the Roman Christian who, along with many of his followers, was massacred in 302 AD for refusing to worship the gods of Rome. Points of interest are the 11th century Abbey church, and the castle, which has a military museum (closed Monday). Trains from Martigny run every 30 minutes (Sfr5.40).

Champéry

Running south-west from Monthey is the Illiez Valley, terminating in the ski resort of Champéry. It's a chalet-style village and shares the vast Portes du Soleil ski region with several other Swiss and French ski resorts. Runs near Champéry are predominantly intermediate although experts have plenty of opportunity for off-piste skiing. Prices in the village are reasonable. The resort is beneath the Dents du Midi, and an excellent view of this mountain range can be achieved from **Croix de Culet** (1963m), a

VALAIS

viewpoint a short walk from the top of the Planachaux cable car.

The tourist office for the Val d'Illiez is on ☎ 024-477 20 77. Another good, inexpensive, and relatively uncrowded resort for skiing the Portes du Soleil is nearby **Morgins**.

From Aigle (20 minutes along the track from Martigny to Lausanne), a train runs via Monthey every hour to Champéry (Sfr11.40, takes one hour).

Orsières

Winding its way south of Martigny is highway 21 (E27), leading to the Great St Bernard Pass and beyond into Italy. The town of Orsières is as far as you can get by rail. From here you can walk (1¾ hours), take the bus or drive to **Champex** and its attractive lake. A cable car ascends above the lake to **La Breya** (2374m). The view from here includes the Grand Combin (4314m) to the south-east, and the cable car operates from mid-June to late November (Sfr12 return).

Bourg St Pierre

South of Orsières is Bourg St Pierre, where Napoleon stayed during one of his incursions over the Alps. Beyond the town, the nine-km St Bernard tunnel, opened in 1964, allows year-round access to Italy. The old road over the **Great St Bernard Pass** is closed in winter and leads to the historic **Hospice**, where the monks have been rescuing travellers stranded in the snows since the 11th century. They have been aided in the task by the famous St Bernard dogs (nowadays Alsatians are used) – it is estimated that over the years, more than 2000 people have been saved by the clerics and their canines.

The first mention of the St Bernard dogs was in 1708. A century later, one of the best-known of the breed, Barry I, toiled for 12 years in the snow drifts. After his death he was rewarded with a visit to the taxidermist, and now stands in the Natural History Museum in Bern.

A more recent Barry (one of a long line) is in the vestibule of the hospice. Some living specimens can be seen in the kennels. The hospice museum (Sfr6, children Sfr4) tells the history of the rescue work and has church relics and ornaments. It is open from June to October, which coincides with the period the bus runs from Martigny (two a day, takes one hour and costs Sfr16.20). Buses are more frequent from Orsières. Buses go as far as the hospice, or you can walk the famous path from Bourg St Pierre in under two hours.

The hospice (☎ 027-787 12 36) has dorm beds (Sfr17) and rooms (Sfr24 per person) available; add Sfr23 for half-board.

MONT BLANC

If there aren't enough mountains in Switzerland to sate your appetite for skiing and scenery, a trip to Mont Blanc makes an excellent and easily arranged excursion. At 4807m Mont Blanc is the highest mountain in the Alps, and with the valley floor some 3800m below the peak, the views are nothing short of spectacular. Unfortunately, by its sheer massiveness the mountain does tend to attract cloudy weather, so choose your day to visit carefully. The two easiest departure points from Switzerland are Geneva and Martigny.

Orientation & Information

Mont Blanc is on the border with France and Italy. On the French side is the resort of Chamonix, one of the oldest in the Alps, which still retains much of its Victorian architecture. The tourist office (☎ 50 53 00 24) at Place du Triangle de l'Amitié, opposite Place de l'Église, is open daily from 8 or 8.30 am to 12.30 pm, and from 2 to 7 pm. In July and August it is open from 8.30 am to 7.30 pm. Useful brochures on ski-lift hours and costs, refuges, camping grounds and parapente schools are available. In winter it sells a range of ski passes, including two-day/seven-day passes, valid for bus transport and all the ski lifts in the valley (except Lognan-Les Grands Montets), for 350/1050FF (325/920FF during discount periods – before Christmas, in January and April). There is also the Office de Haute Montagne (☎ 50 53 22 08), 2nd floor, 109

Circuit of Mont Blanc

It's one of the best known walks in the Alps but only a third of it is in Switzerland. This is an international walk, a three country excursion all the way around the highest mountain in Western Europe. The walk covers 215 km, reaches a maximum altitude of more than 2500m and typically takes 10 to 14 days. The circuit passes through beautiful Alpine scenery and offers stunning views of the mountains along the Mont Blanc range, and undeniably its international nature adds to the pleasure.

The walk can start and finish in any of the three countries. In France the most convenient starting point is Les Houches, in the Chamonix Valley a few km west of Chamonix itself. It's on a railway line and at 1008m it is also the lowest point on the whole circuit. In Italy the select Alpine resort of Courmayeur, close to the southern end of the Mont Blanc tunnel, is the best place to start. In Switzerland there are a number of good places to commence, including the lakeside mountain resort of Champex and the Col de la Forclaz pass, conveniently reached by buses from the town of Martigny.

The circuit is a comfortable walk with *gîtes* (hostel-like bunkrooms) in many villages, mountain refuges in a number of the more remote locations and, for comfort loving walkers, a variety of hotels and guest houses. Unfortunately many places close down in the late autumn for a short break before the winter skiing season. The weather may be fine for walking but at those times you will need to carry camping equipment. There are no border formalities along the route; in fact it can be difficult to know you have crossed a border, but until the Euro comes into use you will need a variety of currencies.

From the Col de la Forclaz starting point the route makes a steep climb to Col de la Balme, marking the border between Switzerland and France. Here the route enters the Chamonix Valley and follows the southern side of the valley, looking across the pricey French mountain resort of Chamonix to the pristine summit of Mont Blanc and its surrounding peaks. West of Chamonix the walk descends to the valley floor at Les Houches then immediately climbs up the other side to round the western end of the Mont Blanc massif and cross the Col de la Seigne into Italy. Passing through some of the most remote country on the route the walk descends along the Veny Valley to Courmayeur, then climbs up the Ferret Valley to the Grand Col Ferret where it re-enters Switzerland. In Switzerland, the walk passes through a series of delightful small villages along the Swiss portion of the Ferret Valley, before climbing to Champex and through the high Alpine pastures known as the Bovine back to the starting point.

Tony Wheeler

Place de l'Église, dispensing information for walkers, hikers and mountain climbers.

Across the Italian border is the resort of Courmayeur. For information contact the tourist office (Azienda Autonoma di Soggiorno e Turismo) on ☎ 0165-84 20 60. The two resorts are connected by the Mont Blanc Tunnel. The country telephone code for France is ☎ 33 and for Italy is ☎ 39.

Things to See & Do

Chamonix Chamonix has exciting if fragmented skiing. A one-day ski pass and equipment rental will cost around 300FF. The most famous area and the world's longest ski run is the **Vallée Blanche**, a 20-km glacier hanging from the shoulder of Mont Blanc. You reach this via the Aiguille du Midi cable railway, and the trip up provides heart-pumping views. A return ticket costs 150FF. There is also the **Mer de Glace Glacier** which can be reached by a cog-

wheel railway or by foot from the village. **Le Brévent** peak on the west side of the valley furnishes more hiking opportunities, fine views of Mont Blanc and some fairly gentle skiing. Chamonix's mix of Victorian and more modern buildings makes the village an appealing place in which to stroll around. For more information about Chamonix, refer to Lonely Planet's *France – travel survival kit.*

Courmayeur The Italian side of the mountain offers a good range of intermediate runs and an excellent ski school. Most of the runs face Mont Blanc (Monte Bianco in Italian) so the views are great. It is also possible to ascend Mont Blanc itself (with a guide) and ski down the other side to Chamonix on the Mer de Glace Glacier, but seek advice before you consider this. The village is atmospheric and reasonably lively, with lots of old buildings to enjoy. For more information about Courmayeur, refer to Lonely Planet's *Italy – travel survival kit.*

Getting There & Away

The narrow-gauge train line from Saint Gervais-Le Fayet (20 km west of Chamonix) to Martigny (42 km north of Chamonix) stops at 11 towns in the Chamonix Valley, including Chamonix itself. There are nine to 12 return trips a day. You have to change trains on the Swiss border (at Châtelard or Vallorcine) because of differing track gauges. Le Fayet serves as a rail head for long-haul trains to destinations all over France, and this is the easiest route to Geneva, about two hours away.

Chamonix bus station is next to the train station. SAT Autocar (☎ 50 53 01 15) has buses to Annecy in France (89FF), Courmayeur (50FF, takes 40 minutes), Grenoble (152FF), Geneva (188FF, 1½ to two hours) and Turin (140FF, three hours).

The road from Chamonix to Martigny follows closely the route of the narrow-gauge railway for much of the distance. From Geneva, the E25 motorway runs all the way to Le Fayet, then an ordinary main road takes over for the last 17 km to Chamonix.

There are two ways to get from Martigny to Courmayeur: either via Chamonix and the Mont Blanc Tunnel, or via the E21a and the Great St Bernard Pass (closed in winter) to Aosta, and the E21b from there. This latter route can be duplicated by a combination of train and bus (the bus section over the pass only runs in summer).

VERBIER

• *pop 2100* • *1500m* • *☎ (027)*

Verbier is a trendy, sophisticated resort that receives hordes of weekend visitors from Geneva, 170 km away, yet its history as a tourist centre is extremely short. In 1945 Verbier had just 27 permanent residents, and the first proper ski lift opened as late as 1947. Nowadays it has one of the largest cable cars in Switzerland, Le Jumbo, which flies up Mont-Fort holding 150 passengers. But skiers still suffer notoriously slow lift queues at peak times.

Orientation & Information

Verbier is scenically situated on a south-west facing ledge above Le Châble, the terminus of the railway. The resort proper is up the hill from Verbier village. The hub of Verbier is Place Centrale, where you will find the tourist office (☎ 771 62 22). It's open Monday to Saturday from 8.30 am to 6.30 pm, and Sunday from 9.30 am to noon. In winter, it's open till 8 pm on Saturday and also on Sunday afternoon from 4 to 6.30 pm. Just off the square is the post office and postbus terminus. Verbier is mostly shut from late October to early December and in May, and that includes the cable cars. The resort has a free bus service. Families, children and senior citizens get substantial discounts on lift prices for skiing and hiking.

Skiing

The ski pass gives access to one of the finest ski areas in the world, comprising 400 km of runs and 100 ski lifts. The pass is also one of the most expensive around, costing Sfr59 for one day, Sfr335 for a week and Sfr1210 for the season. More restrictive, slightly cheaper passes are also available.

The skiing is exciting and varied, and there are many opportunities for experts to flaunt their off-piste skills, particularly at Attelas and Mont Fort. Experienced skiers can also take on the Four Valleys circuit – 80 km of black and red runs which can just about be completed in one day. Mont Fort at 3330m is high enough to allow summer skiing on its glacier (Sfr38 per day, from around early June to early August). Most of the resort runs are too difficult for beginners to handle, but there is a ski school (☎ 771 44 44) behind the post office: Sfr29 for one lesson and Sfr112 for six. Crowds are a definite problem on the less demanding intermediate runs between Les Attelas and the village, yet the Savoleyres area on the other side of the resort is less busy and just as good.

Ski-Mountaineering The ski school has a Bureau des Guides, where you can organise a guide for ski-mountaineering treks along the Haute Route to Zermatt or Saas Fee. The trip takes three to four days and reaches a maximum altitude of 3800m. The charge per day depends upon the number in the group (eg Sfr370 between one/two people, Sfr400 three/four people etc). Equipment hire and cable cars cost extra.

Hiking

The tourist office gives out a map giving brief descriptions (in French) and times of various hiking trails around the resort. From Les Ruinettes, it takes two hours to ascend to the ridge at Creblet, and down into the crater to the lake, Lac des Vaux. For non-skiers, day passes on the lifts cost between Sfr19 and Sfr38 depending upon the validity area. For individual tickets, the basic formula is Sfr8 (Sfr12 return) for each cable station stop.

To get up to **Mont Fort** and enjoy the magnificent view (including Mont Blanc), non-skiers need to take a bus or walk from Les Ruinettes to the Jumbo cable car. Allow around an hour for the full ascent. The non-skiers day pass costs Sfr38. Mont Gelé gives a better view of the valley below Verbier.

Other Activities

Two popular sports are **hang-gliding** and **paragliding**. Solo flights or those with an instructor in tandem are possible: contact the Parapente school (☎ 771 68 18) for details. Max (☎ 771 55 55), based in Hotel Rosa Blanche, offers cheaper tandem flights (Sfr120 to Sfr150). Verbier hosts a paragliding competition every August. There's an 18-hole **golf course** with fine views. Get information from the tourist office or the golf club (☎ 775 21 41).

Places to Stay

Verbier The cheapest option in Verbier is a few private rooms – check with the tourist office. Holiday chalets are also reasonable (book well in advance). Otherwise, prices are high, even in low season, but you should always get a room with at least a private shower. *Hôtel Rosa Blanche* (☎ 771 55), Rue de la Barmettaz, not far from Place Centrale, has singles/doubles from Sfr65/120, except in high season when it's booked by a British

tour operator. *Mont-Gelé* (☎ 771 30 53), by the base of the Les Ruinettes cable car, charges from Sfr95/150. *Ermitage*, (☎ 771 64 77), Place Centrale, starts at Sfr95/130, and has TVs and parking.

Many places offer half-board as standard, like *De La Poste* (☎ 771 66 81), Rue de Médran, which has its own indoor swimming pool and garden terrace. Per person prices range from Sfr89 (hall shower) to Sfr150 (own shower/WC and balcony). One of the best places to stay is *Rosalp* (☎ 771 63 23; fax 771 10 59), a little further along Rue de Médran, with large, well-equipped rooms at half-board starting at Sfr300/470.

Around Verbier The nearest main *camp site* is some distance away at Sembrancher (☎ 785 12 54), open year-round, though Le Châble does have a tiny site (no phone, no pre-booking).

The nearest SYHA *hostel* (☎ 776 23 56) is on the opposite side of the valley in Bruson. In its favour is the fact that it only costs Sfr10 in summer and Sfr11 in winter, there's a good kitchen (no meters) and the doors are always open. Blankets but not sheets are supplied, and there's no breakfast and few showers. Bruson is a pleasant, unspoilt village, full of wooden chalets and traditional storage barns on stilts (with circular stones to keep the rats out). The hostel is around the corner from the café-restaurant, but you need to go to the owner's house, 200m up from the bus stop, to check-in (before 9 am or after 5 pm). It is closed in May and November. Bruson is a 30-minute walk uphill from Le Châble or take the bus from the train station (Sfr2.20).

Le Châble has a few small, cheap hotels. Try *Des Alpes* (☎ 776 14 65) from Sfr40/80 or *l'Escale* (☎ 776 27 07) at Sfr50/100.

Places to Eat

Cheap eating is also fairly problematic in Verbier, unless you're happy resorting to takeaway food from *Harold's*, a burger bar on Place Centrale. There are some supermarkets – the *Denner* on Rue de Verbier is convenient (and it's the cheapest for alcohol!). It has a half-day on Wednesday. Across the road is *Chez Martin*, the most reasonable of several pizzerias in the resort, with pasta from Sfr10.50 and pizzas from Sfr12 (open daily). *Fer a Cheval*, near the Medran lift, has more expensive pizzas (from Sfr14) but is livelier for après-ski. *Hacienda Café*, Route Verbier has pizzas (from Sfr10), Mexican food and other dishes (from Sfr13), happy hour from 5 to 6.30 pm, and live music on weekends in high season. *Channe Valaisanne*, off Place Centrale, has meals from around Sfr20, including fondue. *La Pinte* in the Hotel Rosalp (see Places to Stay) offers stylish dishes for around Sfr25 to Sfr40 (open daily). The same hotel also has the *Restaurant Pierroz*, one of the top restaurants in Switzerland. Creative cuisine and seasonal specialities may tempt you to extend your mortgage: expect to pay around Sfr35 for a starter and Sfr45 to Sfr60 for a main course (closed in summer).

Entertainment
The resort hosts a classical music festival in late July. Nightlife is lively, if expensive. *Pub Mont-Ford*, near the base of the Attelas cable car, is a busy and bawdy après-ski bar, particularly popular with English-speakers. *Farm Club*, on Rue de Verbier and near Place Centrale, is a rather aloof and exclusive nightclub (Sfr20 entry includes first drink). *Tara*, by the pharmacy off Place Centrale, attracts a younger set (open 11 pm to 4 am).

Getting There & Away
From mid-December to mid-April a direct bus goes from Martigny, taking 45 minutes (Sfr13.80). There are three a day on Saturday, and one on Friday evening. Buses only run in Winter.

Trains from Martigny run year-round, hourly, take 30 minutes, and terminate at Le Châble (Sfr9). From there, bus departures are co-ordinated and get you to the resort in 25 minutes (Sfr4.80). In winter, a cable car also ascends from Le Châble (Swiss Pass valid). By car or motorcycle the way is easy; the road from Martigny (27 km) is good and there are car parks at the entrance to the

resort, at the ski lifts, and near Place Centrale.

MAUVOISIN DAM
This dam at the end of the Bagnes Valley reaches a height of 237m and walls in a reservoir of 180 million cubic metres. Postbuses depart from Le Châble. Only a few continue as far as Fionnay and thereafter to Mauvoisin, and this section of the journey is completely closed down from early October to mid-June. From Les Ruinettes above Verbier you can walk along the valley to Fionnay in five hours.

SIERRE
• *pop 15,000* • *540m* • ☎ *(027)*
Sierre (Siders in German) is one of the sunniest towns in Switzerland and lies on the French/German language divide, though French is favoured. The tourist office (☎ 455 85 35) is next to the train station and is open Monday to Friday from 8 am to noon and 2 to 6 pm, and in summer also on Saturday from 9 am to noon.

Things to See & Do
There are several **châteaux** and historic houses in and around the town. Most of these can easily be visited on a walking tour – ask the tourist office for the *Promenade des Châteaux* leaflet. Sierre is surrounded by vineyards and appropriately enough has a **wine museum** (Weinmuseum) in the Château de Villa (sometimes called Manor Villa), north-west of the centre at the end of Ave du Marché. It is open daily except Monday from March to October, and only on Friday, Saturday and Sunday in the winter. Sfr5 gets entry to both parts of the museum – the other part is in the suburb of Salgesch.

Places to Stay & Eat
East of the centre is an area of protected woodland which contains several camp sites, including the TCS site, *Bois de Finges* (☎ 455 02 84), open from mid-April to early October. *La Poste* (☎ 455 10 03), near the train station, has old-fashioned rooms from Sfr65/110 with private shower and doubles

without from Sfr80. There are cheaper places out of the centre, such as *Auberge des Collines* (☎ 455 12 48), to the south, near the river and sports facilities (Sfr45/75 without shower). *Central* (☎ 455 15 66), opposite the station, has renovated rooms with shower (from Sfr90/150).

A *Migros* supermarket and restaurant is five minutes to the left of the station on Ave General Guisan. A *Manora* buffet-style restaurant is in the Centre Commercial to the west of the centre, open daily to 10 pm; take bus No 1 from the station.

Getting There & Away
Around two trains an hour stop at Sierre on the main Lausanne-Brig route. The town is the leaping off point for Crans Montana; take the red SMC bus from outside the station (Sfr10.40). There's a funicular that goes up to Montana, which will be extended to reach the ski slopes in 1998.

ANNIVIERS VALLEY
This valley runs south from Sierre. The inhabitants are known for their nomadic habits, which are gradually dying out. Traditionally, they spend the winter in the mountains and migrate down to homes on the valley floor for the summer.

In the valley there is an enjoyable and scenic six-km **planetary walk** at 2200 to 2500m, starting at Tignousa (above St Luc) and ending at the Weisshorn Hotel. Along the way are models of the planets in the solar system on a scale of one to 100 million. Information boards alongside give a mass of statistics. The distances between the planets are on the scale of one to 1000 million. Near the start of the walk is the François-Xavier Bagnoud Observatory, where telescopes can be used day and night – enquire at the St Luc tourist office (☎ 027-475 14 12). There's a mountain hut by the observatory.

The cable car from St Luc to Tignousa stops running from mid-April to mid-June and late October to mid-December. Around six buses a day depart from Sierre and go as far as Zinal, a mountaineering centre at the end of the valley.

CRANS-MONTANA
• *pop 6000* • *1500m* • *☎ (027)*
This French-speaking twin resort claims to be the sunniest ski area in the country. It's fashionable and affluent and boasts the most famous golf course in the Alps.

Orientation & Information
Crans to the west and Montana to the east together create a large built-up sprawl amid half a dozen lakes. Crans tourist office (☎ 481 21 32) is on the main street, Rue Centrale. This road joins to Route du Rawyl and thence to Ave de la Gare, Montana's main street. Montana's tourist office (☎ 485 04 04) is on this road, backing on to the post office. Local buses are free within this urban area all year. Each tourist office covers both resorts, and they are open daily in high season and weekdays and Saturday morning in low season. Each has a hotel board with free phone outside, or free hotel reservations can be made on ☎ 485 04 44.

Skiing
The skiing is good for all ability ranges, with the majority of runs being at intermediate level. The Plaine Morte Glacier (3000m) allows reasonably testing skiing even in the summer. In all, the skiing area offers 160 km of slopes, 41 lifts and 50 km of cross country tracks. Ski passes cost Sfr45 (Sfr27 children) for one day, or Sfr56 (Sfr38) to include the glacier.

Other Activities
As ever in the Alps, excellent views and **hiking** are presented if you take the cable cars up into the mountains. In the summer there is **golf**, at both a nine-hole course (Sfr43) and an 18-hole course (Sfr86); contact the Golf Club (☎ 481 21 68). The resort hosts the European Masters golf tournament in early September.

There's a strong following for **bridge** games and players meet every afternoon from 3 pm in the Aida-Castel Hotel.

Places to Stay & Eat
The *camp site* (☎ 481 27 87) by Lake Moubra,

VALAIS

open from mid-June to 30 September, also has dorms for Sfr21 per person.

Auberge de la Diligence (☎ 485 99 85), east of Montana, has the cheapest showerless rooms at Sfr40 per person. *Pension Centrale* (☎ 481 37 67), Rue Centrale, has neat, compact singles/doubles for Sfr70/120 with a big bathroom or Sfr60/100 without. It has parking and guests here get a 5% discount off ski passes. *Du Téléphérique* (☎ 481 33 67), at the Crans cable car, is similar in standard and price, but has showers not baths. *Hôtel Régina* (☎ 481 35 22), Ave de la Gare, has cheerful singles/doubles from Sfr85/150 with shower and toilet or Sfr70/120 without. Hall lights flick on automatically, which avoids the familiar hassle of stumbling around in the dark looking for a luminous switch.

Supermarkets include the *Migros* on Route du Rawyl, open daily. Eating is a fairly expensive proposition, unless you stick to the many pizzerias. *Olympic*, just off Place du Rawyl on Ave Louis Antille, has pizzas for Sfr10 to Sfr12 and two menus with soup and dessert for Sfr16. Next door is *Le Vieux Moulin*, serving pizza (from Sfr11.50), fondue (Sfr21), and a daily menu for Sfr16.

Primavera (☎ 481 42 14), Ave de la Gare, has choice meat and fish dishes for around Sfr35, or there's cheaper dining in its terrace café. Rooms cost from Sfr108/184 in this three-star hotel.

Getting There & Away

From Sierre the bus takes around 35 minutes and departs hourly (Sfr10.40). There are two different roads winding up the vineyard-covered hillside to the resort, so you can make it a circular trip either by bus or car. The slow funicular from Sierre takes 30 minutes (Swiss Pass valid).

Upper Valais

LEUKERBAD
• *pop 1500* • *1411m* • ☎ *(027)*
Leukerbad is the largest thermal centre in Europe and has the hottest springs in Switzerland. The Romans had a settlement here, and in the 19th century the town was a popular stopover for travellers negotiating the Gemmi Pass to the Bernese Oberland.

Orientation & Information
Leukerbad, 16 km north of Leuk, is an attractive resort amid a semi-circle of adjacent peaks. German is the main language. The tourist office (☎ 472 71 71, or ☎ 472 71 77 for commission-free hotel reservations) is in the centre, in a new complex incorporating the town hall, post office, a parking garage and the bus station. Opening hours are Monday to Friday from 9 to 6 pm, Saturday from 9 am to 5 pm, and (high season only) Sunday from 9 to 11.30 am. There's a hotel board with free phone inside, and a useful Guest Card. Cars must not be used in the centre at night.

Things to See & Do
There are 10 different places to take to the waters, but the biggest and the best is the **Burgerbad** (☎ 470 11 38). It has many different pools, inside and outside, including whirlpools and water massage jets. The temperature ranges from 28 to 44°C. Entry costs Sfr18 for adults, Sfr13 for students and Sfr9 for children. There are reductions with the Guest Card and for multiple entry tickets. The complex also has a sauna and fitness studio which costs extra. It is open every day until the evening (times vary). The tourist office can give details of training and regeneration programmes and medical treatments that are available in Leukerbad.

The main **skiing** area is the Torrenthorn (2998m), yielding mostly medium-difficulty runs, but there are a few easy ones and a demanding run that descends 1400m. One-day ski passes cost Sfr38 (students Sfr32, children Sfr19), or Sfr49 (Sfr39, Sfr25) combined with entry to a spa. Activities in the sports centre (☎ 470 10 37) include ice-skating (Sfr10 for half a day), curling and tennis.

A cable car ascends the sheer side of the northern ridge of mountains to the **Gemmi**

Pass (2350m). It's a good area for hiking. The cable car costs Sfr20 return, or Sfr14 each way, or it takes two hours to walk up. A summer pass for the cable cars, baths and other facilities costs Sfr32 (students Sfr26, children Sfr16) for one day.

In mid-July Leukerbad hosts a clown festival.

Places to Stay
There is camping (☎ 470 10 37) by the sports arena from 1 May to 31 October. The site has a TV room and a washing machine and it costs Sfr6 per adult, Sfr4 for a tent and Sfr4 for a car.

Dormitory accommodation costs Sfr38 per person (Sfr48 for half-board) at *Touristenlager Bergfreude* (☎ 470 17 61), not far from the Gemmi cable car. They don't speak English. *Weisses Rössli* (☎ 470 33 77), an attractive place off Dorfplatz, has singles/doubles using hall showers for Sfr55/110 and large doubles with own bath for Sfr130. A few doors down is the smaller, slightly cramped *Chamois* (☎ 470 13 57), with rooms for Sfr50/100. *Hotel Derby* (☎ 470 17 27), on the road towards the Gemmi cable car, has rustic-style rooms from Sfr65/130 with shower/WC or Sfr55/110 without.

The four-star *Badehotel Regina Therme* (☎ 472 11 41; fax 470 20 02) is in the north side of the resort and has its own thermal pools. Rooms at half-board start at Sfr150/300.

Places to Eat
Leukerbad has few budget places to eat. Opposite the tourist office is *Heilquelle*, where vegetarians can choose from a number of dishes between Sfr12 and Sfr19. Valais specials cost above Sfr16 (open daily). Diagonally across the road is *Römerhof*, with pizza/pasta from Sfr13. Set menus range from Sfr17 (one course) to Sfr25 (four courses), and there's live music in season. Down the alleyway is a large *Migros* supermarket.

Walliser Kanne, opposite Weisses Rössli, serves cheese specialities from Sfr15;

fondue is Sfr20 (open daily). *Hotel Derby* (see Places to Stay) has a good restaurant where main courses cost Sfr12 to Sfr35. The lunch menu for Sfr16 includes a salad buffet.

Getting There & Away
Leuk is on the main rail route from Lausanne to Brig. A blue postbus goes from outside Leuk train station to Leukerbad at the same time past each hour until 7.38 pm (Sfr8.40 each way; takes 30 minutes). The scenic road winds a bit but is in good condition.

BRIG
• *pop 11,000* • *688m* • ☎ *(027)*
Brig is at the crossroads for various major transport routes, meaning an overnight stay may be necessary at some point. Stockalper Castle is well worth a visit.

Orientation & Information
Brig is the main town in the Upper Valais. The centre is south of the River Rhône and east of its tributary, the River Saltina. The train station has a money-exchange office (with credit card cash advances), open daily. The tourist office (☎ 923 19 01) is on the 1st floor of the station, open Monday to Friday from 8.30 am to noon and 1.30 to 6 pm, and Saturday from 8.30 am to noon and (in summer) 2 to 5.30 pm. It makes free hotel reservations, or use the hotel board with free phone outside. Postbuses leave from outside the train station. Directly ahead is Bahnhofstrasse, leading to the core of the town.

Stockalper Castle
Made out of granite and volcanic rock, this building on Alte Simplonstrasse was formerly Switzerland's largest private residence, and is instantly recognisable by its three onion domes. The central courtyard is particularly attractive. There are hourly guided tours of the interior in summer, lasting 50 minutes (in English if there's the demand). The museum section is interesting, provided you can get the guide to translate the German signs. It is open from 1 May to

31 October and the tour costs Sfr4 or Sfr1 for children.

The main fascination of the castle derives from the man who built it, Kaspar Jodok von Stockalper (1609-91), self-dubbed the Great Stockalper. He made a vast amount of money from salt and other products by controlling trade with Italy over the Simplon Pass. Probably a greater fortune was made from dealing in mercenaries, especially to France. His success allowed him to mix with royalty and helped to build up the reputation and prosperity of Brig itself. He built most of the centre of the town and at one stage owned half of the Upper Valais. In those days a humble maid had to work 10 years to buy a single cow. With only part of his fortune Stockalper could have bought cows stretching from the Furka Pass (the eastern border of Valais) all the way to Geneva.

Small wonder the people of Brig found him and his ostentatious wealth unbearable, and he was overthrown. Much of his wealth was confiscated, and he was eventually forced to flee in fear across the border to Italy. It was six years before he was able to return, to die unmourned shortly afterwards.

Places to Stay

Hotel prices in Brig are comparatively low, and drop marginally in the winter low season. *Restaurant Matza* (☎ 923 15 22), Alte Simplonstrasse 18, has a few simple rooms using hall shower for Sfr35/70; add Sfr10 per person if you want breakfast. *Café la Poste* (☎ 923 12 39), Furkastrasse 23, has renovated rooms with private shower cubicle for Sfr50/100. To get there, turn right from the station and left on Furkastrasse.

At Gliserallee 130, over the Saltina River from the old town, is *Gliserallee* (☎ 923 11 95). Singles/doubles cost from Sfr40/80 with shower or Sfr35/70 without. Nearer town, the three-star *Hotel Central* (☎ 923 50 20), Gliserallee 50, features rooms with private shower and TV from Sfr80/124. *Schlosshotel* (☎ 923 64 55; fax 923 95 36), Kirchgasse 4, offers the best perspective possible of the castle's triple onion domes, and its curved design gives rooms a novel shape

(closed December and January). All rooms have shower/toilet and TV. Singles cost Sfr95, or Sfr150 if two people share the Queen-sized bed. The doubles for Sfr170 are vast.

Places to Eat

There is a *Migros* supermarket and self-service restaurant opposite and to the left of the station. The restaurant is open Monday to Friday from 7.30 am to 6.30 pm and Saturday until 4 pm, but the supermarket section is closed Monday until 1.30 pm.

Matza (see Places to Stay) has pizzas from Sfr12.50 and Valais dishes. The menu with soup costs Sfr14, or Sfr12 for students. Pizzas are similarly priced at *Channa Molino Ristorante*, Furkastrasse 5, but this place has a pleasant rear terrace (open daily).

Restaurant zum Eidgenossen, Schulhausstrasse 2, off Bahnhofstrasse, has Valais meat plates (air-dried cold meat cut into thin slices) for Sfr20 and Sfr21, fondue for Sfr17 and a daily special with soup for Sfr15. The ground floor is a small bar; the dining area upstairs is a plusher affair. *Hotel du Pont*, Marktplatz 1, has a similar refined section beyond the bar area. Grills, fish, and house specialities are upwards of Sfr20 and a four-course menu costs Sfr45.

Getting There & Away

Hourly buses leave for Saas Fee (Sfr17.40) and call at Visp en route. Consider buying the regional bus pass, valid for seven consecutive days (Sfr55, children Sfr33) or for seven days in 15 (Sfr66, children Sfr44).

Brig is an important junction for train users. It is a stop on the Glacier Express line from Zermatt to St Moritz, and it connects the route to Locarno through Italy with the service to Interlaken via Spiez. BVZ trains to Zermatt depart hourly (Sfr58 return, valid for one month) from the track outside the main station entrance.

The Spiez-Locarno rail route is of interest to drivers as it includes vehicle-carrying trains. The Brig-Spiez section passes through the Lötschberg Tunnel and is particularly crucial as there is no corresponding road route. To transport a car or camper van through the tunnel section (Goppenstein to Kandersteg) costs Sfr25 (motorcycles Sfr16, bicycles Sfr8) including occupants. Trains run every 30 minutes from 5.35 am to 11.05 pm (plus a last train at midnight) and the journey takes 15 minutes.

There is a cycling track along the north bank of the Rhône, and bikes can be rented from Brig or Visp train station.

The Simplon Tunnel & Pass From Brig to Locarno via the 20-km Simplon tunnel takes under 2½ hours and costs Sfr48 (passport required as you change trains at Domodossola in Italy).

Vehicles are no longer transported by train through the tunnel; the only option is taking the Simplon Pass (open in winter) at 2005m. This road is steep, winding and time-consuming but does provide excellent views as it passes through the Gondo gorge, and on one stretch the Aletsch Glacier is visible. It was Napoleon Bonaparte who was responsible for building the first proper road through here; it was the strategic importance of this pass that he had on his mind when he set 30,000 men to work upgrading the original track after the battle of Marengo (1800).

BRIGERBAD

Brigerbad has the largest collection of open-air thermal swimming baths in Switzerland. Some pools are curative and others are ideal for just swimming and frolicking, particularly the one with underwater jet propulsion. There are five pools in the open air with a water temperature of 27 to 37°C. Entry costs Sfr10 (children Sfr3) for the whole day and it's open late May to late September, daily from 9.30 am to 6 pm. There's also a unique grotto pool (Sfr8).

Campingplatz Brigerbad (☎ 946 46 88) is part of the thermal complex, so campers get reduced admission to the pools. It's open from mid-May to mid-October and costs Sfr7 per person plus Sfr10 per site. Facilities include a restaurant, shop and washing machines.

Getting There & Away

Hourly postbuses go from both Brig (Sfr3.60; six km, takes 20 minutes) and Visp (four km, 10 minutes).

VISP

• *pop 6200* • *650m* • ☎ *(027)*

Visp stands at the entrance to the valley leading to Zermatt and Saas Fee, but has few tourist attractions in its own right.

Orientation & Information

The tourist office (☎ 946 61 61) is eight minutes' walk from the train station (which has money-exchange daily from 5.15 am to 10 pm), in the La Poste Kulturzentrum. To get there, walk down Bahnhofstrasse and turn left at Kaufplatz. It's open Monday to Friday from 8 to noon and 2 to 6 pm, and Saturday from 8 am to noon. Postbuses depart from outside the post office, which is ahead and to the right of the train station (400m).

Things to See & Do

The pedestrian-only old centre is fairly attractive with its cobbled streets and shuttered windows. You could also make for the cinema on Napoleonstrasse, or the swimming pool near the Mühleye camp site, open June to September. Alternatively, there's the 2½-hour hike up the hill to the wine-growing village of Visperterminen (the highest in Europe at 1336m); an hourly bus does the same trip in 25 minutes. The La Poste Kuturzentrum (☎ 946 76 50) stages several productions per week, including concerts (classical to rock), cabaret, opera and theatre.

Places to Stay & Eat

Mühleye (☎ 946 59 78 or 496 20 84) is one of several camp sites. It's west of the Vispa River, open 15 May to 31 October.

There's a hotel board with free phone on Bahnhofstrasse. *Hotel Bristol* (☎ 946 33 23), at the junction of Kantonsstrasse and Napoleonstrasse, has singles/doubles from Sfr45/80 with use of hall showers. More convenient for the station is *Hotel Adler*

(☎ 946 34 62) on Brückenweg, off Bahnhof-strasse. It's on the 6th floor of a tower block and has rooms from Sfr50/100 with private shower, toilet and TV. Rates without break-fast are possible. Downstairs is *Rendez-vous*, a café with meals from only Sfr8 (closed Sunday). Don't be put off by the tacky letter-ing outside. *Hotel Touring* (☎ 946 47 77) has three stars and is right next to the station; singles/doubles start from Sfr60/110.

Opposite the post office is a *Migros* super-market, which should soon have a restaurant. There are several places to eat on Bahnhof-strasse, including the *Barock Café*, with Asian food (from Sfr20), a lunch menu (Sfr15) and chubby angels on the wall (closed Sunday). Continue along Bahnhof-strasse for Martinistrasse, where *Martini-keller* is at No 1. It has a 1st floor terrace and regional meals for Sfr11 to Sfr30 (open daily). *Bar-Restaurant Commerce*, Kant-onsstrasse, opposite the bus station, has good pizzas from Sfr13 and a garden (closed Sunday).

Getting There & Away
See the previous Brig section for more details. Frequent buses and trains traverse the 10 km to/from Brig (Sfr3.60). Services to/from Zermatt and Saas Fee stop at Visp, but when leaving those resorts you may need to continue to Brig for the quickest onward connection. If you take the Zermatt train, parking is free in Visp at the 'park & ride' car park between the station and the post office; for details call ☎ 923 13 33.

ZERMATT
• *pop 5340* • *1605m* • *☎ (027)*
This skiing and mountaineering resort bathes in the reflected glory of one of the most famous peaks in the Alps, the Matterhorn. On Friday 13 July 1865, a party of seven led by Edward Whymper set out on the first successful ascent of this mountain. The climb up took 32 hours and was completed without problems. But on the way down, one of the team slipped and sent himself and three others crashing to their deaths in a 1200m fall down the North Wall. Only

Whymper and two Swiss guides survived to tell the tale.

Mountaineers still flock here, and some never leave; their names end up inscribed in stone in the town cemetery. Skiers come here to enjoy virtually year-round skiing. The more sedentary come simply to enjoy the awe-inspiring views.

Zermatt doubled in size during the skiing boom of the 1960s and 1970s, but not without its problems along the way – in February 1963 it suffered a wave of typhoid infections and it was a month before the source of the problem was discovered in the water supply. Things have long since settled down. For the rich and stylish, Zermatt is a place to see and be seen. The water is per-fectly safe, although the élite seem content instead to drink alcohol at 'peak' prices in the plusher clubs.

Orientation & Information
The massive Matterhorn stands sentinel at the head of the valley. Zermatt (1620m) is car-free except for electric taxis and buses, and street names are rarely used. The tourist office (☎ 967 01 81), beside the train station on the right, has detailed information in English. It is open Monday to Friday from 8.30 am to noon and 1.30 to 6.00 pm, and Saturday from 8.30 am to noon. During the summer and winter high season it is open weekdays from 8.30 am to noon and 2 to 7 pm, Saturday from 8.30 am to 7 pm, and Sunday from 9.30 am to noon and 4 to 7 pm. Inside and in the station are accommodation boards with a free telephone. Next to the tourist office is Zermatt Tours, a travel agent which changes money (daily in season, oth-erwise closed Sunday) without commission and at the normal bank rate.

The Mountain Guides office or Berg-führerbüro (☎ 967 34 56), on the main street in the same building as the ski school, is another good information source. It is open all day from 1 July to 30 September, and 5 to 7 pm only from mid-February to mid-May. For climbing the Matterhorn they recom-mend previous experience, one week's preparation, and the small matter of a Sfr670 guide fee (plus Sfr140 for accommodation). Also ask here about Haute Route ski-touring and heli-skiing.

The more expensive hotels should charge up to 40% less in low season, though many places close between seasons. Some souvenir shops in the resort are open daily. The post office (3920) is on the main street.

Telephone ☎ 967 20 00 for emergency helicopter rescue.

Things to See & Do

There are excellent views from any of the cable cars and gondolas. The cog-wheel railway to **Gornergrat** (3100m) is a particular highlight. This mountain railway is the most popular in the country and every year around three million people take the trip. It takes 25 to 43 minutes and there are two to three departures an hour. The fare is Sfr33 to go up and Sfr53 return; Inter-Rail and the Half-Fare Card get 50% off and the Swiss Pass, 25% off, but a Eurailpass is as much use as a snorkel to a skier.

Along the way you're rewarded with magical views of the Matterhorn (sit on the right-hand side) and the surrounding peaks. The view from the mid-way station of

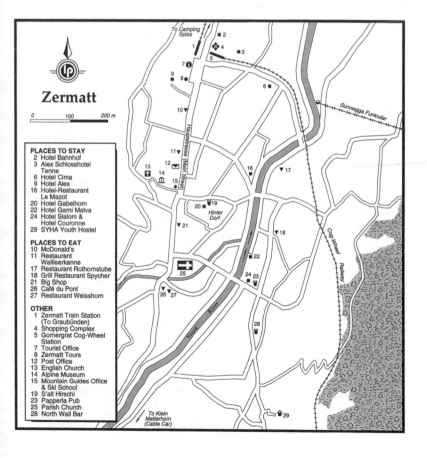

Zermatt

0   100   200 m

PLACES TO STAY
2 Hotel Bahnhof
3 Alex Schlosshotel Tenne
6 Hotel Cima
9 Hotel Alex
16 Hotel-Restaurant Le Mazot
20 Hotel Gabelhorn
22 Hotel Garni Malva
24 Hotel Slalom & Hotel Couronne
29 SYHA Youth Hostel

PLACES TO EAT
10 McDonald's
11 Restaurant Walliserkanne
17 Restaurant Rothornstube
18 Grill Restaurant Spycher
21 Big Shop
26 Café du Pont
27 Restaurant Weisshorn

OTHER
1 Zermatt Train Station (To Graubünden)
4 Shopping Complex
5 Gornergrat Cog-Wheel Station
7 Tourist Office
8 Zermatt Tours
12 Post Office
13 English Church
14 Alpine Museum
15 Mountain Guides Office & Ski School
19 S'alt Hirschi
23 Papperla Pub
25 Parish Church
28 North Wall Bar

Riffelalp to the north is a fine composition of swathes of trees (yellow and green in the autumn) and the mountains ringing the valley. From Gornergrat you get a different perspective of the Matterhorn (but not superior to the view from the village, in my opinion) and a marvellous panorama of the peaks round Mt Rosa. It takes around five hours to walk up from Zermatt.

The village itself is well worth exploring. Glance inside the **Parish church**, where there are good altar pieces and an unusual ceiling mural. **Hinter Dorf**, off the main street, is the oldest part. It's crammed with traditional, tumble-down wooden Valais homes, a world away from the flashy boutiques by the church that sell glass ornaments, figurines and expensive knick-knacks. Notice the stone discs on the stilts of the storage barns in Hinter Dorf: they're intended to keep out rodents.

A walk in the **cemetery** is a sobering experience for would-be mountaineers, as numerous monuments tell of deaths on Mt Rosa and the Matterhorn. The **Alpine Museum** has exhibits on mountain ascents, local fauna, the development of Zermatt, and famous visitors. It's open daily (closed Saturday in winter) and entry costs Sfr3 (children Sfr1). Around the back is the **English church**, where there are more mountaineering epitaphs. A pair from Cambridge University in England were lost in the mountains in August 1959. Their bodies were only found 30 years later.

Helicopter rides(☎ 967 34 87) cost Sfr160 per person for a 20-minute flight.

Skiing
Zermatt has many demanding slopes to test the experienced and intermediate skier in three different skiing areas: Rothorn, Stockhorn and Klein Matterhorn. In all there are 230 km of ski runs, although transferring between the areas can be a bit of a hassle. February to April is peak time, but in early summer the snow is still good and the lifts are less busy. Beginners have fewer options on the slopes. The ski school (☎ 966 24 66) offers group lessons at Sfr65 for one day.

The Klein Matterhorn is topped by the highest cable station in Europe (3820m), and provides access to summer skiing slopes (the highest skiing in Europe). It is also the starting point for skiing in Italy (see the following Cervinia section). With 25 km of runs, Zermatt has the most extensive summer skiing in Switzerland.

A day pass for all ski lifts in Zermatt, excluding Cervinia, costs Sfr60 (Sfr308 for one week). Summer skiing is Sfr58 (Sfr218). Ski shops open daily for rental – for one day, prices are Sfr38 for skis and stocks and Sfr19 for boots. Heli-skiing is a possibility, if you can afford to lay out at least Sfr280.

Cervinia This Italian ski resort is a good day trip from Zermatt. Intermediate skiers can handle the route from Klein Matterhorn (don't forget your passport). A one-day pass to ski Klein Matterhorn and Cervinia costs Sfr62, or if you have a longer-term general pass, pay a Sfr31 supplement to use Cervinia's ski area for one day.

Getting back to Zermatt has been made easier, thanks to a 150-person gondola on the Italian side, installed in the winter of 1992 (last ascent 2.40 pm if you want to return by lifts all the way to Zermatt on the same day). Cervinia offers good, long runs for beginners and intermediates. Food and drink prices in the village are reasonable, too. It's just a pity that visually the resort is a bit of an eyesore, with too many concrete-block constructions looking like building site leftovers. Non-skiers can't get down to Cervinia purely by cable car, and glacier crevasses make attempts to hike down hazardous.

Special Events
On 15 August there's an Alpine Folklore parade and music involving 1200 participants.

Places to Stay – bottom end
Camping *Camping Spiss* (☎ 967 39 21), to the left of the train station, is open from June to September.

Hostels & Hotels The SYHA *hostel* (☎ 967 23 20) has an excellent view of the Matterhorn. Dorm beds at half-board (dinner or lunch packet) are Sfr38, plus Sfr6 in high season – the only hostel in the country to have such a supplement. Laundry costs Sfr8 to wash and dry. Check-in is from 5 pm but the doors stay open during the day. Curfew is at 11.30 pm (or get a key). The hostel is shut from late April to 1 June and early November to mid-December.

Opposite the train station and popular with mountaineers is *Hotel Bahnhof* (☎ 967 24 06), with dorms for Sfr26 or Sfr28. Compact, wood-panelled singles/doubles are Sfr46/76. Unfortunately, there are only two showers, and they're in the basement. Prices are without breakfast but there's a kitchen. The hotel is closed from around mid-October to mid-December.

Hotel Gabelhorn (☎ 967 22 35) is a fine budget choice in the Hinter Dorf area of the village. It's a friendly little place (only 20 beds) with smallish but comfortable rooms for Sfr47/90, plus Sfr1 to use the hall showers. Doubles with shower are Sfr94. On the same lane by the river is *Hôtel Le Mazot* (☎ 967 27 77). This place is booked by a company during the winter; in summer, doubles with shower are Sfr130 and singles using hall shower are Sfr55.

Places to Stay – middle
Hotel Garni Malva (☎ 967 30 33), overlooking the east side of the river, is open year-round. It costs from Sfr55 per person, or doubles with private shower are from Sfr132, and all rooms have a balcony. *Cima* (☎ 966 23 37), in front of the station and halfway to the river, is slightly smaller and has rooms from Sfr75/150 with shower and Sfr55/110 without.

Hotel Slalom (☎ 967 19 77), has an excellent location over the river; rooms with private shower and TV are from Sfr98/190. Its twin in the same building is *Hotel Couronne* (☎ 967 26 81), and has rooms at half-board for Sfr155/290. There's a 1st floor terrace.

Places to Stay – top end
Zermatt offers a wide choice of four-star hotels. *Alex Schlosshotel Tenne* (☎ 967 18 01; fax 967 18 03), near the train station, is architecturally interesting and combines art nouveau and rustic motifs. *Hotel Alex* (☎ 967 17 26; fax 967 19 43), owned by the same family, is behind the tourist office. It also has creative touches in the décor department, and there's an indoor swimming pool, whirlpool and sauna (free for guests of both hotels, Sfr25 for others), and many other facilities including a terrace garden. The bar and disco (free entry) gets busy with people of all ages. Both hotels start at around Sfr200 per person with very appetising multi-course dinners included as standard.

Places to Eat
Get supplies from the *Coop* in the shopping complex opposite the train station. The *Big Shop* is one of the cheapest places for hot food, with eat-in or takeaway food for under Sfr13 (open 11 am to 8 pm daily). Unusually for a ski resort, there's also a *McDonald's*, pretending to be inconspicuous in a chalet. Both places are on the main street.

Beyond the church on the main street, the *Café du Pont* is a rustic place, exuding a red glow from the lampshades. Raclette snacks are Sfr7 and other meals start at Sfr12. The Valais dried meat plate is Sfr22. The next door *Restaurant Weisshorn*, is similar, except that the lampshades throw out yellow light. It's roomier and the choice is wider; fondue is Sfr20. Also recommended is *Restaurant Walliserkanne*, by the post office, which has pizzas, fondue, meat dishes and Valais specialities from Sfr14 to Sfr24. It has a dancing bar below ground level. All three restaurants are open daily in season.

Grill Restaurant Spycher, on the east side of the river by the Hotel Aristella, has interesting and varied dishes from Sfr32 to Sfr46, and English menus. Flambés are a speciality (Sfr90 for two). It's in a small chalet and has an extensive wine list (open daily in season from 6.30 pm). Another quality place is *Rothornstube* in the Perrin hotel on the east side of the river. It has main dishes from

VALAIS

Sfr25 and menus where you can select the number of courses (three courses for Sfr25, up to six courses for Sfr58). It's open daily, but closed at lunchtime in winter.

Entertainment
North Wall Bar, near the youth hostel, is about the cheapest and best bar in the village, and popular with resort workers. It has ski videos, music, good pizzas from Sfr10 and beer at Sfr4.50 for half a litre. The bar is closed during the off season, otherwise it's open daily from 6.30 pm to midnight.

Down the hill, the more expensive *Papperla Pub* is busier for après-ski, aided by live music daily, and has pizzas from Sfr12. *S'alt Hirschi*, in the old part of the village, is a good place for a beer (Sfr4.80 for half a litre) in a less hectic environment. It has limited food in winter (open daily 3 pm to midnight) but not in summer (open from 8 pm; closed Monday and Tuesday). There are many other bars and clubs where you drink, dance and unwind. Just follow your eyes and ears.

Getting There & Away
Train Hourly trains depart from Brig, calling at Visp en route. The steep and scenic journey takes 80 minutes and costs Sfr34 one-way, or Sfr58 return. It is a private railway; Inter-Rail earns 50% off (for those under 26) and the Swiss Pass is good for free travel. Eurailpass offers no discounts. The only way out is to backtrack, but if you're going to Saas Fee you can divert there from Stalden Saas.

Zermatt is the start of the famous Glacier Express to Graubünden, one of the most spectacular train rides in the world. It takes nearly eight hours to reach St Moritz, and costs Sfr127 in 2nd class and Sfr211 in 1st class. In summer, reservations are compulsory whether needed or not (Sfr9 fee, even if you have a railpass). This fee isn't payable on normal trains following the same route, and it doesn't apply on the Glacier Express if you're only going to/from Brig or Visp.

Car As Zermatt is car-free, you need to park cars at Täsch (Sfr3 to Sfr10 per day) and take the train from there (Sfr6.60). There is a road from Täsch, but it's private and tourists are never granted permits to use it. See the Visp section for another parking option.

SAAS FEE
• *pop 1200* • *1800m* • ☎ *(027)*

The self-styled 'Pearl of the Alps' is in the valley adjoining its more famous neighbour, Zermatt. It may not have the Matterhorn, but there are plenty of other towering peaks to overwhelm the senses, and after a hard day's hiking or skiing there are various nightspots to help you unwind. But at night you have to rein yourself in even as you're letting yourself go. A humourless and slightly bizarre notice in the Hotel Walliserhof warns:

Any disturbance of the night's rest is strictly prohibited after 10 pm in the entire village, including on public squares and streets. Our guardians are instructed to denounce marplots and to fine them with Sfr200.

Orientation & Information
Saas Fee is spread out in a long line. The village centre and ski lifts are to the left (south-west) of the bus station. The village extends at least as far as to the right-hand side as well; in this direction there are a few hotels and many holiday chalets.

The tourist office (☎ 957 14 57) is opposite the bus station. Opening hours are Monday to Friday from 8.30 am to noon and 2 to 6.30 pm, Saturday from 8 am to 7 pm, and Sunday from 3 to 6 pm (4 to 6 pm in low season). The office makes hotel reservations (Sfr5 commission) and has a number for direct bookings (☎ 957 51 20). Its hotel list (free) has a functional map. As in other ski resorts, many places shut in November and May. The local Guest Card earns various discounts.

There is a post office (3906) in the bus station.

Things to See & Do
Saas Fee is on a ledge above Saas Grund (1560m), and is surrounded by an impressive

Glaciers

With fears of global warming, glaciers are coming increasingly under scrutiny. Of the world's total supply of fresh water, 80% is stored in ice and snow, and 97% of this is in Antarctica and Greenland. But glaciers are important in the rest of the world, too. Without glacier meltwater, many areas (including Valais) at the foot of high mountain ranges would be desert or steppes. Within Switzerland, the most extensive and highest glacial regions are in Valais and the Bernese Alps. Most glaciers are receding, some at an alarming rate; unless global warming is reversed it is estimated that the Les Diablerets glacier will disappear by 2025.

There's much more to glaciers than lumps of ice. They start off as snow, which over the course of years gets compressed to firn (sometimes called névé). About 10m of fresh snow makes one metre of firn. Ice eventually evolves from firn. Surprisingly, it takes longer to get to ice in 'cold' glaciers (ie those below 0°C, such as the one at Titlis) than in 'temperate' glaciers (like the Obere Glacier in Grindelwald). Glaciers are filled with air bubbles, formed during the transformation of snow to ice, and the gas content of these bubbles may be modified by water-flows in a temperate glacier.

The ice at the bottom of glaciers (in the ablation zone) may be centuries old, and makes it possible to measure past environmental pollution. The eruption of Krakatau in 1883 can be measured in glacial ice, and there are traces of the 1977 Sahara dust storms in Alpine glaciers. The peak of nuclear testing and fallout, 1963, is a benchmark year in dating glacial ice.

Ice avalanches from glaciers account for an average of nearly two deaths per year in Switzerland. The worst recent disaster was at Allalin on 30 August 1965, when 88 people died. Glaciers are always moving. You may think that the movement is so slow as to be insignificant, but owing to the movement of the Titlis glacier, the masts of the ski lifts there have to be repositioned three to four times a year. In the course of the summer huge crevasses are opened up in the ice which have to be filled in before skiing starts again in the winter. But they can still be hazardous – never leave the marked trails when skiing on glaciers.

Much of the information in this passage is based on the displays in the ice pavilions in Saas Fee and Titlis. ■

Former glacial basin

Former glacial valley

panorama of 13 peaks exceeding 4000m. Skiing is the primary activity and winter is the most important season. About 80 km of ski runs favour beginners and experts though intermediates also have sufficient choices. A general lift pass costs Sfr56 (Sfr32 children) for one day and Sfr290 (Sfr165 children) for one week. Ski rental places are open daily (standard prices). The village has two natural ice rinks.

The tourist office has a map of summer walking trails in the region which cover a total of 280 km. Even in winter, 30 km of marked footpaths remain open. The highest underground funicular (metro) in the world operates all year to Mittelallalin at 3500m, giving access to the Feegletscher. This is the centre of summer skiing, with 15 km of runs above 2700m. The funicular was opened in 1984 and ascends 500m in 2½ minutes.

Under the top station is the **Ice Pavilion**, 10m below the surface of the ice. It gives an excellent if slightly erudite explanation of glaciers and the difficulty and importance of surveying them. Dummies enact some of the scenarios expounded. Entry costs Sfr7 (children Sfr3.50) and it's open during metro running times.

Above ground there's a revolving restaurant which is quite expensive (meals from Sfr22) but the views are wonderful. Alternatively, you could try the cheaper self-service restaurant (meals from Sfr14) and take in the view from the stationary terrace. From Saas Fee to Mittelallalin by cable car then funicular costs Sfr42 each way or Sfr54 return (children half-price).

Back down in the village there is the **Saaser Museum**, which tells the history of the resort and gives details about local folklore and building interiors (entry Sfr3). It's open weekday afternoons in winter and daily except Monday in summer. There's also a sports centre near the bus station with swimming, tennis, a gymnasium and a sauna. The mountaineering school (☎ 957 23 48) doubles as the ski school (☎ 957 22 68). Ski-mountaineering is possible along the famous Haute Route all the way to Chamonix.

Places to Stay – bottom end
Camping The nearest camp sites are down in Saas Grund, a 12-minute bus ride away. They're both open year-round; call ☎ 957 29 89 or ☎ 957 20 66.

Hotels The *Albana*, five minutes to the north-east of the tourist office, is an excellent deal. Two to five-bed rooms (singles must share) cost Sfr30 to Sfr50 per person, and each has a shower, toilet and balcony as well as great breakfast-buffets. Half-pension costs Sfr10 extra. It's advisable to book in advance in winter, and it's closed in off-season.

Reception is in the *Hotel Mascotte* (☎ 957 27 24), which has rooms for Sfr55 per person with private toilet and shower. Also ask here about *Chalet Alba*, costing Sfr20 per person. All three places are side-by-side.

Places to Stay – middle
In the south of the village, convenient for the ski lifts, is *Garni Feehof* (☎ 957 33 44), with good-value singles/doubles for Sfr53/106 with shower or Sfr46/92 without. There's a sun terrace and several small TV rooms and kitchens.

Even closer to the lifts is *Rendez-Vous* (☎ 957 20 40), with rooms for Sfr89/168, or Sfr90/190 with half-pension. It has some dorms (Sfr38) but they're nowhere near as good value as Albana's. By the tourist office, try the friendly, family-run *Hotel Bergheimat* (☎ 957 20 30). Wood-panelled rooms with balcony start at Sfr64 per person with shower/WC or Sfr54 without.

About 12 minutes north-east of the tourist office is *Alp Hitta* (☎ 957 10 50). It has two to four-person apartments, each with a TV, telephone, and small kitchen, which are available all year. The price of Sfr39 per person (Sfr36 in summer) includes breakfast in the restaurant.

Zurbriggen (☎ 957 20 50), left of the bus station and next to the swimming pool, has doubles with shower/WC and TV for Sfr190. This place has a fantastic garden, with a huge rock covered in various implements and carved tree trunks.

Places to Stay – top end
Walliserhof (☎ 957 20 21; fax 957 29 10), just down the road, has comfortable rooms finished in wood and floral fabric, with large balconies. As in many other hotels, rooms facing south are more expensive. Prices start at Sfr208/416 (half-pension) for rooms with all the expected amenities, and dinners are gourmet standard.

Places to Eat
The cheapest eating is at the various Metzgerei (butcher shops) where you can get hot takeaways. The best is *Charly's Metzg*, 50m down from the tourist office, which has chips for Sfr3, whole chickens for Sfr8, and a Tagesmenu for Sfr9. There's a supermarket opposite.

Eat pizza from Sfr12 at *Boccalino* near the

ski lifts. It's open daily in season. *Restaurant Vieux Chalet*, off the main street near the tourist office, is good for cheese specialities, ranging from Raclette snacks to filling fondues (Sfr23.50). It's a small cosy place, though there's also seating upstairs (closed Monday). *Restaurant Alp Hitta* (see Places to Stay) has a rustic atmosphere, complete with background Alpine music. Raclette is Sfr6, fondue is Sfr20, and other Walliser meals start at Sfr14. It is open daily, except from mid-April to mid-June and mid-October to mid-December when it closes down.

La Ferme, on the main street near the tourist office, has a satisfying three-course lunch menu for around Sfr25, which is also available in the evening during low season (open daily). Other main courses are Sfr23 to Sfr40. Farm implements hang from walls and ceiling and sledges are used as coat hangers. On the same road towards the ski lifts is *Gletschergarten*, with a wide selection of meals ranging from Sfr13 to Sfr40 (closed lunchtime in low season).

Fletschhorn (☎ 957 21 31) is one of the top 20 restaurants in Switzerland. It's in a quiet location beyond the northern part of the village, about a 10-minute walk from Alp Hitta (or get them to pick you up in their electric car). Special menus cost over Sfr100. It's closed from the end of April to mid-June and mid-☎ October to mid-December.

Getting There & Away
Up until 1951, the only transportation available to Saas Fee from Saas Grund was by foot or mule-train. Things are a little easier now, although you still can't get there by train. Hourly buses depart from Brig via Visp, take one hour and cost Sfr17.40, or Sfr33 for a day return. You can transfer from the Zermatt train at Stalden Saas.

Like Zermatt, Saas Fee is car-free. Park at the entrance to the village, where daily charges are Sfr13. Get a Sfr4 per day reduction thereafter with the Guest Card by validating it at the tourist office.

ALETSCH GLACIER
• ☎ *(027)*
This vast river of ice is an inspiring sight. It's the longest glacier in the Alps, stretching from the Jungfrau (4158m) in the Bernese Oberland to a plateau above the Rhône River. Its southern expanse is fringed by the Aletschwald, one of the highest pine forests in Europe (2000m).

Orientation & Information
There are two resorts on the southern rim, separated from the forest by a ridge of hills. The westernmost is Riederalp at 1925m. Its tourist office (☎ 927 13 65) is open Monday to Saturday from 8 am to noon and 2 to 6 pm. An easy walk to the east is the largest resort, Bettmeralp (1939m). Its tourist office (☎ 927 12 91) is open similar hours. Further east is tiny Kühboden (2212m). All these places are car-free. Ask for the Guest Card (Gästekarte) giving useful discounts.

Things to See & Do
Summer hiking is excellent in the Aletsch forest along numerous marked trails. The tourist office in either Riederalp or Bettmeralp can give details of guided walks around and across the glacier. Riederalp also has an Alpine dairy and an Alpine museum. Kühboden gives access to the Eggishorn (2927m), providing possibly the best view of the glacier. In the Aletsch region there are 75 km of ski runs and 25 lifts. The skiing is mostly intermediate or easy. There are several versions of ski passes costing between Sfr34 and Sfr52 per day.

Places to Stay & Eat
Dormitories are at *Restaurant-Pension Kühboden* (☎ 971 13 77), by the Kühboden cable car, *Touristenlager Seilbahn* (☎ 927 13 96) in Bettmeralp and the *Naturfreundehaus* (☎ 927 11 65) in Riederalp.

In Riederalp, the *Hotel-Restaurant Bergdohl* (☎ 927 13 37), by the Blausee chairlift, has wood-panelled rooms from Sfr68/136 with shower/WC, or Sfr58/116

VALAIS

without (for B&B). In winter, half-pension starts at Sfr114/208 or Sfr100/188.

In Bettmeralp, try *Garni Sporting* (☎ 927 22 52), not far from the Bettmerhorn lift, charging from Sfr60 per person (Sfr75 in winter), or the nearby and comfortable *Alpfrieden* (☎ 927 22 32), starting at Sfr87 per person (Sfr108 in winter).

Both Riederalp and Bettmeralp have a *Coop*. Also look for the Bäckerei (bakeries) and Metzgerei for cheap snacks. Eat pizzas in *Postillon* in Bettmeralp or at *Boccalino* in the Hotel Alpenrose in Riederalp. The Alpenrose also has *Walliser Kanne*, a more expensive restaurant with cheese specialities.

Getting There & Away

The base stations for these resorts are on the rail route between Brig and Andermatt. Cable car departures are linked to train arrivals. Mörel up to Riederalp costs Sfr7.20 each way, the same as from Betten up to Bettmeralp. From Fiesch all the way up to Eggishorn via Kühboden costs Sfr36.60. The Swiss Pass gives you a 25% reduction on these fares. Enquire about combined ski pass and transport deals at Brig train station.

Ticino

Situated south of the Alps and enjoying a Mediterranean climate, Ticino (Tessin in German) gives more than just a taste of Italy. Indeed, it once belonged to Italy. Como and Milan contested control for many years until the Dukes of Milan gained the ascendancy. Swiss encroachment on the area began in 1478 when the canton of Uri annexed the Leventina Valley (Valle Leventina), on the southern side of the St Gotthard Pass.

The Swiss Confederation gradually expanded southwards until by 1513 it had control of the whole area. Except for Bellinzona, which was under the authority of Uri, Schwyz and Unterwalden, Ticino became the joint property of the then member cantons. But the Confederation did little to develop its new acquisition and the region languished. Ticino remained politically tied (and subservient) to the Confederates until 1798 when France imposed its Helvetic Republic. Ticino then became a free canton, and despite the years as a subject territory, opted to officially join the Confederation in 1803, this time on equal terms.

Although Swiss order and efficiency pervades the canton's Mediterranean flavour, the native people are darker skinned than their compatriots in other regions, and the cuisine, architecture and vegetation reflect that found farther south. Italian is the official language in this Catholic canton. Many people also speak French and German but you will find English less widely spoken than in the rest of Switzerland. The region offers mountain hikes and dramatic mountain valleys in the north; water sports and relaxed, leisurely towns in the south.

Orientation & Information

Ticino is the fourth largest Swiss canton. Winters are mild but the best time to visit is spring to autumn, when the flowers bloom, the lakes come alive, and the piazzas become places to watch the world drift by. Average

HIGHLIGHTS

- A taste of Italy, Swiss-style
- Mediterranean climate and flora
- Free summer music festivals
- Castles in Bellinzona
- Museums, piazzas and hill-top views in Locarno and Lugano
- Boat tour of Lake Lugano

Ticino

afternoon temperatures for Lugano are around 28°C in July and August, 17°C in April and September, and 7°C in December and January. Locarno gets over 2300 hours of sunshine per year, with an average yearly temperature of 15.5°C.

Public holidays taken in Ticino, in addition to the normal Swiss national holidays, are:

6 January – Epiphany
19 March – St Joseph's Day
1 May – Labour Day
6 June – Corpus Christi
29 June – Ss Peter and Paul Day
15 August – Assumption

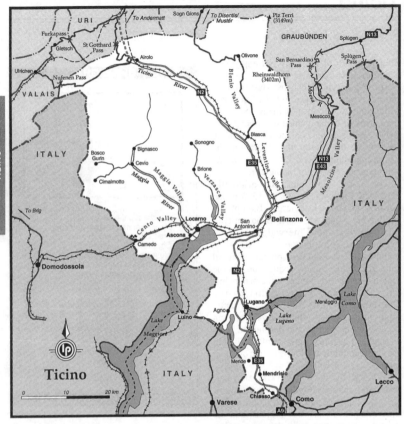

Ticino

0   10   20 km

1 November – All Saints' Day
8 December – Immaculate Conception

The regional tourist office is in Bellinzona (Ente ticinese per il turismo; ☎ 825 70 56; fax 825 36 14) at Villa Turrita, Via Lugano 12, Bellinzona. Opening hours are Monday to Friday from 8 am to noon and from 2 to 6 pm. Postal enquiries can be addressed to the same office via its box number: Casella postale 1441, CH-6501 Bellinzona. The office can provide canton-wide hotel, museum and restaurant brochures, as well as detailed walking descriptions for Upper

Ticino (in the *itinerari* booklet, with English text). For information via the internet try http://www.tourism-ticino.ch.

Local tourist offices sell a fishing permit that covers the whole canton (Sfr50 for 10 days). Fishing is allowed year-round on lakes Lugano and Maggiore, but only from April to September on other lakes and rivers.

The whole canton shares the same telephone code: ☎ 091.

Getting Around

There are two regional travel passes for

Ticinese Cuisine

Pizza and pasta are ubiquitous, but there are many other more specifically Ticinese dishes to try. *Risotto con funghi* is liquidy rice with saffron and mushrooms. It is often served with *osso bucco*, a circular slab of veal or (less expensively) pork, with the bone marrow in the centre. *Polenta* is an accompaniment to all sorts of dishes, particularly braised meat. It's made from maize and looks like yellow mashed potato. *Cazzöla* is a selection of meats with cabbage and potatoes. *Cicitt* are small sausages. *Mazza casalinga* is a selection of delicatessen cuts.

A *trattoria* is a simple, generally family-run *ristorante* (restaurant), and the term *locanda* denotes a trattoria with accommodation. *Birreria* is an establishment where the function of food is merely to provide respite from the main activity of beer drinking.

Osteria is the wine-led equivalent. For authentic eating in rural areas, search out a country inn, called a *grotto* or a *cavetto*. Wherever you eat, consider washing down your meal with a Ticinese Merlot. Around 80% of local wine produced is Merlot, a red characterised by its full-bodied taste. 'VITI' on the label is a seal of very high quality. ∎

Ticino, available in 2nd class only. The Locarno/Ascona Region pass costs Sfr76 (Sfr63 for holders of Swiss railpasses). It gives seven days free travel on boat, train and bus routes around Locarno and the Swiss part of Lake Maggiore, and 50% off boats and trains around Lugano and its lake. A version of the same pass giving three free days and reductions on the other four days costs Sfr50 (Sfr40). The Lugano Region pass gives free travel on Lake Lugano, and on regional public transport in and around Lugano (including the funiculars up Brè and San Salvatore). It also gives 50% off a number of other routes, including transport on land and water around Locarno. The price is Sfr92 (Sfr82 with Swiss railpasses) for seven days, or Sfr70 (Sfr62) for three free days and reductions on the other four. These passes are issued between 1 March and 31 October. Reduced prices for children are available, but get a Family Card instead (see the Getting Around chapter).

Bellinzona

• *pop 16,900*   • *230m*   • *☎ (091)*

The capital of Ticino is a city of castles. It is set in a valley of lush mountains, and stands at the southern side of two important Alpine passes, San Bernardino and St Gotthard.

Orientation & Information

The train station has a money-exchange counter, open daily from 6 am to 9 pm, bike rental, and an Aperto supermarket, open daily to 9 pm. Postbuses depart from Via C Molo, one block away, where there's a postbus ticket and information office. The tourist office (☎ 825 21 31), Via Camminata 2, Palazzo Civico, is open Monday to Friday from 8 am to noon and 1.30 to 6.30 pm, and Saturday from 9 am to noon. It sells maps, including a local hiking map (Sfr7) showing routes and durations. The tourist office is 10 minutes' walk from the train station, and between the two is the main post office (Posta 1, 6500), Viale Stazione 18. The cobbled streets south of the post office, up to and including Piazza Indipendenza, are banned to private vehicles from 7.30 pm to 6 am.

Castles

The three medieval castles which dominate the town are testimony to Bellinzona's historical importance, based on its key location at the crossroads of the major routes through the Alps. All the castles are well preserved and offer marvellous views of the town and surrounding mountains, as well as having their own museum. Each museum is closed Monday and costs Sfr4 (students Sfr2) for entry, or there's a combined ticket for Sfr8 (students Sfr4). The central **Grand Castle** (Castelgrande) dates from around the 6th century, and it's open daily for visits to the grounds (free). The museum covers archaeology and history.

Montebello Castle (Castello di Montebello), slightly above the town, is open daily

PLACES TO STAY
1 Hotel Metropoli
2 Hotel Internazionale
6 Hotel San Giovanni
10 Hotel Croce Federale
19 Tsui-Fok

PLACES TO EAT
4 Ristorante Pedemonte
7 Coop Supermarket & Restaurant
8 Migros Supermarket & Restaurant
11 Ristorante Inova
13 Speranza
14 Snackbar Piazza
16 Birreria Corona

OTHER
3 Train Station
5 Postbus Departures
9 Main Post Office
12 Grand Castle & Archaeological Museum
15 Tourist Office
17 Montebello Castle
18 Sasso Corbaro Castle
20 Cantonal Tourist Office

Bellinzona

from 8 am to 6 pm with free entry. The small museum proffers further archaeological and historical displays. Quite a trek up the hill is the smaller **Sasso Corbaro Castle** (Castello di Sasso Corbaro). The museum is in the dungeon, and exhibits historical clothing, tools and traditional Ticinese crafts. The absence of grounds to explore means that the only thing to tempt you up here when the museum is closed is the sweeping view. No buses go up but it's easy to beg a lift back down again from the car park. The castles are often respectively referred to as that of Uri, Schwyz and Unterwalden, after the bailiffs

of the cantons who ruled the town from the 16th century.

Church

The **Chiesa di Santa Maria delle Grazie**, Via Lugano, features a 15th century fresco of the crucifixion, comparable to the more famous version of the scene in the Santa Maria Church in Lugano. The artist who painted the impressive fresco is unknown.

Special Events

Every Saturday morning there's a **market** that sprawls across the main street either side of the tourist office. There are stalls selling fruit and vegetables, clothes and crafts, plus there's usually a couple of buskers (street musicians) to liven things up. It's very much a social occasion, with locals standing around chatting rather than indulging in any frenzied buying. This relaxed approach to life becomes rather more animated during the **Rabadan Carnival**, which stretches over several days and starts on a Thursday, 7½ weeks before Easter Sunday.

Bellinzona has the happy habit of hosting open-air music festivals. **Piazza Blues** runs for three days in late June, and **Feedback** is three days of 1960s music in early September; both festivals are free. Entry to **Vivi**, a series of open-air rock and pop concerts in late July, costs Sfr15.

Places to Stay
The *camp site* (☎ 829 11 18), Bosco di Molinazzo, costs Sfr6.20 per person, Sfr5.20 per tent and Sfr16 for a car or camper van. It is open from 1 May to early October, and is by the river in the northern suburb of Molinazzo.

Bellinzona hasn't got a very wide choice of hotels, so book ahead if you can. *Tsui-Fok* (☎ 825 13 32), Via Nocca 20, offers oldish rooms but with some quite attractive features. Singles/doubles are Sfr45/70; add Sfr5 per person for breakfast. Convenient for the station is *Hotel Metropoli* (☎ 825 11 79), Via Ludovico il Moro. It looks rundown from the outside, but the rooms are OK and of a decent size. Singles/doubles are Sfr50/90. A lower rate without breakfast is sometimes offered. Reception is in the café/bar downstairs where there's TV, pool and games machines. Also conveniently located is *Hotel San Giovanni* (☎ 825 19 19), Via San Giovanni 7, with singles/doubles for Sfr50/95. The rooms are slightly smarter than those at Metropoli, and the café is calmer. Rooms are with hall shower in all these places.

Ideally situated in the centre is *Hotel Croce Federale* (☎ 825 16 67), Viale Stazione 12, with singles/doubles/triples for Sfr95/130/160. All rooms have shower, toilet and TV, and the hotel has a pizzeria.

Top-of-the-range in Bellinzona are two three-star hotels. One of them is the *Internazionale* (☎ 825 43 33; fax 826 13 59), opposite the station on Piazza Stazione. It's hardly plush, although the stained-glass windows over the stairs are eye-catching. Rooms with private bathroom, telephone, TV and radio are Sfr130/180 or less.

Places to Eat & Drink
Supermarkets with a restaurant are the *Migros*, Piazza del Sole, and the *Coop*, Via H Guisan. A supermarket and the buffet-style *Ristorante Inova* are downstairs in the Innovazione department store on Viale Stazione. You can eat for around Sfr10 in all these restaurants, and they are open weekdays to 6.30 pm and Saturday to 5 pm.

As you might expect, there are plenty of pizzerias around town. Good and cheap (from Sfr9) is *Snackbar Piazza*, via Teatro, with outside tables and a traditional brick oven. *Speranza*, Piazza Collegiata 1, is a bar/café, with cheap but limited food at lunch only. In the section next-door it has free blues concerts on Friday and Saturday nights. *Birreria Corona*, opposite the tourist office at Via Camminata 5, has a café-type front section and a smarter restaurant at the rear. There are pizzas (from Sfr9.50), and other meals from Sfr12 to Sfr32. All the above places are closed on Sunday, so that might be a good day to consider going on a diet.

If you don't fancy making Sunday a day of rest for your stomach, look in at *Ristorante Pedemonte* (☎ 825 33 33), Via Pedemonte 12. It's popular with locals but not many tourists find it as it's on the inaccessible side of the station. You really get personal service in this small place – there's no written menu; instead, the server describes what's cooking tonight. Ordering can be a bit of a gamble as their English is limited, but I've never been disappointed. Expect to pay around Sfr10 for a starter or salad and Sfr30 for a main course. It's closed on Monday. Quality food can also be savoured at the restaurant in the Castelgrande (☎ 826 23 53), which is closed on Mondays.

Getting There & Away

Bellinzona is on the train route connecting Locarno (Sfr6.60) and Lugano (Sfr10.40). The journey takes around 30 minutes in either direction, with two trains an hour. It is also on the Zürich-Milan route. Postbuses head north-east to Chur; you need to reserve your seat the day before, at the train station or on ☎ 825 77 55. The fare is Sfr50, plus a Sfr5 supplement that's not covered by the Swiss Pass. There is a good cycling track along the Ticino River to Lake Maggiore and Locarno.

Car Rental Hertz (☎ 826 10 33) is at Via F Zorzi 40 and Budget (☎ 858 15 10) is at Via Cantonale in nearby Cadenazzo. Avis has no local office.

Lugano

• *pop 28,200* • *270m* • ☎ *(091)*

Switzerland's southernmost tourist town offers an excellent combination of sunny days, watery pursuits and hillside hikes. It's the largest city in Ticino and the fourth most important financial centre in Switzerland.

Before the Swiss arrived on the scene in 1512, Lugano was successively under the jurisdiction of the Bishop of Como and the Duke of Milan. In the days of France's Helvetic Republic it was the citizens of Lugano who started the move for Ticino to officially join the Swiss Confederation, proclaiming themselves 'Liberi e Svizzeri' (Free and Swiss).

Orientation

Lugano is 270m above sea level on the shores of Lake Lugano. The train station is above and to the west of the old town. Take the stairs or the funicular (Sfr0.80, Swiss Pass valid) down to the centre which is dominated by piazzas. The most important one, the Piazza della Riforma, contains the Neo-Classical Municipio building. Paradiso is a suburb to the south; hotels here are slightly better value than in the centre, and it is the departure point for the funicular up to Mt San Salvatore. The other mountain that looms over the town, Mt Brè, is to the east. The airport is three km west of the train station.

Information

Tourist Office The tourist office (☎ 921 46 64), Riva Giocondo Albertolli, is on the lake side of the Municipio building. Opening hours are Monday to Friday from 9 am to 6 pm or later, and Saturday from 9 am to 5 pm. In winter, opening hours reduce to weekdays only from 9 am to noon and 2 to 5 pm. Ask about the Guest Card if you're staying more than three days in the region, and pick up the *Regione Lago di Lugano* official guide which is in four languages.

Foreign Consulates There are a number of consulates in town, including those for Britain (☎ 923 86 06), Via Motta 19, and Italy (☎ 922 05 13), Via Monte Ceneri 16.

Train Station The train information office is open daily from 8.20 am to 6.30 pm (5 pm Saturday and Sunday). The counter for Swissair check-in (for Zürich airport only) also deals with bike rental, and is staffed daily from 8 am to 8 pm. The money-exchange office is open daily to 7.45 pm. The Aperto supermarket is open daily from 6 am to 10 pm. There is also a hotel information and reservation office (Sfr3 fee), open Monday to Saturday from 10 am to 7.30 pm (6 pm in winter). The free telephone outside for hotels is only accessible when the office is shut.

Post & Communications The main post office (Posta 1, 6900) is in the centre of the old town at Via Della Posta 7. Opening hours are Monday to Friday from 7.30 to noon and 1.45 to 6.30 pm, and Saturday from 8 am to 11 am. Services are available during additional hours subject to a surcharge.

Medical & Emergency Services Call the police on ☎ 117, and dial ☎ 111 for a doctor or dentist. The hospital, Ospedale Civico (☎ 805 61 11), is at Via Tesserete.

MARK HONAN

MARK HONAN

MARK HONAN

MARK HONAN

MARK HONAN

Top Left: Bellinzona from Castel
            Grande, Ticino
Top Middle & Top Right: Piazza
            Cioccaro, Lugano, Ticino

Middle: Facade of the tourist office at
          Ascona, Ticino
Bottom: Café, Piazza Della Riforma,
          Lugano, Ticino

Top: Morcote and Lake Lugano, Ticino
Bottom: Chalandamarz Festival, Engadine Valley, Graubünden

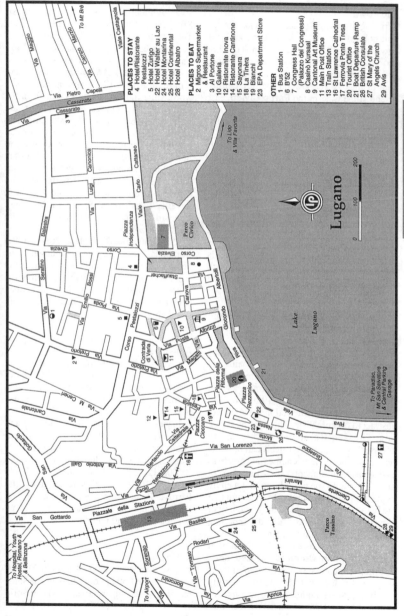

PLACES TO STAY
4 Hotel/Ristorante Pestalozzi
5 Hotel Zurigo
22 Hotel Walter au Lac
24 Hotel Montarina
25 Hotel Continental
28 Hotel Albatro

PLACES TO EAT
2 Migros Supermarket & Restaurant
3 Al Portone
10 Galleria
12 Ristorante Inova
14 Ristorante Cantinone
15 Sayonara
18 La Tinèra
19 Bianchi
23 EPA Department Store

OTHER
1 Bus Station
6 B52
7 Congress Hall (Palazzo del Congressi)
8 Casinò Kursaal
9 Cantonal Art Museum
11 Main Post Office
13 Train Station
16 St Lawrence Cathedral
17 Ferrovia Ponte Tresa
20 Tourist Office
21 Boat Departure Ramp
26 British Consulate
27 St Mary of the Angels Church
29 Avis

TICINO

Lugano

0   100   200

Old Town

Winding alleyways, pedestrian-only piazzas and colourful parks make Lugano an ideal town for walking around. On Tuesday morning from April to October, the tourist office conducts a free guided walk of the centre; make a reservation the day before. Spend some time in the **Parco Civico**, east of the Casino. Magnolias and camellias flower in March, and a month later rhododendrons and azaleas burst forth.

The **St Mary of the Angels Church** (Santa Maria degli Angioli), Piazza Luini, has a pair of frescoes by Bernardino Luini dating from 1529; the most powerful depicts the Crucifixion. Below the train station is the **St Lawrence Cathedral** (Cattedrale San Lorenzo), noted for its Renaissance façade (1517), particularly the three fine doorways that overlook the lake. Inside are frescoes dating from a similar era, and choir stalls with a mini statue protruding from each armrest. The tabernacle at the end of the aisle is 16th century.

Museums & Galleries The **Thyssen-Bornemisza Gallery**, Villa Favorita, Castagnola, is a famous private art collection. In 1992 the Old Masters of the collection were transferred to Spain, but what's left behind is extremely impressive. It constitutes 150 works by American and European artists from the 19th and 20th century, covering all major styles from abstract to photorealism. The wealthy Baron von Thyssen-Bornemisza (the family amassed its fortune from steel) can only get richer, as the gallery charges as much as Sfr10 (Sfr7 for students) for admission, or more if there's a special exhibition. Opening hours are Friday to Sunday from 10 am to 5 pm between early April and the beginning of November. Take the boat from the departure ramp or bus No 1 from Lugano.

Five minutes' walk east is the **Museum of Extra-European Cultures** (Museo delle Culture Extraeuropee), Via Cortivo. It lacks signs in English, but the statues, fertility symbols, masks and photographs are extremely evocative of ancient tribal life-

styles without needing words. Entry costs Sfr5 (Sfr3 for students), and it's open Tuesday to Sunday from 10 am to 5 pm. If you walk back from Gandria (see the Lake Lugano section) you pass by this museum.

The **Cantonal Art Museum** (Museo cantonale d'Arte), Via Canova 10, has a worthwhile modern art collection from the 19th and 20th centuries. Ticinese artists are well represented. It costs Sfr7 (students Sfr5) to get in, or Sfr10 (Sfr5) if there's a special exhibition. Opening times are Wednesday to Sunday from 10 am to 5 pm, and Tuesday from 2 pm to 5 pm. More contemporary art is at the **Modern Art Museum** (Museo d'Arte Moderna), Riva Antonio Caccia 5, towards Paradiso (Sfr8; closed Monday). You can walk or take bus Nos 1 or 9 from Piazza Rezzonico.

The **Alpenrose Chocolate Museum**, Via Rompada, Casalano, gives a rundown of the history of chocolate and its manufacturing process. Visitors can view production in the factory from an elevated walkway. It is open daily from 9 am to 7 pm (5 pm on weekends). Get there by the Ferrovia Ponte Tresa.

Activities

The Lido, just east of the Cassarate River, offers a swimming pool and sandy beaches for Sfr6 a day, and it's open daily from 1 May to mid-September, from 9 am to at least 6 pm.

Places where you can water-ski, sail and windsurf are listed in the official guide; prices are given. The cheapest place for windsurfing is the Club Nautico Sassalto (☎ 606 12 45), Caslano, where two hours costs Sfr10. Caslano is reached by the Ferrovia Ponte Tresa. Pedalos near the boat landing stage can be pedalled for Sfr16 an hour or Sfr8 for 30 minutes.

Courses

The Migros scuola club (☎ 922 76 21), for languages and other courses, is in the same building as the supermarket at Via Pretorio 15.

Special Events

Primavera Concertistica is a series of classical music concerts held during April and May. They are performed in the Palazzo dei Congressi, in the Parco Civico. Tickets cost Sfr20 to Sfr80, with reductions for students and seniors. Enquire at the tourist office. Free open-air **music festivals** are the Estival Jazz in early July and the Blues to Bop and Worldmusic Festival at the end of August. In late July there is a spectacular fireworks display over Lake Lugano.

Places to Stay – bottom end

Camping There are five camp sites by the arm of the lake that loops up near Agno airport. All are open from approximately Easter to the end of October. The Ferrovia Ponte Tresa train from in front of the main station gets you to the vicinity. The cheapest site is *Golfo del Sole*, (☎ 605 48 02), costing Sfr7 per adult, from Sfr7 per tent, and Sfr2 for a car. *La Piodella* (☎ 994 77 88), has many more facilities, is only marginally more expensive and is open year-round. It's south-west of Lugano in Muzzano, reached by postbus, but it's not by the lake.

Hostel The relaxed SYHA *hostel* (☎ 966 27 28), Via Cantonale 13, is a hard 20 minutes' walk uphill from the train station (signposted), or else bus No 5 to Crocifisso (Sfr1.70). Beds are Sfr15 plus (if required) Sfr2 for sheets and Sfr6 for breakfast. There are also private rooms from Sfr20 to Sfr38 per person. It's a refreshing family-run place, with classical music wafting through the reception and breakfast area, CNN (the American news channel) on the TV, and its own extensive grounds, including an outdoor swimming pool. Pity about that 10 pm curfew, though. Reception is shut from noon to 3 pm and but the dorms stay open throughout the day. The hostel closes from 31 October to late March.

Hotels Around the back of the train station is *Hotel Montarina* (☎ 966 72 72), Via Montarina 1, in a pleasant building with a garden. It's less friendly than the hostel but it's more convenient and there's no daytime closing or curfew. Beds in large dorms are Sfr20, plus Sfr2 for sheets. Singles/doubles are Sfr40/80 and triples/quads are Sfr111/148, all with a sink in the room. Singles/doubles with own shower/WC are Sfr50/100. Prices are without breakfast. Reception is until 9 pm and the hotel is closed from 31 October to about two weeks before Easter. Out of the centre (take bus No 5) is *Romano*, Via San Gottardo 103, Massagno, a simple place with rooms for only Sfr38/76.

Hotel Ristorante Pestalozzi (☎ 921 46 46), Piazza Indipendenza 9, has singles/doubles/triples for Sfr88/138/190 with own shower/WC or Sfr54/96/125 without. The top (fourth) floor has newer rooms in a modern, minimalist style; rooms on other floors combine old, solid brown furniture with modern features. There's a lift.

Hotel Zurigo (☎ 923 43 43), Corso Pestalozzi 13, is not quite as good a deal but is also conveniently central and has plenty of parking. Singles/doubles/triples are functional and cost Sfr95/140/169 with private shower and toilet, though there are also doubles with shower only for Sfr100 and singles using hall shower for Sfr60. The hotel is closed in December and January.

Around the bay in Paradiso is *Victoria au Lac* (☎ 994 20 31), Via General Guisan 3, which sometimes has space when places in town are full. Take bus No 1 from Riva G Albertolli. It's old-fashioned and atmospheric; singles/doubles are Sfr65/110, or Sfr95/138 with shower. Parking is no problem, and it's open from 1 April to 31 October. The basement cabaret club is not part of the hotel.

Places to Stay – middle

Hôtel Walter au Lac (☎ 922 74 25), Piazza Rezzonico 7, is centrally situated near Piazza Riforma (closed February). Attractive singles/doubles with TV and big bathrooms are Sfr106/177. Near the station is *Hotel*

TICINO

Continental (☎ 966 11 12), Via Basilea 28, with large if plainish rooms from Sfr98/160, with the same amenities. It closes in winter and manages Beauregard, a cheaper annexe (Sfr80/160), as well as Montarina (mentioned above). Along the road, *Albatro* (☎ 921 09 21), Via Clemente Maraini 8, is a new hotel with garage parking, an outside pool, and air-con rooms for Sfr145/180.

Places to Stay – top end
In four-star hotels, you tend to get more facilities for your money in Paradiso rather than in Lugano itself. *Admiral* (☎ 994 23 24; fax 994 25 48), Via Geretta 15, near the Paradiso funicular, has large, standardised rooms decked out in shades of blue. The indoor and roof-top swimming pools and the fitness room are free for guests but the massage and sauna cost extra. Singles/doubles start at Sfr180/275.

Places to Eat
Self-Service There is a large *Migros* supermarket and restaurant on Via Pretorio. The restaurant is on the 5th floor and is open to 8 pm from Monday to Saturday. It has a salad and dessert buffet, as well as main meals from Sfr6. An *EPA* self-service restaurant in the department store is similarly priced and can be found on Via Nassa at Piazzetta San Carlo. It has late opening till 9 pm on Thursday.

Cheap to Mid-Price Restaurants Any number of restaurants around town offer pizza and pasta; many have outside tables. *Ristorante Cantinone* on Piazza Cioccaro has a large selection of good-sized pizzas from Sfr10.50 and is open daily from 9 am to midnight. Up the stairs from the piazza is *Ristorante Inova*, a buffet-style place where the food is cooked in front of you. An excellent deal is the pizza or pasta for Sfr9.90 where you can select the ingredients for the sauce yourself from the counter. Salad plates are Sfr4.20 to Sfr10.50, and it's open daily to 10 pm.

Also good and cheap for Italian and vegetarian food is *Hotel Restaurant Pestalozzi* (see Places to Stay), open daily from 6 am to 10 pm. It's an alcohol-free restaurant with a wide choice of daily specials from Sfr8.50 to Sfr16, sometimes including soup.

Across Piazza Cioccaro from Ristorante Cantinone is the large *Sayonara*. It has the usual pizza/pasta, as well as local dishes such as polenta from Sfr11 to Sfr35. *La Tinèra*, Via dei Gorini, off Piazza della Riforma, has a typical Ticinese ambience and meals for Sfr11 to Sfr25. Local wines start at Sfr24 a bottle. It's not unusual to have to queue before you can be seated (closed on Sunday).

In Paradiso, the *Ristorante Bar Paradiso*, on Via San Salvatore by the funicular station, offers pasta, including cannelloni and gnocchi from Sfr11.50, and meat and fish dishes from Sfr20. Middle of the road music tinkles in the background, except on Sunday when it's closed.

Expensive Restaurants Eating in Lugano can be a superb if wallet-withering experience. *Bianchi* (☎ 922 84 79), Via Pessina 3, is opposite the elegant shops in the old town and is suitably elegant itself. Waiters dressed in black hover like vultures in reverse – waiting to dispense rather than devour the feast. Main courses are around Sfr35 to Sfr45 (closed Sunday). Similarly priced is the ultimately civilised *Galleria* (☎ 923 62 88) at Via Vegezzi 4, where *sotto voce* waiters whisper over soft music (closed Sunday and Monday).

Also excellent (they're both high up in Switzerland's 'top 100') and similarly expensive are *Santabbondio* – (☎ 993 23 88), Via Fomelino 10, Sorengo, near Agno airport (closed Saturday lunch, Sunday evening, and Monday), and *Al Portone* (☎ 923 55 11), Viale Cassarate 3 (closed Sunday and Monday).

Entertainment
Lugano has plenty of options for a night out although not much within reach of the budget traveller. The tourist office has a list

of discos, nightclubs and piano bars. *B'52*, Via al Forte, is a late-night disco bar (closed Monday). The *Casinò Kursaal* on Via Stauffacher, has dancing, drinking, gambling and a cinema.

Getting There & Away

Agno airport has Crossair flights nonstop to/from Basel, Bern, Geneva and Zürich, with departures several times a day. There are also direct connections to Rome and Munich. Crossair can be contacted on ☎ 604 50 01.

Lugano is on the same road and rail route as Bellinzona. To St Moritz, two postbuses run (daily in summer; only Friday, Saturday and Sunday winter). It costs Sfr54 (plus a Sfr5 supplement, not covered by Swiss travel passes) and takes four hours. You need to reserve your seat the day before at the bus station, the train information office in the train station, or by phoning ☎ 807 95 20. All postbuses leave from the main bus depot at Via Serafino Balestra, but you can pick up the St Moritz bus and many others outside the train station five minutes later.

For further train and boat information see the Bellinzona and Lake Lugano sections.

Car Rental On Via San Gottardo is Hertz (☎ 923 46 75) at No 13 and Europcar (☎ 967 47 65) at No 101. Avis (☎ 922 62 56) is at Via Clemente Maraini 8. Down the road at No 14 is Budget (☎ 994 17 19), located with a local operator, Sud (☎ 994 98 73). International companies have airport offices.

Getting Around

Getting to the airport involves taking the small train in front of the train station, the Ferrovia Ponte Tresa (every 20 to 30 minutes), getting off at Agno, and walking for 10 minutes. The same train goes to the chocolate museum and Caslano; the Swiss Pass is valid, city travel passes aren't. A taxi from the town centre to the airport costs around Sfr25 to Sfr30.

Pick up a bus map from the tourist office. A single trip costs Sfr0.90 to Sfr1.70 (ticket dispensers indicate the appropriate rate) or it's only Sfr4.40 for a one-day pass. Weekly passes are available from transport offices. The Lugano Region pass (see Getting Around at the beginning of the chapter) is valid on the funiculars up to San Salvatore and Mt Brè. It also gets 25% off the trip up to Mt Generoso, as does the Swiss Pass.

Long-term parking is a problem in town – even parking garages usually have a two-hour limit, though Autosilo Central Park on Riva Vela has a 12-hour maximum (Sfr2 per hour). Alternatively, park for free at the Cornaredo sports stadium in the north and take bus No 3 into town.

Call ☎ 971 21 21 or ☎ 971 91 91 for a taxi.

AROUND LUGANO

The tourist office has free guides detailing walks of up to three hours' duration heading south along the lake, or north towards Locarno. Touring the lake itself by boat is an unmissable pleasure on a sunny day (see the following section). Also unmissable – quite literally – are the two peaks soaring over the town, **Monte San Salvatore** and **Monte Brè**. Lugano has dubbed itself the 'Rio de Janeiro of the Old Continent' for the resemblance that Monte San Salvatore (912m) bears to Rio's Sugarloaf Mountain. The funicular from Paradiso up Monte San Salvatore operates from mid-March to mid-November only and costs Sfr11 to go up or Sfr17 return. From the top you get an excellent perspective of the meandering contours of the lake. The walk down takes a little over an hour back to Paradiso or Melide.

Monte Brè (925m) offers a clearer view of the curve of the bay round Lugano. To ascend the peak, you can take the funicular from Cassarate which costs Sfr12 to go up or Sfr18 return; it runs year-round though it's often closed for maintenance in January. A cheaper way to get up Monte Brè is to drive, or take bus No 12 from the main post office to Brè village, and walk about 15 minutes from there.

TICINO

Lake Lugano

There are many points of interest around the lake, easily visited on a day tour if you don't fancy a longer excursion. Boats are operated by the Società Navigazione del Lago di Lugano (☎ 971 52 23). Examples of return fares from Lugano are Gandria (Sfr16), Melide (Sfr16) and Morcote (Sfr24). If you want to visit several places, buy a pass: one day costs Sfr32, three days costs Sfr51 and one week costs Sfr58. There are reduced fares for children, but they go free if you have a Family Card.

The departure point from Lugano is by the Piazza della Riforma. Boats sail year-round, but the service is more frequent and extensive from the end of May to late October. The Swiss Pass is valid and the Half-Fare Card gets reductions.

GANDRIA

Gandria is an attractive village where the houses tumble down the hill right to the water's edge. Piers and boathouses, with small craft dangling from pulleys, stand in lieu of garages as no cars can get near most of these houses; only alleys and stairways separate the compact dwellings. A popular round trip is to take the boat from Lugano and to walk back along the shore to Castagnola (around 40 minutes), where you can visit the Villa Favorita, or simply continue back to Lugano by foot or bus No 1.

From Gandria, take the path by the church. A few minutes after leaving the village you reach a small cove where the main road can be seen winding its own course above. The bare rock here reveals striking patterns in its curved fault lines.

There are a couple of hotels in Gandria. Next to the boat landing stage awaits *Miralago* (☎ 971 43 61), open from 1 April to 31 October. Accommodation costs Sfr76 for compact doubles with sink, available as singles in low season for Sfr48. The restaurant (open daily) offers spaghetti for around Sfr16, and meat dishes ranging from simple cutlets (Sfr18.50) to giant fillets (Sfr78 for two).

Across the lake from Gandria is the **Customs Museum**, at Cantine di Gandria, accessible by boat. It tells the story of the development of customs in the area, using documents, dummies, and confiscated exhibits. An interesting section reveals the ploys used by smugglers over the years. Common tricks include false-bottomed shoes, hollowed out books and modified fuel tanks.

The museum is open from 31 March to late October, daily from 1.30 to 5.30 pm, and entry is free. As there are only minimal notes in English you can get around in 30 to 40 minutes.

CAMPIONE D'ITALIA

This really is part of Italy – a forgotten anomaly surrounded by Switzerland. It's not immediately obvious you're in another country: there are no border formalities, nearly all the cars in the village have Swiss number plates and they still use Swiss francs and Swiss telephones. Not everything is the same, though – the post boxes are red, not yellow as in Switzerland, and the policemen and police cars bear Italian livery. But the main difference is in the gambling laws: there are none of those Swiss restrictions so the casino does brisk business especially, ironically, with Swiss visitors. It is open daily from 3.30 pm (1.30 pm for the slot machines) to around 2 am and smart dress is required for entry. In the evening there is a special bus service from Piazza Rezzonico in Lugano to the casino (Sfr6 each way; travel passes not valid). The casino might lose its appeal when the liberalisation of the Swiss gambling regulations comes into effect (no fixed date yet).

There are no customs formalities, but it is a wise precaution to take your passport. The tourist office (☎ 649 50 51) and the post office are opposite each other. From the boat landing stage, go slightly to the right and about 50m up the hill.

If you want to eat lunch in Italy, there's the *Bar-Pizzeria Rally Club* right next to the boat landing stage, with pizza starting at Sfr11 and other reasonably-priced snacks and meals (closed Wednesday). They want Swiss money but you know you're not in Switzerland when you go to the 'gents' and find a squat-over-the-hole lavatory instead of the usual pristine Swiss porcelain with electronic sensors. Those seeking more elegance and higher quality (and prices) can saunter across the road to *Ristorante Taverna*, also closed Wednesday.

MONTE GENEROSO

The panorama provided by this summit (1701m) includes the lakes, the Alps, and even the Apennines on a clear day. It can be reached by taking the boat, train or car to Capolago, and then the funicular (approximately hourly, Sfr30 up or Sfr42 return, with reductions for children). The funicular and the boat only operate from around the beginning of April to early November.

CERESIO

• ☎ (091)

This is the area south of Lugano, a peninsula created by the looping shoreline of Lake Lugano. There are walking trails dissecting the interior and small villages dotting the lakeside. The tourist office in Melide (☎ 649 63 83), Via Pocobelli 14, covers the whole region. Opening hours are Monday to Friday from 8 am to noon and 2 to 6 pm, and from Easter to October also on Saturday from 9 am to noon.

There is a SYHA *hostel* (☎ 995 11 51), in Casaro, Fignio, open from 1 March to late October. Dorm beds cost Sfr24, and there are cooking facilities. It's near the postbus stop, and boats call at Fignio in the summer. The postbus from Lugano to Morcote goes via either Melide or Fignio, and departs approximately hourly. Year-round boats also connect Morcote and Melide to Lugano.

Some of the roads in Ceresio afford excellent views, particularly the upper road from Melide to Lugano, passing through **Carona** at 602m. Carona (hourly postbus from Lugano) is also a suitable starting point for a number of hikes.

Melide

Melide is on the bulge of the shore from which the N2 motorway slices across the lake. The main attraction of this village is **Swissminiatur** (☎ 640 10 60), where you'll find 1:25 scale models of over 100 national attractions. Children and adults can spend a great couple of hours wandering around the faithfully reproduced replicas. The models are so good that it can help you decide if you want to go on to see the real thing, and there are many boats, cable cars and trains whizzing about the place to complete the picture.

The park is open from mid-March to the end of October, daily from 9 am to 6 pm. If the weather is fine it may also open in the afternoons from November to mid-December. Admission costs Sfr10.50 for adults and Sfr6 for children, and the programme for Sfr2 is essential as there are no other signs. Take advantage of the cheap self-service restaurant inside, or the supermarket by the car park. Boats stop right outside in the summer only.

Places to Stay & Eat *Brandner Garni* (☎ 649 86 02), Via Pocobelli 19, near the tourist office, has a Mediterranean look and singles/doubles for Sfr45 per person (closed in winter). *Al Boccalino* (☎ 649 77 67), Via Borromini 27, is back from the lake. It provides comfortable rooms with shower and toilet for Sfr75 per person in summer and Sfr40 in winter. There's a typical Ticinese restaurant, which is closed on Thursday in winter.

Giardino (☎ 649 79 97) Lungolago G Motta, is an Italian restaurant with many varieties of pizza from Sfr10 (open daily). It has a few rooms using hall shower for Sfr40 per person. Opposite is *Hotel Del Lago* (☎ 649 70 41), at No 9, offering mid-price rooms and meals.

Morcote

This photogenic fishing village clusters at the foot of Monte Abostora. It is graced with well-preserved arcaded houses and quaint alleyways. Narrow stairways lead up to the church of **Santa Maria del Sasso**, a 15-minute climb. The views are excellent, and the church itself has frescoes (16th century), busts of bishops, and carved faces on the organ. Nearby, the cemetery is typically Italian in the way that the faces of the deceased are displayed amid bouquets at their final resting place.

In the village is the **Parco Scherrer**, offering an eclectic collection of architectural styles from around the world, including copies of famous buildings and generic types (eg Temple of Nefertiti, Siamese tea-house). It's all set in subtropical parkland, open 15 March to 31 October, daily between 9 am and 5 pm. Admission costs Sfr7 (students Sfr5, children Sfr1).

By the boat landing stage is a covered arcade where shops offer souvenirs and unusual odds and ends. The walk along the shore to Melide takes around 50 minutes.

Places to Stay & Eat Morcote lacks a budget hotel. The cheapest rooms are at *Oasi* (☎ 996 14 97), open mid-March to 31 October. Singles/doubles are Sfr60/120 with a shower cubicle or Sfr50/100 without. The small café has Ticinese dishes starting at Sfr13. It's not far from the boat landing stage

in the direction of Melide. A little farther on is the *Coop* (early closing on Wednesday).

Della Posta (☎ 996 11 27), right by the post office, has rooms with private shower/WC and TV for about Sfr95/140. It is also a reasonable place to eat, with pizza and pasta starting at Sfr13 and meat and fish dishes around Sfr30. It has the advantage of a sunny 1st-floor terrace and a section on the edge of the lake. The restaurant is open daily but closed from November to March. There are plenty of other restaurants queuing for your custom along the quayside, including some cheap places within the shopping arcade.

MENDRISIO

South of Lake Lugano is Mendrisiotto and Lower Ceresio. It is a fine area for walking tours around the rolling valleys and unspoilt villages. Mendrisio is the district capital (population 6500) and has a tourist office (☎ 646 57 61). It has several interesting old churches and buildings, and is especially worth a visit for the Maundy Thursday Procession or the Wine Harvest in September.

MERIDE

The Fossil Museum in Meride, to the north-west of Mendrisio, displays vestiges of the first creatures to inhabit the region – reptiles and fish dating back 200 million years. The museum is open daily from 8 am to 6 pm (free entry). Near the town is a circular nature trail, complete with periodic information panels.

Locarno

* *pop 15,000* * *205m* * *☎ (091)*

Locarno lies at the northern end of Lake Maggiore and is Switzerland's lowest town. Tourist literature trumpets that it enjoys the country's sunniest climate (2000 hours per year) though several other towns, especially in Valais, make the same claim. Locarno achieved prominence when it hosted the 1925 Peace Conference which intended to bring stability to Europe in the aftermath of WWI.

Orientation & Information

The train station has money-exchange counters (open daily from 6 am to 8.40 pm) and bike rental (daily from 8 am to 7 pm; returns later by arrangement). A few minutes to the west is the core of the town, Piazza Grande. The tourist office (☎ 751 03 33) is here at Largo Zorzi, through the same entrance as the Casino Theatro. It has brochures on many parts of Switzerland and detailed information on the Lake Maggiore region. Various guided tours are offered through the tourist office, such as to Milan (Sfr65), Venice (Sfr100), and Ticino's northern valleys. Opening hours are Monday to Friday from 8 am to 7 pm, and Saturday and Sunday from 9 am to noon and 1 to 5 pm. From around November to March hours reduce to weekdays only from 8 am to noon and 2 to 6 pm.

Piazza Grande also has the main post office (Posta 1, 6600), a shopping arcade and cafés with outside tables. North and west of the piazza is the old part of town *(città vecchia)*, where the streets are small, sometimes confusing, and often pedestrian-only. The hospital (ospedale; ☎ 756 71 11) on Via Castelrotto has a casualty department.

Madonna del Sasso

This sanctuary overlooks the town and lake from a prominent position on the hillside. It was built after the Virgin Mary appeared in a vision to a monk, Bartolomeo d'Ivrea, in 1480. There's a small museum (Sfr2.50, children and students Sfr1.50), a church (chiesa) and several very distinctive statue groups on the stairway. The best-known painting in the church is *La Fuga in Egitto* (Flight to Egypt) (1522) by Bramantino. Also don't miss *Il Transporto al Sepolcro* by Antonio Ciseri (1821-91), with the haunting, mournful face of the central bearer. His silent grief comes across with all the greater intensity for being juxtaposed with the melodramatic swoonings of the women behind him (no matter if one of the women is Mary herself).

Something of a contrast in style are the many naive votive paintings by the church entrance, where the Madonna and Child appear as ghostly apparitions in life-and-death situations.

There is a funicular from the town centre to the sanctuary (Sfr6 return), but the 20-minute walk up is not demanding (take Via al Sasso off Via Cappuccini). At least take the walk down, as you pass some ancient shrines on the way. On the Via Crucis route you're accompanied by the Stations of the Cross.

Old Town

Explore the Italianate piazzas and arcades, and admire the Lombardic houses. At one time the Piazza Grande curved round the actual shoreline of the lake. There are several interesting churches. The 17th century **Chiesa Nuova** on Via Cittadella, has an ornate ceiling complete with frolicking angels, and outside a giant St Christopher with disproportionately tiny feet Peer into the decaying, arcaded courtyard adjoining the east side of the church. The **Sant' Antonio** has paintings by Orelli, as does the **San Francesco Chiesa**.

Off Piazza Grande is the **Castello Visconti**, dating from the 15th century and now housing a museum with Roman and Bronze Age exhibits, and modern art (Sfr5, open Tuesday to Sunday from 10 am to noon and 2 to 5 pm). Locarno was believed to be a glass manufacturing town in Roman times, which accounts for the strong showing of glass artefacts in the museum.

Activities

From the sanctuary, a cable car flies up to **Cardada** (Sfr22 return), and thereafter a chair lift soars to **Cimetta** (Sfr27 combined return fare) at 1672m. The Swiss Pass gets a piffling Sfr2 reduction, the Half-Fare Card gets nothing. From either stop there are fine views and several walking trails, and the transport up runs year round; a day pass for winter skiing is Sfr30. Paragliding is possible up here – enquire at the tourist office.

Locarno's climate is perfect for strolls round the lake. Wisteria, mimosa, azaleas,

TICINO

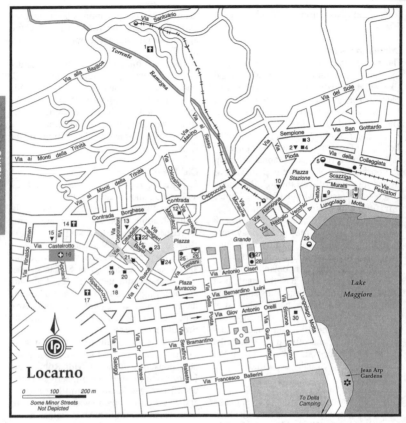

Locarno

0   100   200 m

Some Minor Streets
Not Depicted

PLACES TO STAY
3   Hotel Stazione
4   Hotel Garni
    Montaldi
9   Hotel Ristorante
    Zurigo
12 Pensione Città
    Vecchia
19 Schloss Hotel &
    Visconti
20 Ostello Giaciglio
21 Osteria Reginetta
30 Hotel Arcadia
    al Lago

PLACES TO EAT
2   La Carbonara
8   Ristorante
    Centenario
10 Ristorante Inova
13 Ristorante Cittadella
15 Trattoria Campagna
    Ristorante

OTHER
1   Madonna del Sasso
5   Bus Departures
6   Train Station
7   Postbus Office
11 Funicular Station

14 St Antonio Church
16 Hospital
17 San Francesco
    Church
18 Castello Visconti
22 Nuova Church
23 Coop Supermarket
24 Bar Cantina
25 Sopra Cenerina
    (Conference Centre)
26 Main Post Office
27 Tourist Office
28 Casinò Kursaal
29 Boat Departures &
    Ticket Office

camellias and magnolias bloom as early as March. **Giardini Jean Arp** (Jean Arp Gardens) is a small lakeside park off Lungolago Motta, where sculptures by the surrealist artist are scattered among the palm trees and tulips. It is free to swim in various convenient spots around the lake, though you have to pay at the Lido. Sailing is another popular activity; the tourist office has a list of hiring outlets.

International Film Festival

Locarno has hosted this festival since 1948, and every year it gets bigger and better-known – it received 150,000 visitors in 1995. Cinemas are used during the day, but at night films are shown in the open-air on a giant screen in the Piazza Grande (admission fee). It takes place over two weeks in August. Get advance information from the Festival Internazionale de Film (☎ 751 02 32; fax 751 74 65), Via della Posta 6, CH-6600 Locarno.

Places to Stay

Ask the tourist for the 'Hotels Special' leaflet, outlining discounts and benefits if you book six nights at participating two-star hotels (Sfr480/780 for a single/double with own shower/WC). There are hotel boards with a free telephone at the train station and outside the tourist office. A new SYHA *hostel* is to open in spring 1997; enquire at the tourist office.

Places to Stay – bottom

Camping *Delta Camping* (☎ 751 60 81) is very expensive at Sfr20 (Sfr30 in high season) minimum per site plus Sfr9 (Sfr12) per person. But it is a five-star site with copious facilities, and it's open from late March to mid-October.

Hostels There are two non-SYHA hostels in the old town. *Pensione Città Vecchia* (☎ 751 45 54), Via Toretta 13, is the best. Beds in varying-sized dorms (from three beds) are Sfr22, plus Sfr4.50 each if you require sheets or breakfast. Both are provided with the few singles/doubles at Sfr33 per person (hall showers). Check-in is from 1 to 6 pm (or later

by arrangement) and keys are available. It is open from 1 March to sometime in November; reserve ahead (by telephone is OK) at peak times. *Ostello Giaciglio* (☎ 751 30 64), Via Rustica 7, is expensive at Sfr30 without breakfast in sometimes cramped dorms, but at least it has a kitchen and is open year-round. Enquire at Garni Sempione opposite for reception.

Hotels Opposite the station is *Garni Montaldi* (☎ 743 02 22), Piazza Stazione. Renovated singles/doubles with telephone and cable TV cost from Sfr60/120 with shower, Sfr83/140 with shower/WC, or Sfr52/104 without. It's particularly good value in the low season when they often give the best rooms for the lowest price (closed in January). Reception is also here for *Stazione*, an older building to the rear, which is closed from 1 November to 31 March. It has singles/doubles with shower for Sfr40/80. *Osteria Reginetta* (☎ 752 35 53), Via della Motta 8, has singles/doubles/triples for Sfr39 per person, or Sfr45 including breakfast. Rooms are cheerful and reasonably spacious, and there's a shower/WC on each floor.

Places to Stay – middle

Schloss Hotel (☎ 751 23 61), Via B Rusca in the old town, is a place with character and a slightly regal air, in its own grounds with private parking. All rooms are different but have shower/WC and (usually) TV as standard. Prices start at Sfr65/104, rising to Sfr95/154 in summer. It's open from mid-March to 31 October.

Hotel Ristorante Zurigo (☎ 743 16 17), Viale Verbano 9, offers comfortable accommodation by the lake. Gold-coloured metal bedsteads, tastefully arranged pictures and patterned tiled floors give the rooms some style. Prices start at Sfr87/124 for a single/double in winter, rising to Sfr147/184 in summer. All rooms have cable TV and private shower/toilet, but rooms with lake view are more expensive. The restaurant serves good, low to mid-price food, with a couple of vegetarian choices.

TICINO

TICINO

Places to Stay – top end

Hotel Arcadia al Lago (☎ 751 02 82; fax 751 53 08), Via Orelli 5, is a four-star family hotel overlooking the lake (closed 1 November to late February). It has modern spacious rooms, all with large balcony, satellite TV, private bathroom, mini bar, and telephone. Prices start at Sfr165/284 for single/double occupancy and there are larger apartments suitable for families. The hotel has a roof terrace and an outdoor swimming pool.

Places to Eat

Lake Maggiore yields many different varieties of fish, particularly perch (persico) and whitefish (corigone).

There is *a Coop* supermarket on Piazza Grande with a deli counter. A branch of *Inova* awaits on Via Stazione 1, by the train station, which opens daily to 10 pm. See the Lugano entry for more on this buffet-style restaurant.

The popular *Trattoria Campagna Ristorante* (☎ 751 99 47), on Via Castelrotto near St Antonio Church, has a piatto del giorno (dish of the day) for Sfr14, and pizza and pasta from Sfr11. It is closed Sunday evening, and open until midnight on other days. There are plenty of other places where you can eat cheaply and well on pizza and pasta, such as at *La Carbonara* (from Sfr9) by the station.

The place to go for fish specialities is *Ristorante Cittadella* (☎ 751 58 85), Via Cittadella 18 – its upstairs section serves nothing else. Main dishes are around Sfr30 to Sfr45, although downstairs you can also tuck into pizzas from Sfr11.50 (closed Monday). The *Locanda Visconti* restaurant of the Schloss Hotel (see Places to Stay) is atmospheric, with lunches and pasta for around Sfr15, and other main courses starting at around Sfr25 (closed Sunday).

For a gastronomic feast, where the food is served on sparkling silver salvers, go to *Ristorante Centenario* (☎ 743 82 22), Lungolago 17. It's widely acknowledged as the best restaurant in Ticino, but the prices might make you flavour its French cuisine with the salt of your own tears. Three small courses in the business lunch cost Sfr52,

multi-course evening menus are Sfr80 to Sfr140, and à-la-carte dining is around Sfr40 to Sfr55. The restaurant is closed on Sunday and Monday.

Entertainment

The *Casinò Kursaal* by the tourist office offers a choice of theatre, cinema, gambling (Boule and slot machines) and drinking. Classical concerts are held at the Castello Visconti and the Sopra Cenerina conference centre on Piazza Grande, but especially in the atmospheric environment of the San Francesco church. The tourist office sells tickets for most venues.

Bar Cantina on Piazza Grande has a large selection of different wines stacked up on the shelves and cheap, simple meals at lunchtime. On Friday and Saturday night there's live music of a dance-along accordion-based variety. It attracts a range of ages but particularly an older set, and somehow veers between the authentic and the excruciating. Wine costs from Sfr1.90 a glass.

Getting There & Away

Train There are trains every two hours from Brig, passing through Italy en route. The cost is Sfr48 and it takes around three hours. You change trains at Domodossola across the border, so bring your passport.

Bus Postbuses to the surrounding valleys leave from outside the train station, and there is a postbus ticket and information booth by platform one.

Car The St Gotthard pass provides the road link (N2) to central Switzerland. Hertz (☎ 743 50 50) is at Via Sempione 12. Avis (☎ 791 44 55) is at Via Cantonale in Ascona.

Boat Boats depart from near Piazza Grande, including to Italy. See Lake Maggiore for more information.

Getting Around

There are parking spaces at Piazza Grande, on the square (Sfr2.50 for a maximum one hour) or in the underground garage (Sfr18 for 24 hours). Local buses, including to Ascona, are run by Fart (that's the company name, not the means of propulsion). This unsavoury epithet is well deserved as the company has the cheek to charge for its schedules. Single trips cost Sfr2.40 or Sfr2.80, or it's Sfr5.60 for a day pass. The Swiss Pass is valid.

AROUND LOCARNO
Lake Maggiore

Only the north-east corner of Lake Maggiore is in Switzerland; the rest slices into the Lombardy region of Italy. Navigazione Lago Maggiore (NLM; ☎ 751 18 65) operates boats across the whole lake. Limited day passes cost Sfr10, but the Sfr19 version (Sfr15 for people over 60) is valid for all the Swiss basin, and is also available for seven days (Sfr42). The Sfr33 pass (Sfr66 for seven days) covers the Italian section too. Boats sail from around early April to late October, though there are special services during March to Italy, eg to the Wednesday market in Luino (Sfr23 return from Locarno) and the Sunday market in Cannobio (Sfr21 return). In addition to the steamers, hydrofoils (reservations essential, Sfr2) go to the Italian resorts. Services extend as far as Arona (Sfr33 one way) in the south, where there's an antiques market on the third Sunday of each month. The only car ferry across the lake is in Italy, from Intra to Laveno. The Swiss Pass is not valid on any boats. NLM produces a free brochure in English describing all the Swiss and Italian lakeside resorts.

South-west of Ascona are the **Isles of Brissago**, famous for the botanical gardens (Sfr6, open early April to late September) where subtropical flora thrive. The boat trip costs Sfr9.60 each way (children half-price) from Locarno, or Sfr5 if you embark at Ascona. **Ronco**, beautifully situated opposite the islands, is a great drive from Locarno. The trip by Fart bus (No 21) takes 20 minutes. This region is best known for cigar manufacturing. Ask the local tourist office (☎ 793 11 70) if free tours of the cigar factory have started up again.

Ascona

Ascona is Locarno's smaller twin on the opposite side of the delta of the Maggiore River. The village is known as a centre for arts, and the backstreets are filled with art galleries and craft shops. The beginning of the century saw the arrival of 'back to nature' utopians and anarchists, and the aspirations of this movement is the subject of the **Casa Anatta Museum** on Monte Verità (take bus No 33 from the post office). It's open April to October, every afternoon except Monday (Sfr5, students and seniors Sfr3). **Museo comunale d'arte moderna** in the Palazzo Pancaldi, Via Borgo 34, includes paintings by artists connected with the town, among them Paul Klee, Hans Arp, Ben Nicholson and Alexej Jawlensky. The museum is open Tuesday to Saturday from 10 am to noon and 3 to 6 pm, and Sunday from 10 am to noon, and entry costs Sfr3.

For over 50 years Ascona has hosted **Settimane Musicali**, an international classical music festival lasting from the end of August to early October. It also has **Festa New Orleans**, a jazz festival at the end of June where musicians play from several open-air stages (Sfr5 general entry per night).

The Ascona tourist office (☎ 791 00 90), Casa Serodine, is by the church tower near the waterfront. Opening hours are daily from 9 am to 6.30 pm (6 pm Saturday, 2 pm Sunday), reducing to weekdays only in winter.

Places to Stay & Eat The waterfront is one long parade of mid-price hotels and restaurants with outside tables. Al Porto (☎ 791 13 21) is typical of these, with singles/ doubles for Sfr98/214 or Sfr120/234 with lake view. Rooms have private shower, toilet, TV and direct-dial telephone, and are located in four different buildings. The restaurant has meals for Sfr16 to Sfr30, encompassing pasta, meat, fish and vegetarian choices. Al Porto is closed in January, and the restaurant only is closed on Monday and Tuesday during winter.

TICINO

Garni Silvia (☎ 35 13 14), Via Circonvallazione 7, back from the lake, has large, fresh rooms with hall showers and there's plenty of foliage on the stairway to keep you company. Singles/doubles start at Sfr50/90, plus Sfr5 per person for a single night's stay (closed January and February). Down the road towards the post office is a *Coop* supermarket.

Getting There & Away From Locarno, take bus No 31 from the train station or Piazza Grande; it stops at Ascona post office with departures every 15 minutes (Sfr2.40). Boat services on Lake Maggiore stop at Ascona.

Northern Valleys

The two valleys north of Locarno are dead-ends, but they make enjoyable day trips and allow you to explore areas relatively untainted by tourism. Take refreshment in rustic *grotti* (country inns). Both the Maggia and Verzasca valleys can be visited on a weekly tour (Sfr35) from mid-March to the end of October; reserve at the Locarno tourist office.

All these northern valleys proffer scenic delights, although the minor road winding over the San Bernardino is perhaps the most spectacular (closed from November to May). The motorway is open year-round.

Maggia Valley
Valle Maggia follows the Maggia River, passing small villages, until at Cevio it splits, the first of many divisions into smaller valleys. Take the left branch then a right into the valley that terminates at **Bosco Gurin**. This village was settled by folk from the Valais in the 12th century, and it is the only place in Ticino where German is the principal language spoken. Fart bus No 10 runs

hourly from Locarno to Cevio (takes 50 minutes), but the postbus is less frequent for the 50-minute trip on to Bosco Gurin. The total same day return fare is Sfr30 (available in the summer only); if you stay overnight the fare leaps to Sfr43.20.

Verzasca Valley
Val Verzasca is wilder and less developed than Valle Maggia. **Brione**, where the valley forks, has a castle and a 14th century church. The right-hand fork goes to **Sonogno**, noted for its simple, stone-built houses. Postbuses run from Locarno only every two hours or so; the journey takes 70 minutes and costs Sfr30 return.

Cento Valley
Centovalli (literally 'a hundred valleys'), heading west, is the route to Domodossola in Italy. At **Rè**, on the Italian side, there is a procession of pilgrims on 30 April each year, a tradition that originated after a painting of the Madonna was reported to start bleeding upon being struck by a ball.

Leventina Valley
From Bellinzona, the Valle Leventina is the rail and road route to Andermatt and Zürich. There is the choice of taking the motorway (N2/E35) or a smaller parallel road. En route, the town of **Biasca** has a 12th century Romanesque church with a tall belfry and some fading frescoes. At Biasca, the valley splits: Val Blenio is the route to Disentis, on the Vorderrhein.

Mesolcina Valley
North-east of Bellinzona is the Valle Mesolcina, leading to the San Bernardino Pass and the Hinterrhein. Again, there is a choice of taking a motorway (N13/E43) or a smaller road (highway 13).

Graubünden

Once upon a time, tourists in Switzerland were a summer phenomenon. Then in 1864, Johannes Badrutt, the owner of the Engadiner Kulm Hotel in St Moritz, offered four English summer guests free accommodation if they returned for the winter. He told them they were missing the best time of the year. Although dubious, the English were unable to refuse a free offer. They returned, enjoyed themselves, and winter tourism was born.

Today Graubünden (Grisons, Grigioni, Grishun) has some of the most developed and best known winter sports centres in the world, including Arosa, Davos, Klosters, Flims, and, of course, St Moritz. Tourism is a major earner for the canton; around 50% of the population are directly or indirectly employed in the sector, and it accounts for 20% of overnight stays in Switzerland as a whole.

Away from the international resorts, Graubünden is a relatively unspoiled region of rural villages, Alpine lakes and mountain vistas. In addition to tourism, the generation of hydro-electric power is important to the local economy. It is only the 10th-richest canton, earning Sfr39,646 per capita.

In medieval times the region was known as Rhaetia, and was loosely bound together by an association of three leagues. The modern name for the canton was derived from the *Grauer Bund*, or Grey League. Conquest of the area by an outsider was virtually impossible because of the mountainous terrain – 221 separate communities were scattered within 150 distinct valleys. Graubünden joined the Swiss Confederation in 1803.

Orientation & Information

Graubünden is the largest Swiss canton, covering an area of 7106 sq km, ranging in altitude from 270m (Misox) to 4049m (Piz Bernina). There are two major rivers in this canton; the Rhine and the Inn. The Alps cover most of the terrain, accounting for the

HIGHLIGHTS

- Alpine mountains and lakes
- Top-notch ski resorts – St Moritz and Davos
- Tobogganing and water sports
- Quaint Engadine villages – Zuoz and Guarda
- Switzerland's only national park
- The Romansch-speaking corner of Switzerland

Graubünden

fact that it is also the most sparsely populated canton, with a mere 26 inhabitants per sq km. The Septimber Pass, Julier Pass and Maloja Pass are transit routes through the Alps that have been important since Roman times.

Chur is the cantonal capital, and has the headquarters of the Graubünden tourist office, 2nd floor, Alexanderstrasse 24, with information on the whole canton. Visitors are welcome Monday to Friday from 8 am to noon and from 1.30 to 5.30 pm. The office is in the building marked 'Publicitas', near the train station. The main Graubünden tourist office (☎ 081-302 61 00; fax 302 14 14) is in the Heidiland motorway service

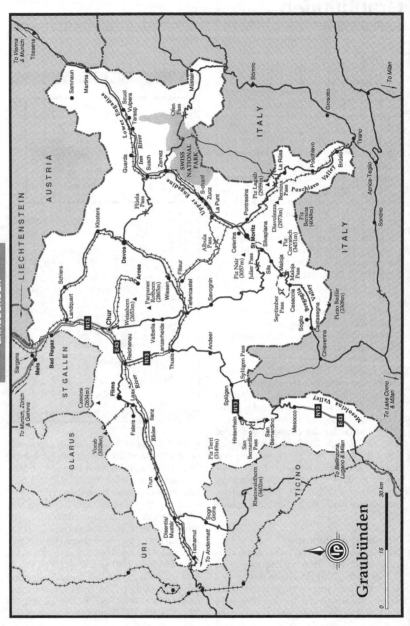

Graubünden

station on the N13 autobahn, north of Chur in the Marienfeld/Fläsch area. Information is available 365 days a year from 8 am to 6 pm (5 pm on weekends).

Holiday apartments abound in Graubünden and are often better value than hotels and pensions. A minimum stay of one week (Saturday to Saturday) is normal and they generally need to be booked up well in advance. Tourist offices compile lists of these, and can inform you about an even cheaper option: private rooms.

The whole canton has the same telephone code: ☎ 081.

Language

The extent to which the mountains have dominated and isolated the region can be heard in the language. In the north (around Chur and Davos) the people speak German, in the south, Italian, and in between (St Moritz, Lower Engadine, Vorderrhein Valley) mostly Romansch. Yet even between neighbouring valleys there can be significant linguistic differences. Take the word 'cup' as an example. In German it's *Tasse*, Italian it's *tazza* and Romansch it's *cuppina*. None of these words for cup are used in the Hinterrhein Valley (where they say *scariola)*, the Albula Valley *(cuppegn)* or the Müstair Valley *(cupina)*.

The use of Romansch is gradually in decline and linguists fear it may disappear altogether, despite efforts to preserve it. Already, German speakers account for 65% of the Graubünden population, with Romansch down to 17%.

When to Go

Most of the Alpine resorts mentioned in this chapter virtually close down in May and November and for one or two weeks either side. It's a good time to go if you hate crowds and just want to do a lot of walking, but bear in mind that most if not all of the cable cars will shut down. Tourist offices will be able to provide exact running times. There will always be a fair selection of restaurants and hotels still open, and the restaurants you find are likely to be pretty good, as they're the ones that can attract the local trade. Hotels may be prepared to negotiate on rates.

Peak season is approximately Christmas to the end of February, and July and August.

Activities

Museums and galleries are not the main reason to visit Graubünden. Instead, it is an area for enjoying the majestic scenery and outdoor activities. There are 10,500 km of footpaths, 1500 km of ski slopes and 870 km of cross-country ski trails. There's a famous five-km toboggan run on the Albula pass from Preda to Bergün (with one-way toboggan rental). Graubünden has over 600 lakes, and those offering the greatest choice of water sports are the lakes at Lenzerheide-Valbella, St Moritz, Sils/Maloja, and Silvaplana. All these lakes have sailing schools. Expect to pay Sfr90 to Sfr140 for one day's sailing boat rental and Sfr45 for a one-hour sailing lesson. One week at a windsurfing school is around Sfr230 (including equipment), or two hours' board and wetsuit rental is about Sfr20. Motorboats are forbidden on all Graubünden's lakes and rivers.

Getting Around

Public Transport Graubünden has a regional transport pass issued between 1 May and 31 October and valid for 15 days. It is good for a 50% discount on main transport routes throughout the region (extending to Bellinzona, Andermatt and Samnaun) and for free travel in five days on selected lines, encompassing Tirano (in Italy), St Moritz, Scuol, Davos, Arosa, Disentis/Mustér and Chur. The price is Sfr133 in 2nd class (Sfr113 with Swiss railpasses) and Sfr210 (Sfr174) in 1st class. The version giving three free days in seven costs Sfr100 (Sfr80) in 2nd class and Sfr164 (Sfr133) in 1st class. Buy them from stations of the Rhätische Railway or Graubünden post offices.

Car & Motorcycle Motorways barely invade Graubünden's territory, but the roads are excellent given the difficulties of the terrain. There are three main passes from northern Graubünden to the southern valleys of

GRAUBÜNDEN

Bregaglia and Engadine; from west to east they are: Julier (open year-round), Albula (summer only) and Flüela (year-round, but may close in bad weather). These approximately correspond to three exit points into Italy: Maloja, Bernina and Ofen (all open year-round). The Oberalp Pass, the route west to Andermatt, is closed in winter, but as at Albula, there is the option of taking the car-carrying train instead. It is advisable to carry snow chains in winter.

Chur

• *pop 32,900* • *585m* • ☎ *(081)*

Chur is the canton's capital and largest town, yet has a very compact centre. It has been continuously inhabited since 3000 BC. The city was virtually destroyed by fire in 1464, and German-speaking artisans poured in to carry out the rebuilding. They rebuilt the linguistic landscape too, for the city had previously been Romansch-speaking. Chur is pronounced *khoor*, which has a rasping, throat-clearing sound.

Orientation & Information

The train station has luggage lockers, bike rental and money-exchange counters (7 am to 8 pm daily). The main post office (Hauptpost, 7001) is by the train station. Five minutes' walk away is Postplatz, where there's another post office (7002) and, 100m down the road, the tourist office (☎ 252 18 18), Grabenstrasse 5. It's open Monday to Friday from 8 am to noon and 1.30 to 6 pm, and Saturday from 9 am to noon. Pick up a free copy of the two walking tours of the mostly pedestrian-only old town, which lies immediately to the south. The office makes hotel reservations for Sfr2 commission and has small free maps. Don't buy their better map for Sfr5 – pop round the corner to the UBS bank which gives them out for nothing.

Many shops in the centre stay open to 9 pm on Friday nights. SSR (☎ 252 97 76), the budget travel agency, is at Untere Gasse. Nearby on Grabenstrasse is a self-service

laundry with English instructions, open daily from 9 am (noon on Sunday) to midnight. It costs from Sfr6 to wash and Sfr3 to dry.

Things to See & Do

Chur has an attractive old town with 16th century buildings, fountains and alleyways. Follow the faded green and red footprints on the pavement that correspond to the tourist office walking tours. Arcas (green walking route) is a photogenic square with the church spire rising in the background.

Augusto Giacometti designed three of the windows in the 1491 **Church of St Martin**. By the church is the **Rätisches Museum**, Hofstrasse 1, displaying a standard provincial collection relating to local history, furniture, crafts and costumes, although the odd Egyptian sarcophagus is an unexpected addition (German signs only). It is open Tuesday to Sunday from 10 am to noon and 2 to 5 pm, and admission costs Sfr5 (students Sfr2.50).

In the impressive **cathedral**, built from 1150, are a number of interesting features, including the carved heads on the choir stalls. The particularly fine **high altar**, made by Jakob Russ from 1486-92, is the largest Gothic triptych in Switzerland. It's just a pity that it's so dark and distant that you can't appreciate it properly. (There are two tiers of alarms to keep you away.) The crypt contains valuable religious reliquaries from the Middle Ages. It can be viewed Monday to Saturday from 10 am to noon and 2 to 4 pm, but you need to get the key from the 1st floor of Hofstrasse 2.

The **Kunstmuseum** on Postplatz contains modern art, including a generous gathering of work by the three Giacomettis: Alberto, Augusto and Giovanni. Note also the sci-fi designs by local artist, HR Giger. If you think the style bears some resemblance to the monster in the film *Alien*, you're right – that beastie with its metallic grin was his brainchild. If you like his stuff, check out his bar (see the Entertainment section). Entry to the museum costs around Sfr6 (students and seniors Sfr4), depending on special exhibitions. It's open the same hours as the

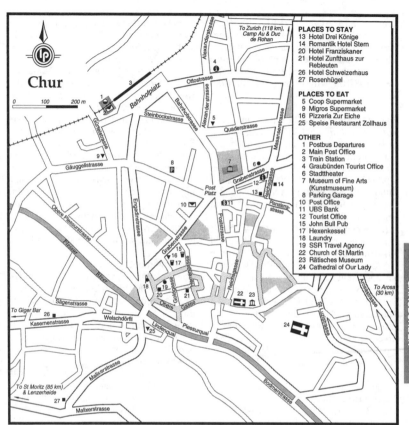

Chur

PLACES TO STAY
13 Hotel Drei Könige
14 Romantik Hotel Stern
20 Hotel Franziskaner
21 Hotel Zunfthaus zur
   Rebleuten
26 Hotel Schweizerhaus
27 Rosenhügel

PLACES TO EAT
5 Coop Supermarket
9 Migros Supermarket
16 Pizzeria Zur Eiche
25 Speise Restaurant Zollhaus

OTHER
1 Postbus Departures
2 Main Post Office
3 Train Station
4 Graubünden Tourist Office
6 Stadttheater
7 Museum of Fine Arts
   (Kunstmuseum)
8 Parking Garage
10 Post Office
11 UBS Bank
12 Tourist Office
15 John Bull Pub
17 Hexenkessel
18 Laundry
19 SSR Travel Agency
22 Church of St Martin
23 Rätisches Museum
24 Cathedral of Our Lady

GRAUBÜNDEN

Rätisches Museum, except for late opening
(8 pm) on Thursday.

To enjoy indoor or outdoor swimming,
tennis and ice skating, look to the **Obere Au
Sportzentrum** (☎ 254 42 88), to the north-
west of town (take bus No 2).

Places to Stay – bottom end

Camping *Camp Au* (☎ 284 22 83), by the
sports centre, costs Sfr6.10 per person and
from Sfr5.50 for a tent. It is open year-round.

Hostel The old SYHA hostel has been closed

down, but a new one should open up in 1997.
Check with the tourist office.

Hotels The best of the cheapies is
Rosenhügel (☎ 252 23 88), Malixerstrasse
32, five minutes' walk uphill from the old
town. Simple but fair-sized rooms using hall
shower are Sfr45 per person, and there's
parking and an inexpensive restaurant. The
English-speaking host has interesting views
about Switzerland. *Hotel Franziskaner*
(☎ 252 12 61), Kupfergasse 18, in the old
town, has adequate singles/doubles for
Sfr50/90 using hall shower; doubles with

shower and toilet are Sfr120. *Hotel Schweizerhaus* (☎ 252 10 96), Kasernenstrasse 10, is a basic bar and restaurant (closed Sunday). Rooms are OK but some could do with a lick of paint; singles/doubles are Sfr58/100 with shower or Sfr50/85 without.

Places to Stay – middle & top end
Hotel Drei Könige (☎ 252 17 25), Reichsgasse 18, has lots of art on the corridors and in the rooms, and an atmospheric bar/café. Singles/doubles (with TV) start from Sfr92/136 with shower/WC or Sfr70/110 without. Garage parking is available and it also stages folk and jazz concerts several times a month.

Hotel Zunfthaus zur Rebleuten (☎ 252 17 13), Kupfergasse 1, is in a 500-year-old building. The rooms are comfortable (Sfr70/110 with shower, Sfr60/110 without), but don't quite live up to the expectations inspired by the frescoed frontage. *Romantik Hotel Stern* (☎ 252 35 55) – with a name like that it also inspires certain expectations – is infused throughout with the fresh scent of Arven wood. All rooms have shower/WC and TV and start at Sfr105/195. Parking is free in the courtyard and it's at Reichsgasse 11.

Top of the range is the four-star Best Western Hotel, *Duc de Rohan* (☎ 252 10 22; fax 252 45 37), Masanserstrasse 44. Prices start at Sfr120/190, and it has a swimming pool and sauna among its facilities.

Places to Eat
There is a *Coop* supermarket and self-service restaurant on Alexanderstrasse, open to 6.30 pm Monday to Thursday, 9 pm on Friday and 5 pm on Saturday. The *Migros* on Gürtelstrasse offers a similar deal and is open the same hours.

There are a couple of pizzerias side by side on Grabenstrasse. Prices start at Sfr11 and both have outside seating. *Trattoria da Gabriele* is closed Sunday. *Pizzeria Zur Eiche* is open daily and also serves Röstis.

Speise Restaurant Zollhaus, Malixerstrasse 1, has two parts (open daily). Biersch-

wemme is the downstairs bar and serves hot meals from only Sfr8.70. The daily special with soup is Sfr10.80 (available from 11 am to 1 pm and 6 to 8 pm), fondue is Sfr15.50 and beer is Sfr4 for half a litre. Upstairs is the calmer and more cultured Bündnerstube, where meals are mostly above Sfr20.

For well-prepared regional food in rustic surroundings, go to *Hotel Stern* (see Places to Stay). Main dishes are around Sfr18 to Sfr40, or you can splash out on the eight-course Bündner menu at Sfr154 for two. Lunchtime eating is cheaper, with three menus (one vegetarian) from Sfr16 including soup (open daily). Also good is the restaurant in *Hotel Zunfthaus zur Rebleuten* (see Places to Stay), with main dishes at around Sfr30 and multi-course menus (closed Saturday lunchtime and Monday).

Entertainment
The *Stadttheater* is opposite the tourist office, which sells tickets for most events. Theatre productions are very occasionally in English, and a variety of musical events are staged. South American buskers (street musicians) are often to be found in the station or on Bahnhofstrasse.

A lively area for nightlife is Goldgasse and Untere Gasse. There are several bars with loud taped music and dancing, including *Hexenkessel*. *John Bull* is part of the same building and has an entrance on Grabenstrasse; a young crowd turns out to play table football and video games. These bars in the city centre close at midnight.

For later fun you need to head to the western commercial district at Freifeld (a stop on bus No 1), where places can stay open till 3 am. By the bus stop is the *Bif* disco (Sfr10 entry). Take the path adjoining the descending garage entrance (opposite Avis) to reach the silver and black *Giger Bar*, Comercialstrasse 23. The place is owned by the artist HR Giger and is a must for anyone interested in sci-fi themes. The décor makes it look like something out of a space movie. You half-expect those skeletal chairs that curve above your head to ingest you at any moment. Beers (0.3 litre) cost Sfr3.50, or

Sfr4.50 after 8 pm, and it's open daily except Sunday from 8 am to midnight. The next street north has *Villa Wahnsinn*, a bar with a DJ and games (open from 8 pm) – Sfr5 entry includes the first drink.

Getting There & Away
There are rail connections to Davos, Klosters and Arosa, and fast trains to Sargans (the station for Liechtenstein, only 22 minutes away) and Zürich (85 minutes, Sfr37). Chur can be visited on the Glacier Express route (see Getting There & Away in the St Moritz section). Postbuses leave from the new terminus above the train station, including the express service to Bellinzona (advance reservations essential on ☎ 252 38 23). Graubünden's one motorway, the N13 (E43), goes north from Chur to Zürich and Lake Constance.

Car Rental Avis (☎ 252 39 73) is at Kalchbühlstrasse 12, and Hertz (☎ 252 32 22) is at Kasernenstrasse 92.

Getting Around
Bahnhofplatz is the hub for all local buses, which cost Sfr2.20 per journey. A strip of 12 tickets costs Sfr16. At around 8 pm routes combine and services are less frequent – some being taken over by postbuses. The fare for these evening buses is Sfr2.40, with services ending at 11 pm or later.

Although the old centre is mostly pedestrian-only, some streets, such as Poststrasse, have vehicle access but only during the day. For parking, look for signs for several parking garages on the edge of the old quarter (eg on Gäuggelistrasse).

Around Chur

Chur is within easy reach of several ski areas.

LENZERHEIDE & VALBELLA
• *1470m & 1540m*   • ☎ *(081)*
These linked resorts are beautifully situated on either side of Lake Heidsee, with surrounding woodland and soaring peaks. Relatively few foreign visitors make it here, but it's a great place for relaxation and sports. It offers a quiet nightlife, and skiing mainly geared towards beginners and intermediates. A one-day ski pass costs Sfr46 (Sfr51 on weekends and holidays) for adults, Sfr37 (Sfr39) for youths and senior citizens, and Sfr28 (Sfr30) for children.

The Parpaner Rothorn (2865m) is the highest point that can be reached by cable car, and has several walking trails radiating from the summit. Contact the Lenzerheide tourist office (☎ 384 34 34) for more information. There is a SYHA *hostel* (☎ 384 12 08), Voa Sartons 41, but it's 30 minutes' walk from the Valbella bus stop and closed in the off-season.

Getting There & Away
Either resort is easily reached by bus (hourly from Chur, Sfr9.60, takes 40 minutes) or car. They're on highway 3, the route from Chur to St Moritz that goes over the Julier Pass.

FLIMS
• *pop 2380*   • *1100m*   • ☎ *(081)*
This well-established ski resort is favoured more by the Swiss than by foreign visitors.

Orientation & Information
Flims has two parts, about one km apart. Except where noted, all the places mentioned are on the main road connecting the two. Flims Dorf is larger, more residential, and slightly closer to the ski lifts. Flims Waldhaus is flanked by woodland and has most of the hotels. It also has the tourist office (☎ 920 92 00), open Monday to Friday from 9 am to noon and 2 to 6 pm, and Saturday from 9 am to noon and (in the high season) from 2 to 5 pm. Postbuses stop at the tourist office, and at the post office (7017) in Flims Dorf.

Activities
Skiing The 'White Arena' skiing area covers Flims, Laax and Falera (225 km of runs). Skiing is mostly intermediate or easy and extends as high as 3000m. A one-day ski pass

GRAUBÜNDEN

includes ski buses and costs Sfr55 (Sfr4 supplement on weekends and holidays, reduction in low season; half-price for children). There are 60 km of cross-country skiing trails.

Hiking In summer, the hiking network covers 200 km, including to the Rhine Gorge (dubbed the Swiss Grand Canyon). At the summit of the Cassons there is a circular walking route, the *Naturlehpfad*, that yields delights of flora, fauna and geology. It takes around 2½ hours to complete the circuit; take the chair lift then cable car from Flims to Cassonsgrat (Sfr33 one way, Sfr39 return). Even in winter there are 60 km of footpaths.

River-Rafting The mighty River Rhine (Rhein in German) has two sources, both in Graubünden: the Vorderrhein and the Hinterrhein. River-rafting is fast and furious on the 17 km stretch of the Vorderrhein between Ilanz and Reichenau. Swissraft (☎ 911 52 50) in Flims Waldhaus offer half/full-day rafting for Sfr99/143 (in summer). The price includes transport to/from Flims – useful as there's no direct bus.

Other Activities Swissraft also offers canyoning, mountain biking, hot air balloon trips and passenger paragliding flights. The nearest lake for summer swimming and hiring boat is Lake Cauma. For fishing in the Rhine and the Caumasee, get a permit from the tourist office.

Places to Stay
There's a Guest Card for staying in the resort. Hotel boards with free telephone are outside the tourist office and the Dorf post office. Camp at *Prau* (☎ 911 15 75), five minutes' walk from the tourist office towards Laax. It is open year-round. The cheapest beds are at *Alte Säge* (☎ 911 28 07), Sulten 187 in Dorf, downhill from the main road. Two to eight-bed rooms are available on a private or mix-and-match basis. Price per person is Sfr23.50 without meals (there's a kitchen), Sfr34 with breakfast or Sfr45 at half-board.

An excellent and inexpensive choice is *Guardaval* (☎ 911 11 19) in Waldhaus. The rooms are a good size, many with a balcony, and the owner is solicitous. Parking is ample and there's a garden with a barbecue. Singles/doubles start at Sfr65/110 with private shower or Sfr52/100 using a hall shower.

One of several four-star hotels, *Crap Ner* (☎ 911 26 26; fax 911 26 75) is immune to puns about its name (*crap* means stone in Romansch). It's near the Dorf post office and provides a free shuttle to the ski lifts. Good facilities include a sauna and indoor swimming pool, and rooms are Sfr161/266 (much less in summer and low season).

Places to Eat
There are supermarkets in both Dorf and Waldhaus. The *Hotel Albana*, by the Cassons chair lift, has an inexpensive but comfortable restaurant on the 1st floor. The Tagesteller (with soup) costs Sfr17.50 and pizzas start at Sfr11.50. Pizzas are about the same price at *Pomodor* in Waldhaus.

Between Dorf and Waldhaus is *Grischuna*, serving a daily menu with soup for Sfr16.50 and regional specialities for Sfr20 to Sfr40 (closed Tuesday and Wednesday in summer). It has rooms as well but they are rather cramped for the price.

Restaurant Giardino is in the hotel Crap Ner (see Places to Stay). There's a salad buffet (Sfr8 or Sfr9.50) and a range of meals, from vegetarian dishes (Sfr16) up to a multi-course gourmet menu (Sfr73). There's live music in the adjoining bar on winter evenings except Monday.

Getting There & Away
Flims is not on a train line (the nearest stations are Reichenau and Ilanz). Postbuses run to Flims and the other villages in the White Arena area hourly from Chur (Sfr11.40 to Flims, takes 40 minutes).

AROSA
• *pop 2600* • *1800m* • *☎ (081)*

Arosa is a relaxing resort at 1800m, spread out in the Schanfigg Valley amid lakes and woodland.

Orientation & Information
Arosa has two parts: Ausserarosa (Outer Arosa) is the main resort and Innerarosa is the older part of the village. Ausserarosa is grouped around the shores of Lake Obersee at the train terminus. The train station has money-exchange counters, luggage storage, and bike rental.

From Oberseeplatz, take Poststrasse, heading uphill in the direction of Innerarosa. After five minutes you'll reach the tourist office (☎ 377 51 51), open in summer Monday to Friday from 8 am to noon and 2 to 6 pm, and Saturday from 8 am to noon and (July to mid-August) 2 pm to 4 pm. Winter hours are Monday to Friday from 9 am to 6 pm, Saturday from 9 am to 5.30 pm, and Sunday from 10 am to noon and 4 to 5.30 pm. Buses in the resort are free until around 7 pm; they cost Sfr3 thereafter. Car drivers should note that there is a traffic ban (except for through traffic) from midnight to 6 am.

The main post office (7050) is at Oberseeplatz.

Activities
Arosa has over 70 km of **skiing** for mixed abilities based on three main mountains. In particular, beginners have a good choice of runs, and the ski school can be contacted on ☎ 377 11 50. The highest skiing point is the Weisshorn at 2653m. Ski passes cost Sfr52 for one day and Sfr239 for one week (children half-price). In addition to cross-country skiing, Arosa features several ice skating rinks (natural and artificial), curling, and tobogganing (from Tschuggen down to the village). Hot air balloon flights (☎ 377 18 43) last about an hour and cost Sfr290 to Sfr360 per person (November to April only).

In the summer, there is a free bathing beach at **Untersee**. The larger **Obersee** is used for rowing boats and pedalos (Sfr10 to Sfr17 per hour). Permits for trout fishing in both lakes can be obtained from the tourist office.

Arosa has 200 km of maintained **hiking** trails. The walk up to Weisshorn from the village takes about 3½ hours and the panorama attained is extensive and elevating (viewing table). The cable car costs Sfr24 or Sfr30 return (no reduction with Eurail or Inter-Rail), but you could consider buying the seven-day general hiking pass for Sfr60. Reserve in advance at the tourist office for the guided nature observation walk (Sfr10).

Other activities include horse-riding, tennis and golf (nine-hole course).

Places to Stay – bottom end
Camping The *camp site* (☎ 377 17 45), is in a quiet location on the edge of the village, down from the tourist office. It is open year-round and costs Sfr9 per adult, Sfr4.50 for a tent and Sfr2.50 for a car.

Hostel For the SYHA *hostel* (☎ 377 13 97), Seewaldstrasse, take a left just beyond the tourist office. Like many hotels, it is closed from mid-April to mid-June and from mid-October to mid-December. Dorms cost Sfr24 (B&B) in summer and Sfr36 (half-board) in winter, and there's no first night's surcharge. Half-board prices for double rooms are Sfr76 (bunk beds) or Sfr102 (double bed). The reception is closed from 10 am to 5 pm but a side door stays open. Get a key for late entry.

Hotels & Pensions Many hotels and pensions have a surcharge for short stays (one or two nights), particularly in winter. *Lindemann's Garni* (☎ 377 50 79), on Oberseeplatz, is convenient and cheap, charging Sfr75 per person (Sfr40 in summer) for rooms using hall shower. There's no street parking but a garage is 200m away.

Bündnerhof & Rössli (☎ 377 16 32) is five minutes' walk east from Hotel Carmenna (see Places to Eat) and open year-round. Singles/doubles are Sfr100/190 with private shower and Sfr88/166 without, reducing in summer to Sfr83/156 and Sfr67/124. Prices include dinner, and rooms have TV. *Pension*

Mezzaprada (☎ 377 12 70), by the children's ski school in Innerarosa, has good-sized rooms with own shower for Sfr85/170, or Sfr65/110 in summer.

Hotel Quellenhof (☎ 377 17 18) has fresh and light rooms, if not overly huge, near to the tourist office. They all have shower, toilet and TV. Prices for half-board are Sfr78 per person in the summer and Sfr118 in the winter, when a Sfr10 supplement applies for short stays.

Places to Stay – middle & top end

Hotel Alpensonne (☎ 377 15 47; fax 377 34 70) is up the hill not far from the Brüggli lifts. The rooms are reasonably spacious, with private shower/toilet, and the south-facing ones have a big balcony with a fine view. Prices start at Sfr75/140 in summer and Sfr135/240 in winter; for half-board add Sfr20 per person. *Hohenfels* (☎ 377 01 01; fax 377 14 89), is a four-star place near the Catholic church. Well-equipped rooms with half-board start at Sfr128/216 in summer and Sfr210/370 in winter. *Posthotel* (☎ 377 01 21; fax 377 40 43), is only marginally more expensive and right by the train station, with its own parking.

Places to Eat

There's a *Denner* supermarket near the train station and a *Coop* by the tourist office. Between the tourist office and Oberseeplatz is the *Café-Restaurant Oasis*, where you can get simple but tasty meals from Sfr10 to Sfr17. It closes at 7 pm and all day Tuesday, except in the winter season when it's open daily to 11 pm.

Opposite is the alcohol-free *Orelli's Restaurant*, offering good vegetarian dishes for around Sfr14 and a salad buffet for Sfr9 to Sfr14 per plate. It has a wide selection of other meals (including children's menus) between Sfr10 and Sfr32, and it's open daily from 7.30 am to 9 pm. Rooms with shower and TV are also available.

By the Obersee, anticlockwise from Oberseeplatz, is the *Hotel Carmenna*, which has a pizzeria open in the evenings from 6 pm to 1 am (pizzas from Sfr11.50), though there's also an inexpensive restaurant with a sun terrace open during the day.

Quellenhof (see Places to Stay) has a good restaurant, where most dishes cost between Sfr15 and Sfr28. It has a daily menu with soup for Sfr17.50. Also worth considering is the restaurant at *Alpensonne* (see Places to Stay), where meals cost from Sfr15.50 to Sfr45. There's a four-course evening menu for around Sfr40. *Hotel Anita* (☎ 377 11 09), near the Catholic church, has a gourmet restaurant.

Entertainment

The tourist office has lists of daily events. The village church is the site for occasional concerts. The *Kursaal* by the tourist office has gambling and games, as well as a restaurant, cinema and nightclub. *Hotel Carmenna* (see Places to Eat) has live piano music in the bar in the evening during the season, as well as a dancing bar with live music (in winter, and usually free).

Getting There & Away

The only way to get here is from Chur: take the narrow-gauge train from in front of the train station (Sfr11.40 each way). Departures are hourly and the trip takes an hour. It's a winding, scenic journey with views of mountains, pine trees, streams and bridges (sit on the right). The road follows the same route. Snow chains are recommended in winter.

Davos

• *pop 11,500* • *1560m* • ☎ *(081)*

Originally known as a health resort, Davos is simply one of the best skiing areas in the world. It includes the legendary Parsenn-Weissfluh area, where ski runs are a vertical mile long.

Orientation & Information

Davos, too large to have a ski village atmosphere, is a four km-long conurbation stretched beside the railway line and the

Landwasser River. It comprises two contiguous areas, each with its own railway station, Davos Platz and Davos Dorf. Both stations have money-exchange counters and lockers but only Davos Dorf has bike rental (in summer).

Davos Platz, to the south-west, is more built up than Dorf and the centre of most of the activity. The main street is Promenade, with one-way traffic from Dorf to Platz. Talstrasse, a parallel street, is one-way in the opposite direction. The main tourist office or Kurverein (☎ 415 21 21) is at Promenade 67, open Monday to Friday from 8.30 am to 12.30 pm and 1.45 to 6 pm, and Saturday from 8.30 am to 12.30 pm and (high season only) 1.45 to 5 pm and Sunday from 9 to 11 am. In winter high season there's no weekday lunch break. Another tourist office (open the same hours) is opposite the Dorf train station, next to a post office (7260). Both tourist offices make room reservations without commission, to personal callers or

via a reservations line (☎ 415 21 31). The main post office (7270) is at Postplatz in Davos Platz.

The Visitor's Card allows free travel on local buses and trains, as does the general ski pass (and the Swiss Pass). A self-service laundry (no English instructions) is at Promenade 102, open Monday to Saturday from 8 am to 8 pm.

Museums

Although Davos is mostly a place for outdoor pursuits, there are four small museums in and around the town. Entry for each of the Mining Museum, the Craft Museum and the Wintersports Museum costs Sfr5 (limited opening hours). A new collection, the Kirchner Museum, displays work by the expressionist painter (Sfr7; closed Monday).

Skiing

Davos offers huge variety for experienced

GRAUBÜNDEN

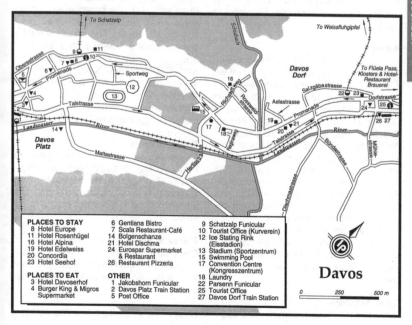

PLACES TO STAY	6 Gentiana Bistro	9 Schatzalp Funicular
8 Hotel Europe	7 Scala Restaurant-Café	10 Tourist Office (Kurverein)
11 Hotel Rosenhügel	14 Bolgenschanze	12 Ice Stating Rink
16 Hotel Alpina	21 Hotel Dischma	(Eisstadion)
19 Hotel Edelweiss	24 Eurospar Supermarket	13 Stadium (Sportzentrum)
20 Concordia	& Restaurant	15 Swimming Pool
23 Hotel Seehof	26 Restaurant Pizzeria	17 Convention Centre
		(Kongresszentrum)
PLACES TO EAT	OTHER	18 Laundry
3 Hotel Davoserhof	1 Jakobshorn Funicular	22 Parsenn Funicular
4 Burger King & Migros	2 Davos Platz Train Station	25 Tourist Office
Supermarket	5 Post Office	27 Davos Dorf Train Station

Davos

0   250   500 m

and intermediate skiers. The Weissfluh ski area goes as high as 2844m, and from here you can ski all the way to Kublis, over 2000m lower and 12 km distant. Alternatively, you can take the demanding run down to Wolfgang (1629m) or the scenic slopes down to Klosters. Across the valley, Brämabüel and Jakobshorn offer equally good skiing for all abilities, and the nearby areas of Pischa and Rinerhorn are also easily within reach of Davos. See also the Klosters section for further skiing areas.

In all there are 315 km of ski runs in the Davos/Klosters region, which are covered by the general REGA pass costing Sfr113 (Sfr68 children) for a minimum two days. Six days cost Sfr259 (Sfr155), discounted to only Sfr207 (Sfr124) during two weeks in January and from late March. One-day passes for specific areas cost between Sfr25 (Sfr21) and Sfr56 (Sfr34).

The Davos ski school (☎ 416 59 51), at the Parsenn funicular, costs Sfr52 for a day and Sfr190 for five days. There are 75 km of cross-country trails open from December to April.

Hiking

The mountains provide extensive hiking options (450 km of paths). Senior citizens get discounts on cable cars. The views of the Alps are excellent from Weissfluh, and you can walk to the top in about 3½ hours in summer. The easy way is to take the Parsenn funicular from near Dorf station up to Weissfluhjoch, and the cable car from there up to Weissfluhgipfel. The combined fare is Sfr27 up, Sfr24 down, and Sfr34 return (25% off with Swiss Pass, half-price with Half-Fare Card). Getting a discount with Eurail or Inter-Rail is as likely as stopping a runaway train with a pocket magnet.

On the other side of the valley, get to Pischa (2465m) by bus and cable car. The walk from there, along the mountain ridge and back down to Dorf, takes about three hours.

Other Activities

Davos Platz has a large natural ice rink where

Royal Race

Every January in Davos an unusual ski race takes place – British members of parliament take on their Swiss counterparts. One would expect that victory for the ski-bred Swiss would be a foregone conclusion against the piste-less British, and so it is, usually. But in 1995 Britain scored a rare victory, aided by Prince Charles who swished over from his holiday in Klosters to lend a hand. Charles, who qualified for the British team as a member of the House of Lords, turned in a sterling performance. ■

---

ice hockey games are staged in the winter. It is complemented by an artificial rink, open all year except in May. Ice skating costs Sfr5 for adults and Sfr4 for children. There's a sports stadium next door. Schatzalp is the place for **tobogganing**, and toboggans (*Schlitten*) can be hired at the lower Schatzalp funicular station (☎ 413 57 26). Contact the Flugschulcentre (☎ 416 55 46), Promenade 111, for **paragliding**. A 'taxi' flight with a pilot costs Sfr160, and tuition costs Sfr100 per day. The indoor **swimming pool** is midway between Platz and Dorf. Entry costs Sfr6.50 (Sfr4.50 students, Sfr3.50 children) or Sfr13 including the sauna. North of Dorf is **Lake Davos** (Davoser See), where there is swimming (free beach) and water sports. Horse and mule trekking is another Davos attraction.

Special Events

Davos hosts an International Music Festival from late July to mid-August, featuring a variety of classical works, held in the Convention Centre (Kongresszentrum). Get information and tickets from the main tourist office.

Places to Stay – bottom end

Camping Camp at *Färich* (☎ 416 10 43), close to Davos Dorf on the road to the Flüela Pass. It is open from mid-May to late September.

Hostel The SYHA *hostel* (☎ 416 14 84) is

nicely situated by woods on the far side of Lake Davos (take bus No 6 or 11 from Dorf to Hochgebirgsklinik, then it's a five-minute walk). Dorms cost Sfr21 and reception is shut from 9.30 am to 5 pm. The hostel is closed from late April to early June and late October to mid-December. Other places with dormitory accommodation are shown in the hotels booklet available from the tourist office.

Hotels & Pensions Except for a few Garni places, all hotels offer half-board as well as B&B. *Hotel-Restaurant Brauerei* (☎ 416 14 88), Dorfstrasse 29, near the Dorf station, has dormitory beds for Sfr45 per person (Sfr40 in summer). Most of the cheaper hotels and pensions are in the Platz side of Dorf. This includes *Hotel Edelweiss Garni* (☎ 416 10 33), Promenade 125. The rooms are nothing fancy in this small-scale place but it's good value, especially for this pricey resort. Singles/doubles start at Sfr61/118 with shower and Sfr48/92 without. Triples and quads (bunk beds) are available, and there's private parking.

On the hill behind the tourist office in Platz is *Hotel Rosenhügel* (☎ 413 54 25). It is instantly recognisable by its giant (fake) roses growing up the side of the building. The interior is decorated with similar flair, with the rose motif constantly reappearing. There is a good view across the town, and a comfortable, welcoming ambience. Prices are Sfr100/180 with shower or Sfr83/150 without, reducing in the summer to Sfr70/120 with or Sfr55/94 without. Half-board is only Sfr10 extra per person.

Also up hill but nearer Dorf is *Hotel Alpina* (☎ 416 47 67), Richstattweg 1, where winter B&B prices are Sfr106/162 with shower or Sfr69/114 without. Summer prices are around 20% lower and half-board is Sfr18 extra. There are parking places and many balconies.

Places to Stay – middle & top end
Concordia (☎ 416 46 66), Promenade 124, has good prices for a three-star place. Rooms start at Sfr120/200 (Sfr90/140 in summer)

and have shower/WC, TV and telephone. There's parking and a bar on site.

There are over a dozen four-star hotels with stacks of facilities. *Hotel Seehof* (☎ 416 12 12; fax 416 61 10), Promenade 159, is by the Parsenn funicular. It has restaurants, a sauna, whirlpool, solarium and fitness room, as well as easy disabled access. Prices start at Sfr236/450 in winter and Sfr126/283 in summer. *Hotel Europe* (☎ 413 59 21; fax 413 13 93), Promenade 63, Davos Platz, lacks the whirlpool but makes up with an indoor swimming pool (free for guests). Rooms start at Sfr200/370 in winter and Sfr126/222 in summer.

Places to Eat & Drink
There is a *Eurospar* supermarket (standard hours) with a self-service restaurant (open Monday to Saturday to 7.30 pm) close to Davos Dorf station. Meals are Sfr10 to Sfr15 and it is licensed. Right by Dorf station is *Restaurant Pizzeria*, where prices for pizza/pasta start at Sfr11 (open daily to 11 pm).

There is also inexpensive eating at Davos Platz station in *Buffet Loki*; meals start at Sfr13 and it's open daily to 9 pm. Just up the hill is the Rätia Centre on Postplatz. Inside is a *Migros* supermarket with hot takeaway food at a deli counter, and a *Burger King*.

Hotel Dischma, Promenade 128, has two inexpensive places to eat, the Röstizzeria, for pizzas and Röstis, and the Chäshütte, for pizzas and cheese dishes, as well as dancing and live music. The music (from 9 pm daily) is easy-listening, except for the first Friday of the month when it's Swiss folk music. *Bolgenschanze*, Skistrasse 1, is a hotel favoured by young snowboarders. It has a restaurant, and in winter there are discos and live music (entry fee on weekends).

By the Hotel Europe on Promenade is *Scala Restaurant-Café*, with outside seating. The décor inside includes huge plants, modern art and a giant portrait of Gorbachev on one wall. Pizza/pasta starts at Sfr13 and other main courses are around Sfr30. The three-course lunch and evening menu is Sfr17.50 (open daily). Upstairs is a Chinese

GRAUBÜNDEN

restaurant where main courses are around Sfr30 (open daily from 6 pm). *Gentiana Bistro*, Promenade 53, is a specialist in snail dishes (Sfr12.80 to Sfr25.80) and meat and cheese fondues (Sfr23.50 to Sfr55.50). It is open daily.

The best place to eat is in *Hotel Davoserhof* (☎ 415 66 66), Postplatz, near Davos Platz station. It specialises in Italian food, with main dishes around Sfr35 to Sfr70. The business lunch costs Sfr49 and evening menus are around Sfr100. The hotel also has a bar where there is a nightly DJ. Another top-notch place is the restaurant in *Hubli's Landhaus* (☎ 416 21 21), midway between Davos Dorf and Klosters at Davos Laret (closed Monday).

Getting There & Away
Davos is on the Rhätische Bahn rail route between Landquart and Filisur, with trains running hourly. Change at Landquart for Chur; the total journey takes up to two hours and costs Sfr26. Landquart is also the junction for trains north and to Zürich. Change at Filisur for St Moritz; the total journey takes 1½ hours and costs Sfr26. En route you might be tempted to alight at Wiesen station, where there's a precipitous gorge and hiking paths.

Postbuses connect Davos to eastern Graubünden and the lower Engadine. Highway 28 follows the same route to/from Davos as the railway. Snow chains are most likely to be needed in winter on the stretch between Klosters and Davos.

KLOSTERS
• *pop 3800* • *1194m* • ☎ *(081)*
Favourite resort of Britain's Prince Charles, Klosters provides the atmosphere of a traditional skiing village that is lacking in neighbouring Davos. Expect fewer diversions in the evening.

Orientation & Information
Like Davos, Klosters is split into two. Klosters Platz is the most important part, and is compactly grouped around the train station. Exit right and turn right for the

tourist office, or Kurverein (☎ 410 20 20), open Monday to Friday from 8 am to noon and 2 to 6 pm, and Saturday from 8 am to noon. Additional hours in winter high season are Saturday from 2 to 5 pm and Sunday from 4 to 6 pm. Staff make commission-free hotel reservations. The post office (7250) is opposite the station.

Two km to the left of the station is the smaller enclave of Klosters Dorf, with several hotels, a tourist office, and the Madrisa cable car. Klosters buses are free with a Guest Card and ski pass.

Activities
The same skiing passes are available as mentioned in the Davos section. Above the village at 2300m is the Gotschnagrat, accessible from the cable car by the train station. It gives access to the fearful Gotschnawang, one of the hardest runs in the world. One of Prince Charles' companions had an accident here in 1988, and they now only open it if conditions are perfect. On the other side of the valley, the Madrisa region has runs favouring beginners and intermediates; a day pass only for this region costs Sfr42 (Sfr24 children). Fifty km of cross-country skiing trails run east from the village. Cross-country rental costs Sfr20 for one day, and the school gives lessons from Sfr58 (Sfr53 for children under 12) for two half-days. Book at the tourist office

The village also boasts swimming pools, tennis courts, and a new sports centre with an artificial ice rink. The tourist office has a leaflet giving times and descriptions (in English) of nearby hikes.

Places to Stay
The tourist office can supply lists of private rooms (from Sfr20 per person) and the numerous holiday apartments.

The SYHA hostel is called *Soldanella* (☎ 422 13 16), and it's at Talstrasse 73, a 12-minute, mostly uphill trek from the station (head right, turn left at the junction and look for the signs). Dorm beds cost Sfr25.50 and singles/doubles/triples are Sfr36.50 per person. Dinners (Sfr11) are sociable, help-yourself affairs. There's a games room and English novels but too few showers for comfort. Reception is shut from 9.30 am to 5 pm but the doors remain open, and there's no curfew. The hostel is closed between seasons.

Minerva (☎ 422 15 62), Gsteinweg 1, is a tiny place near the tourist office with rooms from Sfr45 per person (hall showers). Towards Klosters Dorf is *Malein* (☎ 422 10 88), Landstrasse 120, a cosy chalet with singles/doubles for Sfr52/104; doubles with private shower are Sfr120. *Rufinis* (☎ 422 13 71), Landstrasse, near the Dorf tourist office, is a quaint-looking place with a restaurant and outdoor pool. Rooms are from Sfr55 per person (Sfr35 in summer), and it's a popular haunt for young people, with a bar and dancing. *Bündnerhof* (☎ 422 14 50), Doggilochstrasse 2, across the river from the Platz tourist office, gives more comfort and is family-oriented. Prices start at Sfr75 per person.

Hotel Alpina (☎ 410 24 24; fax 410 24 25), Bahnhofstrasse 1 (opposite the station), has good rooms from Sfr202/354 (Sfr135/230 in summer). Prices are higher in the guesthouse section but the bathrooms are a treat in these rooms – they're fitted with jacuzzis and other luxuries. Use of the swimming pool, sauna and fitness room are included. Apartments (with kitchen, without breakfast) are also available, and garage parking is Sfr15 per night. See Places to Eat for more accommodation suggestions.

Places to Eat
Fifty metres to the right from the train station is a *Coop* supermarket and restaurant. Meals are around Sfr11 (open till 7.30 pm daily).

The most affordable of the other restaurants is *à Porta*, to the right of the station on Bahnhofstrasse. Pizza starts at Sfr12, and it also has pasta, risotto, grills, and a salad buffet. The three-course lunch and evening menu is Sfr22.50 (open daily). Nearby at No 12 is *Chesa Grischuna*, which has piano music at 4 pm for the après-ski crowd. There are some cheapish meals (from Sfr15), including vegetarian choices, on the daytime 'Kleine Karte', though evening dining runs to Sfr30 or more for varied main dishes.

Gasthaus Casanna (☎ 422 12 29), Landstrasse 171, has simple meals from Sfr11 and local specialities above Sfr20, served in the bar section or the plusher adjoining room. It also has standard bedrooms for Sfr60 per person using hall shower. Telephone ahead in off-season as the restaurant (and reception) is closed one day a week. Along the road towards Dorf is *Sonne* (☎ 422 13 49), Landstrasse 155, which usually has tempting smells issuing from the wood-panelled restaurant (closed Monday and Tuesday). The midday Tagesteller is Sfr15; regional main courses are otherwise mostly Sfr25 to Sfr45, though there are cheaper light meals. Rooms cost Sfr60 per person.

The best restaurant is the *Walserstube* in the Hotel Walserhof (☎ 422 42 42), Landstrasse 141. It serves superb seasonal specialities and regional dishes for around Sfr50 – good value considering the quality. It's run by the Bollingers: Mr is in charge of the kitchen and Mrs circulates amongst the guests. Reserve ahead, especially for weekends (open daily, but closed off-season).

Getting There & Away
See Getting There & Away for Davos, as Klosters is on the same rail route between Landquart and Filisur. Klosters to Davos Platz takes 30 minutes and costs Sfr8.40.

Engadine Valley

This valley gets its name from the Inn River (En in Romansch) that meanders along its length. It is divided into two sections, the Upper Engadine (Oberengadin) from Maloja to Zernez, and the Lower Engadine (Unterengadin), stretching from Zernez to Martina, by the Austrian border. The scenery is tremendous, but the mountains don't have the same vertical impact as they do in some other parts of the Alps as the valley floor is

GRAUBÜNDEN

An example of Engadine architecture.

so high, averaging around 1500m. The valley is traditionally Romansch-speaking, although almost everyone also speaks German, and tourist-industry personnel usually speak English too. Turn to the Language Guide at the back of the book for translations of key words.

The Engadine is an excellent valley for exploration by car, bus or train, in part because the contrast between the sophisticated international resorts and the unpretentious rural villages is so marked. In the latter category, many houses display the traditional *sgraffito* design that runs like a floral trim around the edges of building exteriors. These designs, often incorporating arabesques, scrolls and rosettes, are made by scratching off a plaster covering to reveal a different colour underneath. This method of decoration is characteristic of the Engadine.

There is a low, middle and high season in both summer and winter. Hotel prices peak in the winter season; the change can be quite significant for middle-range to top-end hotels or very minimal in budget places. Prices quoted here are for the peak season (usually winter), though for St Moritz summer prices are also given as a comparison. Engadin Reservation (☎ 081-833 74 60; fax 833 69 57), Plazza da Scuola 16, CH-7500 St Moritz, handles hotels, holiday apartments and package deals.

Chalandamarz, a spring and youth festival, is celebrated in the Engadine on 1 March. The **Schlitteda**, an ancient custom

involving a procession of colourful horse-drawn sledges, can be seen in St Moritz, Pontresina and Silvaplana in January.

Skiing
The regional ski pass for the Upper Engadine covers 350 km of downhill runs serviced by 60 cable cars and lifts. It includes skiing in St Moritz and the surrounding resorts such as Sils, Silvaplana, Celerina, Pontresina, Diavolezza and Zuoz. Most of the skiing is too daunting for beginners, but intermediates have endless possibilities. The general pass costs Sfr54 (Sfr42 children) for one day and Sfr286 (Sfr143 children) for one week. Cheaper, more restricted passes are available but the general pass gives huge variety for little extra cost. It even includes train and postbus transport between the different areas and entry for the indoor swimming pools in St Moritz and Pontresina. Rental for skis, boots and sticks is Sfr43 for one day. There's free car parking at all valley stations except at Chantarella and Zuoz.

The region also boasts 160 km of cross-country trails (equipment rental Sfr20). The famous **Engadine Ski Marathon** takes place on the second Sunday in March. It starts at Maloja, crosses over the frozen lakes at Sils and Silvaplana, passes by the south-east side of Lake St Moritz, and finishes between Zuoz and S-chanf, a distance of some 42 km. It's a great spectacle, with around 12,000 professional and amateur skiers taking part. The elite take around one hour 20 minutes to complete the course, but the 'fun' contestants make it last most of the day. If you don't want to join the crowds at the beginning or end of the race, a good place to watch is the approach to Pontresina. There's a tricky bit as they leave the woods where many amateurs are sent tumbling (to sympathetic laughter from spectators), and then a downhill section where they can regain their composure.

Alternatively, Lake Staz (Stazersee, Lej da Staz) allows a clear view of the skiers. It's a pleasant 35-minute walk from St Moritz (clockwise round its lake).

Getting Around

See St Moritz for getting to/from the Engadine. From St Moritz, Rhätische Bahn trains go every hour as far as Scuol (Sfr25, takes 1½ hours). Stops en route include Zuoz (Sfr8.40, 45 minutes), Zernez (Sfr15.80, one hour) and Guarda (Sfr21, 1¼ hours). In the other direction you need to take the hourly bus from St Moritz Bahnhof that goes as far as Maloja (Sfr9, 35 minutes) with stops at St Moritz Bad, Silvaplana (Sfr3.60, 15 minutes), and Sils (Sfr6, 20 minutes). Additional buses go from Pontresina to Sils, via St Moritz. There's a postbus pass that covers the Lower Engadine and the Müstair Valley, giving seven days' free travel within two weeks. It's called the *Fereinkarte* and costs Sfr65 (Sfr50 with Half-Fare Card; Family Card accepted for children's travel). In summer hikers can get a head start with a one or six-day cable car pass. Prices (and itinerary tips) are listed in the free Engadin funicular brochure.

MALOJA

* *pop 300* • *1809m* • ☎ *(081)*

Maloja, a one-street settlement, has Lake Segl to the north. Immediately to the south is the Maloja Pass, which barely rises above the village yet falls away sharply on the far side into the Bregaglia Valley. The local dialect is a mix of Italian and Romansch. The tourist office (☎ 824 31 88) is open Monday to Friday from 8.30 am to noon and 2 to 6 pm, and (in the high season) Saturday from 9 to 11 am and 3 to 5 pm. It can give advice about all day hikes over nearby passes, such as the historic Septimber Pass to the north or the Muretto Pass south to Italy. It even organises excursions itself: hiking the three pass tour with a guide and returning by bus costs Sfr50.

The artist Giovanni Segantini lived in the village from 1894 until his death in 1899, and his studio (*Atelier*) can be viewed (early July to mid-October and early February to mid-April, from 3 to 5 pm except Monday; Sfr2). Paintings are also on display in the Belvedere Tower (accessible in the summer; free),

around which is a protected area of glacial pot holes and flowers.

Places to Stay & Eat

Camp by the lake at *Plan Curtinac* (☎ 824 31 81), open from 1 June to mid-September. The SYHA *hostel* (☎ 824 32 58) is between the post office and the tourist office, in two buildings on either side of the garage. It has a kitchen (Sfr2.50 charge), games room, and dinners for Sfr11. Dorms cost Sfr22 and there are doubles (bunk beds in all but one room) for Sfr58. Reception is only open from 8 to 9 am, 5 to 6 pm, and 8 to 9 pm, though the doors are open through the day (curfew 11 pm). The hostel is closed in May and from mid-October to 30 November.

The elderly Frau Ratti (☎ 824 31 28) has one single, two doubles and one quad (bunk beds) at Sfr28 per person, without breakfast but with use of a kitchen. Her house is the whitish one, back from the road, across the forecourt from the tourist office. Other accommodation is quite expensive. *Schweizerhaus* (☎ 824 34 55), opposite the post office, has rooms for Sfr110/160 with private shower or Sfr75/150 without, reducing in low season. *Villa La Rosée* (☎ 824 31 33), to the north and a left turn, is a smaller place and costs Sfr58/110 without showers; doubles with shower are Sfr135.

Trattoria Cherubini has Italian food from Sfr9.50 and crêpes from Sfr6.50. There's live rock music on Friday and Saturday nights (closed Wednesday lunch and Sunday). Opposite is the calmer *Restaurant Chesa Alpina*, with a nice garden round the back. Local dishes are above Sfr18 (except for the lunch special) and it's closed Monday. There is a supermarket opposite the post office (closed Wednesday afternoon).

SILS

* *pop 600* • *1800m* • ☎ *(081)*

Peaceful Sils (Segl in Romansch) has two parts: Baselgia by the lake, and Maria at the foot of the mountains, where most of the amenities are located (including all the places mentioned below). Postbuses stop at both parts, though through car traffic is

GRAUBÜNDEN

restricted (park in the garage). A cable car ascends to Furtschellas (Sfr12 up, Sfr10 down, Sfr18 return; children half-price) at 2312m, where there is a network of hiking trails and ski slopes. Water sports are also major attractions.

The philosopher Friedrich Nietzsche spent his summers in the resort from 1881 to 1888, and you can look around the **Nietzsche Haus** (Sfr4, students and seniors Sfr2, children free) in summer and winter from 3 to 6 pm, daily except Monday. He wrote several important works here, such as *Also Sprach Zarathustra*. You won't learn much about the man's life unless you can read German, but the many photos are interesting; it's amusing to see how his moustache grew in stature during the course of his life, from a skimpy floss fringing his upper lip in his student days to a bloated hedgehog bristling under his nose at the time of his death.

The tourist office (☎ 838 50 50) is by the street corner, in the same building as the bank. Its opening hours are Monday to Friday from 8.30 am to noon and 2 to 6 pm, and in the high season on Saturday from 9 to 1 am and 3 to 5 pm.

Places to Stay & Eat

Baukantine Kuhn (☎ 826 52 62) provides dorm beds from Sfr15 to Sfr30 per person, and has a kitchen. It is by the river, on the south bank, about halfway towards Lake Silvaplana.

Close to the tourist office is *Pension Schulze* (☎ 826 52 13), with singles/doubles for Sfr70/140 with private shower or Sfr60/120 without. On the other side of the road is *Restorant Survial*, serving pasta from Sfr11, daily specials for Sfr16, and grills and fish from Sfr22. It's open daily in season from 8.30 am to 10 pm. A *Volg* supermarket is nearby.

Close to the post office is *Maria* (☎ 826 53 17), which smells of pine and offers rooms with private shower from Sfr120 per person (half-pension). The restaurant has a cheap lunch card (Sfr8 to Sfr15), although

evening dining is mostly above Sfr30 (open daily in season).

SILVAPLANA
• *pop 850* • *1815m* • ☎ *(081)*

On a bay jutting between the two lakes, Silvaplana (Silvaplauna in Romansch) is a centre for water sports, especially windsurfing. The tourist office (☎ 838 60 00), in the centre at Via Maistra, can give details. Across the causeway is **Surlej**, providing access to skiing slopes and marvellous views from Piz Corvatsch (3451m). The cable car costs Sfr21 up, Sfr14 down and Sfr30 return.

Places to Stay & Eat

Lakeside *camping* (☎ 828 84 92) is available from mid-May to late October. Silvaplana is an easy and pleasant walk around Lake Campfèr from St Moritz Bad, but if you want to stay in the village the best value is *Engiadina* (☎ 828 81 15). This family hotel has singles/doubles with private shower from Sfr86/172, or Sfr73/146 without (rates for half-pension). In Surlej, try the similarly priced *Bellavista* (☎ 828 81 85).

There is a *Volg* supermarket by the campsite. *Restaurant Margun*, in Surlej, serves pizzas until midnight.

ST MORITZ
• *pop 5500* • *1856m* • ☎ *(081)*

St Moritz is where the jet set comes to play and pose. It's one of the world's best-known holiday spots for the wealthy, and has been for a century or more. The not-so-rich who want to linger on the fringes of the elite can stay around the lake in St Moritz Bad. Here you can eat and sleep without taking out a mortgage – there's even a SYHA hostel (gleaming and expensive, but a hostel nonetheless).

Visitors can enjoy a huge variety of winter and summer sports. There is diverse downhill skiing, and probably the best cross-country skiing in the Alps. The toboggan Cresta Run is one of the resort's big draws. If you can't afford to partake in the activities, at least people-watching is fun and free. Health treatments are also part of the St

Top: Schlitteda Festival in St Moritz, Graubünden
Middle: Arosa, Graubünden
Bottom: Soglio village, Graubünden

MARK HONAN

MARK HONAN

MARK HONAN

Top: Rathausplatz, Stein am Rhein, North-East Switzerland
Bottom Left: Shop door with metal-work designs in the windows, Appenzell
Bottom Right: Children in traditional dress, Vaduz, Liechtenstein

Moritz package. The curative properties of its waters have been known for 3000 years.

Orientation & Information

St Moritz (San Murezzan in Romansch) exudes health and wealth from the slopes overlooking the lake that shares its name (St Moritzersee in German, Lej da San Murezzan in Romansch). The train station near the lakeside rents bikes in summer and changes money from 6.50 am to 8.10 pm daily. It also has a hotel board with free telephone. Up the hill on Via Serlas is the post office (7500) and five minutes farther

on is the tourist office or Kurverein (☎ 837 33 33) at Via Maistra 12. It's open Monday to Friday from 9 am to noon and 2 to 6 pm, plus Saturday morning in season. In high season, it's also open Saturday afternoon and (winter only) during weekday lunch times. St Moritz Bad is about two km south-west from the main town, St Moritz Dorf. Local buses run between the two.

Not much stays open during November, May and early June. In winter, St Moritz has plenty of sun and snow, but is colder than might be expected for its altitude. Guests in the resort get a Holiday Pass that earns some

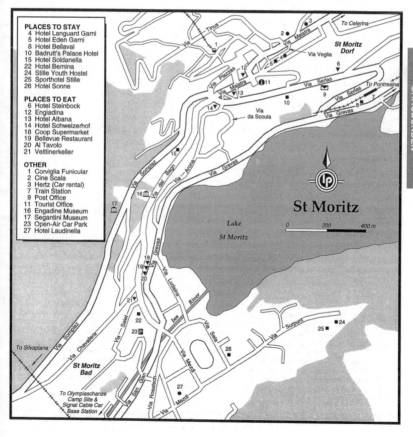

PLACES TO STAY
4 Hotel Languard Garni
5 Hotel Eden Garni
8 Hotel Bellaval
10 Badrutt's Palace Hotel
15 Hotel Soldanella
22 Hotel Bernina
24 Stille Youth Hostel
25 Sporthotel Stille
26 Hotel Sonne

PLACES TO EAT
6 Hotel Steinbock
12 Engiadina
13 Hotel Albana
14 Hotel Schweizerhof
18 Coop Supermarket
19 Bellevue Restaurant
20 Al Tavolo
21 Veltlinerkeller

OTHER
1 Corviglia Funicular
2 Cine Scala
3 Hertz (Car rental)
7 Train Station
9 Post Office
11 Tourist Office
16 Engadine Museum
17 Segantini Museum
23 Open-Air Car Park
27 Hotel Laudinella

St Moritz

useful privileges. Some streets have parking meters (one to four hour maximum on weekdays; Sfr1 per hour), though there is an open-air car park in Bad (see map) that costs Sfr0.50 per hour (10 hours maximum).

Museums

The **Engadine Museum**, Via dal Bagn 39, gives a good introduction to the style of dwellings and simple interiors you may encounter if you explore the Engadine Valley, and some rather patrician interiors you probably won't encounter. The building itself is typical, featuring sgraffito designs on the façade. Traditional stoves and archaeological finds complete the collection. It is open from Monday to Friday from 9.30 am (10 am in winter) to noon and 2 to 5 pm, and Sunday from 10 am to noon. Entry is Sfr5 for adults and Sfr2.50 for children.

The **Segantini Museum**, Via Somplatz 30, is devoted to the local 19th century artist of the same name, who specialised in mountain scenes. The most powerful piece here is the three-part *To Be, To Pass, To Become*. Opening hours are Tuesday to Saturday from 9 am to 12.30 pm and 2.30 to 5 pm, Sunday from 10.30 am to 12.30 pm and 2.30 to 4.30 pm. Winter openings are at 10 am and 3 pm and it's closed Sunday morning.

Admission costs Sfr7 for adults, Sfr5 for students, and Sfr2 for children. A combined ticket for both museums is available.

Skiing

The downhill skiing area adjacent to St Moritz is centred around Corviglia (2486m), accessible by funicular from Dorf. From Bad a cable car goes to Signal (shorter queues), giving access to the slopes of Piz Nair. A ski pass for both areas costs Sfr50 (children Sfr34) for one day. If you ski on Piz Corvatsch, above nearby Silvaplana, you can ski back down to Bad via the demanding Hahnensee run. For tuition in skiing or snowboarding, contact the school on ☎ 833 80 90.

Hiking

There are 120 km of marked hiking paths you can tramp along, and many are open in winter. The tourist office has a map giving suggestions (in English) for walking throughout the Upper Engadine. Above St Moritz soars the Piz Nair (3057m), and the summit provides a marvellous perspective of Alpine peaks and the lakes and valley below. Walking to the top in summer from the village will take three hours or more. The easy way to get up is by funicular then cable

---

St Mo-RITZY Guests

Despite being at the forefront of the winter sports scene in the 19th century, St Moritz hasn't become a mass-market holiday destination in the way that many other resorts have. The main reason for this is its enduring air of exclusivity – one feels the wealthy want to enjoy the facilities without the bother of having to barge the proles out of their path. Average mortals who meander into the rarefied atmosphere of St Moritz Dorf almost feel compelled to apologise that they don't own a wardrobe full of fur coats and a fleet of flashy sports cars. Just about anything you do here costs a pile of money; even window shopping makes you feel nervous about your budget.

St Moritz is by no means ashamed of its snobbish profile. Quite the reverse. 'Class instead of Mass' is its motto. St Moritz's director of tourism describes the typical guest as 'exclusive, chic, elegant, sporty'. Another of the resort's slogans is 'Top of the World'. One begins to wonder whether this refers more to the guest profile than to the physical location. Publicity handouts effuse about the local 'champagne climate' – again, they're probably not talking about the weather. As if the parade of plush shops and fur coats were not enough to underline the message, various events take place that emphasise the champagne-and-caviar angle. There's even curling on Corviglia where the curling stones are shaped like champagne bottles. However, in the third annual Gourmet Festival in February 1996 things went a little over the top, even for St Moritz: two Cigar Gourmet Nights were organised to 'celebrate the art of cultivated smoking'! While the gourmets light up their big ones, the rest of us can merely watch and wonder. ∎

car; the complete trip costs Sfr21 each way and Sfr32 return (25% reduction with Swiss Pass, 50% off with Half-Fare Card, no reduction with Inter-Rail or Eurail).

Other Activities
Among the numerous (and expensive) sports on offer are tennis, squash, horse-riding, sailing and windsurfing. Golf is played on the frozen lake in winter, and in the summer at the 18-hole course in nearby Samedan (☎ 852 52 26), where one day's green fees is Sfr90. For fishing in the Upper Engadine you need a permit (an outrageous Sfr81 for one day for foreigners; the Swiss pay Sfr45). Contact the Bezirkskommissariat (☎ 833 34 04) in the Hotel Eden. In winter, a 'taxi' ride by hang-glider (☎ 833 24 16) costs Sfr220 (Sfr290 in high season); in summer, contact the paragliding school (☎ 828 54 00). For the cresta run, see Celerina below.

Buying a **health treatment** in the spa is another way to spend money. The Holiday Pass gets reduced entry to the Health Spa Centre in St Moritz Bad and a free mineral drink. For information on treatments available there, telephone ☎ 833 30 62.

Places to Stay – bottom end
Hotel prices peak at around mid-December to mid-February. The summer high season, July and August, isn't quite so expensive. Many hotels have reduced seven-day deals.

Camping The *Olympiaschanze* camp site (☎ 833 40 90) is one km south-west of St Moritz Bad; it is open from 1 June to late September and costs Sfr8 per adult and Sfr6.30 per tent.

Hostel The SYHA *Stille Hostel* (☎ 833 39 69), Via Surpunt 60, St Moritz Bad, has good, modern facilities. Compulsory half-board in four-bed dorms is Sfr41.50, or Sfr54 per person in double rooms. Laundry costs Sfr4 per load. Reception is closed from 9 am to 4 pm (but the downstairs doors stay open), curfew is at midnight and the hostel is open year-round. Buses from the station to Maloja

stop at the Hotel Sonne (Sfr2), eight minutes' walk from the hostel.

Hotels The nearest thing to a budget hotel in Dorf is *Bellaval* (☎ 833 32 45), right by the train station. Singles/doubles using hall shower are Sfr62/120 in the summer or winter season. Doubles with own shower and toilet (Sfr156) are reasonably large, if slightly bare. Add Sfr5 per night if staying under three nights. Half-pension costs Sfr20 per person. On Tuesday, when the restaurant is shut, reception is closed from 11 am to 5 pm.

The *Sporthotel Stille* (☎ 833 69 48), next door to the hostel, attracts a young and sporty crowd; in winter it has its own bar and weekly disco. Prices per person are Sfr50 for bed and breakfast in the summer, and Sfr80 for half-pension in the winter, in doubles only (surcharge for single occupancy in busy times). It's open year-round. Also in Bad, but north of the Inn River on Via dal Bagn, is *Hotel Bernina* (☎ 833 60 22). It's only good value in the summer (closed May) when rooms start at Sfr75/145 with private shower or Sfr55/107 without. Prices almost double in winter and these average rooms simply don't merit the increase, though dinner becomes included. The food is not bad.

Places to Stay – middle
Staying in the centre of St Moritz Dorf involves splashing out on at least a three-star hotel. Two good family hotels are close together on Via Veglia, around the back of the tourist office: in summer, *Hotel Eden Garni* (☎ 833 61 61) starts at Sfr100/190 and *Hotel Languard Garni* (☎ 833 31 37) at Sfr100/200. There's little to choose between them in the standard of rooms. Eden has a nice central atrium although Languard's prices rise less in winter (around 30% instead of 35%).

Also worth considering is *Hotel Soldanella* (☎ 833 36 51), with rooms starting at Sfr100/180 in summer or Sfr120/220 in winter. It's a few minutes' walk south from the centre of town at Via Somplaz 17. In Bad is the *Hotel Sonne* (☎ 833 03 62), Via Sela

GRAUBÜNDEN

11, which has singles/doubles/triples with shower/WC, TV, telephone and balcony starting at Sfr85/150/195 in summer or Sfr100/170/210 in winter. Rooms are in the main building or two nearby annexes. There's free private parking and free use of the public swimming pool.

Places to Stay – top end

The place to see and be seen is the renowned *Badrutt's Palace Hotel* (☎ 837 10 00; fax 837 29 99) on Via Serlas. Of course, you have to pay for the privilege, with rooms with half-board costing at least Sfr290/490 in summer and a heart-stopping Sfr600/1200 in winter. The public areas reek of class and taste (men must wear a jacket and tie after 7 pm), but the cheaper rooms aren't as lavish as you might expect.

Places to Eat

The cheapest restaurants are between Dorf and Bad. There is a *Coop* supermarket in Via dal Bagn. Next door there's *Bellevue*, a self-service restaurant with meals from Sfr10, and salad and dessert buffets. It is open until 7 pm on Monday to Thursday, 8 pm on Friday and 5 pm on Saturday. Beside it is *Al Tavolo*, with light meals from Sfr10, although à la carte dishes are mostly above Sfr20. It is open daily until 11 pm (kitchen until 9.30 pm).

Veltlinerkeller, nearby at Via dal Bagn 11, features Engadine sgraffito outside and beheaded animals inside. If the hunting trophies don't put you off your food, tuck into a wide choice of pasta, grills, omelettes, fish or schnitzels for Sfr10 to Sfr40 (closed Sunday in off-season). The popular *Hotel Sonne* (see Places to Stay) has pasta, salads and grills. Tasty pizzas, cooked in a traditional wood-burning oven, are available from 5 pm (costing Sfr12 or more). It is open daily from 7 am to midnight, and has a bar area.

Eating in Dorf is not necessarily an asset-stripping experience if you stick to lunchtime specials, which many good-quality restaurants offer. *Hotel Albana*, Via Maistra 6, has lunch with soup for Sfr16, or for Sfr19

with an additional starter. The four-course evening menu costs Sfr40 to Sfr55, and main courses top Sfr30 (open daily). The restaurant of the *Hotel Schweizerhof*, Via dal Bagn 54, has a lunch menu with starter for Sfr16. In the Stübli (bar area) there is live music nightly (from 10 pm), and for the winter après-ski crowd (4 to 6 pm).

The restaurant of the *Hotel Steinbock*, opposite the post office at Via Serlas 12, is good value and popular with locals. Light meals start at Sfr16 but most dishes are around Sfr28 to Sfr40, and it's open daily during the season. *Engiadina*, around the corner from the tourist office at Plazza da Scuola 2, is famous for fondue, and that's the best thing to eat here (from Sfr25.50 per person). It is closed on Sunday.

Try an expensive taste of the high life at the top of the Corviglia funicular by sampling the truffles, caviar and desserts at *La Marmite* (☎ 833 63 55). Queue or reserve ahead in season, when it's open daily. On the floor above there's a reasonably cheap self-service restaurant, with a terrace.

Entertainment

Nightlife is lively and varied, but unless you have plenty of money, forget it! Over 20 bars and clubs have dancing and/or music. One of the most elegant places is the *King's Club* in Badrutt's Palace Hotel. This disco is open nightly from 10 pm and entry costs Sfr30. *Cine Scala* by the Schiefer Turm (the Leaning Tower) shows films in the original language; seats cost from Sfr15.

Concerts, theatre and other events are staged by Pro Cultura (☎ 832 21 31), based in the Laudinella Hotel in St Moritz Bad.

Getting There & Away

Train Nine daily trains travel south to Tirano in Italy with connections to Milan. The famous Glacier Express links St Moritz to Zermatt (Sfr125) via the 2033m Oberalp Pass. The majestic, scenic route takes 7½ hours to cover the 290 km and crosses 291 bridges. Novelty drink glasses in the dining car have sloping bases to compensate for the hills – but you must remember to keep turning them around! Reservations (Sfr9, not covered by railpasses) are compulsory on these trains, but only in the summer and only for the stage between Disentis and Brig. This is not required for normal trains following the same route.

Bus To Lugano, two postbuses run (daily in summer; only Friday, Saturday and Sunday in winter). The cost is Sfr54 (plus a Sfr5 supplement, not covered by Swiss travel passes) and the seat must be reserved the day before; ☎ 833 30 72. To get to Austria, see Scuol later in this section.

Car & Motorcycle The roads around St Moritz are good, if winding. See the Getting around section in the chapter introduction for details of which passes are open in winter.

Car Rental Hertz (☎ 833 27 84) is at Via Maistra 46 and Budget (☎ 837 36 34) is at Via Somplaz 33. Europcar (☎ 833 80 25) is at Saluver garage in nearby Celerina.

CELERINA
• *pop 1100* • *1730m* • ☎ *(081)*
This resort (Schlarigna in Romansch) by the Inn River is 30 minutes' walk from St Moritz and shares the same ski slopes. In the winter it is known for its famous Olympic **bob run** and **cresta run**. The bobsleigh run is the oldest in the world and the only one made from natural ice. It starts by St Moritz lake and one trip costs Sfr200. The cresta run (a toboggan course enticingly known as the skeleton run) was created by British tourists in 1885 and starts near the Schiefer Turm in St Moritz; it's over one km long and five rides costs Sfr450. The finish for both runs is the western end of Celerina.

The tourist office (☎ 833 39 66) is in the village centre at the corner of Via Maistra and Via da la Staziun. It is open Monday to Friday from 8.30 am to noon and 2 to 6 pm, and Saturday from 9 to 11 am and 3 to 5 pm.

Places to Stay & Eat
Except for the many holiday apartments and few private rooms, the cheapest lodgings are at *Hotel Trais Fluors* (☎ 833 88 85). It could do with a lick of paint outside, but the interior is OK. Singles/doubles start at Sfr51/98 and it's north-east of the tourist office on Via Samedan. Between the two is the comfortable *Arturo* (☎ 833 66 85) on Via Maistra. Rooms are Sfr80/160 and have private shower/WC, TV and telephone. The restaurant has a good selection of food (Sfr12 to Sfr45) and wine (open daily). Opposite, the *CCC Café* provides cheaper meals.

Demont Garni (☎ 833 65 44), on Via Maistra in the direction of the cresta run, has smallish but pleasant doubles for Sfr150 with shower/WC or Sfr110 without. Single occupancy costs Sfr80 or Sfr60. Two doors away is *Veltlinerkeller*, where pasta starts from Sfr10 and grills and cutlets from Sfr18 (closed Sunday). It also has rooms (hall showers) for Sfr60/110. There are two supermarkets, a *Coop* beyond Arturo and a *Volg* opposite the tourist office.

Getting There & Away
Celerina is easily reached from St Moritz by train (Sfr2.40), which takes you to the village centre, or postbus (Sfr2.80), which you leaves by the cresta run or in the centre.

ZUOZ
• *pop 1300* • *1750m* • ☎ *(081)*
Zuoz has some undemanding skiing (day pass Sfr35, or Sfr27 for children), but a greater attraction are the beautiful Engadine houses sporting traditional sgraffito designs. The main square looks suitably immune to contamination by modern life, and features a fountain bearing the coat of arms of the influential Planta family. The bear's paw motif reappears in the church, which also has windows in the chancel designed by Augusto Giacometti. The small prison tower next door contains some torture implements – don't annoy the tourist office (☎ 854 15 10) staff, because they look after the key. Office opening hours are Monday to Friday from 9 am to noon and 3 to 6 pm, and (high season) Saturday from 9am to 1 pm. There is a post office at the train station.

GRAUBÜNDEN

Places to Stay & Eat

There are a few private rooms, such as at *Chesa Walther* (☎ 854 13 64) opposite the tourist office (Sfr35 per person without breakfast, though you can use the kitchen for Sfr5). The restaurant downstairs offers a range of meals (Sfr12.50 to Sfr40; open daily). Near the main square, *Pension Albanas* (☎ 854 13 21) has singles/doubles for Sfr60/100 using hall showers, and a simple restaurant. Virtually opposite is *Crusch Alva* (☎ 854 13 19), where comfortable rooms are Sfr120/190. It also has a restaurant with excellent, pricey food.

Supermarkets are by the train station and the tourist office. *Restaurant Dorta*, on the far side of the train station, offers a traditional Engadine experience, with regional food (from Sfr19) and live music (usually on Friday; closed Monday). A little farther, by the river, is *Sur En Restorant*, providing cheap self-service fare (Sfr4 to Sfr12). It's open daily from 8 am to 7 pm and has a sun terrace.

ZERNEZ

• *pop 980* • *1474m* • ☎ *(081)*

Zernez is another attractive Engadine village, but its main claim to fame is as the headquarters of the Swiss National Park.

Orientation & Information

By the Zernez entrance to the park is the National Park House (☎ 856 13 78), open from around June to October, when the park itself is open. It can give details of hiking paths, route descriptions, the best locations to see particular animals, and other information. A similar low-down can be picked up at the Zernez tourist office (☎ 856 13 00), on the main street leading from Zernez train station (five minutes' walk). Look for the *infuormaziun* sign; opening hours are Monday to Friday from 8.30 to noon and 2 to 6.30 pm, and Saturday from 2 to 4 pm. Winter opening reduces to weekdays from 2 to 5.30 pm. There's no charge to enter the park, and parking is free. S-chanf (pronounced Sh-kanf), to the south-west of the

park, also has a tourist office (☎ 854 22 55), only open weekdays from 8 to 10 am.

Swiss National Park

The park comprises 169 sq km of woodland and mountains where flora and fauna flourish in a stringently protected natural environment. Ibexes, chamois and marmots are left to roam at will. You can roam the park too, but not at will, as deviating from the paths is not permitted. Numerous other regulations prohibit camping, littering, lighting fires, cycling, picking flowers, bringing dogs into the park, or disturbing the animals in any way. Less relevantly for tourists, you also may not allow cattle to graze. Fines of up to Sfr500 may be imposed for violations.

A three-hour walk south from Zernez is the scenic Cluozza Valley, where there's cheap accommodation (see below). Another three-hour walk goes from S-chanf to Trupchun. This is especially popular in October when you can get close to large deer. The Naturlehrpfad circuit near Il Fuorn gives an opportunity to see bearded vultures, which have been released into the wild since 1990.

Places to Stay & Eat

Camping *Cul* (☎ 856 14 62) is around the back of Zernez station and open from 1 May to late October. *Hotel Bär-Post* (☎ 856 11 41), in the

The chamois has crook-shaped horns and a reddish-brown summer coat with a black stripe along the spine.

centre, has dormitory beds for Sfr15 (Sfr25 including breakfast), a kitchen, and parking spaces. Rooms with shower/WC are Sfr75 per person and its restaurant has food for Sfr12 to Sfr35.

Near the station on the main street is *Filli* (☎ 856 10 72), with newly-built rooms with shower/WC and TV from Sfr64/116. The restaurant has a good choice of meals from Sfr10. *Adler* (☎ 856 12 13), towards the park, costs Sfr75 per person with shower or Sfr45 without.

Alpina (☎ 856 12 33), and the next door *Spöl* (☎ 856 12 79), in the centre of the village, are both fresh, attractive buildings where rooms with private facilities including TV start at Sfr75 per person. Both have decent restaurants. Across the street is *Pizzeria Mirta*, where prices start at Sfr13.50. There is a *Coop* opposite the tourist office, with no half-day closing.

Il Fuorn (☎ 856 12 26), in the middle of the national park by the main road, has rooms for Sfr90 per person with shower or Sfr55 without. It also has dorms (Sfr18 without breakfast). Also in the park is *Chamanna Cluozza* (☎ 856 12 35), sometimes called the Blockhaus. It has dorm beds for Sfr25 (reductions for children) and can only be reached by foot.

Getting There & Away
From Zernez, the train fare is Sfr5.40 to S-chanf, Sfr8 to Zuoz (takes 25 minutes) and Sfr8.40 to Scuol (30 minutes).

The main road through the park, highway 28, goes from Zernez, over the Ofen Pass (2149m; Pass dal Fuorn in Romansch), and into Italy. This route is covered by postbus: there are six to nine departures a day between Zernez and Müstair. The park can also be entered on foot from close to S-chanf and Scuol.

MÜSTAIR
The village of Müstair, at the far side of the park by the Italian border, has the Abbey of St John the Baptist, founded in the 8th century. Inside there is a unique series of wall paintings from the Carolingian period

(around 800 AD), and a statue of Charlemagne from the 12th century.

GUARDA
• *pop 200* • *1653m* • ☎ *(081)*
This is one of the best preserved villages in the Engadine, with tiny, cobbled streets, fountains, and many houses bearing sgraffito engravings. It easily merits an hour or so exploring its confines. The village is on a belvedere above the valley floor and has expansive views (Guarda means 'look' in Romansch – that's good advice). Guarda is 20 minutes' walk from the train station by the footpath (40 minutes by road), or you can take the fairly infrequent postbus. The train station is 15 minutes from either Zernez or Scuol-Tarasp. Contact the tourist office (☎ 862 23 42) for information on accommodation.

SCUOL
• *pop 2060* • *1250m* • ☎ *(081)*
The approach along the valley towards Scuol is very scenic, and you pass Tarasp Castle rising impressively on a ridge to the south. Scuol is close to the smaller resorts of Vulpera and Tarasp, which are on the south side of the Inn River.

Orientation & Information
Scuol is the main resort in the Lower Engadine. The train station is over one km west of the village centre. Take the postbus (Sfr1 in summer, or the ski bus is free for everyone in winter) or walk down the hill in around 15 minutes. The tourist office (☎ 864 94 94) is in the new Bogn bathing centre: from the main street, take the covered circular stairway opposite the Hotel Quellenhof. It is open Monday to Friday from 8.30 am to 6.30 pm, Saturday from 10 am to noon and 2 to 6.30 pm, and Sunday from 2 to 6.30 pm. In low season, hours reduce to weekdays only from 9 am to noon and 2 to 6 pm. The post office (7550) is halfway between the station and the centre.

Things to See & Do
Lower Scuol displays some typical Engadine

dwellings, and has a museum (Sfr3, children Sfr1) devoted to the Lower Engadine which is open only limited hours during the season – check with the tourist office. **Tarasp Castle** (☎ 864 93 68) was built in 1040 and was controlled by the Austrians until 1803. It can be visited by guided tour (Sfr6, children Sfr3).

There is **skiing** above Scuol up to 2800m, a total of 80 km of runs, the longest being 12 km. A one-day pass costs Sfr41 for adults, Sfr32 for youths and senior citizens, and Sfr24 for children. Two companies offer **white-water rafting** down the river to Martina (18 km); prices start at Sfr100. Book through the local travel agency, Viadis Reisen (☎ 864 94 97).

Scuol is a **health spa**, and there are around 25 mineral springs in the vicinity. At The Bogn bathing and health centre, 2½ hours in the pools, sauna and steam bath costs Sfr20. Its Roman-Irish Bath is a regimen of hot and cold baths also lasting 2½ hours (Sfr49). The Schneebade Pass (Sfr54 for one day) covers skiing, bathing and other facilities.

Places to Stay & Eat

There is camping at *Gurlaina* (☎ 864 15 01), by the southern banks of the Inn. It's open year-round and costs Sfr7.90 per adult and Sfr8 for a tent.

Contact the tourist office about the many holiday apartments. *Hotel Garni Grusaida* (☎ 864 14 74) is on the east side of Scuol and has rooms for Sfr50 per person, or Sfr56 with private shower. *Hotel Garni Engiadina* (☎ 864 14 21) is a typical Engadine building in Lower Scuol and has rooms with private shower from Sfr65 per person.

Café Collina (☎ 864 03 93), opposite the post office, costs Sfr65 per person for pleasant, non-standardised rooms with TV, using private shower (doubles) or hall shower (singles). The restaurant serves pizza and pasta from Sfr12 (closed Sunday). *Hotel Traube* (☎ 864 12 07), on the main street, has comfortable rooms with shower/WC, TV and telephone from Sfr80 per person. Add Sfr20 for half-pension (four-course dinner).

Its restaurant serves good food above Sfr30 (open daily).

There is a *Coop* supermarket on the main street, with no half-day closing. *Hotel Quellenhof*, along the road, is better value for food than rooms. Its four-course daily menu (Sfr18) is available lunch and evening, and there are pizzas from Sfr11 and steaks and grills for around Sfr20 (open daily).

Getting There & Away

The train from St Moritz terminates at Scuol-Tarasp station. Postbuses from the station continue year round to Martina, Samnaun (a duty-free area in Switzerland), and Austria (as far as Landeck). From early June to late October, several buses a day run to/from Davos (Sfr26; takes under two hours).

Bernina Pass Road

This road runs from Celerina in a south-easterly direction, leading to Tirano in Italy. It links the Bernina and the Poschiavo Valleys by way of the Bernina Pass at 2323m. There are some great hiking trails in the surrounding mountains, and these are identified and described in the *Summer Panorama Map* available for Sfr2.50 from the tourist office in Pontresina. This map also details winter skiing in the valley. The ski lifts are covered by the Upper Engadine ski pass (see the Engadine Valley section).

Getting There & Away

Trains run every one to two hours from St Moritz to Tirano, stopping at all stations en route. Postbuses operate either side of the Bernina Pass but there's no through service, even though the pass is open for traffic year-round. Buses from St Moritz to Lagalb and Diavolezza run only from late December to early April.

Rhätische Bahn offers an excursion from the Upper Engadine, over the Bernina Pass and into the Poschavio Valley. Sfr45 (Sfr35 children or with Half-Fare Card) includes return rail fare, a lunch of *pizzoccheri* (a type of dumpling that is a speciality of this valley) and entry to Poschavio's folk museum.

PONTRESINA
• *pop 1750* • *1800m* • ☎ *(081)*
Pontresina is at the mouth of the Bernina Valley, close enough to the Engadine for the Engadine Ski Marathon to loop down to the village en route to Zernez. Interesting features in the village are the pentagonal Moorish tower, and the Sta Maria chapel with frescos dating from the 13th and 15th centuries. There's also an Alpine museum.

Orientation & Information
The train station is to the west of the village, changes money, and has a hotel board with free telephone on platform 1. Cross over the two rivers, Rosegg and Bernina, for the centre and the tourist office (☎ 842 64 88), open Monday to Friday from 8.30 am to noon and 2 to 6 pm, and Saturday from 8.30 am to noon and (in the high season) Saturday and Sunday from 4 to 6 pm.

Skiing
Like most of the resorts in the vicinity, Pontresina has plenty of sports facilities to offer the visitor. There's not very much skiing from Pontresina's own mountain, Alp Languard (2261m), but it's feasible to use the resort as a base for exploring the slopes farther down the valley, at Piz Lagalb and especially Diavolezza (summer skiing possible). A one-day ski pass to cover these areas costs Sfr44 (children Sfr31).

Hiking
In the summer, hiking trails wind away from Alp Languard in all directions; the chair lift to the summit runs from the end of May to mid-October and costs Sfr13 each way and Sfr19 return (children half-price). It takes 2½ hours to walk to Muottas Muragli (2453m), overlooking the junction of the Bernina and Engadine Valleys. This is the best spot for a view of the course of the Inn River.

Mountaineering
Pontresina is well known as a mountaineering centre. Its mountaineering school (☎ 842 64 44) is the largest in Switzerland and has a programme of touring weeks year-round, either on skis or on foot. Prices for the week including half-pension are typically around Sfr870, and one-day excursions are also available from Sfr70. For details, write to the Schweizer Bergsteigerschule, CH-7504, Pontresina.

Places to Stay & Eat
There is camping at *Plauns* (☎ 842 62 85), about two km to the south, open from 1 June to mid-October.

The SYHA *hostel* (☎ 842 72 23) is right next to the train station, and is closed from mid-April to early June and from mid-October to mid-December. Reception is shut from 9 am to 4 pm (check-in up to 9 pm) but there's day time access to the building. Six-bed dorms cost Sfr29 per person and two-bed rooms Sfr54 per person. Taking dinner (Sfr11) is compulsory in the main season, but this is no hardship as the food is good (three courses, and there's plenty of it). The hostel runs the alcohol-free *Restaurant Tolais* from the same premises, providing cheap meals (open until 9 pm daily).

Between the tourist office and the post office is *Pension Valtellina* (☎ 842 64 06), Via Maistra, where old-fashioned rooms with hall shower cost Sfr52/100. There are many places to eat along Via Maistra, but the only inexpensive option is searching for daily specials, or compiling a snack at the *Coop* supermarket near the post office (no half-day closing). *Bahnhof* (☎ 842 62 42), by the station, has meals from about Sfr15 and cosy rooms for Sfr70 per person. The *Sportpavillon* has an inexpensive pizzeria (open daily).

Steinbock (☎ 842 63 71; fax 842 79 22), south of the post office, is a good choice for mid-price food. It also has singles/doubles for Sfr180/300 with shower/WC and TV, at half-board. Singles without shower are Sfr125. Guests have free use of the indoor

GRAUBÜNDEN

swimming pool and sauna of the next-door Hotel Walther.

Getting There & Away

Hourly trains from St Moritz take 11 minutes and cost Sfr4.20. Postbuses leave from the centre of Pontresina by the post office, and run about every 30 minutes to St Moritz, via Celerina.

CHÜNETTA

This is a well-known belvedere above the Morteratsch train station and below the Morteratsch Glacier. It can be reached in only about a 30-minute walk from the station and the views are more than worth the effort.

DIAVOLEZZA

Diavolezza (2973m) offers testing skiing on the glacier and inspiring views of the Bernina Massif. Take the train to Bernina Diavolezza and then the cable car (Sfr18 up, Sfr14 down or Sfr25 return). Alternatively, get off the train at the previous stop, Bernina Suot, and take the trail up, which gets steep after a gentle start (takes 2¾ hours). A summer ski pass to cover the cable car and ski lift costs Sfr33 (children Sfr25) for one day.

PIZ LAGALB

This peak (2898m) is on the opposite side of the valley and gives comparable views of a landscape of mountains, glaciers and lakes. Take the cable car from the Bernina Lagalb station which costs Sfr15 up, Sfr11 down and Sfr20 return (children half-price). The walk down from the peak to the next station along, Ospizio Bernina, takes 1½ hours.

ALP GRÜM

This viewing point at 2019m provides a tremendous view over the Poschiavo Valley to the south, with the lake shimmering below and the mountains glowering above. The *Hotel Ristorante Belvedere* provides refreshment. From here you can walk down to Caviglia in one hour or back to Ospizio Bernina in 1½ hours.

Getting There & Away

The train from St Moritz takes one hour and costs Sfr28 return. The closest you can get by car is Ospizio Bernina; walk or take the train from there.

Bregaglia Valley

From the Maloja Pass (1815m), the road spirals downwards to the Bregaglia Valley (Bergell in German), cutting a course running south-west into Italy. The road then splits: one arm leads north and back into Switzerland via the Splügen Pass, and the other goes south to Lake Como and on to Milan. The postbus from St Moritz to Lugano branches off from the Milan road to circle the western shore of the lake.

As the valley proceeds in a south-westerly direction, the villages betray an increasing Italian influence. **Stampa** was the home of the artist Alberto Giacometti (1901-66), and is now the location of the tourist office (☎ 081-822 15 55) for the Bregaglia.

SOGLIO

* *pop 220* • *1095m* • ☎ *(081)*

This tiny, idyllic village (La Soglina in Italian) is close to the Italian border and has no tourist office. It commands excellent views over the valley, and faces the smooth-sided Pizzo Badile (3308m). Soglio rests on a south-facing ledge, reached from the valley floor by a narrow, winding road.

The village is a warren of small lanes and alleys overlooked by picturesque stone-built houses, and there is a church with an Italianate bell tower. Soglio is the starting point for several **hiking** trails, most notably the historic **Panorama Hochweg**, which easily lives up to its name. It takes around four hours to reach Casaccia, 11 km distant and down in the valley. Stampa, also on the valley floor, takes 1½ hours.

Places to Stay & Eat

It is worth visiting Soglio if only to stay in the *Palazzo Salis* (☎ 822 12 08). This place really is like a palace, with paintings and portraits on the walls, suits of armour, hunting trophies and fine old furniture. There are several lobbies, an open fire, and a private garden. The rooms are grand, too, with porcelain stoves and stucco or wooden ceilings. Singles/doubles are Sfr80/115 with shower or Sfr65/100 without. You would expect to have to pay a lot more for such a place. It's open Easter to 31 October. It is 50m up from the post office, and has parking places at the front. The restaurant has pasta from Sfr16 and grills from Sfr30.

The three other choices for accommodation are all owned by the same family.

Rooms are slightly cheaper (from Sfr60/95 with shower or Sfr58/88 without) but have much less character. Enquire at the hotel/restaurant *Stüa Grande* (☎ 822 19 88) by the church, which is open daily in summer and closed on Wednesday in winter (and for the whole of November). Meals there cost Sfr12 to Sfr40.

Getting There & Away
Buses from St Moritz to Castasegna run along the Bregaglia Valley. Alight at the post office at Pomontogno and take the bus to Soglio from there (Sfr2.40 each way; six to 10 departures per day).

GRAUBÜNDEN

North-East Switzerland

The north-east of Switzerland is often over-looked by visitors. That's a pity, because although it doesn't have the scenic grandeur of the southern areas, the rolling green hills are equally enticing. The region is over-loaded with castles (most of them private) and attractive town centres. Stein am Rhein has probably the prettiest main square in all Switzerland. Lake Constance (Bodensee) is another big draw, providing summer re-creation possibilities and access to attractions in neighbouring Germany and Austria.

History

Glarus was one of the earliest converts to the Swiss Confederation, joining in 1352. Schaffhausen joined in 1501 after the Swabian War, and Appenzell in 1513 during the Swiss attempts to subjugate Milan. During this period of expansionist policies by the Confederation, Thurgau became a sovereign territory and St Gallen an 'allied canton' (with inferior rights). Both became full cantons in Napoleon's 1803 reorganisa-tion of the Helvetic Republic.

The north-east could easily have become larger than it is; in 1510 the German town of Constance would have been admitted, had not the Confederates shied away from alter-ing the urban/rural balance, and in 1918 the Austrian state of Vorarlberg wanted to join the Confederation, a request turned down by the great powers in 1919.

Orientation & Information

The north-east tourist region includes the cantons of Schaffhausen, Thurgau, St Gallen, Appenzell and Glarus. It also takes in the Principality of Liechtenstein which is dealt with in a separate chapter.

Most of the land is fairly flat, making it suitable for dairy and arable farming. The Appenzell region is famous for the produc-tion of the cheese of the same name. Textiles

HIGHLIGHTS

- Picturesque town centres in St Gallen, Appenzell and Stein am Rhein
- Cheese-making in Stein
- Boat cruise along the River Rhine
- Water sports on Lake Constance
- Open-air parliaments in April and May

Appenzell Innerrhoden
Appenzell Ausserrhoden
Glarus

Schaffhausen
St Gallen
Thurgau

are also important, particularly in St Gallen, where embroidered lace has an international reputation. The metal and machine industries also make a significant contribution to the local economy.

The north-east is also noted for the high concentration of small and medium-size breweries. Liquid assets to look out for

332

include Falkenbier (brewed in Schaffhausen), Löwengarten Bier (Rorschach) and Locher Bräu (Appenzell).

The region's best-known mountain is Säntis (2503m), although there are some higher peaks in the southern part. Aside from Lake Constance, which it shares with Germany and Austria, the largest lake in the north-east is the Walensee. The Rhine Falls, near Schaffhausen, are a noisy, often dramatic spectacle.

The local people in rural parts have a reputation for being traditional, parochial folk. This is reflected in the fact that the ancient practice of the *Landsgemeinde* (open-air parliament) is still conducted in two cantons. This annual meeting, where citizens vote by show of hands on local matters, is well worth viewing. Citizens in Glarus vote on the first Sunday in May. Appenzell is split into two half-cantons so there is a meeting at two locations on the last Sunday in April: in Appenzell village and either in Trogen (even years) or Hundwill (odd years).

Information for the north-east is covered by the St Gallen tourist office (see the following St Gallen Canton section). There are

North-East Switzerland

fewer brochures available in English than in most other regions.

Getting Around

The canton of Thurgau has a regional one-day pass, the Thurgauer Tageskarte. It covers a 1000-km network of rail, bus and boat travel, and costs Sfr26, or Sfr16.50 for children (six to 16 years) and those with the Half-Fare Card. This is bound to save you money, particularly if you're planning a boat trip on the Rhine River or Lake Constance – merely the fare from Kreuzlingen to Schaffhausen would cost the same price. Towns bordering Thurgau, like St Gallen, Winterthur and Schaffhausen are covered, as is the route to Engen in Germany (using the white Thurgau trains only). The pass is issued year-round. Parents travelling with children should acquire a Family Card (see the Getting Around chapter).

Another regional pass covers some of the routes in the Säntis region, including Appenzell, Ebenalp, Gamsalp and Buchs. This pass is worth considering if you intend to spend several days mountain-hopping in this small area. The price is Sfr75 (Sfr60 for Swiss railpass-holders) for three days' free travel in seven, or Sfr95 (Sfr75) for five in 15. It's issued from 1 May to 31 October.

St Gallen Canton

ST GALLEN
• *pop 73,000* • *670m* • *☎ (071)*
In 612 AD, an itinerant Irish monk called Gallus fell into a briar. Relying on a peculiar form of Irish logic, the venerable Gallus interpreted this clumsy act as a sign from God and decided to stay put and build a hermitage. He was helped in this task, according to legend, by a bear. From this inauspicious beginning, the town of St Gallen evolved and developed into an important medieval cultural centre, reaching the peak of its influence in the 10th century. The Reformation was brought to St Gallen

in 1524 by Vadian, the mayor of the town, whose statue stands in Marktgasse.

Orientation & Information

St Gallen is the seventh largest city in Switzerland. The train station has the usual facilities, including train information, lockers, money-exchange counters and bike rental. The main post office (Bahnhofplatz, 9001) is opposite the train station, and is also the departure point for postbuses. The transport hub for city buses is also by the station.

Two minutes away is the tourist office (☎ 227 37 37; fax 227 37 67), Bahnhofplatz 1a, which is open Monday to Friday from 9 am to noon and 1 to 6 pm, and on Saturday from 9 am to noon. The office has a free hotel booking service for personal or telephone callers. Pick up its *Tourist Information* booklet in English, which has a map and coupons for shopping discounts. A few minutes to the east is the pedestrian-only old town, dominated by the twin spires of the cathedral. Most of the main sights are clustered in this area.

The budget travel agency, SSR (☎ 223 43 47) is at Frongartenstrasse 15, open from Monday afternoon to Saturday morning.

Pedestrian Centre

St Gallen has a distinctive old-city centre. It's full of interesting buildings with colourful murals, carved balconies and relief statues. The most striking feature of the centre are the oriel windows; some of the best are on Gallusplatz, Spisergasse and Kugelgasse. Look out also for the busy market on Marktplatz on Wednesday and Saturday.

Cathedral

The twin-tower cathedral cannot and should not be missed. It's the final incarnation of Gallus' original hermit's cell and the subsequent monastery. Work was begun in 1755 and the 68m towers were erected in 1766. Completed in 1768, it's immensely impressive and impressively immense. The ceiling frescoes are by Josef Wannenmacher; unfortunately, in poor light the detail of the

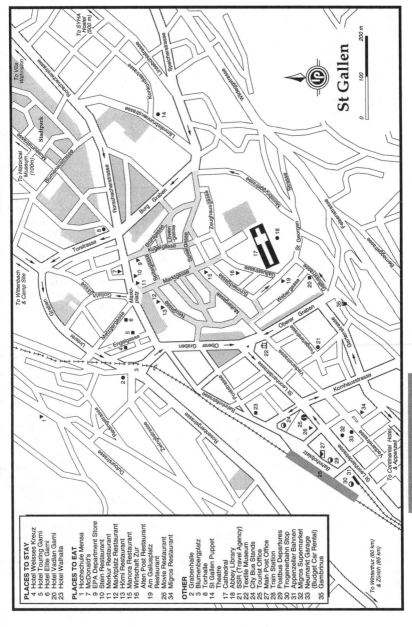

St Gallen

PLACES TO STAY
4 Hotel Weisses Kreuz
5 Hotel Touring Garni
6 Hotel Elite Garni
20 Hotel Vadian Garni
23 Hotel Walhalla

PLACES TO EAT
1 Hochschule Mensa
7 McDonald's
9 EPA Department Store
10 Stein Restaurant
11 Merkur Restaurant
12 Marktplatz Restaurant
13 Hörni Restaurant
15 Manora Restaurant
16 Wirtschaft Zur
 Alten Post Restaurant
19 Am Gallusplatz
 Restaurant
26 Movie Restaurant
34 Migros Restaurant

OTHER
2 Grabenhalle
3 Blumenbergplatz
8 Tonhalle
14 St Gallen Puppet
 Theatre
17 Cathedral
18 Abbey Library
21 SSR (Travel Agency)
22 Textile Museum
24 City Bus Stands
25 Tourist Office
27 Main Post Office
28 Train Station
29 Postbus Departures
30 Trogenerbahn Stop
31 Appenzeller Bahnen
32 Migros Supermarket
33 Neumarkt Garage
 (Budget Car Rental)
35 Gambrinus

To Winterthur (80 km)
& Zürich (85 km)

paintings is masked by the darkness of the colours. The stucco embellishments are the work of the Gigi brothers. Look out also for the pulpit, arches, statue groups and wood-carvings around the confessionals. It's open daily except during services.

Abbey Library

Adjoining the cathedral is the Stifts-bibliothek, containing some beautifully etched manuscripts from the Middle Ages and a splendidly opulent Rococo interior. The graceful lines of the wooden balustrades in the main hall show rare artistry. In total, the library contains 140,000 volumes. There's even an Egyptian mummy dating from 700 BC. Entry costs Sfr5 or Sfr3 for students and children. Opening times are: May to October, Monday to Saturday from 9 am to noon and 1.30 to 5 pm and Sunday from 10.30 am to noon and (June to August only) 1.30 to 4 pm; December to March, Monday to Saturday from 9 am to noon and 1.30 to 4 pm; April, Monday to Saturday from 9 am to noon and 1.30 to 5 pm. It's closed for most of November.

Museums

St Gallen has several museums vying for the attention in the Stadtpark, off Museum-strasse to the east of the old town. The most significant is probably the **Historical Museum**. Of particular note are the models and maps of the town, illustrating the succes-sive versions of the monastery-turned-abbey. Elsewhere in the museum there are some excellent tiled stoves and panelled state rooms, as well as portraits, uniforms, ceramics and ethnological exhibits. Entry costs Sfr6 (children Sfr2) and it's open Tuesday to Saturday from 10 am to noon and 2 to 5 pm, and Sunday from 10 am to 5 pm.

The **Textile Museum**, Vadianstrasse 2, displays an extensive collection of intri-cately-worked lace and embroidery, spanning three centuries. It's open Monday to Saturday from 10 am to noon and 2 to 5 pm (closed Saturday from 1 November to 31 March) and costs Sfr5 (free for children and students).

Places to Stay

Exhibitions and conferences can make beds scarce and prices high; busy times are usually April and October.

Camping The nearest camping is north of St Gallen at *Leebrücke* (☎ 298 49 69) in Wit-tenbach, accessible by postbus. It's open April to October.

Hostel The SYHA *hostel* (☎ 245 47 77) is a signposted, 15-minute walk east of the old town at Jüchstrasse 25 (pedestrians should follow the hostel signs with the adult and child – the other hostel signs are a less direct route for drivers). However, it's easier to take the orange Trogenerbahn from outside the station to 'Schülerhaus' (Sfr2.40) and walk a few minutes up the hill until you see the hostel on the left. Beds are Sfr23 in a dorm or Sfr32 in a double room. Reception is closed from 9 am to 5 pm but there's usually daytime access to communal areas. Get a key to avoid the curfew. The hostel closes from mid-December to early March, though it's sometimes open in January.

Hotels & Pensions *Hotel Weisses Kreuz* (☎ 223 28 43) on Engelgasse is the best value, though some walls are thin. It has varying singles/doubles from Sfr40/75 using hall showers, or from Sfr55/80 with private shower. A few rooms have TV. The reception is in the metallic blue-lit bar downstairs.

If you can't get in there, *Hotel Touring Garni* (☎ 222 58 01) is virtually opposite. Singles for Sfr54 have a shower cubicle in the room, and doubles for Sfr95 have an en suite bathroom. Rooms for Sfr44/75 have a sink but no access to a shower. *Hotel Elite Garni* (☎ 222 12 36), Metzgergasse 9-11, is slightly better but also slightly more expen-sive, with rooms from Sfr68/108; singles using hall shower start at Sfr54. This place has a lift. *Hotel Vadian Garni* (☎ 223 60 80), Gallusstrasse 36, has attractive modern-looking rooms with TV, from Sfr70/100, or Sfr85/135 with own shower and WC.

The best mid-price deal is *continental* (☎ 277 88 11; fax 278 33 80), Teufener Strasse

95. It's a little bit out of the way, but bus No 5 stops out the front (stop: Ruhbergstrasse) and goes to Bahnhofplatz every 10 minutes. Comfortable rooms with TV and bath or shower start at Sfr100/185. The cheaper rooms face the main street and there is garage parking for Sfr12. The restaurant (closed Sunday) is reasonable value, with Swiss dishes for Sfr13 to Sfr38.

The Best Western *Hotel Walhalla* (☎ 222 29 22; fax 222 29 66) is a conveniently situated four-star place on Bahnhofplatz, and has a fish-speciality restaurant. Standard, renovated rooms with all facilities start at Sfr165/250.

Places to Eat

Eating can be pretty good in St Gallen across the range. At the basic level, look out for various fast-food stalls selling St Gallen sausage and bread for around Sfr4. The university *Hochschule Mensa*, east of the rail tracks at Dufourstrasse (take bus No 5), offers cheap weekday lunches.

A large *Migros* supermarket and restaurant is near the tourist office on St Leonhardstrasse. Self-service food is also available in the restaurant of the EPA department store at Bohl 6. A *Manora* restaurant is in the Manor department store on Marktgasse. All are open until 6.30 pm weekdays (9 pm on Thursday) and 5 pm on Saturday.

On and around Marktplatz are several options, including a McDonald's and a branch of Merkur (for reliable, inexpensive food). There's also *Stein*, which, if building renovations don't alter the menu, has tasty but cheap fare. Close by are two places straddling Marktplatz and Neugasse, *Hörni* and *Marktplatz*. Both are similar, open daily, and offer food for a range of prices. Hörni has a wide selection of beers, but you can only get the cheaper draught stuff on the ground floor. Marktplatz restaurant also has an upstairs section, where prices are slightly higher.

Near the tourist office is *Movie Restaurant*, St Leonhardstrasse 32, with movie memorabilia and menus written on cinefilm canisters. It's busy, and youngish, and has

meals for above Sfr18. During weekday lunch times, a similar price will include a starter and soft drink.

A good mid-price place is *Wirtschaft Zur Alten Post* (☎ 222 66 01), Gallusstrasse 4. The food is typically Swiss, with meat and fish dishes mostly above Sfr30. Lunch menus (Sfr16 to Sfr29) are more affordable. Small and cosy, this restaurant fills quickly, so reserve ahead. It's closed on Sunday and Monday.

Top-of-the-range in prices and quality is *Am Gallusplatz* (☎ 223 33 30), Gallusstrasse 24. You can construct your own multi-course feast from a number of options (from Sfr69 for four courses), or go with one of the set menus. Main dishes are about Sfr40, or Sfr25 at lunch. The style is French and it's closed Saturday lunchtime and all day Monday.

Entertainment

The *Grabenhalle*, Blumenbergplatz, is a major venue for rock and jazz concerts, and other arts events. Buy tickets at the venue on the night. *Gambrinus*, Wassergasse 5, is a bar/restaurant with live jazz nightly (around Sfr15 cover on Friday and Saturday, free other nights). It also has a lunch menu for Sfr12.50 (closed Sunday).

Villa Wahnsinn, Rorschacherstrasse 150, is in the Silberturm (silver tower), east of the centre – take bus No 1 or 11 to Grossacker, or it's walkable from the hostel. This busy, darkish late-night bar and disco has dancing, games and competitions. Sfr5 entry includes your first drink. It's closed on Monday and Tuesday.

There are several theatres in the city, including the *Puppet Theatre* at Lämmlisbrunnenstrasse 34. Classical concerts are often performed at the *Tonhalle*, Museumstrasse 25. The tourist office has details, and sells tickets for some events.

Getting There & Away

St Gallen is the transport hub for the northeast. It's just a short train or bus ride to/from Lake Constance. There are also regular trains to Bregenz in Austria (Sfr12), Constance

(Sfr15.80), Chur (Sfr32) and Zürich (Sfr26; takes 70 minutes, via Winterthur).

By car, the main link is the N1/E60 motorway, which runs from Zürich and Winterthur to the Austrian border. It passes close to the centre of town, just slightly to the north.

For car hire, go to Avis (☎ 277 35 77), Zürcherstrasse 246, Hertz (☎ 278 84 74), down the road at No 63, or Budget (☎ 222 11 14) at the Neumarkt garage, Vadianstrasse.

Getting Around

Journeys on the bus cost Sfr1.90, though you could also pay Sfr19 for 12 tickets, Sfr6 for a day pass, or Sfr22 for one week. Buy tickets from dispensers; there's a fine of Sfr50 if you're caught without one. Individual bus tickets are not valid on the Trogenerbahn, where the fare depends upon distance, but the general day passes and the 12-strip tickets *are* valid.

There are many parking garages in town, including by the tourist office. To park all day in a blue zone, buy an 'Erweiterte Blaue Zone' ticket for Sfr5.50 from the tourist office or a police station. Otherwise, blue zones are free and subject to a 90-minute limit (no limit from 7 pm to 7 am and at weekends).

RAPPERSWIL
• *pop 7400* • *405m* • ☎ *(055)*
This small town on the north bank of Lake Zürich is in the canton of St Gallen. The tourist office (☎ 210 70 00) is three minutes from the train station, by the lake at Fischermarktplatz, and is open Monday to Friday. The town has a castle which dates from the 13th century and provides a good view from its terrace.

But the main reason to stop off is for the **Knie Kinderzoo** (children's zoo), situated behind the station (signposted). There are animal rides and other attractions such as a Noah's Ark. Best of all are the performing dolphins who show off their stunts several times a day. Entry costs Sfr7 for adults and Sfr3 for children, and it is open mid-March to early November, from 9 am to 6 pm (7 pm

July and August). The Knie circus is a travelling show that visits many Swiss towns from March to November. Ask the tourist office about Rapperswil's new circus museum.

Places to Stay & Eat

The S Y H A *hostel* (☎ 210 99 27), Hessenhofweg 10, is close to the lake in the suburb of Jona. It costs Sfr27 and it is closed from early November to the end of January. In the sports complex near the children's zoo is the *Familien Herberge Lido* (☎ 210 33 98). Beds in two, four or eight-bed rooms with shower cost Sfr15 (children to age 12 Sfr11), plus Sfr4 for sheets. Breakfast is Sfr4 to Sfr9. If you stay here, entry to the swimming pool is just Sfr1.50.

Hotel Eden (☎ 210 12 21), Seestrasse, has a couple of singles for Sfr50, and good doubles for Sfr90 to Sfr140. It also has a quality restaurant (closed Sunday and Monday).

Tower of Rapperswil Castle. Built by the Counts of Rapperswil around 1230, the castle served as the museum of the Swiss Society for the Conservation of Castles from 1962 to 1973.

Bahnhof Buffet in the train station has cheap self-service Swiss and Italian dishes, and mid-price Chinese food (open daily). Opposite the station is a large *Migros* supermarket, open until 6.30 pm weekdays (9 pm Wednesday) and 4 pm Saturday; its restaurant is also open on Sunday from 10 am to 6 pm.

Getting There & Away
Rapperswil is 50 minutes by train from St Gallen (Sfr22). From Zürich (Sfr13.60), the S5 takes 30 minutes; S7 takes 40 minutes but it's a more scenic lakeside trip. Zürich's cantonal tickets are valid. Rapperswil can also be reached by boat from Zürich (Swiss Pass valid).

WALENSEE
This lake at 419m is flanked by impressively steep mountains to the north. Wedged between the crags and the water on this side is **Quinten**, a tiny place with just a couple of guesthouses. There's no road there – you have to walk from Walenstadt (one hour) or take a boat. Boats go year-round from Murg on the south shore, though other boat tours of the lake are in the summer only. Contact Schiffsbetrieb Walensee (☎ 081-738 12 08) for details. The main rail route from Zürich to Sargans passes along the southern shore of the lake.

Appenzellerland

If you ever hear a joke in Switzerland, the inhabitants of Appenzellerland are likely to be its target. They are known for their parochialism and are considered (a little unfairly) to be several stages lower on the evolutionary ladder than the rest of humanity. Politically, Appenzellerland is divided into two half-cantons, Innerrhoden and Ausserrhoden. Appenzell itself is in Innerrhoden. Women were finally allowed to vote for the first time in Innerrhoden cantonal affairs in 1991, and then only after the supreme court ruled their exclusion by the men unconstitutional. The men of Ausserrhoden, reluctantly but without coercion, allowed the women to have their say the year before.

Such resistance to change has its advantages for the tourist in that Appenzellerland has a quaint air of being unaffected by modern life. It is a region of farms, verdant hills and villages with characteristic gabled houses. Several mountains enliven the hiking possibilities.

Activities
Hiking Pick up the hiking map (Sfr1) from one of the local tourist offices, which gives a summary of routes and average walking times. All the peaks in the region can be ascended by foot if you don't want to take the cable car. There's a **geological path** (*geologischer Wanderweg*) linking Hoher Kasten, Stauberen, Saxerlücke, Fälensee lake and Brülisau. There are 14 information boards along the several alternative routes, detailing geological features. Start at the highest point by taking the train to Weissbad, the bus to Brülisau, and the cable car to Hoher Kasten (Sfr18 up, Sfr13 down, Sfr23 return). See the Säntis section for more walking suggestions.

Skiing Skiing is not a major activity, but it's still possible. The main area for downhill is the **Kronberg** (1663m) with 10 km of runs, reached by cable car from Jakobsbad. There are also some slopes on Ebenalp and above Appenzell. A three-day lift pass costs Sfr70 (children Sfr50), available from the Appenzell tourist office. There are also some ski schools and cross-country skiing trails.

APPENZELL
• *pop 4800* • *785m* • ☎ *(071)*
The smell of the countryside – cows and their waste products – permeates the air in pastoral Appenzell. The village is a delight to wander around (albeit crowded with tourists on summer weekends), with traditional old houses, painted façades and lush surrounding pastures.

Orientation & Information

The train station (with money-exchange and bike rental) is five minutes from the centre of town. The tourist office (☎ 788 96 41) is in the centre on Hauptgasse, a mostly pedestrian-only street. It has information on all of Appenzellerland and is open Monday to Friday from 8 am to noon and 2 to 5 pm (6 pm in summer), and Saturday from 9 am to noon and (in summer) from 2 to 4 pm.

Things to See & Do

Hauptgasse is an attractive main street, with wrought-iron hanging signs, and souvenir shops selling (including on Sunday) locally-made wares, such as embroidery and decorated confectionery. Take a look inside the village **church** on Hauptgasse and admire the gold and silver figures flanking the Baroque altar. The **Appenzell Museum**, in the same building as the tourist office, has folklorish exhibits (Sfr5, Sfr3 students; closed winter Mondays); ask for the extensive English notes. Over the river lies the **Alpenbitter Distillery** (☎ 787 17 17). It offers free tours for groups from Monday to Saturday, which you may be able to join if you telephone ahead. Otherwise, there are open tours at 10 am on Wednesday.

The streets are bedecked with flags and flowers on the last Sunday in April. This is when the locals vote on cantonal issues by a show of hands in the open-air parliament, the Landsgemeinde. It takes place, not surprisingly, in Landsgemeindeplatz. People wear traditional dress for the occasion and many of the men carry swords or daggers as proof of citizenship.

Places to Stay & Eat

There is year-round camping at *Eischen* (☎ 787 50 30). *Gasthaus Hof* (☎ 787 22 10), off Landsgemeindeplatz, has dorms (Sfr21, or Sfr25 including breakfast), rooms (from Sfr60/100), a restaurant and private parking.

Hotel Taube (☎ 787 11 49), by the corner of Postplatz, has singles/doubles for Sfr55/110 using hall shower, or Sfr70/140 with private shower. Its restaurant has good food, including vegetarian dishes, for about Sfr18.

By the station is *Big Ben Pub & Pizzeria*, where pizzas start at Sfr10.50 (closed Tuesday). Other restaurants are quite pricey, though there is a *Coop* supermarket in town. *Gasthaus Traube*, just off Hauptgasse, has meals for Sfr11, but most dishes top Sfr18 (closed Monday).

Restaurant Sonne, on Landsgemeindeplatz, has daily specials from Sfr15 (closed Thursday and Friday), and cheaper 'senior' meals. *Hotel Säntis* (☎ 787 87 22; fax 787 48 42), also on Landsgemeindeplatz, provides more expensive options for both eating and sleeping; rooms start at Sfr115/180.

Getting There & Away

The red, narrow-gauge Appenzell train leaves from outside the St Gallen station (Swiss Pass and Eurail valid; Inter-Rail gets half-price). It meanders along, criss-crossing the course of the road, and takes around 40 minutes. There are two routes so you can go back a different way. Departures from St Gallen are approximately every half hour, via Gais (Sfr9.60) or Herisau (Sfr12.20).

STEIN

Appenzell culture and crafts are highlighted in this small village. The **Appenzell Showcase Cheese Dairy** (Appenzeller Schaukäserie) provides the opportunity to see the famous cheese undergo a 10-stage progress from pure milk to a ripened cheese wheel. A viewing gallery allows you to watch every move made by the white-clad workers as they rush around manipulating gleaming metal vats and presses. (There's no sneaking a quiet fag behind the churns for these people.)

It's free and open daily from 8 am to 7 pm (6 pm from 1 December to 31 March), but it's more interesting to go when the various processes are instigated, from 9 to 11 am and (sometimes) 1 to 3 pm. A brochure in English explains the different stages and contains cheese recipes on the reverse. There's a restaurant on site.

Swiss Cheese

Switzerland has 1200 village cheese dairies producing around 130,000 tonnes of cheese per annum. The most popular variety is Emmental (55,000 tonnes), followed by Gruyère (23,000 tonnes). It all starts with fresh milk, which is heated and stirred. At the correct temperature rennet is added: this curdles the milk. After further heating, stirring and slicing (eg with a cheese harp), the resultant cheese grains are extracted from the watery mass (in traditional dairies, by lifting it out with a cheesecloth). The cheese is pressed into circular moulds to form 'wheels'. The size of the cheese wheel depends on the type of cheese – they're as heavy as 60 to 130 kg in the case of Emmental. When cooled, these are immersed in a saline bath, within which the cheese discharges water, absorbs salt, and forms its rind.

The cheese is then stored in a cool cellar, though Emmental cheese also has several weeks in a warm, moist fermenting cellar (this causes gas pockets of carbonic acid to form, which creates Emmental's distinctive holes). Months will pass before the cheese attains its full flavour and is allowed to reach the plate and the palate. Semi-hard cheese (eg Appenzeller) matures the quickest. Hard cheeses, with a lower water content, take the longest (up to three years in the case of Sbrinz cheese). ■

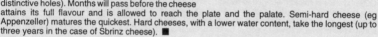

Next door is the **Folklore Museum** (Volkskunde Museum). In addition to the periodic weaving demonstrations, displays include furniture, cowbells, decorated harnesses and traditional pipes. The best exhibit is the collection of simple, childlike, yet evocative pictures of village life, usually showing herders leading lines of cattle. Cows in the foreground are often the same size as those in the distance – the newfangled notion of artistic perspective obviously hadn't reached Appenzellerland at the time (19th century!).

It takes only an hour or so to get round, and costs Sfr7 (Sfr6 students, Sfr3.50 children). It's open April to October, 10 am to noon and 1.30 to 5 pm from Tuesday to Saturday, 10 am to 6 pm on Sunday, and 1.30 to 5 pm on Monday. The rest of the year it's open Sunday only from 10 am to 5 pm.

Getting There & Away

The St Gallen bus (direction: Herisau) passes through woodland and rolling countryside, takes 15 minutes, and drops you right opposite the cheese dairy. The fare is Sfr4.80 and departures are every one to two hours.

SÄNTIS

Although a mere tiddler in Swiss terms, the Säntis mountain (2502m) is the highest peak in the vicinity, and accordingly offers a marvellous panorama that encompasses Lake Constance, Lake Zürich, the Alps and the Vorarlberg Mountains. To get there, take the train to Urnäsch (on the Appenzell to Herisau line) and transfer to the bus (approximately hourly) to Schwägalp. From Schwägalp, a cable car ascends to the summit every 30 minutes (7.30 am to 6.30 pm in summer, 8.30 am to 5 pm in winter). The fare is: Sfr19.20 up, Sfr16.40 down, and Sfr27 return.

From Säntis, you can walk along the ridge to the neighbouring peak of **Ebenalp** (1640m) in about 3½ hours (4½ hours going the other way). On Ebenalp there are prehistoric caves at Wildkirchli, showing traces of Stone Age habitation. The descent to Seealpsee lake on foot takes 1½ hours. Alternatively, a cable car runs between the summit and Wasserauen approximately every 30 minutes (Sfr16.60 up, Sfr12 down, Sfr21 return). Wasserauen and Appenzell are connected by rail.

Schaffhausen Canton

SCHAFFHAUSEN
• *pop 34,300*   • *404m*   • ☎ *(052)*
The capital of the canton that bears its name, Schaffhausen joined the Swiss Confedera-

tion in 1501. It is known as a heavy industry, communications and arms centre. During WWII, in 1944 and 1945, it was accidentally bombed by the USA (see the boxed aside). Thankfully its medieval town centre survived the shelling, and today merits a leisurely exploration.

Orientation & Information
Schaffhausen is an enclave of Swiss territory surrounded by Germany on the north bank of the Rhine. The train station is adjacent to

WWII and the Schaffhausen Bombings

Quite how Switzerland managed to avoid getting sucked into the 1939-45 war is a question without an easy answer. Swiss pilots shot down Allied and German planes that violated its air space with equal diligence, yet Swiss neutrality also involved covert help to both sides too. Switzerland would have survived whichever side won – somehow the Swiss managed the trick of backing both horses in a two horse race.

The country's civil defence was not so developed in those days, and it would have been relatively easy for Hitler to sweep in and take the northern cities, if not the Alpine regions. Indeed, in July 1940 General Guisan realised that the borders could not be held against attack, and re-deployed the army from frontier posts to entrenched positions in the Alps. There was even plenty of support for Nazi Germany (not least from the president of the Federal Council) boosted by the common border and language, which would have made Hitler's task easier. Nazi party members numbered 4000 in Basel alone.

When Paris fell in 1940 the Nazis discovered a secret agreement for the exchange of military information between Switzerland and France. This could easily have been used by Hitler as a pretext for invasion. But a neutral Switzerland had its uses to the Nazis, not least in providing a safe haven for the art treasures and assets pilfered from conquered lands (a fortune in assets still remains in Swiss banks, secured by both metal vaults and a veil of secrecy).

To keep Germany at bay, Switzerland also used negotiation and bluff. In a famous (and probably aprocryphal) conversation between a member of the German military and General Guisan, the German asked what would happen if the Nazis sent down a force to take Switzerland. Guisan told him that he could have over 500,000 men mobilised to defend the country within a few hours. 'And what would happen if we sent down a force double that size?' probed the German. Guisan replied simply, 'Then each man would have to shoot twice.'

Diplomatic relations were kept open with both the Allies and the Nazis, allowing Switzerland to be a conduit through which the belligerents could communicate, and the country undertook tasks like exchanges of prisoners of war. Exactly how far Switzerland had to go to pacify Hitler is not in the public domain, but it is accepted that some arms (tank parts, etc) produced by the town of Schaffhausen ended up in Germany. Whether this was by intent or 'accident' is also not clear.

Strange and secretive things happen in wartime. Perhaps it is a coincidence that American bombers, on a mission to southern Germany on 1 April 1944, 'mistakenly' identified Schaffhausen as a German target and unloaded their bombs. The town suffered about 100 casualties, with most bombs falling around the train station and in the nearby woods. The Americans' excuse to the outraged Swiss for this error was that there were navigational difficulties induced by bad weather. Swiss outrage was merely inflamed by this explanation, as weather conditions on the day in question were extremely clear.

The Americans later supplemented their account of the incident with the information that the divisional leader had been shot down earlier, and the winds they encountered were much stronger than expected. The USA paid full compensation to Switzerland, and created guidelines that no target would be bombed within 50 miles of the Swiss frontier, unless positively identified. Curious, therefore, that on 22 February 1945 Schaffhausen again suffered 'accidental' bombing, this time leaving 16 dead. ■

the old town, and has lockers, bike rental, and money-exchange counters (open daily from 6.50 am to 7.10 pm). There are also information offices for both Swiss and German trains. The tourist office (☎ 625 51 41) is in the heart of the old town at Fronwagturm. It is open Monday to Friday from 9 am to noon and 2 to 6 pm, and Saturday from 9 am to noon, reducing in winter to weekdays only from 2 to 5 pm. Postbuses depart from the rear of the station and local buses from the front. The main post office (8201 Schaffhausen 1) is also opposite the station.

Things to See & Do

The attractive old town is bursting with oriel windows, painted façades and ornamental fountains. The best streets are Vordergasse and Vorstadt, which intersect at Fronwagplatz. From May to October the tourist office organises a guided walking tour of the centre on Monday, Wednesday and Friday afternoons (Sfr10, children Sfr5).

Vordergasse has the most distinctive house in the centre, the 16th century **Haus zum Ritter**, decorated in scenes from mythology and Roman history. These drawings are a relatively recent copy of work done by Tobias Stimmer in 1570. Fragments of the originals can be seen in the **Allerheiligen Museum**, by the cathedral in Klosterplatz. The rest of the collection ranges from ancient bones to modern art. Entry is free and it's open from Tuesday to Sunday from 10 am to noon and 2 to 5 pm.

Get an overview of the town from the **Munot**, a fortification atop a vine-covered hill. The summit can be attained in under 15 minutes from the centre. Aside from the impressive view, this 16th century keep boasts a couple of old canons. It's free and open daily: 8 am to 8 pm in summer and 9 am to 5 pm from October to April.

The Rhine Falls (see the Around Schaffhausen section) is an easy excursion from the town. Another essential excursion while in the area is a trip along the river. The 45 km from Schaffhausen to Constance is considered one of the Rhine's most beautiful

stretches, passing by meadows, castles and ancient villages. See the Stein am Rhein and Lake Constance Getting Around sections for more details.

Places to Stay

Camp by the river at *Rheinwiesen* (☎ 659 33 00), a couple of km east of the town in Langwiesen, and accessible by postbus. It's open from 1 May to mid-September.

The SYHA *hostel* (☎ 625 88 00) is 15 minutes' walk west of the train station (or take bus No 3 to Breite), at Randenstrasse 65. Dorms cost Sfr21.50, and the reception is closed from 9 am to 5.30 pm. The hostel closes from 1 November to late February.

The best budget deal in the town centre is *Steinbock* (☎ 625 42 60), Webergasse 47, with singles/doubles for Sfr48/75, and triples for Sfr100, all without breakfast and using hall showers. It's above a fairly noisy café but the rooms are clean and reasonably sized.

Lowen (☎ 643 22 08), Im Hösli 2, has rooms for Sfr55/95, or Sfr65/110 with private shower. It's three km north of town in Herblingen, reached by city bus No 5.

Park Villa (☎ 625 27 37; fax 624 12 53), Parkstrasse 18, south of the station by the west side of the tracks, costs from Sfr105/159 for comfortable rooms with shower/WC, or Sfr70/100 without. Some rooms in this friendly, atmospheric place have luxurious antique furnishings, and there's plenty of parking.

The only four-star hotel is the convenient *Hotel Bahnhof* (☎ 624 19 24; fax 624 74 79), Bahnhofstrasse 46. Rooms are quiet and large with all amenities, and cost from Sfr130/190.

Places to Eat

You can eat for under Sfr12 at either the *Migros* supermarket and restaurant at Vorstadt 39, or the *EPA* department store and restaurant at Vordergasse 69. The food is self-service and good value. Both places are open until 6.30 pm on weekdays and 4 pm on Saturday. The Manor department store near Fronwagplatz has quite a good *Manora* self-service restaurant, which has great salad and dessert buffets (open same hours). There are also several reasonable cafés with outside seating on Fronwagplatz, that are ideal on a sunny day.

Restaurant Falken, Vorstadt 7, has Mexican and Swiss food from about Sfr13 (open daily). The best Italian food (from Sfr13) is at *Pizzeria Romana*, Unterstadt 18 (closed Wednesday).

For a taste treat, go to *Rheinhotel Fischerzunft* (☎ 625 32 81), Rheinquai 8. It is acclaimed as one of the top 10 restaurants in Switzerland, a justification for spending around Sfr50 per main dish. It combines Oriental and European styles, particularly incorporating fish, and it's open daily. Rooms (also expensive) are available, too.

Getting There & Away
There are hourly trains to Zürich (Sfr15.80; takes 40 minutes). Basel can be reached by either Swiss (Sfr43, via Zürich) or German (Sfr19.40) trains. To Constance by German train (via Singen) costs Sfr12.

Steamers travel to Constance several times a day in summer, and the trip takes four hours; they depart from Freier Platz (☎ 625 42 82 for information). Schaffhausen has excellent road connections radiating out in all directions.

THE RHINE FALLS (RHEINFALL)
This is the largest waterfall in Europe, and makes a tremendous racket as the Rhine crashes down a 23m drop. The average flow of water is 600 cubic metres per second in summer and 250 cubic metres in winter. The highest ever recorded was 1250 cubic metres per second in the summer of 1965. Impassable to shipping, the falls contributed greatly to the past expansion of Schaffhausen, three km up-river, as boats were forced to unload cargo there.

From the north bank of the river the falls are less steep and less violent. You need to cross the bridge to the south side to get a true impression of the power of the water flow. The viewpoint from the Schloss Laufen is best. A stairway leads right down to the edge,

where the water leaps and boils and sprays the edge of the platform. You need to pay Sfr1 to the Schloss souvenir shop (open daily) to gain access to the staircase. It seems surprising that they should bother to charge, because when the shop shuts in the evening you can walk down for nothing.

Places to Stay & Eat
Within the Schloss is an ageing *SYHA hostel* (☎ 052-659 61 52) where the doors are locked from 10 am to 5 pm and there's a 10 pm curfew. Dorms cost Sfr22 and the hostel is closed from late November to the end of February. Kitchen facilities are available for a Sfr2 charge.

Stock up or eat in the *Migros* supermarket/restaurant in Neuhausen (no half-day closing). Schloss Laufen has two restaurants, where main courses cost Sfr17 to Sfr45 (closed Sunday evening, Monday and Tuesday in low season).

Getting There & Away
From Schaffhausen, the falls can be reached by a 40-minute stroll westward along the river. Alternatively, take bus No 1 or 9 to Neuhausen and get off by the Migros in the centre; then follow the brown signs leading to the north bank of the river (five minutes).

STEIN AM RHEIN
• *pop 2940* • *407m* • ☎ *(052)*
Stein am Rhein, commonly known as Stein, is quite simply delightful, its medieval centre completely captivating. Unused film in your camera stands no chance – the Rathausplatz will claim it before you have time to draw breath. Inevitably, such beauty has its down side. Stein receives 32,000 overnight visitors annually – quite manageable for its small population. However, over *one million* people per year visit on day trips. The tour buses rolling through are in danger of choking the place to death. If possible, try to visit outside the summer crush.

Orientation & Information
Stein reclines on both sides of the Rhine River. The train station is on the south side,

and has money-exchange, bike rental and left luggage facilities. Take Bahnhofstrasse and turn right then left to cross the river for the old town (a 10-minute walk). Leading off the pivotal Rathausplatz is Oberstadt (both are pedestrian-only), where awaits the tourist office (☎ 741 28 35) at No 10. Its opening hours are Monday to Friday from 9 to 11 am and 2 to 5 pm and (April to September) Saturday morning. The small post office is on Brodlaubegass.

Things to See & Do

The first thing to do is to admire the splendid façades of the buildings all around the **Rathausplatz** It is the most photogenic square in Switzerland. Many of the murals depict the animal or object after which the house is named, such as the Sun, Red Ox or White Eagle. A particularly good pairing of pictorial scenes is at Nos 14 and 15. The former was painted by Thomas Schmid from 1520-25; it is the oldest fresco in the Rathausplatz. No 15 displays the most recent work, painted by Alois Carigiet in 1956. The town hall opposite has some historical exhibits on the second floor. No 17 contains a small museum of phonographs (Sfr3 entry; open March to October).

The streets round the square are worth exploring, too. There are several gate towers dating from the 14th century, including one at the end of Understadt. **Kloster St Georgen** is a well-preserved former Benedictine monastery dating from the 12th century. It houses a museum of local history and art, open March to October from 10 am to noon and 1.30 pm to 5 pm (closed Monday; Sfr3, children and students Sfr1.50). The **Puppet Museum**, Schwarzhorngasse 136, features 500 antique puppets going back 150 years. It's open mid-April to mid-October from 11 am to 5 pm (closed Monday) and costs Sfr5, with reductions for students.

On the hill above the town, the **Hohenklingen Castle** offers a commanding view of the town and river, and a restaurant (closed Monday and the months of January and February).

Places to Stay

Stein camp site, *Grenzstein* (☎ 741 23 79), is about two km from the village by the Rhine. It is open year round and costs Sfr5 per adult, Sfr3 per child, Sfr4 for a tent and Sfr2 for a car. Good facilities on site include washing machines, camp shop and restaurant.

The SYHA *hostel* (☎ 741 12 55) is 1½ km out of the centre at Hemishoferstrasse 711. This road is the continuation of Understadt to the west, and the hostel is two minutes from the beach. It's closed from 31 October to late February (reception closed 9 am to 5.30 pm; beds cost Sfr23.)

Gästehaus Garni Bleichehof (☎ 741 22 57) costs Sfr45/75 using hall showers but it's not really viable unless you have your own transport or don't mind walking over two km; head towards the Hohenklingen castle then follow the brown signs (no street name).

Staying in the centre is a budget-busting proposition. *Gasthof Mühlethal* (☎ 741 27 25), Öhningerstrasse, 200m east of the tourist office, is the cheapest, with singles/doubles for Sfr70/100. *Hotel Adler* (☎ 742 61 61), Rathausplatz 15, has comfortable rooms for Sfr120/160 with own shower, toilet, TV and telephone; garage parking costs Sfr10 and it has a quality restaurant. It is also the reception and breakfast site for the *Motel Roseberg*, on the south side of the river. Rooms here are slightly smaller and lack the TV; prices start at Sfr95/120 and there's ample free parking.

Places to Eat

As if to deliberately counterbalance the splendour of the old centre, the *Migros* supermarket and restaurant is housed in a dreary concrete block with all the flair of a bombshelter; it defaces Di Gross Schanz, a few minutes north of the Obertor gate tower. It's open Monday to Friday from 9 am to 6.30 pm and Saturday from 7.30 am to 4 pm.

Restaurant Jumbo, Öhningerstrasse, is a Chinese place with two-course lunches for Sfr12. Evening meals are expensive, as they are at most of the other restaurants. Fish dishes are a speciality at a number of places in the centre, including at *Salmenstübli*,

Understadt 15. Prices are in the range of Sfr19 to Sfr35 and it is closed Monday.

For top quality, look to *Sonne* (☎ 741 21 28) also on Rathausplatz. It's the oldest restaurant in town (the building dates from 1463) and it is closed on Tuesday and Wednesday . It serves fish dishes and seasonal specialities for around Sfr40 to Sfr50, and open (decanted) wines.

Getting There & Away
To Zürich (S-Bahn S29) costs Sfr19.40. It is also on the hourly train route linking Schaffhausen (Sfr6.60) and Rorschach (Sfr18.20). The easiest way to St Gallen (Sfr23) is via this route, changing at Romanshorn. Regular buses to Singen (in Germany) depart from the train station.

A boat trip along this stretch of the Rhine is a real pleasure (see Getting Around in the Lake Constance section). The same sights can be perused by car on highway 13, which runs along the south bank of the river. Although the other towns and villages en route aren't as perfectly preserved as Stein am Rhein, many feature attractive church spires, half-timbered houses and hilltop castles. Places to look out for, and perhaps linger a while, are Ermatingen, Mannenbach and Steckborn to the east, and Diessenhofen to the west.

Lake Constance

Lake Constance (or Bodensee in German) is a giant bulge in the sinewy course of the Rhine and offers a choice of water sports, relaxation or cultural pursuits. Constance (Konstanz) the town achieved historical significance in 1414 when the Council of Constance was convened to try to heal huge rifts in the Catholic Church. The consequent burning at the stake of the religious reformer, Jan Hus, as a heretic, and the scattering of his ashes over the lake, failed to halt the impetus towards the Reformation.

Lake Constance is a summer area, too often foggy or at best hazy in winter. On the German side of the lake, the pre-Lent Fasnacht celebrations can be lively, helped along by Constance's large student population.

Orientation
The lake is shared by Switzerland, Germany and Austria and is 395m above sea level. Constance (Konstanz) is the largest town on the lake and sits on the end of the peninsula between the two western arms, the Überlinger See and the Unter See. Constance proper is in Germany, although the adjoining town of Kreuzlingen is Swiss and really all part of the same conurbation. Border controls between the two are very low key. Romanshorn and Rorschach are the other two main towns on the Swiss side, but plenty of other enjoyable resorts dot the shoreline in between.

In addition to Constance, the German stretch of the lake features two other main tourist centres, Meersburg and the island of Lindau. The only town of note in the Austrian part of the lake is Bregenz.

Information
Local tourist offices often have information that covers the whole lake, though there's also a general office: Internationales Bodensee-Verkersverein (☎ 07531-90 94 0), Schützenstrasse 8, D-78462 Constance. Resorts in all three countries are covered in this section, and prices listed are given in the local currency. One Swiss Franc is worth around DM1.2 (Deutschmarks) and 8.5AS (Austrian schillings). In Germany and Austria, post offices provide the most cost-effective money-exchange facilities, though as you'll pay commission, try to change money in Switzerland. Most shops and restaurants will accept neighbouring currencies, but perhaps at an unfavourable rate. The telephone country code for Germany is ☎ 49 and for Austria it is ☎ 43.

Things to See & Do
Although there is some sightseeing to be done, the main point of being here is to enjoy the lake and the many water sports on offer.

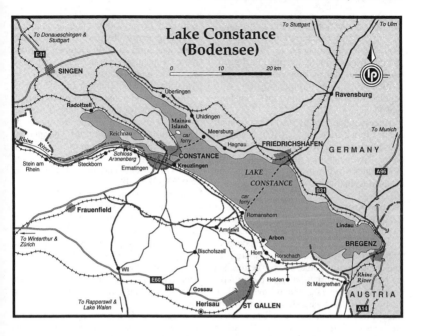

Lake Constance (Bodensee)

In Switzerland, there are sailing schools at Kreuzlingen (☎ 071-688 80 20) and Romanshorn (☎ 071-463 51 21)). Other schools are mentioned below. Swimming is at swimming pools, private beaches (entry fee) or free public beaches. The international **Bodensee Festival** takes place from early May to early June. Most of the events (concerts, cabaret, theatre, etc) are on the German side of the lake. Get information from the Bodensee-Festival GmbH (☎ 07541-92 32 0; fax 33 32 3), Olgastrasse 21, D-88045 Friedrichshafen.

Places to Stay & Eat

Accommodation and food are cheaper in Germany and Austria than in Switzerland, so it could make sense to use one of those two countries as a base for exploring the whole lake. Most places round the lake are smaller-scale establishments, so book ahead in season. Contact tourist offices well in advance for lists of holiday apartments.

Other places to stay include pensions, and cheap private homes (usually a three-day minimum stay is required), as well as many camp sites (generally closed from November to March) and hostels. Hostel prices in Germany are lower for people under 27 (so-called juniors). There is no junior/senior distinction in Bregenz or the Swiss hostels. All hostels mentioned under the following towns are HI-affiliated.

Places to eat with a lakeside view are invariably more expensive. Be sure to sample some of the Bodensee's aquatic inhabitants on your dinner plate, such as trout (Forelle) or whitefish (Felchen).

Getting There & Away

Direct trains run hourly from Schaffhausen to Kreuzlingen and the journey takes one hour. Excursions to the lake are easy from St Gallen: direct trains go to Romanshorn and Rorschach, and a direct bus goes to Arbon and Rorschach Hafen (Sfr7.20). Constance has train connections every one to two hours to Zürich and Donaueschingen (DM21). Trains from Munich go to Lindau (2½ hours). Trains from Switzerland to Bregenz go via St Margrethen. Bregenz is on the main express rail route through Austria, with regular direct trains to Innsbruck, Salzburg and Vienna.

Access to the lake by road is good on all sides. From Zürich, the N1 (E60) motorway runs north-east via Winterthur and St Gallen, to the Austrian border near Rorschach. The N7 branches off just after Winterthur and leads to Kreuzlingen.

Getting Around

Train & Bus Although trains link Bregenz, Lindau, Friedrichshafen and Constance, buses often provide the easiest land connections between these places. Meersburg isn't even on the railway line, and can be reached by bus from Friedrichshafen or by car ferry from Constance (see the following Boat section). On the Swiss side, train or bus is equally convenient. Single rail fares from Rorschach Hafen are: Horn Sfr2.40, Arbon Sfr2.80, Romanshorn Sfr5.40 and Kreuzlingen Sfr11.40.

Car The B31 hugs the northern shore of the lake but it can get busy. Likewise on the southern shore, where highway 13 shadows the course of the railway line around the lake, linking all the Swiss resorts mentioned in this section.

Cycling A 270-km bike track encloses the lake and is well signposted. The Cyclists' Touring Club in Britain (see the Getting There & Away chapter) produces useful notes to accompany a circular tour.

In Constance, Aktiv-Reisen Velotours (☎ 07531-5 20 85), Mainaustrasse 34, rents bikes (DM20 per day or DM100 per week). Bregenz (AS100 per day) train station also rent bikes, as do the stations of all the places mentioned on the Swiss side (except Horn), and the larger stations on the German side.

Boat The most enjoyable way to get around

is by boat. Ferries follow a number of routes, travelling across, along, or around the lake from late April to early October, with the more frequent services starting in late May. Eurail and Inter-Rail passes get 50% off. The Swiss Pass and the Thurgau Tageskarte (see Getting Around in the chapter introduction) are valid only for the Swiss side of the lake (with the exception of the Romanshorn-Friedrichshafen ferry with the Thurgau day pass). For boat information in Romanshorn ring ☎ 071-463 34 35, in Bregenz ring ☎ 05574-42 868 and in Constance ring ☎ 07531-28 13 98.

A Lake Constance (Bodensee) Pass (Sfr40 for 15 days) entitles the holder to purchase half-price tickets within the validity period on boats, trains and buses. Holders can buy transferable day passes (Sfr28 per set of three) valid for free travel on boats. Purchasers of the Bodensee Pass can also get a special boat-only version of the Family Card (see the Getting Around chapter), free of charge.

Bregenz to Constance by boat (via the German shore) takes three hours 30 minutes with up to six departures per day. Boats also cruise along the Rhine from Kreuzlingen and Constance all the way to Schaffhausen, via the island of Reichenau and Stein am Rhein. The total journey takes three hours 40 minutes heading downstream to Schaffhausen and 4½ hours going the other way (Sfr26).

Between Meersburg and Constance there's a car ferry that sails all year round; every 15 minutes in the day, every 30 minutes in the evening and hourly all through the night. The fare is DM2.20, plus DM10 per car. In Meersburg, boats depart only a few minutes' walk from the centre, but in Constance, you need to get to/from Staad (bus No 1 from the Bahnhof). Another car ferry sails during the day between Romanshorn and Friedrichshafen. Departures are hourly in the summer and every two hours from mid-November to mid-March. The fare is Sfr7 per person plus Sfr6 per bicycle, Sfr16 per motorcycle and from Sfr20 per car, and the journey takes 40 minutes. The boat landing stage in Romanshorn is directly outside the train station.

CONSTANCE
• *pop 170,000* • ☎ *(07531)*
In Constance, the tourist office (☎ 13 30 30) is to the right as you leave the train station. The SBB counter in the station changes money without charging commission.

The town's most visible feature is the Gothic spire of the **cathedral**, added only in 1856 to a church that was started in 1052. The views from the top are excellent. Follow the walking tour of the historic centre prescribed in the tourist office leaflet, lingering in the **Stadtgarten** and the Bohemian **Rheingasse** quarter. If you have time, head across the footbridge to **Mainau Island**, a tropical garden that was established by the royal house of Sweden (entrance DM16, or DM5 in winter). Constance has a casino, where Swiss gamblers can lose the large amounts of money that restrictive laws (soon to be changed) prevent them from losing in their own country. Constance has a public beach at **Strandbad Horn**, open May to September.

Places to Stay & Eat
The DJH *hostel* (☎ 3 22 60) at Zur Allmannshohe 18 is open from March to October and costs DM19.50/24.50 for juniors/seniors. Take bus No 1 or 4 from the station. There's an accommodation board outside the tourist office. Central places include *Pension Graf* (☎ 2 14 86), Wiesenstrasse 2, with singles/doubles for DM48/87, or *Barbarossa* (☎ 2 20 21) charging DM55/98 with own shower.

Seekuh, Konzilstrasse 1, is a student-type bar that dishes up great food and company. Salads, pasta and pizza cost DM6 to DM11; it's open every evening until about 1 am. Also try *Sedir*, Hofhalde 11, another young, cheap place but with Turkish food. The university *Mensa* provides cheap lunches. For more class and atmosphere visit *Graf Zeppelin* (☎ 2 37 80), on Untere Laube by Stephansplatz. Fish dishes are around DM25 (open daily).

KREUZLINGEN
• *pop 16,200* • ☎ *(071)*
Kreuzlingen has a tourist information counter in the TCS travel agent (☎ 672 38 40), Hauptstrasse 39. Opening hours are Monday to Friday from 8.30 am to noon and 1.45 to 6 pm.

There's not very much to see in the town, except perhaps the 17th century **St Ulric's Church** on Hauptstrasse. Most of the attractions are on the German side of the border. The main crossing points are at Hauptstrasse and Konstanzerstrasse. There's a smaller crossing by the east side of the railtracks that is usually unattended in the evening; using this route you can walk to the centre of Constance from Kreuzlingen youth hostel in 20 minutes, rather than messing around taking two trains.

A possible excursion when the weather is poor is to nearby **Frauenfeld**, where the cantonal museums of Thurgau are located: the Historisches Museum in the Schloss, the Naturmuseum in the Luzernerhaus, and the Kunstmuseum (Fine Arts Museum) on the outskirts of town. About 10 km west of Kreuzlingen is the Napoleon Museum in Schloss Arenenberg.

Places to Stay
Fischerhaus camp site (☎ 688 49 03) is by the lake, 1½ km from the tourist office. The SYHA *hostel* (☎ 688 26 63), Promenadenstrasse 7, is 10 minutes' walk from Kreuzlingen Hafen station (turn left, then left again over the tracks). It features communal showers and good buffet breakfasts in a stately old building situated in parkland. Dorm beds cost Sfr21 and it is open from 1 March to 31 November.

For hotels, you could just as easily stay in Constance, or try *Schweizerland* (☎ 672 17 17), Hauptstrasse 6, by the German border. Pleasant singles/doubles with TV are Sfr55/94, rising to Sfr66/120 with private bathroom. To get there from the main station, walk left then take the first left. *Bahnhof-Post* (☎ 672 79 72), Bahnhofstrasse, has more facilities and is right opposite the main station. Singles/doubles cost Sfr48/90, or Sfr75/115 with private shower/WC.

Places to Eat

In Kreuzlingen there's a huge *Coop* supermarket five minutes from the main station; head left then look for the Coop sign down the sidestreet. Its restaurant is even open Sunday (to 5 pm). Ultra-cheap is the self-service restaurant in the *EPA* department store, on the corner of Hauptstrasse and Parkstrasse. Nearby at Hauptstrasse 82 is the *Park Café*, with food, including vegetarian dishes, for Sfr14 to Sfr18 (closed Monday). *Restaurant Seeburg* (☎ 688 47 75), by the youth hostel, offers quality cuisine in a cultured setting. Main dishes start at Sfr18 (closed Tuesday and Wednesday).

ROMANSHORN

• ☎ *(071)*

About 20 km south-east of Kreuzlingen, this industrial town is of minimal sightseeing interest, but is a convenient base thanks to the direct ferry service to Friedrichshafen (see the Lake Constance Getting Around section above for details). The tourist office (☎ 463 32 32) is in the train station, open daily in summer, Monday to Saturday in winter.

Places to Stay & Eat

Camping is at *Strandbad Amriswil* (☎ 463 47 73), west of Romanshorn at Uttwil. The SYHA *hostel* (☎ 463 17 17), Gottfried Keller Strasse 6, is five minutes from the station and has a kitchen. Dorm beds are Sfr20 (no first night's surcharge) and it is closed from November to mid-February.

Hotel Garni (☎ 461 23 61), Bahnhofstrasse 56, one km from the station, has ample parking. Newly-built rooms with shower/WC are Sfr40/70, and breakfast costs from Sfr6.50 per person. Next-door is a large *Migros* supermarket and restaurant.

Bodan (☎ 463 15 02), opposite and to the right of the station, has singles/doubles for Sfr45/90 using showers in the hall. Doubles with private shower/toilet are Sfr90 (Sfr60 for single occupancy). Its restaurant is open

daily and has plenty of fish and vegetarian dishes (meals from Sfr12). The vicinity of the station has several other places to eat.

ARBON

• ☎ *(071)*

The tourist office (☎ 446 33 37), to the left of the station at Bahnhofstrasse 26, is in a travel agency. Walk 10 minutes in the same direction for the historic centre of town. With its castle and old churches it certainly merits a stroll. The castle was built in the 16th century and is home to an historical museum that is open daily from May to September (plus Sundays in spring/autumn; entry Sfr2). There are also a number of eye-catching, half-timbered houses in the vicinity.

Places to Stay & Eat

Camp at *Strandbadcamping Buchhorn* (☎ 446 46 65 45). *Hotel Krone* (☎ 446 10 87), Bahnhofstrasse 20, has rooms for Sfr30/60, or AS50/88 with private shower. It also offers cheap meals from Sfr9. *Pension Garni Sonnenhof* (☎ 446 15 10), Rebenstrasse 18, a residential street, has kitsch garden statues and rooms from Sfr40 per person. *Hotel Restaurant Park*, (☎ 446 11 19), Parkstrasse 7, behind Hotel Krone, charges Sfr85/140 for rooms with shower, toilet and TV.

By the station is a *Migros* restaurant and supermarket, with a lake terrace and late opening till 8 pm on Friday. *Gasthof Frohsinn*, Romanshornerstrasse 15, brews its own palatable beer; eat from Sfr14 in the downstairs bar (the upstairs restaurant is plush and expensive). Those on a spending spree can wander into *Wirtschaft zum Römerhof* (☎ 446 17 08), Hauptstrasse, in a distinctive old building attached to the ancient town fortifications. Main courses are around Sfr30 and it is closed on Tuesday and Wednesday.

HORN

• ☎ *(071)*

This resort is a pleasant 50-minute amble north of Rorschach (see below). It has the Shipper's Shop (☎ 841 56 68), Seestrasse

64, with a sailing school, boat and yacht charter and all sorts of water sports gear for sale. Frau Baumann (tel 841 26 52) at the bakery (Bäckerei), Seestrasse 72, sometimes offers very cheap rooms in summer (phone ahead). The *Hotel Restaurant Schiff* (tel 841 30 40), Seestrasse 74, provides a welcome change from the usual with its South America and Spanish specialities (Sfr13 to Sfr30). It also has a lakeside garden and rooms with shower/WC for Sfr65 per person (closed on Sunday in the off-season, and in December).

RORSCHACH
• *pop 9900* • ☎ *(071)*

The main points of interest are around the Rorschach Hafen train station; the main Rorschach station, which is on the St Gallen-Bregenz route, is a couple of km to the east of the centre. The Hafen station is also the departure point for the hourly cogwheel train which climbs a scenic route to the health resort of **Heiden**. The tourist office (☎ 841 70 34), is opposite the Hafen station and near the post office. It's open weekdays except Monday morning from 9.30 am to noon (closed in winter) and 2 to 5 pm, plus (in summer) Saturday morning.

Exit the Hafen station and turn left down Hauptstrasse to see some fine oriel windows, particularly Nos 33, 31 and 29 (the town hall).

By the station and by the lake is the **Heimat Museum**, housed in the old Kornhaus. It has a good scale model of the town in 1797, lace and embroidery displays, and temporary exhibitions. It is open daily except Monday from mid-April to mid-November (Sfr4, Sfr1 for students and children). Close by is a new **Motor Museum**, open daily from 1 May to 15 November (Sfr7, children Sfr4).

Rorschach has three sailing schools, including Delfino Segelschule (☎ 866 23 20), St Gallerstrasse 1.

Places to Stay & Eat
Rorschach's SYHA *hostel* (☎ 841 54 11) is for groups only. The cheapest hotel in the centre of Rorschach is *Hotel Löwen* (☎ 841 38 87), Hauptstrasse 92, with fair-sized singles/doubles for Sfr40/80. Each has a shower cubicle in the room. Downstairs there's a British-style pub with cheap lunches and live piano music nightly. A couple of doors along the road at No 88 is *Hotel Rössli* (☎ 844 68 68), with nicely proportioned rooms from Sfr65/130 with own shower, toilet and TV.

Rorschach has a better than average, licensed *Coop* restaurant with menus from Sfr10 and a salad buffet. It's around the back of the post office on Poststrasse. It has late opening to 9 pm on Friday and is also open on Sunday to 7 pm (unlike the supermarket section). Opposite the tourist office is *Pizzeria Krone*, with 25 types of pizza from Sfr8.80 to Sfr15.80, plus pasta and fish dishes. *Kornhausstube*, next to the tourist office, is typically Swiss (meals from Sfr13; closed Tuesday and Wednesday.).

BREGENZ
• *pop 24,700* • ☎ *(05574)*

Bregenz is the provincial capital of Vorarlberg, Austria's smallest state. The tourist office (☎ 43 39 10), Anton Schneider Strasse 4A, is open Monday to Friday from 9 am to noon and 1 to 5 pm and Saturday from 9 am to noon, except in July and August when hours are extended. The post office is on Seestrasse (Postamt 6900).

The old town is worth a stroll. Its centrepiece and the town emblem is the bulbous baroque **St Martin's Tower** built in 1599. Follow the walking route described in the tourist office leaflet. The **Pfänder Mountain** (1064m) offers an impressive panorama over the lake and beyond. Walk up or take the cable car (AS77 up, AS55 down and AS110 return). The **Bregenz Festival** takes place from late July to late August. Operas and classical works are performed from a vast water-bourne stage on the edge of the lake, but you need to book months in advance from the Kartenbüro (☎ 49 20 223), Postfach 311, A-6901. Like Constance, Bregenz has a casino that attracts many gamblers from Switzerland.

NORTH-EAST SWITZERLAND

Places to Stay & Eat

Seecamping (☎ 71 8 95/6), Bodangasse 7, is three km west of Bregenz train station. The HI *hostel* (☎ 42 8 67), Belruptstrasse 16A, Bregenz, is open 1 April to 30 September. Dorm beds cost AS116 and there's a place to leave bags during the day.

Private rooms are the best bargain (ask the tourist office), though *Hotel Krone* (☎ 42 1 17), Leutbühl 3, has good-value, central doubles (AS500, or AS640 with private shower). *Pension Traube* (☎ 42 4 01), Anton Schneider Strasse 34, has rooms for AS350/660 using hall shower, and it's closed in winter. *Hotel Kinz* (☎ 42 0 92), Kirchstrasse 9-11, has good rooms with private shower/WC for AS480/800.

The GWL shopping centre has a *Familia* supermarket with cheap self-service restaurant. *Restaurant Charly*, Anton Schneider Strasse 19, serves Italian food from AS65 (closed Thursday). For slightly pricier Austrian food, try the atmospheric *Alte Weinstube Zur Ilge*, Maurachgasse 6 (open daily).

LINDAU

• *pop 25,000* • ☎ *(08382)*

Lindau is just inside Bavaria in the east, near the Austrian border. Tourist information (☎ 2 60 00) for the island and environs is directly opposite the station, open weekdays, and Saturday mornings in summer.

This island village spills over onto the adjoining north shore. Take a walking tour along **Maximilianstrasse**, **Ludwigstrasse**, and the **harbour** with its Bavarian Lion monument and lighthouse. Also note the murralled **Altes Rathaus** at Reichsplatz. Hermann Kreitmeir (☎ 2 33 30) has windsurfing schools and equipment rental at Strandbad Eichwald.

Places to Stay & Eat

Campingplatz Lindau-Zech (☎ 7 22 36) is three km south-east of Lindau. The *hostel* was due to re-open in December 1996 – enquire about its status at the tourist office. As it's in Bavaria, only juniors may stay.

On the island, the best deal is *Gästehaus Limmer* (☎ 58 77), In der Grub 16, with

singles/doubles for DM36/70. *Gasthof Inselgraben* (☎ 54 81), Hintere Metzgergasse 4-6, has rooms with TV for DM70/130 with shower and DM60/100 without.

For food, budget travellers should head to *Früchtehaus Hannes*, In der Grub 36; it offers fruit, vegetables, meats, fish, pastas and prepared salads, all sold by weight. There are tables inside (open weekdays to 6 pm and Saturday to 1 pm). The touristy *Goldenes Lamm Restaurant* (☎ 57 32) on Paradiesplatz has filling meals from DM12 and occasional live music.

FRIEDRICHSHAFEN

Graf Zeppelin was born in Constance but first built his overgrown cigar-shaped balloons in this town, an endeavour commemorated in the **Zeppelin Museum** (DM8, concessions DM4; closed Monday and February), Adenauerplatz 1. Friedrichshafen's DJH *hostel* (☎ 07541-7 24 04) is at Lindauer Strasse 3 (DM19.80 for juniors, DM23.70 for seniors).

MEERSBURG

• ☎ *(07532)*

Meersburg is the prettiest town on the lake, with terraced streets and vineyard-patterned hills. The helpful tourist office (☎ 43 11 11) is up the steep hill at Kirchstrasse 4. It's open Monday to Friday from 9 am to noon and 2 to 5.30 pm, and Saturday morning in summer.

Marktplatz offers great vistas and leads to **Steigstrasse**, lined with lovely half-timbered houses. The 11th century **Altes Schloss** is the oldest structurally intact castle in Germany and houses ancient weaponry (open daily; DM8, students DM6). The adjacent **Neues Schloss** is classic baroque and contains an excellent staircase (open daily April to October; DM4, students DM2).

Überlingen, about 14 km to the west, features the astonishing **Cathedral of St Nicholas**. This has a dozen side altars and a wooden four-storey central altar dating from the 17th century, bedecked in intricate carvings. Another impressive baroque church can be found at **Birnau**.

Meersburg is a good base for water sports. The Surfschule Meersburg (☎ 53 30) at Uferpromenade 37 is well organised and hires out windsurf boards (with wetsuit) for DM20 per hour. Yachtschule Meersburg (☎ 55 11) offers five-day sailing courses for DM350. Call Motorboot-Charter (☎ 3 64) for sailing boat and motorboat rental.

Places to Stay & Eat

Four km east of Meersburg are three camp sites side-by-side, including *Camping Hagnau* (☎ 07545-64 13). The DJH *hostel* (☎ 07551-42 04), Alte Nussdorfer Strasse 26, in Überlingen, costs DM21/26 for juniors/seniors.

In Meersburg centre, the cheapest place is the cosy *Hotel Zum Lieben Augustin* ☎ 65 11), Unterstadtstrasse, charging DM40/80 (showers are DM2). Not far out of town is *Gasthaus zum Letzten Heller* (☎ 61 49), Daisendorfer Strasse 41, with rooms for DM45 per person (great food, too). For more expensive options, try Uferpromenade.

For hearty food from DM14, go to *Gasthof zum Bären*, at Marktplatz 11. A more upmarket alternative, the *Alemannen-Torkel* (☎ 10 67), in an old wine cellar at Steigstrasse 16-18, has Baden vintage wines and serves specialities priced from around DM23 (open daily).

Liechtenstein

In some ways you could be forgiven for thinking Liechtenstein is part of Switzerland. The Swiss franc is the legal currency, all travel documents valid for Switzerland are also valid for Liechtenstein, and the only border regulations are on the Austrian side. Blink and you might miss it; the country measures just 25 km from north to south, and an average of six km from west to east. Switzerland also represents Liechtenstein abroad and in foreign policy (subject to consultation).

But a closer look reveals that Liechtenstein is really quite distinct. The ties with Switzerland began only in 1923 with the signing of a customs and monetary union. Before that, it had a similar agreement with Austria-Hungary from 1852 to 1919. Unlike in Switzerland, there is no military service and no army. In fact, the country last went to war in 1866; soldiers guarded an Alpine pass, and never once made contact with the enemy. The armed might of Liechtenstein, numbering 80 men, was disbanded in 1868.

It also has its own reigning monarch. The present dynasty of rulers has controlled lands here since 1699, mostly by remote control from their estates in the former Czechoslovakia. Prince Franz Josef II was the first ruler to actually live in Liechtenstein, in the castle above Vaduz, the capital and seat of government. He died in 1989 after a reign of 51 years and was succeeded by his son, Prince Hans Adam II.

Although it shares the Swiss telephone and postal system, Liechtenstein issues its own postage stamps. It is a prosperous country and the people are proud of their independence.

Facts about the Country

Liechtenstein was colonised by the Rhaetians after 800 BC and conquered by the

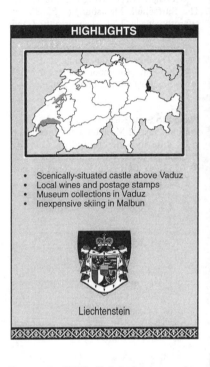

HIGHLIGHTS

- Scenically-situated castle above Vaduz
- Local wines and postage stamps
- Museum collections in Vaduz
- Inexpensive skiing in Malbun

Liechtenstein

Romans in 15 BC. Christianity appeared in the region in the 4th century. The country's modern history began when Prince Johann Adam of Liechtenstein purchased the Lordship of Schellenberg (1699) and the County of Vaduz (1712) from the impoverished German nobles who had previously governed them. Although he already owned vast tracts of land in Austria, Hungary, Bohemia and Moravia, the purpose of this purchase was to qualify for a vote in the Diet of Princes. It became a principality on 23 January 1719 by decree of the Holy Roman Emperor, Charles VI.

Liechtenstein remained a principality under the Holy Roman Empire until 1806, when Napoleon took it into his Confederacy

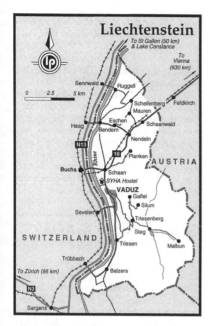

tional affairs, and campaigned actively for EEA (European Economic Area) membership, even threatening to renew the family tradition of living abroad if this policy was rejected. In December 1992, shortly after the Swiss 'No' to the same issue, 55% of Liechtensteiners voted in favour of EEA membership. The country was formally admitted to the EEA in 1995. Despite going separate ways over the EEA issue, the open border between Liechtenstein and Switzerland remains intact. Liechtenstein has no plans to seek full EU membership.

Despite its small size, Liechtenstein has two political regions, Upper and Lower, yielding a total of 25 parliamentary members. As in Switzerland, local communities (11 in number) have a fair degree of autonomy. There are three distinct geographical areas: the Rhine valley in the west, the edge of the Tirolean Alps in the south-east, and the northern lowlands. The current population is 30,600, with a third of that total made up of foreign residents.

Liechtenstein is well known as a tax haven, and a significant proportion of national income is derived from this status. The late infamous entrepreneur Robert Maxwell was one person who took advantage of the discretion and secrecy of the banking services. The government is understandably sensitive about bad press from acceptance of funds from dubious origins. Although the banks have agreed to tighter controls, there are no plans to do away with numbered bank accounts.

Wine production is also important to the economy. Liechtenstein is one of the richest countries per capita in the world, and unemployment is only an isolated phenomenon (in 1996 it was unusually high: 1.1% – 227 people!). Such is its economic strength, that it even employs guest workers from affluent Switzerland! Inflation had crept up to nearly 2% in 1996.

The abbreviation for the country is FL (standing for Fürstentum Liechtenstein), which is used on vehicle registration plates. Nearly 90% of the population are Catholic. The official language is German, although

of the Rhine as part of his machinations against Prussia. Following Napoleon's fall and the Congress of Vienna in 1815, it joined the German Confederation, before achieving full sovereign independence when that fell apart in 1866. The modern constitution was drawn up in 1921. Even today the prince retains the power to dissolve parliament and must approve every act before it becomes law. As in Switzerland, the people can initiate or reject legislation by referendum.

Prince Hans Adam (full title: His Serene Highness Prince Johannes Adam von und zu Liechtenstein) succeeded Franz Josef II in November 1989, although he had effectively been running the state since 1984. He has always tried to stamp his own authority on the government, going as far as to dissolve parliament in 1989 when politicians failed to give support to his plan to build a new museum for his art collection. The prince is also keen to ensure that the country doesn't blindly follow Switzerland's lead in interna-

The Alpine marmot can be seen most during autumn; it prefers the sunny, grassy slopes at very high altitudes.

most people also speak French and English. The Austrian greeting *Grüss Gott* is more common than the Swiss *Grüezi*. Women were given the vote only as recently as 1984 (the men claimed they didn't want it). In September 1990, Liechtenstein became a member of the United Nations.

Facts for the Visitor

See the Switzerland Facts for the Visitor chapter for practical details not covered here.

Tourist information abroad is distributed through Switzerland Tourism. Local offices in Liechtenstein are well organised and you can pick up the excellent and free *Tourist Guide*. This is updated annually and tells you everything you might want to know about the country. A hotel and pension list is given out that covers the whole country.

Prices are comparable to those in Switzerland (VAT at 6.5% was also introduced in 1995). Shops are usually open Monday to Friday from 8 am to noon and 1.30 to 6.30 pm, and Saturday from 8 am to 4 pm. Banks share the same weekday hours except they shut around 4.30 pm.

Liechtenstein does not celebrate Switzerland's National Day (1 August) – it has its own National Holiday on 15 August (Franz Josef II's birthday). It also has a public holiday on all the main Catholic feast days, as well as on Labour day on 1 May. Although the stamps are different, postal rates are the same as for Switzerland. The telephone code for all Liechtenstein is ☎ 075.

It would be slightly unfair – but not very far removed from the truth – to say that if Liechtenstein was not a separate country, few people would bother to visit. As it is, many people come here only for the stamps – a stamp in the passport and stamps on a postcard for the folks back home. But it's worth lingering to appreciate the prince's art collection, and to enjoy the scenery.

Getting There & Away

Liechtenstein has no airport (the nearest is in Zürich), and only a few trains stop within the country (at Schaan). Getting there by postbus is easiest. There are usually three buses an hour from the Swiss border towns of Buchs (Sfr2) and Sargans (Sfr3) which stop in Vaduz. The express train from Zürich to Sargans takes one hour (Sfr48). Buses run hourly from the Austrian border town of Feldkirch, but you must change at Schaan to reach Vaduz (the Sfr3 ticket is valid for both buses).

By road, route 16 from Switzerland passes through Liechtenstein via Schaan and ends at Feldkirch. The N13 follows the Rhine along the Swiss/Liechtenstein border; minor roads cross into Liechtenstein at each motorway exit.

Getting Around

Postbus travel within Liechtenstein is cheap and reliable; fares cost Sfr2 or Sfr3, with the higher rate for journeys exceeding 13 km (such as Vaduz to Malbun). The only drawback is that some services finish early: for example, the last of the hourly buses from Vaduz to Malbun leaves at 4.20 pm (6.20 pm in summer). Get a timetable from the Vaduz tourist office.

For car hire, contact Avis (☎ 232 59 44), Winkel Garage, Im alten Riet 23, Schaan, or Budget (☎ 392 13 88), Reisebüro Linsi Tours, Landstrasse 221, Triesen. There are seven taxi companies in the country; in Schaan, ring ☎ 233 35 35 or ☎ 232 18 66.

For bicycle hire, go to the Swiss train station in Buchs or Sargans, or try Melliger AG (☎ 232 16 06), Kirchstrasse 10, Vaduz. Prices are Sfr20 per day, and bikes can be picked up the evening before rental begins. It is open weekdays to 6.30 pm (except for half-day closing on Tuesday) and Saturday to 2 pm.

Vaduz

• *pop 5070* • *455m* • ☎ *(075)*
Although the capital of Liechtenstein, Vaduz is little more than a village. But it still contains most of the points of interest in the country.

Orientation & Information
Vaduz is the geographical and political centre of the country. Two one-way streets, Städtle and Äulestrasse, diverge and then rejoin, thereby enclosing the centre of town. Everything of importance is near this small area, including the bus station. There's also car parking within this loop (Sfr0.50 per hour, maximum three hours).

The Vaduz tourist office (☎ 232 14 43; fax 392 16 18), Städtle 37, has a room-finding service for personal callers (Sfr2) and information on the whole country. It is open Monday to Friday from 8 am to noon and 1.30 to 5.30 pm. The office is also open May to September on Saturday from 9 am to noon and 1.30 to 4 pm; and July and August on Sunday from 9 am to noon and 1.30 to 4 pm. Staff members are kept busy putting surprisingly dull souvenir stamps in visitors' passports (Sfr2).

The main post office, (FL-9490) Äulestrasse 38, is open Monday to Friday from 8 am to 6.30 pm, and on Saturday from 8 to 11 am. The post office has an adjoining philatelic section that is open similar hours.

Things to See & Do
Although the **castle** is not open to the public, the exterior graces many a photograph and it is worth climbing up the hill for a closer look. At the top, there's a good view of Vaduz and the mountains, and a network of marked walking trails along the ridge. The **National Museum** (Landesmuseum), Städtle 43, has coins, weapons, folklore exhibits and an informative slide show in English of the history of Liechtenstein. Unfortunately, it's closed till around the end of the century.

The **State Art Collection** (Staatliche Kunstsammlung) at Städtle 37 is wholly devoted to temporary exhibitions that invariably contain something special. It includes parts of the art collection that the princes of Liechtenstein have acquired over the centuries. It is open daily from 10 am to noon and 1.30 to 5.30 pm (5 pm November to March). Admission costs Sfr5 (students Sfr3).

The **Postage Stamp Museum**, next to the tourist office, contains 300 frames of national stamps issued since 1912. Located in just one room, it is free and open daily the same hours as the state art collection.

A **Ski Museum** awaits at Bangarten 10 (Sfr5; open weekday afternoons). Look out for processions and fireworks on 15 August, Liechtenstein's national holiday.

It is possible to sample the wines from the prince's own vineyard, but only for groups of 10 or more people. Advance reservations are essential; contact the Hofkellerei (☎ 232 10 18), Feldstrasse 4.

Places to Stay
Vaduz has no camping. The only sites are at Bendern (☎ 373 12 11), by the river in the north, and *Camping Mittagspitze* (☎ 392 26 86), south of Triesen. Both are open year-round.

LIECHTENSTEIN

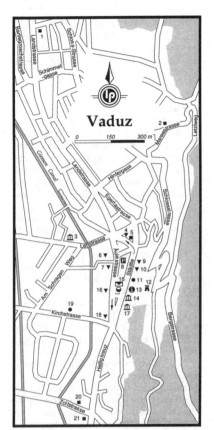

Vaduz

PLACES TO STAY
1   Hotel Falknis
2   Parkhotel Sonnenhof
5   Hotel Engel
20   Landhaus Prasch
21   Gasthof Au

PLACES TO EAT
4   City-Snack
6   Azzurro & Denner Supermarket
7   Old Castle Inn
9   Au Premier
10   Café Wolf
16   Café Amann
18   Linde

OTHER
3   Ski Museum
8   Car Park
11   Liechtenstein State Art Collection
12   Vaduz Castle
13   Tourist Office
14   Postage Stamp Museum
15   Post Office & Postbus Station
17   Liechtenstein National Museum
19   Melliger AG

The SYHA *hostel* (☎ 232 50 22; see the Liechtenstein map), Untere Rütigasse 6, is open from 1 March to 31 November, and dorm beds are Sfr26.30. Reception is closed from 10 am to 5 pm, when the doors are also locked. It is 30 minutes' walk from Buchs or 10 minutes' walk from Schaan. Take the road to Vaduz and turn right at Marianumstrasse.

Hotel Falknis (☎ 232 63 77), Landstrasse, is a 15-minute walk (or take the postbus) from the centre of Vaduz towards Schaan. Reasonable singles/doubles are Sfr50/100 with a shower on each floor.

Gasthof Au (☎ 232 11 17), Austrasse 2,

south of the centre, is the only other budget option in Vaduz. Singles/doubles with private shower are Sfr80/120, or Sfr60/95 without; triples are Sfr145. Eating is pleasant and fairly inexpensive in its garden restaurant. *Landhaus Prasch* (☎ 232 46 63) is opposite. It has good facilities (indoor swimming pool, sauna and fitness room) but is closed from November to April; rooms with shower are Sfr100/120.

Hotel Engel (☎ 232 03 13), Städtle 13, has singles/doubles with private shower and TV starting at Sfr99/135, or Sfr120/160 if you want a bath and balcony. Prices rise slightly in summer.

Parkhotel Sonnenhof (☎ 232 11 92; fax 232 0053) is more luxurious and has an indoor swimming pool (free for guests) and sauna (Sfr25). There are good views from its elevated perspective and the rooms are bright and cheerful (closed from Christmas to mid-February). Prices start at Sfr190/270 and it has a guests-only restaurant. It's in the north-east of the village on Grasiger Weg.

Places to Eat

Restaurants are expensive in Vaduz, so look

out for lunchtime specials. Opposite the car park on Äulestrasse is *Denner* supermarket, open to 6.30 pm weekdays and 4 pm on Saturday. It has a deli counter with some hot snacks. Next door is *Azzurro*, with decent-sized pizzas from just Sfr7.50, plus sandwiches and salads. This stand-up place is open daily to 7 pm (8 pm in summer; 5 pm on Sunday).

City-Snack, Städtle 5, is a combination bar and souvenir shop (open daily till around 11 pm). It's rather basic, but does provide the cheapest sit-down meals in town, with tables inside and out. Snacks and meals are Sfr5 to Sfr14, often with a soft drink included. Another budget possibility is the new *McDonald's* restaurant, 1½ km south of Gasthof Au in Triesen.

Linde, Kirchstrasse 2, is a bar and restaurant, popular with local young people. It offers Latin American décor and Mexican food (Sfr14.50 to Sfr35); it's open daily from 8.30 am to at least 11 pm.

Hotel Engel (see Places to Stay) has Swiss meals from Sfr17; look out for *Schwingerhörnli*, a filling pasta dish usually available in winter. It also has Chinese specialities.

Old Castle Inn, Äulestrasse, a British-style pub with an outside terrace, has main meals starting from Sfr16 (open daily). Another good place to try is *Café Amann* at No 56. Its daily lunch menu with soup is Sfr15.50, and other meals and snacks cost Sfr5 to Sfr20. It is open until 7 pm on weekdays and 12.30 pm on Saturday.

Café Wolf, Städtle 29, has lunch menus with soup from Sfr21.50, and occasional live piano music on winter evenings. In the shop on the ground floor you can gorge on quality confectionery. One of its specialities is cognac-filled chocolate snail-shapes (Sfr11.90 for seven). It's open daily.

Hotel Real, Städtle 21, has *Au Premier* (☎ 232 22 22), the best restaurant in Liechtenstein. Enjoy seasonal specialities and locally produced wine in an interior where the lighting comes from dozens of shimmering cylinders. Main courses top Sfr40 and it is open daily.

Around Vaduz

The lowland (Unterland) of northern Liechtenstein is dotted with small communities. There's little to do except enjoy the quiet pace of life and view the village churches. Pottery-making is demonstrated at Schaedler Keramik (☎ 373 14 14) in **Nendeln**. Admission is free and opening hours are Monday to Friday from 8 am to noon and 1.15 to 6 pm. The Rofenberg in **Eschen-Nendeln** was formerly a place of public execution and is now the site of the Holy Cross Chapel. **Schellenberg** has a Russian monument, commemorating the night in 1945 when a band of 500 heavily armed Russian soldiers crossed the border. They had been fighting for the German army, but they came to defect, not attack.

Triesenberg, on a terrace above Vaduz, commands an excellent view over the Rhine valley and has a pretty, onion-domed church. There's also a museum devoted to the Walser community which journeyed from Valais to settle here in the 13th century. It is open every afternoon except Monday (and Sunday from September to May) and admission costs Sfr2 or Sfr1 for students. The Walser dialect is still spoken here.

In the extreme south of the country is **Balzers**, which is dominated by the soaring sides of Gutenberg Castle. The interior of the castle is closed to the public, but there are plans in the long term to make it a museum.

Malbun
• *pop 100* • *1600m* • ☎ *(075)*
Nestled amid the mountains in the southeast, Malbun is Liechtenstein's ski resort. The skiing is inexpensive if not too extensive. The runs are for beginners and intermediates, with just a couple of stretches for experts. There are two ski schools in the resort. A pass for all ski lifts and chair lifts costs Sfr22 (children Sfr14) for half a day, Sfr33 (Sfr22) for a day or Sfr143 (Sfr90) for one week. One day's equipment rental costs

Sfr43 including skis, shoes and poles, from the sports shop (☎ 263 37 55) or ski school (☎ 262 29 34). Two km from Malbun is the Väluna Valley, the main area for cross country skiing. The road from Vaduz terminates at Malbun. The tourist office (☎ 263 65 77) is by the bus stop and is open daily except Sunday from 9 am to noon, and 1.30 to 5 pm (1 to 4 pm on Saturday). It's closed during the off-season from mid-April to mid-May, and 1 November to mid-December. For recorded snow reports in German, call ☎ 263 80 80, or ask at the tourist office.

The sports shop changes money (normal rates), but the village Bancomat doesn't accept Visa cards for cash advances.

Places to Stay & Eat There are seven hotels in this small village, nearly all with restaurants. By the bus stop is *Alpenhotel Malbun* (☎ 232 11 81), which is under the same management and has the same telephone number as the nearby *Galina*. Prices per person start at Sfr40 for a basic room or Sfr70 for one with private bath. Half and full-pension are available at favourable rates, and there is an annex with a swimming pool.

Turna (☎ 232 34 21), by the Sareis ski lift, has singles/doubles starting at Sfr40/70, or Sfr60/90 with private shower and toilet; add Sfr10 in winter. All three places have inexpensive restaurants with outside terraces, and Turna also has a bar and disco.

Appendix I – Alternative Place Names

The following abbreviations are used:
(E) = English
(F) = French
(G) = German
(I) = Italian
(R) = Romansch

Basel (E, G) – Basle (E), Bâle (F), Basilea (I)
Bern (E, G) – Berne (E, F), Berna (I)
Bernese Mittelland (E) – Berner Mittelland (G), Le Plateau Bernois (F)
Bernese Oberland (E) – Berner Oberland (G)
Biel (G) – Bienne (F)
Brig (E, G) – Brigue (F)

Chur (E, G) – Coire (F)

Fribourg (E, F) – Freiburg (G), Friburgo (I)

Geneva (E) – Genève (F), Genf (G), Ginevra (I)
Graubünden (E, G) – Grisons (F), Grigioni (I), Grishun (R)

Lake Brienz (E) – Brienzersee (G)
Lake Constance (E) – Bodensee (G)
Lake Geneva (E) – Genfersee (G), Lac Léman or Lac du Genève (F)
Lake Geneva Region (E) – Genferseegebiet (G), Région du Léman (F)
Lake Lucerne (E) – Vierwaldstättersee (G)
Lake Maggiore (E) – Lago Maggiore (I)
Lake Thun (E) – Thunersee (G), Lac de Thoune (F)
Lake Zug (E) – Zugersee (G), Lac de Zoug (F)
Leuk (E, G) – Loeche (F)

Leukerbad (E, G) – Loeche-les-Bains (F)
Lower Valais (E) – Unterwallis (G), Bas Valais (F)
Lucerne (E, F) – Luzern (G), Lucerna (I)

Matterhorn (E, G) – Cervino (I)
Mont Blanc (F) – Monte Bianco (I)

Neuchâtel (E, F) – Neuenburg (G)

Rhine River (E) – Rhein (G)

Sarine River (E) – Saane (G)
Schaffhausen (E, G) – Schaffhouse (F), Sciafusa (I)
Sierre (E, F) – Siders (G)
Sion (E, F) – Sitten (G)
Solothurn (E, G) – Soleure (F), Soletta (I)
St Gallen (E, G) – St Gall (F), San Gallo (I)
St Moritz – Saint Moritz (F), San Murezzan (R)
St Peter's Island (E) – St Peterinsel (G), Île de St Pierre (I)
Switzerland (E) – Suisse (F), Schweiz (G), Svizzera (I), Svizzra (R)

Ticino (E, I) – Tessin (G, F)

Upper Valais (E) – Oberwallis (G), Haut Valais (F)

Valais (E, F) – Wallis (G)
Vaud (E, F) – Waadt (G)
Visp (E, G) – Viége (F)

Winterthur (E) – Winterthour (G)

Zug (E, G) – Zoug (F)
Zürich (G) – Zurich (F), Zurigo (I)

Appendix II – Acronyms

The following abbreviations are used:
(F) = French
(G) = German
(I) = Italian

ACS (G)	Automobile-Club der Schweiz – Swiss Automobile Club
AHV (G)	Senior Citizens
ATMs	Automatic Teller Machines, also known as Bancomats or Bankomats
AVS (F)	Senior Citizens
BIJ (F)	Billet International de Jeunesse – Card for those under 26 giving discount on international rail travel
CFF (F)	Chemins de Fer Fédéraux Suisse – Swiss Federal Railway
EC	EuroCity trains
EPA	Name of an inexpensive chain of department stores
FIYTO	Federation of International Youth Travel Organisation
FFS (I)	Ferrovie Federali Svizzere – Swiss Federal Railway
HI	Hostelling International
IC	InterCity trains
ICE	InterCity Express trains
IDP	International Driving Permit
ISIC	International Student Identity Card

RADAR	Royal Association for Disability & Rehabilitation
SAC	Swiss Alpine Club
SBB (G)	Schweizerische Bundesbahnen – Swiss Federal Railway
SBC	Swiss Bank Corporation – Société de Banques Suisses (F), Schweizerischer Bankverein (G), Società di Banca Svizzera (I)
SCCV (G)	Swiss Camping & Caravanning Federation
SSR-Reisen (G)	Swiss student travel agency
SSCV (G)	Swiss Ski School Federation
SYHA	Swiss Youth Hostel Association – Auberges de Jeunesse Suisses (F), Schweizer Jugendherbergen (G), Alberghi Svizzeri per la Gioventù (I)
TCS (G)	Touring Club der Schweiz – Swiss Touring Club
TGV (F)	*Train à grande vitesse* – very fast train
UBS	Union Bank of Switzerland – Union de Banques Suisses (F), Schweizerische Bankgesellschaft (G), Unione di Banche Svizzere (I)
Voyages-SSR (F)	Swiss student travel agency
WWOOF	Willing Workers on Organic Farms

Language Guide

HIGH GERMAN

Pronunciation Unlike English or French, German does not have silent letters: you pronounce the **k** at the start of the word *Knie*, 'knee', the **p** at the start of *Psychologie*, 'psychology', and the **e** at the end of *ich habe*, 'I have'.

Vowels As in English, vowels can be pronounced long, like the 'o' in 'pope', or short, like the 'o' in 'pop'. As a rule, German vowels are long before one consonant and short before two consonants: the **o** is long in the word *Dom*, 'cathedral', but short in the word *doch*, 'after all'.

a	short, as the 'u' sound in 'cut', or long, as in 'father'
au	as in 'vow'
ä	short, as in 'act', or long, as in 'hair'
äu	as in 'boy'
e	short, as in 'bet', or long, as in 'day'
ei	as the 'ai' in 'aisle'
eu	as in 'boy'
i	short, as in 'in', or long, as in 'see'
ie	as in 'see'
o	short, as in 'pot', or long, as in 'note'
ö	as the 'er' in 'fern'
u	as the 'u' in 'pull'
ü	like the 'u' in 'pull' but with stretched lips

Consonants Most German consonants sound similar to their English counterparts. One important difference is that **b**, **d** and **g** sound like 'p', 't' and 'k', respectively, at the end of a word.

b	normally as the English 'b', but 'p' at the end of a word
ch	the 'ch' in Scottish 'loch'
d	normally as the English 'd', but 't' at the end of a word
g	normally as the English 'g', but 'k' at the end of a word, and 'ch', as in the Scottish 'loch', at the end of a word and after **i**
j	as the 'y' in 'yet'
qu	'k' plus 'v'
r	as the English 'r', but rolled at the back of the mouth
s	normally as the 's' in 'sun'; as the 'z' in 'zoo' when followed by a vowel
sch	as the 'sh' in 'ship'
sp, st	's' sounds like the 'sh' in 'ship' when at the start of a word
tion	the **t** sounds like the 'ts' in 'hits'
ß	as in 'sun' (written as **ss** in this book)
v	as the 'f' in 'fan'
w	as the 'v' in 'van'
z	as the 'ts' in 'hits'

SWISS-FRENCH

Pronunciation French has a number of sounds which are notoriously difficult to produce for Anglophones. The main causes of trouble are:

1. The distinction between the 'u' sound (as in *tu)* and 'oo' sound (as in *tout)*. For both sounds, the lips are rounded and projected forward, but for the 'u' the tongue is towards the front of the mouth, its tip against the lower front teeth, whereas for the 'oo' the tongue is towards the back of the mouth, its tip behind the gums of the lower front teeth.

2. The nasal vowels. During the production of nasal vowels the breath escapes partly through the nose and partly through the mouth. There are no nasal vowels in English; in French there are three, as in *bon vin blanc*, 'good white wine'. These sounds occur

where a syllable ends in a single 'n' or 'm'; the 'n' or 'm' in this case is not pronounced, but indicates the nasalisation of the preceding vowel.

The standard 'r' of Parisian French is produced by moving the bulk of the tongue backwards to constrict the air flow in the pharynx while the tip of the tongue rests behind the lower front teeth. It is quite similar to the noise made by some people before spitting, but with much less friction.

SWISS-ITALIAN

Pronunciation Italian is not difficult to pronounce once you learn a few easy rules. Although some of the more clipped vowels, and stress on double letters, require careful practice for English speakers, it is easy enough to make yourself understood.

Vowels Vowels are generally more clipped than in English.

a   as the second 'a' in 'camera'
e   as the 'ay' in 'day', but without the 'i' sound
i   as in 'see'
o   as in 'dot'
u   as in 'too'

Consonants The pronunciation of many Italian consonants is similar to that of English. The following sounds depend on certain rules:

c   like 'k' before 'a', 'o' and 'u'. Like the 'ch' in 'choose' before 'e' and 'i'
ch   a hard 'k' sound

g   a hard 'g' as in 'get' before 'a', 'o' and 'u'. Before 'e' and 'i', like the 'j' in 'job'
gh   a hard 'g' as in 'get'
gli as the 'lli' in 'million'
gn   as the 'ny' in 'canyon'
h   always silent
r   a rolled 'rrr' sound
sc   before 'e' and 'i', like the 'sh' in 'sheep'. Before 'h', 'a', 'o' and 'u', a hard sound as in 'school'
z   as the 'ts' in 'lights' or as the 'ds' in 'beds'

Note that when 'ci', 'gi' and 'sci' are followed by 'a', 'o' or 'u', unless the accent falls on the 'i', it is not pronounced. Thus the name 'Giovanni' is pronounced 'joh-**vahn**-nee', with no 'i' sound after the 'G'.

Stress Double consonants are pronounced as a longer, often more forceful sound than a single consonant.

Stress often falls on the next to last syllable, as in *spaghetti*. When a word has an accent, the stress is on that syllable, as in *città*, 'city'.

ROMANSCH

Useful words are:

tourist office	*societad* (or *biro*) *da traffic*
Please.	*Anzi.*
Thank you.	*Grazia.*
Hello.	*Allegra.*
Good morning.	*Bun di.*
Good evening.	*Buna saira.*
Good night.	*Buna notg.*
Goodbye.	*Adieu./Abunansvair.*
house	*chesa*
room	*la chombra*
bed	*il letg*
closed	*serrà/serrò*
left	*sanester*
right	*dretg*

east	*ost/orient*	Monday	*Lündeschdi*
west	*vest/occident*	Tuesday	*il Mardi*
north	*nord*	Wednesday	*Marculdi*
south	*sid*	Thursday	*la Gievgia*
woman	*la dunna*	Friday	*Venderdi*
man	*l'um*	Saturday	*Sanda*
snow	*naiv*		
cross-country skiing	*il passlung*	**Numbers**	
food	*mangiar*	1	*in*
bread	*il paun*	2	*dus*
cheese	*il chaschiel*	3	*trais*
fish	*il pesch*	4	*quatter*
ham	*il schambun*	5	*tschinch*
drink	*baiver*	6	*ses*
milk	*il Latg*	7	*set*
wine	*il vin*	8	*och*
		9	*nouv*
Sunday	*Dumengia*	10	*diesch*

ENGLISH	GERMAN	FRENCH	ITALIAN
Basics			
Hello.	*Guten Tag.*	*Bonjour.*	*Buon giorno./Ciao.*
Goodbye.	*Auf Wiedersehen.*	*Au revoir.*	*Arrivederci./Ciao.*
Yes./No.	*Ja./Nein.*	*Oui./Non.*	*Si./No.*
Please.	*Bitte.*	*S'il vous plaît.*	*Per favore./ Per piacere.*
Thank you.	*Danke.*	*Merci.*	*Grazie.*
You're welcome.	*Bitte sehr.*	*Je vous en prie.*	*Prego.*
Excuse me.	*Entschuldigung.*	*Excusez-moi.*	*Mi scusi.*
Sorry. (excuse me, forgive me)	*Entschuldigung.*	*Pardon.*	*Mi scusi. Mi perdoni.*
How much is it?	*Wieviel kostet es?*	*C'est combien?*	*Quanto costa?*
Language Troubles			
Do you speak English?	*Sprechen Sie Englisch?*	*Parlez-vous anglais?*	*Parla inglese?*
Does anyone speak English?	*Spricht hier jemand Englisch?*	*Est-ce qu'il y a quel-qu'un qui parle anglais?*	*C'è qualcuno che parla inglese?*
I understand.	*Ich verstehe.*	*Je comprends.*	*Capisco.*
I don't understand.	*Ich verstehe nicht.*	*Je ne comprends pas.*	*Non capisco.*
Just a minute.	*Ein Moment!*	*Attendez une minute.*	*Un momento.*
Could you write that down?	*Können Sie es bitte aufschreiben?*	*Est-ce-que vous pouvez l'écrire?*	*Può scriverlo per favore?*
Signs			
Camping ground	*Campingplatz*	*Camping*	*Campeggio*
Entrance	*Eingang*	*Entrée*	*Ingresso/Entrata*
Exit	*Ausgang*	*Sortie*	*Uscita*
Full/No vacancies	*Voll, Besetzt*	*Complet*	*Completo*
Guesthouse	*Pension, Gasthaus*	*Pension de Famille*	*Pensione*
Hotel	*Hotel*	*Hôtel*	*Albergo*
Information	*Auskunft*	*Renseignements*	*Informazione*
Open/Closed	*Offen/Geschlossen*	*Ouvert/Fermé*	*Aperto/Chiuso*
Police	*Polizei*	*Police*	*Polizia/Carabinieri*
Police station	*Polizeiwache*	*(Commissariat de) Police*	*Questura*
Rooms available	*Zimmer Frei*	*Chambres libres*	*Camere libere*
Toilets	*Toiletten (toilet)*	*Toilettes, W.C.*	*Gabinetti/Bagni*
Railway station	*Bahnhof (Bf)*	*Gare SNCF*	*Stazione*
Youth hostel	*Jugendherberge*	*Auberge de Jeunesse*	*Ostello per la Gioventù*

ENGLISH	GERMAN	FRENCH	ITALIAN
Getting Around			
What time does.... leave?	Wann fährt ...ab?	À quelle heure part...?	A che ora parte ...?
What time does.... arrive?	Wann kommt ...an?	À quelle heure arrive...?	A che ora arriva....?
the boat	das Boot	le bateau	la barca
the bus	der Bus/der (Überland) bus	l'(auto)bus/l'(auto) car	l'autobus
the tram	die Strassenbahn	le tramway	il tram
the train	der Zug	le train	il treno
next	nächste	prochain (m) prochaine (f)	il prossimo (m) la prossima (f)
first	erste	premier (m) première (f)	il primo (m) la prima (f)
last	letzte	dernier (m) dernière (f)	l'ultimo (m) l'ultima (f)
I would like ...	Ich möchte ...	Je voudrais ...	Vorrei ...
a one-way ticket	eine Einzelkarte	un billet aller simple	(un biglietto di) solo andata/un biglietto semplice
a return ticket	eine Rückfahrkarte	un billet aller-retour	(un biglietto di) andata e ritorno
1st class	erste Klasse	première classe	prima classe
2nd class	zweite Klasse	deuxième classe	seconda classe
Where is the bus/ tram stop?	Wo ist die Bushalte-stelle/Strassen-bahnhaltestelle?	Où est l'arrêt d'autobus/de tramway?	Dov'è la fermata dell'autobus/del tram?
I'm looking for ...	Ich suche ...	Je cherche ...	Cerco ...
Can you show me (on the map)?	Können Sie mir (auf der Karte) zeigen?	Est-ce que vous pouvez me le montrer (sur la carte)?	Me lo può mostrare (sulla carta/pianta)?
far/near	weit/nahe	loin/proche	lontano/vicino
Go straight ahead.	Gehen Sie gerade-aus.	Continuez tout droit.	Si va (vai) sempre diritto.
Turn left ...	Biegen Sie ... links ab.	Tournez à gauche ...	Gira a sinistra ...
Turn right ...	Biegen Sie ... rechts ab.	Tournez à droite ...	Gira a destra ...
Around Town			
I'm looking for ...	Ich suche ...	Je cherche ...	Sto cercando ...
a bank	eine Bank	une banque	un banco
the city centre	die Innenstadt	le centre-ville	il centro (città)

ENGLISH	GERMAN	FRENCH	ITALIAN
the ... embassy	*die ...Botschaft*	*l'ambassade de ...*	*l'ambasciata di...*
my hotel	*mein Hotel*	*mon hôtel*	*il mio albergo*
the market	*den Markt*	*le marché*	*il mercato*
police office	*die Polizei*	*la police*	*la polizia*
the post office	*das Postamt*	*le bureau de poste*	*la posta*
a public toilet	*eine öffentliche Toilette*	*des toilettes*	*un gabinetto/ bagno pubblico*
the telephone centre	*die Telefon-zentrale*	*une cabine téléphonique*	*il centro telefon-ico/SIP*
the tourist informa-tion office	*das Verkehrsamt*	*l'office de tourisme/ le syndicat d'in-itiative*	*l'ufficio di turismo/ d'informazione*
beach	*Strand*	*la plage*	*la spiaggia*
bridge	*Brücke*	*le pont*	*il ponte*
castle	*Schloss*	*le château*	*il castello*
cathedral	*Dom*	*il dumo/la cathédrale*	*il duomo/ la cattedrale*
church	*Kirche*	*l'église*	*la chiesa*
hospital	*Krankenhaus*	*l'hôpital*	*l'ospedale*
island	*Insel*	*l'île*	*l'isola*
main square	*Hauptplatz*	*la place centrale*	*la piazza principale*
mosque	*Moschee*	*la mosquée*	*la moschea*
old city	*Altstadt*	*la vieille ville*	*il centro storico*
palace	*Palast*	*le palais*	*il palazzo*
ruins	*Ruinen*	*les ruines*	*le rovine*
sea	*Meer*	*la mer*	*il mare*
square	*Platz*	*la place*	*la piazza*
tower	*Turm*	*la tour*	*il torre*

Accommodation

Where is a cheap hotel?	*Wo ist ein billiges Hotel?*	*Où est un hôtel bon marché?*	*Dov'è un albergo che costa poco ...?*
What is the address?	*Was ist die Adresse?*	*Quelle est l'adresse?*	*Cos'è l'indirizzo?*
Could you write the address, please?	*Könnten Sie bitte die Adresse auf-schreiben?*	*Est-ce vous pouvez écrire l'adresse, s'il vous plaît?*	*Può scrivere l'indi-rizzo, per favore?*
Do you have any rooms available?	*Haben Sie noch freie Zimmer?*	*Est-ce que vous avez des chambres libres?*	*Ha camere libere?/ C'è una camera libera?*
I would like ...	*Ich möchte ...*	*Je voudrais ...*	*Vorrei ...*
a single room	*ein Einzelzimmer*	*une chambre pour une personne*	*una camera singola*
a double room	*ein Doppelzimmer*	*une chambre double*	*una camera matri-moniale/per due*

ENGLISH	GERMAN	FRENCH	ITALIAN
a room with a bathroom	*ein Zimmer mit Bad*	*une chambre avec douche et W.C.*	*una camera con bagno*
to share a dorm	*einen Schlafsaal teilen*	*coucher dans un dortoir*	*un letto in dormitorio*
a bed	*ein Bett*	*un lit*	*un letto*
How much is it per night/per person?	*Wieviel kostet es pro Nacht/pro Person?*	*Quel est le prix par nuit/par personne?*	*Quanto costa per la notte/ciascuno?*
Can I see it?	*Person?*	*Je peux la voir?*	*Posso vederla?*
Where is the bathroom?	*Kann ich es sehen?*	*Où est la salle de bain?*	*Dov'è il bagno?*
	Wo ist das Bad?		

Food

bakery	*Bäckerei*	*boulangerie*	*panetteria*
delicatessen	*Delikatessengeschäft*	*charcuterie*	*gastronomia*
grocery	*Lebensmittelgeschäft*	*épicerie*	*negocio di alimentari*
restaurant	*Restaurant, Gaststätte*	*restaurant*	*ristorante*
breakfast	*Frühstück*	*petit déjeuner*	*prima colazione*
lunch	*Mittagessen*	*déjeuner*	*pranzo/colazione*
dinner	*Abendessen*	*dîner*	*cena*
I would like the set lunch.	*Ich hätte gern das Tagesmenü bitte.*	*Je prends le menu.*	*Vorrei il menu turistico.*
Is service included in the bill?	*Ist die Bedienung inbegriffen?*	*Le service est compris?*	*È compreso il servizio?*
I am a vegetarian.	*Ich bin Vegetarierin (f)/Vegetarier. (m)*	*Je suis végétarien (m)/ végétarienne. (f)*	*Sono vegetariano/a. Non mangio carne.*

Time & Dates

What time is it?	*Wie spät ist es?*	*Quelle heure est-il?*	*Che ora è/ Che ore sono?*
today	*heute*	*aujourd'hui*	*oggi*
tomorrow	*morgen*	*demain*	*domani*
yesterday	*gestern*	*hier*	*ieri*
in the morning	*morgens*	*le matin*	*di mattina*
in the afternoon	*nachmittags*	*l'après-midi*	*di pomeriggio*
in the evening	*abends*	*le soir*	*di sera*
Monday	*Montag*	*lundi*	*lunedì*
Tuesday	*Dienstag*	*mardi*	*martedì*
Wednesday	*Mittwoch*	*mercredi*	*mercoledì*
Thursday	*Donnerstag*	*jeudi*	*giovedì*
Friday	*Freitag*	*vendredi*	*venerdì*
Saturday	*Samstag, Sonnabend*	*samedi*	*sabato*
Sunday	*Sonntag*	*dimanche*	*domenica*

ENGLISH	GERMAN	FRENCH	ITALIAN
January	*Januar*	*janvier*	*gennaio*
February	*Februar*	*février*	*febbraio*
March	*März*	*mars*	*marzo*
April	*April*	*avril*	*aprile*
May	*Mai*	*mai*	*maggio*
June	*Juni*	*juin*	*giugno*
July	*Juli*	*juillet*	*luglio*
August	*August*	*août*	*agosto*
September	*September*	*septembre*	*settembre*
October	*Oktober*	*octobre*	*ottobre*
November	*November*	*novembre*	*novembre*
December	*Dezember*	*décembre*	*dicembre*

Numbers

0	*null*	*zéro*	*zero*
1	*eins*	*un*	*uno*
2	*zwei* (*zwo* on the phone)	*deux*	*due*
3	*drei*	*trois*	*tre*
4	*vier*	*quatre*	*quattro*
5	*fünf*	*cinq*	*cinque*
6	*sechs*	*six*	*sei*
7	*sieben*	*sept*	*sette*
8	*acht*	*huit*	*otto*
9	*neun*	*neuf*	*nove*
10	*zehn*	*dix*	*dieci*
11	*elf*	*onze*	*undici*
12	*ölf*	*douze*	*dodici*
13	*dreizehn*	*treize*	*tredici*
14	*vierzehn*	*quatorze*	*quattordici*
15	*fünfzehn*	*quinze*	*quindici*
16	*sechzehn*	*seize*	*sedici*
17	*siebzehn*	*dix-sept*	*diciassette*
18	*achtzehn*	*dix-huit*	*diciotto*
19	*neunzehn*	*dix-neuf*	*diciannove*
20	*zwanzig*	*vingt*	*venti*
30	*dreissig*	*trente*	*trenta*
40	*vierzig*	*quarante*	*quaranta*
50	*fünfzig*	*cinquante*	*cinquanta*
60	*sechzig*	*soixante*	*sessanta*
70	*siebzig*	*soixante-dix/septante*	*settanta*
80	*achtzig*	*quatre-vingts/huitante*	*ottanta*
90	*neunzig*	*quatre-vingt-dix/ nonante*	*novanta*
100	*hundert*	*cent*	*cento*
1000	*tausend*	*mille*	*mille*
one million	*eine Million*	*un million*	*un milione*

Index

MAPS

Basel (Bâle) 180
Bellinzona 286
Bern (Berne) 88
Bernese Mittelland 85
Bernese Oberland 101
Biel (Bienne) 96

Cantons 16
Chur 307

Davos 313

Engelberg 147

Fribourg 194
Fribourg, Neuchâtel & Jura 192

Geneva 216
   Old Town 220
   Station Area 225
Graubünden 304

Interlaken 104

Jungfrau Region 108

La Chaux-de-Fonds 210
Lake Constance (Bodensee) 347
Lake Geneva Region 231
Lake Lucerne
   (Vierwaldstättersee) 139
Lake Lugano 295
Language Areas 29
Lausanne 234
Liechtenstein 355
Locarno 298
Lucerne (Luzern) 133
Lugano 289

Martigny 261
Meiringen 125
Montreux 242

Neuchâtel 205

Sion 258
St Gallen 335
St Moritz 321
Switzerland 14
   Central 131
   North-East 333
   North-West 177
   Rail Routes 78

Thun 119
Ticino 284

Vaduz 358
Valais 255

Winterthur 173

Yverdon-Les-Bains 246

Zermatt 275
Zürich 158-9
   Central 164

TEXT

Map references are in **bold** type.

Aare Gorge 124
Aargau Canton 188-90
accommodation 55-8
Affoltern 99
Aigle 251
air travel 63-8, 76-7
   to/from continental Europe 65
   to/from Africa 68
   to/from Asia 68
   to/from Australasia 68
   to/from Canada 65
   to/from the UK 64
   to/from the USA 65
airport taxes 63
Albula pass 305
Aletsch glacier 117
Aletschwald 281
Alp Grüm 330
Alpenrose Chocolate Museum 290
Alpes Festival, Leysin 252
Alpine Folklore parade,
   Zermatt 276
Alpine Museum, Zermatt 276
Andermatt 154

Anniviers Valley 269
Appenzell 339-40
Appenzell Showcase Cheese
   Dairy 340
Appenzellerland 339-42
Arbon 350
army 19
Arosa 311
arts 27
Ascona 301
Augusta Raurica 185
Avenches 199

Baden 189-190
Bahnhofstrasse, Zürich 170
Bâle, see Basel
ballooning 53, 251
Balzers 359
bank accounts 25
bargaining 38
Basel 176-85, **180**
   getting there & away 184
   places to eat 183
   places to stay 181
   tourist offices 178
Beckenried 143

Bellinzona 285-8, **286**
Bern 85-95, **88**
   entertainment 93
   getting around 95
   getting there & away 95
   museums 89
   places to eat 92
   places to stay 91
   shopping 94
   special events 91
   sport 94
   things to see 87-90
   tourist office 86
Bernese Mittelland 84-99, **85**
Bernese Oberland 100-29, **101**
Bernina Pass Road 328
Bettmeralp 281
Bex 253
Biasca 302
bicycle travel 73, 76-82
Biel 95-8, **96**
Black Forest 185-6
Blue Lake 127
boat tours
   Bernese Oberland 118
   Lake Constance 348

boat travel 74, 76-82
bob run, Olympic 325
Bodensee Festival 347
Bodensee, *see* Lake Constance
books 41
Bosco Gurin 302
Bourg St Pierre 264
Bregaglia Valley 330
Bregenz 351
Breitlouwina 111
Brienz 122
Brienzersee, *see* Lake Brienz
Brig 271
Brigerbad 273
Brione 302
Broc 202
Brunnen 143
Brunni 147
Bruson 267
budgets, *see* money
Bulle 202
bungy jumping, Mt Titlis 147
Burgdorf 99
Burgerbad 270
bus travel 68, 76-7
    Eurobus 69
    Eurolines 68
    youth fares 68
business hours 50
Byron 242

camping, *see* accommodation
Campione d'Italia 294
cantons 16-17, 218
car & motorcycle travel
    Alpine passes 80
    road rules & signs 80
car travel 71, 79
    camper van 72
    car purchase 81
    car rental 81
    International Driving Permit
        (IDP) 72
    motorway tax 73
    parking 76-80
    petrol 71
    Swiss Touring Club 76-9
Carona 295
casinos
    Constance 349
    Montreux 243
Casino de la Rotonde,
    Neuchâtel 207
Castle Waldegg 188
caves
    prehistoric 341
    St Beatus 121
    Vallorbe 249
Celerina 325

Cento Valley 302
Central Switzerland 130-55
Ceresio 295
CERN 222
Chamonix 264
Chamossaire 253
Champéry 263
Champex 264
Chaplin, Charlie 240
Château d' Oex 251
Château de Chillon 242
Chaumont 208
cheese-making
    Château d'Oex 251
    Gruyères 200
chess, Zürich 162
children 49
chocolate 202
Chünetta 330
Chur 306-9, **307**
Cima Museum 248
cinema 61
climate 20
cog railway
    Mt Pilatus 140
Coire, *see* Chur
Combat de Reines 262
Constance 349
Coppet 239
Corviglia 322
costs, *see* money 36
Courmayeur 265
courses 54
cow fights 262
Crans-Montana 269
cresta run, Celerina 325
crime 49-50, 161
Croix de Culet 263
currency, *see* money
customs 35
cycling, Lake Constance 348

Dada 157
Danube River 185
Därligen 121
Davos 312-16, **313**
Dents du Midi 263
departure tax, *see* airport taxes
Diavolezza 330
dinosaur 188
disabled travellers 48
diving
    Därligen 121
documents 35
Domodossola 302
Doubs Falls 212
drinks 61
driving, *see* car travel
drugs 50, 161

Ebenalp 341
ecology 21
economy 24
education 27
Einsiedeln 151
Einstein, Albert 90
electricity 43
embassies 35
Emmental cheese 341
Emmental Region 99
Engadine Valley 317
Engelberg 145-9, **147**
entertainment 61, 227
environment 21
Eschen-Nendeln 359
Estavayer-le-Lac 197-8
exchange rates 36
Expovina 165

Fasnacht
    Lucerne 135
    Zürich 165
Faulensee 121
fauna 22
fax services, *see* postal services
festivals
    Bellinzona 287
    Bregenz 351
    clown 271
    Engadine 318
    Golden Rose Television
        Festival 243
    International Alpine Film
        Festival 252
    International Comedy Film
        Festival 240
    International Festival
        of Music 135
    Lugano 291
    Montreux Jazz Festival 243
    Montreux-Vevey Music
        Festival 243
    Settimane Musicali 301
fishing 53
    Lake Joux 250
Flims 309
flora 22
Folklore Museum, Stein 341
fondues, Château d'Oex 251
food 58
    Swiss cuisine 59
    Ticinise cuisine 285
Fossil Museum, Meride 296
Franches Montagnes 213
Frauenfeld 349
Freiburg, *see* Fribourg
Freilichtmuseum Ballenberg 123
French, *see* Swiss-French

Fribourg 193-6, **194**
  getting there & away 196
  places to eat 196
  places to stay195
  things to see 193
Fribourg Canton 193-203
Friedrichshafen 352
Furka Pass 126

Gandria 294
gay travellers 48
Gemmi Pass 271
Gemsstock 155
Geneva 214-29, **216**
  activities 222
  Genève Plage 222
  getting around 229
  getting there & away 228
  Jet d'Eau 219
  museums & galleries 220
  old town **220**
  places to eat 225
  places to stay 223
  shopping 228
  station area **225**
  St Peter's Cathedral 219
  tourist offices 215
  walking tour 219
Genfersee, *see* Lake Geneva
geography 19-20
geological path,
  Appenzellerland 339
German, High 31, 363, 366-70
Gersau 143
Giacometti, Alberto 27
Giardini Jean Arp 299
Giessbach Falls 122
Giger, HR 306
glaciers 279, 280
  Aletsch 117
  Mer de Glace 265
  Plaine Morte 269
  Rhône 126
  Stein 126
Glacier Express 278
Glacier Gorge, Grindelwald 111
Golden Rose Television
  Festival 243
golf
  Arosa 311
  Crans-Montana 269
Gornergrat 276
Gotthard Pass 126
government 23
Grand Combin 264
Grande Dixence Dam 260
Grandson 248
Graubünden 303-331, **304**
Great St Bernard Pass 264

Grimsel Pass 126
Grindelwald 109
Grisons, *see* Graubünden
Gruyères 200-1
Gryon 253
Gstaad 128
Guarda 327
Gunten 121

Habsburg family 13
hang-gliding 53
health 44-7
helicopter flights, Jungfrau
  Region 109
Helvetic Republic 16
Hérens Valley 260
Hesse, Hermann 27
hiking 53, 82, 149
  Appenzellerland 339
  Arosa 311
  Black Forest 186
  Ceresio 295
  Crans-Montana 269
  Davos 314
  Flims 310
  Franches Montagnes 213
  Grindelwald 110
  Gstaad 128
  Kandersteg 127
  Kleine Scheidegg 117
  Mont d'Or 250
  Pontresina 329
  Soglio 330
  St Moritz 322
  Verbier 267
  Weissenstein 188
  see also walking
history 13
hitching 74, 82
Hodler, Ferdinand 187
Hohenklingen Castle 345
holidays, *see* public holidays
Honegger, Arthur 27
Horn 350
Hornussen 62
horse-riding
  Arosa 311
  Franches Montagnes 213
hostels, *see* accommodation
hotels, *see* accommodation

ice hockey, Zürich 170
ice palace 117
Ice Pavilion 280
ice skating, Davos 314
Interlaken 100-7, **104**
  entertainment 106
  getting around 107
  getting there & away 107

  places to eat 106
  places to stay 103
  things to see & do 102
International Alpine Film
  Festival 252
International Comedy Film
  Festival 240
international dialling, *see*
  telephone services
International Festival of Music,
  Lucerne 135
International Film Festival,
  Locarno 299
International Jazz Festival 165
International June Festival 165
International Motor Car
  Museum 220
International Olympic
  Committee 236
International Red Cross & Red
  Crescent Museum 221
Isles of Brissago 301
Italian, *see* Swiss-Italian

Jass 61
Jenisch Museum 240
Jet d'Eau 219
Julier Pass 309
Jung 160
Jungfrau Region 107-18, **108**
Jungfraujoch 117
Jura Canton 213

Kandersteg 127
Kiesen 99
Klee, Paul 27
Kleine Scheidegg 117
Klosters 316
Klus Gorge 127
Knie Kinderzoo 338
Kreuzlingen 349
Kronberg 339
Kühboden 281
Kunstmuseum 306
Kyburg Castle 174

La Breya 264
La Chaux-de-Fonds 208-11, **210**
Lac Léman, *see* Lake Geneva
  Region
La Côte 239
Lake Biel 98
Lake Brienz 118
Lake Constance 346-53, **347**
Lake Geneva Region
  230-53, **231**
Lake Lucerne 138-45, **139**
Lake Lugano 294-6, 295

Lake Maggiore 301
Lake Neuchâtel 204
Lake Oeschinen 127
Lake Thun 118
Lake Uri 144
Langnau 99
language 29, 305, 363-70
l'Art Brut 232
laundry 44
Lausanne 232-9, **234**
    consulates 232
    entertainment 238
    getting there & away 238
    Palais de Rumine 235
    places to eat 237
    places to stay 236
laws 50
Le Brévent 265
Le Châble 267
Le Chasseron 248
Le Corbusier 209
Le Fayet 266
legends 140
Lenzerheide 309
Les Diablerets 252
lesbian travellers 48
Les Marécottes 263
Leukerbad 270
Leventina Valley 302
Leysin 252
Liechtenstein 354-60, **355**
Lindau 352
Locarno 296-301, **298**
Loeche-les-Bains, see Leukerbad
Lommiswil 188
LSD 182
Lucerne 132-8, **133**
    entertainment 137
    getting there & away 138
    Kapellbrücke 134
    Lion Monument 134
    museums 134
    places to eat 137
    places to stay 135
    things to see 134
    tourist office 132
Lugano 288-93, **289**

Maggia Valley 302
Malbun 359-60
Maloja 319
Männlichen 116
Marin 207
Martigny 260-3, **261**
Matterhorn 274
Maur 172
Mauvoisin Dam 268
medical kit 44
Meersburg 352

Meiringen 124-6, **125**
Melide 295
Mendrisio 296
Mer de Glace Glacier 265
Meride 296
Mesolcina Valley 302
mineral springs 247
money 36-8
Mont Blanc 264
Mont Fort 267
Monte Brè 293
Monte Generoso 295
Monte San Salvatore 293
Montreux 241-4, **242**
    getting there & away 244
    jazz festival 243
    places to eat 244
    places to stay 243
    things to see & do 242
Montreux-Vevey Music
    Festival 243
Morcote 296
Morges 239
Morgins 264
motorcycle travel 71-3, 79
mountain biking, Engelberg 147
    see also cycling
mountain transport 82
mountaineering 53
    Pontresina 329
Mt Berneuse 252
Mt Rigi 141
Mt Rosa 276
Mt Titlis 146
Murten 198-200
Musée de l'Art Brut 234
Museum of Art & History,
    Geneva 220
Museum Oskar Reinhart am
    Stadtgarten 173
music 27-8, see also festivals
music boxes 248
müsli 60

Napoleon 264
national character 26
national service 19
Nendeln 359
Nestlé-Caillers Chocolate
    factory 202
Neuchâtel 203-7, **205**
Neuchâtel Canton 203-12
Neuchâtel Montagnes 211
newspapers & magazines 42
Niesen 127
Nietzsche, Friedrich 320
nightclubs 61
Nocturama 208
North-West Vaud 245-250

Nurfenen Pass 126
Nyon 239

Olympic Museum, Lausanne 236
online services 42
orchestras 61
Orsières 264

paddleboats 53
Paléo Festival 239
Papiliorama 207
paragliding 53
Parpaner Rothorn 309
Parsenn-Weissfluh 312
Payerne 199
Petit Palais, Geneva 221
Pfänder Mountain 351
Pfingstegg 111
photography 43
Piz Lagalb 330
Plaine Morte Glacier 269
planetary paths
    Anniviers Valley 269
    Uetliberg 172
politics 23
Pontresina 329
population 25
Portes du Soleil 263
postal services 39-40, 356
public holidays 50, 283, 356
public transport network 171
puppet museum 345

Quinten 339

Rabadan Carnival 287
radio 42
rafting 53
    Flims 310
Rapperswil 338
Rathausplatz, Stein am
    Rhein 345
recycling 21
Reformation 15
Reichenbach Falls 124
Reichenbach Valley 124
religion 29
Rhine Falls (Rheinfall) 344
Rhône Glacier 126
Riederalp 281
Rochers de Naye 245
Rolle 239
Romansch 31, 318, 364-5
Romanshorn 350
Ronco 301
Rorschach 351
Rothorn Bahn 123
rowing 53
    Lucerne 135

rules 50
Rütli Meadow 144

safety, *see* crime
Saignelégier 213
sailing 53
  Horn 351
  Lake Joux 250
  Locarno 299
Sainte Croix 248
Sammlung Oskar Reinhart am
  Römerholz 173
Säntis 341
Schaffhausen 342-4
Schaffhausen Canton 342-6
Schellenberg 359
Schlitteda 318
Schloss Hünegg 122
Schloss Oberhofen 121
Schwingen 62
Schwyz 149
Schwyz Canton 149-52
Schwyzertütsch 30
Scuol 327
Sechseläuten 163
Sembrancher 267
senior travellers 48
Sherlock Holmes Museum 125
shopping 62
Sierre 268
Sigriswil 121
Sils 319
Silvaplana 320
Simplon Pass 272
Simplon Tunnel & Pass 273
Sion 256-60, **258**
ski marathon, Engadine 318
ski run, world's longest 265
ski-mountaineering, Verbier 266
skiing 31
  Andermatt 154
  Appenzellerland 339
  Arosa 311
  Axalp 123
  Champéry 263
  Crans-Montana 269
  Davos 312
  Engadine Valley 318
  Engelberg 147
  Flims 309
  Franches Montagnes 213
  Graubünden 305
  Grindelwald 110
  Gstaad 128
  inferno run 115
  Jungfrau region 109
  Klosters 316
  Les Diablerets 252
  Leukerbad 270

Leysin 252
Locarno 297
Mont d'Or 250
Pontresina 329
Portes du Soleil 264
Saas Fee 279
Sinte Croix 248
St Moritz 322
Verbier 266
Villars 253
Weissenstein 188
Soglio 330
Solothurn 186-8
Sonogno 302
special events 51, *see also*
  festivals
Spiez 120
Spitteler, Carl 27
sport 29, 62
St Bernard dogs 264
St Gallen 334-8, **335**
St Gallen Canton 334-9
St Maurice 263
St Moritz 320-5, **312**
Stans 142
steam trains, Realp 154
Stein 340-1
Stein am Rhein 344-6
Stockalper Castle 271
Stockhorn 126
Student travellers 47
sulphur springs, Baden 189
Susten Pass 126
swimming
  Locarno 299
  Lugano 290
Swiss Confederation 13
Swiss-French 31, 363-4, 366-70
Swiss-Italian 31, 364, 366-70
Swiss Museum of Games 240
Swiss Museum of
  Gastronomy 122
Swiss National Museum 162
Swiss National Park 326
Swiss Path, Lake Uri 144
Swiss Riviera 239-45
Swiss Technorama 174
Swiss wrestling 111
Swissminiatur 295

Taubenloch Gorge 98
taxes, consumer 39
telephone services 40
Tell, William 145
tennis
  Arosa 311
  Saas Fee 280
  Swiss Open 128
Tessin, *see* Ticino

theatre 27-8, 62
theft, *see* crime
thermal centre, Leukerbad 270
Thomas Cook 110
Thun 118-20, **119**
Thunersee, *see* Lake Thun
Thyssen-Bornemisza
  Gallery 290
Ticinese cuisine 285
Ticino 283-302, **284**
time 43
tipping 38
tobogganing,
  Grindelwald 110
toilets 47
tourist offices 34
tours 75
train travel 69
  European Railpasses 70-1
  Glacier Express 77
  information & tickets 77
  luggage 78
  Panorama Express 77
  platforms & trains 78
  Swiss Federal Railway 77
  to/from Asia 71
  to/from Europe 69
travel passes 76
Triesenberg 359
trotting 245
Trubschachen 99

Uetliberg 172
United Nations 222
Unspunnenstein 62

Vaduz 357-9, **358**
Valais 254-82, **255**
  getting there & away 256
  tourist office 256
Valais Regional Fair 262
Valbella 309
Vallée Blanche 265
Vallorbe 249
Vaud 230, *see also* Lake Geneva
  Region
Vaud Alps 253
Verbier 266
Verzasca Valley 302
Vevey 240
video, *see* photography
Vierwaldstättersee, *see* Lake
  Lucerne
Villars 253
visas 35, *see also* documents
Visp 273

Waadt, *see* Lake Geneva Region
Walensee 339

walking
    Locarno 297
    Lugano 293
    Saas Fee 279
    see also hiking
Wallis, see Valais
watch-making 212
water sports 53
water-skiing 53
    Därligen 121
Weggis 142
weights & measures 44
Weissenstein 188
West Bernese Oberland 126
William Tell Chapel 144
windsurfing 53
    Därligen 121
    Faulensee 121
    Lake Joux 250
wine 256

wine museum, Aigle 251
wine-growing, Lavaux 240
Winterthur 173, **173**
women travellers 47
woodcarving school,
    Brienz 123
work 54
World Snow Festival 111
WWI 17-18
WWII 18, 342
Wynigen 99

Yehudi Menuhin Festival 128
yodelling festival
    Grindelwald 111
    Mürren 115
youth hostels, see
    accommodation
Yverdon-les-Bains 245-8, **246**

Zermatt 274-8, **275**
Zernez 326
Zofingen 190
Zug 152-4
Zuoz 325
Zürich 156-75, **158-9** , **164**
    Bahnhofstrasse 162
    entertainment 169
    getting around 171
    getting there & away 170
    Grossmünster Cathedral 162
    Lindenhof 162
    museums 162
    places to eat 167
    places to stay 165
    shopping 170
    special events 163-5
    tourist offices 157
    zoo 163
Zürich Canton 156-75

LONELY PLANET JOURNEYS

JOURNEYS is a unique collection of travel writing – published by the company that understands travel better than anyone else. It is a series for anyone who has ever experienced – or dreamed of – the magical moment when they encountered a strange culture or saw a place for the first time. They are tales to read while you're planning a trip, while you're on the road or while you're in an armchair, in front of a fire.

JOURNEYS books catch the spirit of a place, illuminate a culture, recount a crazy adventure, or introduce a fascinating way of life. They always entertain, and always enrich the experience of travel.

THE GATES OF DAMASCUS
Lieve Joris
Translated by Sam Garrett

This best-selling book is a beautifully drawn portrait of day-to-day life in modern Syria. Through her intimate contact with local people, Lieve Joris draws us into the fascinating world that lies behind the gates of Damascus. Hala's husband is a political prisoner, jailed for his opposition to the Assad regime; through the author's friendship with Hala we see how Syrian politics impacts on the lives of ordinary people.

Lieve Joris, who was born in Belgium, is one of Europe's leading travel writers. In addition to an award-winning book on Hungary, she has published widely acclaimed accounts of her journeys to the Middle East and Africa. *The Gates of Damascus* is her fifth book.

'Expands the boundaries of travel writing' – Times Literary Supplement

---

KINGDOM OF THE FILM STARS
Journey into Jordan
Annie Caulfield

Kingdom of the Film Stars is a travel book and a love story. With honesty and humour, Annie Caulfield writes of travelling in Jordan and falling in love with a Bedouin. Her book offers fascinating insights into the country – from the traditional tent life of nomadic tribes to the first woman MP's battle with fundamentalist colleagues. *Kingdom of the Film Stars* unpicks some of the tight-woven Western myths about the Arab world, presenting cultural and political issues within the intimate framework of a compelling love story.

Annie Caulfield, who was born in Ireland and currently lives in London, is an award-winning playwright and journalist. She has travelled widely in the Middle East.

'Annie Caulfield is a remarkable traveller. Her story is fresh, courageous, moving, witty and sexy!' – Dawn French

LONELY PLANET PHRASEBOOKS

Building bridges,
Breaking barriers,
Beyond babble-on

Listen for the gems

Speak your own words

Ask your own
questions

Master of
your
own
image

- handy pocket-sized books
- easy to understand Pronunciation chapter
- clear and comprehensive Grammar chapter
- romanisation alongside script to allow ease of pronunciation
- script throughout so users can point to phrases
- extensive vocabulary sections, words and phrases for every situations
- full of cultural information and tips for the traveller

'...vital for a real DIY spirit and attitude in language learning' – Backpacker

'the phrasebooks have good cultural backgrounders and offer solid advice for challenging situations in remote locations' – San Francisco Examiner

'...they are unbeatable for their coverage of the world's more obscure languages' – The Geographical Magazine

---

Arabic (Egyptian)
Arabic (Moroccan)
Australia
  Australian English, Aboriginal and Torres Strait languages
Baltic States
  Estonian, Latvian, Lithuanian
Bengali
Burmese
Brazilian
Cantonese
Central Europe
  Czech, French, German, Hungarian, Italian and Slovak
Eastern Europe
  Bulgarian, Czech, Hungarian, Polish. Romanian and Slovak
Egyptian Arabic
Ethiopian (Amharic)
Fijian
French
German
Greek

Hindi/Urdu
Indonesian
Italian
Japanese
Korean
Lao
Latin American Spanish
Malay
Mandarin
Mediterranean Europe
  Albanian, Croatian, Greek, Italian, Macedonian, Maltese, Serbian, Slovene
Mongolian
Moroccan Arabic
Nepali
Papua New Guinea
Pilipino (Tagalog)
Quechua
Russian
Scandinavian Europe
  Danish, Finnish, Icelandic, Norwegian and Swedish

South-East Asia
  Burmese, Indonesian, Khmer, Lao, Malay, Tagalog (Pilipino), Thai and Vietnamese
Spanish
Sri Lanka
Swahili
Thai
Thai Hill Tribes
Tibetan
Turkish
Ukrainian
USA
  US English, Vernacular Talk, Native American languages and Hawaiian
Vietnamese
Western Europe
  Basque, Catalan, Dutch, French, German, Irish, Italian, Portuguese, Scottish Gaelic, Spanish (Castilian) and Welsh

---

LONELY PLANET TRAVEL ATLASES

Lonely Planet has long been famous for the number and quality of its guidebook maps. Now we've gone one step further and in conjunction with Steinhart Katzır Publishers produced a handy companion series: Lonely Planet travel atlases – maps of a country produced in book form.

Unlike other maps, which look good but lead travellers astray, our travel atlases have been researched on the road by Lonely Planet's experienced team of writers. All details are carefully checked to ensure the atlas corresponds with the equivalent Lonely Planet guidebook.

The handy atlas format means no holes, wrinkles, torn sections or constant folding and unfolding. These atlases can survive long periods on the road, unlike cumbersome fold-out maps. The comprehensive index ensures easy reference.

- full-colour throughout
- maps researched and checked by Lonely Planet authors
- place names correspond with Lonely Planet guidebooks
  – no confusing spelling differences
- legend and travelling information in English, French, German, Japanese and Spanish
- size: 230 x 160 mm

Available now:
Chile & Easter Island • Egypt • India & Bangladesh • Israel & the Palestinian Territories •Jordan, Syria & Lebanon • Kenya • Laos • Portugal • South Africa, Lesotho & Swaziland • Thailand • Turkey • Vietnam • Zimbabwe, Botswana & Namibia

---

LONELY PLANET TV SERIES & VIDEOS

Lonely Planet travel guides have been brought to life on television screens around the world. Like our guides, the programmes are based on the joy of independent travel, and look honestly at some of the most exciting, picturesque and frustrating places in the world. Each show is presented by one of three travellers from Australia, England or the USA and combines an innovative mixture of video, Super-8 film, atmospheric soundscapes and original music.

Videos of each episode – containing additional footage not shown on television – are available from good book and video shops, but the availability of individual videos varies with regional screening schedules.

Video destinations include: Alaska • American Rockies • Australia – The South-East • Baja California & the Copper Canyon • Brazil • Central Asia • Chile & Easter Island • Corsica, Sicily & Sardinia – The Mediterranean Islands • East Africa (Tanzania & Zanzibar) • Ecuador & the Galapagos Islands • Greenland & Iceland • Indonesia • Israel & the Sinai Desert • Jamaica • Japan • La Ruta Maya • Morocco • New York • North India • Pacific Islands (Fiji, Solomon Islands & Vanuatu) • South India • South West China • Turkey • Vietnam • West Africa • Zimbabwe, Botswana & Namibia

The Lonely Planet TV series is produced by:
Pilot Productions
The Old Studio
18 Middle Row
London W10 5AT UK

For video availability and ordering information contact your nearest Lonely Planet office.

Music from the TV series is available on CD & cassette.

PLANET TALK

Lonely Planet's FREE quarterly newsletter

We love hearing from you and think you'd like to hear from us.

*When...*is the right time to see reindeer in Finland?
*Where...*can you hear the best palm-wine music in Ghana?
*How...*do you get from Asunción to Areguá by steam train?
*What...*is the best way to see India?

For the answer to these and many other questions read PLANET TALK.

Every issue is packed with up-to-date travel news and advice including:

* a letter from Lonely Planet co-founders Tony and Maureen Wheeler
* go behind the scenes on the road with a Lonely Planet author
* feature article on an important and topical travel issue
* a selection of recent letters from travellers
* details on forthcoming Lonely Planet promotions
* complete list of Lonely Planet products

To join our mailing list contact any Lonely Planet office.

Also available: Lonely Planet T-shirts. 100% heavyweight cotton.

LONELY PLANET ONLINE

Get the latest travel information before you leave or while you're on the road

Whether you've just begun planning your next trip, or you're chasing down specific info on currency regulations or visa requirements, check out Lonely Planet Online for up-to-the minute travel information.

As well as travel profiles of your favourite destinations (including maps and photos), you'll find current reports from our researchers and other travellers, updates on health and visas, travel advisories, and discussion of the ecological and political issues you need to be aware of as you travel.

There's also an online travellers' forum where you can share your experience of life on the road, meet travel companions and ask other travellers for their recommendations and advice. We also have plenty of links to other online sites useful to independent travellers.

And of course we have a complete and up-to-date list of all Lonely Planet travel products including guides, phrasebooks, atlases, Journeys and videos and a simple online ordering facility if you can't find the book you want elsewhere.

www.lonelyplanet.com
or
AOL keyword: lp

LONELY PLANET PRODUCTS

Lonely Planet is known worldwide for publishing practical, reliable and no-nonsense travel information in our guides and on our web site. The Lonely Planet list covers just about every accessible part of the world. Currently there are eight series: *travel guides*, *shoestring guides*, *walking guides*, *city guides*, *phrasebooks*, *audio packs*, *travel atlases* and *Journeys* – a unique collection of travel writing.

EUROPE

Amsterdam • Austria • Baltic States phrasebook • Britain • Central Europe on a shoestring • Central Europe phrasebook • Czech & Slovak Republics • Denmark • Dublin • Eastern Europe on a shoestring • Eastern Europe phrasebook • Estonia, Latvia & Lithuania • Finland • France • French phrasebook • German phrasebook • Greece • Greek phrasebook • Hungary • Iceland, Greenland & the Faroe Islands • Ireland • Italian phrasebook • Italy • Mediterranean Europe on a shoestring • Mediterranean Europe phrasebook • Paris • Poland • Portugal • Portugal travel atlas • Prague • Russia, Ukraine & Belarus • Russian phrasebook • Scandinavian & Baltic Europe on a shoestring • Scandinavian Europe phrasebook • Slovenia • Spain • Spanish phrasebook • St Petersburg • Switzerland • Trekking in Greece • Trekking in Spain • Ukrainian phrasebook • Vienna • Walking in Britain • Walking in Switzerland • Western Europe on a shoestring • Western Europe phrasebook

Travel Literature: The Olive Grove: Travels in Greece

NORTH AMERICA

Alaska • Backpacking in Alaska • Baja California • California & Nevada • Canada • Florida • Hawaii • Honolulu • Los Angeles • Mexico • Miami • New England • New Orleans • New York City • New York, New Jersey & Pennsylvania • Pacific Northwest USA • Rocky Mountain States • San Francisco • Southwest USA • USA phrasebook • Washington, DC & the Capital Region

CENTRAL AMERICA & THE CARIBBEAN

Bermuda • Central America on a shoestring • Costa Rica • Cuba • Eastern Caribbean • Guatemala, Belize & Yucatán: La Ruta Maya • Jamaica

SOUTH AMERICA

Argentina, Uruguay & Paraguay • Bolivia • Brazil • Brazilian phrasebook • Buenos Aires • Chile & Easter Island • Chile & Easter Island travel atlas • Colombia • Ecuador & the Galápagos Islands • Latin American Spanish phrasebook • Peru • Quechua phrasebook • Rio de Janeiro • South America on a shoestring • Trekking in the Patagonian Andes • Venezuela

Travel Literature: Full Circle: A South American Journey

ANTARCTICA

Antarctica

ISLANDS OF THE INDIAN OCEAN

Madagascar & Comoros • Maldives • Mauritius, Réunion & Seychelles

AFRICA

Africa - the South • Africa on a shoestring • Arabic (Moroccan) phrasebook • Cape Town • Central Africa • East Africa • Egypt • Egypt travel atlas • Ethiopian (Amharic) phrasebook • Kenya • Kenya travel atlas • Malawi, Mozambique & Zambia • Morocco • North Africa • South Africa, Lesotho & Swaziland • South Africa, Lesotho & Swaziland travel atlas • Swahili phrasebook • Trekking in East Africa • West Africa • Zimbabwe, Botswana & Namibia • Zimbabwe, Botswana & Namibia travel atlas

Travel Literature: The Rainbird: A Central African Journey • Songs to an African Sunset: A Zimbabwean Story

MAIL ORDER

Lonely Planet products are distributed worldwide. They are also available by mail order from Lonely Planet, so if you have difficulty finding a title please write to us. North American and South American residents should write to Embarcadero West, 155 Filbert St, Suite 251, Oakland CA 94607, USA; European and African residents should write to 10 Barley Mow Passage, Chiswick, London W4 4PH; and residents of other countries to PO Box 617, Hawthorn, Victoria 3122, Australia.

NORTH-EAST ASIA

Beijing • Cantonese phrasebook • China • Hong Kong • Hong Kong, Macau & Guangzhou • Japan • Japanese phrasebook • Japanese audio pack • Korea • Korean phrasebook • Mandarin phrasebook • Mongolia • Mongolian phrasebook • North-East Asia on a shoestring • Seoul • Taiwan • Tibet • Tibet phrasebook • Tokyo

Travel Literature: Lost Japan

MIDDLE EAST & CENTRAL ASIA

Arab Gulf States • Arabic (Egyptian) phrasebook • Central Asia • Iran • Israel & the Palestinian Territories • Israel & the Palestinian Territories travel atlas • Istanbul • Jerusalem • Jordan & Syria • Jordan, Syria & Lebanon travel atlas • Lebanon • Middle East • Turkey • Turkish phrasebook • Turkey travel atlas • Yemen

Travel Literature: The Gates of Damascus • Kingdom of the Film Stars: Journey into Jordan

ALSO AVAILABLE:

Travel with Children • Traveller's Tales

INDIAN SUBCONTINENT

Bangladesh • Bengali phrasebook • Delhi • Hindi/Urdu phrasebook • India • India & Bangladesh travel atlas • Indian Himalaya • Karakoram Highway • Nepal • Nepali phrasebook • Pakistan • Rajasthan • Sri Lanka • Sri Lanka phrasebook • Trekking in the Indian Himalaya • Trekking in the Karakoram & Hindukush • Trekking in the Nepal Himalaya

Travel Literature: In Rajasthan • Shopping for Buddhas

SOUTH-EAST ASIA

Bali & Lombok • Bangkok • Burmese phrasebook • Cambodia • Ho Chi Minh City • Indonesia • Indonesian phrasebook • Indonesian audio pack • Jakarta • Java • Laos • Lao phrasebook • Laos travel atlas • Malay phrasebook • Malaysia, Singapore & Brunei • Myanmar (Burma) • Philippines • Pilipino phrasebook • Singapore • South-East Asia on a shoestring • South-East Asia phrasebook • Thailand • Thailand's Islands & Beaches • Thailand travel atlas • Thai phrasebook • Thai audio pack • Thai Hill Tribes phrasebook • Vietnam • Vietnamese phrasebook • Vietnam travel atlas

AUSTRALIA & THE PACIFIC

Australia • Australian phrasebook • Bushwalking in Australia • Bushwalking in Papua New Guinea • Fiji • Fijian phrasebook • Islands of Australia's Great Barrier Reef • Melbourne • Micronesia • New Caledonia • New South Wales & the ACT • New Zealand • Northern Territory • Outback Australia • Papua New Guinea • Papua New Guinea phrasebook • Queensland • Rarotonga & the Cook Islands • Samoa • Solomon Islands • South Australia • Sydney • Tahiti & French Polynesia • Tasmania • Tonga • Tramping in New Zealand • Vanuatu • Victoria • Western Australia

Travel Literature: Islands in the Clouds • Sean & David's Long Drive

THE LONELY PLANET STORY

Lonely Planet published its first book in 1973 in response to the numerous 'How did you do it?' questions Maureen and Tony Wheeler were asked after driving, bussing, hitching, sailing and railing their way from England to Australia.

Written at a kitchen table and hand collated, trimmed and stapled, *Across Asia on the Cheap* became an instant local bestseller, inspiring thoughts of another book.

Eighteen months in South-East Asia resulted in their second guide, *South-East Asia on a shoestring*, which they put together in a backstreet Chinese hotel in Singapore in 1975. The 'yellow bible', as it quickly became known to backpackers around the world, soon became *the* guide to the region. It has sold well over half a million copies and is now in its 9th edition, still retaining its familiar yellow cover.

Today there are over 240 titles, including travel guides, walking guides, language kits & phrasebooks, travel atlases and travel literature. The company is the largest independent travel publisher in the world. Although Lonely Planet initially specialised in guides to Asia, today there are few corners of the globe that have not been covered.

The emphasis continues to be on travel for independent travellers. Tony and Maureen still travel for several months of each year and play an active part in the writing, updating and quality control of Lonely Planet's guides.

They have been joined by over 70 authors and 170 staff at our offices in Melbourne (Australia), Oakland (USA), London (UK) and Paris (France). Travellers themselves also make a valuable contribution to the guides through the feedback we receive in thousands of letters each year and on our web site.

The people at Lonely Planet strongly believe that travellers can make a positive contribution to the countries they visit, both through their appreciation of the countries' culture, wildlife and natural features, and through the money they spend. In addition, the company makes a direct contribution to the countries and regions it covers. Since 1986 a percentage of the income from each book has been donated to ventures such as famine relief in Africa; aid projects in India; agricultural projects in Central America; Greenpeace's efforts to halt French nuclear testing in the Pacific; and Amnesty International.

'I hope we send people out with the right attitude about travel. You realise when you travel that there are so many different perspectives about the world, so we hope these books will make people more interested in what they see. Guidebooks can't really guide people. All you can do is point them in the right direction.'

– Tony Wheeler

LONELY PLANET PUBLICATIONS

Australia
PO Box 617, Hawthorn 3122, Victoria
tel: (03) 9819 1877 fax: (03) 9819 6459
e-mail: talk2us@lonelyplanet.com.au

USA
Embarcadero West, 155 Filbert St, Suite 251,
Oakland, CA 94607
tel: (510) 893 8555 TOLL FREE: 800 275-8555
fax: (510) 893 8563
e-mail: info@lonelyplanet.com

UK
10 Barley Mow Passage, Chiswick,
London W4 4PH
tel: (0181) 742 3161 fax: (0181) 742 2772
e-mail: lonelyplanetuk@compuserve.com

France:
71 bis rue du Cardinal Lemoine, 75005 Paris
tel: 1 44 32 06 20 fax: 1 46 34 72 55
e-mail: 100560.415@compuserve.com

World Wide Web: http://www.lonelyplanet.com
or *AOL keyword: lp*